Miss Manners'
Guide to Excruciatingly
Correct Behavior

ALSO BY JUDITH MARTIN

Star-Spangled Manners

Miss Manners' Guide to Domestic Tranquility

Miss Manners' Basic Training: The Right Thing to Say

Miss Manners' Basic Training: Eating

Miss Manners' Basic Training: Communication

Miss Manners Rescues Civilization

(A Citizen's Guide to Civility)

Miss Manners on (Painfully Proper) Weddings

(Miss Manners on Weddings)

Miss Manners' Guide for the Turn-of-the-Millennium

Common Courtesy

Miss Manners' Guide to Rearing Perfect Children

Miss Manners' Guide to Excruciatingly Correct Behavior

Style and Substance

Gilbert: A Comedy of Manners

Miss Manners'

Guide to Excruciatingly Correct Behavior

FRESHLY UPDATED

JUDITH MARTIN

Illustrated by Gloria Kamen

W. W. NORTON & COMPANY   NEW YORK · LONDON

Copyright © 2005, 1982, 1981, 1980, 1979 by Judith Martin
Illustrations copyright © 1982 by Gloria Kamen

For information about permission to reproduce selections from this book, write to
Permissions, W. W. Norton & Company, Inc., 500 Fifth Avenue, New York, NY 10110

Manufacturing by RR Donnelley, Harrisonburg, VA
Illustrations by Gloria Kamen and Mike Wood.
Illustration on page 14 by Mike Wood.
Book design by Dana Sloan
Production manager: Anna Oler

Library of Congress Cataloging-in-Publication Data
Martin, Judith, 1938–
Miss Manners' guide to excruciatingly correct behavior / Judith Martin ; illustrated by Gloria
Kamen.— Freshly updated.
p. cm.
Includes index.
ISBN 0-393-05874-3 (hardcover)
1. Etiquette. I. Title.
BJ1853.M294 2005
395—dc22

2005000264

W. W. Norton & Company, Inc., 500 Fifth Avenue, New York, N.Y. 10110
www.wwnorton.com

W. W. Norton & Company Ltd., Castle House, 75/76 Wells Street, London W1T 3QT

1 2 3 4 5 6 7 8 9

FOR NICHOLAS AND JACOBINA

Contents

List of Illustrations 13

Preface 15

1. Introduction 19

    Some Thoughts on the Impulse Rude and the
        Mannerly Way of Life 21

    Gentle Readers Wrestle with Philosophical Problems
        Arising from the Great Study of Manners 31

    On Manners and Morals 31

2. Birth 35

    Prebirth Manners for Parents and Others 37

    Showers 44

    Announcements 47

    Names 52

    Baptisms and Circumcisions 58

    Social Life Begins 61

    Social Life Resumes 67

3. Basic Civilization 71

  Concerning Children 73

    Manners toward Children 73

Manners for Children 80

Children's Social Events 89

COMMON COURTESY FOR ALL AGES 96

Introductions and Greetings 96

Handshakes, Kisses and Other Introductory Gestures 109

Saying No: Silence as a Social Skill 115

Common Annoyances 118

Relations between the Genders 127

The Virtuous Life in Wicked Cities 137

Transportation 147

TABLE MANNERS 154

Methods 162

Family Dinner 172

Manners for Particular (and Ornery) Foods 179

SOCIAL INTERCOURSE 204

Vocabulary 204

Conversing (Rather than Communicating) .213

Conversational Hazards 230

ELECTRONIC COMMUNICATION (PERSONAL) 234

The Domestic Telephone 236

The Itinerant Telephone 242

The Internet 246

FAMILY RELATIONS 251

Family Crises 258

VISITING 268

HOUSEGUESTS 274

House-Sitting 282

UNPLEASANT FACTS OF LIFE 284

    Major and Minor Illnesses 284

    Messy Emotions and Minor Emotional Distress 290

    Disgusting Habits 293

    Citizen Participation 298

4. RITES DE PASSAGE 303

BAR AND BAT MITZVAHS, COMMUNIONS AND CONFIRMATIONS 305

GRADUATIONS AND REUNIONS 309

DEBUTS AND DANCES 317

COURTSHIP 325

    Love Problems (from Bad to Worse) 344

    Breaking Up 350

5. MARRIAGE (FOR BEGINNERS) 355

ENGAGEMENTS 357

FAMILIES AND FRIENDS 371

    The Bride's Family 373

    The Bridegroom's Family 377

    New Family Nomenclature 379

    The Attendants 381

WEDDINGS 385

    Invitations and Responses 390

    Announcements 404

    Wedding Clothes 408

    Wedding Procedure 416

    Wedding Receptions 423

    Photographs 428

    Wedding Presents (and Of Course Thank-You Letters) 431

THE TROUSSEAU 444

    Silver 444

    China 448

    Glass 449

    Linens 451

THE WELL-APPOINTED HOUSE 454

6. WORK 457

    INTERVIEWS, RECOMMENDATIONS AND RAISES 459

    WORKPLACE ETIQUETTE 467

    BUSINESS ENTERTAINING:

        NEITHER BUSINESSLIKE NOR ENTERTAINING 477

    BUSINESS COMMUNICATIONS 482

        Business Letters 482

        Telephones 484

        Email 487

        Notebooks and Laptops 488

    CUSTOMER SERVICE 490

        When Things Go Wrong 498

        Common Complaints 501

    THE JOB ENDS 505

7. INTERMEDIATE CIVILIZATION 511

    SOCIAL FORMS, SOME STUNNING AND OTHERS GHASTLY 513

    INVITATIONS AND REPLIES 528

        Responding 536

        The Social Unit 541

        Breaking Social Engagements 545

SOCIAL PROCEDURE 546

    Social Disasters 556

    Apologies 562

DINNER PARTIES 566

    The Guest List 569

    At Table 571

    Adding the Guests 576

    The Menu 581

    Correct Service 584

SOCIAL CORRESPONDENCE 591

    The Form 591

    The Content 604

    Greeting Cards and Christmas Letters 609

PRESENTS 614

DECENT DRESS FOR LADIES AND GENTLEMEN 622

    Dressing for the Occasion 625

    Controversial Clothing 631

    Confusing Clothing 635

    Children's Dress 641

    Jewelry and Other Adornments 642

8. EVER AFTER 649

DIVORCE 651

    Announcements and Demeanor 653

    The Children 663

MARRIAGE TWO (PREREQUISITE: MARRIAGE FOR BEGINNERS) 669

ANNIVERSARIES 677

9. ADVANCED CIVILIZATION 685

    PROTOCOL 687

    THE WHITE HOUSE 699

    THE LARGE HOUSEHOLD 708

    CELEBRITY AND PUBLICITY 713

    PLAY 724
        Culture 724
        Sports 732
        Clubs 741
        Alcohol, Tobacco and Other Stimulants 743
        Restaurants 750
        Travel 764
        Vacation Trips 776
        Holidays 780

10. DEATH 797

    FUNERALS 802

    BEREAVEMENT 806

    CONDOLENCES 811

11. ANSWERS TO QUESTIONS NOBODY ASKED 823

    ACKNOWLEDGMENTS 827

    INDEX 829

List of Illustrations

THE AWFULS CONSIDER BECOMING PERFECT • 14

THE ANNOUNCEMENT OF A BIRTH • 48

A CHILD'S LETTER OF THANKS • 88

THE FORMAL DINNER TABLE • 155

DESSERT SERVICE • 156

THE DISSECTION OF A FISH • 188

AN INVITATION TO A BAR MITZVAH • 306

INVITATIONS TO A DEBUT • 319

WEDDING INVITATIONS (WITH VARIATIONS) • 397, 398

THE REPLY • 400

A WEDDING ANNOUNCEMENT • 407

LADIES' WEDDING CLOTHES • 410

GENTLEMEN'S WEDDING CLOTHES • 412

PLACEMENT OF THE WEDDING PARTY • 418

A BRIDE'S LETTER OF THANKS • 440

A FORMAL ALL-PURPOSE INVITATION • 537

THE REPLY • 538

A NOTE OF APOLOGY • 563

A LETTER THAT SHOULD NOT HAVE BEEN WRITTEN • 593

SOCIAL AND BUSINESS CARDS • 597

AN INVITATION TO A SECOND WEDDING • 671

LETTERS TO DIGNITARIES • 688, 689

THE PROPER WAY TO ADDRESS DIGNITARIES • 693

AN INVITATION TO THE WHITE HOUSE • 701, 702

THE REPLY • 704

A LETTER OF CONDOLENCE • 816

A REPLY • 817

Preface

"WHAT WOULD Mother think?" was a question that had accompanied Daffodil Right for her entire life. She knew she was growing old when it no longer set off the thought "And how can I keep her from finding out?"

The change did not occur when that lady, Clara Grace Perfect (née Proper, and equipped with crisp little cards that announced her as Mrs. Geoffrey Lockwood Perfect) departed this world for a more nearly correct one. Mrs. Perfect had what was known as Presence, the dignified precursor of what deteriorated to Poise during Daffodil's youth and then disappeared into a pottage of Assertiveness and Sensitivity from which it has not yet managed to surface.

Mere death did not soften Mrs. Perfect's august influence. Indeed, during her declining years, if a lady so upright may be said to decline, she served as a stalwart example of what the family called Clara Grace under Pressure. Her memory had gently receded, but her manners had not. When Daffodil came to visit, Mrs. Perfect never failed to introduce herself and to add, "And I hope your dear mother is well. Please remember me to her." If Daffodil attempted a mild correction, Mrs. Perfect would manage a sweet smile with just a dollop of reproach in it as she said, "Well, of course I know that, dear. What do you take me for?" And she would continue, seamlessly, with a polite inquiry after Daffodil's husband. Not Teddy Right, who was usually standing right there holding out a box of her favorite liqueur-laced chocolates, but Rhino Awful, Daffodil's first husband, who had long ago acquired a wife of more nearly his brain power, although not nearly his age.

The increasing appreciation of her mother's view that only a strict code of manners can keep civilization from descending into chaos began as reverie during work.

As a judge in Domestic Court, Daffodil spent hours listening to evidence against society's panacea for bad behavior. It was generally believed that what people needed to get along was love and communication skills. Even business colleagues were thought to work better if they spoke their minds and really got to know one another personally, from which affection would follow—only not too much affection, because that might be illegal. Yet here was Judge Daffodil Right, listening all day long to people who were only too familiar with one another, who had certainly loved at one time and whose communication skills were so well honed that she sometimes had to threaten them with contempt of court.

At the same time, she knew, to her sorrow, that the law was not going to solve their problems. She could offer some protections and retributions, but she was helpless to stop them from being plain mean, and from going out and repeating these horrid situations among themselves or in new domestic arrangements. At times she heard her mother's voice coming out of her own mouth, delivering etiquette orders: "I want you to apologize right now" and "Don't speak of your father that way" and "Do you consider yourself properly dressed?" and "I would appreciate it if you would show more respect." But she decided that the day she heard herself sentencing someone to have his mouth washed out with soap would be the day she retired.

Still, Daffodil was surprised to hear the old question from another source: "What would your mother think?"

It was Zoe and Zachary, her favorite grandchildren, notwithstanding that she would have sworn on her own courtroom Bible that she had no favorites among her many descendents and step-descendents. She seemed to be a favorite of theirs as well, and they had come to show her the outfits they had put together for their high school prom.

What would her mother think of Zoe in a black dress so tight and slashed that those body parts pushed up into the décolletage must be her knees? And of the over-the-elbow black gloves with bracelets and a ring worn over them? And of the two-toned, upswept hairdo achieved with gel instead of hairpins? What would she think of Zachary wearing a tailcoat with a black tie and black chino pants? And of the red cummerbund and matching hankie stuck into a pocketed shirt?

Awful, awful, is what Clara Perfect would have thought. There would have been some validity to this, quite aside from the sartorial angle, as the two children were also, through no fault of their own, descended from Jonathan Rhinehart Awful, 3rd.

Daffodil lacked the heart to dampen their pleasure, but she also knew that she was the children's only source of information about etiquette, a subject toward which they harbored none of the antipathy that their parents' generation had shown. Because they so often visited, she was able to teach them the once-common amenities, such as table manners and greetings and expressions of gratitude without criticizing their parents. The cover was simply that this was the way she and Teddy did things, which Zoe and Zachary learned as a sort of second language of behavior. She was both proud and appalled to watch them cash in on this knowledge—getting the best summer jobs, impressing college interviewers and taking in a significantly better haul of family presents than their cousins who never wrote letters of thanks.

"You'll be the best-looking people there," she declared with misleading truthfulness that failed to mislead them. "But don't even ask what Mamma would have thought. She went by an entirely different standard."

So of course they did ask. "Well, for Mamma, evening clothes were serious. No, that's not quite right. They were also a game, but the game had rules, and the object was aesthetic—to stand out because your clothes were beautiful or stylish or even daring, although I suppose not what you would consider daring. For gentlemen, it was to have clothes that were perfectly tailored.

"What you're doing is putting together different elements from this style and that, the fancy along with the trashy, as a kind of satire. Your friends will be doing that too, and I'm sure you'll both be the hits of the evening.

"It is what we used to call postmodernism," she continued, making it sound unattractively dated. "But you mustn't expect that your great-grandmamma would think it funny. In her way, she had a sense of humor, but she would not have been amused to have formality satirized by people who didn't know the rules they were trying to make fun of."

That came out harsher than Daffodil had intended, so she quickly moved on, saying, "I see that movie stars are beginning to wear serious evening clothes again. The women, anyway. Some of them."

"I love period movies," said Zoe. "Don't you?"

"No, I hate them," said her grandmother. "The costumes are lovely, but the period manners are ridiculous. Just once I'd like to see an historical movie, or play, or opera, where the women don't eat with their gloves on. And the way they all use first names and—oh, don't get me started."

In the hope of avoiding that, Zachary said, "I suppose you wish you'd lived back in the good old days." He was addressing Daffodil, but Zoe, who had been tugging off her gloves, piped up saying, "Oh, I do."

"Well, I don't," said Daffodil. "I mean, I did, sort of, and that was enough. When people carry on about how awful—I mean dreadful—manners are nowadays, they forget the extraordinary strides we've made. I went to law school late, but my college roommate went when we were young and she was constantly being taunted in class—not just by the men but by the professors, who all resented her taking the place of a man who would have to support his family. Which didn't stop them from making it dangerous to see them in their offices. And ask your Uncle Gregory what he and Uncle Lars had to endure in the way of insults—and they're the only couple in the family since my parents who never changed partners. If your own godparents had gone to restaurants with us, the service would have been suddenly nonexistent. What about your cousin Che? He would have been labeled a bastard."

"Actually, he is," said Zoe.

"Sure, but that's personal. He earned it; it's not because his parents weren't married when he was born," Daffodil replied. "I mean, don't say that about your own cousin. He's just going through a rough period. He'll grow out of it. Someday. We hope. But no, I don't want to go back to the old days. I just want people to behave better nowadays."

"There's still plenty of discrimination," said Zachary. "But what's changed was changed by law."

"And how does law get changed?" Daffodil asked, peering over her reading glasses in a manner cultivated to remind witnesses of their school principals. "Social pressure. If you try to do it without some sort of consensus about what constitutes good and bad behavior, you're never going to be able to enforce it. We still have discrimination because society isn't doing a good enough job. But we've come a long way from the times when people tolerated—practiced, chortled over, actually relished—outright bigotry."

"Grammy!" said Zoe, waving her hand to get her attention. "Speaking of change, I'm going to run up and change. You'd better too, Zack. We're due at Grandpa's— you know Aunt Kristen's getting married again, don't you, Grammy? And we have to be in it. Now that's going to be strictly formal. She was asking us etiquette questions, like how she should tell people to give cash instead of dumb presents, and whether her ex-husband should give her away. Gramps says he's tired of doing it and having her bounce back, it was getting to be like a bad tennis match. I told her she should talk to you."

"Don't you know the answers by now?"

"Not exactly. I mean, I think I know what your mother would say, but you always admit that etiquette and law do change with the times, and I'm not sure anymore."

"Well, in both, the moral principles don't change, but the surface rules adjust when there is a compelling reason to alter tradition, which . . . Never mind, dear. Run along, both of you. We'll get to it another time."

It is in case they don't, and for those who can't or don't listen to wise grandmothers, that this book is written.

I. *Introduction*

Some Thoughts on the Impulse Rude and the Mannerly Way of Life

WHEN PEOPLE complain about the rudeness of others (and surely you don't think they are lining up here to turn *themselves* in), they like to generalize. It is apparently less satisfying to be battered by a rude individual than by a whole class of them. Thus it is that Miss Manners keeps being alerted to two categories of rude people:

1. People Who Should Know Better (as in, "They're professionals, so they should know better").
2. People Like That (as in, "What else can you expect of People Like That?"). Surprisingly, this is less often a reference to the downtrodden than to that perennially popular target "the newly rich," which has come to include such specialties as "corporate pigs," "baby billionaires" and "trophy wives."

Etiquette crimes committed in both categories are pretty much the same. It is reported that these people don't know the basic decencies of how to eat, dress or talk, respond, reciprocate or thank, but have mastered infinite ways of enraging decent folk. Yet the first set's behaving this way is met with shock, while the second's doing so causes not the least surprise.

Miss Manners can't for the life of her figure out the distinction between them. Aside from its apparently being considered decorous to halt at a modest rung of the pay scale, what does this have to do with acquiring manners?

Perhaps you remember a phantom category, no longer polite to mention, which went by such names as People of Property, Well-Bred, Used to Good Things, Our Sort, We Know the Family and, of course, Old Money (which Miss Manners thinks of as New Money: The Sequel). The notion was that people who grew up with

21

money were also amply supplied with manners. That neither truth nor logic accompanies this proposition has never discouraged the rich or their distant admirers from believing it.

Manners are not inheritable goods, and therefore every individual starts with a clean—meaning rude—slate. Furthermore, Old, New and No Money learn their manners from the same people. In the case of No Money, it is their own parents, usually their mothers. In the case of the moneyed, it's the same mothers who, being short on money, take on the challenging job of civilizing the children of the rich.

The rich make the argument that they are exposed to a greater variety of manners, including formal and foreign varieties, and that they have a tradition of *noblesse oblige*. The non-rich make the argument that they are left more exposed to the human elements and that knowing how it feels to be mistreated makes one manners-conscious. So in theory, the newly rich should have all the benefits of the latter as well as the opportunity to develop the former. In fact, Miss Manners has found politeness and rudeness to be unpredictably scattered among all these groups, the way intelligence is. Similarly, there is far too little to go around.

It would help if they all stopped calling one another names and used the time to learn to behave like Miss Manners. Miss Manners is unfailingly polite. Even when Miss Manners is treated badly, she responds courteously. This is known as Not Stooping, or Shaming Them, or Setting a Good Example.

It is not that she has never felt the Impulse Rude. You wouldn't trust a preacher who never experienced the temptations of sin, would you?

How one longs to strike back. But two wrongs make a blight, and if rudeness begets rudeness, which begets more rudeness, where will it all end? (And why is Miss Manners speaking like a preacher? The verb "to beget" was never in her daily vocabulary before.) There are now many practitioners of the art of getting back, and many books, classes and discussions on techniques for doing so. Miss Manners often receives letters from people who assume that she is such a one and can supply a method for "putting down" this person or that.

Alas. At the risk of sounding unbearably saintly, Miss Manners spurns these methods. Nevertheless—and this is the interesting part—she does not suffer from the indignities that an undignified assertiveness asserts it can correct. No one takes advantage of Miss Manners without her consent. (What happens when she consents is also interesting, but another story.) She does not allow rude people to spoil her life, but she does not seek satisfaction in spoiling theirs.

For one thing, they outnumber her. One can easily encounter a dozen provoking rudenesses on the way to work in the morning, and a matching set on the way home. A lunch hour spent shopping, or, for that matter, buying lunch, can increase the total tenfold. For another thing, counter-rudeness is escalating, sometimes beyond rudeness itself into violence. Even the lexicon of rudeness one hears these days is explicitly violent, although the specific words are usually sexual. (Does anyone know why such a nice practice as sex should have to supply the words for uncontrolled hostility? Maybe it would be better that this not be explained to Miss Manners.)

What, then, does one do with one's justified anger? Miss Manners' meager arsenal consists only of the withering look, the insistent and repeated request, the cold voice, the report up the chain of command and the tilted nose. They generally work. When they fail, she has the ability to dismiss inferior behavior from her mind as coming from inferior people.

You will perhaps point out that she will never know the joy of delivering a well-deserved sock in the chops. True—but she will never inspire one, either.

～ On Class Consciousness ～

There are three social classes in America: upper middle class, middle class and lower middle class. Miss Manners has never heard of an American's owning up to being in any other class. However, if there is one thing that all Americans agree upon, no matter what their background, it is that the middle class is despicable. The shame of having been born into it is sufficient excuse for a lifelong grudge against one's parents and the entire society. This is not a happy state of affairs.

The problem, in Miss Manners' opinion, is that the classes have traditionally behaved badly—either oppressively or obsequiously—to those below or above them. Being in the middle, the middle class has the opportunity to do both. Being a democracy, we extend this opportunity to everyone.

One would think, therefore, that an entirely middle-class nation would stop despising people on the basis of middle class–hood, or that everyone who could make or lose enough money would quickly scurry into one of the other classes. Miss Manners' mother always told her to travel either first or third class, but never second, when crossing. (Not crossing class lines, silly; crossing the Atlantic Ocean, in the days when that was done properly, with bouillon at eleven on the promenade deck and tea at five in the salon.) In first class, in those days, you had luxury; in third class, you had fun. This is the proper distribution of the world's blessings. In second class, you had neither. Naturally, then, someone invented the one-class ship, where the advantages of second class could be enjoyed by all, which is probably why we have those overanxious things called airplanes for crossings these days.

You see the problem. Here are Miss Manners' solutions: First, some people must volunteer to be in the upper class, and others must volunteer to be in the lower class. This is a democracy, so admission will be based solely on ability to pay. But, then, people must behave according to the class they have chosen. We will have no confusion with upper-class people wanting to be earthy, or loved for themselves alone, or lower-class people coveting status symbols. Nor will members of any class be allowed to be ashamed of their own class. We have a fine new example of pride in the enthusiasm, during the last few decades, of Americans for their racial and ethnic origins. All Miss Manners is asking is that people who now own up proudly to their grandparents be willing to own up to their parents, as well.

The last rule is the most important of all. Miss Manners will not tolerate the classes' taunting one another in any way. Not even at recess.

~ On Making Others Comfortable ~

At a great London banquet, dear Queen Victoria lifted her finger bowl and drank the water. She had to. Her guest of honor, the Shah of Persia, had done it first.

At a Washington embassy dinner party, the king of Morocco plunged his fingers into his teacup and wiped them on his napkin. He had to. His guest of honor, President Kennedy, had done it first.

Then there was the time that Mrs. Grover Cleveland attempted to engage a tongue-tied guest in conversation by seizing on the nearest thing at hand, an antique cup of thinnest china. "We're very pleased to have these; they're quite rare and we're using them for the first time today," she is supposed to have said.

"Really?" asked the distraught guest, picking up his cup and nervously crushing it in his hand.

"Oh, don't worry about it," said the hostess. "They're terribly fragile—see?" She smashed hers.

Mr. Grover Cleveland, on another social occasion, carefully added sugar and cream to his coffee, stirred it and poured some into his saucer. Observing this, all his guests felt obliged to do the same. There they all were, pouring their coffee into their saucers, when the President leaned down and put his saucerful on the floor for his dog.

Miss Manners relates these alarming incidents to illustrate a great danger. It is not the peril of serving watery tea, engaging in diplomacy with foreigners, permitting dogs in dining rooms or other such grand-scale hijinks. It is the terrible burden one assumes when attempting the practice of Making Others Feel Comfortable.

Miss Manners is sensitive to this because she often hears the great and subtle art of etiquette described as being "just a matter of making other people feel comfortable." As if etiquette weren't magnificently capable of being used to make others feel uncomfortable.

All right. Miss Manners will give you an example, although you are spoiling her Queen Victoria mood: If you are rude to your ex-husband's new wife at your daughter's wedding, you will make her feel smug. Comfortable. If you are charming and polite, you will make her feel uncomfortable. Which do you want to do?

～ On Making Others Uncomfortable ～

Miss Manners cannot be expected to experience embarrassment firsthand, but it is something for which she has a moderate amount of sympathy. The correct use of embarrassment is as a conscience of manners. As your conscience might trouble you if you do anything immoral, your sense of embarrassment should be activated if you do anything unmannerly. As conscience should come from within, so should embarrassment. Hot tingles and flushes are quite proper when they arise from your own sense of having violated proper standards, inadvertently or advertently.

However, Miss Manners hereby absolves everyone from feeling any embarrassment deliberately imposed by others. The less scrupulous of those who sell wedding or funeral services try to embarrass people with the suggestion that anyone who cares about the bridal couple or the recently deceased will "spare no expense," an emotional non sequitur if ever there was one. The same tactic has been adopted by other professions. The whole posture of being what is termed, in the vernacular, "snooty" is cultivated by those wily headwaiters, real estate salespeople, boutique clerks and others who hope to embarrass honest customers into spending more than they wish to spend.

This should be seen as a commercial ploy, not a challenge of manners. It is perfectly good manners to check over one's bill and ask for an explanation if it seems to be wrong; it is good manners to spend what one wishes to spend and not what one doesn't want to or cannot afford; and it is good manners to ask for what is coming to one if it does not seem to be forthcoming. What is dreadful manners is to attempt to embarrass anyone into spending money. That is a matter that ought to make those who practice it feel horribly embarrassed.

～ On Improving Others ～

As if self-improvement weren't bad enough, we now have a world full of new, improved people who are ready to move on to improving others. This had better stop before there are no good people left, to say nothing of no decent social intercourse.

Miss Manners has been accosted by a variety of people who do missionary work under the pretense of friendship, generously spreading their newly acquired insights in the hope of making others as attractive as themselves. There are those who offer to explain to Miss Manners how to deal with her guilt, although guilt is an emotion unknown to Miss Manners, who took the simple precaution of always doing everything right. Others want to teach her to be free of her inhibitions. Miss Manners does have a few inhibitions, as it happens, but she needs them and is, if anything, hoping to develop a few more. People have even offered to help Miss Manners find God, Who Miss Manners hadn't realized was lost.

The zeal of such people is so great that they will spare nothing, not even the feelings of those they want to save, in this quest to make others feel good. If you are skeptical about their solutions working for you, they affect a patronizing smile and say, "That's the way I felt once." If you protest that you have no problems, they offer to help you with the problem of not being able to recognize your problems. If you admit that you are happy, they reply, "Ah, but perhaps you only think you are happy." What the difference is between being happy and thinking yourself happy Miss Manners has never been able to figure out.

⌒ On De-proving Others ⌒

"Relax!"

"Don't go to so much trouble!"

"Why don't you use plastic glasses?"

"Take off your jacket!"

"Why don't you use paper napkins?"

"Don't be so formal!"

"Sit down!"

"Why don't you use paper plates?"

"You don't have to impress us!"

Guests who make such remarks to their hosts must fondly imagine the effect they produce:

"Whew," the host must think. "I don't have to strain myself pretending to be something I'm not. These people love me just as I am, without all this fancy stuff."

Or maybe not. Miss Manners is afraid that the effect might be more like this:

"Try and do something nice for people, and look what you get. They come into my house, call me pretentious to my face, criticize my stuff, complain about the way I do things, bark orders at me and try to foist their own slobby standards on me. How would they like it if I came to their houses and suggested that they try a little harder?"

Yet the Etiquette-Busters are out in full force. If they attack their own friends who are in the very act of showing them hospitality, you can imagine that no one is safe. Not even little children, whom they taunt for politeness and tempt to rudeness:

"Did your mother make you wear that?"

"Don't call me 'Mr.,' that's my father."

"You don't have to thank me."

"You must be bored having to listen to the adults."

"'Ma'am'? Do I look that old?"

"I bet you'd rather be watching television."

What is the problem here? Could it be, Miss Manners wonders, that they fear that the world is not rude and crude enough as it is? And believe that it is their mission in life to stamp out niceties wherever they find them?

Miss Manners has heard of motives that are more altruistic, if no more attractive.

The face-value one is, indeed, that they are saving their friends trouble and rescuing them from false values. The presumption that nobody really likes doing things "nicely" is paired with the revelation that nobody—or at least not they—even likes to have things done this way for them by others.

In countermanding the courtesies that children exhibit, the idea is to form a sympathetic alliance with children against their parents' strictures. Whether this stems from a belief in preserving the natural soul from civilization or is merely a grab for popularity with the young, the effect is to undermine the parents and confuse the children.

A wider argument is sometimes made on behalf of an element of society other than the parties directly involved. "It intimidates people," the critics will say of those benighted folks who, unlike themselves and the criticized, are too primitive to be exposed to any but the crudest way of doing things. These people are not up to being treated with any luxuries, so it is considered a kindness to hold back on them.

But sometimes one hears an Etiquette-Buster's confession that rings true: "You make me feel guilty." I'm not going to bother, this argument goes, so we need to lower the standard so I don't look bad.

∼ On Correcting Others ∼

Can Miss Manners, whose vocation, whose calling, is correcting etiquette transgressions, condemn the practice? Certainly.

Miss Manners corrects only upon request. Then she does it from a distance, with no names attached, and no personal relationship, however distant, between the corrector and the correctee. She does not search out errors like a policeman leaping out of a speed trap. When Miss Manners observes people behaving rudely, she behaves politely to them, and then goes home and snickers about them afterward. That is what the well-bred person does. The only way to enjoy the fun of catching people behaving disgustingly is to have children. One has to keep having them, however, because it is incorrect to correct grown people, even if you have grown them yourself. This is the mistake that many people make when they give helpful criticism to their children-in-law, who arrive on the scene already grown.

Miss Manners is constantly besieged by people who want to know the tactful manner of pointing out their friends' and relatives' inferiorities. These people, their loved ones report to Miss Manners, chew with their mouth open, mispronounce words, talk too loudly, crack their knuckles, spit, belch and hum tunelessly to themselves. They have bad breath and runs in their stockings. They are too fat, dress badly and do their hair all wrong.

How can those who love these people dearly, for reasons that are not clear, and who wish to help them, for reasons that unfortunately are clear, politely let them have it?

The answer is that they cannot, certainly not politely. There are times, in certain trusting relationships, when one can say, "Cracking your knuckles drives me up the wall and if you do it one more time I'll scream," or "Have a mint—there's something wrong with your breath," or "What's that thing on your left front tooth?" No reasonable person should take offense at these remarks. Because they are so frank, they do not seem to carry a history of repulsion long predating the offense. Also, they deal with matters that are more or less easily correctable (although Miss Manners knows some determined knuckle-crackers she suspects aren't half trying to stop), and which it is plausible to assume the offenders hadn't noticed.

What is unacceptable is to criticize things a person cannot easily remedy or may not want to. People who you think are too fat either disagree about what too fat is, are trying to do something about it, or are not trying to do something about it. In no case is it helpful for them to know that other people consider them too fat.

Even if it be proven that the mistakes of others come from gross ignorance or from maliciousness, it is not the place of anyone except God, their mothers or Miss Manners to bring this to their attention. As dear Erasmus said, "It is part of the highest civility if, while never erring yourself, you ignore the errors of others." Besides, it is a law of nature that he who corrects others will soon do something perfectly awful himself.

On Profiting from Others

"I'll scrub floors before I'll accept charity."

"We may be poor, but we have our pride."

"I've always been independent, and I always will be."

"Thank you, but I wouldn't dream of taking your money. I'm sure I'll manage."

"I may not be legally responsible, but I consider this a debt of honor, and I'll pay off every cent if I die in the attempt."

"I don't accept tips."

When was the last time you heard any of these statements? If ever. The young must think that allowing pride to trump avarice dates back to a long-distant age of romance and stupidity.

Miss Manners does not exactly complain that she misses what were, after all, responses to difficult, perhaps tragic, circumstances. But she sorely misses the quaint attitude they represented. The rapidity with which begging and bankruptcy shed any sense of shame and took on an air of insouciant cleverness astonishes her.

In the social realm, pleading financial need and requesting assistance have become so commonplace that the techniques are cited as "traditional" by the clueless, as well as by the financially irresponsible. Not a day goes by that Miss Manners doesn't receive several questions about how to do something—throw a party, take a trip, buy household items, entertain in a restaurant—that the writer states being unable to afford.

Various schemes are proposed, with the expectation that Miss Manners will explain the proper way to do them. How do you politely tell your guests to give you money so you can buy what you want? What is the correct wording to invite people while letting them know that they are supposed to pay? How do you graciously state your desire that guests contribute payments toward your vacation or house?

Miss Manners' favorite Scheme of the Week is a postal card sent to members of a church congregation asking them to celebrate the marriage of their pastor with "monetary gifts for the honeymoon. If you like, do it anonymously to eliminate the need for thank you cards." She can't wait to hear his sermon about how charity begins at home. Or the one on gratitude.

Nevertheless, Miss Manners saw it all coming. Once the commercial gift registry (originally kept only in case customers inquired about a bride's silver or china pattern) expanded to put generosity under the control of its beneficiary, the rest was inevitable. Now would-be beneficiaries are saving others the trouble of volunteering by listing demands—whether directly or through web sites, gift registries and notations on invitations—without waiting to be asked.

Stripping sentiment from the custom of giving presents naturally prompted the question of why the giver should be entrusted—or encumbered, depending on the degree of hypocrisy exercised—with the purchasing. It is all very smart to sneer at the notion that it is the thought that counts, brazenly declaring that no, it's the take that counts. But the whole symbolic basis of exchanging presents, hospitality and favors refers to our longing to be noticed thoughtfully by others. (True, the possibility of error is always there, which is why etiquette allows thoughtfulness to be assisted by sneaky tactics. If observation fails to suggest what presents might be welcome, it is fair to ask people who are in a better position to observe. If that doesn't work, the unfortunate present may be discreetly exchanged, sold or given away after thanks have been rendered.)

The next step was for the recipient to examine overhead costs involved in entertaining the donors, which would have to be subtracted from the take. Prospective guests often ask Miss Manners whether etiquette requires that the cost of a present be dictated not by their resources or impulses, but by the amount spent on their food and drink. Hosts, especially those who like to entertain at places they frankly announce they cannot afford, are inclined to see these as two different obligations, and ask how to explain that the guests should both pay their own way and give a (directed) present.

But why bother with guests at all? The virtual community is larger and less trouble than the relatives and friends upon whom self-fundraisers had been drawing. The pioneers in using the Internet to ask strangers for money patterned themselves on the causes of reputable charity—such as donating toward education or helping the ill—except for designating themselves the sole beneficiaries. A breakthrough was achieved when it was discovered that asking for money for luxuries also brought results.

These practices are no less vulgar for having become commonplace. There is no polite way to tell people to give you money or objects, and no polite way to entertain people at their expense. Begging is the last resort of the desperate, not a social form requiring others to help people live beyond their means. Miss Manners fails to understand why philanthropists would turn from the needy to the greedy, but she is not in the business of laundering rudeness to make it seem acceptable.

Gentle Readers Wrestle with Philosophical Problems Arising from the Great Study of Manners

DEAR MISS MANNERS:
Who says there is a "right" way of doing things and a "wrong"?

GENTLE READER:
Miss Manners does. You want to make something of it?

ON MANNERS AND MORALS

~ *Talking Back* ~

DEAR MISS MANNERS:

I've been told that etiquette is used as a means to exclude "outsiders," i.e., those not in the class of the group that observes certain etiquette rules. If I were to attend a function hosted by an upper class group, I would not know all of the etiquette rules and everyone would know I was not a member of that social status. To me, that makes etiquette rules seem mean and snobby, which would make etiquette unmannerly. Therefore etiquette is rude, isn't it?

GENTLE READER:

Nice try. If etiquette is rude, Miss Manners really ought to apologize for coercing people into behaving better than their etiquette-free instincts—such as running slow drivers off the road, and demanding that people send them cash for getting married—dictate.

But wait. Apologizing is also an invention of etiquette. So what she should really tell you is to—never mind. Being terminally polite, she can't bring herself to say anything of the kind.

It is true that specific forms of etiquette vary enormously among societies and subsets of society. If you were to attend a function in a foreign country, or if you were to attend a teenagers' club meeting, you probably wouldn't know the etiquette rules either. If any of those people attended a function of yours, they probably wouldn't know the rules by which you operate, consciously or not.

This hardly means that everybody else's customs exist to make you feel bad. If you want to participate in a group with whose behavior you are unfamiliar, then you should make the effort to learn it.

Here is a major etiquette rule you need to learn right now: The use of specialized knowledge of whatever kind to embarrass those who cannot be expected to know it is an etiquette violation. This is why we have a rule that the lapses of newcomers who are making an honest effort—including young children, by the way—should not be an excuse to humiliate them.

Looking Back

DEAR MISS MANNERS:

Sometimes I wish we were back in 18-something where everyone was mindful of their manners. I'm a 21-year-old woman and even though I love to joke around and be mannerless with my friends, I still enjoy politeness. I'm writing you for advice on how to be goofy and classy at the same time. And also how to extract manners from other people. People nowadays don't think its necessary to be polite, they consider it "old fashioned."

GENTLE READER:

You weren't around in 18-something, were you? Not even in novels or history books?

Much as we would love to believe that we saucy and imaginative moderns are responsible for introducing misbehavior into a previously fun-free world, Miss Manners is afraid that the population, even back then, consisted of actual human beings. Some of them behaved none of the time and the rest behaved some of the time.

Perhaps you misunderstand what manners and etiquette are. Surely you do not mean to say that you are mannerless with your friends. Do you shove them out of the way to get to the food? Do you tell them they are boring you and you wish they would go home? Do you respond to their problems by saying, "So what?"

Miss Manners doubts it. Some people do, perhaps the very people about whom you are complaining, but they tend not to have friends. She suspects you mean that you and your friends tease one another in ways you know will not hurt, and that when you get together, you dress, eat and speak in ways you would not do, even with them, on formal occasions such as their weddings or their relatives' funerals.

In other words, you observe informal etiquette on informal occasions. That is perfectly consistent with being mannerly, which means showing respect and consideration for others while practicing the etiquette—the specific rules on how to do this—that apply to the particular situation and era in which you find yourself.

What bothers you is that many people do not. Miss Manners has not failed to notice this either, which is why she has devoted her career to urging them to do so. On a nonprofessional level, one can only properly do this by example—the example of behaving politely yourself and of avoiding those who do not.

It is true that there are etiquette rules that have been updated, so that the principles on which they are based are served in different ways. We no longer spend the morning calling upon others, hoping not to find them in so that we can just leave engraved cards and get credit for touching base. Instead, we call around leaving voice mail, hoping their telephones are turned off so that we can just leave messages and get credit for touching base.

But Miss Manners supposes that what you are hearing is that while your obligations to others are not in question, their reciprocal duties—including thanking and reciprocating—have expired. The people who tell you that are not etiquette historians; they are just plain, old-fashioned rude.

~ *A Rule of Thumb* ~

DEAR MISS MANNERS:

Do you have any guidelines that will help me to feel correct in all situations?

GENTLE READER:

Yes, two, both of which were given to her by her Uncle Henry when Miss Manners was a mere slip of a girl. They have served her well in all the vicissitudes of life ever since. They are:

1. Don't.
2. Be sure not to forget to.

2. *Birth*

Prebirth Manners for Parents and Others

LONG AGO, ladies who found themselves in a delicate condition were supposed to refer to it, sartorially as well as conversationally, only with the greatest delicacy. And if young people today can't even imagine what is meant by "a delicate condition"—well, that was the idea.

Naturally, people today regard this as an insult to motherhood, womanhood and everyone else in the 'hood. Childbirth itself being natural, why shouldn't it be out in the open? After all, the event that led up to it pretty much is.

Miss Manners can think of a reason that birth parties for friends are not in the best of taste: They interfere with the decorum that requires ladies who are appearing in company to keep their ankles demurely crossed. She also retains the prudery of believing that expectant mothers, no matter how justifiably proud of their expectations, should be discouraged from posing nude for general distribution.

However, she finds herself surprisingly charmed by the new maternity fashions that are more up front, so to speak, than in previous eras. Formerly, the declared purpose of such wardrobes was to hide the condition. The unfortunate tactic employed was to cover the lady in question with what appeared to be great rolls of wallpaper left over from decorating the nursery. This was a failure, both aesthetically and as camouflage.

Dresses, trousers, sweaters and blouses that frankly follow the emergent shape but are otherwise unexceptionable are surely an improvement. (That qualifier should be noted, however. The belly button is mistaken if it thinks itself a treat for all eyes, and displaying the place it has disappeared along a stretched belly is not an improvement.)

Frank discussions are another matter. The reticence by parents-to-be in talking about pregnancy has disappeared, but this had a purpose beyond protecting innocent children from speculating about where babies come from. It helped protect innocent mothers from adults not only speculating about where these particular babies have come from, but asking the mother, as well as offering her scary warnings, making horrid remarks and poking and patting the work in progress.

There is no barrier left—certainly not taste—to inhibit the curious from annoying pregnant ladies, now that the social silence on this subject is gone. The most these only-too-obvious targets can hope to do is to freeze out their tormentors by refusing to make the subject of pregnancy open to discussion. Not announcing it with startling immediacy to anyone except one's intimates is a start. Those who need to know before they can see for themselves, such as prospective grandparents and supervisors who need to schedule maternity leave, should be told in confidence. Others can wait until the second trimester.

The late announcement also puts some distance between the fact of the pregnancy and the visual associated with its cause. A lady should take time to comb her hair before she announces her pregnancy. Not only can this cut a good three months off the time of public attack, but it saves making emotionally difficult explanations if anything goes wrong.

Once the pregnancy is observable, it means curbing one's natural exuberance and limiting the conversation to saying how happy one is and how fine one feels. (The version of the latter suitable for use by those being sick all over the place is, "Oh, I'm a little uncomfortable, but basically I'm fine, thanks.") Never mind that the answer "We're so happy" does not exactly address the question "was this intentional?" and that "I'm fine, thanks" is an odd answer to "How come you're so huge?" It is time to learn that one does not have to explain everything—prenatal practice for saying, "Because I say so, that's why."

Remarks about women's breasts are as vulgar at this time as at any other, and unsolicited appraisal of the fruitful body is no more adorable than other such critiques. Patting the pregnant stomach is in the same category as other bodily contact: except for the prospective father, who has reason to assume that his advances are acceptable, no one may be certain, without inquiring, that physical attentions are welcome. Such people should be told that you will be glad to let them hold the baby if they will be kind enough to wait until it is born.

Naturally, carrying a baby about under one's dress is an open invitation for advice from everyone. If a lady does not want others to tell her how to run her life, she should not be having a baby, because it is only a matter of a few years before that baby will consider this one of his or her chief duties.

∼ *Proper Responses* ∼

DEAR MISS MANNERS:

When I was growing up, I was always taught that "Congratulations!" was the proper response upon learning that a woman was pregnant. Even if the mother-to-be was being forced by her family to marry the seventeen-year-old father, one was supposed to rejoice with her in the creation of a new life and utter disapproving remarks about modern morality well out of her hearing. What I need to know, Miss Manners, is has this rule of polite behavior changed?

I am twenty-nine and am more than five months pregnant. My husband and I are looking forward with joy and excitement to the birth of our first child. When casual acquaintances and colleagues at work learn of my condition, however, their typical response is to open their eyes wide and blink at me, saying "Oh!" or "Well!" After a few moments of awkward silence, I feel compelled to assure them that yes, it was wanted and, of course, planned. At this point, the startled listener has recovered enough to mumble, "Well, good!" still staring in confusion and embarrassment.

What is the correct response upon learning that a woman is expecting a child?

Have you any snappy comebacks which would serve to alert the other person(s) that the situation suits me fine and I don't wish to pursue its more personal aspects casually? I tried telling one woman that my husband and I were appalled by the high cost of meat and were growing our own, but this just prolonged the blinking stage.

GENTLE READER:

First, congratulations. Miss Manners is very happy for you. She is also puzzled to find that it is usually the same people who claim to have a special interest in sex who are most horrified by its natural consequence.

Too bad for them. Miss Manners happens to believe that children are a joy (if you have no descendants, how do you expect to have the pleasure of being an ancestor?) but has no wish to force her views on others and is, in fact, reassured by the idea that people who don't want children often don't have them.

The best you can do at the moment is to alert people to the fact that you consider it a matter for congratulation by saying "I'm so thrilled" when you speak of your pregnancy. Soon you will be too busy to care.

DEAR MISS MANNERS:

What do you say to congratulate a friend on a pregnancy that you know was an unwanted accident? A friend of mine who has three small children had been planning to return to school as soon as her youngest was in school himself. Now she is pregnant again. When she told me about it, she did not look like the picture of a joyous young madonna, to say the least. Apparently she is not considering abortion, but I can tell that she is resentful. In fact, she kept saying to me things like, "We certainly didn't plan on this," and "I can't face doing diapers again." Do I try to talk her into being more accepting, or do I commiserate with her, or what?

GENTLE READER:

Contrary to the credo of this society, Miss Manners firmly believes that there are certain honest, understandable, deeply felt emotions that ought never to be expressed by anyone. First among them is that one does not want a child one is going to have.

It is a sad fact of nature that such a statement, unlike other carelessly confided remarks, will never be forgotten. One day, someone who heard it will repeat it to the child, and it will poison whatever maternal devotion the reluctant mother may have lavished from that moment on. Any sensitive person can understand that it is possible for a good woman to feel negative or ambivalent about being pregnant.

The best thing to do when someone has spoken the unspeakable is to fail to hear it. The greatest kindness you can do your friend is to pretend that you do not understand, or even catch, her feelings. When the baby is born, treat it as a joyous event. By that time your friend's feelings may have come around to that view; if not, at least you will be expressing the sentiments of a brand-new friend, who will be badly in need of someone to share them.

DEAR MISS MANNERS:

I have a sister who has told other siblings that she plans on being artificially inseminated this year. I cannot think of anything polite to say about this, as for a variety of reasons:

I think my sister will make a horrible parent. I do not want to give her the impression that I approve of her having a child, but she is my sister and I don't want to alienate her. What can I say without being rude when she tells me she is pregnant?

GENTLE READER:

"Congratulations."

~ *Improper Responses* ~

DEAR MISS MANNERS:

I am happily pregnant with my first child. Until recently, people around me have been blissfully (to me) unaware of my condition, and I heard nothing but congratulations from those with whom I decided to share my good news.

However, since I have begun to "show" the signs of pregnancy, I have run into a certain group of people I will call the "Pregnancy Police." These people, whether I know them or not, have no qualms about coming up to me and telling me I should not be drinking my coffee, eating my chocolate, or enjoying my hot dog.

I am an educated and informed adult who has thoroughly researched all of my pregnancy-related decisions, and am doing what I and my doctor think is best for my unborn child. What can I say to these people that will fall far short of how rude I secretly wish to be?

GENTLE READER:

Let's skip ahead for a minute, to when your child is socially active. If you catch him being rude and he points to his target and says, "She started it," are you going to reply, "Oh, in that case, go ahead"?

Granted, you had already decided not to be rude. Please forgive Miss Manners for not being able to resist enforcing that point. So now let's skip ahead to where your child thinks he knows how to run the family better than you do. This is not as far off as you might imagine. Some time between the stage when you say, "I'm the mommy around here" and the one where you realize he knows more about computer programming or tax law than you do, you will learn to listen patiently, thank him for his suggestions and go right ahead doing what you had already decided. You might as well start developing this now.

DEAR MISS MANNERS:

My sister has recently given birth to her fourth daughter. It's no secret that they were trying for a boy, and yet I know it hurts her when people keep mentioning this fact when they come to visit the new baby. I mean, she's not going to send it back, so what's the point?

GENTLE READER:

Indeed, but what was the point in her expressing her preferences beforehand? Unless there is a throne to be filled, the official position of prospective parents should always be that they don't care which sex the baby is. (The phrase "so long as it's healthy" is an optional extra.) However untrue this may be, there is nothing to be gained by stating the first choice. Refusing to do so may discourage rude postnatal evaluations on the part of others. It will also deprive the baby of a lifetime of attributing her every discontentment to the idea that "I was supposed to be a boy."

DEAR MISS MANNERS:

I've just found out I am pregnant. Of course I'm keeping my job and I'm insulted by people who would presume to ask the question. Men don't get asked that question. In fact, my husband's salary is roughly half of mine, so if anyone were going to stay home, it would be him, not me.

How can I answer this very intrusive question?

I'd like people not to make the assumption that I would be the one staying home. Even people who know me and our financial situation quite well (like my sister) have asked this question. What can I say?

GENTLE READER:

You can say, "Yes, I'm taking a short maternity leave and then I'll be back at work."

Miss Manners considers herself alert to nosy questions and to patronizing questions, but neither of these sounds an alarm. What would be both nosy and patronizing would be if people assumed, as you seem to, that spouses rate each other by earning power and the loser has to stay home with the child.

DEAR MISS MANNERS:

A very close couple of friends of my husband and myself just had a baby boy. Their new baby has a rare birth defect, and is currently blind and there is seemingly little hope that he will ever have vision. Do we still send them a congratulatory card and buy a baby gift to celebrate his arrival? We don't want to send the wrong message, yet we do want to help them celebrate the joy of their first child.

GENTLE READER:

Trying to imagine what "wrong message" it would possibly send to congratulate your very close friends and give the baby a present has upset Miss Manners dreadfully.

In spite of your acknowledgment that you should be rejoicing with them, you seem to be suggesting that a baby with a birth defect somehow doesn't count, and that it might be tactful not to notice his birth.

This is a horrid thought, and Miss Manners urges you to banish it. Your friends have a new baby. Tell them unreservedly that you are happy for them, and go over there and say "kitchy-kitchy-koo" to him.

Showers

~ Clouds ~

DEAR MISS MANNERS:

I'm in a quandary. I'm nearly seven months pregnant with my first child, and my friends have not hinted at a baby shower. I've already bought the basic furniture but wanted to shop earlier for other things as well. Should I be asking my best friend about this?

Also, in the past I'd been invited to showers by relatives of the mothers-to-be. Should I be inviting the people who invited me or the recipients to whom I gave the gifts to? Me and my husband have a budget so we cannot afford to invite everyone from the church that we attend!

GENTLE READER:

Miss Manners' response will help you with your budget. It is that you cannot properly give yourself a shower, your relatives should not be doing it either, nor should you be prodding your best friend to do so. Therefore, you can take the money you were going to spend and use it to buy the rest of the things you need for your baby. Then if anyone is planning to surprise you, you will have no trouble acting surprised—and, Miss Manners hopes, grateful.

~ Continuing Showers ~

DEAR MISS MANNERS:

Does it really matter if a friend gives a baby shower for someone who is having her second child? Isn't a baby shower just a nice thing to do for a friend? I find it hard to believe there could be a rule saying only the first child receives a shower.

GENTLE READER:

So does Miss Manners, who was a second child. However, there is a rule. If you will be patient while Miss Manners explains the reason for the rule, Miss Manners will help you circumvent it.

A shower is held for the purpose of showering a novice (at marrying or mothering) with the equipment she did not need in her previous state (of spinsterhood or childlessness) but which is essential in the life she is about to enter. That is why Miss Manners and her friends at college always gave "lingerie showers"; in those days, no nice girl needed pretty underwear before marriage. This is also why showers are not needed for women having their second, or eighth, babies. It is why members of the family are not supposed to give showers when they could just equip the honoree themselves and not ask her friends to do it.

However, it is a charming custom to entertain a lady who is about to do something again, even though she has a good idea of what it is all about. Miss Manners merely suggests you not call it a shower, and therefore get around the rule, while also leaving the question of presents vague so that the guest of honor is not trying the feelings of friends who attended earlier showers.

∼ *Thunderstorms* ∼

DEAR MISS MANNERS:

You seem intolerant—and justifiably so—of nonsense masquerading as correctness. But what about sexism and oppression disguised as polite tradition? I'm referring to wedding and baby showers. Do these traditions not have considerable sexist and oppressive components? Are they not designed to reinforce women who accept the roles society deems most acceptable for women, rewarding them with vacuum cleaners, kitchen utensils, and baby paraphernalia when they assume their rightful roles as wives and mothers?

Are you sympathetic to such thinking? How should a person with such views respond to an invitation to attend a shower? A simple "No, thank you" seems too unfriendly or, worse, cheap. A political discussion is probably counter-productive.

GENTLE READER:

Few of our social institutions can bear severe philosophical scrutiny. Neither can using an invitation to participate in other people's pleasures as an opportunity for dampening them with one's disapproval. It is not impolite simply to decline an invitation that goes against your principles, provided you do not explain that fact.

In the matter of showers, things are changing. Miss Manners can't help noticing that your signature indicates that you are a man, and pointing out that a few years ago you would not have been invited to showers. Presumably, the bridegroom or father will also be a guest of honor at such a shower, and your present should be given to both husband and wife. Vacuum cleaners and baby clothes are not, in themselves, sexist objects. They become so when it is presumed that only the woman should put them on the rug or the baby.

(For bridal showers, please see p. 365.)

DEAR MISS MANNERS:

My unmarried niece gave birth to a little girl last month. Earlier in her pregnancy, her family sent out invitations for a baby shower. Since she lives several states away, I sent a monetary gift and received a lovely thank-you note in return. I was later quite surprised to learn the baby was given up for adoption. Is it appropriate to have a shower when the baby is to be given up for adoption? If this was a last minute decision, should I not have been sent a note of explanation? I do not wish my gift returned, I just feel as if I should have been informed.

GENTLE READER:

As a matter of family news, Miss Manners agrees that you should have been informed, but you seem to relate this courtesy to your contribution to the shower. That is a mistake: The baby was born, you gave her a present and you were graciously thanked. Now—could we not look too closely into the question of whether there should have been a shower? The decision about adopting might have been made subsequently, as you realize. But even if not, perhaps your niece simply craved this small ritual and wanted to send the child off with things from her family. Miss Manners is not able to grudge her that.

Announcements

— Vivid Announcements —

DEAR MISS MANNERS:

I received several emails (as one of over 50 on the address list of family, friends, neighbors, and co-workers) during a friend's admission to the hospital and through her labor. I assume the expectant father had a laptop at the hospital.

I read more details than I cared to know, and I about got ill when the email regarding the mother's delivery mentioned that she was doing well but suffered a vaginal tear and episiotomy. Whatever happened to the long-awaited phone call stating "It's a boy"?

The baby and mother are home and doing well, and I am very happy for them and their family and share in the excitement—but now we receive weekly emails with pictures to be downloaded. This is a special time in their lives, I know, but I think that the new parents might want to cool it.

I hope that people will think about what they are sharing with the world before they punch the address book button and send personal information to their entire list. Our mothers' custom of sending out birth announcements via snail mail was a nicer touch than these mass produced communications, and I prefer getting an annual card with a picture of the kids instead of weekly downloads. Am I just being too prudish and old-fashioned?

GENTLE READER:

Here's what happened to "It's a boy":

They already told you. Don't you remember, weeks ago, receiving an email with a prenatal picture pointing out the telltale sign? While all of this is on a taste level with publicizing the conception, Miss Manners trusts you have resisted the temptation to go along with the idea of sharing symptoms by emailing back a picture of your reaction.

~ Proper Birth Announcements ~

DEAR MISS MANNERS:

Even though our baby's due date is three months hence, we have begun to inquire about birth announcements. (We may not need them if you reply in the negative.) I have been informed that the proper announcement is as follows:

Baby Newborn Couple
Birth date
Mr. and Mrs. Happy New Couple

These are separate cards, joined with a pink or blue ribbon, whichever is appropriate. Unfortunately, the company that engraves these announcements takes four weeks. The only other company that does the new "pseudo engraving" cannot guarantee quality. Secondly, engraving costs four times what the other costs. We could

---

321 Primrose Path

Mr. and Mrs. Geoffrey Lockwood Perfect

We are delighted to announce the birth of our daughter, Daffodil Louise, on April first at Merciful Good Hospital.

The announcement of a birth, written on a married couple's engraved message card. (The card, which can also be made with the woman's name only from the same plate, may be used for any informal note, invitation, reply to an informal invitation or message accompanying flowers or a present.) Any plain or marked writing paper is suitable for announcing a birth, but in that case it must be written in the form of a letter. (Most people include the baby's birth weight; Mrs. Perfect omitted it because she does not care to have the Perfects judged by the pound. However, on some cards she included such additional comments as "She has the Perfect expression already!" or "Do come and see us at home next week.")

have a single sheet of paper pseudo-engraved with the words I previously wrote, and without the ribbon. A company could have them in approximately two weeks.

I realize that perhaps we shouldn't be having a baby if we have to ask how much birth announcements cost. However, being a young couple, money does enter into many of our decisions. Should we get as close to propriety as we can afford, or do nothing?

GENTLE READER:

Do go ahead and have the baby. Miss Manners is fond of babies, provided they don't leak on visitors, and to help you along in this venture will now save you a pile of money.

Order no announcements. The engraved baby announcement you describe is, in Miss Manners' opinion, a silly misuse of formality. The rationale is that the tiny card with the baby's name, attached to the parents' card, is the little one's "card," in case it should decide to pay formal calls or send flowers to hostesses. This is not only pretentious and expensive, but impractical, because, as you point out, it arrives so much later than the baby. A poor-quality substitute for it would be even sillier.

Nor is Miss Manners fond of informal, fill-in announcements which strain to be cute and which include a line for the baby's weight to show whether you have produced something substantial.

The solution is simple, gracious and cheap. Take a box of pretty paper to bed with you, and a roll of stamps. It is an agreeable and restful occupation to write brief letters to your friends, informing them that you have a new baby. Two lines are enough, and if you don't feel up to it, make the papa do it. The time involved is less than that for ordering or choosing cards. Now take that money you were to have given to the engravers and put it in a college fund for the baby.

DEAR MISS MANNERS:

I am expecting my first child, but I have been informed by a knowledgeable acquaintance that because I am an unmarried woman, I should not send out birth announcements when the baby arrives because, I guess, my situation is too shameful to be broadcast to my friends and family. Many of them already know, but perhaps they've been too kind to say anything.

This acquaintance also let me know that women in my condition do not get baby showers (really, I wasn't expecting a shower—a relative with small children has generously given me more baby things than I need).

I replied, "That's very interesting. Thank you."

I live in a liberal area, so my condition doesn't seem all that exceptional to me. Am I out of touch with the rest of the country's mores? Have I utterly disgraced myself? (I admit that part of me is looking for approval here, but part of me genuinely wants to know, so I can start working on the appropriate facial expressions.)

May I send out birth announcements when the baby arrives (it will be soon), or do I truly risk offending people with my brazen unmarried-mother-ness? As a side question, more than one person has commented on my future child's "illegitimacy." I have responded with a joking "Hey, if anyone is illegitimate here, it's me; let's not insult the baby!" Do you have a better response?

GENTLE READER:

As there are two parts of you, Miss Manners will address them separately. One part might be happier about that than the other.

The purpose of birth announcements is to announce the birth. (That needs to be said because there are those who believe that the purpose—probably of the birth, as well as of the announcement—is to extract presents.)

So of course you should announce the birth to anyone you think will be interested. Or perhaps to anyone you think will be not just interested, but pleased.

That brings us to the part of you looking for approval. Don't.

To do so is to acknowledge that others are invited to give their opinions—and you have already answered your question about whether mores have changed to the point that you can expect everyone's opinion to be favorable.

What you should expect is tolerance, and you are quite right to be insulted when you are the target of mean remarks. The reply to such is a frosty "How kind of you to point that out."

~ *Announcing Requests* ~

DEAR MISS MANNERS:

Is it considered good taste to send birth announcements? I am expecting my second child in June. I did not receive announcements from many of my friends for their first child and very few for the second. Is an announcement considered a request for a present?

GENTLE READER:

Only by the cynical, although Miss Manners realizes that this describes most of the population. No announcement, whether it is for a first or second child, first or second marriage or first or second attempt to be graduated, requires the recipient to send more than congratulations (please see "Presents," which begins on p. 614).

Failing to Announce

DEAR MISS MANNERS:

I am sorely puzzled. This past season, four different couples I know all produced their firstborn children. During the pregnancies, I asked at various times how the mother was, etc. But in each case, once the baby was born, no one bothered to let me know about the actual birth, and whether they had a boy or girl. Have birth announcements vanished from our culture? Is it proper to ask: "Did Marilyn finally have the baby?" I feel a bit put out at the parents in question for not letting me know of their blessed event.

GENTLE READER:

What has vanished is the simple, guileless note telling people something they might like to know. Why bring children into a world where no one writes letters?

The best way to find out is to tell an expectant father, "Please put me on your list of people to call when the baby is born." Telephoning is considered a new father's first duty. You take the risk of his assuming that you are awake when he is.

Otherwise, you can certainly ask, but do it kindly or you will some day ask with that "put-out" tone in your voice and be told, "The baby was stillborn." Miss Manners has her reasons for objecting to heavy sarcasm.

Names

ACCORDING TO the law, you may change your name at will, provided you do not do so with the intention of escaping justice. According to Miss Manners, you may change your name at certain specified times, provided you are merciful in judging those who have allowed the changes to escape them.

The wise parent will bestow an adolescent nickname upon an infant and a grown-up name upon a child. The tenderest of babies will soon sprout hair in unlikely places, and the gangliest of teenagers will some day sprout some unlikely desire for dignity. It is well to stay ahead in the nomenclature.

But ultimately, each person is responsible for fashioning his or her own name. The first opportunity comes with entry into the educational system. Anyone allowing himself to be announced at roll call in nursery school by the nickname his parents fashioned from his own inability to pronounce his name in infancy will be marked for life.

Daffodil Louise Perfect made the mistake, at the age of fourteen months, of referring to herself as "Doopsie" instead of employing the personal pronoun. Although her blood relatives will continue to call her this until the day she dies, partly from fondness, partly from bad memory and partly for the annoyance value, she had the sense to announce herself as Daffodil when she first went to school.

Two years later, another Daffodil showed up in her school as a transfer student, and Daffodil was told she had to be called Daffodil P., to distinguish her from Daffodil R. Our Daffodil did not like this one bit, but it opened to her a world of possibilities. At summer camp, she went for her middle name, and told everyone she was called Louise. That fall, she endeavored to get her old classmates to call her Lou, but, this not being as natural a breaking point as was camp, it didn't work. So she waited until she moved from lower school to middle school, and successfully grafted her new choice, becoming Daffodil-Lou.

Tiring of this as soon as it had taken, she tried to continue the evolution, but was unable to budge her teachers or classmates. Fortunately, the school tired of her at this time, and at boarding school she was able to effect a complete break and persuade everyone that she should be called Samantha.

After a year at Miss Waffles' School, she was sent home to complete her education at Midtown Country Day School, where her uncle was a benefactor, and there she began to style herself D. Louise. At the next changing point, entry into college, she became known as D. L., until her engagement, when she resumed the full dignity of Daffodil Louise. In tender moments, her fiancé called her his Doopsie. When they were divorced, she became Daffy, to her new friends.

You see here the possible, as well as the impossible, times that changes may be made in given names. And that's even without changing last names, through marriage, divorce, hyphenation and the desire to depart from, or return to, one's point of ethnic origin.

The general rule is that a change of location or legal status is always good for a fresh start, but that one cannot expect the same people to acknowledge more than one change each in given name and surname (and that many people will not be able to master even that). Grateful that her mother has made the transition from her infant nickname to her baptismal names and that her bridesmaids were able to memorize her married surname, Daffy accepts as a natural accompaniment to life's development that her chum from seventh grade still writes her as Daffy-Lou. It is only because of her own poor memory that she addresses this woman, now a federal judge, as Poo-Poo instead of Prudence.

There is nothing wrong with children playing with their names, provided that they clean up the mess when they are finished. Miss Manners even recommends that parents give their children the proper equipment—middle names, good combinations of initials, nicknames, names that have alternate spellings—to use when the children inevitably decide that they can no longer tolerate their childhood identities.

What Miss Manners objects to is grown-up people who continue to play with their names and then are insulted when their friends can't keep up with the changes. Changing names around always has been an American habit, but it's getting worse. Take, for example, a typical American family of four generations. The family's American history began with a man who Americanized his surname when he arrived and a woman whose last name reflects a misspelling by an immigration officer. In the next generation, there is a daughter who married three times, changing her name successively to the full name of each husband, preceded only by "Mrs."; and a son who is a movie star and was issued a completely new name when he signed a studio contract. After that, there is a daughter who has a hyphenated last name, consisting of her maiden name and her husband's last name. She is no longer married to him and has, in fact, married someone else, but she must retain that hyphenated name because she has made her professional reputation with it. Also in this generation is a son who has had an attack of ethnic nostalgia and changed his name to that of the family name in the old country. These people's children are already plotting to change their names because they have found that all the other children in their respective homerooms share the same names their parents thought were unique.

Miss Manners has decided, for the sake of order, to put some limits on all this.

Here are the new rules:

Up to the age of seventeen, children are allowed free play with their names. They are even allowed to change the names that end in *y* to *i* and vice versa, which of course they always do anyway.

Upon leaving high school, they must each pick a permanent first name. On beginning college or employment, they may tell everyone the new name, pretending they have always had it, but they are not allowed to chastise relations and childhood friends for using the old one.

When they either marry for the first time or settle on a first serious career, they must pick a permanent last name. It is wise not to associate these names with philosophies or spouses who are likely to prove fleeting, because this is the surname they must keep. Miss Manners suggests sticking to the original family surname—but in the female line. The basic family unit has now become the mother and children of whom she has been awarded custody, and it is simpler if they all have the same name and keep it, no matter who happens to join them later. The system of the matriarchal line worked fairly well in ancient societies, before women made the mistake of telling men that they had any connection with the production of children.

∽ *Continuing Names* ∽

DEAR MISS MANNERS:

Will you please settle two burning issues that recently arose in our family. The problems are as follows:

1. William Wellborn has a son, William Wellborn, Jr., who has a son William Wellborn, III. Young William, wishing to ensure his son's inheritance, names the first of his 2.3 children William Wellborn, IV. When William, Sr., passes on, how are the rest to be called? I believe the American custom is that the oldest living person of that name is William Wellborn, his son William, Jr., and so on. My interlocutor says that William, IV stays William, IV, even if he is the oldest living person of that name. I believe that the system of continuing Roman numerals from generation to generation should be reserved for reigning monarchs and that ordinal numbers are reserved for marquesses and the like. Will you please settle this?

2. William Wellborn marries Miss Elizabeth Gotbucks. She is Mrs. William Wellborn, and, upon his untimely death, so remains. If she wises up and divorces him, she is Mrs. Gotbucks Wellborn until her remarriage. When, if ever, is she Mrs. Elizabeth Wellborn? This is a matter of curiosity, not politics.

GENTLE READER:

Politics always enters into problems of nomenclature, and being a reigning monarch does not ensure a neat succession of Roman numerals. Just when you think it is perfectly clear that you are William III, for example, everyone starts calling you William and Mary.

In the examples you give of the proper names for non-reigning Americans, you are absolutely correct. The oldest living William Wellborn is numberless, and one starts counting junior, III, IV (or 3rd, 4th, a form Miss Manners prefers) and so on from there. You are also correct in your intimation that no one is ever correctly styled "Mrs. Elizabeth Wellborn," come death, divorce or famine.

However, let us now consider the politics of the matter. The above rules are correct. You know it and Miss Manners knows it. Popular opinion is often against us nevertheless, and the populace has a great deal to say about it, particularly when people are talking about their own names. Ask any reigning monarch whether it is safe to disregard public opinion.

Many men consider that the word indicating their place in the family line at birth is actually part of their full name; 4th gets used to being called 4th, and even if he is willing to become 3rd when great-grandpa dies, his father doesn't know what to do about his dear old widowed grandma, who has all those cards engraved Mrs. Grandpa, only to be told that that title now belongs to her daughter-in-law, the former Mrs. Jr., who never uses cards anyway, and what a waste of good money that would be. Such people may refuse to change, and you must respect their wishes, even if they start producing Williams the 12th.

Then there are the people who want to change when no change is necessary, as in the case of a widow who has always used her husband's name. And then (things are never simple when you are dealing with popular opinion) there are the people who, for a variety of reasons, dislike a traditional form (such as Mrs. Gotbucks Wellborn for a divorcée) or a useful modern form (such as Ms. Elizabeth Wellborn for a woman of whatever marital status who wishes to use her own name—please see p. 56). Such a person may insist on being addressed as Mrs. Elizabeth Wellborn, whether you and Miss Manners like it or not.

DEAR MISS MANNERS:

My grandfather, Thomas, lost his first son, whom he named Thomas. He named my father George after his bachelor brother who died at thirty. I am also named George. Question: Is my son George, III, or is he legitimately George, IV?

GENTLE READER:

If your father is alive and calls himself George II, your son is George IV, God save him. (God save Miss Manners too, who has a wastebasket full of sketches of your family tree.) However, commoners tend to get lopped off the tree when they die. Your father could therefore be George, senior, which would make you junior and your son III. If your father is dead, then you are senior and your son is junior. In any case, George IV was unquestionably legitimate, but the same unfortunately cannot be said of all of his children.

∽ Parents' Names ∽

DEAR MISS MANNERS:

My husband and I have been married almost two years. For personal, as well as professional, reasons, I didn't change my name when we married. We now have a child whose last name is a combination of my last name and my husband's, hyphenated.

My problem: Neither of our families fully approves of these circumstances, and therefore call not only me, but also our son, by the wrong name. How can I tactfully tell them I don't want our child growing up not knowing his or his mother's correct name?

GENTLE READER:

The important thing is for your child to grow up knowing that, as we live in confusing and changing times, and probably always will, it behooves us all to be flexible and tolerant. Your families are admittedly being inflexible, but this gives you the opportunity of setting an example of tolerance. Miss Manners does not doubt that your son will find out his name some time before he has to fill out his college entrance applications.

DEAR MISS MANNERS:

My twenty-year-old niece lives out of state and is doing the usual twenty-year-old things, college and all that. Last week, I got a casual letter from her mother, and, just as a mention, word that the niece is giving birth soon and "Harvey" and niece are very happy.

I seem to have missed out on some in-between events, except I now understand that Harvey is a forty-year-old divorced father of some others. Niece and Harvey's marital status is left hanging, but later news told me that they had a boy, and used Harvey's middle name and last name in the baby's name. My problem: I want to send a gift. Just looking at baby clothes is a lot of fun. But how to address the package? I feel funny calling my niece Mrs. Harvey Whatever. Miss sounds dumb for a new mother. And Ms. doesn't fit the bill, either. Help!

GENTLE READER:

Indeed, "Ms." does exactly fit the bill, in Miss Manners' opinion, as it was designed to skip over the question of whether a woman is married, which is apparently what you mean when describing your niece's behavior as "the usual twenty-year-old things . . . and all that." However, if you don't like it, Miss Manners will not attempt to force it on you. Instead, she will give you special dispensation to address the present to the baby himself, since you have been supplied with his name. Ordinarily, Miss Manners finds this rather too cute, but something tells her that your niece is not a stickler for formalities.

DEAR MISS MANNERS:

We are about to have our first child. I am fairly young, younger actually than my wife, and I think it would be appropriate for our child to call us by our first names. I had to call my father "Sir," and it didn't help the relationship any.

My wife has no strong objection to this, although she sometimes says she likes the thought of being somebody's "Mommy." We don't have to have matching titles, of course. She could be "Mommy" and I could be "Frank." But my in-laws have hit the ceiling. They maintain that it is bad taste for a child to call his father by his first name. I would appreciate your telling them that it is common enough these days to be considered proper.

GENTLE READER:

Indeed, a Mommy and Frank household is quite usual these days, but there is generally a Daddy and Jessica household for the same child somewhere else. Be prepared for people not so much thinking that you are young, but that you arrived late on the scene.

First names for parents are in vogue from time to time, as people think they sound sporty. Miss Manners has no violent objection to this on the grounds of etiquette, although she can't for the life of her see why a grown person would want to seek the semblance of equality with an infant or an adolescent, or, for that matter, an unruly middle-aged child.

Baptisms and Circumcisions

~ The Christening ~

THE CHRISTENING of newborn Christian babies is one of only two social events that most people have in a lifetime in which they can be both the undisputed center of attention and completely free from responsibility for either the arrangements or their own behavior. The second such event comes at the extreme other end of life.

The baby who is having a christening may cry and yell, turn purple in the face or drop off to sleep in the middle of the festivities—actions we have all been tempted to perform at other social events, but mustn't—without being disgraced.

The burden of behaving well thus falls on the parents, the godparents and the guests. What the parents must do, in addition to producing the baby, is to:

- Arrange with a clergyman the appropriate time and place for the ceremony. A church christening usually takes place during the church's off hours, although some churches also include them in Sunday services. A home christening, if permitted, requires that a formal table be set up with a bowl, usually silver, to be used as a font.
- Send out informal invitations—that is, individual letters giving the time, place and baby's name and a sentence of urging, such as "We hope you will be able to join us"; or the information may be written on the parents' card—to relatives and close friends. This is not an occasion for casual acquaintances.
- Give a small party afterward, such as a luncheon or tea party. Caudle, a hot eggnog punch, and white cake iced with the baby's initials or other such fancies are traditional, but most people prefer champagne to a heavy glug.
- Decorate the house in flowers and the baby in white. When the baby wears the traditional elongated christening dress, the whole thing takes on the charming look of a postscript to the wedding, or, as happens nowadays, a precursor.

- Choose the godparents from among their extremely close friends, whose general outlook on life they would not object to the baby's sharing.

The godparents' duties are to:

- Hold the baby at the christening.
- Present it with a present of some permanence, such as one of the many adorable silver objects of unknown utility on which names and the date can be engraved.
- Act as second-string parents to the child, providing moral and religious instruction, birthday and Christmas presents and asylum when the child has had a teenaged quarrel with its parents.

The duties of guests are to:

- Put on dressy street clothes (no black for women) and attend the ceremony and party.
- Declare convincingly that the baby, though alternately dozing noisily and yelling itself purple, is perfectly beautiful.

The Bris, Naming Ceremony and Circumcision

DEAR MISS MANNERS:

Can you tell us about the ritual of circumcision if our baby is a boy? When my husband was born, it was just done at the hospital, but we would like some celebration. Also, what about if it's a girl? We are joining a local synagogue, but I don't want to start out by asking questions whose answers the rabbi would expect us to know, and I also want to know about the rules of etiquette for making this a social occasion that everyone will enjoy.

GENTLE READER:

Well, not everyone. The Berith Milah, or Bris, like all the great ceremonies of life, is designed to be enjoyed by everyone except the guest of honor.

The actual circumcision could be done at a hospital, but as traditionally it must be performed on the eighth day after birth and as maternity wards no longer encourage lengthy confinements, this is not a down-the-hall convenience. One can return to the hospital and have the reception there, or, as is customary, do both at home.

Miss Manners needn't explain that this cannot be done for a girl. A daughter is formally named at services on the Sabbath after her birth, and you may give her a reception in the temple or at home afterward.

Since the baby will be your firstborn, a son may also have a Pidyon Raben ceremony, in which he is dedicated to the service of God and then redeemed by his parents. This, too, is followed by a reception. Only close friends and relatives are invited, and usually just wine and cake are served. This is to give your extended circle and the caterer time to prepare for the child's bar or bat mitzvah.

⟡ Age Requirement ⟡

DEAR MISS MANNERS:

What is the proper age for baptism?

GENTLE READER:

It varies, depending on a variety of factors. For example, have you just been born or were you born again?

Social Life Begins

~ *The Proper Infant* ~

SURELY WE are all agreed now that children cannot begin too young to learn manners. Miss Manners does not any longer expect an argument.

There used to be parents who believed that a child should be allowed to develop naturally, with no artificial standards of behavior imposed on his or her innocent instincts, but we have all had a gander at the results of that. A child who is able to express his true feelings without the restraints of convention is a menace to society, and Miss Manners trusts that no one will deliberately attempt to rear such a creature in the future.

That decided, when do we begin to torture the baby? The first formal social occasion in a person's life is generally the call that friends pay on him and his mother when they return from the hospital. Friends of the family customarily telephone as soon as they hear of the birth and ask when they may be permitted to visit, a request that should not be refused. Recent childbirth is no excuse for either participant to avoid social duties.

The round of visits to newly enlarged families can be charming if the baby understands the rules. Some allowances are made for error on account of the baby's youth and inexperience, but an ambitious baby will not count on excessive indulgence outside the immediate family. New parents can be of great assistance in displaying the baby to his best advantage. This does not include pretending to speak or write for the baby. Parents should never issue birth announcements or write letters of thanks that pretend to be coming directly from the baby; they should write in their own names on his or her behalf. Speaking for someone else is a vile practice that the baby will resent increasingly over the years.

One thing parents can do is to schedule visiting so that the baby's less attractive functions can be accomplished privately. Hours may be suggested by parents so that the baby has a decent chance of freshening up between onslaughts.

Unlike other members of the family, the newborn baby is permitted to sleep while visitors are present, and even to have a meal without offering whatever he is enjoying to everyone else. But he must be made to understand his obligation: to allow visitors to satisfy their curiosity as to his looks. For example, if he wishes to sleep on his stomach, he should turn his head toward the room so that he presents a three-quarter view of his face.

A child who is less than a month old is not expected to produce social smiles, but neither should he produce anything else with his mouth, such as food or excessive noise. He should expect to be passed around to visitors and should remember to bring some protective covering with him. Wetting or otherwise inconveniencing well-wishers is not a good way to begin a social career. He should never show a negative reaction to a compliment or a present. Crying in response to an innocent remark or shifting one's head when a new bonnet is placed there are both bad form. A baby who receives, say, a silver toothbrush with his initials on it, should never volunteer that he has one already or that he has no teeth.

Parents who think of these visits as occasions for encouraging their children to cater to the comforts of guests, rather than the other way around, will be getting their children off to a good beginning.

⟶ *The Beautiful Baby* ⟵

DEAR MISS MANNERS:

You wrote about visiting newborn babies, but you didn't say what the visitor should say if the baby is a mess. I mean, really ugly. I have seen some terrible looking babies, believe me. And there are the parents, standing there, waiting for me to say something. I heard someone suggest "My, that *is* a baby!" but that's an old one, and I think the parents are on to it. Can you suggest something for people who don't want to lie and say the baby is beautiful?

GENTLE READER:

It is not a lie. All babies and all brides are beautiful by definition. That is a fact of nature.

～ The Beautiful Adopted Baby ～

DEAR MISS MANNERS:

We have recently adopted a beautiful baby boy, whose arrival we happily announced, and many of our friends have sent him nice presents. But most of them behave embarrassingly when they come to visit. Some of them say, "Who does he look like?" and then stop short when they remember he's adopted. Others ask who his real parents are or make remarks that suggest that it must be a deep mystery where he came from. As a matter of fact, we know who his natural parents are, but we don't want to talk about them, and we find the term "real" insulting. Why do people behave so strangely with an adopted baby?

GENTLE READER:

Actually, people behave strangely, in one way or another, about any new baby, because there is so little to say about a person of such limited experience. After "How long were you in labor?" and "I think he has your eyes," neither of which is really first-rate conversation, there isn't much left to say, which is why people are at a loss with an adopted baby. As the standard comments are not much less dumb than the ones you are getting, you might as well accept the verbal paucity of the situation and resolve not to be offended. Telling people pleasantly that there are things you refuse to discuss with them sets an excellent example for your baby.

～ The Anonymous Baby ～

DEAR MISS MANNERS:

What do you do when you are talking to a friend who just had a baby, and all of a sudden you cannot remember the child's gender, let alone the name?

I don't mind admitting that I've forgotten a name so much, but you can't even ask "What's his name?" without running the risk of being wrong about the child's gender. It's possible to get around this by addressing the baby and saying, "Well, what's YOUR name?" but I find it a bit cutesy to talk to an infant like that.

GENTLE READER:

All newborn babies are cutesy by definition, and therefore may be correctly addressed as either "Sweetie Pie" or "Honey Bunch."

Furthermore, they never leap out at you shouting, "I bet you don't remember who I am!" Miss Manners thinks it a shame that they so quickly outgrow this polite restraint.

∽ *The Hungry Baby* ∽

DEAR MISS MANNERS:

What is your opinion of women who nurse their babies in public?

GENTLE READER:

Miss Manners is fully aware of what will follow her answer. Lactation apparently stimulates the flow of ink in the pen, and nursing mothers emit great cries about the naturalness and beauty of this function and therefore its appropriateness under any circumstances. These cries tend to be louder than the original cries of the babies.

Nevertheless, Miss Manners is against the public nursing of babies (or anyone else). There seems to be a basic confusion here between what is natural and/or beautiful, and what is appropriate in public. The two often have very little to do with each other. When people carry on about their right to perform perfectly natural functions in public, Miss Manners suspects them of wanting to add interest to functions normally of interest only to the participants, by performing them in unnatural settings.

DEAR MISS MANNERS:

I believe your opinion of breastfeeding in public was a bit simplistic in that it failed to distinguish between nursing per se and exhibitionism, which a minority of nursing mothers practice while they feed their babies. It is hard to understand why you would oppose discreet public breastfeeding (it can easily be done so discreetly that the only obvious sign of it is the swallowing noise) any more than you would oppose bottle feeding in public. I feel etiquette is rather poorly served by social pressure either to bottle-feed (known to be nutritionally and medically inferior to breastfeeding) or to remove oneself from society.

GENTLE READER:

Miss Manners knew, when she took up the subject of public breast-feeding, that she was going to end up accused of depriving hungry infants of warmth, love and sustenance. This was not her intention. Nor does saying a thing is inappropriate in public constitute "social pressure" against its being performed at all; if so, the human race would have ended some time ago.

Exposing the female breast for any purpose other than getting a suntan on southern French beaches is considered an exhibition, which is not to say it should not be done when that is the intent. You are asking about mothers whose intent is only to feed their babies. In that case, Miss Manners' only objection about doing it discreetly is the fear that babies don't breathe well under ladies' sweaters.

～ *The Soiled Baby* ～

DEAR MISS MANNERS:

My mother-in-law and I had always been friends until my baby was born. It seems mom-in-law excels in giving advice, and though I appreciate some helpful hints, I'm up to my diaper pins in hers.

I admit that she slowly needles me into feeling totally inadequate. (I have a degree in child care.) Now, for the nitty-gritty. Is it proper to change one's baby in mixed company? I feel there is nothing vulgar about diapering; m-in-l swiftly disagrees. In fact, she goes as far as snatching my naked child away from me and rushing into an empty room to complete the diapering. Isn't this a bit perverted?

GENTLE READER:

Perverted? On the contrary, it is a normal instinct for a new grandparent to needle a new mother, and just as normal an instinct for the new mother to have to defend herself.

On the actual issue, Miss Manners must side with your mother-in-law, unless the mixed company consists only of father and grandfather. You would be surprised at how uncute people who are not closely related to the baby think it is to watch a wet or soiled diaper being changed. This is especially true since most babies take the opportunity to hit the fresh diaper before it is even pinned.

In the larger problem, you are right. Degree or no, it is up to you to decide how to rear your baby. The usual way is to thank the grandmother for her advice but not follow it; but as this one seems to be a baby-snatcher, perhaps you had better explain gently that you must learn to do the best you can.

～ *The Baby as Performer* ～

DEAR MISS MANNERS:

People keep asking me if my infant son does things "yet." "How come he doesn't sit up yet?" "Does he eat solids yet?" "Does he recognize you yet?" "He doesn't have much hair yet, does he?" Things like that. The implication seems to be that he is behind what he ought to be doing at his age, and I don't like it. Why should he have to conform to their timetables? Am I wrong to take offense?

GENTLE READER:

As it is difficult to ask a newborn baby if he has seen any good movies lately, one does what one can in the way of conversation. You are free to turn the conversation away from the baby. Miss Manners does not, however, recommend doing so by asking visitors, "Is your daughter married yet?" or "Have you found a new job yet?"

The Baby as Attractive Nuisance

DEAR MISS MANNERS:

What can you do about people who make a fuss over your baby in a public place, such as a bus or the supermarket? People will lean into the baby's face, talk baby talk, and grab her hand. First of all, that's a good way for a baby to get a cold, and anyway, it seems to me the baby is entitled to as much privacy from people we don't know as I am. Nobody tries to get cute with me when I'm on a bus without the baby.

GENTLE READER:

In one sense, all babies are the property of the human race. In another sense, it is the parents, rather than the human race, who stay up with them at night when they have colds. If you accept restrained admiration gracefully, you may ward off close contact with the placid remark, "I hope it's not something catching that Baby has."

Social Life Resumes

~ *Entertaining the Parents* ~

DEAR MISS MANNERS:

It seems that all my friends are having babies these days. How soon after the birth is it polite to ask them out? Should we allow them to bring the baby with them?

We don't have children, and are not sure we ever will, but we don't want to drift away from our friends who do. What adjustments should we make for them in our social lives?

GENTLE READER:

The chief kindness is to remember that your friends now have children and to try not to hold it against them. That is, you must appear to sympathize with both their admiration for their babies and their difficulties in parking them with responsible people so that they can get away from them.

Of course, you have paid a visit to each newborn and expressed your appreciation of its beauty; and of course, you will continue to include your friends in your usual social activities, giving them time to make arrangements for baby-sitters.

Allow Miss Manners to suggest some other social niceties:

Soon after the baby is born, before the mother is prepared to go out, you might invite the new parents to a dinner in their own home. You cook, you serve—on trays, if necessary—and you clean up. This can be counted as a baby present.

If you have several friends with new babies, you might give a party at which you provide a baby-sitter. Each couple brings its baby and turns it over to your sitter, in a part of your house as remote from the festivities as possible.

Schedule interruptible social events to which your friends may bring their babies. A relaxed Sunday teatime, for example, isn't marred if a parent has to get up at feeding or crying time, but a seated dinner is.

~ *Entertaining the Family* ~

DEAR MISS MANNERS:

Pamela and I have been best friends all our lives, and I hope always will be. We survived lots of squabbles when we were little kids, living two blocks from each other, and a big problem when she left college, where we shared a room, to marry a boy I didn't then like. Now he's a best friend of mine, too, and was the main one who helped me two years ago, when my father died. One problem I had at their house has now been solved—they used always to be urging me to get married, and if I brought a boyfriend there, they would go into this newlywed happiness act, holding hands, etc., to give the boy the idea, and I had to stop taking anyone there who might scare easily. I say that's solved now, because I am getting married, and there's no reason that the four of us can't be best friends, as my fiancé likes them very much.

Now we have a new, similar problem. Pamela and Richie have a four-month-old baby. We have great times when they get a babysitter and we all go out together, but that's all there is to the friendship anymore. If I go over to the house during the day, Pamela is always too busy to talk to me, even if the baby is asleep. If I go there in the evening, with or without my fiancé, they make the baby the center of attention, and then they do a new act—about how wonderful it is to be parents and how we ought to have lots of babies. We're not even married yet, and anyway, I'm not sure I ever want to have children. Not if it dominates my life like it does theirs.

Are Pam and Richie always going to be one step ahead like that? Should we forget about them and find friends who share our interests now?

GENTLE READER:

1. Yes. 2. No.

Indeed, the great milestones of life, such as marriage and parenthood, are fascinating to those who are in them and less so to those who are not. It is interesting that Richie was of particular comfort to you during another, less attractive, such time; perhaps he had known what it was, before you did, to lose a parent, as he has known before you the joys of marriage and parenthood.

This time difference will sometimes be an annoyance to you, and sometimes an advantage. Are we to have only temporary friends whose experiences happen, at the moment, to match ours? Miss Manners sometimes fears that we live in a society where friends, and even spouses, are supposed to be relevant, like college courses in the 1960s, or else discarded.

Her suggestion to you is to make a new friend—of that baby. If you do have children of your own, you will find the experience useful, and if you don't, you may be especially grateful some day to have a friend in a generation younger than your own. One should not wait to begin such a friendship until the child reaches whatever stage of development you now consider interesting. If you begin to enjoy that child now, either while the mother is there or, giving the mother a chance to get away, by yourself or just with you and your fiancé, you will enrich your friendship with her parents and probably develop a new lifelong friend.

⟶ Parking the Children ⟶

DEAR MISS MANNERS:

I can handle my social life fine—the part when I'm out, that is. It's before I go out and after I come home that the etiquette problems occur. With the baby-sitter. I've had them ranging in age from twelve to eighty-two, and the problems range from the one I found asleep in our bed with a friend (and this wasn't one of the teenagers, either) to the one who rearranged everything in the kitchen cabinets. I've been told to provide special foods, transportation to and from their homes, and a new television set because ours doesn't get enough channels. Over one thing or another, most of them have gone away mad, including two who were the children of friends of mine, or rather, ex-friends. Could you please tell me what the proper behavior is toward baby-sitters, not forgetting to include the correct thing to say when you come home and find comparative strangers making love in your bed.

GENTLE READER:

There is no use deciding what the correct thing would be to say under those circumstances, because you will undoubtedly say anyway, "Hey—what are you doing?" This isn't even a sensible question, because it is perfectly obvious what they are doing, but it is always asked on such an occasion.

As for the rest of it, you can minimize the problems by spelling out beforehand what the working conditions are. Baby-sitters should not be expected to do housework, other than cleaning up after themselves, unless there is extra compensation, but they should not be able to use your house as a free motel either. The employer is generally expected to provide transportation and some food; the employee to enjoy some mild amusement, such as watching television, after the children have been put to bed. You might spell out your resources and expectations when you provide the standard information, such as feeding and disciplining instructions, emergency numbers, your whereabouts and the hour of your return. "I don't feel that this is a job that allows you to entertain others during working hours" is the way you phrase the rule about not messing up your sheets.

⁓ *Parking Fees* ⁓

DEAR MISS MANNERS:

I am divorced with three small children, ages two through eight years. When I go out on dates, I am usually stuck with paying the baby-sitting bill.

Is it proper for the man to offer to pay for the sitter? After all, I would not be out this money if it were not for going out on the date. All my dates are far more well off than I am financially. Having three children and being single, I am on a very fixed budget. Sometimes I have to turn down dates because I cannot afford to pay the sitter.

Is it proper to let the person know you cannot go out with him unless he volunteers to pay for the baby-sitting? I have talked with a lot of other women in my same situation. Please let us know what is the best way to handle this problem.

GENTLE READER:

Please do not think Miss Manners unsympathetic to single mothers with financial problems. Nevertheless, she must tell you that the sort of thinking that begins with "After all, I would not be out this money if it were not for . . ." can lead to no good.

You would also possibly not be out the money for the dress you wore; and you are missing any money you could be earning by working that evening. However, you have transferred your food and entertainment costs to someone else.

Do you see how detestable that type of calculation is? However, Miss Manners wouldn't dream of leaving you the poorer for being proper. She has a suggestion. Get together with all those other women in the same plight, and take turns baby-sitting for one another free.

3. Basic Civilization

Concerning Children

MANNERS TOWARD CHILDREN

⟶ *Adults vs. Children* ⟵

HATING CHILDREN did not used to be a respectable option. Perhaps as many people always did as seem to now, but they had to satisfy themselves with smiling weakly and saying, "Oh, I'm afraid I'm no good with children" and "Don't you want to go outside and play?"

Anyone who so much as called out "Scat!" was suspected of being crazy. Making a big deal of an occasional baseball through the window or a habitual shortcut through the flowerbed marked one as a crank. How could anyone seriously condemn the generation that represented the future and the hope of civilization?

Wait—Miss Manners suspects that might account for the animosity right there. Several decades of being told that everything that everybody else wants to make you do or to prevent you from doing has the compelling moral motivation of being for the sake of our children and their children—that alone is enough to make people weary of the righteous little folks.

In any case, there is no more free ride, kids. People are stating outright their dislike of children and their unwillingness to be anywhere in their vicinity. In general desirability, a child-free environment is considered somewhere between smoke-free and germ-free.

Miss Manners finds this ugly, and would like to remove child-bashing once more from positions that can be safely uttered in public. Never mind that hope-of-the-future business. She thought we were past permitting whole categories of people to be insulted for the sake of efficiency. The old days of getting away with doing this by gender, race, nationality and such are thankfully gone, and legitimate insults are supposed to target individuals.

That did not exactly come out right, Miss Manners fears. She is not in the business of drumming up one-on-one meanness; people seem to manage that quite nicely without her. What she is trying to say is that airing prejudice should be socially unacceptable. If it is wrong to make cracks about the elderly, and an aging population is working hard on that, then it should be wrong to make cracks about the young.

People are people, and one can't like them all, but surely age should not be the disqualifying characteristic. It strikes Miss Manners as equally undiscriminating, although not as rude, to declare that one simply adores children. It reminds her of those dreadful sorts who used to go around announcing "I'm a people person," as though one had another choice.

She recognizes one exception to the ban on group reactions, however. To dislike the rude is a sensible position personally, and to join in social condemnation of the rude is a favor to society.

That is what is behind open season on children, she suspects. There seems to be a high number of rude children around, courtesy of parents who ignore their children and of parents who ignore everyone else's needs on behalf of their children. It is all right to come out and state a dislike of rude children. And it is even better to do the same in regard to rude parents.

~ Children vs. Children ~

DEAR MISS MANNERS:

My sons are 8 and 4. My dilemma with teaching my children politeness has been teaching them when it is ok not to be polite.

My husband and I were both raised to be extremely polite. Because of this, it took us years to "stand up for ourselves" and learn to be assertive. I am an adjunct professor with a background in counseling school children and my concerns are twofold: It is the meek and mild mannered, polite children that often get bullied. The same children are often at risk for being victimized by adults.

It is very difficult to teach your children to be polite yet not allow themselves to be violated. Teaching children to protect themselves is a challenge when I have to overcome my mindset that children should be taught only respect and politeness.

GENTLE READER:

Okay not to be polite? Quick! Where are Miss Manners' smelling salts?

Your mistake is in positing a choice between being polite and put upon, or being impolite and assertive. If those were true alternatives, perhaps even Miss Manners would grudgingly admit that it might be better to rear rude bullies than pathetic patsies. You would save on bandages, although perhaps not, in the long run, on bail.

Fortunately, such is not the case. If etiquette demanded that its adherents surrender their interests, always yielding to the rude, they would have been Darwin'd out of existence long ago. Nor is rudeness an effective form of self-defense. It only inspires more rudeness, and still, the bigger child wins.

The only known protection against bullying that children can muster is the polite but devastating weapon of feigned indifference. It is no fun to pick on people without getting visible results. Miss Manners does not pretend this is a cure-all for bullying, which can be serious enough to require adult interference. Even then, however, the technique of aloofness will serve your child against those accusations of tattling that restart the horrid cycle.

~ Parents vs. Children ~

A well-bred person always takes the side of the weak against the strong, but nevertheless Miss Manners has promised to say something on behalf of children against their parents. Namely: Rudeness to children counts as rudeness. The fact that people are smaller and blood relatives does not mean that it is open season on insulting them.

Besides, it teaches them the technique and thus leads to such tedious exchanges as "Don't you dare talk to Mommy like that," "But that's what you said to me," "That's different," "Why is it different?" and so on. What makes it different is that when children do it, parents call it "sassing," and when parents do it, parents call it "discipline."

Heaven knows that Miss Manners is not against the disciplining of children. We are all born charming, frank and spontaneous and must be civilized before we are fit to participate in society. In a fit of exasperation, Miss Manners once demanded of a six-year-old person how it could be so childish and was forced to admit the justice of its reply, "I'm a child." Admission of this state is a temporary excuse at best, and one that one's loved ones should help one to overcome. However, humiliation is neither a proper nor an effective method of disciplining children. Personal insults and public rebukes should be avoided.

~ The Look ~

DEAR MISS MANNERS:

Once my son was really acting up at a birthday party and he wouldn't listen to me, so I yelled for him to stop his behavior. Everyone got very quiet and stared at us.

My husband pointed out that I can correct him quietly—that everyone has a child that misbehaves every once in a while. I have since learned to do it subtly.

Gentle Reader:

And a very good lesson that is. In contrast, the lesson that you can get results through yelling and public humiliation, if only you are big enough, is one that Miss Manners sincerely hopes you do not care to teach.

You are in dire need of The Look, a code that parent and child understand but outsiders do not (similar to the pleasant expression you or your husband direct at each other at parties, meaning "I want to go home! Now!"). It consists of a tight little smile, in which the mouth curves upward but the eyes are fixed on the child with a decidedly unhumorous intensity. You may need to practice, but Miss Manners assures you that it is worth the effort. Done properly, it freezes an errant child in his tracks and dampens his desire for defiance with the dread of what is to come.

One also needs a way of staring brightly at the child that prompts him to search his mind for the phrase, such as "How do you do?" or "Thank you" or "I'm sorry I broke your lamp," that he has neglected to utter. This look is more pointed, and enables the parent to stop the child from whatever he is doing wrong, while alerting others that he is not getting away with it (just enough to prevent them from doing it too); and then to continue with the planned activity, reserving punishment for the first private opportunity.

~ *The Double Insult* ~

Dear Miss Manners:

My father always criticizes me when my little sister does something wrong. I don't mean he blames me for what she has done, but he says things like "Why are you two always breaking things?" or "Children—stop that this instant."

But I wasn't doing anything wrong! It's so unfair! Don't you think it's insulting to do that to a person who wasn't at fault?

Gentle Reader:

Yes, but it's an interesting category of insult, which may be taken as offhandedly as it is given. What your father is administering is known as the Double Insult.

Technically, only one insult has been delivered—to you—because what your sister has received is a reprimand. The trick is to include in one's remark as many innocent people as possible. If your father were more advanced in this specialty, he might say, for instance, "You children are always so clumsy, just like your mother." Presuming that you and your mother were both minding your own business when the act that set him off was committed, he will have gotten two extra people for the price of one. Or he could say "like your mother's side of the family," which would, with four extra words, extend the insult to countless numbers of other people, depending on how many generations you consider this to include. Or he could say "your generation" instead of "you children," thus including people who aren't even related to him. As you see, it is a great art, and your father is practicing only a mild version of it.

∽ Relatives vs. Children ∽

DEAR MISS MANNERS:

I have a 13 year old daughter who I believe is well mannered and well behaved. Many people have complimented me for this. When I go to family affairs, it seems to me that the children—especially the boys of my brother, sister and cousins—are a little wild. I believe that my siblings think that it is OK or even cute.

I feel it is semi-important for extended families to get together and get to know one another; but is it acceptable for me to comment to my sister, brother, cousins (and their spouses) that the behavior of their children is other than what I really want my daughter to be associated with? It wouldn't be that big of a deal, except that they routinely ask me if my daughter can spend a week with them during summer vacation.

GENTLE READER:

Criticizing other people's child-rearing methods, or the absence of them, is rude. If you do this, your brother, sister and cousins might consider you the sort of person with whom they don't want their children to be associated.

Unless by "a little wild" you mean physically or morally dangerous, Miss Manners would advise your sending your daughter off on that visit. She might learn some important manners lessons you have failed to teach her: that some people have higher standards than others, that she should practice good behavior whether others do or not, and that relatives should be cherished, in spite of their shortcomings.

But if you really want to improve the cousins' behavior, you might arrange occasions to consort with them individually so that they, too, could observe other standards. You could invite one to your house and gently explain the "rules of the house" when she or he exhibits poor manners. Invite one out for a treat, such as lunch in a restaurant, and insist on proper behavior. The privilege of individual attention from an adult other than a parent should be enough to compensate for the expectation of manners.

Meanwhile, you may want to keep them from knocking your drink into your lap while you are attending obligatory family dinners. Assuming these children are not bigger than you are, grab an offending child by the arm and say, with a firm voice and hypocritical smile, "I think you'd better stop that—you might get hurt." It helps if you have a tight grip on the arm while saying this.

～ Neighbors vs. Children ～

DEAR MISS MANNERS:

I live in a townhome development. My neighbors consist largely of five-years-removed-from-the-trailer white trash, and Title 8 welfare trustees, both of whom basically let their packs of darling offspring run wild.

They and their darling offspring seem to have firmly bought into the notion that it isn't really vandalism/theft if you destroy/steal the property of someone you perceive as better-off than you.

As a result, I have recently installed a video surveillance system outside my unit, to catch them in the act of tearing up and stealing my flowers, bird feeders, etc.

My etiquette question is this: Should I alert their parents to the video tapes I've made of their actions first, or should I just turn the tapes directly over to the police, and let the police deal with them?

GENTLE READER:

Without condoning vandalism, Miss Manners is suspicious of anyone who uses the word "darling" to refer to other people's children. Oddly enough, it is only child-haters who refer to the young as "the little darlings."

If you have already voiced your complaint to the parents and they have refused to do anything, Miss Manners has no quarrel with your taking the next step to protect yourself. But yes, she thinks you should inform the parents that you are turning over evidence to the police, and furthermore, you should do so in a tone of regret that you are forced to take such a measure.

There is a practical, as well as a courteous, reason for doing this. The police may come in and help you by issuing warnings (just a guess, but they are not likely to jail children for picking flowers), but after they leave you will still have to live near these people. So it would be a good idea to drop the offensive terms you used about them as well.

⌒ *Hosts vs. Children* ⌒

DEAR MISS MANNERS:

I don't allow bad language in my house, and I believe my children have learned our standards enough not to say those words elsewhere either, although I know that most people do. Last night, my son's friend, who was having dinner with us, said a four letter word at the table. It slipped very casually into the conversation, but I was stunned. Too stunned, I'm afraid, to say anything. And yet when I thought about it afterwards, I felt as if I had set a bad example to my children in permitting another child to do what I would not let them do. How should I have handled this?

GENTLE READER:

Exactly as you did—by looking stunned but saying nothing. It is one thing to teach children to behave better than the rest of the world, and quite another to teach them to teach the rest of the world. If you make their task that heavy, they are likely to abandon it.

⌒ *Strangers vs. Children* ⌒

DEAR MISS MANNERS:

I am tired of being treated like a child. My father says it's because I am a child— I am twelve-and-a-half years old—but it still isn't fair. If I go into a store to buy something, nobody pays any attention to me, or if they do, it's to say, "Leave that alone," "Don't touch that," although I haven't done anything. My money is as good as anybody's, but because I am younger, they feel they can be mean to me. It happens to me at home, too. My mother's friend who comes over after dinner sometimes, who doesn't have any children of her own and doesn't know what's what, likes to say to me, "Shouldn't you be in bed by now, dear?" when she doesn't even know what my bedtime is supposed to be. Is there any way I can make these people stop?

GENTLE READER:

Growing up is the best revenge.

MANNERS FOR CHILDREN

⌐ *Toward Other Children* ⌐

What a pity it is that most children have become too hardened by life to be capable of imagining what it is like to be a grown-up. The wonder and the innocence with which parents regard the early years of schooling is something that children are simply unable to understand.

The harsh truth is that there is no more hostile and humiliating social environment than grades K through eight. There is no ambiguity in the insults; descending the scale of popularity is not like stepping on a down escalator but rather like stepping into an empty elevator shaft; and there is no escape, either, into new circles or old philosophy.

Yet parents, bless their hearts, see it as a rosy time of laughter and irresponsibility. That is why the most loving of them will pooh-pooh the announcement of a social stomachache—the child's equivalent of the social headache—or cut off a story of full-scale social warfare with, "Oh, I'm sure it'll all be forgotten by tomorrow and you'll be as good friends as ever." There is charm to this naïveté, and the thoughtful child will take care to preserve parental illusions. Let those dear people be, in their own happy world, and come and listen to some tough social truths from your own Miss Manners.

You have heard, perhaps, of such advantages as beauty, brains, wealth or charm. Forget them. It may be accepted, in your class, that this person is "pretty" and that one "smart"; it may be known that one has a big allowance and another is always nice enough to share. In this age group, none of these characteristics has anything to do with popularity, and often they have nothing to do with the people who are supposed to have them.

The child who is thought good-looking is merely one (often a plain one) who is smart enough to make people think so. The one with a reputation for being smart is dumb enough to think that if he or she cultivates the teacher, class favor will result. Those who flash money or press their possessions on others are taken for suckers.

The only social skill worth having in this unpleasant milieu is the ability to appear indifferent to the opinions of others, neither seeking their love nor noticing their scorn. Those who can manage this will be rewarded with popularity, and those who seem anxious to possess popularity will be either slaves or outcasts, the toadies or the victims of those who have it. Popular children often behave badly because, as we know, power corrupts. But those who commit the sin of wanting to be popular usually behave scandalously, competing in their cruelties to one another for the favor of those above.

Miss Manners begs you, whatever your rank, not to indulge in the practice of taunting or maligning others. She would not dream of appealing to your moral sense with this plea, but advances it on strictly practical grounds. Excessive meanness, like excessive generosity, is correctly interpreted by children as anxiety to please, which they consider the greatest of social crimes. It is also a terrible gamble. The cards are shuffled every summer in this age group, with many people smartening up over the holidays through new experiences or having read Miss Manners. The person it was safe to taunt last year may be the ruling power this year.

Calm, cheerful, pleasant, unruffled indifference, no matter how severe the provocation, is your only hope of achieving popularity. Even if you fail, you will be loved later in life by those to whom you recount your brave attempts. Confessing to having been a bully is worth nothing in the tame adult world.

⌒ Learning Compassion ⌒

DEAR MISS MANNERS:

The mother of a boy in my class is a friend of my mother's. This boy is also a creep and no one likes him. My mother wanted me to invite him to my birthday party, but I told her it would spoil everything, and she said it was my birthday, so I didn't have to, but I did have to be nice to him in some way. So I offered to show him my report card if he would show me his, but he ran away and told his mother I was mean to him and she told my mother. Now I'm in trouble. Do you believe me that I was being friendly, or do you think I was being mean, or what?

GENTLE READER:

Or what. Miss Manners hopes you are in sufficient trouble now so that you will not grow up to offer to compare paychecks with people you believe to be earning less than you.

⌒ Learning Wariness ⌒

DEAR MISS MANNERS:

I told my closest friend a deep dark secret that I didn't want anyone else in the world to know, and she went around blabbing it to everyone. Don't you think that's disgusting and wrong? I don't feel I can trust anybody now.

GENTLE READER:

One can never learn to trust others until one has learned to trust oneself. Who blabbed first, you or she?

◦— *Toward Grown-Ups* —◦

A well-behaved grown-up is a credit and a joy to his or her child. It distresses Miss Manners to see so many children carelessly trampling on their grown-ups' tender feelings when a little courtesy and attention would transform sullen and edgy adults into cheerful and cooperative parents.

The sensitive child will notice that grown-ups worry endlessly about the judgment of their peers and can be thrown into agonies of embarrassment by trivial transgressions of conventionality. It does not take much effort to cater to these little prejudices, and the returns, emotional and otherwise, are enormous.

Adults are full of secrets. They find it humiliating to have people know the most basic, and often the most obvious, facts about themselves. A child is expected to reveal his age and grade level whenever asked, and he is constantly asked. But adult society pretends to make a mystery of such things as age and income, and the polite child will respect this, no matter what he thinks of it. He will steadfastly claim ignorance of what birthday a parent just celebrated, what was paid for the house and what was said at the dinner table discussion of who is getting ahead of whom at the office.

Loyalty also demands that the child suppress any knowledge of behavior that makes his parents look bad. Cute stories about their squabbles and their party behavior should not be repeated outside the family, no matter how amusing. On the contrary, the child has an obligation to defend his family against any disparagement, no matter how justified he believes it to be. To know, better than anyone, how impossible your relatives are, and to be ready to kill the outsider who suggests such a thing, is the essence of family chivalry.

Respect must be shown to the grown-ups' peculiar ideas of what is proper and what improper in matters of dress and behavior. The intelligent child knows that such customs are not questions of right and wrong but of transitory group standards, and he is able to master more than one standard. To dress as your parents prefer when going out with them or appearing before their friends should entitle one to adopt the fashions of one's contemporaries when one is among them. Observing their social rituals, including pretending to be interested in their friends, is extremely important. The child who greets his parents' guests, engages in small talk with them and excuses himself politely when he can bear no more of their silliness has earned the right to have his own friends made appropriately welcome.

None of this is difficult to perform, although it requires some patience to make parents understand that courtesy is reciprocal. In the end, a parent who is continually exposed to high standards of politeness and consideration cannot fail to be the better for it.

Challenging Authority

DEAR MISS MANNERS:

I am currently working on a research paper, on the parental right to censor music. My question for you is, Should a parent censor or monitor their children's listening habits? And if so, how should they go about doing so?

GENTLE READER:

Such a harsh word—"censor." All freedom-loving people, even small ones, bristle when they hear it and rise to protect their liberties from those who would usurp them under the guise of benign paternalism.

But wait. Isn't benign paternalism what parents are supposed to provide? What else are they there for, besides providing the wherewithal to purchase disgusting music?

Miss Manners realizes that parents cannot hope to protect their children for long against outside influences, however nasty. The protection they can provide them is to teach them that there are other, higher standards, and that they subscribe to these and expect their children to do so.

Are the children actually going to do so? Of course not. But the parents can make rules against buying and bringing into the house what they consider to be vulgar or otherwise objectionable. They can also use the issue to discuss why they feel the way they do, thus making their resentful children aware that there are people—including people they love and respect in spite of their differences in taste—who maintain their own standards instead of succumbing to whatever is out there.

Will their rules and arguments be challenged, ridiculed and broken? Of course. That is why parents do need to do some reasonable monitoring.

DEAR MISS MANNERS:

What is the proper dress for school?

GENTLE READER:

Miss Manners knows a loaded question when she sees one. You have already heard what your parents consider to be proper dress for school. You have already heard what the school considers proper dress. And you have seen what your most daring classmates consider proper dress.

Miss Manners is sorry to inform you that proper school dress is what your parents and teachers deem proper dress, modified by whatever you can manage to do to it that they fail to notice.

Challenging Patience

DEAR MISS MANNERS:

I didn't realize I hadn't taught my kids properly until one night they were wiping their faces on their sleeves! We have seven children, ages 2–15, and dinner is frequently on the way to ball games, etc. How can they learn to put their napkin in their laps when we aren't around the table enough?

So, though the off season is brief, I have made a point not only to make sure they have napkins in their laps, but also to require help with setting the table, so they'll know how. I also use this time to teach, "Please pass the salt" because I've noticed they will reach over their sibs or just say, "Give me the salt."

Smacking has also reared its ugly head, and I'm quick to correct them, no matter if we're in the car or around the table.

Sometimes I really consider sending them to manners class, which I've noticed is offered through continuing ed. at the local university. I am really considering it this coming summer, but at the same time I am almost embarrassed it has come to needing a manners class. I'm just afraid I will forget to teach them something.

GENTLE READER:

Your children are already enrolled in a manners curriculum, and even the eldest is far from finished. Packing them off to reform school because of a few flubs strikes Miss Manners as rather harsh.

Nor would it turn them into instant ladies and gentlemen, relieving you of that great maternal burden of nagging. A quickie course might familiarize them with a few surface rules, but even those you would still have to keep reinforcing, and there are bound to be others a mere summer course would miss.

That part of etiquette that has to be learned by rote, such as table manners, requires years of practice. The part that requires judgment, such as how to square your own wishes with the consideration due others, requires endless discussions and examples. It's called child-rearing.

You have associated your discouragement with not holding the most important class—family dinner—often enough. This suggests that your children need fewer outside commitments, not more.

(For the behavior of children in a divorce, please see p. 663.)

⌁ Conversation ⌁

The idea that children should be heard, as well as seen, has been abroad in the land for some time now, and just look at the place. Miss Manners believes that civilized society as we know it will come to an end on the day the present fourth-graders are let loose upon the world.

If the wise adage needed amendment, it might be added that some children should never be seen either. Most, however, merely need to be taught to listen. Miss Manners has noticed many well-meaning parents doing their children a disservice by encouraging them to express themselves, particularly when the adults are trying to talk. It would be more in the children's interest if they were encouraged to listen to adult conversation. They might pick up something they can use against their elders later.

The current school of child-rearing is based on two mistaken notions: that children are naturally good and that they are naturally creative. If children are naturally good, why do they teach themselves to walk by holding on to the edge of the dining room tablecloth? If they are naturally creative, why do they all draw alike?

Miss Manners is not, however, advocating switching to suppressing rudely the spontaneity of little children. It can be done politely. (Miss Manners is a non-allied power in the war of the generations and also attacks adults who are rude to children.)

Rather than zipping up their wee mouths, Miss Manners suggests that adults stun babbling children into silence by asking them nicely to explain what they mean. If they are being truly natural and creative, they have neglected to figure out this point. One hopes that the more promising ones may therefore be shocked enough by this question to rummage around in their minds, sort out the mess and endeavor to express themselves with clarity and supporting evidence. This should not only make it possible for the adults to hear themselves think, but for the children to be forced to think. As a by-product, we may get some creative adults from these children. Haven't you noticed that all artistic people brag about having been suppressed as children?

⌒ *Conversation Stoppers* ⌒

DEAR MISS MANNERS:

I would like to share with you some comments made to my tall and lovely thirteen-year-old daughter—comments made by well-bred, usually courteous adults:

"Good grief! You're so tall for your age!"

"You've grown so much since I saw you three weeks ago!"

"How on earth does your family keep you in clothes?"

Never do these adults consider their negative remarks about another's physical appearance to be the least bit rude. But how would these same individuals like to hear some of the following remarks about their physical appearance:

"What's left of your hair is getting so gray!"

"You've gained so much weight since I saw you three weeks ago!"

"Why are your teeth so brown?"

"My, but you're flabby for your age!"

"Do you dye your hair?"

Several facts need to be faced.

1. Kids are getting taller and healthier and more physically fit than previous generations. Thank goodness!

2. One's size is determined at the time of conception. There is, therefore, little that one can do about height.

3. Constantly hearing negative utterances about one's height can only make a child feel that there is something very wrong, in spite of parental assurances that tall is beautiful and normal. The end result will be self-consciousness, shyness, poor posture, and a negative self-concept. Please, if you've ever made negative remarks about a child's size—think about it. Say something positive to the child or buzz off!

GENTLE READER:

Indeed. Miss Manners hopes you will not for a moment accuse her of arguing with your principle—that personal remarks addressed to individuals of any age should be complimentary—if she quibbles with your examples.

The expressions of surprise that children grow taller, rather than smaller, are not stunning instances of observation and tact. Miss Manners does not see them as insults either. It is generally agreed upon in society that aging is an excellent thing from birth to, say, thirty, but a terrible misfortune from then on. Miss Manners has never understood why this is. To watch individuals change with the years can be interesting, if predictable, but to regard it as either a miracle or a shame seems naive and futile.

However, that is society's attitude, and Miss Manners is normally given to accepting conventions rather than fighting them. Given this assumption, comments on your daughter's growth should be taken as compliments. Miss Manners suspects you see in them an attitude that she hopes and believes has been discarded by society—that boys, but not girls, should be tall. Without arguing genetics with you, she endorses your policy of conveying a positive attitude to your daughter, and suggests that you extend this by teaching her to reply properly. Not, "And I see you're getting to be a little stooped over as you get older," but, "Why, thank you very much."

⟶ Interruptions ⟶

DEAR MISS MANNERS:

Should you tell your mother something if it is important when she is talking to company? I am six.

GENTLE READER:

Yes, you should (after saying "Excuse me"). Here are some of the things that are important to tell your mother, even though she is talking to company:

"Mommy, the kitchen is full of smoke."

"Daddy's calling from Tokyo."

"Kristen fell out of her crib and I can't put her back."

"There's a policeman at the door and he says he wants to talk to you."

"I was just reaching for my ball, and the goldfish bowl fell over."

Now, here are some things that are not important, so they can wait until your mother's company has gone home:

"Mommy, I'm tired of playing blocks. What do I do now?"

"The ice-cream truck is coming down the street."

"Can I give Kristen the rest of my applesauce?"

"I can't find my crayons."

"When are we going to have lunch? I'm hungry."

~ Giving Thanks ~

DEAR MISS MANNERS:

I have tried to adopt a policy for myself and my children of sending thank-you notes promptly and consistently; however, I have run into a possible gray area when it comes to the spontaneous gifts my mother bestows on my kids. She lives about 10 minutes away from us and regularly drops by with little surprises for my girls (aged 8 and 9), gifts rang-

> *Christmas Day*
>
> Dear Aunt Patience,
>   Now I can hardly wait for snow so I can use your nice present! Thank you very much.
>   I hope you are having a wonderful Christmas, too, and are getting lots of things you need.
>
>   Love,
>   Daffodil

A letter from a child, thanking the giver of a present. Children may use almost any colorful or fanciful writing paper, and are therefore excellent recipients of the paper that adults sometimes buy on impulse or receive from others, which is too silly for them to use. Note the date on this letter.

ing from candy bars to new CDs or outfits. My kids always give her their verbal thanks, of course, and for larger gifts I've sometimes had them send notes as well.

In an intimate relationship such as the one between grandchild and doting grandparent, especially with the parties having frequent contact with each other, is there ever a time when a thank-you note is not required? I understand that relaying written gratitude is never inappropriate, but is it ever unnecessary? And is the value of the gift really the determining factor? In this instance, my mother—the Miss Manners of my childhood—is the one who thinks I go overboard on thank-you notes, so it's a bit of a quandary for me!

GENTLE READER:

That is nothing compared to the tizzy in which you have put Miss Manners. Accustomed to a world of ingrates, she is astonished at the concept of excessive letters of thanks.

But yes, a written letter of gratitude for a candy bar from Grandmamma down the street would be excessive. Except for extraordinary items (measured in terms of sentiment more than money), presents enthusiastically received firsthand do not require such letters.

Far be it from Miss Manners, however, to discourage children from the practice. Wouldn't it be charming if you just had them write their grandmother an occasional letter, unattached to any particular little treat, saying how lucky they feel to have her nearby?

CHILDREN'S SOCIAL EVENTS

⌒ Birthday Parties ⌒

A certain amount of childish behavior is to be expected at parties given in celebration of the birthdays of minors. However, Miss Manners would just as soon that it not come from the parents. Some of them she would not trust, even blindfold, to play pin the tail on the donkey. They are already far too eager and inventive about skewering one another.

Of course, she understands that everything parents do is motivated entirely by the desire to please their children. Can it be their fault that it makes their children happy for them to vie at outclassing other parents, to make a point of excluding certain children, and to encourage forms that foster social irresponsibility?

Only partly, Miss Manners acknowledges.

Children do appear to be born with some scary social inclinations. It is a parental obligation to disabuse them of the idea that they can get away with this. The chief excuse for the birthday party, one of the most hazardous social forms in existence, is as a laboratory for teaching counter-intuitive, and therefore civilized, behavior.

The young host or hostess has the difficult job of pretending that the guests were invited for their company as much as for the packages under their arms, and that they are there to have a good time, rather than to form an audience for whom the birthday child can be the center of attention. All of this being against every natural human inclination, it takes a lot of training.

But there are parents who seem to be training their children, instead, in acquisitiveness and self-centeredness. The forms that have burgeoned put an increasing emphasis on presents, including not just the present-opening ritual, but posting wish lists or demanding college fund contributions in lieu of gifts, and on glorifying and indulging the birthday child, regardless of the effect on guests. A particularly nasty innovation, for example, is to award the host prizes in any competitive games, regardless of performance.

What this training is supposed to prepare them to become, it could not be decent, hospitable, considerate people. Maybe it is to become medieval lords, whose relationships with others consist of extracting tributes and exercising privileges.

In their own future interests, and that of the society on which these people will be unleashed, Miss Manners recommends that parents set limits. Children being traditionalists, it would be wise for parents in the same neighborhood and school circles to agree on them.

Well-meaning ones have already made some moves toward doing this in regard to the guest list, for example decreeing that everyone in a child's class be invited. (The less altruistic form, of demanding that all one's own children be invited regardless of acquaintanceship, is a bad one; one Gentle Reader whose parents demanded that said the result was that the entire family was dropped socially.) Another method is reverting to the old rule of inviting only the number of guests equal to the child's age, thus limiting it to so few that being left out is no distinction.

Care should be taken that parties do not get big enough and expensive enough to put an undue burden on the hosts and frighten the children. One solution is joint parties, for children born in the same month, but then care has to be taken not to put a burden on guests in supplying multiple presents when they might not be acquainted with all the honorees. An agreement on low-key parties and a low ceiling on present expenditures would help.

The most important lesson to be learned by the host parent is what it feels like to:

1. Look out the window with a child at the appointed time of arrival and not see anyone at all running up the steps with a package under the arm.
2. Look out the window, at the appointed time of departure, your living room full of chaos behind you, and not see any parents trudging up the steps.

If the parent learns to deliver and fetch his own children on time when they are attending another child's birthday party, it will have been a successful learning experience. And if they all learn to replace competition with cooperation, they may find they can also make rules for their own convenience in regard to transportation, for example. If anyone is entitled to have a special day, they are the ones who earn it.

The Parent's Departure

DEAR MISS MANNERS:

How do you word a birthday party invitation for a child so that his or her parents do not assume that they are invited to stay for the party? A friend who is planning her son's fifth birthday party wants to have a lovely time for the kids, but does not want to have to deal with essentially running two parties, one for the kids and one for their parents.

GENTLE READER:

Before answering, Miss Manners wants to extract a promise from your friend: When some five-year-old starts crying inconsolably, or suggests a game of jumping up and down on her sofa, or retroactively announces an allergy to whatever he just ate, she won't blame Miss Manners because she will have to deal with it alone. The two-party system may be worth the effort.

If she thinks not, she should put only the starting time of the party on the invitation and then "Pick-up time, 7 P.M." Birthday invitations are informal by nature, and there is no reason to use the cocktail formula of "5 to 7." In addition, Miss Manners would suggest her opening the door with her child and welcoming the child-guest while thanking the parent for dropping her off and reminding her when to come back.

⸺ *The Child's Departure* ⸺

DEAR MISS MANNERS:

I am trying to teach my child, a precocious five-year-old, to be natural in company, but what do I do about getting him to be polite? The case in point is a birthday party at which I prompted him, when I picked him up, to tell his hostess that he had a nice time. I was mortified, because he said, "I didn't!" It later turned out that he had gotten into a quarrel at the table with the birthday child and another little boy, and a lot of tears were shed. Obviously, he didn't have "a nice time." Is there something else he could say, which is polite but not dishonest?

GENTLE READER:

"Thank you for inviting me." However, this is not going to solve your basic problem, which is that you have given the child an impossible task by asking him to express his true feelings and, at the same time, to be gentle with other people's feelings. Miss Manners would choose the latter. Teaching a child to "be natural" seems a silly endeavor, but teaching him to say a big booming "Thank you" will serve him forever.

⸺ *The Classroom Party* ⸺

DEAR MISS MANNERS:

I have received invitations to parties that include a demand for money with the explanation that it is needed to defray expenses. Naturally, I decline such "invitations."

Unfortunately, this type of invitation has made its way to the public school system where my child attends third grade: "You are invited to a pizza party for returning your reading records. You did a great job and you should be rewarded. Please bring $2 for the cost of the pizza. I will provide the drink and dessert. You did a great job!"

These parties are held during the school day. While I have used this as an opportunity to teach my child that this is bad manners, I am in a quandary as to how to respond. I don't want my child to be ostracized by not being able to participate if I refuse to pay, but I feel these invitations take advantage of me. So could you please advise me how to let the teacher know I don't approve, but not be rude in doing so? Other parents have no problem with these invitations, so a petition would not be possible.

GENTLE READER:

It would be if you gave those other parents a problem. No one wants to be the one to seem stingy, so Miss Manners suggests providing them with a loftier reason.

Unfortunately, she knows only too well how hard it is to make anyone under-stand what is wrong with charging people when you announce that you are giving them a treat. So here are two other ideas:

1. "Trifling as the amount may seem to most of us, I'm afraid these collections penalize people who find all that nickel-and-diming a strain, but are embar-rassed to speak up."
2. "Can't we think of another way to praise the children? We don't want them to think that the only rewards involve fast food and, for that matter, collecting money."

⌒ The Play Date ⌒

DEAR MISS MANNERS:

I am nine years old. When I call a friend and they're not home and I leave a message on their answering machine, how long should I wait till I call a different friend? How many hours should I wait till I call a different friend without hurting the first friend's feelings? Then when my other friend returns my call and I already have a friend over, what should I do?

GENTLE READER:

If you are old enough to issue invitations, Miss Manners believes you are old enough to learn a secret that many adults get into trouble for not knowing:

Invitations do not have to be open-ended to be gracious. Now is the time to learn to put time limits. Your message should be, "I'm hoping you can come over to my house. Call me by three if you can come today, but if you can't, please call me tomorrow and let's pick another day."

⌒ The Overnight Visit ⌒

Children dear, if you don't learn now the proper way to behave when you spend the night with a friend, how do you expect to have any fun when you grow up?

Staying overnight is the second most common major social activity among medium-sized children and therefore second among the opportunities they have to disgrace their own parents and disgust the parents of their friends.

The first rule is to bring the proper equipment and to take it home with you when you leave. It is not at all cute, at any age, to expect to share a toothbrush or hairbrush with a friend. Children should inquire whether they should bring their own sleeping bags, if they have them. Leaving things behind, whether from the hope of being asked back or the failure to double-check the room, is a nuisance for hosts.

The guest must be friendly to everyone there, not just the person who invited him. That includes parents, siblings and other guests. The child who doesn't look his friend's parents in the eye and talk to them will grow up to pretend a friend's roommate doesn't exist. In both cases, he will have induced reluctance to have him there again.

By law, guests of any age enjoy doing and eating whatever their hosts want to do and to eat. Some wily people attempt to throw children off by asking them to say what they want to do or whether they like what is being served for dinner. The clever guest admits to no food dislikes, short of things that give him violent physical reactions—and those should be explained at the time of accepting the invitation—and will name a preferred activity only when given a multiple choice by the hosts. Instructions to leave the bed unmade are in the same category with invitations to forget about going home. Nobody is ever revolted by a guest's excessive neatness.

Thank everything that moves. Not only the host and his parents, but the sibling who may have given up his room, the housekeeper who may have to do the sheets and the goldfish who may have had to move his bowl to give you somewhere to put your hairbrush.

⟶ The Restaurant Visit ⟶

DEAR MISS MANNERS:

I have very bright children who are simply lovely to be around. One problem my wife and I have encountered is that when we are in restaurants, our smallest children, ages 1.5 and 4 years, refuse to remain seated. They want to run around the table, stopping for bites at anyone's place who will hold out a hand with food in it.

When we attempt to enforce table manners, and rules, they create an awful scene. Other guests become nervous, and their eating out experience is all but ruined by the cries of children. I have recently begun taking each child out of the eating area before too much damage to guests has been done. I talk to them, and on occasion I have swatted them, albeit quite gently, yet firm. This method lasts momentarily, however, a repeat scene is always in the offing. I have almost decided not to take them to adult restaurants anymore until they are capable of following basic rules. We are not lazy parents, but may be going through a time of relaxed standards so we stand to be corrected.

Gentle Reader:

You have almost decided not to take them to adult restaurants until they are capable of handling the situation? Almost?

Miss Manners is not questioning your parenting skills, because no one can turn toddlers, however bright and lovely, into adults, not even for an evening. However, she would like to say a word or two about parental judgment.

You are being unfair, not only to the other restaurant patrons, but to your own children. If this were a situation where you had no choice about taking them—a family occasion, or a roadside food stop during a trip—your method of removing them when they caused trouble would have to do. But there is no reason to take them to restaurants where adults go for pleasant, quiet, leisurely meals. These outings may be a treat for you and your wife, at least before the children act up, but they are a treat that you must postpone unless you can hire or persuade someone to take the children so you can have a night out.

Do not mislead yourself, however, into thinking these outings are a treat for the children. If your idea is to use the setting to teach them manners, you need to make it into a treat—and the way to do that is to refuse to take them. Talk up how much fun restaurant-going is, but stop short of inviting them, on the grounds that such places are for big people who know what they are supposed to do. Then teach them the manners at home and let them practice until they are old enough to master and enjoy the experience.

Common Courtesy for All Ages

INTRODUCTIONS AND GREETINGS

INTRODUCTIONS, THESE DAYS, range from perfunctory to perfectly dreadful. It is not just the proper form that is missing, but the names. People who take the trouble to say "Hey, guys, meet my friend" seem to think they have done the job.

Miss Manners remembers who should be introduced to whom, but then she also remembers the difference between "who" and "whom." The formula is simple: One introduces inferiors to their superiors. Thus, gentlemen are introduced to ladies, young people to old, unranked ones to those of exalted stature and your own relatives to everyone else.

It only becomes complicated because there are actual human beings involved. Suppose you have to rank an assistant curator of Japanese beetles and a mechanical engineer specializing in the rolltops of desks—especially if you are not certain what sex they are, let alone what vintage? One would have to quiz them so thoroughly that the introduction, when it was finally performed, would be an anticlimax.

Fortunately, Miss Manners has an all-purpose solution. Let us begin with the classic introduction, and then she will explain how to adapt this to baffling circumstances.

Rory Hoppity, who used to be married to your stepsister, has parlayed his experience making license plates into a new job with the snow lobby and persuaded you to introduce him to your friend the First Lady, whom he has long admired for her unusual ability to reach the President. Although consorts carry no official rank, it is safe to assume that she outranks him in every possible way.

"Mrs. Eagle," you say, "may I present Mr. Hoppity?" Politics being what they are, Mrs. Eagle restrains herself from replying "No," and the introduction is complete. Now, suppose you had said, "May I present Mr. Hoppity, Mrs. Eagle?" That's the same thing, isn't it? The name of the person addressed could really go on either end.

The fill-in words could also be "I have the honor to present," or "I would like to introduce you to," or "this is," or even "do you know," the last being a useful form in introducing apparent strangers when you can't remember if they were once married to each other.

We don't always say all the fill-in words, though, do we, in this speedy age? A person who says "Ham on rye" to a waitress is understood to be saying, "I wonder if you would be so good as to ask the chef to prepare me a sandwich, using rye bread, perhaps moistening it a bit with mustard, with a filling of ham in it, please?" Therefore, the introduction, "Ms. Perfect, Ms. Awful," has become common. Everyone understands that this is short for "Ms. Perfect, may I present Ms. Awful?" and knows you would never mean to say "This is Ms. Perfect, Ms. Awful."

So there you are: a foolproof introduction—unless, of course, you have forgotten the name of one of the people you are introducing. In that case, the form is "May I present Ms. Smelt-Hargrove?" A person whose name you have forgotten always takes precedence over one whose name you remember.

⌁ An Example ⌁

DEAR MISS MANNERS:

I would like to introduce a friend of mine that is 80 years old (Helen) to a friend that is 26 years old (Jennifer). Would I say to Helen, "Helen, I would like to introduce you to Jennifer"? Or would I say, "Jennifer, I would like to introduce you to Helen"? Is it age above all? And what would be proper information to include in the introduction? Would the relationship that Helen and Jennifer have to me be appropriate?

GENTLE READER:

Either way, Helen is not going to like this. She is old enough—as apparently you are not—to remember when people had surnames and young things were not encouraged to assume cheeky familiarity with their seniors.

Younger people are introduced to older people, except in cases of extraordinary rank being held by the younger person. If Jennifer is on the Supreme Court, you could make a case for presenting an older lady to her. Family relationships or another clue as to who the person is are mentioned in an introduction, although one does not introduce someone as "my friend" because it implies that the other person isn't.

It is even more essential to give these people each other's names, surely the purpose of the introduction, and this should be in the form in which they would properly address each other. Thus, you would say, "Helen, this is my college roommate, Jennifer Fox, who's just moved to town; Jennifer, this is my second cousin, Mrs. Hound." (And yes, Miss Manners realizes that Jennifer is a grown-up too, but she trusts Mrs. H. to call her Ms. F.)

~ *Completing the Incomplete Introduction* ~

DEAR MISS MANNERS:

What is the polite way one goes about eventually learning the last name of a new acquaintance?

As much as it used to be the case that one would first introduce one's self by one's last name and only reveal one's first name under more intimate circumstances, it is now the custom in most social circles to introduce one's self solely by the first name. I find myself generally reduced to the subversive tactics of finding some list in which the name is written or asking a third mutual acquaintance who happens to know, but surely etiquette has a better solution.

GENTLE READER:

You might ask at the time of the introduction. Miss Manners finds that most people remember their own surnames when prompted, even if they haven't used them for years.

~ *Introducing Servants* ~

DEAR MISS MANNERS:

I have read that it is improper to introduce the maid to one's friends, even if the friends are staying overnight and need to know her name. I read that you perform a half-introduction, such as "Mary will look after your needs; Mary, Mr. Brown will be here two nights." I feel funny about this. I don't want to do the wrong thing in front of a friend, yet I don't want to embarrass my maid, either, or do anything that is undignified toward anyone.

GENTLE READER:

People who are lucky enough to have servants should realize how comparatively easy it is to find a good friend. Miss Manners' inclination, therefore, is to worry about the dignity of the employee before the dignity of the friend. Unless the employee is committed to the old-fashioned method you describe, Miss Manners would prefer that you perform a decent introduction, which includes providing everyone with a last name. "This is Mary Jewel; Mary, Mr. Brown will be occupying the Queen's Bedroom."

∽ Introducing Children ∼

DEAR MISS MANNERS:

I have taught my children to introduce their friends to me, but sometimes they forget. If a child is visiting here, should I, as the lady of the house, greet him first or expect him to greet me?

GENTLE READER:

As you have noticed how hard it is to train one's own child, Miss Manners is astonished that you are contemplating waiting for someone else's child to carry the social burden. She recommends your saying, "I'm Christopher's mother; you must be Scott," rather than waiting, perhaps forever, until your visitor says, "I'm Scott; you must be Christopher's mother."

Children should be taught to start with the most formal form appropriate (Mr. and Ms. or Mrs. to nonrelatives, family titles to relatives), and then to accept modifications as offered by the person being addressed. It leaves them with an odd collection of usages, but the lesson that respect has to do with respecting the wishes of others.

∽ Introducing Oneself ∼

DEAR MISS MANNERS:

Some years ago, an elder relative told me one should not announce oneself as Mr. Soandso, because "Mister" is a title and "one does not give a title to oneself."

Having been around for some time and traveled a lot, I have come to know a number of persons with titles of nobility, from the heir apparent of an ex-maharaja to American women who had married European title holders and who, after these men had shed or been shed by the women, went on calling themselves the Baroness von This or the Contessa di That forever. In the British Isles, I once had occasion to telephone Lord Suchandsuch; he answered simply "Suchandsuch here!" Thus he followed my kinsman's system. But at a convention in England last year, a man in the elevator recognized me, stuck out his hand, and said, "Hello! My name's Lord Thusandso!" He did not obey my relative's rule.

Now, what is the drill on this, if, indeed, there is any rule for (a) "Mister" and (b) titles of nobility? Not that, as an American, I shall ever have a title of nobility; but it would be nice to know.

GENTLE READER:

Your kinsman is obviously one of nature's noblemen. Isn't it nicer to have Miss Manners say that than for him to have to announce it himself?

Why? Because a person who uses a title in reference to himself or herself, whether the title is grand duchess, doctor, maharaja, or even mister, seems suspiciously anxious to establish that he is entitled to that title. People naturally adore addressing others by fancy titles, but they grudge even the simplest to those who insist on them.

The correct British peer would no more dream of using his own title than he would of using his own umbrella, although he carries both and is proud of their age. Your Lord Thusandso probably has a new title and a new umbrella, too, which he enjoys opening in people's faces. Miss Manners has been trying for years to get people who have doctoral degrees to understand this principle of modesty, but they keep protesting that they earned their titles and want to show them off. They fail to understand the greater impact there is in being discovered to have a title that one has not bothered to show off.

People who have titles that are not officially recognized should be even more careful in doing this. Your Baroness von This and Contessa di That are badly in need of such a lesson. Never mind what happened to the baron or the conte—the German and Italian titles themselves have been legally abolished and are only used socially, by courtesy. The best way to ensure their use is by protesting, "Oh, no, we're just plain Habsburgs now, like everyone else." Your ladies could try the now fashionable Proud American routine that goes, "Please, I can't bear to be called princess—why, I was born and bred in Grand Forks, North Dakota." Either of these approaches will have people on their knees; but an American woman who calls herself "contessa" is assumed to be in the boutique business.

This is true on down the line. The person who announces stiffly, "I'm Mr. Ipswich" has undoubtedly given you his highest claim to dignity; but the one who says quietly, "My name is Isabel Bourbon" has left some room for grander assumptions.

∽ Introducing the Unknown ∽

DEAR MISS MANNERS:

Is it so awful not to be able to remember people's names? I've tried all kinds of systems, and it never seems to work. I find that if I fake a person's name when I don't know it, I get caught, but I'm afraid to admit right off that I don't know a name because people get insulted.

GENTLE READER:

We have a great deal of admiration in this country for people who have the ability to remember names. It is considered enough of a talent to qualify an otherwise undistinguished person for public office. If one votes for a candidate because he has remembered one's name from one minute of a campaign appearance to another, it is not reasonable to expect such a feat from every private citizen. Miss Manners promises not to be offended if you ask her what her name was again.

DEAR MISS MANNERS:

Suppose I'm talking to someone I'm supposed to know, but I can't remember his name. Another person joins us. Can I get them to tell each other their names?

GENTLE READER:

Certainly; who would be in a better position to know what they are? If you know the name of one of them, you can address the other with a firm statement, "This is Hollister Stranger," and then adjust your shoe, thus removing yourself from view and leaving the field clear for the unknown to complete the introduction. If you know neither name, it is wise to remove yourself from the scene entirely, after saying brightly, "I'm sure you two know each other!"

DEAR MISS MANNERS:

Whatever do you do when a person from your long-ago past unexpectedly confronts you with, "Do you know who I am?" This is really confounding, particularly when you are at a social gathering, with others around you, enjoying the joke on you.

It happened again yesterday when a woman whom I had not seen in over twenty-five years, whom I did not then know particularly well, and who is not aging with much grace, confronted me, as I was at a function, chatting with some recently-met acquaintances.

"No, you look too old and too fat for me ever to have paid attention to you" came to mind, but I didn't want to be that rude. As I am now in my 70th year, with all my faculties good and sound, I sound like a stumbling idiot as I stand there, fumbling with what to say. What should I say?

GENTLE READER:
"How could anyone forget you?"
Should the lady be so rash as to pass up the opportunity to accept this gracefully and ask "Well, then, who am I?" Miss Manners gives you leave to say gently, "Surely you can tell me." Your only error is to feel foolish when approached by foolish people.

Name Tags

DEAR MISS MANNERS:
Where is the correct place to pin a name tag? We use them at our club parties, and I hope you don't disapprove of this practice, because it's very useful. But it looks odd to see everyone bending over, reading one another's bosoms.

GENTLE READER:
Miss Manners disapproves of name tags only at strictly social functions, because she believes they make things too easy and thus take away the fun. When they are used, they should be placed at collar level, for the reason you mention, and they should be on the right-hand side of the wearer. This makes it possible for people to sneak a quick look halfway between the handshake and the face, and then to pretend to have remembered the other person's name.

Introducing the Roof Principle

DEAR MISS MANNERS:
While boarding a bus on my way home from work recently, I noticed on the same bus a fellow with whom I was graduated from law school last June. Although we attended many of the same classes for three years, we never spoke to one another (both being true gentlemen, it could not have been otherwise, since we were never properly introduced). Now that it appears that we will be riding the same bus home, it seems a bit silly to continue ignoring one another, particularly should we ever end up sharing the same seat. Could you arrange an introduction?

GENTLE READER:

Allow Miss Manners to introduce you to a principle: "The roof constitutes an introduction." This does not apply to every roof. It does not apply to a bus, for example, although it does apply to a ship. It does, however, apply to an academic institution. Therefore, it is as proper for you to say, "I believe we were in class together" as it would be, if you had been "properly introduced," to say, "I believe we met at the Wintergreens' last Christmas."

A Gay Introduction

DEAR MISS MANNERS:

What am I supposed to say when I am introduced to a homosexual "couple"?

GENTLE READER:

"How do you do?" "How do you do?"

Honorifics

Just when Miss Manners had despaired of ever again hearing an honest-to-goodness honorific, a new formal courtesy title sprang into use. A whole generation now believes that the respectful way to address one's elders is "You guys," the plural form of "Yo."

Although this would not have been Miss Manners' choice, it beats tugging on people's sleeves to get their attention. And something is needed. The first-name-only system has long suffered from the apparent requirement that all children who go through school together must share names. The convenience of knowing exactly how old each Lisa, Jason, Kelly, Emily, Zachary and Madison is no matter how far into adulthood one encounters them is offset by the problem of distinguishing among the bearers of these names.

Miss Manners has kept an iron grip on that "Miss" of hers and refused to let go. You never caught her trying to con some toddler into thinking she was his age and therefore required no deferential treatment. Had she been either older or younger, she would have taken the more sensible title of Ms., which was the traditional abbreviation for the title of Mistress before that word slipped from respectability and bifurcated into the remnants, Miss and Mrs. Once everyone has gotten over mistakenly condemning Ms. as a modern invention, she would still need to make the touchy point that Mrs. is correctly used only with the lady's husband's name, and that it makes no difference whether the husband is dead or alive (as regards nomenclature, whatever other difference it may make to the wife). Mr. is suitable for most of the rest of the population.

But there is also rank, and the rule is that the higher the rank, the less likely its bearer is to give you a clue about how to use it in address. We call this modesty. And because usage grows haphazardly as a result of ancient, melded and whimsical customs, do not expect to be able to reason it out. Here are a few handy particulars:

The President of the United States is addressed by nickname (his or his enemies') before the election and "Mr. President" after taking office. Everybody else in Washington is styled "The Honorable" to make up for what everybody outside of Washington calls them.

"Your Majesty" is used for reigning sovereigns, pretenders whose presence is being sought to posh up your board of directors or charity event and children who don't pick up after themselves. Lesser royalty and younger children who don't pick up after themselves are called "Your Royal Highness."

The correct use of military titles is taught by force to those who need to know. Religious titles are taught gently to those who need to know, as a result of which most congregates mistakenly believe that "Reverend" can be used alone or with the surname, whereas it must be preceded by "the."

The system for addressing different varieties of European aristocrats should also be on a need-to-know basis, except that few people who feel they need to know have grasped the fact that "Lady" is not used before the lady's first name unless she is the daughter of a duke, marquess or earl; those who come by the title through marriage use it before the husband's name.

Fortunately, we do have all-purpose titles for direct address, as a foolproof way of conveying the respect due to people whose names escape you. These are "Madam" (or "Ma'am") and "Sir." True, they specify the gender, but Miss Manners figures that you guys are not in a position to complain about that.

Doctors

DEAR MISS MANNERS:

I have several physician friends and when I introduce them and their wives at formal gatherings, the "Doctor and Mrs." title seems just fine. But I have a more troublesome set of friends—a couple in which she is a doctor and her husband is not.

I introduced them as "Doctor and Mr." at our last dinner party and he winced as if his hiatal hernia were acting up. How can I properly introduce this couple without discriminating against my female friend or doing irreparable damage to her husband's ego?

GENTLE READER:

Miss Manners fails to understand why a female doctor is any more troublesome to society than male doctors naturally are, or why a gentleman should be more abashed than a lady at being married to someone who takes money from the sick. You introduced him properly. Perhaps his hiatal hernia *was* acting up, in which case he should see a doctor.

Doctorates

DEAR MISS MANNERS:

I was introduced to a Dr. Soandso at a party and was embarrassed to have him say, after I had discussed at length an interesting disease in my family, that he didn't know anything about medicine. I suppose he was a doctor of philosophy, but should he then call himself a doctor?

GENTLE READER:

What you have there is either an honest medical practitioner or an uncertain Ph.D. Only people of the medical profession correctly use the title of doctor socially. A really fastidious doctor of philosophy will not use it professionally either, and schools and scholarly institutions where it is assumed that everyone has an advanced degree use "Mr.," "Mrs.," "Miss" or "Ms."

Many people feel strongly possessive about their scholarly titles, however, and it is Miss Manners' principle to allow them to call themselves what they want. She will only offer them a story: Miss Manners' own dear father, who would never allow himself to be addressed as doctor, used to say that a Ph.D. was like a nose—you don't make a fuss about having one because you assume that everyone does; it's only when you don't have one that it is conspicuous. For sheer snobbery, doesn't that beat insisting on being called doctor?

⌒ *Honorary Doctorates* ⌒

DEAR MISS MANNERS:

I have recently received an honorary doctorate and am especially pleased about it as I have had no formal higher education, and so this is my first degree. However, it seems to be show-offy to use the title of "doctor" under these circumstances. Many of the doctors of philosophy I know don't even use theirs. Yet what good does the title do me if nobody knows about it?

GENTLE READER:

You are in the position of a woman who has invested in silk underwear. She must derive her satisfaction from knowing that she has it on, and perhaps the knowledge of an intimate or two. To let everyone know cheapens the effect. However (to drop the underwear), you might look out for the chance to ally yourself with the doctors of philosophy who do not use the title by telling those who do, "I would never dream of calling myself 'doctor'—after all, I'm not a physician."

⌒ *The Clergy* ⌒

DEAR MISS MANNERS:

Is it true that I shouldn't introduce our pastor as "Reverend Jones"? Maybe I wasn't paying close attention at church, but it seems to me I've always heard it done that way.

GENTLE READER:

Maybe you weren't paying close attention at school. "Reverend" is an adjective. The correct introduction is, therefore, "*the* Reverend Cotton Pious."

DEAR MISS MANNERS:

What is the correct way to address a Protestant clergywoman? What about when she is with her husband, who has no title?

GENTLE READER:

The form is the same as for a clergyman—the Reverend Angela Mather for her alone, adding "and Mr. Mather" when they are both present. Miss Manners is scandalized by those who believe that God is more interested in sex than service when contemplating those in His or Her ministry.

～ *Omitting Honorifics* ～

DEAR MISS MANNERS:

Is it now considered appropriate for everyone to address everyone else by first names, without even asking permission? Is this no longer considered taking a liberty? In the past few months, my insurance salesman, a man who sold me a car part, and a man who sold me a pair of shoes have all considered it their privilege to address me by my first name. My name is on my credit cards, etc., and cannot be kept from the world. How do I inform people, particularly prospective employers, that I do not wish to be addressed in this manner, without appearing rude myself? I am not from a bygone age. I am twenty-six years old and appalled by this rudeness, which passes for casualness or friendliness. Please help.

GENTLE READER:

The answer to your question is, Miss Manners regrets to say, that yes, indeed, it is commonplace to use first names promiscuously. The answer to your plea for help, however, is that yes, we will fight this unfortunate practice together, with anyone else who cares to join this noble cause. Such usage is not only undignified, but makes a sham of the ideas of friendship and equality. There is no such thing as instant intimacy.

As you recognize, however, the ticklish part of the fight for good manners is to exhibit them oneself during battle. One cannot go around correcting others. However, one can go about driving others crazy in a perfectly polite fashion. One method of doing this is to keep saying, "No, no, I'm terribly sorry, you must have misunderstood—Geoffrey is my first name. My last name is Perfect." Another is to address the offenders by their last names, no matter how many times they urge you not to. If they tell you only a first name or say, "Call me Sam," then address that person as "Mr. Sam." Miss Manners is not guaranteeing that this will teach others respect, but it will pay back some of the irritation you have experienced and serve to alert them that something is wrong, even if they can't figure out what.

DEAR MISS MANNERS:

I have never adjusted to the everyday assumed intimacy by acquaintances and strangers. When I am asked my first name, I find that answering "Mrs." is very helpful—the other person will then ask for my last name and nothing more is said. This usually solves my problem and often brings a smile.

GENTLE READER:

Is it possible that you and Miss Manners are related? She has never countenanced instant intimacy either, preferring the voluntary kind; she also imparts this information gently to people who assume otherwise—and she has the good fortune to bear the given name of Miss.

~ *Advancing Past Honorifics* ~

DEAR MISS MANNERS:

You have many times pointed out that it is presumptuous, rude, annoying, and everything else short of illegal to call people by their first names when you hardly know them. How do you properly get on a first-name basis with someone you are beginning to know well?

Suppose you find yourself with an acquaintance you have always addressed as "Mrs." at a social gathering where everyone else is on first-name basis? Or you want to indicate to an older person that you consider him a friend, rather than just an object of respect? Or you meet, for the first time, the spouse of someone whose first name you have been using? If you just plunge right in and use that person's first name, will Miss Manners write you off as a clod who doesn't know any better?

GENTLE READER:

Now, now. You don't know Miss Manners very well if you think she goes about applying the name of clod to people who are earnestly trying to get the nuances of behavior right. Therefore, you may continue to call her "Miss Manners."

One reason Miss Manners stresses waiting to address people by their first names is that the little ceremony involved is so charming. The woman who goes around announcing herself to strangers as "Hi, I'm Brook," will never have the pleasure of blushing and saying, "Oh, I do wish you would call me Brook, now that we're friends." In a heterosexual situation, so to speak, this is the privilege of the woman; among people of the same gender, it should be done by the elder.

~ *. . . or Not* ~

DEAR MISS MANNERS:

I have recently moved to a neighborhood peopled largely with retired couples and older widows. I am considerably younger than these neighbors, but they have been very helpful and kind to us. I want my children to call them "Mrs." or "Mr." but, in these days of informal manners, how should I address them? They have introduced themselves by first names and I want them to call me by my first name, but I'm not comfortable calling someone considerably older than myself by a first name. I now call them by their titles and most of them appear a little uncomfortable with this—but they haven't suggested otherwise. What do you suggest?

GENTLE READER:

Asking someone to use your first name is a gesture of warmth and friendship, but it cannot be made unless titles are used before the request. Continue to address them as you do, and if they get really uncomfortable, they will request you to do otherwise. If they want to stay uncomfortable, that's their problem.

HANDSHAKES, KISSES AND OTHER INTRODUCTORY GESTURES

Watch out! Someone is coming at you with the clear intention of saying hello.

Will your shoulder be thumped, or your fist be bumped? Will your hand be slapped? High five? Low five? Will you receive a pat on the cheek or a pinch on the cheek? A grabbing of the forearm or a full leap into both arms? Will you be hugged or kissed? Kissed on the cheek or the mouth? Which cheek? How many times?

The chances of receiving a curtsey are not big unless you make a living teaching ballet, running debutante balls or reigning. But the bow and namaste are not uncommon, although not necessarily performed by, respectively, Japanese or Hindus.

The handshake is more of a rarity these days, unless performed with four hands, either in a pile-up, patty-cake style, or sandwich style, with one set taking the outside and the other the inside. The hands may also be used to grab or snap a finger, curl the fingers together or execute some combination of such gestures.

What will be said, or will you be expected to say? "How're you doing?" "Pleased to meetcha?" "Wassup?"

You have to chose among the correct things to say on being introduced: "Good morning" or "Good evening," which requires checking the position of the sun; or "Hello" or "How do you do?" depending on the formality of the occasion, and whether you can count on the other person to understand that the answer to "How do you do?" is "How do you do?" even though that makes two questions in a row.

(Etiquette opposes any declaration of being pleased to meet someone on the cynical grounds that it may not turn out to be a pleasure.)

The simple part is supposed to be the handshake, which Miss Manners would have thought to be quite warm enough as a start for an acquaintanceship or an evening. True, the lady/older/ranking person should initiate the gesture, but we have to wrestle with identifying which one that is.

There are exceptions and objections to hand-shaking, religious, physical and hygienic, and exemptions are granted. But the gesture itself has been so well known that a refusal to participate has to be explained ("I'm so sorry, but I can't shake hands") because a refusal to shake hands is a symbolic insult (and thus a handy gesture when faced with tyrants and outlaws).

Unless, of course, you are too busy thumping, bumping and kissing, or positioning yourself to dodge or return whatever may be thrown your way.

⟶ Shaking What Is Offered ⟵

DEAR MISS MANNERS:

What is the proper way to shake hands when being introduced to someone who has accidentally lost his/her right hand? This situation occurs often enough to me in my work (sales and management) to risk embarrassing the less fortunate person. If he extends his right (artificial or stump), do you extend your right and shake his (a) artificial hand or (b) his right forearm or shoulder? Several people have the same question and none of us has found a satisfactory answer; "social graces" columnists have usually responded with "do whatever you think is right" or some such nonresponsive answer. I'd like to know what you think.

GENTLE READER:

Miss Manners is fully sensible of the fact that if everyone did whatever she or he thought was right, Miss Manners would be out of business. Please do not take it as non-responsiveness, therefore, if she tells you that neither she nor you is the person who knows best what the amputee would feel most comfortable doing.

That individual—the one with the hand missing—must therefore take the lead in this common social situation. Some people extend a left hand, others extend the right arm or artificial device affixed to it. All you need to know is that you always shake hands with your right hand. What you shake is whatever is offered to you.

⌒ Social Kissing ⌒

There is a great deal of kissing going on these days among people who do not especially like one another. Miss Manners is not referring to the popular teenage pastime of this description, but to what is known as social kissing, an activity common among consenting, if unenthusiastic, adults.

Why everyone is doing it when no one can agree on how it should be done is a question that could also be asked of more invigorating forms of bodily contact. The consequences of kissing improperly range from having one's cheek hanging jilted in midair, to getting one's lip neatly severed by a diamond ring.

In administering a kiss of greeting to someone one knows (it is improper to kiss people upon meeting them for the first time, and this includes baby-molesting on the part of political candidates), the following surfaces may be employed:

Lips.

The right cheek only.

The right cheek, followed by the left cheek.

The hand.

This is a complete list of acceptable places for the social kiss. If you intend to use any other, Miss Manners requests that you and the object of your intentions step quickly behind the nearest curtain for the purposes. If you should unintentionally deliver the kiss on another area, such as the nose or the ear, it is just as bad. Good intentions count for nothing here.

Much of the confusion comes because each participant assumes he or she is choosing the type of social kiss to be performed, and the two choices don't match.

Remember that we are talking about a formal, public gesture, and the fact that parts of the body and ways they are used may duplicate private expressions of emotion is irrelevant.

Just because gentlemen no longer have the exclusive right to initiate private kissing does not mean that they may now share in the ladies' privilege of initiating—or withholding—public kissing. If a lady presents her lips by tilting her face upward without moving it to either side, the gentleman has no choice but to perform. A gentleman's choice is the hand kiss, although there must be some excuse of a continental background. Charter trips of twenty-one to forty-five days are not enough.

Cheek-kissing, in this country, requires a minimum of one lady, but the partner may be either a lady or a gentleman. All cheek kisses begin with the presentation of the right cheek by the ranking lady. The recipient also presents the right cheek. The first presenter gets to choose whether they will actually kiss each other's cheeks, make a smack-smack noise in the air, or simply bump cheeks. That person should also decide whether to proceed with the European version, of repeating the adventure using left cheeks, or whether to call it a day. The partner's job is still to be alert in order to follow suit and not go after someone who doesn't mean it or walk away from someone who does.

Eye Contact

DEAR MISS MANNERS:

Please bring the issue of eye contact into focus for me. I am a twenty-five-year-old unmarried half-Oriental female. My entire life has been spent in the Far East, where staring into the pupils of another is the height of impropriety (or come-and-get-it-ness). I have, since coming here, been accused of avoiding the issue, and now feel that my adjustment to the United States will never be complete without some kind of "code of looks."

GENTLE READER:

What pretentious people call "body language" and make fortunes writing paperback books about, Miss Manners considers merely details of etiquette that vary from culture to culture. In a way, it is more important to learn these when going from one society to another than it is to learn the more obvious forms, such as table manners, because people often fail to realize that such behavior as eye contact is learned, and they pounce on it as being psychologically revealing.

Miss Manners once had a similar problem, when she was a girl. After a year's residency in South America, she found she was standing closer to people when she conversed with them than is customary in North America, and that her perfectly decent behavior was being interpreted as flirtatious. The solution was merely to relearn the North American standard for the proper distance between conversing acquaintances.

Miss Manners advises you to learn the American etiquette with regard to eye contact for use here, rather than to endure the handicap of being misinterpreted by people who are unaware of foreign customs. In this country, it is considered polite to look people in the eye when conversing with them. If you find this difficult, an alternative is to look away but maintain a smile, in which case your behavior will be misinterpreted as charming demureness. That, at least, is better than being considered shifty.

~ Speaking When Spoken To ~

DEAR MISS MANNERS:

Would you please give me the correct etiquette on speaking or greeting people when entering a room of people, and when meeting on the street. Should the person entering the room speak first? Should the youngest speak first, respecting their elders? I have relatives in their late teens and also young adults (married) who will never speak unless spoken to first. I was brought up differently.

GENTLE READER:

Even Queen Elizabeth gave up the rules about speaking first, and she was brought up differently too. Many years ago, when she visited America, she greeted with regal silence anyone who presumed to speak to her before being spoken to; on her later visits, while she was not up to calling out "Howdy" to everyone, she at least returned all greetings. Miss Manners feels that it is always gracious to address another person civilly and to acknowledge civil addresses, and is pleased to see anyone master this ability, whatever her upbringing and however late in life.

~ Removing the Hat (If Any) ~

DEAR MISS MANNERS:

Does a gentleman's "tipping" his hat look too much like a military salute? Since I seldom see any male wearing a real hat, I'd almost forgotten this gesture. I think it's been at least twenty years since this has meant grasping the hat brim and either lifting the hat an inch or two, or just grasping and releasing the brim.

GENTLE READER:

You have obviously not met a polite cowboy for twenty years. The rule is the same now as it always was: A gentleman removes his hat when speaking to a lady or sharing an elevator with one, and lifts his hat as a gesture to a stranger from whom he receives a courtesy or thanks for a courtesy of his. As you have noticed, however, it does require a hat and is therefore seldom performed. The military salute is much more energetic, but it also comes with PX privileges.

∼ Offering an Arm ∼

DEAR MISS MANNERS:

When does a gentleman offer his arm to a lady as they are walking down the street together?

GENTLE READER:

Strictly speaking, only when he can be of practical assistance to her. That is, when the way is steep, dark, crowded or puddle-y. However, it is rather a cozy juxtaposition, less compromising than walking hand in hand, and rather enjoyable for people who are fond of each other, so Miss Manners allows some leeway in interpreting what is of practical assistance. One wouldn't want a lady to feel unloved walking down the street, any more than one would want her to fall off the curb.

∼ Failure to Yield ∼

DEAR MISS MANNERS:

An act of public rudeness that I encounter frequently, if not daily, is a condition I have come to call "sidewalk selfishness." Two or more people walking down the street do not make space for someone walking in the opposite direction. Once I was actually forced off the sidewalk by three people walking abreast, who barely acknowledged my presence.

My girlfriend and I like to take walks, and when we see people coming the other direction, we will form a single-file line to make room for the others to pass. Surprisingly, the people coming from the other direction often do not follow suit. I can only guess as to the cause. Please tell me what I can do to address the issue without being as rude as the perpetrators of this selfishness.

GENTLE READER:

The cause is simple. The people you encounter are using the sidewalk to walk on, but in the opposite direction to you, and they are confident that they do not need to disturb themselves because they can disturb you. As you point out, this is selfish. There is a lot of that going around, Miss Manners has noticed.

If you want to make a point of this without encountering a lot of other unpleasantries that are going around, you can stay on the sidewalk rather than yield. Presuming they don't mow you down, they will have to notice you when you say, "Excuse me, please, coming through."

~ *Failure to Follow* ~

DEAR MISS MANNERS:

I hope you will give me the answer to a problem that confronts me every now and then: Two people (a male and a female) walk toward each other on a sidewalk. As they pass each other, should each step to the right, even though the curbside is on the female's right, or should the male step to the curbside and the female to the inside, even though the inside is to the female's left? If two females pass each other, no problem—each steps to the right. I presume the same holds true for two males.

It is so embarrassing to step to the right and have the other person step to the left at the same time—and then to have each reverse. This impromptu "Turkey Trot" can be repeated three or four times, with both parties apologizing profusely, until one or the other stands still and lets the other go by. If both were to stand still simultaneously, I can visualize the problem recurring, but this is unlikely.

Once I "danced" with a dog. I didn't have time to notice whether it was male or female, but after three times going from side to side, it barked at me and passed me by stepping off the curbing. I wonder why I didn't think of stepping off the curbing before the dog did. Right or wrong, that dog made a fool of me. I'll very much appreciate your advice as to the accepted directions in which a male and female pedestrian should step when passing each other on the sidewalk.

GENTLE READER:

Miss Manners advises you not to get into a chess game with that dog, because the dog will win. The idea in chess, as in life, is to see what is coming before it arrives and plan ahead to avoid undesirable confrontations. The basic move is that everyone steps to the right on uncheckered sidewalks—ladies, gentlemen, dogs, knights and bishops.

SAYING NO:
SILENCE AS A SOCIAL SKILL

Mindful of etiquette's injunction to please others, nice people have trouble saying no. This is a good way to get a bad reputation.

Miss Manners knows, because she has one. Not personally, of course, because she says "No, thank you" so touchingly that petitioners pity her for being unable to comply with their demands. It is etiquette itself that has a bad reputation, stemming from the mistaken belief it requires a perpetual sacrifice of one's own wishes and judgment in favor of others'. As the naive invariably put it, "Isn't etiquette always a matter of making other people feel comfortable?" This would make politeness an activity exclusively for suckers and wimps. And, of course, sluts.

In fact, etiquette has no such requirement. The mistake arises from the fact that it does recognize that one has duties toward others, which is why it will not put up with such duty-dodging attempts as "Why should I thank Grandma for the check just because she wants me to?" And it does require being polite to others, even when they are no role models themselves.

But that is a far cry from declaring that courtesy means taking everybody else's orders. And orders are being constantly issued, now that reticence and modesty are no longer considered the virtues they once were. From the selfish and the philanthropic alike, we are bombarded with requests to do, donate, attend, volunteer, eat, drink and buy.

With the best of will, the biggest of purses and the freest of schedules, one could never fulfill all these orders. And much as Miss Manners appreciates any inhibitions at all that are inspired by courtesy, she hopes that people will make these important choices with more discrimination than is involved in surrendering whenever they happen to be cornered.

This is why the ability to say no politely is an essential social skill. All that is really needed is the ability to repeat "No, thank you," interspersed with such small politenesses as "I'm so sorry" and "You're kind to ask" and "I wish you luck."

Elaborating is what gets people into trouble. Excuses that are false are traps one sets for oneself, but even true excuses encourage the audacious to argue: "Can't you do that another night?" "One little piece of cake isn't going to kill you." "But this helps more people."

Yet most people can't help blabbing on to soften the "no," which is apt to be so softened as to give way. So here is a small supply of supplementary sentences:

"I'm afraid I'm not taking on anything else right now."

"Sorry, I never discuss my finances."

"I'm sure it's wonderful, but I'm not going to have any."

"We never go to balls, but we'd love to see you privately."

"I'm so sorry, but that's not something I can help you with."

"If you care to send me some written material, I'll get in touch if I find it interests me."

"I didn't realize what this involved, and I think I'd better bow out."

And the ultimately correct, no-excuses refusal:

Dr. Peony Wiley
regrets that she is unable to accept
the exceedingly kind invitation of
Mr. and Mrs. Popinjay
for Saturday, the first of June

⌒ When "No" Is Kinder than "Yes" ⌒

DEAR MISS MANNERS:

I feel frustrated when I make a request of a friend or coworker and they answer my question in a vague manner, avoid answering the question altogether or even sometimes say yes, and then back out at the last minute with an excuse like they did not have enough time to fulfill the request.

It seems pretty clear to me that sometimes people simply do not want to honor a request made of them but do not respond in an honest manner. I feel it is okay to decline the request of a friend or colleague so I do not understand why people just don't say no in the first place.

Is telling a person "no" in nonverbal communication more appropriate than straightforward communication? Is indirect communication more appropriate than direct communication in professional and personal relationships?

GENTLE READER:

In some societies, it is. Elaborate conventions exist to enable people to field or ignore a request so as to make clear that it has been refused—while also conveying how much pain it costs to refuse.

We don't go in for that sort of subtlety; we pride ourselves on our frankness. Yet Miss Manners is amazed and touched that in a society that suffers from only-too-straightforward communication, often in the form of a raised finger, many people still feel that it is rude to refuse any request. Also, they think they have to supply an excuse, which will be led into a tangle of implausible lies.

So they hedge. As you have noticed, this causes more trouble to those who mistakenly think their requests have been granted than if they were refused outright.

The polite way to refuse is to precede the denial with an apology but no excuse:

"Oh, I'm terribly sorry, but I can't." "I'd love to, but I'm afraid it's impossible." "Unfortunately, I can't, but I hope you can find someone."

It is not more polite to say, "Well, sure, if I can finish up my other stuff and I don't have another assignment, only my stepson may be in town then and I'm having trouble with my car, so I don't know."

∽ An Example ∼

DEAR MISS MANNERS:

How do you say no—without appearing stingy—to someone who wants to borrow your cell phone to make a call? On several occasions, friends, acquaintances, and once a complete stranger at a bus stop have asked to use my phone. They may see it as a simple call, but it ends up draining my battery and inflating my bill.

GENTLE READER:

Was the stranger at the bus stop lying on the sidewalk bleeding? There are circumstances under which you must let people use your cellular telephone, although that is the only one that comes to Miss Manners' mind.

Otherwise, the best way to say no is with much regret but no explanation: "Oh, I'm afraid not, I'm so sorry, I can't let you, I wish I could." No polite person would argue with this, but an impolite one could be told "It's a restricted line." Indeed it is. You are restricting its use to yourself.

<h1 align="center">COMMON ANNOYANCES</h1>

∽ Annoying Those with Disabilities ∼

It was the popular belief that etiquette is simply a matter of acting naturally that drove Miss Manners from her comfortable chaise longue into this business. Miss Manners does not want people to act naturally; she wants them to act civilly. Nowhere is the difference more evident than in the uncivil way most people naturally treat those with disabilities. You turn a well-meaning, good-hearted, average, sensitive citizen loose on someone who is not as able-bodied as himself, and just watch the well-meaning, good-hearted insults fly.

Why do the Temporarily Able-bodied, as they have been called, behave so unpleasantly to others? Perhaps out of fear that such a fate could befall them, but Miss Manners is not interested in hearing excuses. Insults to those with handicaps seem to be based on the absurd assumption that they are not full-functioning adults and therefore—like patients or children—must do as others think best for them. That is why people cheerfully invade their privacy, address them with patronizingly false good cheer and blithely overrule their expressed wishes.

A typically sympathetic person will think nothing of accosting another human being, if he or she is in a wheelchair, demanding to know what is "wrong." This is personal information which someone may or may not want to volunteer. As a lady with disabilities of Miss Manners' acquaintance put it, "You wouldn't go up to a person and ask, 'Hey, why are you so ugly?'" Nor should you lean close into the face of someone you hardly know with what she describes as "that gooey smile."

Miss Manners fails to see why a person seated in a wheelchair should be approached differently from one seated in an ordinary chair—one leans at an acceptable distance or sits nearby, and does not clutch the arm of another's chair—or why the ordinary rules of conversation, as to taste or lack of it, should not apply.

Along with the presumption about lack of privacy there is an assumption about a lack of sexuality. Miss Manners has long since learned not to make such assumptions about anyone.

Another area of offensiveness is the matter of offering assistance. A polite person will offer assistance to anyone who seems in need of it, but the key word here is "offer." People with disabilities often find, to their peril, that assistance is given to them after they have declined it or contrary to their instructions on what assistance would be helpful. If such a person has some aid, such as a cane or a Seeing Eye dog, it should be entirely under his or her control. Attempts to grab the cane arm or to pet a dog on duty are as helpful as playing with the controls of a car someone else is driving. If there is an accompanying companion, that assistant is not to be presumed to be a guardian. You address all people directly, instead of talking about them in the third person in their presence, and when you talk to a deaf person, you face him, not his interpreter.

Some leeway is allowed to children when they ask "What is wrong with you?" or "How do you operate that thing?" But this is only because everybody understands that children don't know any better than to act naturally.

Dear Miss Manners:

A new family moved in next door to us with a daughter who is about the same age as my roommates (early twenties) and I. We want to be friendly, but don't know anything about how to be helpful to the blind, which she is. For instance, when I was introduced, I blurted out, "You must come see us sometime," and then nearly died because I realized that, of course, she can't see.

GENTLE READER:

You may well be embarrassed. A woman in her twenties who does not know the difference between the literal and figurative use of a simple word like "see" ought to be ashamed of herself. Blindness means that a person literally cannot see and nothing more. When dealing with the blind, therefore, one makes some adjustments relating to lack of vision, but no others. One does not, for example, change one's manner of speaking. Blind people use and understand the language like everyone else.

For some strange reason, people often assume that a blind person must have other disabilities, physical and mental. This is rude, as well as illogical. One does not shout at the blind, one does not ask their companions about them as if they did not understand, one does not touch them without permission and one does not assume that they are lost or helpless as a matter of course. One of the greatest handicaps the blind have to deal with is the number of people who will pounce on them while they are minding their own business and start pushing them around, literally as well as figuratively.

There are, however, things you can do if you want to be helpful to your neighbor. (Do not expect Miss Manners to congratulate you on initiating the friendship; it is neither more nor less charming than welcoming any new neighbor, for the purpose of giving friendship the chance to develop or not as it will.)

Identify yourself when you see her. She may learn to recognize your voice, but "Hi" is a short sample to go by, guessing games are atrocious for all people under all circumstances and a friendly wave is no help at all. You should also announce your departures, so that she is not left talking to you after you are gone. Do as you would in a telephone conversation.

Mention whatever you see that might be useful or amusing for her to know. "There's a plate of cucumber sandwiches on the table to your right," "Here comes Mrs. Awful heading straight for you, and does she look furious," "You dropped your napkin near your left foot," "Erica's pearls don't look real," "We've moved the piano across the room since you were here last," "The man who keeps bumping against you is General Nuisance, whose wife is over by the bar."

When she really does seem to need help, offer it orally: "Do you want to take my arm going down the stairs?" Miss Manners should not have to remind you it is always considered polite to take no for an answer. If your neighbor asks for help, it is helpful to give it without unsolicited advice or editing. If you read a menu to her, read the whole menu, with prices, not what you think she might like; and if you read her mail to her, do not interpret it.

The basic rules of identification, offering specific information, and refraining from molestation also apply to blind strangers. "I'm waiting for the bus too, and the T-7 is coming" is preferable to mugging a person silently to shove him on the bus; and "Stop! There's a pothole in front of you!" is more useful than a general "Watch out!" which could apply literally to an escaped lion's coming down the street or figuratively to the idea that inflation is going to get us all. Do you see?

DEAR MISS MANNERS:

All right, my day is now complete. I just got yelled at by a white-haired old lady in a wheelchair for trying to help her into the intersection when the light turned green. You know what she said? "F—— off, buddy." Nice? No doubt, I am a pig for trying to help her, and also a racist and an oppressor of the poor, handicapped, and elderly. I have learned my lesson about that. I promise never to try to be a gentleman again. But you know what else? *I am damn sick of people hating me for trying to be a nice guy. And I can't stand it any longer.* I am going to go out and punch the first sweet little old lady I see right in the mouth. What do you think of that? Hurrah for modern manners.

GENTLE READER:

There, there. Please try to calm yourself. Miss Manners doesn't hate you. Miss Manners knows you meant well. You just sob quietly on Miss Manners' shoulder for a minute, and when you feel up to it, she will explain to you what happened.

All right? Feel a little better now? The desire to help people is a noble one. But you must first make sure that they are in need of help. Surely the smallest Boy Scout has learned by now that it doesn't count as a good deed to help an old lady across the street if she doesn't want to cross the street—or if she doesn't want to be helped. You made an assumption that the old lady in the wheelchair must be in need of help; must be, in a word, helpless. But how do you suppose that she got to the intersection where you saw her? Did she fall out of a nursing home window, wheelchair and all?

No, you have to assume that she got there after having set out, knowing, as all rational beings do, the extent of her own capabilities. You also have to realize, when you think about it, that a wheelchair occupant is bound to know more about how to handle a wheelchair than you, as a passerby. Your assistance may have endangered not only her dignity, as a person entitled to be considered in control of herself unless she specifically asks for help, but it may also have endangered her safety.

Miss Manners dearly hopes you will not discontinue helping damsels in distress, and mensels too, for that matter. Just make sure, before you do so, that they are in distress. Helping someone into distress, however courteously, is not a good deed.

⌒ *Annoying the Stricken* ⌒

DEAR MISS MANNERS:

Someone in our office collapsed suddenly, and a crew of paramedics had to be called. They gave him assistance right there and then took him to the hospital on a stretcher. We were all terribly concerned, and many of us stood around until he was taken away, only to be told later, by some co-workers, that it was awful of us to watch what was going on. This was not a stranger who had an accident on the street—this was someone we work with, and we were there because we wanted to see if he would be all right.

GENTLE READER:

Nevertheless, the same rule applies as at accidents. If you cannot fulfill the need for medical or practical assistance, help fill the need for privacy. The discipline required for studying medicine is nothing compared to that needed to stifle one's curiosity.

⌒ *Annoying the Pious* ⌒

DEAR MISS MANNERS:

When entering my Episcopal Church, we have traditionally knelt in silent prayer and kept quiet before the service starts. Recently it sounds more like a cocktail party than a sanctuary.

A whispered "good morning" I can accept, but I was recently subjected to details ranging from what was cooking at home to a thoroughly explicit medical report of the innards of the man behind me, plus his home improvement project.

This seems to be happening all over the country. At my niece's church, ballet performances are part of the service. A friend hears business contracts all but signed-sealed-and-delivered while waiting to worship.

Good Lord, deliver us.

GENTLE READER:

First, He is going to have to get the churchgoers' attention. Miss Manners would think that the clergy might feel obliged to point out to those who consider their churches to be social, entertainment and business centers that occasionally someone does go there to pray.

DEAR MISS MANNERS:

As a child, I was taught never to applaud in church. Now it is very common in my church and others I have attended. It seems that everything—singing, speeches or any type of performance—is followed by someone saying "Let's give them a big hand." Everybody applauds except me. Is this right or wrong?

GENTLE READER:

You are right, but brace yourself. A lot of angry churchgoers are going to come at you with that quote about making a joyful noise unto the Lord.

Miss Manners is delighted that they have the joyful noise idea, and is all for music, speaking and other decently appropriate forms of worship. But she is afraid the good people missed that part about its being directed unto the Lord, and not unto themselves. Their pleasure may be great, but it is incidental to the purpose of worship, and they should not attempt to usurp the Lord's power of passing judgment on those who are worshipping Him. If God wishes to applaud in church, He may, but it is inappropriate for anyone else to do so.

Annoying the Literary

DEAR MISS MANNERS:

When I read the newspaper at the breakfast table, my wife, who has another section of the paper in front of her, starts reading the back of the section I am holding up. So do my children, who ordinarily wouldn't read anything. It's not just a family problem, either. People do it when I'm reading on the bus. I find it annoying to have people lurking behind me while I'm trying to read, shifting about if I happen to drop the paper down slightly to hold my coffee cup or whatever. If I then offer my section to my wife, she always says, "Oh, no, I don't want it, I was just looking at that one little thing that caught my eye." Do you consider it legitimate for people to read the backs of other people's papers?

GENTLE READER:

Within reason, yes. Miss Manners believes it is one's duty to contribute to an informed public. However, when they start asking you to turn the page, reason and duty end.

DEAR MISS MANNERS:

Once you loaned a book, or someone has loaned you a book, what is the appropriate length of time for returning it? I'm not talking about a $6 paperback; I would

not expect that to be returned to me (although I'd probably return it if I were the "loanee"). I'm talking about your average $25–$35 hardback. And then, is it appropriate to ask for it back after that length of time has passed?

GENTLE READER:

The time to get the book back is when the borrower no longer mentions the book, either with literary pronouncements or with the excuse of being about to get to it any day now. It is then that you know it is on its way to being no longer considered yours. In the first instance, Miss Manners recommends saying, "If you're finished with it, I'll take it back," and in the second, "Why don't I take it back now, in case I need it, and you'll let me know when you have time."

Annoying Animals

DEAR MISS MANNERS:

I hate it when animals jump on me, but other people's pets are always doing so. Dogs, particularly, are such sycophants that they always ignore the guests who are trying to pet them and throw themselves at animal haters, such as myself. I'm not flattered by this repulsive attention. I'm not above kicking a pesky pet, either, when the owner isn't looking, but what can I do to get rid of it when my host is looking right at me?

GENTLE READER:

The most tactful thing to do would be to announce an allergy. This is not strictly a lie if you define "allergic" loosely, the way sophisticated children have learned to do, as in, "I think I'm allergic to vegetables." And stop kicking animals. Miss Manners assures you that while vague references to medical conditions elicit sympathy, viciousness does not.

DEAR MISS MANNERS:

This problem may be outside your bailiwick. It concerns the neighbors' dogs and the stretch of sidewalk and grassy parking that I am responsible for. When the dogs are out on their own, a well-aimed missile, the business end of the garden hose, or just a loud, threatening noise can usually discourage them. The dog walkers, when the dogs have them out on a leash, could probably be discouraged in the same fashion, but this doesn't seem quite—well, quite.

If the proper procedure is to speak to them, what is the proper thing to say? I hesitate to try speaking ad lib, because it makes me so doggone mad I don't know what I would end up saying. If they are so certain that using the area I mow, rake, and walk on for a canine latrine is so unobjectionable, why don't they do themselves a great big favor and train their dogs to use their own front lawn? Signs tacked on the trees saying "Please curb your dog" are not the answer. I have to get in and out of my car along that curb.

GENTLE READER:

If refraining from defecating on other people's property is not a matter of basic manners, Miss Manners would like to know what is. However, you seem to be dealing with two species who do not realize this, and while your method of notifying the unaccompanied dogs is working, Miss Manners agrees that turning a garden hose on a neighbor is not a good way of asking for his consideration. You must do so in words, and should do it as pleasantly and neutrally as possible, when you are first informing him of your feelings. "Please don't have your dog use my property," for example. If this is ignored, the problem is no longer one of correcting ignorance, and you may allow yourself to inject some of your feelings into your words.

~ Complaining ~

DEAR MISS MANNERS:

In an attempt to beat the heat last night, I went to my local coffeehouse and camped out in the air-conditioning with an iced chai and a book.

A woman sat down three chairs away. She flipped open her laptop, and suddenly the speakers began playing an Italian language tutorial. Since I don't speak Italian, and have no desire to learn, I found this frustrating.

After 30 minutes of this, she treated us to music from her laptop. The establishment had been playing Nina Simone over the loudspeakers—quietly—but she drowned it out with her discordant heavy metal. Glares and dirty looks failed to elicit a response. Finally, frustrated, I got up and stalked out into the heat.

Oddly enough, the gentlemen sitting next to me had a conversation at almost the same decibel level, but I didn't find this offensive at the least.

Both you and my mother have always said it's rude to tell someone when they are being rude. But is there anyway to inform this young lady that she is impinging her will upon the rest of the customers and that this is not done in polite society? Perhaps she honestly didn't know any better—her mama didn't teach her the same things mine did.

Ok, that's ingenuous, but it was the only approach I could think of and stay within the bounds of manners. Thoughts, possible future solutions? The weatherman says it's going to be hot again next week and this may happen again.

GENTLE READER:

Sorry, but neither your mother nor Miss Manners considers the pseudopitying comment that the offender doesn't know any better to be exempt from the rule against calling people rude.

You do not inform the offender; you inform the coffeehouse management. As these become more like sixteenth-century coffeehouses, each will have to decide whether it wants to be a home for the noisemakers or the quiet types, and customers will have to choose.

~ *Correcting* ~

DEAR MISS MANNERS:

What does one do when the bearded gentleman you may be talking with at a cocktail party has a few crumbs of cake or quiche in his beard? Likewise, when a person you know, perhaps but slightly, has spinach stuck between his or her front teeth? Do we gently tell them, ignore it all, or, in the case of the beard, lean over and brush it off?

GENTLE READER:

You are talking about a problem of such complex delicacy that it requires exquisite tact to judge each individual instance. Miss Manners can see that you realize that there can be no one solution applicable to all such situations. You do not, for example, suggest leaning over and picking the spinach out of someone's front teeth.

Here are some guidelines for making a judgment:

1. Is this something that others are likely to notice?
2. Is this something that the victim is likely to realize after it's too late to do anything about it?
3. Is there a way of correcting the problem without seeming to take it seriously?

For example, one of the severest cases of That Sinking Feeling is brought on when one returns home, satisfied that one has been unusually witty and merry at a dinner party, and then sees, in the bathroom mirror, that one has spinach on the teeth. It does not take long to calculate when the spinach was consumed and for how long afterward one displayed one's triumphant smile. This is not a nice feeling. In the case of a crumby beard, one may possibly assume, especially if one has a quiche-colored beard, that no one else has noticed it.

Miss Manners would therefore point out the spinach but ignore the crumb, unless the crumb could not possibly have gone unnoticed—if it were an inch square, say, and covered with tomato sauce.

Now we get to how to do this. The corrector should seem to have some doubt, in order to convince the sufferer that the problem is only barely noticeable. "Excuse me—I can't quite tell. Is there something on your tooth?" Or perhaps the brushing off of a crumb could be accomplished with a slightly flirtatious gesture. (You begin to see why delicate individual judgment is required.)

If you think your examples are difficult, what about the lady of Miss Manners' acquaintance who only realized *after* a tea at the State Department, in the days when pants were considered dressy, that her fly had been open all the time and nobody had told her? She still holds this against each and every woman at that tea.

Dear Miss Manners:

Can you tell me a tactful way of letting a friend know that she is getting too fat?

Gentle Reader:

Can you tell Miss Manners a tactful reason for wanting to do so?

RELATIONS BETWEEN THE GENDERS

~ Taking Offense ~

Technically, there is no such thing as accidental rudeness. Try to remember this when you are stabbed with an umbrella, trodden on, given a dial tone after being told to "hold" on the telephone, greeted by a name that is not yours, stood up by a dinner guest or sneezed upon. However, a true insult, Miss Manners believes, must be intentional. The insulter must understand what is expected, and do either something else or nothing at all.

Today, however, the insult threshold seems to have lowered below this standard. All sorts of people are running around sulking, pouting, acting huffy or retaliating as the result of kindly meant actions. This is most apparent in the relationships between gentlemen and ladies, partly because these are still open to misinterpretation, and also because everything always becomes more apparent when it's between gentlemen and ladies.

A gentleman holds the door open for a lady, and she sails through, insulted by the suggestion that she is too weak to manage the door herself. A lady gives her seat in the subway to a gentleman many years her senior, and he haughtily rejects it because it seems to suggest that the power of his manhood is past. A married woman is insulted by being considered socially as half a couple, so that she is not invited when her husband cannot or will not attend. An unmarried man is insulted by being invited socially without his live-in lover's being included.

Some women are insulted by being styled "Ms.," others by "Mrs." or "Miss." Couples are insulted by being addressed conventionally by those who do not know which name they have decided is to come first, or how they have used their mutual inheritance of surnames for themselves and their children.

All this has got to stop. There is little enough courtesy in the world, Miss Manners has observed; we cannot afford to go around rejecting what attempts to pass for it. In chaotic times, a consideration of motivation becomes important. Complete ignorance of prevailing manners is not much of an excuse, but perhaps it is a little—in unfortunate children whose parents brought them up to be free rather than civilized. But ignorance of revisions in manners since one was reared, or of the custom-made preferences of individuals, is more of an excuse.

It is true that manners grow and change, as does language, but also true that traditional usage has a special sweetness to those who have long known it. What social reformers must realize is that there can be a gap between reason and habit. It is rude to subject tiny courtesies to philosophical scrutiny.

The polite thing to do has always been to address people as they wish to be addressed, to treat them in a way they think dignified. But it is equally important to accept and tolerate different standards of courtesy, not expecting everyone else to adapt to one's own preferences. Only then can we hope to restore the insult to its proper social function of expressing true distaste.

⸺ *Taking History* ⸺

DEAR MISS MANNERS:

In my eighth grade history class, we came upon the subject that women have equal rights to men. We talked about how men used to be the dominators and that women were known as wives, end of sentence.

Women have come far in their fight for equal rights. But men still pull out the chairs for women to sit down in and they still open doors for women and say, "Ladies first." So for the sake of manners, is it still right that men are treating women better than women are treating men?

GENTLE READER:

Are they? Surely someone in your class must be arguing that such gestures of deference are actually bad treatment, intended to humiliate and handicap women by marking them as helpless.

Not that Miss Manners is taking that position, or yours either. But then, she has had enough advanced etiquette history to know that both have elements of truth and neither tells the full story. (Nor does your conclusion that women were "wives, end of sentence." Many managed to distinguish themselves in various fields in spite of barriers and prejudices.)

Chivalric etiquette was an improvement on the previous system of "Ladies never." Nevertheless, symbolically declaring women too superior to run the everyday world had an amazingly similar effect to declaring them too inferior. And by the way, chivalry originally applied only to upper-class ladies, and while a version of it was extended to the middle class in the nineteenth century, it never inspired anyone to defer to the lower classes.

In order to debate whether remnants of this system should still be practiced, you must understand the cultural and sentimental part that tradition plays in history. The manners at any given time are not an exact fit with a society's philosophy, nor should they be. It takes a while for consensus to build, even—or especially—for the most morally sound changes, and progress is not helped by the abrupt condemnation of familiar ways.

Still, everything evolves, and sometimes needs help to do so sensibly. The trick is to be able to distinguish practices that might be harmful from those that are merely graceful. If the boys in your class opened doors for the girls and pulled out their desk chairs for them, it would emphasize gender differences just when you are supposed to try to forget them and concentrate on your work. But would you welcome a rule that as everyone is equal, you all have to dress alike for the prom?

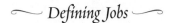

Defining Jobs

DEAR MISS MANNERS:

I understand that the practice replacing gender specific terms with neutral ones, for instance, "waiter" and "waitress" being replaced with the generic "server," began to prevent gender-based exclusion. And I appreciate substitutes such as "letter carrier" for "mailman," "fire fighter" for "fireman," "police officer" for "policeman," and "chair" for "chairman," as each of the traditional terms implies that a woman could not take up that vocation.

But I find it troublesome to think that perfectly acceptable and commonly used gender specific phrases have become politically incorrect. What is degrading about being a "waitress" or a "stewardess"? And why are actresses now calling themselves female actors? It seems as though women would hate to be taken as feminine and so they are adopting gender neutral titles.

I affirm the need for neutrality when it excludes the other gender from a given profession. But why must we fall to the least common denominator when there are perfectly familiar and comfortable gender specific terms? I realize that this inquiry may seem a bit old-fashioned. For what it's worth, I am 24 years old and simply hate to think that I'm living in a world where I must keep my womanhood under wraps.

GENTLE READER:

If you are puzzled, you can imagine the bewilderment of a sweet, old-fashioned feminist like Miss Manners. She has no problem with the gender-neutral terms, such as "server"; what bothers her is when male terms are used to replace female ones. Little did she think that, as part of the effort to assert female dignity by disallowing grown-ups to call them "girls," women would then endorse being addressed as "guys."

The nomenclature we have been using for ladies and gentlemen of various professions is the haphazard result of meandering tradition. That's the way it is with many things in the charmingly wayward discipline of etiquette. Why has it been considered dignified to call women actresses and hostesses but belittling to call them poetesses or lady doctors? Miss Manners can't tell you, but she knows it to be true.

Stodgy as she is, she is not for changing just for the sake of uniformity. But if there has to be change, she would rather it be in the direction of establishing more female titles, rather than making the male ones universal.

Miss Manners' intent here would be the same as those going in the opposite direction—to make the point that ladies are just as legitimately members of the profession as gentlemen. But it strikes her that using only masculine titles says symbolically that these are jobs for gentlemen, although they may now be filled by ladies, where using both puts the factor of gender with the job-holder, rather than the job itself, which should be gender neutral.

～ Defining Job Etiquette ～

DEAR MISS MANNERS:

My husband, who works in engine research, mostly works with men, although the company hires women engineers and chemists. He has always wanted me to do my very best, encouraged me through school and to full time work, and is also caring and encourages other women to seek their potentials.

At work, he's going through a door and a woman walks up behind him. He opens the door and allows her to go ahead of him. "I've got two good arms," she retorts.

My husband was speechless. Still is. He resisted the urge to run inside and hold the door shut, but how does one respond in this situation?

GENTLE READER:

Miss Manners finds this question discouraging. She has been trying for decades now to get across two not-so-simple ideas, and if she had succeeded, this problem would have been stamped out by now.

Not rudely, of course. That's one of the two lessons.

Deliberately interpreting an obviously kindly meant courtesy as an insult is something Miss Manners classifies as a high crime. The society really does not need vigilantes to go around stamping out the pitifully few remaining attempts to be polite. Anyone who is eager to be pushed aside—and to have any genuine need for help met by "Whatsa matter, lady, your arms broke?"—can surely get her fill.

At the same time, Miss Manners has been trying to teach the idea that gender-specific manners are out of place in professional life. Manners that seem to say "Oh, my, stop everything, there's a lady here!" may be charming socially, but they are a handicap to those who are trying to be identified primarily as, in this case, engineers.

So if your husband had held the door because the engineer behind him had her hands full, or he always steps back and helps others, he was entirely in the right. If he did it to show gallantry to a lady, his courtesy was misplaced.

None of this remotely excuses another's being rude. Miss Manners trusts that your husband's fantasy about retaliatory rudeness is just a soul-satisfying fantasy. Because if he did what he suggested, he would be adopting exactly the bad manners he has just asked Miss Manners to condemn.

(For more about workplace etiquette, please see p. 467.)

⌒ *Being Ladylike* ⌒

DEAR MISS MANNERS:

Those of us working for women's rights have been advised to take a "ladylike" approach. We tried emulating the behavior of our opposition, but this hardly seemed ladylike. Could you provide a precise definition of "ladylike"?

GENTLE READER:

A lady is, above all, someone who is passionately concerned that others be treated with dignity, fairness and justice. It has always been considered ladylike, for instance, to fight for these things on behalf of children, animals and one's husband. The difficulty you are encountering on the subject is that many people do not consider it ladylike to fight that battle on one's own behalf. Therefore, if a woman truly wishes to be ladylike, she will fight for dignity, fairness and justice not for herself but for all other women.

⌒ *Being Gentlemanly* ⌒

DEAR MISS MANNERS:

I was brought up as a gentleman and attempt to be one as much as I can. I have frequently been disappointed at the lack of manners from my fellow gentlemen. At a formal event in Washington, D.C., with mostly southerners in attendance, I did as I was supposed to by standing when a lady rose from my table and standing when she returned as well as getting the chair of the woman next to me.

To my horror, none of the other men at the table stood nor at other tables. I also noticed men starting to eat their dinners immediately after it was placed in front of them when some of the ladies have not yet been served. What do you make of all this?

At one event, I was seated with an old southern congressman who was physically capable of standing yet ignored his manners completely. I wasn't sure whether to continue with my manners and risk embarrassing the senior member present or follow his lead. I chose the latter only to learn later that I should have ignored his senior status. It just disappoints me that men are unsure and awkward in showing their proper manners. Are old fashioned manners dead and if so, do I risk being ostracized for continuing them?

GENTLE READER:

As a native Washingtonian, Miss Manners can assure you that flouting the rules to meet the lowest general standard is a dreadful idea that regularly backfires.

Whatever camaraderie this produces quickly evaporates when the behavior is called into question. For example, if a high-ranking lady complained of rude treatment, a canny congressman would explain that he had a medical reason for not rising or waiting to eat, but that you must be a lout.

Of course, Miss Manners believes you should do the right thing because it is the right thing, not because you might get caught. But as she mentioned, she is a Washingtonian.

~ Gender-related Gestures ~

DEAR MISS MANNERS:

Is there an etiquette rule concerning the crossing of knees? I ask because I must soon take oral comprehensives to qualify for my master's degree at a local university. During these interviews, appearances are important. Unfortunately, I recently skinned my right knee playing Frisbee, and I would like to cross my left leg over my right knee to hide the rather unattractive scab. Slacks are out of the question, and I do not believe the board of examiners would appreciate it if I stood for the entire interview. (My skirt would be long enough to cover the scab if I were standing.) Can you offer me any guidance?

GENTLE READER:

Miss Manners will refrain from pointing out that your problem arises from the fact that you were out playing Frisbee when you should have been studying for your orals. Here is a quick course in knee-crossing:

Neither gentlemen nor ladies properly cross their knees, and the fact that this is universally done does not make it right. A gentleman's at-ease posture while seated is to place one ankle upon the opposite knee. A lady's is to cross her ankles. Take care that the examiners do not uncover other such areas of ignorance in you.

~ Opening Doors ~

DEAR MISS MANNERS:

My friend is always very sweet and opens doors for me. I was wondering what to do in a situation where there are two doors in a row. He opens the first for me and I walk through. Should I stand at the next door and wait for him to open it for me or should I open it myself? When I open it myself, he rushes up and holds it open for my last few steps through the door. Would it be more polite for me to just wait for him?

GENTLE READER:

It seems to Miss Manners that you are going to have to wait for him, on one side of that door or the other. Surely you don't contemplate tearing ahead and leaving him behind. A gentleman who performs graceful gestures without belligerently objecting on the grounds that they are not fair is worth keeping. What you need to learn is a ladylike pause between the doors, where you seem to be advancing and may even hold up a delicate hand as if you plan to fend for yourself, but allow him to overtake you, half-turning your head as he does to give him a grateful smile.

∽ Opening Car Doors ∽

DEAR MISS MANNERS:

What should an enlightened male do to help a (presumably also enlightened) female into his (or her) car? My boyfriend feels that it is demeaning to the woman when the man opens her door, waits around until she gets all tucked in (probably fuming impatiently), and then closes the door after her. At present, I notice he unlocks and opens my door for me, leaving me to close it for myself. I find this quite satisfactory and I agree that most women have no difficulty mustering the strength to close a car door. (We both feel that mothers and grandmothers should be treated in the traditional manner if they are accustomed to it.) My boyfriend wonders if not shutting the woman's car door after her would be frowned upon at a formal occasion.

I also feel it is a gesture of respect to open a friend's door first if I am taking someone into my car, but I notice that most men are uncomfortable with this. It seems to me that women are let off too easily where manners are concerned. Equal rights demand equal courtesy from us. But rarely do I see another woman so much as reach across to unlock her escort's door from the inside—something that seems a basic courtesy.

GENTLE READER:

Miss Manners has a puzzling time trying to decide why one courtesy is "demeaning" and another is a "gesture of respect," and therefore would like to forget the entire symbolic aspect of this ritual. Once we agree that the opening and shutting of car doors will not be a test of character or physical strength, we are left with two methods of accomplishing the opening: the traditional and the practical.

If the traditional is performed, it should not be half done. The gentleman who has opened a door for a lady must also close it, preferably after waiting for her to pull her leg inside the car. It is also permissible for men and women to open doors for themselves and unlock them for each other. The difficulty comes only when the two methods are employed at the same time, as when the lady waits patiently inside the car because she is following the first method, while the gentleman, who is following the second, departs from the parking lot and enters, say, a restaurant, only noticing that something is wrong when the captain asks if he wants a table for one. The other consequence of mixed methods that you mention, the discomfort of some men when women attempt to be helpful and courteous to them, is very low down on Miss Manners' list of things to fret about.

Pushing Chairs

DEAR MISS MANNERS:

A waiter in a fancy restaurant tried to push my chair in for me, and nearly catapulted me into the sharp edge of the table. Not many men perform this service anymore, which is probably just as well for the hospitalization insurance rates, but what does a woman do if they attempt it?

GENTLE READER:

This is a confusion between the performance of a courtesy and the performance of a useful function, and Miss Manners is not surprised that the result of so basic a misunderstanding may be fractured kneecaps. The proper procedure for a man pushing in the chair of a woman has nothing whatever to do with moving her chair physically. It goes as follows: She approaches the chair. He puts a hand on the back of the chair. She sits on the chair. She scoots along toward the table, surreptitiously dragging the chair with her by means of her own hand, placed stealthily behind her knees to grip the front of the chair seat. The gentleman allows his hand to move along with the back of the chair as she scuttles toward the table. She then turns and gives him a half-smile to acknowledge her indebtedness for his contribution to her comfort.

Using Stairs

DEAR MISS MANNERS:

A young woman from my office who lives near me takes the same bus to work every day that I do. We have even occasionally paid each other's fares when one or the other of us doesn't have the exact change. Since we work at the same place, naturally we get off at the same stop. I want to be correct with her, but always letting her go first has been awkward. When we get on, does it depend on who pays the fares? How about getting off? She seems to stand back then, and one of these days we're going to miss our stop.

GENTLE READER:

A lady gets off a bus after the gentleman with her, although she boards the bus before. The same is true of any staircase they ascend or descend together. That way, if she can't make the steps in either direction, he will be there to catch her, or, failing that, to provide a soft surface on which she can fall. This order need not be violated if she pays both fares. She merely fixes the bus driver's attention with a half-smile and nods toward the accompanying gentleman to indicate the financial relationship.

～ Making Overtures ～

DEAR MISS MANNERS:

Usually, lots of men I pass by on the street say "hi" to me. I assume it's flirting. Most of the time I just ignore it and walk right by, since I don't want to stop walking and say "hi" to a stranger, I don't even know what his intentions are! But lately I've felt that what I do seems pretty rude and I think I'm coming off as unapproachable, and I was wondering what is the best way to deal with this kind of situation without being rude.

GENTLE READER:

If you want to seem approachable—which Miss Manners understands to be the same as not wanting to seem unapproachable—you might respond, "Hi, honey. Are you lonesome?"

She does not recommend this. What you were already doing is the correct behavior, not because you don't know what a strange man's intentions are toward you, but because you do.

～ Dueling ～

DEAR MISS MANNERS:

Even in the best of company and the most genteel of circumstances, it can happen that a man hideously insults one's wife. Given that dueling, alas, is outmoded, what is the best approach for the gentleman? Just how forceful can and should one become?

GENTLE READER:

Even in the heyday of the duel, there were gentlemen who preferred the cutting remark, or the cut direct of refusing to acknowledge the existence of a cad, to playing around with swords or pistols, which can be dangerous. Such cutting is still legal. Let Miss Manners give you a warning, however. A gentleman who attempts to defend his wife's honor without obtaining her full agreement to the idea that she has been hideously insulted will soon find that his life is no longer worth living.

THE VIRTUOUS LIFE IN WICKED CITIES

⌒ Urban Neighbors ⌒

Good fences may or may not make good neighbors, but shared walls, particularly when the people living on different sides park their electronic equipment against them, certainly do not. Miss Manners would therefore like to spell out some special rules of neighborliness, based on city living.

Urban neighborliness means that one has an obligation to notice disreputable characters who seem to be fooling around with a neighbor's house, and to report them. Urban neighborliness also means that one has an obligation not to notice disreputable characters whom one's neighbor has invited to his house for purposes of fooling around.

A person who lives in the city should take in his neighbor's mail and newspaper when requested, so that the house whose tenant is absent will not seem deserted. A person who lives in the city should not take in the papers or magazines of those living in nearby apartments if the owners are merely late risers.

Friendly gossip about the neighbors is as much a part of city as country living. It is not, however, friendly to pass on possibly damaging speculation about one's neighbors, particularly if interviewed about them by the Federal Bureau of Investigation.

Greater individuality is permitted in the city than in small towns or suburbs. Provided that your hours, your taste in music and the color you paint your house suit the wishes of the person next door, there should be no conflicts. And if there are, an impartial arbitrator is no farther away than the corner squad car.

⁓ *Territorial Disputes* ⁓

DEAR MISS MANNERS:

Every spring and fall, when the evening weather is fine, we have a problem with our neighbors. We live in a first-floor apartment and all of our windows open immediately onto the backyards and patios of a group of individually owned town houses. Most of these town house types we never see or hear, but one family, the one whose patio is directly off our bedrooms, uses its patio continually in good weather. For four springs and autumns, we have had to shut ourselves up in our apartment or have these people hold their parties, discipline their children, and shush their barking dog virtually in our bedrooms.

It is especially galling because they are very well off, we are not, and their attitude toward us has always been contemptuous and condescending. My complaints about parties have been met with, "Well, you see, we are getting together with old friends from Harvard, and I am sure that whatever momentary discomfort you feel is outweighed by our pleasure in seeing these wonderful old friends."

We'd like to move, but really can't afford to. I've thought of calling the police, but I can't say that, objectively speaking, they are so very noisy; it's just that they're in our laps when we want peace. We tried playing loud and horrible music, but there's a limit to how much Schoenberg I can listen to, and seemingly no limit on how much they can stand. We no longer care about maintaining any semblance of neighborliness; we just want them to hold it down. They are not stupid or evil people, just remarkably callous and thoughtless. If you have no ideas, I'm afraid my husband is going to pour battery acid on their car.

GENTLE READER:

That is not a good idea. You would only be giving them the opportunity to sic the police or Schoenberg on you.

Please recognize that the villains here are not your neighbors, or even Harvard (unless you can trace the problem to the School of Design), but your architects, whoever they were. People should be able to entertain friends from the college of their choice and discipline their children and dogs in the free air without annoying their neighbors.

This is why Miss Manners recommends a semblance of neighborliness. Approach them again, preferably with other apartment dwellers who have been bothered by the noise. Miss Manners feels certain that they will sympathize if you explain to them how awkward it is for you to be the unwilling auditors of their family secrets and the indiscretions of their guests.

DEAR MISS MANNERS:

We live in an apartment in a large apartment building and try to be considerate of our neighbors, in part by not making loud noises during inappropriate times of day. Please tell us, when exactly are those times?

After what hour of the morning and before what hour of the evening is it appropriate to run the vacuum cleaner in an apartment? Also, are these times the same all seven days of the week, or are there extended hours on weekends? We assure Miss Manners that we do avoid making loud noises at all times throughout the day, but would like some advice for those times when it is unavoidable.

GENTLE READER:

The advice is: Talk to the people who live in the apartment next to yours on the right. Talk to the people who live in the apartment next to yours on the left. Talk to the people who live in the apartment above you. And talk to the people who live in the apartment below you. If you know their habits, you may be able to work out a vacuuming schedule that suits them without unduly inconveniencing yourself.

Miss Manners realizes that this involves making four inquiries as opposed to the one that you made to her. But she can only tell you the generalities—that reasonable quiet should be maintained approximately from ten at night until eight in the morning and until ten on weekends. It may turn out that your neighbors are on the night shift, have invalids or babies who keep odd hours or were hoping themselves to vacuum at midnight.

DEAR MISS MANNERS:

We live in a nice apartment complex with two assigned parking spaces in the garage, which are used by my wife and me. My daughter consequently has no choice but to park on the residential street next to our building. She has a convenient and favorite parking place close by that she usually uses.

Yesterday, there was a note on her car that rudely, ending with an exclamation point, asked her to make use of the apartment building's parking area. This note was presumably left by the people who live in the house behind her usual parking spot. The local police station advised my daughter that use of the street and all parking spaces is available to the public.

My daughter would like to leave a strongly worded note on the porch of the house in question to advise them of her rights, and then not park there anymore to avoid further confrontation. What would Miss Manners advise her to say?

GENTLE READER:

It seems to Miss Manners that your daughter does want confrontation; indeed, that she wants it even more than she wants a parking space. She is willing to give up the space, to which she is legally entitled, but can't resist snapping back at the people who complained.

So what your daughter apparently means by avoiding "further confrontation" is that she wants to have the last word with the neighbors. This would be the first time in the history of the world that rude people became cowed and ashamed when counter-attacked, rather than spurred on to new rudeness.

Unless she wants both a parking problem and hostile neighbors, the only thing left for her to try is politeness. Here is the sort of note she should leave:

"I am so sorry to have inconvenienced you, especially as I share your frustration with the neighborhood parking problem. Unfortunately, I am unable to get a parking place at the apartment complex, and the police had nothing to suggest beyond reminding me that we are supposed to share street spaces on a first-come, first-served basis. Please accept my assurances that I will not park by your house when I am able to find space elsewhere. Your neighbor . . ."

DEAR MISS MANNERS:

After large parties, I find my garbage cans filled to capacity. Is it acceptable to place my empty whiskey bottles in a less social neighbor's trash can?

GENTLE READER:

There are two possible problems here. First, your neighbor may suddenly take to drink and find that he has no room in his trash can for his own whiskey bottles. Second, he may be hit by sudden fame and find that the contents of his garbage can have become of interest to trashy publications or government departments, in which case the profiles of him they reconstruct as a result of your deposits will be misleading. Perhaps you could place your empty soda bottles in his trash can, thus leaving room in your trash can for your whiskey bottles. It would be a special nicety to ask his permission, if you are planning to do this on a grand scale—"Would you be so kind as to allow me to share your garbage can?"

~ *Acknowledging Others* ~

"Every time you walk down the street, everybody says hello."
This is a statement that Miss Manners has heard in a variety of tones of voice:

Proud, as in "I come from a charming place! Folks here are soooo rude."

Plaintive verging on petulant, as in "I come from a village. Just don't expect me to be as sophisticated as all you cos-mo-pol-itan types."

Exasperated, as in "Is there no privacy around here at all?"

Rattled, as in "Who are these people, and what do they want from me?"

But if attitudes are contradictory about greeting and being greeted, etiquette rules are even more so. Hikers properly greet those approaching them on the trail, but tourists who happen to be visiting the same site do not. Passengers on airplanes used to introduce themselves, but no longer do; bus passengers sometimes do, only to find their seatmates making sudden departures.

It is not always a question of the friendly approach being polite and its omission being rude. It would be rude, for example, to greet someone you know who is having a hilarious time with an incongruous-looking person and who covers his face with the menu when he sees you coming. This acquaintance is probably conducting important business and cannot spare the time for social niceties. Nor would it be polite to roam around parking lots at night offering greetings to strangers as they unlock their cars. Or for unrelated adults to hang around school yards saying hello to stray children.

Yet the excuse of "I'm just trying to be friendly" always resonates with Americans, for whom being open to friendship is a virtue. This is not necessarily because we are bigger hearted than others, although Miss Manners does not rule out that happy possibility. A country that began by staking out sparsely populated territory and has continued ever since to be an unusually mobile society has to condone making friends fast.

That was a huge departure from European customs, which Americans then began to ridicule as snobbish. It is not a fair charge, even though we needn't feel sorry for people who were having such a good time ridiculing Americans for being open.

Friendliness toward strangers is necessarily context dependent. When you live in crowded cities, very likely spending your entire life in the same one with all your nursery school classmates, you don't need to make new friends at every turn. What you need from strangers is for them to please keep out of your way. And to refrain from scaring you.

You still must acknowledge those you know, those whom you frequently encounter, and those with whom you have even fleeting business transactions. In small towns or other restricted areas, such as a campus, that may mean nearly everyone; in large cities, it may mean very few, but it does include neighbors and shopkeepers.

Yet the tendency is either to chat up everyone including the express checkout clerk trying to move the line ("And what about your cousins, are they fine too?") or to ignore next-door neighbors and tablemates at large social gatherings.

To cover these different situations, there is a range of greetings:

Dearest friends and close, but not necessarily dear, relatives: kiss air near cheek, once or serially, depending on local custom. Next circle, handshakes or equivalent gestures, depending on generation.

Same encountered where silence is expected, for example at the movies or a funeral: meaningful nod.

Household companions, neighbors, co-workers: acknowledgment upon arrival and departure, ranging from "Good morning" and "Good evening" to "Hi, is there some coffee made?" and "Okay, I'm out of here."

Acquaintances glimpsed on the street: pleasant nod without breaking stride.

Strangers: maintain stride without breaking into a smile.

Strangers with whom one is trapped, as at a wedding dinner or shipwreck: full introduction.

⸺ Tourists ⸺

DEAR MISS MANNERS:

Please, sometime, offer some put-downs for people who seek instant information from complete strangers who are going about their business and not bothering anyone. I seem to be the born victim of such people, who stop me on the street wanting to know the time (because I am wearing a highly unreliable watch) or when the shops open or, in the case of tourists (with cameras for identification as such), where one can get a good breakfast. This always seems a particularly stupid question to fire at an obvious resident (without a camera) who has to get up and make it herself. What's the best way to squash such people? They usually ask for directions when your arms are full of bundles so a blunt instrument isn't too practical.

GENTLE READER:

Miss Manners is not in the business of disseminating "put-downs" for the purpose of humiliating problem-ridden strangers. It seems to Miss Manners that even with a bad watch and full arms, the quickest way to dispense with the problem is to say "Sorry—I don't know." May you never be lost in a strange city where everyone else is busy minding her own business.

~ *Picketers* ~

Although Miss Manners is a great believer in fresh air and acting out one's beliefs, she cannot say that she is happy to see so many people out picketing these days. The weekly sums that unions are able to allow to members who engage in this activity do not seem to Miss Manners to be commensurate with the strenuousness of the job and the working conditions on most sidewalks.

It is for this reason that Miss Manners would especially urge consideration to picketers on the part of the public, quite aside from the moral or social issues. Miss Manners also expects picketers to treat the public with courtesy. So does the law, for that matter.

The conventions of picketing allow the striking workers to make known their views through ritualistic marching in an orderly oval pattern, the carrying of signs and distributing of leaflets. Miss Manners expects them to observe the amenities by not making their signs obscene or forcing leaflets on those who do not wish to take them.

Proper dress for picketers is either outdoor apparel appropriate to the weather, or the working clothes of the striking profession. Miss Manners was once glad to see Washington striking musicians wearing white tie, and was even willing to waive for the occasion the general rule about not wearing evening dress during the day. In return, Miss Manners expects the public to remember the dignity of labor and not engage in undignified behavior toward its representatives. This means no shouting at them, no throwing of fruit or other objects and no deliberate jostling. It also means that while one can decline to accept a leaflet, one may not take it and then visibly treat it with contempt, such as tearing it up or throwing it on the sidewalk. Ideological differences are no excuse for rudeness.

~ *Pamphleteers* ~

DEAR MISS MANNERS:

A lot of kids stand along the streets where I walk to work, handing things out. Usually it's religious pamphlets, but sometimes it is advertising of one kind or another, or political flyers. There I am, walking along, and someone shoves paper at me so that I have no choice but to be a litterbug or carry a bunch of literature with me through my whole walk until I get to a wastebasket. Can I just refuse to take it? It seems rude to turn one's head away from a church person, and I hate to hurt people's feelings. I've never done this sort of work myself, but I can imagine how awful it must be to have to stand on the street all day being rebuffed by strangers.

GENTLE READER:

If one takes a job, for spiritual or other reasons, which involves accosting strangers on street corners, one must accept the possibility of being rebuffed. The papers you mention are, regardless of their content, in the category of personally delivered junk mail and may be as properly refused as that which has been delivered by post.

～ Panhandlers ～

DEAR MISS MANNERS:

I live in a large city, with people asking strangers for handouts everywhere you go. If it is a homeless person approaching me, I will normally either give them a bit of cash, or reply with a shrug and a "Sorry." However, there are people collecting for all kinds of "charities" who wait just outside (or inside) the front doors of many grocery stores and such, so that you cannot avoid them. I find this approach so annoying that I usually just keep walking, but once in a while they will call out a sarcastic comment in response to being ignored. I don't want to be rude, I just want them to leave me alone. What's the proper way to respond to being "cornered" like this?

GENTLE READER:

Miss Manners is having trouble understanding the geography here. How did you manage to get cornered after walking away? Did you get so upset that you walked into a wall?

Never mind, let's extract you, and set you walking on. If you don't want to accede to these people's requests to donate money, why would you want to stop to accept their insults? By their reaction, they have provided you with public justification at having ignored them in the first place. By yours, you will provide them with the additional frustration of not knowing whether you chose to ignore them again or were safely out of earshot.

～ Waiting ～

Many things in life are worth waiting for, but not all that long. Miss Manners would put a time limit on how long one should wait for salespeople to finish their conversations with each other before writing up one's order, or for a spouse who has departed with someone else to realize what a terrible mistake that was.

Nevertheless, waiting is now in a class with working as a popular pastime. A waitologist has estimated that the average adult spends one-tenth of his or her waking time waiting. There are waits for buses, banks, stores, theaters, gas stations, court cases, elevators, driver's licenses, dentist appointments and on telephone hold. One could easily pass one's life enduring just such basic waits. But there are also intermediary waits, such as waiting for the rain to stop, and advanced waits, such as waiting for your ship to come in. Some of these go in fashions. There was a time when all of America was waiting to be discovered by a movie talent scout in a drugstore, and now everyone is waiting for a television camera to come along and ask him to tell the world what he thinks.

It is the elementary and comparatively short-term wait with which Miss Manners is concerned at the moment. (If you want to hear about the others, you will just have to wait.) There are correct ways to wait and correct ways not to wait, as well as incorrect ways to wait and incorrect ways not to wait. For example, it is perfectly correct, although not many people realize it, to refuse to wait on the telephone. When Miss Manners is asked "Can you hold on for a minute?" she often replies, "No, sorry," and it is too bad that the person on the other end ties up his own line by putting her on hold anyway, because that person has not waited for Miss Manners' reply. One should also refuse to wait for inefficient or indefinite service. A restaurant should be able to tell you how long the wait will be, and a service person should not keep you waiting except to attend a previous customer.

It is rude to refuse to wait by announcing that one's needs take precedence over those of other waiting people. Miss Manners can think of no circumstances in which a person transacting the ordinary business of life can plead with legitimacy that it is more outrageous to expect him to wait than to expect it of others. "Let me go through, please—I'm in labor," perhaps, but what are you doing at the stockings sale then anyway?

The only polite way to wait, if one must do so, is to bring one's own portable work or amusement. An unoccupied person waiting in line is by definition a potential raving maniac. A nice Jane Austen novel, ready to go, has preserved even the naturally tranquil spirits of Miss Manners. Using conversation as a means to pass the time is tempting but dangerous. Two people quietly discussing what a shame it is to have to wait are, by that same definition, a potential mob.

 Eating

DEAR MISS MANNERS:

Is it proper for one to eat while in the public right of way? Are fruits and vegetables fine, but not fried chicken? Of course I carry a napkin and do not litter with my leftovers, but what is really correct? Tomorrow's breakfast may depend on your response.

GENTLE READER:

Dessert is the only course that may be properly eaten while strolling on the sidewalk, and only certain desserts at that. Apples, bananas and pears are acceptable; mangoes and grapefruit are not. Ice-cream cones and chocolate bars are fine, but pineapple upsidedown cake is out. You will notice that dessert means that no meats or vegetables are permitted, nor are the usual breakfast foods, such as pancakes with maple syrup or eggs once over lightly.

~ *Dodging the Elements* ~

DEAR MISS MANNERS:

I have very delicate skin, and have never even tried to get a suntan, after dreadful childhood troubles with burns, and I now realize this is just as well, as I have been reading that sun can be damaging and drying to the skin. I am considering using a parasol this year. When does one carry a parasol and how?

GENTLE READER:

Anyone who can master the use of the umbrella can master the parasol, which is easier because it is not raining. That is, one keeps it close to the body when furled, and out of other people's faces when unfurled. One also takes care to do the furling and unfurling in an open space. The important thing to remember is that this instrument is not a weapon as is, for instance, the walking stick.

DEAR MISS MANNERS:

While walking through shopping crowds on a rainy Saturday afternoon and while maneuvering through rush-hour crowds at subway stops on drizzly mornings, I have narrowly missed being speared by many an out-of-control umbrella. I assume that common sense should prevail, but just what are the rules for opening, closing, carrying, and otherwise manipulating this potentially lethal accessory?

GENTLE READER:

Managing an umbrella is just like managing a parasol, only it is raining out.

DEAR MISS MANNERS:

When two people are walking down the street together, sharing an umbrella, who should hold the umbrella? The man? Suppose it is the woman's umbrella?

GENTLE READER:

The taller of the two should hold the umbrella. This is not a matter of etiquette so much as it is having the sense to come in out of the rain.

TRANSPORTATION

⌣ *Motoring* ⌣

Machines do not have feelings. There is no use trying to tell Miss Manners how bad your answering machine feels when someone hangs up on it, or to engage her in a discussion of whether the elevator is hurt if you keep pushing its button when it heard you the first time and is rushing up and down as fast as it can.

This is not to say that no inanimate objects have feelings—toys are loaded with feelings, for instance, and only a monster would break the heart of a rag doll—or that property should not be treated with care. But if you are faithfully courteous to your fellow human beings, Miss Manners does not mind if you tell off your toaster or your computer.

What she does mind is the way people crawl inside machines and then start behaving rudely to others. You may kick your automobile, if it deserves it, but you may not park your own manners outside when you get into it. Miss Manners is amazed at the number of otherwise gentle souls who turn nasty when they are driving. And they all suffer from the wonderful, ostrichlike delusion that they cannot be identified because they are safely inside their cars.

It seems silly to her to have to say what good driving manners are. They are the same as the simplest, most obvious of nondriving manners, except that each person is surrounded by thousands of dollars in treacherous metal. You do not shove your way in front of others, and so you do not break into parking lot lines or force your way into crowded lanes. You do not occupy two seats in a bus, and so you do not allow your car to occupy more than the marked-off space of one parking place. You do not leave your things about in ways that block the progress of other people, and so you do not double-park or cut off people's driveways. You do not shoplift, even if no one is looking, and so you do not break traffic laws, even if no one is looking. You do not breathe down the necks of people who don't walk as fast as you do, and so you do not tailgate slow cars. You do not yell at people, except in emergencies, and so you do not honk at people, except in emergencies. You don't scream insults at passing strangers—so you don't scream insults at passing strangers.

Why isn't all this obvious? Probably it is because all the foolish anthropomorphizing that is done has led people to envy the capricious, aggressive, irresponsible lives led by machines, and tempted them to disguise themselves as machines and do likewise. This Miss Manners cannot allow. For one thing, it sets a bad example to dishwashers and garbage disposals.

Carpooling

DEAR MISS MANNERS:

How should I handle grown adult men in my carpool who get in my car in the morning without saying "good morning" or any other type of polite greeting? At the end of the day, some of them won't say anything unless I provoke them to speak. I'm not sure if it's got anything to do with me being Black and them White or not. It's usually only one guy that does this.

GENTLE READER:

Miss Manners appreciates your giving this problem general and moral importance by applying it to males in general and suggesting that it may have racial undertones. Exploring the depths of society through surface behavior is what she does best.

But as far as she can see, what you have there is one lout in your carpool, along with one or two others (after all, how many does your car hold?) who sometimes slip.

This is still a problem, Miss Manners agrees—it is unpleasant to start or end your day in the company of a silent grouch—but a less complex and intractable one. By all means, provoke him. If you keep greeting him firmly and by name, occasionally responding to silence by concern ("Keith? Are you okay?"), he will eventually succumb.

Vigilantism

DEAR MISS MANNERS:

I will soon have handicap license plates on my car, and I have been warned that as a member of the "invisible" handicapped, I will be the target of much abuse. What is a mannerly response to the people who will inevitably confront me?

I know this is none of their business, but I am a lady and do not wish to be rude by ignoring these ignorant judges of parking spaces. I would happily change places with them, even for a day, to be pain free and "abled."

GENTLE READER:

Miss Manners deeply appreciates your supplying your own answer. This saves her a lot of work. The only addition she needs to make, on her way out to the porch swing with a mimosa and the new Henry James novel, is to caution you to use a pleasant tone when you voice your willingness to change places with the vigilantes.

⌁ *Public Transportation* ⌁

Even the most unenlightened of men are now allowing women to stand up on crowded buses while they, offering no argument at all, sit in comfort. This is a complete triumph for equality because it is extended to all women. Elderly, disabled and pregnant women are accorded the same standing privilege as their stronger sisters.

The bus situation is far from solved, however. Buses are now full of resentful faces and overactive elbows, because no system of precedence has been instituted to replace the old one based on gender. Thoroughly disliking an approach based on every man for himself and every woman for herself, Miss Manners proposes precedence based on ability. It is the reverse of the present method, by which seats go to those most able to push their way into them. Standing room should be the reward going to those most able to stand comfortably.

It works simply. Any person who would obviously find it a hardship to stand, because of advanced age (or extremely unadvanced age, for that matter), infirmity or such temporary burdens as born or unborn babies, has first claim on a seat. After these people have been accommodated, the next opportunity goes to people who have burdens that are not acts of God but willfully incurred, such as groceries. (Miss Manners considers pregnancy an act of God and will not listen to your argument for putting it in this second category.) After that, the strong may seat themselves wherever they like.

⌁ *Boarding and Exiting* ⌁

DEAR MISS MANNERS:

Is there a convention that subway exits and entrances should both be from the right? One usually sees only pushing and shoving. But even where people try to be courteous to each other, every time doors open to load and unload passengers, there's a jam-up.

GENTLE READER:

The American subway conventions have always consisted precisely of pushing and shoving. Those who practice it think of it as a challenging social form and pride themselves on adroit maneuvering during jam-ups. However, Miss Manners thinks you raise a valid point when you question whether more courteous subway riders should not develop their own conventions for the situation. In that case, yes, the sensible thing would be for those disembarking to precede those embarking, and for each to keep to the right.

～ Backpacks ～

DEAR MISS MANNERS:

Could you say something about people who wear backpacks in crowded places, such as elevators, public transit, and cafeteria lines?

These people don't seem to realize that their appendage makes them cut a wide swath whenever they turn around, and I am forever getting hit by their baggage. I believe the proper thing is for these wearers to put their packs in front of themselves when they are in a crowded area. Mail carriers do it, although they are mainly interested in protecting their letters.

GENTLE READER:

Miss Manners trusts that you are not implying that mail carriers ought to be better motivated. Surely protecting the mail is their sacred trust, and it is not their fault that most of it consists of duplicate catalogues.

Backpackers or ladies with purses may be perfectly well motivated, and yet go around smashing people. This is why etiquette, unlike the more forgiving social sciences, is interested in action as well as motivation. Good-hearted people who hit others with their burdens are rude.

～ Striking Back ～

DEAR MISS MANNERS:

What is the proper etiquette on a crowded bus? If some little old lady with a pointy umbrella hits me in the shins first, may I kick back?

GENTLE READER:

It is rare, nowadays, to have a deep-seated, well-motivated sensual urge that you are forbidden ever to gratify. However, Miss Manners must tell you that kicking little old ladies in the shins is one of them. Scream "Ow!" and stare at her with a frightened expression.

~ *Self-Protection* ~

DEAR MISS MANNERS:

My question is on subway etiquette. I often meet a co-worker whom I do not like on the subway platform; we are heading for the same destination. May I say hello and go farther down the platform in order to read my book? Saying, on a sunny day, that I must run back to the office for my umbrella is losing its credibility.

GENTLE READER:

The instrument you require is in your hands, and it is not an umbrella. All travelers should carry books, whether they read or not, as weapons of defense against conversational assault. You need not move along the platform after you have greeted your colleague politely; merely move your nose downward toward your open book. If the person says anything more than a return hello, you pause, look up with a puzzled smile and say slowly, "What?" as if awakening from a deep sleep. If the statement is repeated, you reply "Oh," with another vague smile, and then return to the book. Two or three rounds of whats and ohs should polish off even a determined talker.

~ *Escalators* ~

DEAR MISS MANNERS:

In the office building where I work, we have escalators and elevators. I sometimes become annoyed when arriving or departing the office via escalator and I get stuck behind someone who stands still, blocking the entire path. I know that in Europe and other countries, it is customary to stand to the right (or to the left, as in Australia) so that others may pass.

Sometimes one person can hold up an entire horde of people trying to get someplace. Maybe they're tired or have an unseen handicap, but isn't that where the elevator comes in? Maybe I am at fault and I need to be more patient and easygoing.

GENTLE READER:

This isn't the stress test department, but yes, since you ask, Miss Manners does think that anyone who makes no distinction between staircases and escalators, and who believes that anyone who doesn't hike on escalators must be disabled, ought to learn to take it easy.

But this has nothing to do with the fact that you ought to be allowed, if you wish, to race up or down, rather than to stand there in a pleasant stupor and let the machinery do the work. Yes, the riders should stand to the right to make a left lane for the passers. Should they fail to do so, however, you needn't stand fuming behind them. There is a magic phrase that can be invoked politely to get them to move. It is "Excuse me, please."

⌒ Elevators ⌒

DEAR MISS MANNERS:

When the elevator stops at your floor, but you don't know whether it's going up or down, do you ask the people inside which direction it is going by saying the one you want, or the one you assume? Let me try again: Do you say "Up" if you want to go up, or if the elevator seems to be going up, even if you want to go down? You only get a second to ask the question, of course, because the doors shut right away, but I've had it happen that I say "Down" and the people inside say, "No, up," and close the doors when I really want to go up; and I've also had it happen the other way around.

GENTLE READER:

You should pronounce the direction that is your goal interrogatively. In a confusing world, we must all be able to state our own intentions, without taking on unbidden tasks such as second-guessing mechanical contrivances about their whimsical intentions.

DEAR MISS MANNERS:

What is the proper way to enter an elevator, please? By the time all inside come out, the door is closing on those trying to enter. Why can't those inside come out on one side, so those going in can enter more easily? I ride elevators all day long for a delivery service, and some folks just won't give you room to get into it or hold the door. You should ride some with me—it would make you a drinking person.

GENTLE READER:

Thank you, but Miss Manners does not mix drinking with elevator travel because, for the reasons you describe, she considers it dangerous. While acknowledging your problem, she sees only additional problems in your solution, what with all the people inside pushing one another to get ready for their one-sided landings. The key courtesy here is door-holding. If the person nearest the button panel keeps the doors open long enough for the exiting, followed by the entering, more people would travel on the same side of the doors as their limbs.

DEAR MISS MANNERS:

Who should get out of an elevator first?

GENTLE READER:

The person nearest the doors. Provided, of course, it is his or her floor.

Table Manners

～ The Implements ～

IF MISS MANNERS hears any more contemptuous descriptions of etiquette as being a matter of "knowing which fork to use," she will run amok with a sharp weapon, and the people she attacks will all be left with four tiny holes in their throats as if they had been the victims of twin vampires.

Knowing or caring which fork to use is regularly cited as proof that one is narrowly fixed on a detail of life that is probably a deliberate booby trap set by the snobbish to catch the unsuspecting, and that therefore one has no time or heart left for the great spiritual values of life. The Great Fork Problem is used to ridicule the holy subject of etiquette, but the defenders of etiquette use it too, when they claim that manners are "a matter of being considerate of others, not which fork to use." In either case, this is like declaring that as long as you truly have love for humanity, it is not important that you happened to put your left shoe on your right foot and your right shoe on your left foot.

Forks are not that difficult. It is possible that anyone who has learned to operate a computer, kitchen appliance or washer with delicate fabric cycles may also be capable of being trained to operate as many as three forks.

Why is this important? Because the person who has not mastered the fork is going to make a mess, miss the last course of dinner, or make the hostess get up from the table. Also, the forks may get tired some day of being bad-mouthed, and may cut off your food supply. Therefore, we will now take a minute to learn everything there is to know about Which Fork to Use.

Use the one farthest to the left.

That's it. That's all there is to know. Now run outside and cultivate the spirit until dinnertime. When you come in to dinner, you will find, typically (if you are dining with Miss Manners), that there are three forks to the left of your plate, three knives to the right, a soup spoon, and a teeny-weeny little forklet lying on the diago-

Formal place setting. The fork resting in the soup spoon is for oysters, which will be followed by soup. Then comes fish (use the outer fork and outer knife), then meat (the center fork and knife), then salad and cheese (the inner fork and knife). Above the soup spoon is a glass for sherry, to be drunk with the soup. The front center glass is for white wine (with the fish), and the glass at left is for red wine (with the meat). Behind that is the water goblet; to its right, the champagne glass (with dessert).

nal, resting its head in the bowl of the spoon. What does this tell you? It tells you that you are not going to go to bed hungry; that's what it tells you.

The wee little fork is the oyster fork, which may not actually be farthest to the left, but is pointing left, to give you a hint. Use it to eat your oysters, dear. For the next course, you may relax from the fork question, and just eat your soup. With the spoon, dummy. The third course is a fish, which you will recognize immediately from the funny look in its eye. If you remember your lesson, you will reach for the fork farthest to the left, the outside fork, and guess what? That is the fish fork! Then will come the meat, and the next fork you will discover will be . . . ? Show of hands, please. That is correct; the meat fork. Now we will eat salad, and the fork we will find will be . . . yes, it will be the salad fork.

This is presuming that the hosts set the table correctly and did not, for example, set out the forks in order of size rather than usage. Of course, if your hosts set things

Formal dessert service. Dessert equipment is a spoon, a fork and a finger bowl with doily, all on a plate. The guest moves the spoon to the right of the plate, the fork to the left and the finger bowl and doily to the left. The gentleman has done so, but the oblivious lady has left the footman to contemplate dumping the mousse on her lap.

incorrectly they can hardly sneer at you for using the wrong fork. If they have to fetch you a fresh one because you ran out by following their system, it should teach them a lesson.

Naturally, the knives to the right of the plate will be moving right along at the same time. Miss Manners has not mentioned them because no one ever complains of not knowing which knife to use. They don't dare make nasty remarks about knives, because knives don't fool around.

There will now be a moment of panic in which you will become aware of the fact that you have no forks left, nor knives, nor spoons, and you haven't eaten your dessert. Have you done something wrong? Is it so wrong that you will be sent to bed without any dessert? No indeed. All is well. The dessert plate is about to arrive. On it will be, of all things, a dessert fork and a dessert spoon. You will remove these, putting the spoon to the right of your dessert plate and the fork to the left, so you'll know just where they are when you need them.

That wasn't so hard now, was it?

A Reply

DEAR MISS MANNERS:

A dessert fork or spoon is *never* served on the dessert plate unless you are eating in a "hash house," or "greasy spoon" restaurant. I have worked in some of the finest restaurants and hotels in the country, in the dining room, and have been served dinner in elegant homes and have never seen silver served on the plate. That's as bad as a steak knife being shoved under your steak on a dinner plate at a fast-service steak house.

GENTLE READER:

If good manners were what is done in "some of the finest restaurants and hotels in the country," instead of what Miss Manners tells you, filled plates would be plopped in front of guests, sugar would be served in little packets with advertising on them and conversation would be continually interrupted by such remarks as "Coffee now or later?" and "Is everything all right?"

Although a dessert fork and spoon may be placed above the dinner plate, strict formal service does indeed mean that the dessert fork and (not or) the dessert spoon are brought on the dessert plate. Often the finger bowl is placed between them, although there should really be a fruit course after the sweet dessert, in which case the finger bowl is brought in on the fruit plate, between the fruit fork and the fruit knife. Want to make something of it? If hash houses and greasy spoon restaurants wish to follow this correct procedure, so much the better for them. The rich have no monopoly on manners.

(For more complete instructions on formal service, please see p. 587.)
(For a complete list of silver for formal service, please see p. 444.)

A Lapse

DEAR MISS MANNERS:

I was at a dinner party the other night where a lot of silver was spread out at each place, for many courses. I know you taught us which fork to use when, but I forgot. Kill me. My question concerns the next step after one uses the wrong fork. I realized, by looking at the hostess' place, that I would never come out even, and, in fact, I had to ask for something to eat the salad with. If I promise to go back and study fork order, would you consent to tell me what to do about mistakes?

GENTLE READER:

Miss Manners is a tolerant soul, but feels that you are concealing from her the extent of your mistake. If, for example, you ate the fish with the salad fork, why did you not have the fish fork left, with which to eat the salad? Miss Manners is always ready to receive back a sinner, but not those who steal the forks. However, she will let you in on the secret of correcting mistakes, if you promise not to tell anyone she said so. Lick clean the wrong fork you have just used and slip it back on the table-cloth while no one is looking.

~ Napkins ~

DEAR MISS MANNERS:

My brother brought his fiancée to dinner at my house for the first time, after telling me how much my mother would like her because of her good manners. I served a formal dinner, or at least not a casual one, in our dining room with nice table linens.

When I was doing the laundry afterwards, I found that the fiancee's dark lipstick was smeared all over the hand-embroidered napkin she had used. After several launderings with different stain removers, I've had no success in removing the offending stain. As a hostess, should I expect this to occur and simply throw away the napkins after a meal, or should I offer paper napkins instead? (Or perhaps I need laundry tips?) I've had many dinner parties without encountering this problem. My brother is now married to her and I haven't yet invited them for dinner.

GENTLE READER:

Miss Manners' mind has flashed ahead, to when you and your sister-in-law are old ladies and she finally works up the nerve to say to you, "I had always hoped we would be close, and all these years I've racked my brain trying to think what possible thing I could have done to offend you. You gave that lovely dinner for me forty years ago, when I was first engaged, and then never again from that day to this. I understand your house is lovely."

What are you going to say? "Well, sure, except for that napkin you ruined, that hand-embroidered napkin! You didn't think I was going to give you a chance to do that again, did you?"

True, hosts should not have to expect their guests to use their napkins as makeup towels, and you have not had others who did so. Still, let's see if this relationship can be saved without having to resort to paper napkins. Miss Manners doesn't do laundry tips, but you could ask your sister-in-law for one. Enough time has gone by that it should not seem pointed if you get into a cozy household discussion, during which you confide that you have had a lipstick stain problem and inquire whether she knows a remedy.

⌒ Paper Napkins ⌒

DEAR MISS MANNERS:

Why can't I use paper napkins—the heavy kind—at a dinner party? They look all right, do the job, and it's more practical to be able to throw them away instead of cleaning them, but some people are fussy about them.

GENTLE READER:

The identical claims are made for paper underpants. How come you don't wear them?

⌒ Napkin Rings ⌒

DEAR MISS MANNERS:

What about napkin rings?

GENTLE READER:

Yes, what about them? Napkin rings are not, as many seem to believe, decorative items for the formal table. They should be used only at the family dinner table but even there are a complicated subject, involving many levels of reasoning. Miss Manners would like to explain the complexities before reaching a judgment. Let us start from the top:

1. The highest level of thinking about napkin rings is that they are horrible, because they presuppose that not everyone is issued a freshly laundered napkin at every meal.
2. Next, we have the school of thought that this is an imperfect world, and one ought to make the best of it by at least ensuring that one person does not have to suffer for the sins of another, as would happen if a fastidious person and a greasy one regularly ate together without benefit of napkin ring.
3. At the bottom of the social level, we have people who habitually use paper napkins. These people do not object to napkin rings, but are puzzled about what they are for.

Miss Manners finds herself in the unusual position of favoring the middle course. She feels that napkin rings promote social morality by forcing people to live with the consequences of their behavior.

A cloth napkin that is not to be reused before being laundered is left looking like a paper airplane—pointed at the top, and the sides both extended to form an elongated triangle. Actually it is always politely presumed that napkins are never reused, the only exception being the family dinner, at which each person folds his or her napkin and inserts it into the proper napkin ring. A houseguest may follow this procedure also. Not doing so suggests the presumption of fastidiousness on the part of one's hosts, but they will probably not appreciate this fine point.

As for paper napkins, whatever is left of them at the end of the meal should be left as neatly as possible at one's place. Miss Manners refuses to think about the prospect of their being refolded for possible reuse.

~ Pushers ~

DEAR MISS MANNERS:

We have an important question to ask you about "pushers"—the nondrug variety. When our four-year-old succumbs to our pleas to use eating utensils, he sometimes runs into the problem of needing something—other than his fingers—for pushing his food onto his fork. We've run into a family crisis: I was taught to use a small piece of bread as a pusher. My husband (although brought up at table with silver pushers that looked like little hoes—ugh!) insists it's more practical, proper, and less caloric to teach our son to use a knife. What would you push?

GENTLE READER:

Using the knife to push food onto the back of the fork is a European custom. Using bread to push food onto a fork is also a European custom. Both date from the time that Europe needed all the help it could get.

What do we Americans do? We have a marvelous time chasing the food merrily around the plate with a fork turned tines upward; or we use the fork to sneak up on the food unawares and scoop it up before it knows what hit it.

This is indeed a difficult motor skill, but lots of fun once you get the hang of it. Toddlers may be issued special silver pushing instruments, but they love learning to balance lots of little funny things, as you no doubt realize every time you try to pick up the marbles and Lincoln Logs on the floor. Eventually, your child should be able to master no-push eating. Nothing in life worth having, including plump garden peas, comes easily.

⌒ The Salad Bowl ⌒

DEAR MISS MANNERS:

Where exactly does the salad bowl go?

GENTLE READER:

Directly under the salad. Where this combination is then placed on the table depends on whether the salad is being served by itself, in which case it takes center stage, or whether it is in a crescent-shaped plate, in which case it is served on the side. The left side.

⌒ The Carry-out Box ⌒

DEAR MISS MANNERS:

What is the proper way to serve carry-out Chinese food or pizza? I don't want you to think that I don't know how to serve a proper meal that I cook myself, but what about impromptu gatherings, when you just send out for something? Should I try to pass it off as mine—which is difficult if everybody hears the doorbell ring when it's delivered—or should I just put it out the way it arrives?

GENTLE READER:

Many Americans are under the mistaken impression that small paper cartons with metal handles are correct serving dishes in China (or Taiwan), and that large flat cardboard boxes are in Italy. Transfer the carry-out food into your own serving dishes. This does not imply that you cooked it yourself. The cow gets credit for having produced the milk, even if it is put into a glass before serving.

⌒ Dessert Service ⌒

DEAR MISS MANNERS:

I think it's ridiculous to put out both a fork and spoon just to eat dessert, as a number of people do for dinner parties, to show off their silver, I suppose. If it's a cake-type thing, all you need is a fork, and if it's a pudding-type thing, you just need the spoon.

GENTLE READER:

Miss Manners knows what type-thing you are: You are the type-thing that is more often discovering that you don't have enough equipment with which to eat. If there is no fish knife, you want to use a meat knife on the fish instead of making do with your fork, and if there is no salad knife, you think you have the right to use your butter knife on the lettuce. Be grateful for bounty. Besides, Miss Manners saw you sneaking cake crumbs into your mouth with a wet fingertip. Between the dessert fork, in the left hand, and the dessert spoon, in the right hand, you could have fed your greed gracefully.

(If you are still confused, please turn to p. 444 for an exhaustive explanation of the employment of silver flatware.)

METHODS

⌁ American vs. European Eating ⌁

DEAR MISS MANNERS:

Is one style of eating, European or American, considered proper in our western culture? My father thought eating European style was wrong, whereas my wife thinks that American style eating is fine at the local cafeteria, but if we are at a highfalutin joint we should be eating European style. I try to be open minded, seeing advantages in both styles. I even try using chopsticks when eating Chinese food.

Your answer to this question is of utmost importance. My anniversary is coming up and I do not want to be an embarrassment to my wife when I spring for an expensive dinner.

GENTLE READER:

It sounds as if being American, or being seen with an American, embarrasses your wife, in which case nothing Miss Manners can say will help. Nevertheless, she will try by serving a small helping of civics:

The American style of using the fork in the right hand, which requires parking the knife after cutting, and then transferring the fork from the left hand, used to be the European style. It has retained its basic form, dating from the time it was imported, while the Europeans sped ahead and developed the method of keeping the fork in the left hand, so as to get their food down faster.

Meanwhile, America exported the notion that the class system is wrong. It also let the world know that it is a mistake to think that America's comparative youth as a country and its devotion to egalitarianism mean that Americans are bumpkins who may be insulted with impunity. Yet there are many, not only abroad but in America, your wife among them, who do not seem to have mastered this lesson.

The answer is that it is proper for you and your father to eat American style if you are Americans, and for her to eat European style if she is a European. Whatever her nationality, however, it is rude to assume that Americans are less presentable than Europeans.

(For more information on American behavior abroad, please see p. 764.)

⌒ An Original Method ⌒

DEAR MISS MANNERS:

To me, the cut-and-shift American way of using a fork is silly and I find the tines-down English way to be inefficient.

I hold my fork mainly in my left hand when there is food to be cut or pushed onto the fork with my knife. The tines are up, and the handle rests on my ring finger and first knuckle, with two fingers and the thumb on top. I hold the fork the same way in my right hand for certain foods. On several occasions, remarks have been made about this alleged peculiarity of mine. I respond by making it clear I know the alternatives. You may say that people who make such remarks have more to learn about manners than what they assume I do not know. Would you, however, advise me to change a comfortable habit just to earn the good opinion not only of those who question me about it, but also of people with the decency to be quiet?

GENTLE READER:

You, sir, are an anarchist, and Miss Manners is frightened to have anything to do with you. It is true that questioning the table manners of others is rude. But to overthrow the accepted conventions of society, on the flimsy grounds that you have found them silly, inefficient and discomforting, is a dangerous step toward destroying civilization.

Unfolding the Napkin

DEAR MISS MANNERS:

Is there a rule of etiquette that covers when one should place a dinner napkin on the lap? Recently, a friend corrected me on this. He feels it is correct, when in a restaurant, or club, to unfold the napkin and place it across the lap the moment one sits down at table. I feel that when planning to spend some time over cocktails before ordering, common sense rules that I place the napkin on my lap as the dinner is ordered—or better yet, when dinner is served.

GENTLE READER:

Common sense has nothing whatever to do with etiquette, but in this case, it happens to coincide with the hard-and-fast rule that one puts one's napkin on one's lap immediately upon sitting down at the dinner table, regardless of whether it is a cocktail or soup that one is first planning to spill onto one's lap.

Waiting to Begin

DEAR MISS MANNERS:

In households where people still observe the custom of waiting for everyone to be served before anyone can start eating, thus making all the people who were served early eat their dinners cold, what are you supposed to do while waiting? Just pretend the food isn't there in front of you and sit with your hands folded, trying not to let your mouth water?

GENTLE READER:

Miss Manners senses a negative feeling from you about this custom, which was instituted on the principle that no one should be ready for seconds before everyone has had firsts. The violation of this principle leads to the uneven distribution of food in the world which, in turn, brings on famine, war and other things too unpleasant to mention at the dinner table. While waiting for your hostess to signal the beginning, you may break open your potato, and even butter it. That is quite enough excitement before dinner.

DEAR MISS MANNERS:

My husband, who is in all other respects a gentleman and a scholar, is extremely incorrect in one particular. When we give an occasional dinner party, he always sits down and serves himself and begins eating, sometimes even before the other guests have been alerted to the fact that dinner is ready. There is almost always enough food to go around, and it's not that good anyway, so I can't understand his behavior. I tell him the guests should be served (or allowed to serve themselves) first and then we should all begin eating together, but he says this is old-fashioned and silly, and it's every man for himself these days.

GENTLE READER:

Your husband's justification is the second worst explanation Miss Manners has ever heard for the rudeness of eating before one's guests. The worst was from a gentleman of Miss Manners' acquaintance who explained the fact that his wife had eaten her dessert in the kitchen before giving the guests theirs by saying, "She doesn't believe in delayed gratification."

If you can persuade your husband to reverse his barbaric practice, do so. If not, allow Miss Manners to suggest to you a better excuse. As he begins eating, say to your guests, "Wait a minute, please. Rhino always likes to make sure the seasoning is just right before he lets our guests have this dish." As your meals are "not that good anyway," this will be a convincing explanation.

DEAR MISS MANNERS:

Is it considered bad manners to take a sip of your drink at dinner, before everyone has been served food?

GENTLE READER:

It is considered an act of survival.

◝ The Sin of Not Waiting ◜

DEAR MISS MANNERS:

What is the procedure when one has the first bite of potato halfway to the mouth and then discovers that everyone else is waiting for the host to say grace? Do you proceed and pop it into the mouth, or lay the fork down at once? If the former, does this invalidate the grace?

GENTLE READER:

God will forgive all sins, even gluttony, but to talk with your mouth full—even to say "Amen"—is unforgivable in this life. Therefore, Miss Manners considers it theologically safer to put down the fork, gracefully.

⌒ *Passing Directions* ⌒

DEAR MISS MANNERS:

Which way does one pass the food, to the right or the left?

GENTLE READER:

Food platters should travel left to right, as most people are right-handed and can serve themselves more easily with the right hand reaching over to the left side. If more people at the table are left-handed, however, the food should travel from right to left. Guests have no responsibility for such decisions, as they will encounter a platter already marching along as whoever launched it has seen fit. If you try to reverse whatever pattern is under way, you will end up with the most dreadful traffic jam, to say nothing of gravy all over your lap.

⌒ *The Full Mouth* ⌒

DEAR MISS MANNERS:

It seems that whenever I have just popped a bite of food into my mouth, I am asked the title of my master's thesis or my views on the world situation—nothing, in short, that I can get out of with a simple nod of the head. What is the correct response in this situation? Must I force my questioner to wait until I've chewed and swallowed that bite? If it was almost completely chewed, can I stash that last morsel in a spare cheek and answer—provided the answer is short? When I am dining with someone I wish to impress, my boss for instance, I take small bites just in case.

GENTLE READER:

In today's hectic world, one is often faced with the choice, at business lunches or dinners, of losing the opportunity to make a statement or losing one's unfinished plate to an impatient waiter. Small bites and cheek stashing are, indeed, two legitimate solutions.

Another is to develop a facial expression that, without opening the busy mouth, suggests that wonderful words are about to come out of it, well worth the waiting. The eyes brighten, the lips smile knowingly and a hand is raised slightly. If you will practice this expression before a mirror, you will find that you can develop it into something mesmerizing that will buy you the time to swallow your food in silence.

⌒ *Elbows and Arms* ⌒

DEAR MISS MANNERS:

Why was it considered rude to put elbows on the table? Are those reasons still valid?

GENTLE READER:

Did you hear Miss Manners issue a retraction? No? Then the rule is still valid. Actually it applies only when one is eating, not when one is lingering over a completed meal or attending a meeting around a conference table. Etiquette, being custom, is not obliged to provide reasons, but confidentially, it is repulsed by the sight of an arm hovering, cranelike, over the plate—or circling around the plate, even if you have to protect your food from predators.

⌒ *Fingers* ⌒

DEAR MISS MANNERS:

I have acquaintances who seem to remember the teaching that crusts or other "pushers" to assist food onto a fork are taboo beyond the nursery table. Their solution is to use one or more fingers for the purpose, with fingers busy in their plates throughout a meal. This could be something that developed from the proliferation of dips and fast foods, but I find it somewhat distressing to see. Would you please say whether I am just slow in moving with the times, or whether I may be permitted to shudder?

GENTLE READER:

Yech. Distressing it certainly must be, to see all your friends with their busy little fingers in their plates, but when they claim to be doing this in the sacred name of manners, bragging that they are not using bread for the purpose—well, that is truly disgusting.

Using bread to sop up sauces or help spear difficult foods is a middle-European custom of dubious class origins. The way to do it, if you must do it at all, is to put a small piece of bread on the dinner plate, spear it with the fork as if it were a food legitimately domiciled there and then quickly mop up.

It is Miss Manners' belief that Americans with pure minds and bodies are perfectly capable of triumphing over any article of food without calling in assistance from the breadbasket. Sopping up sauces with bread should be confined to the nursery—"nursery," in this sense, meaning the family, of whatever age, at home enjoying garlic butter in privacy. Using the fingers should be confined to oblivion.

～ Declining Food ～

DEAR MISS MANNERS:

We are supposed to go to a relative's house for Thanksgiving, and I am tired of people making derogatory remarks to me about us vegetarians. Since when is it all right for someone to impose his/her views and lifestyle on others? Some of them even go so far as to dump meat on my plate in order to make me eat it. What should I do and say?

GENTLE READER:

What you should say is "No, thank you," and what you should do is not eat it. And you should steadfastly continue doing both, until New Year's, if necessary.

Miss Manners realizes that she is serving you a bitter portion, and apologizes for it. It is extremely difficult, not to mention unfair, for the victim of blatant rudeness to have to be the one who calmly refuses to react. And it is rude, not hospitable or funny, to attempt to force people to eat or drink after they politely refuse. (Note to minors: This rule cannot be invoked when your parents tell you to eat your vegetables or drink your milk. Miss Manners is sorry about that, but don't even try.) Retaliatory rudeness will only get you into that debate that you politely and sensibly wish to avoid.

～ Disliking Food ～

DEAR MISS MANNERS:

We were invited to a neighbor's for dinner last week. Their company was delightful, but the fish was extremely undercooked. I realize that I like my meat cooked more than most, and I am willing to choke down meat cooked less than I'd like. But this fish was two inches thick and only the outside 1/8″ was opaque. I ate the cooked portion but was physically unable to swallow the rest. There was not a lot of food available, so I was unable to hide the raw stuff under a lettuce leaf. I'm afraid they noticed me not eating the food, although I raved about the salad. What does one do in this situation?

GENTLE READER:

Rave about the salad. What else did you have in mind—sending it back with instructions to cook it properly?

Miss Manners hopes it will be of comfort for you to know that for a host to draw attention to what the guests do or do not eat would be rude and that there are so many food fusses going about nowadays that your hosts would be more likely to blame you than themselves.

~ Second Helpings ~

DEAR MISS MANNERS:

My grandmother always said "You must never ask anyone, 'Would you like a second cup of coffee?' or 'Will you have some more dessert?'" She said it should always be, "Would you like a cup of coffee?" or "Will you have some dessert?" no matter how many portions the person has had already. The other way, she said, only calls attention to the fact that the person is having a lot to eat or drink and is therefore impolite. Is this a general rule?

GENTLE READER:

It should be. There is something less than gracious about being urged, "Oh, come on, have a fifth slice of pie—you've hardly eaten anything." Consider this wisdom from dear Lewis Carroll's *Alice in Wonderland*: " 'I've had nothing yet,' Alice replied . . . 'so I can't take more.' 'You mean you can't take *less*,' said the Hatter: 'it's very easy to take *more* than nothing.'"

~ Parking the Roll ~

DEAR MISS MANNERS:

First, presuming there is no butter plate, do you place your roll on the cloth or the side of the plate? If there is no butter knife, do you use your own?

GENTLE READER:

One does the best one can with the available materials. If there is no bread-and-butter plate, use the tablecloth for parking the roll, and the luncheon plate for parking the butter. Bread, or rolls, with butter are not correct at a formal dinner (please see p. 582). If the hosts serve bread and butter, they should provide butter plates and knives. If there is no butter knife, use your main knife. If you don't have one, call it quits. An essential of good manners is knowing when to give up.

⟶ Parking the Napkin ⟵

DEAR MISS MANNERS:

My significant other and I travel quite a bit, and we have come up with a perplexing situation. When dining out and we leave our table for a few minutes, upon our return the napkins are placed back in the seat, not on the chair arm or beside the plate on the right hand side where we originally placed them. We don't want to appear unmannerly, so we politely pick up our napkins and continue with our meal.

Please tell me what is the correct way to address this matter. We do not wish to put our mouth on a napkin that has been laying on a chair that a person's behind has sat on millions of times.

GENTLE READER:

Miss Manners has a wish too. She wishes not to hear of the journey that you believe takes place between the metabolism of previous occupants of your chairs and your own. Maybe etiquette is just attracted to danger, but the chair is the correct place for you to leave your napkin if you get up in midmeal; it is at the end of the meal that it is left to the side of the plate.

⟶ Parking the Silver ⟵

DEAR MISS MANNERS:

My fourteen-year-old daughter says her teacher said it's wrong to place your silverware on the dinner plate with knife, fork, and spoon neatly across the top of the plate, the knife blade turned in, after you finish eating. My parents were bugs on manners and table setting, and I was brought up that way, so I've always told my children the same.

My daughter never did say what the teacher thought was proper. What do you do with the silverware—put it on the tablecloth and possibly stain it? Whatever—I will be gracious, even if corrected.

GENTLE READER:

Miss Manners hopes that the teacher will be equally gracious. Your method is essentially correct. That disclaimer, "essentially," is put in because Miss Manners wonders what the spoon is doing there. A spoon and fork may be used together for eating dessert, but the presence of the knife indicates that you are talking about a meat course and there is no business for the spoon's intruding, even if the meat was swimming in béarnaise sauce.

The knife blade should, as you say, be turned toward the eater, but there is a difference of opinion, among those of us who care, about whether the fork prongs should be up or down. Some leeway is also permitted in the angle at which the fork and knife are to be placed—straight across the plate, or diagonally across, usually from eleven o'clock to five o'clock. Perhaps the teacher was confused by two positions associated with the unfinished meal. If one is pausing while eating, the fork and knife placed in a crossed position—the handle of the fork to the left and the handle of the knife to the right, with the two instruments crossed at the center of the plate—signals the waiter or footman or host that you have not finished. Another position, knife and fork at right angles to the table edge, but off to the right-hand side of the plate, is used when passing the plate to a host for seconds, as it leaves the central part of the plate bare to receive more food.

Whew. They teach—or mis-teach—this subject in schools these days?

⌣ Outdoor Eating ⌣

One reason that picnics are popular is that many people believe that the rules of table behavior do not apply to tables made out of moss or worse. So here comes Miss Manners, like a queen bee on a rare royal tour, anxious to spoil your pleasant little outing by telling you that they do too.

It is true that some rules for eating outdoors are different from those that apply indoors. For example, it is permissible to execute extraneous wildlife found crawling across the picnic table, while any such creature making an appearance at a private, indoor dinner table must be ignored by the guests. At picnics, one may kill ants, but not complain of their presence. Accepting discomfort cheerfully is the basic rule of picnic behavior. If one is unalterably opposed to being bitten, sunburned, and having sand mixed with one's food, one should not go picnicking. The exception is that a small child drowning in a creek may call out to the adults at the picnic table, even if it means interrupting their conversation.

Nevertheless, it is important not to introduce the discomforts of civilization into a picnic to compete with nature's own discomforts. Radios, plastic forks and knives, paper plates and napkins, and tin cans are among the abominations that one has no right to bring to the countryside. The well-supplied picnic basket must include implements with which food may be served and eaten in dignity, and no one can eat decently from a paper plate with a plastic fork, since when the side of the latter is applied to the center of the former, they both buckle, with disastrous results.

Food should be chosen that can be served at its proper temperature, and it should be repackaged so that it may be served with no commercial containers appearing on the table or grass. If food is cooked at the picnic area, no more allowances are made for the chef's ruining it than would be made at a dinner party indoors.

The differences between indoor and outdoor manners are:

- One may never spill food accidentally indoors, but it is permissible to spill outdoors onto the grass, although not the blanket, tablecloth or dog.
- Children may be served first at picnics in the hope that they will then go play in the poison ivy.
- One may perform such normally unacceptable acts as reaching across the table, reclining at one's place and licking one's fingers, provided that they are done with grace.
- Everyone gets to help clean up, this not being, as indoors, the sole privilege of the hosts.
- There is no seating plan, so that people may sit where they wish, although it is customary to ask permission before putting one's head on someone else's lap.

FAMILY DINNER

~ *The Procedure* ~

DEAR MISS MANNERS:

Another big family dinner! I can't stand it, I can't stand it, I can't stand it! First of all, they'll all show up looking like slobs because "it's only family." The kids will be dirty before they get here, and it won't be ten minutes before they'll get a good fight going, and then the various grown-ups will start one by making remarks about how this child or that one was brought up (meaning they weren't). It's all right to insult people, you see, because families should be frank.

I don't even want to think about the table manners. The children don't have any, and the grown-ups do but don't use them because "among family" it's fine to hunch over the table, talk with your mouth full, eat with your fingers, and discuss your digestion problems. Also, they'll turn on the television during dinner, and in the interests of "saving work," they'll offer to lick their dinner forks and use them for dessert, and ask for paper napkins. Believe it or not, these people—my relatives!—are not animals when they take clients out to dinner or see their friends. Just when they're with family. I keep hearing that "the family is dying" in America. Any chance of this happening before dinner today?

GENTLE READER:

It is family dinner that has died, probably for the reasons you state, and Miss Manners is struggling to revive it. Properly practiced, the family dinner is a pleasure that makes keeping the family together worthwhile. People who know only the company dinner table and the kitchen counter, with nothing in between, don't know what they're missing. Your relatives are apparently among these unfortunates. If each household representing part of the greater family were to learn the ritual through daily practice, you might even be able to save the extended family, which sounds as if it is heading straight for extinction, probably today.

Here are the rules:

- Family dinner is regularly scheduled every night of the week, and delays or absences must be registered in advance.
- A reasonable attempt is made to make the table and the participants presentable. It's amazing what cloth napkins can do for the one and washcloths for the other.
- Entertainment is live, not electronic. First, each person gets a turn to present his or her news of the day, and then general conversation is held. Television and telephone interruptions are not allowed, but bragging is, and even encouraged.
- Good table manners are practiced, but they are good family table manners, as opposed to good company table manners. The chief difference is that chicken, spareribs and other such messes may be picked up and thus enjoyed in a way they never satisfactorily are with knife and fork. Spoons may even be used for getting up all of special sauces—but only in the privacy of the family, with a strict pact never to tell outsiders. This delicate blend of politeness and piggishness is extremely pleasant. Neither eating out nor eating directly from stove top or refrigerator can compare with it. It even justifies keeping one's family alive.

DEAR MISS MANNERS:

My father refuses to let me take telephone calls during dinner. I think it's rude to ask people to call back at a time that might not be convenient for them, and even ruder to ignore a ringing phone.

GENTLE READER:

You have a wonderful sense of the courtesies and conveniences due others. Have you thought of applying these to your father?

❦ *The Teaching Method* ❦

DEAR MISS MANNERS:

My husband is a fanatic about table manners. Every evening he comes up with a new rule. This is very nerve-racking to my daughter and me.

Will you please give me a list of the absolute no-no's? I have tried to convince him that some of the strict rules have been relaxed. Our daughter is eight years old, and our son is five. They are expected to eat perfectly or the dinner becomes a fiasco. I say that nagging and disrupting what should be an enjoyable family time is bad manners. What do you say?

GENTLE READER:

Is the choice between family harmony and teaching the children table manners? If so, Miss Manners would like to be excused from your table.

There are two social purposes to family dinner: the regular exchange of news and ideas, and the opportunity to teach small children not to eat like pigs. These are by no means mutually exclusive. Mrs. Perfect, for example, merely has to maintain a patient and cheerful tone: "Cutlip, dear, do tell us about your class trip to the zoo. . . . Now, swallow what's in your mouth first, and then we'll all listen. . . . Daffodil, dear, take your fingers out of your plate. How did your social studies report go? . . . Mommy's going to tell you what she said to the traffic policeman. Just pick it up quietly, Cutlip, and say excuse me and take it into the kitchen and throw it away and then come back and finish your vegetables. . . . Don't interrupt, darling. It'll be your turn to talk in a minute. Sit up, please, and put your left hand in your lap. So, the policeman came up and Mommy said, 'Wait a minute, officer' . . ." And so on. One can become quite proficient at this amiable patter; the trick is to omit the instructive parts when attending formal dinner parties outside the house.

It would be a mistake for Miss Manners to provide you with a list of no-no's. It may never have occurred to your children to laugh with a mouthful of soup, for instance, or to discharge unappreciated salad ingredients into the napkin. Here, instead, are a few yes-yes's:

Small children should be expected to wait until their mother begins eating; to use their forks, knives and napkins as God meant them to be used; to refrain from mentioning their dislikes on the menu; to pretend to listen attentively when others are speaking; to ignore the toy potential of various food items; and not to leave the table without permission. Older children should be expected to have table manners as good as or better than their parents'.

Expectations are not always fulfilled, of course. What Miss Manners really means is that children should be repeatedly reminded to do these things in such a way as not to interfere with the opportunity for pleasant family conversation, but as to make basic table manners such a constant requirement that they become automatic before the children reach maturity. Then you and your husband can dine in peace.

～ *Showing Up* ～

DEAR MISS MANNERS:

How promptly should one respond after being called to the family dinner table? The chef, who has so lovingly prepared the meal, believes that the diners should take their seats as soon as they are summoned, even if this means that the food is still arriving at the table while or after everyone is being seated. This ensures that the food, which is intended to be eaten while still hot, will be placed on the table at the temperature most likely to compliment the cooking and please the diners.

The non-culinary principals involved believe that an effort to arrive at the table is not necessary until the food has been placed on the table in its entirety and the chef is seated and remains seated. Once this is achieved, the non-cooking family members often take five or more minutes before arriving at the table, taking the time to do one or more of the following: dress for dinner, wash hands, select and open a bottle of wine. Once arriving at the table, a request to say grace is then made. Food is now growing cold and it is difficult to restrain hungry children, not to mention the chef. Giving all diners a five-minute warning prior to calling everyone to the table has not seemed to help.

GENTLE READER:

As Miss Manners does not find it difficult to detect a point of view in the way this question is presented, she thinks you will be pleased with the answer. You win on two counts. The cook is entitled to be tyrannical about setting dinner time; even George Washington claimed to be afraid of his cook and went to table at the appointed time without waiting for tardy guests. Parents are also empowered to require mealtime promptness. Miss Manners is afraid that you will have to insist upon exercising your double authority. She can validate it for you, but she cannot come over and round everyone up.

~ *Staying Put* ~

DEAR MISS MANNERS:

Can you please give an opinion to help settle a problem before somebody gets diced with my electric carving knife?

I say that when you sit down to eat, you should eat without getting up and deciding that you have to have some added condiment or item. I set the table thoroughly and prepare good and varied meals three times a day. But it seems that there is always something missing and that somebody has to get up and go to the refrigerator. I tell them that if they were in a restaurant they would not go into the kitchen and retrieve something and their reply is that they are at home and want to feel comfortable. Getting up reminds me of teen-aged boys who push their chairs back from the table and have to go get a Coke or pickles or something like that. I have suggested eating in front of the refrigerator with the doors open so that one could reach right in, but the layout of our kitchen won't permit this.

When we are invited to somebody's house for a meal, I am satisfied with what is on the table. I wouldn't think of asking for something or going to help myself to something additional. I was told that "everybody does it" but I don't believe it. I realize that we are in the age of Slobus Americanus Rex, but surely there must be some set of manners or standards. We are all waiting for a reply and you better hurry otherwise I might be writing to you from behind bars the next time one of my family decides they have to get up and get some sliced cheese to put on my home-made chili.

GENTLE READER:

There, there. You're a little overworked, aren't you? And perhaps a little hurt that those for whom you cook want to make adjustments to the food?

Miss Manners begs you to put down the carving knife and be reasonable. It is true that people would not pop up from the table when eating out, but also that in a restaurant they would have ordered what they wanted and asked a waiter to fetch anything that was missing, while in someone else's house, they would have had to accept what they might not like.

Things should be different at home, but not because family members needn't have manners. It would be the greater part of politeness for these people to set the table with whatever they might require, thus relieving you from some of the work, as well as from their absences.

∽ *Ranking Relatives* ∾

DEAR MISS MANNERS:

Could you elaborate on family etiquette regarding meals? Who serves? Who is served first? What is served first? Also, who is served second, etc., when the family is alone, and when the family has one or two guests?

GENTLE READER:

In a simple, family-style meal, consisting of perhaps six people—a grandparent, two parents, two children and a guest—it is possible to combine four different ranking systems, so that everyone gets his just desserts, except, of course, children who don't deserve them. The systems are blood, age, gender, and ability.

The privilege of serving dinner should go to the adult (age) in the family (blood) who is most likely to get the food divided and transferred from platter to plate without its lingering along the way on the tablecloth (ability). The first portion goes to the oldest (age) unrelated (blood) female (gender). Within the family, adult women are served by generation (first Grandmama, then Mama), and then adult men by generation (Grandpapa after Mama but before Papa). As one of these people is likely to be doing the serving, that person is removed entirely from the order of precedence. Serving oneself last not only looks modest, but gives one a clean place in which to work.

The youngest generation should be served last, by the same rules, beginning with unrelated females, and so on. However, many adults have noticed the advantage, in large family gatherings, of serving children first and then "excusing" them from the table. Ability is an important factor in children's ranking, as a person who lacks the ability to restrain his wailing when he sees food on the table but not in front of him is likely to find that he has rapidly passed the entire ranking system. There is an unfortunate moral in that.

∽ *Respecting Relatives* ∾

DEAR MISS MANNERS:

When asking someone to pass an item, say the butter, my mother says "Pass the butter." I correct her to "Pass the butter, please."

She maintains that if she is going to say "Thank you," she is not required to say "please." Please clarify this so we can have closure to an argument that has been going on for years.

GENTLE READER:

Did your poor mother grow up when there were wartime shortages? Does she think that politeness is rationed? So if you've said "Good morning," you've used up your allotment for the day and can't say "Good night"? Actually, "please" and "thank you" come as a set, like—well, Miss Manners realizes that it would no longer be understandable if she said like love and marriage. Like salt and pepper.

DEAR MISS MANNERS:

Would you please comment on the proper etiquette for reading at the dinner table? In particular, is it considered proper to prop a letter against the salt shaker or to lean the newspaper against a carton of cottage cheese, in order to free the hands for eating?

GENTLE READER:

Miss Manners was about to duck this question, on the grounds that it is never proper to read at the dinner table if anyone else is present and that what you do when you eat alone is between you and your God, and not a matter of etiquette. Then she came to the cottage cheese container. No decent person would put a food package—including ketchup bottles, milk cartons or cereal boxes—on the table, even at home alone with the shades drawn.

~ *Feeding Miss Manners* ~

DEAR MISS MANNERS:

When you want to take the last of anything from the serving plate, can you just take it? Or should you say, as a courtesy, "Would anyone else care for the last piece of chicken?"

I am trying to teach my children decent table manners. If you ask, must each of your siblings say, "No, you go ahead," out of courtesy, even if s/he actually wanted it? If your brother says, "Yes, I want it," must you gracefully allow him to take it, even though he pulls this on you every night? Does it make a difference if the food is something difficult to split (say, a chicken wing) versus something easy to split (mashed potatoes)? Does it make a difference whether you are dining at home with your family (still mannerly, of course, but more casual) or a guest at someone else's table (maybe the hostess would consider it rude of you to interrupt the conversation with the question)?

Gentle Reader:

The rule is that you must leave the last item on the dish for—you'll never guess whom.

Miss Manners!

At least that was the rule in better days. (Better for Miss Manners, that is; worse for everyone else.) It was considered greedy looking to polish off all available food, and children were taught to "leave some for Miss Manners."

A fellow etiquetter, Eleanor Roosevelt, was the one to break the news that Miss Manners' meal ticket had been cancelled. In her *Book of Common Sense Etiquette*, Mrs. Roosevelt reported that her grandmother had reversed the rule when she noticed that it wasted food.

Now that you are probably in tears over Miss Manners' travails, she apologizes for digressing. (And thank you, but she always carries her own handkerchief.) As much as she appreciates your teaching your children table manners, Miss Manners is wary of this little routine. It does not apply in company, because if there is a guest present, the guest should be offered the last piece (without its being called such) and when they are guests they should wait to be offered. Within the family, you could allow some latitude, while being on the lookout to prevent grabbiness and encourage consideration.

Better yet, teach your children that not everything on the platter has to be finished, and that good children who clear the table and do the dishes are entitled to consume leftovers in the kitchen.

MANNERS FOR PARTICULAR (AND ORNERY) FOODS

It is the opinion of many people who never attend formal dinner parties that to be obliged to eat under such circumstances is a dreadful ordeal. (Many people who do attend such events also consider them an ordeal, but that is a different matter; these people are referring to the conversation.) Actually, the formal dinner is one of the easiest ways there is of taking sustenance. When a waiter appears at your left with a platter of carefully apportioned food, and you have trouble taking some, he apologizes and serves you. You are provided with a variety of sturdy tools with which to attack the food: large china plates, solid silver knives and forks, a huge damask napkin to protect you from your own mistakes. Should you select the wrong implement, a whispered word will bring you a replacement. (In any case, such errors are less serious than popularly supposed. Most formal dinner tables are not patrolled by fork-enforcement officers, and unless you use three implements at a time, it is hard to come out short at the end.)

What is impossible to eat, without covering yourself with embarrassment or worse, is fast food. To attack, for example, a chiliburger, spareribs or hot dog, you are issued a paper plate that sops up juice and sags, a plastic fork that breaks and leaves its tines in your food, and five inches of thin paper with which to wipe up the mess. Why people are not frightened of informal meals, Miss Manners cannot understand. Any fool can sit at a mahogany table and eat breast of guinea hen.

⌒ Artichokes ⌒

DEAR MISS MANNERS:

What is the most efficient way of eating artichokes?

GENTLE READER:

For those who want to eat efficiently, God made the banana, complete with its own color-coordinated carrying case. The artichoke is a miracle of sensuality, and one should try to prolong such treats rather than dispatch them speedily.

An important part of sensuality is contrast. First pull off a leaf with a cruel, quick flick of the wrist, dip it in the sauce and then slowly and lovingly pull the leaf through the teeth, with the chin tilted heavenward and the eyes half closed in ecstasy. If the sauce drips, a long tongue, if you have one, may be sent down to get it. When the leaves are gone, the true subtlety of the artichoke reveals itself: a tender heart, covered with nasty bristles. To contrast with the fingering, there should be a sudden switch to cool formality. The fuzzy choke should be removed with dignified precision and a knife and fork, so that the heart may then be consumed in ceremonial pleasure.

⌒ Asparagus ⌒

DEAR MISS MANNERS:

The other night at the dinner table, my eight-year-old son started to eat his asparagus with his fingers. When I brought this to his attention, my wife informed me that it is considered good manners to eat this with the fingers. Good etiquette tells me you don't use the fingers for this vegetable.

GENTLE READER:

Miss Manners tells you that you do. Asparagus is, indeed, correctly eaten with the fingers, in a very old tradition of which few modern people seem aware. Those who do know can therefore have a marvelous time doing this in company or in restaurants and being reprimanded or at least stared at, only to have the disapproving people find out later that they were in the wrong. What Miss Manners wonders is how an eight-year-old boy found out about this. Would he like to meet a refined Victorian lady?

DEAR MISS MANNERS:

I am afraid that I must take exception to your response to the reader who asked if it was proper to eat asparagus with your fingers. I have it on good authority that one's fingers should never be eaten with any other food. I suspect that you misunderstood the question.

GENTLE READER:

How right you are. But after the fingers convey the asparagus to the mouth, the fingers may then be eaten with whatever remains of the hollandaise sauce.

～ Bacon ～

DEAR MISS MANNERS:

When I am eating breakfast out, or when I'm staying at someone's house, how do I eat breakfast bacon—with the fingers or a fork?

GENTLE READER:

The correct way to eat bacon is with a fork. Limp, greasy bacon is easily eaten this way, but is not worth the eating. Crisp bacon is delicious, but impossible to eat correctly. Life is often like that, but it's a shame it has to be that way at breakfast time.

～ Bread and Butter ～

DEAR MISS MANNERS:

Why can't bread be buttered all at once instead of in the time-consuming method of breaking off small pieces, buttering each one, and then eating it before breaking off another piece?

GENTLE READER:

It is not for nothing that bread has earned itself the title of Staff of Life, as anyone will verify who has failed to catch a waiter's eye in a restaurant. Good bread deserves respect and must be eaten in the traditional fashion out of reverence. Poorly made bread is consumed only as a pastime by people whose meals are inadequate or late, and therefore should be eaten in as complicated a manner as possible to fill the time. Children who make little balls out of bread have the right motivation, although the wrong method.

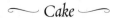

Cake

DEAR MISS MANNERS:

How do you eat cake?

GENTLE READER:

So that you can have it too. This is done by cutting a bite-sized piece with the edge of the fork and lifting it up to the mouth in such a way that crumbs drift down and lodge themselves in the shirtfront. These may be furtively picked up and eaten later.

Candy

DEAR MISS MANNERS:

How do you take a piece of candy when a box is passed around? How can you tell which are the kind you like? Can you take more than one? Do you take the paper frill it comes in along with the candy, or just the piece of candy?

GENTLE READER:

Of course you know that "Take the one you touched" used to be the first rule of social behavior. Well, it still applies to candy. So does taking one at a time. As for the paper frill: Never leave behind evidence of how much you have taken.

DEAR MISS MANNERS:

When you advised a reader to throw away the paper frills that boxed candy comes in, you said, "Never leave behind evidence of how much you have taken." Clearly this means that I must kill the person sitting next to me if he saw me take a piece of candy. Tell me, Miss Manners, what is the proper way to kill another house-guest? Please rush your answer, as I plan to attend a party in the near future and I may want some candy while I am there.

GENTLE READER:

People are not "evidence"; they are witnesses. Killing witnesses is a dreadful idea. Miss Manners hopes she has caught you in time.

~ *Chips and Dips* ~

DEAR MISS MANNERS:

Please be kind enough to give me the correct way of eating chips and dip. I was recently at a party and was very upset when quite a few of the guests repeatedly put the same chip they had taken a bite out of back into the dip. The bowl that con-tained the dip was for everyone. Was this proper?

GENTLE READER:

Your reading of the law—that one does not put food from one's mouth back into a communal dish—is correct. However, consider the circumstances of the defense. The path of chip to dip to mouth is a treacherous one. The chip may be broken into the dip. The dip may slide off the chip. A full chip, laden with dip, is apt to end up on the lip. Half a dip makes a safer trip.

Allow Miss Manners to propose one compromise, and one rhetorical question, as soon as she can stop babbling. The compromise: Suppose we require people to rotate their half-eaten chips, presenting a fresh edge for the refill? The question: How many germs can balance on the end of a potato chip anyway?

 ~ *Clams* ~

DEAR MISS MANNERS:

What are long-necked clams, and how do you eat them?

GENTLE READER:

Long-necked clams are a comma-shaped creature of the sea that God invented for people who can't sop up enough garlic butter with snails. To eat them, you need the following equipment:

- Bowl of long-necked clams
- Bowl of nasty, gray, watery broth
- Bowl of garlic butter
- Washable tablecloth
- Towel disguised as napkin
- Bathtub (optional)

Grab the slippery little devil firmly by its neck and rip away its shells. Holding on to the base of the neck, pull back the tough outer skin covering the neck, stripping the thing naked. All of this has a hostile tinge, but now comes the caring part. Holding on to the edge of the neck, dip the clam, as if it were Achilles, into the broth for a wash. Then dip it again into the garlic butter. All of these activities are exciting in different ways, but the challenge is to get the clam into the mouth before all the butter is absorbed into the tablecloth. The fastidious clam eater will take a complete bath after each clam.

~ Corn ~

DEAR MISS MANNERS:
   What is the proper way to eat corn on the cob?

GENTLE READER:
   Left to right.

~ Éclairs ~

DEAR MISS MANNERS:
   How does one properly serve chocolate éclairs for a bridge party dessert?

GENTLE READER:
   Chocolate éclairs are too good to waste on clothes, upholstery or bridge hands, however poor. Everyone should be issued a plate, fork and napkin with the éclair, and probably also a more stable surface on which to cut it than a lap.

~ *Eggs* ~

DEAR MISS MANNERS:

Is the proper way to cut a friend egg using a knife and fork or just a fork? The knife seems like overkill to me.

GENTLE READER:

Miss Manners is in the habit of tactfully correcting typographical errors, but she couldn't bear to change "friend" to "fried." It sounds like such a pleasant way to start the day. Well, not knifing a friend, exactly, but being greeted by a friendly egg.

Even a hostile egg should not be attacked with a knife, however. Since the days when people did most of their eating with their knives (the fastidious first wiping off any blood stains left from hunting), it has been the rule to use knives as little as possible, certainly not with anything so pliant as an egg.

~ *Fake Food* ~

DEAR MISS MANNERS:

What can one do about the increasingly common problem of fake food? In a restaurant, it is easy. I simply ask the waiter or waitress to remove the nondairy creamer and bring me real milk for my coffee. At a private home, the situation is more difficult. A week ago, a friend asked if I would like strawberries and whipped cream. However, when the dessert arrived, it turned out to be strawberries and canned whip, quite a different thing from what had been promised. I scraped the offending stuff off and ate the berries only, while receiving puzzled looks from my friend. My husband says I should have choked it down to be polite. Was I so obligated, having been trapped into accepting it?

Also, I am frequently offered butter for rolls, etc., and the so-called butter turns out to be margarine. I can think of several reasons why people serve fake food—financial, medical, atrophied taste buds—but can think of no reasons why they could not admit what they are serving and let their guests decide if they want to accept or reject said foods. How should one deal with this problem politely?

GENTLE READER:

Miss Manners will uphold your right to truth in advertising if you promise to apply it to commercial transactions only, and not to social ones. She does not want you claiming fraud when your friends ask you to dinner to meet what they say are interesting people you will be crazy about.

In restaurants you are certainly allowed to insist upon getting what was on the menu. In people's houses, you accept what you are given, but you do not have to eat it. It is rude to point out to people that they have allowed their language to deteriorate and their words have spoiled.

⟨ Fast Food ⟩

CHEESE SNACKS

If a finger bowl is not served with these, it is best to find a water fountain afterward for the same purpose. Do not shake hands with anyone directly after eating cheese snacks.

FRENCH FRIES

A quick motion of the wrist, such as one uses to shake down a thermometer, will remove excess ketchup.

FRIED CHICKEN

The fingers are of great use here, in prying off the huge globs of fried fat and placing them quietly on the side of the plate so that the chicken itself may be eaten.

HOT DOGS

While the hot dog in a bun is finger food, this does not include using the finger to push the meat along so that it will come out evenly with the bun at the end. The way to eat a hot dog is to accept the fact that nothing—not the mustard, nor the relish, nor the meat—will come out even, so a wad of tasteless bun must be consumed at the end.

PIZZA

This may be lowered into the mouth by hand, small end of the triangle first, taking care that the strings of cheese also arrive in the mouth.

SLOPPY JOE

The only way to eat this neatly is to eat the paper plate on which it is served; lifting the food out of it is a mistake.

⌁ Fish ⌁

Fish think they're so smart. Just because they get to loll in the water all the time, while the rest of us have to get out when our lips turn blue or our two weeks' holiday runs out, they think they deserve special treatment in everything.

At the dinner table there are special rules for the eating of fish that friendly animals, such as veal and mutton, wouldn't dream of requiring. Take the matter of bone and pit removal. Miss Manners is always telling people the simple rule about removing undesirable material from the mouth: It goes out the way it came in. A bit of chicken bone that went in by fork goes out by fork; a grape seed that went in by hand goes out by hand. But that's not good enough for fish. Fish have to be the exception, and fish bones that go in by fish fork are nevertheless entitled to a return trip by hand.

This unwillingness to go along with the crowd does not make fish popular. Some people won't eat them at all because they don't want anything to do with them, and others who, out of kindheartedness, don't eat agreeable animals, don't mind eating fish, whom they think of as being cold. You might call someone a "cold fish," but you wouldn't call a different sort of person "a hot, passionate fish."

This may be the reason that fish is often served with the head still on. No one would have the gumption to dig into a turkey while its beady eye was staring up from the plate, but a fish head is not considered to have a reproachful expression, so many people are able to ignore it. They have enough troubles dealing with the body.

Characteristically, fish require special tools. The old-fashioned equipment was two forks, which were used to rake the fish meat as if it were gravel in a Japanese garden. In Victorian times, the fish fork and fish knife were invented, which makes them considered déclassé by people who already had their family silver. The knife blade has an interesting shape, as if someone had ironed an obelisk and bent it off to one side. The fish knife and fish fork should be enthusiastically adopted by brides, restaurants and anyone else who expects fish in his life. By grabbing the fish fork firmly in the left hand and the fish knife in the right, pencil style, one arms oneself for a fair contest with any fish. Without them, the fish, using its tiny white bones as darts, is likely to win in the end.

Some people believe in decapitating the fish first and detailifying it too; others preserve its form, placed across the plate, head to the left and tail to the right. To eat a whole fish that is facing to the right is disgusting and vulgar. The method of attack, which dear Evelyn Waugh called ichthyotomy, is to use the knife to slit the fish from gill to tail just above the middle of its side, where it keeps its backbone, before it has a chance to realize what is going on. If you then lift the fish meat off carefully, it

To bone a fish

The proper dissection of a fish under social conditions. Anchor fish with fork and cut along dotted line with fish knife or a second fork. Pry flesh open at C–B, and lift top section. Eat, starting at A; then lift B section and eat, from left to right, or head to toe—no, tail. Remove skeleton with knife and eat underside. The fish may be decapitated before eating. Squeeze lemon with right hand, using left hand as umbrella to protect dinner partner's eyes.

should be bone-free. If not, see above method of bone removal. If the bone has gone too deep for that, see a doctor.

After that half has been eaten, the backbone may be removed so that the entire fish skeleton may be placed to the side of the rest of the food. Sometimes that doesn't work, however, so one waits until no one is looking and then flips the fish until it again presents a whole side, which is slit as the first side was.

If you can accomplish all this, you have the satisfaction of knowing that you have fought by the fish's own rules, and won. You may then proceed to the meat course, glowing with triumph.

~ *Fruit* ~

DEAR MISS MANNERS:

I am uncertain about the correct way to eat fruit, although I like nothing better. Does it depend on what the fruit is, or the circumstances under which it is served, or is it a matter of individual preference? I am referring to such questions as peeled vs. unpeeled, and hand vs. fork. More and more often, probably because of everybody's dieting, I see bowls of fruit used as centerpieces for dinner parties and then being passed as the dessert course.

GENTLE READER:

Fruit occupies the place in the food world that the ingenue does in society. That is, it is usually fresh (but occasionally stewed), and although welcome anywhere for its charm and simplicity, it requires more complicated treatment when going about socially than it does when it is just hanging around the house.

Also, it is a mistake to treat individual members of this group in the same fashion, because some of the strongest-looking ones are frank and adaptable, while others look soft but have hearts of stone.

The least formal way to eat fruit is to pick it from a tree or fruit stand and pop it into your mouth with your hand. It is customary to secure the permission of the owner, and a good rinsing doesn't hurt either.

The most formal method is to attack it with fruit knife and fork until it is halved, then quartered and, if you wish, skinned. As all this fierceness might be considered overkill with, say, a grape; small fruits are formally eaten by hand, with the pits quietly transferred from tongue to hand to plate.

Here are the details:

APPLES

Informal: Grasp at ends, bite, and rotate.
Formal: Stab with fork, quarter and peel (optional); eat with fork.

APRICOTS

Informal: Same as apple, but with emergency napkin poised, and rotating from left to right, as well as back to front.
Formal: Halve, cut out pit and eat with fork.

BANANAS

Informal: Strip peel gradually, using bottom part as holder.

Formal: Strip peel entirely away, cut slices and eat with fork. N.B.: Eating a banana with a knife and fork is almost as funny to spectators as slipping on a banana peel.

BERRIES

Informal: Grasp stem with hand and pull with hand while securing berry with teeth.
Formal: Use a spoon.

CHERRIES

Informal: Same as berries, then remove pit with hand.
Formal: Use a spoon, especially if the cherry is nestling in ice cream.

GRAPES

Informal: Grape goes in by hand, and seed comes out by hand.
Formal: Cut cluster with grape scissors and then follow same procedure.

ORANGES

Informal: Cut in quarters and hold by peel while slurping noisily. Better yet, squeeze into glass.
Formal: Peel and then cut, or cut and then peel, whichever is easier (both are nearly impossible), and eat sections with fork.

PEACHES

Informal: Same as apricots, but with more absorbent napkin.
Formal: Cut in quarters around pit, peel and eat with fork. Apologize to hostess for staining tablecloth.

PEARS

Informal: Same as apples.
Formal: Fresh, same as apple; stewed, with dessert spoon and fork.

PINEAPPLE

Informal: Same as formal. It is a mistake to hold an unpeeled pineapple in the hand and bite into it.
Formal: Quarter, cut from peel, slice and eat with fork. Wonder why hosts didn't perform this in pantry.

WATERMELON

Informal: Same as pineapple, but flecking away seeds with knife.
Highly informal: Put face into watermelon and see who can spit the seeds farthest.

Garnishes

DEAR MISS MANNERS:

Do I or do I not? There are many of the garnishes that I really enjoy. Is it considered appropriate to eat them? Please enlighten me.

GENTLE READER:

Whether you do or do not is hardly something Miss Manners would consider to be her business. Garnishes, however, are. You may eat them.

 Grapefruit

DEAR MISS MANNERS:

What is the best way to eat grapefruit?

GENTLE READER:

Carefully, if at all. The grapefruit is a particularly vicious piece of work with a sour disposition, just lying in wait to give someone a good squirt in the eye. If the grapefruit sections have not been loosened with a grapefruit knife before serving, or if you are not armed with a pointed grapefruit spoon, give up. It will get you before you get it.

 Ice Cream

DEAR MISS MANNERS:

Is it proper to mush ice cream that is served in a bowl? I prefer to eat it soft.

GENTLE READER:

No, it isn't, but it does taste better that way, doesn't it? The proper method is to become vivaciously engaged in conversation as soon as the ice cream has been served, and then, when it has turned into a puddle on its own, to eat it.

Ice-Cream Cones

DEAR MISS MANNERS:

Admittedly, it sounds silly to have to ask how to eat an ice cream cone. But I always end up with a mess dripping all over myself. Can it be that there is a right and a wrong way to eat ice cream cones?

GENTLE READER:

Much more than that, it is an art. Many parents mistakenly think that there is a natural instinct for the eating of ice-cream cones, and then they make a dreadful fuss about the upholstery.

The problem is a seemingly insoluble one, namely that the cone is served empty with the scoop or scoops of ice cream on top of its fragile rim, but the eater is expected to place the frozen substance inside the cone during the course of his eating. It may be done, but it requires the ability to plan, manual and lingual dexterity, and a knowledge of physics and geometry.

First, lick the ice cream in a clockwise motion (counterclockwise for left-handed people), until the scoop is not wider than the rim of the cone. No overlap is permitted. Then, placing the tip of the tongue in the center of the remaining scoop, push gently downward. This requires much skill because if you apply too much pressure, the cone will burst in your hand like a crystal goblet. After each such push, additional edge licking will be needed, as the pressure forces the scoop outward. With careful planning, you should be able to fill the cone at the same time that you are filling your stomach. The cone, once full, is nibbled clockwise down to the tip, which is put whole into the mouth. This sounds like a great deal of work, but once mastered, the ability will serve you well in other, more sophisticated areas of life, such as frozen yogurt cones.

⌒ Ice-Cream Sodas ⌒

DEAR MISS MANNERS:

There are so few places where ice cream sodas are still made—I mean the kind where the syrup and ice cream and soda have to be mixed right there at the soda fountain, by hand—but I still love them. My question is how to eat the soda properly, when I get the chance, without spilling it all over the place. There is a certain amount of mixing that has to be done by the person who is eating it, and that's what I have the problem with.

GENTLE READER:

Miss Manners quite agrees with you about the value of the ice-cream soda, which is one of the great gastronomical treats of the American cuisine. A true artistic creation goes by its own rules, some of which would be considered scandalous if practiced in connection with lesser achievements.

First eat the cherry alone with the spoon. Next, remembering Archimedes' principle, eat the whipped cream with the spoon, without attempting to force it into the full glass. You then have a slight amount of space between the level of the drink and the rim of the glass, which is your working space. Insert the spoon into the glass and poke at the ice-cream scoop.

The first sip may be taken through the straw. It will not be a perfect blend of soda, ice cream and syrup, but will serve as a prelude to the perfection that occurs when, through hard work and the natural consequences of putting ice cream into soda water, full blending may take place.

The great paradox here—and fine art is full of ironic contradictions—is that the soda begins to disappear just as it reaches its perfect state. How like life itself. It is for this reason that Miss Manners has given the ice-cream soda a unique privilege. And that is that the drinker may take three—he is entitled to no more than three—noisy slurps to get up those few last drops.

⌒ *Lobster* ⌒

DEAR MISS MANNERS:

Lobster bibs make people look silly. I hate them. I have actually been ignored, however, by waiters who fasten them around my neck, without asking, when I tell them I want to eat my lobster without one, taking my own chances about soiling my clothes. Do I have to order something else at a restaurant unless I am willing to wear their bib?

GENTLE READER:

The reason that God made the lobster delicious, messy and expensive, all at once, was to reserve for humanity one treat that is better enjoyed in the privacy of the home. There is nothing better than boiled lobster with garlic butter, but you pay a restaurant a considerable markup for something that is simple to make, and as it is impossible to eat neatly, you expose yourself to public ridicule. Eat your lobster at home, wearing washable clothes, and you will not need a bib.

⌒ *Nuts* ⌒

DEAR MISS MANNERS:

Could you please tell the correct way to eat nuts at the dinner table and at a buffet.

GENTLE READER:

Is there a nut spoon?

Of course not. It is Miss Manners who must be nuts to inquire, as she is the only person left on earth who puts these out so that the nuts can be spooned into the eager fist. Failing this nicety, people must use their bare hands, she is afraid. Under such conditions, fastidiousness consists of not taking all the choice ones and leaving the peanuts, and not licking the salt from the fingers and then plunging them back into the nut dish.

Peas

DEAR MISS MANNERS:

I know that peas should not be eaten with a knife, but how do you eat them? I have trouble getting them on my fork. Should I mash them first?

GENTLE READER:

Peas are unique in that they are the only vegetable with a herd instinct. Thus it is easily possible to catch them when armed only with a fork if they are crowded together and feeling safe; but impossible by conventional means to catch one or two that have strayed from the herd and are therefore on their guard. Don't even try. You will only work yourself into a rage and end up with one or two peas dancing around the rim of your plate, laughing at you.

Pickles

DEAR MISS MANNERS:

I love eating pickles, but I'm afraid that eating them whole, as I often do, might not be considered proper. I know that it's all right to put pickle slices on hamburgers and sandwiches, but I am not sure if they should be eaten by themselves. Do you know of a correct way to eat them?

GENTLE READER:

Pickles should be eaten with relish. No—not that kind of relish—enjoyment. A large, slurpy pickle is eaten from the hand under informal circumstances, while the more dressed-up pickle, which is either small or sliced, may find its way to more formal meals, where it should be eaten by fork.

⌒ *Pomegranates* ⌒

DEAR MISS MANNERS:

A friend says there is no polite way to eat pomegranates in public. I say that providing they have been completely peeled and the seeds separated, one can eat them, singly or in groups, and discard the pits via a spoon, on one's plate. Please don't answer that a squeezer would solve the problem by allowing you to have pomegranate juice.

GENTLE READER:

Why not? Why should you have all the fun? If you are eating pomegranates, it seems to Miss Manners that you are having about as much fun as a human being can stand. The pomegranate is nature's little tease, inviting you to guess which parts of it are edible and which are not. Some people throw out the seeds and are sorry afterward, and some people eat the pulp and are sorry about that. The key skill here is knowing how to admit defeat gracefully, which is to deposit mistakes neatly in the spoon and then on the plate, as you describe.

⌒ *Potatoes* ⌒

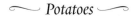

DEAR MISS MANNERS:

I am extremely fond of baked potato, and the heck with the calories. I eat so many, the least I can do is to eat them correctly. But if you slice into the potato, you get a smooth surface and the butter slides right off it. Everybody knows that baked potato tastes best with the butter mashed right into it, but I can't find anyone who knows how to do this politely.

GENTLE READER:

Well, now you have. Baked potato is properly broken up with the fingers, from which we get the expression "a hot potato." (Considerate cooks cut an X on the top before serving, so that the heat escapes somewhat, but how many considerate cooks are there?) This gives an irregular surface. Then the butter is put on it—not with the knife, as you might expect, but with the fork. A flick of the wrist mashes some of the butter, and no one will be the wiser. You may do this one half at a time, eating from the shell, which you may steady with the left hand. Shell eaters may then cut up the shell with fork and knife.

⌒ *Potato Chips* ⌒

DEAR MISS MANNERS:

What is the proper way to eat potato chips?

GENTLE READER:

With a knife and fork. A fruit knife and an oyster fork, to be specific. For pity's sake, what is this world coming to? Miss Manners doesn't mind explaining the finer points of gracious living, but feels that anyone who doesn't have the sense to pick up a potato chip and stuff it into his mouth probably should not be running around loose on the streets.

⌒ *Prunes* ⌒

DEAR MISS MANNERS:

When eating stewed prunes, where is the proper place to put the pits? I am assuming that the whole prune is put into the mouth. Is the pit eased as unobtrusively as possible back onto the spoon and then put in—on—where?

GENTLE READER:

Stewed or not, you must take inedibles out the way you put them in. If you put it in with the spoon—and let's hope that in the case of stewed prunes, that is what you did—it comes out onto the spoon. The skill is to get the pit clean while it is still in your mouth, so that what comes out has no food attached to it. It is fun to watch the facial maneuvers of a person trying to do this. Now, where do you put the pit? On the plate under the dish in which the prunes were served.

⌒ *Salt* ⌒

DEAR MISS MANNERS:

You wouldn't think that something so common and ordinary as table salt would require training to use, but I have several unresolved problems.

1. What is the formal way to serve salt? I am thinking of where it should be put on the table, and in what. Also, how much—that is, how many guests to a salt shaker?

2. When someone asks me to pass the salt, it is often a reminder that I haven't yet salted my own food. May I do so before passing the salt?

3. If there is a salt and pepper set, do I pass both together, even if only the salt was requested?

GENTLE READER:

Common salt may be, but ordinary it is not, being truly a seasoning for all.

1. The really fastidious person will serve salt in tiny open dishes, with salt spoons, at a formal dinner, and not use a salt shaker. Almost no one except Miss Manners is that fastidious, however. Such salt cellars are placed between every two guests, or, if you want to go all out, one in front of each guest.

2. No, you may not. That is like using a friend's engagement announcement to notice how suitable a partner the betrothed would make for yourself.

3. Keep them together. Like many couples, one is sought after and the other generally ignored, but the polite person will treat them as a couple and invite them together.

~ Sandwiches ~

DEAR MISS MANNERS:

I like to have a club sandwich for lunch, but my mouth isn't big enough to get all the layers in at one bite. Should I try to eat it with a knife and fork?

GENTLE READER:

The club sandwich is typical of the club decision, usually thought of by a committee that tries to fit in everyone and ends up making a mess. You will never manage to pack all that stuff onto a fork. Save the fork for eating whatever has dropped out of the sandwich when it is eaten, as a civilized sandwich is intended to be eaten, with the hands.

DEAR MISS MANNERS:

When a multistory sandwich is served, such as a club sandwich, and it is held together with frilled toothpicks, what do you do with the toothpicks?

GENTLE READER:

You take them out of the sandwich. What did you think: You eat them?

⌒ Shish Kebab ⌒

DEAR MISS MANNERS:

When eating shish kebab, are the pieces of meat, onion, etc., left on the stick, or are they removed before eating, and if so, how?

GENTLE READER:

Are we talking about a vicious metal skewer, or about an oversized toothpick at a cocktail party? Miss Manners needs to know these things. There is no use coming in here and claiming you want help until you are ready to bare your very soul. The metal weapon served for a meal is held daintily by one end in the left hand, while the other hand (right), wielding a fork, slides the goodies off onto the rice. The wooden portable variety is eaten from, as ice cream is from a stick, with about the same lack of success in the areas of neatness and grace.

⌒ Shrimp ⌒

DEAR MISS MANNERS:

I have a recipe for broiled shrimp with garlic that doesn't say anything about peeling the shrimp before cooking. Can unpeeled shrimp be served at a luncheon? How do people peel them? Do I provide a dish for the peelings? How are you supposed to eat this dish?

GENTLE READER:

You are supposed to eat this dish while sitting in a Spanish café, sipping sherry. Peeling the shrimp is half the fun. You grab each shrimp by its wee little legs, tugging to pull them all off as an unpleasant child would pull the wings from a fly. You then dig the thin shell away from the shrimp and eat the shrimp. Then you find that the shrimp is so delicious that you attempt to catch a waiter's eye to reorder. In the forty-five minutes before the new order comes, your eyes and fingers gradually wander toward the shrimp shells, which smell of garlic. Surreptitiously, you slip a shell into your mouth. The shell tastes like fingernail parings, but the garlic is so good that you eat the remaining shells. You then crumple your napkin on top of your plate so the waiter won't look around to see what became of the shrimp shells.

As you can see, all of this is such an adventure that you could hardly conduct a decent luncheon party while it is going on. Miss Manners suggests you save this recipe for the privacy of your family.

⌒ *Snails* ⌒

DEAR MISS MANNERS:

What is the proper equipment necessary to eat snails? And then, how do you use it?

GENTLE READER:

Surely you mean to ask: What is the maximum equipment you can use to eat snails, and how can you make the biggest fuss and have the most fun doing it?

Snails, after all, may be prepared in many delicious ways and served in a sauce on a plate or on toast that is, in turn, on a plate. All you need then is a fork, and some dexterity in cutting the sodden toast with the edge of the fork. To make the most of the dish theatrically and still have something slurpy to eat, you can buy snail plates, tongs and forks, hide the snails in shells to give them a sporting chance and then attack them with both hands and all this metal.

The snail plates are ceramic or metal, with indentations for the snail shells, in which are put the snails themselves, usually floating in garlic butter. The whole mess has probably been broiled as a unit, so slyly steadying your plate with your fingers, never proper, is in this case promptly and severely punished. Snail tongs have a bowl that opens when you press the handle and closes around the snail shell, anchoring it. The fork is narrow, with two prongs that pierce the snail and drag it out of its lair. As the tongs are held in the left hand and the fork in the right, it is permissible to empty the shell of its sauce over the extracted snail.

Now comes the real conflict of the conscience. As you know, Miss Manners does not approve of sopping up sauces with bread. However, she approves of garlic butter. That is why you see her turning discreetly away from you at the table, and also why you hear her offering to clear the snail dishes from the table.

⌒ *Soup* ⌒

Do you have a kinder, more adaptable friend in the food world than soup? Who soothes you when you are ill? Who refuses to leave you when you are impoverished and stretches its resources to give you hearty sustenance and cheer? Who warms you in winter and cools you in summer? Yet who is also capable of doing honor to your richest table and impressing your most demanding guests?

Why, then, do people so mistreat this inestimable friend? They dump it unceremoniously into all the wrong containers, pay no attention to its modest preferences in spoons, tilt it from side to side until it is afraid of perishing in an oceanic storm, make frightful noises at it and leave spoons pitched into it, like daggers in trusting hearts.

Soup does its loyal best, no matter what undignified conditions are imposed upon it. But soup knows the difference. Soup is sensitive. You don't catch steak hanging around when you're poor or sick, do you? Soup deserves to be treated well. If soup could talk—and it doesn't, because it feels there is quite enough unpleasant noise made in its immediate vicinity—here is what it would say:

Not all soups are alike, and if possible, we would like you to distinguish among us. Like you, we enjoy going differently to different occasions; what is appropriate at home with the family is not at a formal dinner. So don't just put us all in cereal bowls and attack us with teaspoons. We like soup spoons, which have large, oval bowls, although we are perfectly happy to lend these to desserts when we are finished with them. If you can manage it, we also like smaller, round-bowled spoons for soups served in cups.

Handled cups are what all jellied soups like, and cold soups prefer. We generally like cups at luncheon, with little matching plates underneath. At dress-up dinners, we prefer soup plates, which are wide, and have broad, flat rims for the same reason that you are required to have a concrete apron around a swimming pool. You can put the soup plate right on the place plate, if you like, or on an underliner. The only thing we really can't bear, even in the kitchen or on the sickbed tray, is not having any plate at all beneath the soup plate or cup.

As for serving soup, we are really very accommodating about that, even for formal dinners. We could insist that soup be passed at the table, as every other food does, but passing a soup tureen on a platter is madness, we recognize, so we agree to the easier method of serving up in the kitchen and putting the soup plates on the table, already filled. We love tureens for family-style service, however.

We have become very modern about allowing you to tilt the soup plate gently away from you at the finish of the soup course, knowing what a shame it would be to force you to leave good soup uneaten. Handled soup cups we encourage you to pick up and drink from, while cautioning you that it is wiser to eat the fishballs, mushrooms, or noodles first with your spoon.

Now, about that spoon. Please hold it parallel to your mouth. It is the side of the spoon that should kiss the mouth, not the oval tip. The soup is gently and quietly poured from the soup spoon bowl, over its side, into the mouth. It is not inhaled. If you knew how often people do dreadful things to soup, kind, caring soup, you would weep. And even as the tears rolled from your cheeks, your faithful soup would expand in response.

⁓ *Spaghetti* ⁓

DEAR MISS MANNERS:

How do you eat spaghetti with a spoon?

GENTLE READER:

Bite your tongue. This is not an eating instruction, but an old-fashioned reprimand to anyone who would even entertain such an outrageous idea as eating spaghetti with a spoon.

Actually, there simply is no easy, foolproof way to eat spaghetti, and that is just as well when you think of how gloriously fat we would all be if there were. The inevitable slippage of spaghetti from the fork back onto the plate is Nature's way of controlling human piggishness. A fork is the only utensil that may be used to eat spaghetti while anyone is looking. It must make do with whatever cooperation it may muster from the plate and the teeth. The fork is planted on the plate, and the spaghetti is then twirled around the tines of the fork. If you can manage to use the grated cheese to add grit to the mixture for better control, so much the better. The twirled forkful is then presented to the mouth. If this were an ideal world, all the spaghetti strands would begin and end in the same place, so that the mouth could receive the entire forkful at once. However, we have all learned that compromises must often be made, and the fact is that one will often find a few long strands hanging down outside the mouth.

As you may not spit these parts back onto the plate, what are you to do with them? Well, for heaven's sake. Why do you think God taught you to inhale?

DEAR MISS MANNERS:

Eating spaghetti is a two-handed exercise, and it does employ the use of a spoon. But consider first your proposed method, the fork perched like a flagpole on the plate, twirling the spaghetti around its base as though to drill a hole in the china. Ugh. Proper, perhaps, for a Roto-Rooter man. The correct way to eat spaghetti is with a fork and a soup spoon. The soup spoon is held in the right hand, the fork in the left. One cannot eat spaghetti properly without a soup spoon. Shame on you.

GENTLE READER:

That many people use spoons to assist forks in eating spaghetti, Miss Manners is well aware. That correct spaghetti eating, with fork only, is not easy, Miss Manners also knows. (Why Miss Manners is suddenly writing her sentences backward, she does not know.) The most rewarding things in life require patience and diligence. In the civilized world, which includes the United States and Italy, it is incorrect to eat spaghetti with a spoon. The definition of "civilized" is a society that does not consider it correct to eat spaghetti with a spoon.

Steak

DEAR MISS MANNERS:

Would you please tell me, is it proper to put your steak sauce on the steak, or off to the side and dip your meat?

GENTLE READER:

If you are asking about *sauce béarnaise*, which is Miss Manners' idea of a steak sauce, the answer is to ladle it right onto the meat, where it will do the most good. If, however, you are talking about bottled steak sauce, you must allow Miss Manners to beg you, fervently, to have it decanted from the commercial bottle into something fit for the table before you even think about putting any on your steak. It, too, may then be ladled directly on the steak.

The principle about putting things to one side is to avoid using a community utensil, such as the butter knife that travels with the butter—as opposed to your very own butter knife—on your individual portion. Ladles and even (Miss Manners is closing her eyes and pretending not to see this) bottles dribble onto your portion, rather than touch it.

Taffy

DEAR MISS MANNERS:

What is the correct way to eat saltwater taffy?

GENTLE READER:

With the mouth closed. Actually, that is the way to eat all food, but taffy is the only food capable of enforcing the rule.

⁓ *Tomatoes* ⁓

DEAR MISS MANNERS:

Will you please tell me the proper way to eat cherry tomatoes (large and small ones)? I like them very much, but don't eat them when eating out for fear of being embarrassed.

GENTLE READER:

The cherry tomato is a wonderful invention, producing, as it does, a satisfactorily explosive squish when bitten. This sensation must, however, be confined to the inside of the mouth, not shared with one's friends or one's tie or blouse. Small tomatoes should be chosen for one-bite consumption in a closed mouth. Large ones may be treated as ordinary tomatoes and sliced, which is not as much fun. Medium-sized ones are neither here nor there.

Social Intercourse

VOCABULARY

ETIQUETTE WENT to a lot of trouble to invent short code words and expressions to indicate goodwill in the daily give and take of life. The prime examples are "please" and "thank you," which your mother annoyingly called The Magic Words.

Miss Manners will thank you to remember that these are merely grace notes intended to soothe and excuse the jostling of one person's needs against another's. To subject them to psychological and sociological analysis is not just silly but tedious.

Nor should they be put to a truth test. It is their job to create the fiction that people who use them do not wish to disturb others and are grateful for even the smallest favors.

So naturally, during the Age of Querulousness, people started objecting to them as not just unnecessary but degrading. Even now, when society has become as graceless as they might wish, some still do.

Because the expressions ceased to be universally taught, generations grew up without learning how to use them. As the need to get along with others remains, people of goodwill are stumbling along as best they can, often with awkward or easily misunderstood substitutes. Here, then, is a glossary of, ah, magic words. Just learn them. Please.

Please. Precedes any request, however trivial or perfunctory. Unauthorized replacements: "I need you to . . ." or "You want to . . ."

Thank you. Follows any granted request, however trivial or perfunctory. (Note to Gentle Reader who argues that he is "not obliged to be profusely grateful for a person's actions or requests in the normal course of their work": No, but you are obliged to say "please" and "thank you" to them.)

You're welcome. Response to "thank you." Unauthorized replacements: "No problem" and "Thank *You*." (Note to Gentle Reader who argues that "we need to assure customers that there is not anything that cannot be done to assist them": Yes, there probably is, but you can create that impression by saying "Certainly, I'd be happy to . . ." when the request is made and then cheerfully fulfilling it.)

No, thank you. Negative response to offers, typically of refreshments. Unauthorized replacement: "I'm fine."

Yes, please. Positive response to offers. Unauthorized replacement: "Okay."

Excuse me. Preface to interrupting or otherwise inconveniencing someone.

Unauthorized replacements. "Hey," "Coming through!" "I'm just going to sneak by you here," "Let me just steal that" and "Well, excuse *You*." (Note to numerous Gentle Readers who point out that "Excuse me" is often the immediate prelude to grabbing and shoving: Deplorably true, but would you really be happier with the unannounced rude action?)

Pardon Me. Pseudoapology when one believes one is in the right. Unauthorized replacement: "I'm really more of a victim."

I'm sorry. Response to complaints about mistakes made by oneself or one's place of employment. Unauthorized replacements: "I'm sorry you feel that way," "I can see you're upset," "I wasn't here that day," "Okay, here's what you have to do."

That's quite all right. Acceptance of apology, can be said graciously or grudgingly. Unauthorized replacement: "Well, you ought to be." (Authorized replacement of traditional rejection of apology, from "My seconds will call you in the morning" to "You'll hear from my lawyer.")

Sir, Madam, Ma'am, Miss. Courtesy titles to people whose names are not known to the speaker. Unauthorized replacement: "You guys." (Response to argument of "It makes me feel old": Perhaps you are, but whatever your age, you can't alter it by being rude to people who treat you with dignity.)

DEAR MISS MANNERS:

Must you say please to your dog when commanding him to sit? "Sit!" sounds so dictatorial.

GENTLE READER:

How else are you going to teach him to say "Thank you"? If you do not wish to act as a superior to your dog, even "Please sit" is somewhat strong. What about "Oh, do sit down and make yourself comfortable"?

∽ *Conventional Phrases* ⌁

Whether it is a deficiency in abstract reasoning or of language skills, Miss Manners is not certain. But she does know that people who insist on taking social idiomatic expressions literally have a problem. Two problems, actually. The second one is being tiresome.

"Why did she ask me how I feel if she didn't want to hear about what I've been through?"

"I'm not going to address him as 'dear' or sign myself 'Yours truly' or 'Sincerely,' when he's certainly not dear to me and I'm not truly or sincerely or any other way his."

"They told me I could stay with them any time I'm in town, and when I wrote them about next weekend, they said they already had plans and didn't offer to cancel them."

Naturally patient and tolerant, not to say saintly, Miss Manners nonetheless grows testy with people who make such arguments. She cannot believe that they honestly don't understand what a conventional phrase is. She thinks they want to strip these remarks of their usefulness and then laugh at their nakedness. What a nasty urge that is.

However, it does occasionally happen that an expression of that sort can change its meaning somewhat, or that it could have more than one meaning, depending on how and by whom it is said. Here, therefore, is a short glossary of social idioms:

How do you do? How are you? Both of these mean "Hello." The correct question, when you want to know how someone's digestion or divorce is getting along, is "Tell me, how have you really been?"

Call me. This can mean "Don't bother me now—let's discuss it on office time" or "I would accept if you asked me out" or "I can't discuss this here" or "Don't go so fast."

I'll call you. This has opposite meanings, and you have to judge by the delivery. One is the notoriously ephemeral declaration "Let's start something," and the other is "Don't call me."

Let's have lunch. Among social acquaintances, this means "If you ever have nothing to do on a day I have nothing to do, unlikely as that is, let's get together." Among business acquaintances, it means "If you have something useful to say to me, I'll listen."

Let's have dinner. Among social acquaintances, it means "Let's advance this friendship." Among business acquaintances, it means "Let's turn this into a friendship."

Please stop by some time and see me. Said to someone who lives in the same area, it means "Call me if you'd like to visit me." Genuine dropping in disappeared with the telephone, so if you want to encourage that, you have to say "I'm always home in the mornings. Don't bother to call; just drop by."

Please come and stay with me. Missing a date and said to someone from another area, this means "I would consider extending an invitation at your convenience if it coincides with my convenience."

We must get together. Watch out here, because there are several similar expressions. This one means "I like you but I'm too busy now to begin another friendship."

We really must see more of each other. One of the tricky ones, this actually means "I can't make the time to see you. "

We must do this more often. Another variation, it means, "This was surprisingly enjoyable, but it's still going to happen infrequently."

Yours truly, Yours sincerely. The first is business, the second distant social. Both mean "Well I guess that's all I've got to say so I'll close now."

Is all that clear? Oh, one last thing. People who say "I only say what I really mean," really mean "I am about to insult you."

⟶ Greetings ⟵

DEAR MISS MANNERS:
What is the difference between "Good morning" and "Good day"? Is there any?

GENTLE READER:
Yes, indeed. "Good morning" is an opener, and "Good day" is a closer. Although "Good morning" can be purely a greeting, to which only the same words are expected as a reply, this function has, for the most part, been replaced by "Hi." Therefore, "Good morning" usually leads to "How are you?" and other such mild conversational excursions.

"Good day," an extremely useful expression, is less often employed. With the proper tone, perhaps expanded to "I wish you a good day, sir," it means "Get out of my sight this instant" in the language of irreproachable manners.

⟶ Growth ⟵

DEAR MISS MANNERS:
My children hate it when adults say, "My, how you've grown!" or something like that. People do it all the time, of course, and I tell them they just have to expect it. Yet I find myself at a loss when confronted with other people's children. There is some kid, hiding behind his parents' legs, and I find myself saying things just as bad

as what others say to my children. What should grown-ups say to children on such occasions?

Nothing that would be considered rude if the child said it back. A child of Miss Manners' acquaintance who was brought along to an adult party and told, when he left, that he had "behaved like a perfect gentleman," replied to the host, "So did you." Miss Manners feels that the child came out ahead in this encounter. All basic social remarks are silly; the best one can do is to keep them from being patronizing as well. "How do you like this weather?" and "Stock market killing you?" may not be brilliant, but they are better than "The last time I saw you, you were only so high."

Unauthorized yet Common Remarks

Genuinely dumb remarks are those that sound insulting, even though no ill will went into them, or sound nosy, even though no real curiosity prompted them. They are uttered just because the speaker felt inclined to say something, and never thought to analyze how it might strike the target.

The most popular dumb remark now seems to be "You look tired," beating out the "Smile!" command, which had a long run. This replacement is at least more likely to produce results. Telling someone he or she looks tired has the effect of making the person look even more tired, the original state being compounded by the wearying knowledge that one's dragginess is so obvious. But then, instructions to cheer up generally produced the same effect.

The appearance of other people, almost always a dangerous subject for commentary (the exception being when someone you love gets dressed up and it becomes dangerous not to comment), is a major inspiration for dumb remarks. To point out to others that they are short, tall, fat, thin, pregnant, using a wheelchair, looking anxious or blushing is not as informative as many people imagine, and to inquire why is not likely to enlighten or amuse even the one who asks.

When it comes to unsolicited suggestions for improving the appearance and such, the merely thoughtless are often confused with proselytizers, who are as purposeful as they are rude. But instead of recommending therapists and handing out exercise plans, the former just deliver offhand remarks, such as "You could stand a haircut," "That's a terrible neighborhood you live in," "You should get married," "Are you still in that same job?" or a simple "Yuck!" at the sight of what someone else is eating.

Birth, marriage, divorce and death seem to move practically everyone to astonishing dumbness. Nobody much cares if prospective parents want a boy or a girl, but people keep asking them. This is about as useful as asking engaged couples if they know what they are doing, and about as suitable to casual conversation as asking divorcing couples what went wrong. When there is a death, people don't ask the bereaved if they are pleased; they tell them they should be: "It's better this way."

Commenting on children who are present, guessing and asking people's ancestral origins and assessing their possessions are other rich sources of dumb remarks. Miss Manners is regularly besieged by the victims who beg or suggest a response in case it happens again. Something witty and withering, they specify. A putdown.

But while Miss Manners has nothing against wit, she refuses to resort to using rudeness against the rude, and certainly not against those who parrot thoughtless remarks without intention to hurt. Fortunately, she has also found that the most effective reaction to dumb remarks is dumbfoundedness. Looking at them wide-eyed and saying nothing has the simple charm of leaving the dumb remark echoing in the air for everyone to hear how dumb it was. Sometimes even the person who said it.

"Ladies," "Women" and "Girls"

"Lady," "woman" and "girl" are all perfectly good words, but misapplying them can earn one anything from the charge of vulgarity to a good swift smack. We are messing here with matters of deference, condescension, respect, bigotry and two vague concepts, age and rank. It is troubling enough to get straight who is really what. Those who deliberately misuse the terms in a misbegotten attempt at flattery are asking for it.

A woman is any grown-up female person. A girl is the un-grown-up version. If you call a wee thing with chubby cheeks and pink hair ribbons a "woman," you will probably not get into trouble, and if you do, you will be able to handle it because she will be under three feet tall. However, if you call a grown-up by a child's name for the sake of implying that she has a youthful body, you are also implying that she has a brain to match.

Ladies come in three varieties: ladies, old ladies and young ladies. The term "lady," meaning a woman who behaves herself and is considerate of others, is the most difficult to use. You must not be influenced by having noticed that Miss Manners refers to all females as ladies (and all men as gentlemen) in the hopes that they will become so. Miss Manners is prim and old-fashioned, which is part of her considerable charm, and can get away with anything. For anyone else to use the term "lady" when "woman" is meant would be vulgar or even insulting.

What restricts the use of the word "lady" among the courteous is that it is intended to set a woman apart from ordinary humanity, and in the working world that is not a help, as women have discovered in many bitter ways. "Lady" is, there-fore, a word that should be used sparingly, and never in ways that interfere with a woman's livelihood. Because it should be a term of respect, its potential for sarcastic use is staggering, and snideness is always presumed when the word is used inappro-priately, as in "lady lawyer" or "saleslady."

Because respect should be accorded to the aged, an elderly female is called an old lady, not an old woman, unless she is a particularly nasty old thing and you think you can get away with it. "Young lady" is also a special category. A young lady is a female child who has just done something dreadful.

~ *Age Sensitivity* ~

DEAR MISS MANNERS:

My husband and I disagree on the use of the expression "older person." His point, and it is well taken, is that one should not use a comparative form when no actual comparison is being made. I accede that the expression is grammatically incorrect, but it serves a social purpose. No one wishes to be called elderly or (God forbid) a senior citizen. I use "older" to spare the tender feelings of those forever young at heart. What is your opinion please?

GENTLE READER:

Miss Manners' venerable opinion is that there is nothing wrong with the word "old," but a lot wrong with the phrase "young at heart." It suggests that young hearts are the only ones capable of harboring love and enthusiasm, while old hearts are fit only for cholesterol deposits.

DEAR MISS MANNERS:

My son and his wife have six children. They are all through college, some mar-ried, except two girls still at home. One of them is getting married in June. Last night, I said to my daughter-in-law, "Well, how will it feel with only one child at home?" She said, "She is not a child." That was her only reply. I said, "Well, all mothers say 'children' if speaking to one about their family." It wouldn't sound right to say, "Well, how would it feel to have one adult left?" What would be the correct phrase?

GENTLE READER:

The word "child" means offspring of any age, as well as meaning a minor. What is incorrect here is the use of semantic double-talk for the purpose of putting down one's mother-in-law.

⌁ Commercial Terms ⌁

DEAR MISS MANNERS:

A friend of mine always corrects me when I say the word "drapes." She says that is vulgar, and that the right word is "draperies." Which of us is correct?

GENTLE READER:

You are both hopeless. The word for material that hangs on the sides of windows is "curtains."

DEAR MISS MANNERS:

Please stand corrected. The sheer fabric made up to cover a window is named a curtain. A solid fabric made up into window covering or decoration is named drapery.

GENTLE READER:

This is true for commercial purposes, but in ordinary conversation the word "drapery" is never used for anything that covers or decorates a window. All such materials are called "curtains." Other such words to be eschewed outside of commerce, where they serve the purpose of making the item seem fancier, include "hose" for stockings, "tuxedo" for dinner jacket and "limousine" for car. Please stand recorrected.

DEAR MISS MANNERS:

What is the proper and correct term to use when referring to a lady's lower undergarment? Is it—"panties" or "underpants"? I've always called them "panties," but recently I've noticed that most of the women I know here call them "underpants" and they laugh at me when I say "panties." Which is correct?

GENTLE READER:

"Panties" is the nickname for underpants and, like "tummy" for stomach, has a certain childish charm. But not very much. Miss Manners is not vehemently opposed to "panties," as she is to "lingerie," a silly way of referring to the perfectly respectable institution of underwear. She loves to drive department store clerks crazy by inquiring for the "Underwear Department" and watching them look puzzled.

~ Naughty Words ~

It was a sad day when Miss Manners lost the capacity to be shocked. Such a delicious feeling it used to be—that tingle while one thought, "He doesn't really mean *that*" or "She *can't* have said what I thought she said." Nowadays, there is no doubt that that is what he meant, and that is what she intended. It certainly does take the fun out of conversation. Miss Manners is thinking of buying a jumbo-family-size box of detergent and washing out everyone's mouth with soap, so we can all start talking dirty afresh.

It is a common misconception that shocking conversation is that which reveals to the hearer ideas that were previously unknown. Not at all. There are only so many ideas in that area, and everyone over the age of eight knows what they are. To hear them uttered aloud—that used to be something. Papas who used vile expressions were understood to have been pushed beyond human endurance. Mamas given to such extremes had three-generation families quailing. Young gentlemen and young ladies who exclaimed "damme" (with the "e" on it; that was important) were taken seriously; if they said worse, they were treated as dangerous madmen, a useful way to be regarded when you require quick action.

Now every babe in arms can reel off the whole vocabulary, and nobody pays them the slightest attention. There is nothing more infuriating, when you are furious, than to have people shrug off your severest expressions of displeasure. The fact is that through overuse of three or four words, we no longer have language that adequately describes such situations as being splashed with mud by an empty taxi that one has tried in vain to hail. On such occasions, Miss Manners has been driven to exclaiming, "My goodness gracious!" or "Upon my word!" These are not nice, as she is the first to acknowledge, but desperate times call for desperate measures.

~ *"Vase"* ~

DEAR MISS MANNERS:
When is a VASE a VAHZ?

GENTLE READER:
When it is filled with DAH-ZIES.

CONVERSING
(RATHER THAN COMMUNICATING)

Could you people try talking to one another?

Oops. The last thing Miss Manners ever thought she would do would be to encourage what was known, in its faddish heyday, as "communication." That was the nonelectronic version, when people were encouraged to face one another to divulge all their deepest thoughts and feelings. The premise was that we were naturally so virtuous and compatible that all human friction resulted from a "failure of communication" worse than the kind that the power company promises to fix if you'll only stay home and wait for a week. It was believed that any personal conflict could be cleared up, if only we turned off that artificial, if not dishonest, inhibitor, tact.

There were, however, small miscalculations in this formula that began to appear when it was eagerly adopted. It turns out that not every thought or feeling we have, even about those we love, is benign. Furthermore, there are people whom we do not love, and when they reveal their innermost souls to us, we care for them even less.

Poor Miss Manners was still cleaning up the mess left by free and frank communication when along came email. Now we could reveal ourselves to total strangers. We could say what we really think of people we know but had meant to tell others, not them—until we hit the wrong button. We could pass along everything we got from other sources. We could bombard people with communication until they howled for mercy, and they do.

Miss Manners' hope is that, having learned to communicate, people have now rid themselves of their emotional and anecdotal backlogs and are willing to return to talking like civilized people.

Conversation consists of developing and playing with ideas by juxtaposing the accumulated conclusions of two or more people and then improvising on them. It requires supplying such ingredients as information, experience, anecdotes, and opinions, but then being prepared to have them challenged and to contribute to a new mixture.

Conversation is not:

Gossip about oneself. The preliminary to conversation may include asking and stating some limited personal information, but that is only for the purpose of choosing a real topic. As soon as a common interest has been found, the quizzing should be stopped and the development of conversation begun.

Recitals. Conversation being an exchange, long stories, such as jokes or travelogues, cannot be included unless they are abbreviated and offered in illustration of the conversation's idea.

Position statements. Buttons, T-shirts and bumper stickers are available ready-made to announce one's politics, preferences and availability, so there is no need to devote time to them that could otherwise be pleasantly spent in conversation.

News. Startling bulletins may be effective in suggesting ideas, but the popular notion that being able to recite current political and cultural news accurately makes one a conversationalist is erroneous. The person who has actually read the book that everyone is supposed to be talking about is a menace unless everybody is really talking about it.

Advertisements. From the direct sales pitch to a play for the goodwill of influential people, the rule is that if it is designed to advance your career, it isn't conversation. The same is true of public service announcements, such as recommending one's therapist or one's diet.

DEAR MISS MANNERS:

What do you consider a good conversation opener?

GENTLE READER:

Almost anything except, "I've been on a wonderful journey of self-discovery lately, and I'd like to share it with you."

⌒ Hazardous Topics ⌒

"What are we supposed to talk about—the weather?"

Miss Manners hears this question often, delivered in a tone that is not at all nice. It is intended as an indictment of etiquette as being either so draconian as to repress all but the blandest conversation, or so wimpy as to be unable to tolerate discussion on any but the least controversial subjects.

She is thinking of barring these people from discussing the weather. With that contentious attitude, they are bound to make themselves socially impossible, hectoring everyone about the environment and pointing out that their listeners are stupid and immoral for, depending on their point of view, ruining it, or ruinously protecting it.

But does not Miss Manners' reaction prove the accusations against etiquette? Questioning free speech in a free society, where airing conflicting opinions is not just a Constitutional right but the means by which we decide how to run the country! And not just shying away from talk about sex, religion and politics, but now—the weather!

Hold on. This is Miss Manners pontificating, not the United States Supreme Court. She couldn't abridge free speech if she wanted to, and she doesn't want to. Nor does she want to restrict the exchange of ideas and opinions. On the contrary. Far from squelching substantive discussion and debate, etiquette is what makes them possible. Admittedly, it does tell people when to keep their mouths shut and what they should not say. Is that what people mean by repressive?

Without such rules, there are no exchanges of ideas, only exchanges of set positions and insults. People who disagree rapidly move from talking over one another to shouting one another down, and from expressing their opinions on the matter at hand to expressing their opinions of the intelligence and morality of those who disagree with them. It is only by adhering to strict etiquette that any controversy can truly be aired, whether it is at a legislature governed by *Robert's Rules of Order*, a courtroom governed by the judge's sense of decorum or a dinner party governed by social etiquette. The rules vary, but the idea is always to protect the assemblage's ability to accomplish its purpose.

It is true that at a dinner party, the purpose (aside from food, drink and those forlorn hopes of meeting someone new and interesting) is conversation. So why shouldn't people talk freely about things they feel strongly about?

Because Miss Manners doesn't trust them. She has seen them when they really get going on something they care deeply about. People who pooh-pooh the rule against discussing sex, religion and politics at the dinner table, under the impression that these areas are so overexposed that they have lost their former ability to inflame the passions, should recall the last time they heard people disagree about war, abortion, the death penalty, gay marriage and other such tepid topics.

Was there a true exchange of opinions? That needn't mean that anyone ended up changing positions, only that they listened respectfully to one another's point of view and debated the argument and not the goodwill of the person making it. Occasionally, she concedes, there is. People with manners have been known to participate in stimulating dinner conversation about hot topics—but only if they have the self-control to wait until getting into the car before saying, "I had no idea those people were such morons."

⌒ *Occupations* ⌒

Miss Manners has observed that when people meet one another they now say, "What do you do?" instead of "How do you do?" It is the grown-up version of that snappy opener at college mixers, "What are you majoring in?"

As successful people are afraid of being used, unsuccessful people are afraid of being snubbed, interesting people want to talk about something different from their jobs and boring people won't stop talking about their jobs, this approach has its limitations. The chief use that she sees is that once you ascertain someone's occupation, you can choose a conversation topic that is entirely unrelated to it. One asks a housewife who is really running the city government, and a corporation president which is the best of the new kitchen machines. That is what we call charm.

DEAR MISS MANNERS:

I'm a somewhat (well, actually a very) introverted and quiet person who is willing to be sociable pretty much only when I have to. (Rest assured I know that I should be mindful to show interest in others, and I work hard at being a gracious listener.) My husband has a great job which allows me to stay home. We have a grown son and grandchildren, so I really am not hampered by work/family obligations. We enjoy our life and routine, and I have no desire to change a thing.

So how do I handle the demanding (and I mean demanding—the body language, facial expressions and tone of voice indicate this) questioning I sometimes receive when new acquaintances or recently reunited old friends ask what I do for work, and then ask if I'm bored staying home?

There is plenty to do at home and I have many, many deep intellectual interests, though I do not earn a wage by the knowledge in my head. I also create a warm, caring atmosphere for my family.

I blush and stammer and answer so apologetically when this question arises that I have developed an irrational fear of the question because my response is so weak. I feel that I have to justify my choice to these pushy people who want to know more than just the simple response that I prefer to give.

Help! It's so impossible to just live in this world sometimes.

GENTLE READER:

Now, now. Let's not make it harder than it is. Yes, there is plenty of nosiness around, and yes, people are always telling ladies at home that they belong at work, and those at work that they belong at home.

But please allow Miss Manners gently to remind you that they are not from the Department of Homeland Security. Many of them may be asking out of foolish curiosity, but some are trying to do what you work at doing—to be good listeners. Knowing that most people like to talk about themselves, they are trying to draw you out. Whatever their motivation, there is no need for you to blush and stammer—and certainly not to justify yourself.

The people who enjoy society most are those who love conversation, by which Miss Manners means talk that goes beyond the personal, and the personal may just be a way of getting to a subject of mutual interest. As you have many, many interests, try trotting one of them out as an answer to questions about what you are working on.

DEAR MISS MANNERS:

As a member of a college English department, I share a distressing problem with many of my colleagues: Whenever we are introduced at social gatherings and our profession is indicated, we are greeted with at least one gleeful shout of "Oh, dear; I'm certainly going to have to watch the way I talk in front of you—you're an English teacher!" To a man (or woman), we cringe. Is there a correct response?

I have toyed with both "Yes, and as a specialist in the eighteenth-century novel, I intend to pounce on any error you may utter regarding that field, embarrassing you in front of all these people, because, as you have correctly assumed, I have no manners or tact whatsoever" and the more concise "Thank you, but I'm perfectly capable of forming a low opinion of you on completely different grounds." Neither, however, seems entirely satisfactory. You would oblige us all greatly by advising us of the proper etiquette for managing these situations.

GENTLE READER:

Thank you. You have hit on the one problem that drives Miss Manners bananas in her own life. People are always saying to her, "Oh, dear; I'm certainly going to have to watch the way I eat in front of you. . . ."

As you can imagine, Miss Manners does not care to solve the problem with rude remarks and cannot endorse the ones you suggest. Her own rejoinder is that they are safer with her than with anyone else because if they make mistakes, she'd be too polite to notice. Every profession attracts its particular stupid remark, and the correct thing to say when being told someone's profession is simply, "Oh, how interesting." An all-purpose response to silly accusations of policing others is "But I'm off-duty tonight."

~ *Personal Questions* ~

There is a bizarre notion around that it is both charming and beneficial to force a person to yield, for general consumption, everything there is to know about himself. Social interrogators are thus able, while indulging their base nosiness, to maintain a complacent air that is part compassionate glow and part scientific inquiry.

Widespread as the practice is, Miss Manners knows that those questioned feel neither charmed nor benefited, but are often cowed into answering. They have to be reminded that they need not allow trespassers on their privacy. "I'd rather not talk about that, if you don't mind," or "I'm afraid that's too private for me to discuss" may be said, accompanied by anything from a pleasant, regretful smile, suggesting that this policy will change when you know each other better, to a raised-eyebrow stare, suggesting that you had better not try that again.

The two big questions you must never ask and never answer are, according to Miss Manners' grandmother:

1. "How old are you?"
2. "How much money do you have (or make)?"

Miss Manners' grandmother was not, as you can imagine, the sort of lady who fooled around. Another of her maxims was "Colored stones are vulgar," and so she gave away any family jewelry with rubies or sapphires, thus saving Miss Manners herself from the temptation of eventually falling into such vulgarity. All her descendants naturally bless her for this. The family was never rich, but we try to behave ourselves.

With such sensitivity, it is fortunate that Grandmother Manners did not live to hear of a whole world of other unanswerable questions that modern ladies are asked. Let us assemble, then, a beginner's sampler of personal questions to be avoided in all beginning, and probably also intermediate, relationships:

Age. "That was an awfully nice young man you brought over the other night, but tell me, isn't he a little young?"

Birth Control. "Isn't this your third? Did you plan it that way?"

Children. "Shouldn't he be talking by now?"

Divorce. "And we thought you were the ideal couple. What went wrong?"

Energy. "Don't you think you keep this house too hot?"

Food. "I'm surprised to see you eating that. Didn't you tell me you were on a diet?"

Good Works. "Our development officer has figured out what a person of your income level can afford to give. Would you like to hear what it is?"

Health. "You didn't tell us what that test was you went into the hospital for. But let me just ask this: Was it benign?"

I. "I think you ought to . . ."

Enough of this alphabet stuff. When you keep going with this sort of thing, you get to X, and then you have to try to make xylophones seem relevant. They aren't. It's permissible to ask a perfect stranger about his xylophone, or his zither.

◟ Responding ◞

DEAR MISS MANNERS:

Some months ago, I was mugged. I've spent weeks going around replacing everything in my purse, filling out forms, and so on. As if that isn't enough of a nuisance, everywhere I go, everyone—friends, credit department clerks, people at the office—asks me for details about what happened. Why do they do this? It was a nasty experience and I would like to forget it.

GENTLE READER:

Because they are dying to know if you were raped. Do not tell them.

DEAR MISS MANNERS:

What is the proper response to the question "Are you going to have children?"

My husband and I are at a painful loss for words, as we have had two miscarriages and do not know if we will be able to have children. Is there a polite way to signal that this question is inappropriate, or are we being thin-skinned?

GENTLE READER:

One can hardly exaggerate the rudeness of inquiring into the contents of someone else's womb, but Miss Manners is gratified that you do not consider that it therefore requires a rude answer. Nor should you be bullied into giving a substantive answer. Miss Manners suggests merely "We don't know," accompanied by an uninvitingly blank look and a remark on another topic.

DEAR MISS MANNERS:

When, if ever, is absolute, stony silence the proper response to a question or a comment?

GENTLE READER:

Whenever those questions and comments are—or rather ought to be—unspeakable, which is to say unfortunately often.

⌒ *Money* ⌒

Frankness about money, like frankness about sex, sounds like a good idea to everyone except Miss Manners. When something assumes such great importance in life, why not admit it? Why not openly exchange information and feelings, instead of leaving everyone guessing and worrying? Why be coy?

She can tell you why: Frank talk soon turns to frank schemes, and these are not distinguished by the observance of another requirement of etiquette, namely taking other people's feelings into consideration. Apparently this is hard to do while taking other people's pockets into consideration.

Miss Manners has noticed that a great many people now believe that their relatives and friends are obliged to pay them to move through life, so they frankly set the payment they expect for their birthdays, graduations, weddings, babies, anniversaries and—if not their own deaths, then the deaths in their immediate families.

The habit of requiring a tangible return from guests has become so widespread that those who still have qualms seek to quiet them by suggesting that the payment be rerouted to charity.

What this tells Miss Manners is that things are so far gone that the option of merely minding their own financial business does not occur even to the well-meaning. To others, the idea of hospitality freely offered, or presents freely given, is unimaginable. All she is asking is for them to consider what they do imagine to be unmentionable.

Discussing your own money—how much you paid for your house, how much the other houses in the neighborhood are going for now, how much your silver is worth, how much it's costing you to insure it, how much it would cost you to replace it and what they are charging these days for a decent pair of shoes—is not only vulgar but boring. Yet Miss Manners detects the same two underlying statements being made through all these statistics, and both of them are among the most satisfying communications one human being can make to another. They are:

1. My, I was clever.
2. My, things have changed for the worse since I was younger.

The first covers all accounts of things the speaker has purchased that are now more expensive; the second, all things he didn't buy when the prices were lower than they are now. Therefore, no one is excluded from such conversations; they are, indeed, tempting. Would you like Miss Manners to tell you what her dear mother paid for the handmade silver tea service, now Miss Manners', which Mama bought in 1948? No, you really wouldn't. Let her tell you, instead, how erratic the weather has become since she was a girl (My, things have changed for the worse), and how she is nevertheless able to avoid ever catching cold (My, she is clever).

⌒ Sex ⌒

DEAR MISS MANNERS:

I have failed at the art of conversation and most desperately need your help! While my husband and I were sitting at dinner the other night with another married couple, the other man turned to me and, apropos of nothing in the conversation, declared that he was now "safe." Naive as always, I asked, "What do you mean by "safe?" "A vasectomy," he proudly announced. Nearly speechless, I frantically searched for the proper response, but a splutter and a giggle were all I came up with.

GENTLE READER:

Ah, isn't it wonderful what passes for conversation these days? You can hardly sit down at dinner anymore without being told what everyone does with the parts of the body that cannot be seen above the table. Miss Manners is going to take to shocking perfect strangers by looking them deep in the eyes and saying, "Beastly weather we've been having lately, don't you think?" But she cannot improve on your response, which was perfectly proper—unless it would be by accompanying your splutter and giggle with the appropriate gesture of staring the man straight in the napkin.

DEAR MISS MANNERS:

What is your response to a lewd remark?

GENTLE READER:

People do not make lewd remarks to Miss Manners. If they did, her response would be a sweet smile, accompanied by a naive but earnest request to explain exactly what the remark meant. The result would be that even if a person made a first lewd remark to Miss Manners, he would never make a second.

⌒ Dreams ⌒

DEAR MISS MANNERS:

Is it polite to tell other people your dreams? A man in my office who is, I believe, in analysis, recites his in a loud voice the first thing every morning to whoever will listen, and all of us around the coffee machine can plainly hear every word. Sometimes they involve sexual fantasies about women at the office.

I reached the breaking point yesterday, when he made dirty remarks about a woman I am seeing regularly, and I was about to punch him in the nose, but she took me aside and said that wasn't fair, because they're only dreams, and discussing his dreams is an important part of his recovery. Frankly, it makes me wonder about her, in regard to him.

GENTLE READER:

It makes Miss Manners wonder about a society in which such privilege is given to illness, provided it is not identifiable physical illness. Would people feel equally tolerant about the spreading of cold germs or, for that matter, other regurgitation?

~ *Accomplishments* ~

"I apologize for boasting," says Nicholas Devize in *The Lady's Not for Burning* by dear Christopher Fry, "but once you know my qualities, I can drop back into a quite brilliant humility."

He says it in verse, but you do see his problem. Humility is easy, although Miss Manners much admires brilliant humility. The usual variety, with its claims about feeling awed and hoping to be worthy, is tiresome. But it is extremely difficult to make others acquainted with how very much one has to be humble about. No, that's not quite what Miss Manners meant to say. What is difficult is to establish gracefully that one has cause to be proud and haughty, before one can be contrastingly humble.

The ideal solution is to get others to broadcast one's achievements, so that the achiever has only to handle the humility. Only a few boastworthy matters can be counted on to attract such assistance. If you are elected President, you can generally get the networks to announce it for you. Enlisting your relatives for such a job is, however, tricky. Miss Manners has seen few family acts in which the boast ("Alexandrina has been chosen to play the Madonna in the Christmas pageant because she's the most popular girl in the school") is followed by a convincing amount of humility ("Oh, Mo—ther! Pul—*eeze!*"). Besides, the person who has the role of boaster then seems to be boasting on his or her own behalf for having amazing relatives. This sabotages the separation of the two functions.

The safest thing is to do it all oneself, but to blend the two parts. In artful boasting, one states all the information necessary to impress people, but keeps the facts decently clothed in the language of humility. Useful approaches include Disbelief,

Fear and Manic Elation. For some reason, these are considered to be more attractive human emotions than justifiable pride or self-satisfaction. Probably because they are not as much fun.

Here are some samples of each. The dots stand for the listener's predictable questions and responses. The best-prepared social speeches always allow for such interruptions.

Disbelief. "There must be some mistake. . . . My test scores—I can't believe it. . . . I know I couldn't have done that well—the number must have been copied wrong, because I know I messed up. . . . What did you get? . . . You see? There's a mistake. I know you had to do better than I because you know more. . . ."

Fear. "Oh, oh, now I've had it. . . . Well, you see, I—uh, I got the promotion. . . . Yes, I'm going to be the supervisor. . . . I know, but I'm not sure I can handle it. . . . I don't think they thought enough about how young I am and how little time I've been there. . . . Yes, I suppose so, but I'm terrified I can't handle it. . . ."

Manic Elation. "I can't stand it! . . . It worked! It worked! . . . They bought my idea! They bought it! I'm going to be rich and famous! . . . Well, listen to what they're going to pay me! It's wild! You know what this could lead to? Let me tell you how they're going to promote it! . . . Isn't this the most fantastic thing you ever heard of? . . ."

Miss Manners doesn't claim that any of this dialogue is sparkling. But at least it doesn't inspire the dislike that bald boasts do. Plain statements, such as "I just inherited a million dollars" or "I got three proposals this year—from a congressman, a movie star and a president of a bank," do not arouse unmixed admiration.

~ *Autobiography* ~

Can you say a few words about yourself?

"A few," Miss Manners says. "Well chosen" also comes to her mind.

Going about your business and assuming that others will be aware of your essential qualities no longer seems to be an option. The most you can expect is that at your funeral, your friends will wax poetic about how much they contributed to your life. If you achieve public attention before that, half the people asked will describe you as "kinda normal, I guess" and the other half as "I dunno, kinda strange."

On numerous ordinary occasions, people are required to provide some background information about themselves. Typically, they attend meetings where people who are drawn together by work, interests or problems go around the table telling their qualifications for being there. They find themselves at the sort of large social gatherings where the roof provides an introduction (which is etiquette's quaint phrase for encouraging guests to talk even without the host's prompting), but the roof fails to provide material for conversation.

They receive questionnaires from their schools asking them what they have been doing since graduation. They meet—or become—a new neighbor, colleague or client and need to provide some biography to launch the relationship. They are stranded with strangers, in airports and other waiting rooms, and turn to conversation as one of the few available amusements.

True, the life story of an honest person is presumably always the same, but each such situation requires that it be edited to fit the circumstances. Miss Manners has observed, however, that many people have developed a single set piece about themselves, which they deliver in full at each of these opportunities, and sometimes when no such opportunity exists. Furthermore, the forms used are suspiciously reminiscent of patterns intended for specific circumstances that have nothing to do with the way they are used.

The daytime talk-show format is particularly popular: "Mother loved the other children best, which led to my substance abuse, but now, with your help, I'm finally going to get my life together." Suitable for support group meetings, but a bad choice for first dates.

Others favor the professional résumé: "I became a vice president at twenty-five, and naturally I expect compensation commensurate with my talents, but I've gotten bored and am looking for something more challenging." Should be confined to job interviews and clueing in prospective in-laws, but never trotted out at social events.

Despite its bad reputation, the Christmas letter survives as a biographical format: "Here are pictures of the children on our rafting vacation—as you can see, they are great athletes, and they star on their school teams, but they are also tremendous students, which I suppose comes naturally because we . . ." Should be reserved for people from whom an equivalent saga would be not only tolerated but welcomed.

The Academy Awards have a big influence: "I feel so humbled and grateful, and I couldn't have done it without the love and faith that my family and God and my wonderful dog have shown in me." Should be edited down for public consumption, but can be expanded for strictly family occasions.

The Miss America Pageant is also influential: "These are my ideals, and I believe that I can help make the world a better place because I can be anything I want if I have faith and work hard." Excellent for private, late-night talks with intimates and for professional ethical discussions, but should never be unleashed on strangers.

The protest rally format keeps gaining: "I see how things really are, and you're making the world a worse place because you don't." Fine for public discussions, but should never been unleashed on family and friends.

⟡ Ancestors ⟡

DEAR MISS MANNERS:

I have a friend who talks all the time about his ancestors. He didn't used to, but now he's involved in what he calls a "history project" about his family, and we're never going to hear the end of it. It sounds to me like plain old bragging. Isn't this topic considered taboo among polite people?

GENTLE READER:

Among polite people descended from the upper classes, yes. But bragging about one's ancestors is quite fashionable now if one can claim to be descended from the lower classes. Many such claims are exaggerated, of course.

⟡ Gossip ⟡

The question to ask oneself before indulging in gossip is not so much "Is it true?" or "Is there any useful reason for repeating it?" (no, and no again), but "Is this likely to come around again and hit me in the face?" Yes, it is. But applying some discipline to the exercise will minimize the blow. Let us consider the different types of gossip, with the safeguards that should be used for each.

1. Gossip about oneself. This is a peculiar form of gossip, as the gossiper does not call it that—he calls it a "confidence"—and does not understand that it becomes gossip the minute it has left his mouth. The only precaution one has against making one's confidences known is to keep them confidential. Promises extracted from the hearer mean nothing; if you haven't been able to resist telling, why should he? As dear Erasmus said in *De Civilitate*, "It is safe to admit nothing that might embarrass one if repeated."

2. Gossip one has heard firsthand from and about someone one knows. This is the receiving end of the first category and is considered quality gossip because it is presumed to come from an informed source. However, it is the worst gossip to repeat, as the subject can also trace the gossip source. Repeating it and asking one's listener not to do the same is ridiculous. Skip this category and move on to the next.

3. Gossip received secondhand about someone one knows. This is better than the first two, as you can pass it on along with the name of your source, who will then be blamed for blabbing. Gossip this far removed from original research also makes better stories, as the facts are flimsy enough to be bent

into whatever shape you need to make the story illustrate a larger truth about human nature. Just make sure you're not telling it to someone who is in a position to know the information better than you do. In other words, find out first if your listener is the brother-in-law of the person you're gossiping about.

4. Gossip received secondhand about someone you don't know. This is celebrity gossip, and the best kind. It is highly unlikely to be true, as all celebrity gossip is made to fit a pattern of simple irony and assumes that people are always the opposite of what they seem, but it's a lot less likely than the other to get back to them and inspire them to get back at you.

⌒ Revenge ⌒

"You'll ruin your reputation" had a long run as a scary threat acting as a deterrent to bad behavior, but now it has to be explained to the young. The concept that they find difficult to believe is that we didn't once admire people who made mistakes. We didn't praise them for their courage and pronounce them all the better for having had the chance to learn from experience and declare that it would be unfair to penalize them because everybody deserves a fresh start, even those who have been given fresh starts before.

Miss Manners is afraid that we considered deed a greater clue to character than declarations, and presumed that those who fell into error once might well do so again.

People who were called "courageous" were the ones who didn't fall into error, and who performed their ordinary duties as human beings—what we call a "hero" nowadays when such a person is called to our attention.

Having a bad reputation did not make people sought after socially, even though it was as true then as now that the bad are more interesting to talk about than the good. They talked about them, all right. They just didn't invite them to dinner.

What Miss Manners is leading up to with all this is not a plea to bring back the use of reputation as an instrument for condemning people, but a warning that, in fact, it is back. Where once people could count on mobility as a way of escaping disapproval, cyberspace gives them nowhere to hide. Instead of crying alone, a jilted lover posts those grievances and disillusions in a chat room frequented by people who might otherwise have been future prospects of the jilter's.

A worker gives in to the temptation to trash the boss before leaving the job, and hits the wrong button, spreading it throughout the workplace and—as colleagues amused at the mistake pass it along to their friends—to the entire industry. A traveler who decides not to waste time on an acquaintance is similarly rebuffed the next day by an important contact who had been of use before. The unknown factor is that the two share an email correspondent back home, and a comment about climbing has already gone halfway around the world and back.

People are getting labeled by their misdeeds faster and more bluntly than the most dedicated town gossips could ever have condemned them. In many respects, it is no longer possible to start fresh by keeping quiet or moving on. Miss Manners finds the new use of reputation worrisome. She still believes that the way people have lived their lives is the best indication of who they are, and that society should register its disapproval of bad behavior. But it strikes her that the new method of taxing people with their faults has not only retained but magnified its own faults.

It tells only one side of the story, and a far from disinterested one. Checking it out is difficult, but passing it on is easy. It favors titillating or embarrassing incidents rather than serious ones. And the test of whether it is suitable for passing on is not whether others need to know but whether they would find it amusing. Come to think of it, that was what was wrong with the previous era's use of reputation—people spread and believed scandal carelessly. Miss Manners is hoping we will be more careful this time around.

Bigotry

DEAR MISS MANNERS:

What do you do when someone makes a bigoted remark or tells a joke with a slur in it? These offend me—and not only when my own race is the target. Should I show that I am offended? Should I keep quiet—doesn't silence indicate some kind of endorsement? Are there any guidelines about how to behave in connection with such remarks or jokes?

GENTLE READER:

Certainly there are. There are guidelines for everyone, regardless of . . .

1. Bigoted jokes or expressions are properly used only by members of the group being slurred, addressed to other members of that group. A nonmember would be well advised not to join in the fun. When an ethnic joke is told among nonmembers of the group, disapproval may be expressed by a stony face and a frosty smile.

2. If a nonmember slurs a group of which you are obviously a member, you may walk haughtily out of the room; inquire menacingly, "Just what do you mean

by that?"; or otherwise indicate that you are insulted. Not enough ladies take advantage of this opportunity.

3. If a nonmember slurs a group without knowing you are a member or have some other close connection, you may convey this information ("Perhaps you don't know that my wife is black"). In this case, there is no need to emphasize it with angry behavior—the statement is more devastating if given in a simple, factual way.

4. The only effective recovery that the offender may offer is a counterclaim. "Oh, really? So am I." If that is not even remotely possible, one must at least dredge up a second cousin; "best friends" won't do. Nor will the common mutter "I was only kidding." Bolstering this remark with "Don't you people have any sense of humor?" only compounds the problem.

5. If you are running for political office or are contemplating ever running for political office, train yourself never to let any such words pass your lips.

6. Dirty jokes in unmixed company—that is to say, jokes that depend on a shared belief in the inferiority of the other gender—are not safe any longer either. Nowadays you can never tell when people might care more for those with whom they live than those with whom they share public bathrooms.

7. Jokes that make fun of the teller's own wealth, ancient lineage or prestigious school or neighborhood are successful only among those who share these handicaps.

8. Jokes about other people's proper names are never successful. For one thing, the people have all heard every possible one before. You will never manage to satirize anybody's name in a fashion he has not heard since nursery school, and Miss Manners isn't even going to tell you the name of the person who first told her that.

9. The only truly safe and proper subject for a joke is oneself. Many a person who thought this privilege extended to his or her spouse, parent or child, has lived—but not very long—to find otherwise.

⁓ Compliments ⁓

DEAR MISS MANNERS:

I have had the same podiatrist for about fifteen years, a very pleasant man of uncertain age who has worn a quite obvious hair piece as long as I have known him. He also has been clean-shaven. Recently this nice gentleman had open heart surgery and was away from his office for about four months. Upon his return, I made an appointment and to my astonishment was greeted by someone I scarcely recognized, but who was indeed the same dear man. The voice wasn't different, but the hair piece has been discarded, revealing a mostly bald pate surrounded by a soft, curly fringe (much more attractive than the phony toupee), and a great tan was embellished by a mustache. The whole image was improved by new, stylish gold-rimmed spectacles.

My question is—in such a situation, is a comment appropriate, or does one ignore the transformation? I can't imagine saying, "Oh, I see you're not wearing your toupee now," or "I never *did* like that hair piece, you could *tell* it wasn't yours. . . ." I couldn't decide if it would be unmannerly to comment, or if the improvement should be noted by a compliment.

GENTLE READER:

It is not at all uncommon for people to be absent from their usual circles for a few months and to return looking improved. There was a time, for instance, when it was common for unmarried young ladies whose stomachs stuck out to disappear for a few months and come back looking slim. Now one more often sees older people of both sexes returning from unspecified vacations wearing their faces or other parts of their bodies higher than before. No true friend can ever figure out the cause of such a change for the better, except a change of scenery or rest, both of which can do wonders. It is not necessary to supply this observation, however. One should merely mention the improvement. The conventional compliment is, "Why, you look marvelous! I don't know what it is, but you look fabulous."

DEAR MISS MANNERS:

After attending a recital in which a friend had taken part, I was asked by the friend what I thought of his performance. What would be the proper response for a poor performance? Should one give a detailed criticism of the faults and merits, or simply a pat on the back, "very good," etc.? And for an exceedingly good one, is bubbling enthusiasm appropriate, or merely a standard compliment?

GENTLE READER:

Bubbling enthusiasm is appropriate for poor and exceedingly good performances alike, the idea being deliberately to confuse the performer about which one he gave. This is what friends are for. Music teachers and music critics exist for other purposes.

~ *Receiving Compliments* ~

DEAR MISS MANNERS:

I find it difficult to accept compliments or congratulations. What should I say that is appropriately modest without seeming to question the judgment of the person complimenting me?

GENTLE READER:

"Thank you." Or if you feel that is not enough, "Why, thank you very much, how kind of you to say so."

Actually, you already know that. What you don't know, Miss Manners suspects, is how to leave it at that. You then babble on to explain that the achievement was nothing anyone couldn't have done, the article of clothing is old and valueless, and that whatever is admired compares unfavorably with the equivalent quality or possession of the admirer.

To put this under the heading of modesty is absurd. It actually serves to prolong the compliment by treating it as the topic sentence in a speech rather than, as is more likely to be the case, a passing pleasantry. The only advantage of debating a compliment one has received is to reduce the chances of its recurring.

DEAR MISS MANNERS:

What do you say if someone you don't like gives you a compliment?

GENTLE READER:

"Thank you."

CONVERSATIONAL HAZARDS

DEAR MISS MANNERS:

I am basically a nonpushy, nonaggressive conversationalist. For a long time, I just called myself "a good listener." There are times, though, when I'd like the chance to talk myself. Yet so many people just talk right over me. Sometimes I'm halfway into a sentence or an idea when they burst in with their own. I have tried politeness, patience, and even, once, repeating a sentence over and over again (six times) till that person finally listened. Is there a polite way to deal with conversation hogs?

GENTLE READER:

Conversation, which is supposed to be a two-way street, is treated by many people as if it were a divided highway. They may acknowledge that traffic must go in both directions, but speed independently on their own way, expecting you to do the same on your side.

If you are, in fact, a practiced "good listener," you have not been traveling through life in silence. You have been asking questions, inserting relevant information and providing commentary on what the chief talkers to whom you have been listening are saying. A good listener is not someone who has to be checked every now and then by the speaker to see if he or she is awake.

Presuming, therefore, that you have been doing some of the talking (and if you have not, you might begin by adapting your listening method), you need only to make the transition from supporting role to leading role. It is unfortunate that this (if Miss Manners may drop the new metaphor and go back to her original one, which was more clever) is often like trying to drive over a grassy highway divider.

The way to get across is to say something related, however vaguely, to what has been said before. While lulling the speaker into believing that you are responding as a listener, this tactic can be a shortcut to the main highway. (Getting back to that metaphor was not as easy as Miss Manners anticipated. She now feels lost and is considering staying right where she is until someone comes and finds her.) Once in the driver's seat (to go bravely and recklessly on), you should try to be a good talker. That is to say, you must allow proper interruptions that are in the tradition of good listening, and even encourage them by asking occasionally and perhaps superfluously, "Don't you think so?" or "What do you think?"

If people persist in trying to wrest the controls away from you, put up warning signs. "Just a minute—I haven't finished" is one, "But wait—I haven't told you the point yet" is another. (All right. If everyone will now stop talking for a minute, perhaps we can find a volunteer to go and rescue a lady caught out there in the verbal traffic jam.)

Quotations

DEAR MISS MANNERS:

A gentleman's language should be easy and unstudied, marked by graceful carelessness that never oversteps the limits of propriety. The art is, in truth, the very soul of good breeding, which renders us agreeable to all with whom we associate. A friend of mine, by all measures well bred, has a verbal affectation that is annoying. He has a mania for Greek and Latin quotations. I believe this is particularly to be avoided. It is like pulling up stones from a tomb wherewith to kill the living. How can I let him know his pedantry is wearisome?

GENTLE READER:

A gentleman does not let another gentleman know that that gentleman's conversation is wearisome. However, there is nothing to prevent a gentleman from arming himself with Chinese or Sanskrit quotations with which to answer another gentleman's remarks.

∼ Mispronunciations ∼

DEAR MISS MANNERS:

Can you suggest a graceful way of calling a friend's attention to a word that has been egregiously mispronounced? I am thinking especially of a well-educated person with a reasonably good vocabulary at his or her command who makes this kind of gaffe in a conversational circle. I recall someone saying "reticent" as if it were "re-tie-cent" with the accent on the "tie." Just recently a friend spoke of "maniac-depressive." Trying to be objective, one would like to help a friend, to help avoid a repetition of the mistake, but at the same time one would not want to seem to be putting on airs.

GENTLE READER:

Nobody knows better than Miss Manners the joy of "helping a friend" by graciously indicating how much more one knows than he or she. For example, Miss Manners would adore pointing out that your "someone saying 'reticent' " ought to be "someone's saying 'reticent,' " but is reticent about doing so because of the unlikely chance you may then catch Miss Manners in a tiny error and the whole thing might never end, with each of us becoming increasingly bitter. At best, you may inquire of your friend, "Oh, is that the way you pronounce that? I've always heard . . ." However, you do this at your own risk.

∼ Repetitions ∼

DEAR MISS MANNERS:

When an elderly person tells a joke that has been heard before or repeats something previously said, what should the other person say—"I've heard that before," or "You told me that," or simply act as if it had not been heard before?

GENTLE READER:

It is not only the elderly who tend to repeat themselves, as Miss Manners often says. There is one method of heading off a repeated story, but one must be quick about it. Jump in right at the beginning, and say, "Oh, I love that story" or "Is that that hilarious joke you told us—I've been trying to tell it myself."

Sometimes, a "Yes, so you were telling us" works if it is accompanied by an interested expression, as if the listener were waiting for the talker to tell a sequel. However, often nothing works, in which case you should listen gracefully. We should all be tolerant of the foibles of age; with luck, we will achieve them ourselves.

⌒ Eavesdroppers ⌒

DEAR MISS MANNERS:

Would you be so kind as to advise me in choosing between hypocrisy and nonhypocrisy? My office is so arranged that phone calls (business and nonbusiness) may be overheard by several neighboring workers. I pretend not to hear the content of personal conversations, but I am often tempted to chime in later to give business information to individuals whom I have overheard. Should I pretend that I cannot overhear any call?

GENTLE READER:

Yes. Hypocrisy is a higher form of human behavior than eavesdropping. Besides, you have only overheard one side of the conversation, and that can be misleading. And besides that, such information is more valuable when stored up for private use than when given out freely as if it had been legitimately acquired.

⌒ Bores ⌒

DEAR MISS MANNERS:

When an acquaintance interrupts himself while telling an uncompelling story to ask, with sincere concern, "Am I boring you?" what is the proper reply?

GENTLE READER:

"Good heavens, no. I hope you don't think I was yawning because I'm bored. Not in the least. Please go on."

The morally alert will now seize on the possibility that this may not be the rigid truth. Miss Manners does not apologize for that. The virtue of truth-telling does not always trump the necessity for kindness.

Electronic Communication (Personal)

ALL RIGHT, you've had enough fun now. Put that thing away and pay attention to what's going on around you. And the rest of you—will you please stop taunting them?

Miss Manners has been watching this pattern for decades now. Every time an item is invented for everyday use—preferably an electronic item pertaining to that babbling we glorify under the name of Communications—we run through a predictable succession of etiquette skirmishes.

Cellular telephones, email, and handheld digital organizers triggered the last round. Before that, it was the beeper and the laptop. Perhaps there are still people around who remember even longer ago, when it was the answering machine and the personal computer.

When each item becomes available, the first on their blocks to get them are beside themselves with delight. Perhaps they can be said to flaunt them, but they are encouraged by the curiosity of others. Friends put up with lectures on how backward they are not to have their own, and perfect strangers ask for demonstrations. This encourages the owners to believe that they are welcome to take these attractions wherever they like.

At the next stage, the novelty is wearing off and the mood begins to sour. More and more people own these items, and those who got them earlier are being told by latecomers how much better and cheaper the new versions are. This does not improve their dispositions.

Meanwhile, the admiration of those who don't have them is turning to annoyance. There are dark murmurings that the only real use of this item is to show off. "They just want to make themselves feel important," people say, discounting any possibility that anyone would buy such a thing to send or receive messages.

The users begin to swagger. They had been patient, even modest, with the curious, assuring them that they, too, should have this wonderful item and offering reams of advice about how to buy and use it. But their sudden loss of popularity makes them turn away from onlookers and concentrate on their absent friends.

Now the murmurings erupt into public declarations that these people are a nuisance and ought to be forcibly restrained. They are causing accidents and ought to be outlawed. Consequently, they grow more defiant. Social warfare erupts.

Mind you, at the very first stage, while the ink on the patent is barely dry, Miss Manners will have declared new etiquette rules governing their use. She shouldn't have to do this, because the old rules about not interrupting events or ignoring people who are present or pestering people who are absent should prevent these items from being used rudely. But she takes the precaution of pointing out that those rules still apply, and of issuing whatever specific ones might be required.

Alas, she suffers the fate of the diplomat caught between belligerent parties. Although at first, both sides cite their own devotion to etiquette's rules, a moral fervor takes over and they soon escalate to a war of morality. Harmony is only restored when the item becomes more easily available, at which point the people who declared its only purpose was showing off find they can't live without it either.

And then the next thing comes along, and we run through the whole routine over again. Miss Manners would like to communicate the fact that she is getting really tired of this routine.

 Dodging It

DEAR MISS MANNERS:

I have an unlisted telephone number because I live alone and hate being bothered by calls when I am apt to be in the bathtub or watching a television program. If it's someone I really want to hear from, I do give out the number. But I resent it when people expect me to tell them my telephone number as a matter of course. Can I just make up a number and give it to them?

GENTLE READER:

At the other end of that made-up number lives a person who is lying in the bathtub or watching television, and not anxious to hear from your acquaintances. When people ask you for your telephone number, write down your email or street address.

THE DOMESTIC TELEPHONE

⌒ *The Announcement* ⌒

DEAR MISS MANNERS:

If you are answering the telephone in the home of Patty and Pete Magpie, is it true that it is NOT correct to say "Mr. Magpie's residence"?

And it IS correct to say "Mrs. Magpie's residence"? I read this idea in a book written in 1960.

GENTLE READER:

That is because it was the assumption, in 1960, that Mr. Magpie was off at work and Mrs. Magpie was in charge of the household.

Nowadays, we assume that Mrs. Magpie is off at work and still charged with running the household. Therefore, the form "Mrs. Magpie's residence" is still current among traditionalists unless Mr. Magpie will make such a fuss as to not make it worth Mrs. Magpie's while. ("Mr. Magpie" was never correct, and now it would be foolhardy as well.) Judging from the choices of more advanced folk, they would prefer you to say, "You've reached Patty and Pete. They can't take your call right now, but if you leave a message they'll get back to you just as soon as they can. Have a good one."

⌒ *Caller ID* ⌒

DEAR MISS MANNERS:

When I foolishly, perhaps, let it slip that I have Caller ID, a friend said, "So this means that if I call you and you aren't home, you will know that I have tried to reach you and I can expect you to return my call."

I was caught off guard and mumbled something along the lines of "I will return your call as soon as it is convenient." My friend was a bit miffed and said that I wasn't a very good friend if I chose not to return the call as soon as was physically possible. I let the matter drop though I was thinking, "How about as soon as it is mentally possible?"

Often, when I return home from a long day's work, the last thing I want to do is to talk on the telephone. I prefer to spend my evenings in solitude unless I choose to go out. Now, however, when I opt not to answer my telephone, a record of who has called is available. If I do not return the call until a later date, perhaps on the weekend, my friend will be insulted.

I suppose this is akin to having an answering machine and not returning calls straight away—or is it? Is there any relation between these new technologies and a butler's duties in days past? What is the proper way to utilize Caller ID other than to screen out telemarketers and other unsolicited businesses?

GENTLE READER:

Miss Manners can point out some differences between a butler and Caller ID: cost, health insurance, vacations and judgment. There is also a big difference between an answering machine and Caller ID: the ability to convey the intent of the caller.

Any of these items should enable you to chat on the telephone when it is convenient to you, as well as to the caller, without that person's having a legitimate reason to take insult. Both butlers and answering machines can register the fact that the caller said that the call was urgent, and the former might even be able to make a shrewd guess as to whether that was an exaggeration.

But while Caller ID has many uses—alerting you not only to calls you might want to avoid, but to those that you might be just as happy to take later—it has less judgment even than the answering machine. It cannot let you know whether the call was made by pushing the wrong speed dial number, and it cannot let you know whether the need to talk to you has now passed, because the caller reached someone else who was free to play viola in his quartet that night.

DEAR MISS MANNERS:

How should someone with Caller ID answer the phone? I know that many people find it an essential part of maintaining their privacy but I think it has also raised a new manners issue.

Because their phone identifies me as the caller, some of my friends don't just say "Hello," they say "Hello, Peter." I assume they think this is friendly, but to me it has the opposite effect. To me, it seems—I really don't know how to describe it—jarring, startling, a bit off-putting, almost rude. I guess that somewhere in there I sense a bit of "I'm letting you know that I already know who you are"—a bit of Big Brother. I prefer the traditional way, which gives me the opportunity to introduce myself and lets the recipient express pleasure: "Hello?" "Hello, Melanie, this is Peter." "Peter! It's good to hear from you. How are you?"

My wife, who is somewhat more techno-oriented than I am, thinks I'm being silly and not a little paranoid.

GENTLE READER:

"Paranoid" is rather a strong word for someone who can't yet let go of the idea that telephone calls are intended to be a surprise. But once you get over the novelty, you might ask yourself why.

A person who opens the door can immediately see who is there, and may know before that by means of a window or peephole. A letter or an email should at least have an identifying address. Surely it behooves someone seeking admission to another's house to submit his or her name first. Indeed, in many societies, a polite caller does so before guessing who has happened to answer.

Which brings Miss Manners to the question of poor Melanie. How do you know it was she answering the telephone? And if she did, you have given her—according to your own thinking—a sense of "I'm letting you know that I already know who you are"—a bit of Big Brother.

Old-Fashioned Caller ID

DEAR MISS MANNERS:

What do you think about people who ask you, on the telephone, "Who is calling?" before telling you if the person you asked for is there?

GENTLE READER:

Miss Manners thinks that they are mouthing your name at a person who is wildly shaking his head and hands at the very mention of it. The same purpose can be accomplished politely by asking the question after expressing doubt: "Let me see if he is in. Who may I say is calling, please?"

Mistaken Identity

DEAR MISS MANNERS:

A question of etiquette that has been bothering me for many years is, What is the proper response to "I'm sorry, I have the wrong number"?

GENTLE READER:

Miss Manners feels that "That's quite all right" is sufficient, although she realizes that there will always be those who say, "That's all right—I had to get up to answer the phone anyway."

⁓ *Call Waiting* ⁓

DEAR MISS MANNERS:

I have three children and, naturally, Call Waiting! My problem is that sometimes I will be talking to someone and they will be offended if I click over just to see who the other caller is. Sometimes it is important, other times it isn't. If it isn't, I just return that call later. I don't mind if someone does it on their end because I know there is a purpose. As a mature mother, wife and friend, I would never just leave the person hanging or decide I'd just rather visit with the other caller. What is an appropriate way to handle this?!

GENTLE READER:

By canceling the service and limiting the time that your children spend on the telephone. Call waiting operates on the principle of Last Come, First Served, and Miss Manners is afraid that people will always find that offensive. Having three children does not constitute a perpetual state of emergency in which others may routinely be brushed aside.

⁓ *Answering Machines and Voice Mail* ⁓

DEAR MISS MANNERS:

I hang up whenever I reach an answering service, as I hate talking to a machine. I know this is not proper, but what is?

GENTLE READER:

It is perfectly proper to hang up on a machine. In fact, the whole concept of proper and improper behavior does not apply between people and machines. Miss Manners has enough trouble getting people to be polite to one another, without worrying about whether they are treating machines with consideration.

DEAR MISS MANNERS:

I must take issue with your statement that "it is perfectly proper to hang up on a machine." You wouldn't dream of hanging up on someone's secretary, would you? Hanging up on an answering machine is tantamount to hanging up on the person who owns it.

I do a lot of free-lance work which takes me away from home at odd hours. The only way I can stay in contact with business associates and friends is through an answering machine. If someone calls and hangs up without leaving a message, I have no idea of who tried to reach me or why, and have to listen to several seconds of dial tone instead of a friendly voice. Therefore, I maintain that the proper response to an answering machine is to state, at the sound of the tone, a message such a "Hello, this is Anastasia, at Winter Palace 2362. Rasputin was mad over the cherry cheesecake you served last week, and I wondered if I could get the recipe." If it is worth the trouble to pick up the telephone and dial someone's number, then it is certainly worth the trouble to stay on the line long enough to say who you are. I submit that it is the same, in modern terms, as leaving one's card with the footman.

GENTLE READER:

Miss Manners is sorry to be stubborn, but cannot be persuaded to take an anthropomorphic view of answering machines. "Someone's secretary" has feelings. "The footman" has feelings. Your answering machine does not. Rasputin, Miss Manners is willing to argue about.

~ *Multitasking* ~

DEAR MISS MANNERS:

It is bad enough to have to put up with someone smacking food when talking on a cordless phone, but it has reached the point where people are relieving their bodily functions while talking to others.

Maybe I am wrong, but I have always been taught that if you must use the restroom, you must excuse yourself, even if you have to make something up, such as that someone is at the door and may I call you back? I feel so degraded and disrespected hearing what they are doing, then hearing the toilet flush.

GENTLE READER:

As these people are not polite enough to excuse themselves, Miss Manners suggests that you excuse yourself—if possible before the flush.

It is never necessary to invent a reason—"Oh, I'm terribly sorry, I'll have to call you back" is enough—but in this case, you have an excellent one. Say, "I can hear you're busy, so why don't we talk later?" That is, if you are still willing to take a chance.

~ *Signing Off* ~

DEAR MISS MANNERS:

Of all the geegaws invented in our modern language that people readily take into their daily usage, I don't think any competes with the words many use to conclude a phone conversation: "I'll have to let you go now."

Invariably, this is said by the person instigating the call, so the person called has the option of various interpretations, i.e.:

1. "I'm sick and tired of listening to you so hang up!"
2. "I've spent quite enough money on this phone call, so shut up!"
3. "Stop talking, for heaven's sake, and let me do something worthwhile."

Almost any words to end a phone conversation would be more palatable. "There's someone at the door," "My timer just went off on the oven" or "I have to let my dog out" would all be kinder. Anything you can say to get this phrase erased from phone lines would improve the air. "I'm gonna let you go now" is just like a slap in the face.

GENTLE READER:

Could Miss Manners persuade you to go back to picking on the misuse of "hopefully"? Or "loan" used as a verb instead of "lend"?

It so happens that she finds "I'll let you go now" to be a rare example of a new conventional phrase—a fresh cliché if you will—that serves a hitherto neglected polite purpose. What she hears in it are not the insults you suggest, but an acknowledgment that one has chattered long enough at someone whose time is important.

This is in contrast to the I Think I Hear My Mother Calling Me sort of excuse you recommend, in which the emphasis is on one's own commitments. Besides, those may bring on an even more dreaded phrase, "Then I'll call you back later."

~ *Baby Talk* ~

DEAR MISS MANNERS:

Friends of ours have a daughter who has just learned the joys of speaking. Lately, when I've been speaking to the mother on the phone and little Olga has been in the vicinity and has expressed a desire to speak to me, mother immediately puts her on the phone. I am then obliged to say "Hi!" to which the reply is a knowing "Hi!" Unless I continue asking questions or otherwise blubbering something to which the reply is never anything but a monotonic blurt, there could be minutes of silence.

I have reached the point where I dread calling my friend, for having to experience the above-described delight. I have learned from this and will never attempt such a thing with my future children and friends. Help, if you would be so kind. My friend does not work, so there is rarely an opportunity to talk with her when Olga is not nearby.

GENTLE READER:

Miss Manners is pleased to hear that you have learned from this experience. No one except a grandparent should be expected to hold telephone conversations with people who have not yet learned conversation (as opposed to learning "to talk"), and even they should not be pushed too far. You might try making the child feel important by entrusting her with a message. The message is, "Tell Mommy I said bye-bye."

THE ITINERANT TELEPHONE

"I'm crossing the street now."

"I'm on the train."

"I'm at the bistro, having lunch."

The air has been filled with these and similar statements ever since the cellular telephone enabled people to keep others constantly informed of their whereabouts. A remarkable number seem to be doing this, supplying running reports of their progress:

"Okay, now I'm going up 10th Street."

"We're stopping now, and a lot of people are getting on so I'll probably have to move my briefcase."

"I'm still waiting for my coffee."

Miss Manners is astonished that so many people appear to be on parole, and that parole is so strict. It is apparently no longer a question of checking in at set periods, but of not being permitted to make a move without simultaneously reporting it.

She is pleased, however, that everybody seems to be telling the truth. If she looks up when these statements are being broadcast, she observes that the sign really does say 10th Street, the train really is stopping and the coffee really is slow in coming. Exciting though it might be to hear someone spinning a story—pretending to be on 12th Street, for example, or claiming to be traveling while waiting in line at the movie theater, or describing ordering coffee while digging into a hot fudge sundae—it might necessitate a citizen's arrest. Fortunately, everyone within her hearing has been scrupulous about confessing every move.

Yet she has begun to worry about the people to whom these reports are being made. They are not being lied to, but they are surely being bored senseless. Miss Manners recognizes the possibility that the reporting parties are not reformed criminals, but honest citizens, beloved by their families and friends, to whom they are confiding their every move.

On the other end of the line, there may be a voice laden with emotion saying, "I miss you so much I can't stand it. Tell me where you are so I can at least picture you there. I want to know every move you make, every bite you take. Oh, why did we part? We were so happy at breakfast, weren't we? Weren't you as happy as I? And now it's hours before we'll see each other again. Where are you now? I know, but you must have moved since you said that. Please don't hold back. Tell me everything! Nobody will ever love you as I do. Has the coffee arrived yet? I can't stand to have you suffer. What street are you on now? I want to know if you're closer to me."

What Miss Manners fears is that it may be a person who, although equally filled with love and kindness, is saying, "Okay, great, I really appreciate your calling. Uh-huh. Really? Mmmm. Yes, I see. So listen, I'll talk to you when you get home, okay? What's that? Oh, that's great. I mean, that's too bad. Look, it's kind of busy here. I'm glad to know you're all right, but you can tell me the rest later. Okay, good. Okay. Fine. Okay. Okay, okay, okay. We'll talk when we see each other.

"You what? Guess what? I don't care! No, wait, I don't mean that, of course I care, but I mean I've got things to do. I'm glad to know you're fine. You didn't hear a word I said, did you? How do you know I'm not being run over this very minute? How do you know that *I* got any lunch? Listen to me! Don't you think I have anything to do with my time? Can you hear me?"

An Example

DEAR MISS MANNERS:

There is nothing nicer, most would agree, than having a friend say that he or she is thinking of you. Lately, I seem to be having friends and acquaintances tell me this more and more.

They are doing so from their cellular phones, generally from the line at the bank, the service station or on their way to dinner with a more deserving friend. It's becoming increasingly clear to me that their intention is not to tell me that they are thinking of me, but to kill time during their tedious routines. More often than not, when I receive these calls, I am involved in a routine myself, but my routine often consists of eating dinner, reading a book or playing with my dog.

Miss Manners, how can I, without sounding utterly harsh, tell them that I would be glad to hear from them when they return home or schedule a time to meet for coffee so that I am not barraged by background noises of honking horns or bank tellers noting that post dated checks are not acceptable.

GENTLE READER:

Miss Manners' idea of progress is when the invention of potentially intrusive gadgets is matched by the invention of protective gadgets. That way, with a little effort and a lot of money, we can end up where we were before the cycle started.

Thanks to the cellular telephone, your friends are now able to reach you wherever they happen to be. But thanks to the little button on your telephone, you can turn yours off and let it take their "Thinking of you—oops, dropped my deposit slip" messages.

~ The Rules ~

DEAR MISS MANNERS:

A friend and I were catching up at a local coffee shop when the person at the table next to us pulled out his cell phone and talked on it non-stop for 20 minutes. He was loud enough to be heard by most everyone around him and was very annoying. I see more and more people using cell phones in grocery stores, shops, restaurants, movie theaters, and all kinds of public places. What are the new etiquette rules about cell phone use in public?

GENTLE READER:

Why do you people keep asking for new rules when you haven't yet used the old ones?

Oh dear, please forgive Miss Manners, who didn't mean to turn testy. It's just that when the telephone was invented, we kept it tethered with a cord for nearly a century in the hope that during that time, people would get the idea that it shouldn't be taken everywhere. Even before that, we had rules against shouting in public, making noise in theaters, ignoring the people one is with, spoiling the atmosphere of a quiet and dignified place and appearing to do business under social circumstances. These are still in effect.

So are the old rules about minding one's own business. Miss Manners is afraid that these would preclude interesting oneself in the conversations of people who are using cellular telephones reasonably. In grocery stores, shops and possibly your coffee shop, unless it is frightfully atmospheric, chatter is permitted, and unless you can invoke the shouting rule, you can have no reasonable objection.

⸺ *Applying the Rules* ⸺

DEAR MISS MANNERS:

I was eating lunch in a mall restaurant a few days ago, when a woman who was eating alone a couple of tables to my right paused in her eating/reading, reached into her purse, and pulled out a cell phone. She looked at the screen, put down her fork, and, as she raised her phone to her right ear, she raised her left hand to her mouth and cupped the phone.

The resultant conversation was only barely distinguishable from the restaurant background noise and much quieter than the live conversations around us.

As I was leaving, I thanked her for her courtesy and said I would pass her practice on. She thanked me.

GENTLE READER:

Did you get her telephone number? Miss Manners only asks because she would be happy to thank the lady too, if only she knew how to reach her.

⸺ *The Camera Telephone* ⸺

What with all the commotion made by people screaming into cell phones and people screaming about cell phones, the camera function may not be immediately suspected by its targets. And they could be anyone—household members thinking they were at leisure, guests caught off guard, strangers assuming shared privacy in gyms and anonymity in the streets.

Not that there is a lot of pictorial privacy to lose. We are all already starring on numerous security films, presumably caught in the act of going about our lawful business. Some who claim to have been going about lawfully find that the traffic-regulating film on which they have made cameo appearances argues otherwise.

Most people seem to be used to being on camera, although Miss Manners has to remember not to stop and use video monitors to pat her hair into place as she passes through surveillance.

This does not excuse amateur paparazzi. In the days when being photographed involved fitting the head against an iron clasp and going immobile until the photographer scared the daylights out of you with a burst of sound, light and possibly smoke, you were at least not caught unawares. Nowadays if the subjects do not give permission in advance, they should at least be offered the chance to delete.

THE INTERNET

All right, hands off the Send button, everyone. There is the problem, right there: Send before Think. Not to mention Send before Spell Check.

For all the interest there has been in developing an etiquette for person-to-person (Cc: everyone else) computer communication—and don't think Miss Manners doesn't appreciate this—we have not yet arrived at a standardized style for the email letter. The rules have been concerned with content, all of them attempting to discourage the sending of boring or nasty material to people who don't want to read it.

Leaving aside the question of "Heck, isn't that what the Internet is for?" this puts the burden on each letter-writer of inventing a suitable format. Such freedom of choice always inspires paeans to the liberty of cyberspace and the creativity of those who frequent it. But after years of examination, Miss Manners has observed that this opportunity has inspired nothing more than variations on a sideways smiley face. Inventing new etiquette, unless it is of immediate self-serving use—in which case Miss Manners has to bat it down—is nobody's idea of fun except hers.

So what email users have done is to avail themselves of the forms associated with other systems of communication. Some of them copy that of snail mail, complete with more or less formal salutations and closings; others copy the forms of graffiti, with their more direct attempts to hook attention.

One drawback is the strain of not automatically knowing what to use, freeing available creativity to be concentrated on the message itself. Another is not being able to assume that whatever one uses will be neutrally received by the reader, rather than being interpreted as being too cumbersome, too cheeky, too cute or too curt.

There is already enough misunderstanding from the content of email, Miss Manners is aware, although she has trouble with the explanation. People are always saying that without body language, one cannot convey emotional tone through mere words, even with the addition of tiny clusters of punctuation passing itself as signals.

Doesn't Miss Manners recall that we used to use writing before to say everything we had to say from a distance? And that it was thought to be more carefully written, and therefore clearer, than extemporized speech?

Anyway, here are the new rules:

Business communications should follow the format of the memorandum. If they are formal enough to justify the letter form, complete with Dear Mr. or Ms. Whoever, and Yours very truly, then they should be letters, and the instant way to send them is by fax.

Personal communications should borrow from such succinct predecessors as the telegram and the postal card. Although the sender and recipient must be fully identified, salutations and signatures require no more than a name or an initial and a dash; pronouns are often omitted (as in "Having wonderful time" or "Arriving Wednesday stop"); and abbreviations or initials—provided one is sure the reader will be able to interpret them—help protect the privacy of the persons or issues mentioned.

Miss Manners trusts these matters of form will help with the larger etiquette problems that have been identified. People didn't used to blather on when they paid by the word, or when they had two inches square in which to write.

⁓ *Spamming* ⌁

DEAR MISS MANNERS:

What is the kindest way to tell someone you do not want them to have your email address? My husband and I have hedged, demurred, etc., but his sister is most persistent. She's really a nice person, very strict about etiquette, but is a little pushy sometimes. We keep in regular touch by cards, calls and visits, but for various reasons do not want what we consider an intrusion by her and others she might give it to. But we don't want to hurt her feelings or make her mad.

GENTLE READER:

What? You don't want to receive reams of jokes passed on by your sister-in-law's colleague's cousin's college roommate? Not even if everybody else in the country is also getting them from six different sources and passing them on to everyone else on their lists?

Your sister-in-law cannot be stricter about etiquette than Miss Manners, who nevertheless allows people some leeway about methods of keeping in touch. Attempts to say that it is rude not to be always available by telephone, email, fax and every other means of communication available do not receive her endorsement.

You may be relieved to hear that Miss Manners does not expect you to explain this to your sister-in-law. It would most certainly annoy that lady, as it implies, erroneously, that email is not a proper means of informal correspondence.

You avoid that if you suggest a method that would be almost as easy for her, yet more convenient for you. "Oh, email is such an unreliable way to reach me," you might say—without specifying whether this is because you are having trouble with your email, confine its use to work or are fast on the delete button—"but you could leave a phone message, or just print out the message and pop it into the mail."

DEAR MISS MANNERS:

How do you tell friends and relatives to stop sending you nonsense email that is frequently batched out to all their closest friends and enemies? Not only do I not have time to read these missives or better yet missiles but I have better things to do with my spare time.

My mother never had this problem so I was never taught how to deal with junk email and to date I've never seen it addressed. I have a very favorite relative who thinks these are hilarious and sends us and her fifty other addresses daily nonsense. How do I tell her to take me off her batch list?

GENTLE READER:

If your mother doesn't have these problems, isn't it about time you got her on the Internet? It is not that Miss Manners is concerned that your mother may miss out on those same silly jokes that have been cycling cyberspace for years now. It is only that she hopes that the novelty will eventually wear off, as it did when everyone got used to answering machines, and people will stop using email as a toy. In the meantime, hit Delete.

∼ Googling ∼

DEAR MISS MANNERS:

As it's become easier than ever to keep up with the events in the lives of people one has known, even if one has fallen out of touch with the actual person, I hope you can help me understand what the rules of etiquette are for the practice of typing someone's name into an Internet search engine and seeing what entries result from the search.

I came across information that a high school classmate and friend, whom I haven't spoken with in years, recently lost his wife, whom I did not know. This information prompted a flurry of searches, and I discovered that another classmate has also passed away and a third has been jailed for repeated alcohol-impaired driving offenses.

How does one (indeed, should one?) admit to having this information, without causing undue distress? I would like to contact my old friend whose wife died to express my sympathy, but I simply don't know how to initiate the contact. It seems one thing to say, "I was talking with Christine, who told me about your wife . . . I'm so sorry for your loss" while it's quite another to admit that I came by the information through a practice that's not far removed from stalking. What would Miss Manners do?

GENTLE READER:

What she is doing at the moment is wondering whether this will always be considered delicate, or is, even now, other than by you and Miss Manners.

It is true that as a people, we are fiercely protective of our privacy. But that is only to make others stop bothering us while the population is busy posting everything it does, thinks or feels, accompanied by pictures, on its personal web sites. Perhaps not in the situations you mention, however. Presumably, people do not post their own arrests, deaths and bereavements. Yet these are matters of public record, and there are many ways you could have found out about them.

How you actually did is not that important. You need only begin your letter to your friend who lost his wife—and the survivor of your other classmate, should you be prompted to send condolences—with "I was so sorry to learn of your loss."

As for your other unfortunate classmate, Miss Manners suggests checking his web site and your school's self-submitted alumni notes, and offering sympathy only if it appears to be solicited by his telling his version of what happened.

Instant Messaging

DEAR MISS MANNERS:

Can you please address the topic of etiquette for Instant Messenger correspondents? Many is the time I have been in the middle of an exchange of messages, only to have the other person simply stop responding without explanation.

This is understandable in cases where the ISP or the computer has crashed, but entirely too often my correspondent resumes the chat after 10 or 15 minutes (and sometimes longer) with "Sorry, had to answer the phone" or just "Hi, I'm back!" It is my feeling that the departing party is obligated by courtesy to inform the other party of his/her imminent departure. I use the shorthand "brb" (be right back) if I have to answer the phone, the door, or nature's call, and sign off instant message chats in much the way I end telephone conversations.

I have been told, however, that this medium is NOT the telephone, so the courtesies don't apply, and it is acceptable to simply stop responding and go do something else without warning to one's correspondent. What is your view of the subject?

GENTLE READER:

That phrase, "the courtesies don't apply," chills Miss Manners' otherwise tender and glowing heart. It usually means that the anti-etiquette forces have a new toy and erroneously assume that it may be operated etiquette-free. But if your informants only mean that the rules for telephone calls should not apply to instant messaging, Miss Manners is open to hearing their case.

Although instant messaging is reciprocal, as are telephone calls, it has in common with other written means—not only email, but letters, if anyone remembers what they are—that there is some leeway in choosing when to write or read. In telephoning, we assume we have the other person's full attention, although goodness knows that this is now rarely the case. At the computer, you may be sure that there are other distractions. So while Miss Manners admires your alerts when you momentarily leave, she is not ready to insist that others issue them when turning their attention to a boss or parent who assumes that they have been working.

— *Busy Signals* —

DEAR MISS MANNERS:

Several friends go online with their computers, but have neither call-waiting or voicemail, nor a second line, and calling their phones often results in a busy signal, a situation that can last for several hours.

If they have called and left a message for me, is it incumbent on me to keep trying to call them back until they are no longer on the phone? Is it rude not to return such calls if one has tried several times to get through? I presume the situation would be the same for a person who spends a lot of time talking on the phone, but using the phone to go online seems to be a far more common occurrence.

GENTLE READER:

It depends upon how much you want to reach these people. If you are miffed and don't mind waiting until they realize someone is wrong, Miss Manners admits that you can claim you tried repeatedly, and let it go at that.

Fortunately, we have other means of communication available should you actually want to be in touch. Depending on whether you are more technologically advanced than your friends or less, you could dash off an email or a post card to say, "Tried to reach you but couldn't get through—call me when you get a chance."

Family Relations

THE ESSENTIAL thing to know about a family, when predicting its chances of survival in these perilous times, is not whether it is nuclear, multigenerational, single- or double-parented or tied together by bonds of blood, marriage, passion or mortgage. A more useful clue is whether each member of the family who uses up a roll of paper in the bathroom immediately fetches another roll and puts it in place, even if he or she is not planning to return to the house for the rest of the day. Is there, in other words, a prevailing family etiquette?

Miss Manners is horrified when she hears "company manners" defined as not just more formal etiquette but a higher standard of politeness than family manners. One can always go out and corral a new set of friends to be company, if one has offended the old ones beyond repair. One can begin a new family too, of course, after one has hopelessly clogged the old one with hurt feelings, and many people do, but it is considerably more expensive.

It strikes Miss Manners as misguided to believe that home is a place where you can relax because you needn't bother to be polite. Home should be a place where you can relax because you know that there, unlike in the rest of the world, no one will be impolite to you. There is enough rudeness in the streets without inviting it indoors.

Here are some of Miss Manners' basic rules of family etiquette:

- Newspapers and magazines may not be mutilated until everyone in the house has had a reasonable chance to see them.
- People do not enter the rooms of those beyond toddlerhood without knocking or use one another's property without asking. However, all such requests should be kindly considered.
- No questions are asked about letters or telephone calls, not even "I see you got a letter from . . ." or "What'd she want?" All such information is voluntary, with no prompting allowed.
- Under no provocation may the secrets of a family member be revealed by other members outside the family.

- Unless otherwise arranged, everyone shows up at dinner, prepared to make general conversation and looking reasonably appetizing. As for what you consider appetizing looking in your relatives, Miss Manners is not prepared to decide.
- Rudeness that is introduced under the name of informality or intimacy is still rudeness.
- True family informality includes the use of first names, even between husband and wife, and the wearing of dressing gowns on Sunday morning, a designation that applies to any period of time when members of the family are home alone.
- Family intimacy means not having to disguise the announcement of one's triumphs or fiascoes with modesty or with the pretense that it didn't really hurt.
- Everyone says "Good morning" to all members of the family encountered before noon and "Good night" before retiring.
- When preparing food for oneself, one offers to make some for whoever else is hanging about the kitchen.
- A person who did not participate in a given meal or snack should not be expected to clean the resulting dishes.

An Example

DEAR MISS MANNERS:

My wife objects if I use her bath towel when mine isn't handy by. Don't you think that kind of "formality" is a bit much?

GENTLE READER:

Certainly not. Your wife is quite right. Marriage is no excuse for that sort of intimacy.

Principles of Marriage

Our vast cadre of social scientists is focusing its attention on marriage with the intention of rescuing that institution from a wayward predilection for extra-legal cohabitation and divorce. This strikes Miss Manners as only fair, considering what these folks accomplished with their last generation of techniques for improving marriage.

True, today's experts are mostly not responsible for the previous go-around. It is just that Miss Manners has witnessed so many cycles in which solutions to social problems were trumpeted, tried and then trounced that she pictures all experts as members of the same guild, taking turns keeping their profession going and the public entertained by alternately issuing alarming warnings and counterwarnings.

Appreciating their dedication and concern for public welfare, she hopes they take comfort from knowing that when they are not able to help, at least they are not unduly upsetting the public. Millions of people drift into a good night's sleep when they hear the soothing tones of a favorite announcer proclaiming "New studies show . . ."

One cannot be told often enough to be careful not to ingest household cleaning solutions and to be nice to one's spouse. Miss Manners only objected to these study-based findings when they turned out not to suggest being nice to one's spouse, stressing, instead, the need for total, frank, open communication. Whatever else that is, it is not nice.

Loyal, loving spouses sometimes think "I'm so lucky I married you" and "You get cuter all the time," both of which should be stated, although preferably not while the person in question is trying to recover accidentally deleted work that is due the following morning. But those loyal, loving spouses may also have such thoughts as "I suppose you can't help it, but how can any human being be that clumsy?" and "If you died, nobody would mind my leaving my stuff where I want it." These thoughts and feelings should not be shared.

Miss Manners does not have the experts' confidence in teachable "marriage skills" that can be applied to all couples. She once heard one such expert ask in despair, "Why is it that we teach high school kids how to drive, and yet we don't even try to teach them how to have a happy marriage?" Her timid reply was, "Maybe it's because we know what makes cars work?"

Yet she does know something that always helps domestic life, although she would hardly classify it as a skill. It is (surprise!): ordinary politeness. A myth exists that one of the pleasures of private life is the ability to drop manners and—as people always put it when they assert the desire to be repulsive—be themselves. On the contrary, that rapidly becomes one of its drawbacks.

True, family manners are less formal than those that are supposed to be applied outside the home. In family privacy, it is not improper to gnaw the chicken bones and walk around in bunny slippers. But when no manners are practiced—when people start licking their plates or living in their underwear—things usually go bad. And when the manners of personal respect disappear, and couples feel free to insult each other when they happen to harbor unflattering feelings, they get rapidly worse.

So if the new skill that experts are vaunting is politeness, Miss Manners would be willing to forget that it is the very one that their predecessors advised jettisoning.

DEAR MISS MANNERS:

It's a little scary to be getting married when so many marriages end in divorce. Do you have any more etiquette advice for a new husband and wife to each other?

GENTLE READER:

Give your spouse the courtesy of not being embarrassed on his or her behalf. Marriage is no excuse for installing yourself as the resident critic of another person's behavior. There is no surer way of ending one than the habit of saying, "You shouldn't have done that" or "Why did you have to say that?" If you resolve not to feel that it reflects on you if he makes an ass of himself, and extract a promise that he will allow you to make an ass of yourself without feeling that it reflects on him, you will be off to a very solid start.

DEAR MISS MANNERS:

We have a quarrel about married couples who order different food at restaurants. I can't stand to kiss my husband when he has garlic or onions, which I don't eat, on his breath.

GENTLE READER:

Well, Miss Manners is not going to do it for you.

~ Substituting Business Principles ~

How much are you charging Granny for Christmas dinner? Consider how poor her appetite is these days. Should you yield to the spirit of the season and offer her a discount? Or a senior rate if she promises to eat early and leave?

Deciding such delicate questions should be the etiquette of the twenty-first century, if Miss Manners were to listen to some of her more practical Gentle Readers. Family life has much to learn from the marketplace, they believe. These are the people who have recently discovered soliciting corporate sponsors for their weddings, promising that they will tout whatever wares they receive free to their guest list of potential customers. They throw anniversary parties for their parents, for which the invitation states how much the meal will cost the guest and how much should be contributed toward a present. They teach their children both the technology and the psychology for informing and embarrassing people into giving them exactly the things they want.

But even Miss Manners was shocked when a gentleman reported that he and his mother were billed for the Easter dinner to which his brother and sister-in-law had invited them. In turn, Miss Manners' old-fashioned reaction shocked one of those practical Gentle Readers. This lady snapped back: "Holiday dinners for all the relatives get to be expensive!! And no one wants to do them!! With half a honey baked ham running $35, I can see the brother's point. Perhaps constant holiday dinners should be shared. Some (almost all) relatives are freeloaders and Miss Manners should have pointed that out!"

Actually, in a way, Miss Manners had pointed this out. She had speculated about whether the brother had credited his mother for the meals he had consumed during his upbringing. Talk about freeloaders! If toddlers knew the price of strained peas . . . !

Nevertheless, the objection was valid, in that Miss Manners actually does disapprove of celebrating religious holidays, or any other occasion, by selling meals to one's relatives and friends.

She does not deny that there is sharing involved in offering and accepting hospitality, which can take the form of helping out and/or alternating being the host. But this is done on a most unbusinesslike basis. Rather than keeping strict accounts, people who are fond of one another exercise tolerance in understanding and accepting one's another's abilities and wishes. That is typical of the unbusinesslike way in which families are run. They carry unproductive people, including children and old people. They share their resources on the basis of need rather than contribution. They admit affection as a factor in decision-making. Admittedly, this is no way to run a business. But, then, business is no way to run a personal life.

⌒ *Shared Spaces* ⌒

Gather 'round the hearth, everyone, and Miss Manners will tell you stories of how things used to be, back when everyone used to gather 'round the hearth.

Dear Nathaniel Hawthorne is responsible for bringing to mind the simple but great pleasures of the hearth, cut short in his day by the introduction of the "cheerless and ungenial stove." As he tells it in an essay called "Fire Worship," the hearth of his youth conferred countless blessings on mankind—inspiring love, kindness, patriotism, religion. The dear man predicted, in 1854, that "social intercourse cannot long continue what it has been, now that we have subtracted from it so important and vivifying an element as firelight." Future generations, he said, "will never behold one another through that peculiar medium of vision—the ruddy gleam of blazing wood or bituminous coal—which gives the human spirit so deep an insight into its fellows and melts all humanity into one cordial heart of hearts. Domestic life, if it may still be termed domestic, will seek its separate corners and never gather itself into groups.

The easy gossip; the merry yet unambitious jest; the lifelike, practical discussion of real matters in a casual way; the soul of truth which is so often incarnated in a simple fireside word—will disappear from earth. Conversation will contract the air of debate and all mortal intercourse be chilled with a fatal frost."

Well, was the gentleman right? Does your family gather together in the evening, to warm one another with merry jests and simple truths, or doesn't it? The fact is that modern households have no centers to attract family members, let alone wayfarers, who are considered to be getting a warm welcome if they are squinted at through peepholes and interrogated through doors, rather than shot on sight. Miss Manners does not count those squabbles over entertainment centers and computers around which families may gather if they do not have enough to allow each to operate one in privacy.

Nevertheless, there are houses that actually have fireplaces, and Miss Manners recommends that their lucky owners use them as much as possible, in the way that Mr. Hawthorne described, to help restore the amenities whose passing he so rightly mourned. If a fire is lit in the home of an evening, and perhaps supplied with optional extras, such as dinner meat gently roasting on a spit or grill, or a bowl of marshmallows and a supply of long forks for after dinner, perhaps those people who have slunk away into their individual rooms and lives will begin to venture forth once more and reestablish the family circle. Especially if you turn down the thermostat.

DEAR MISS MANNERS:

When many people in the same family have to share the same bathroom, and all have to go off to work or school about the same time in the morning—who gets to go first, and how do you decide how long people can take? This is a major question in our household.

GENTLE READER:

There's no problem answering this question. People should go in order of need and stay there only until that need is met. Now, all you have to do is to define "need," judge the relative needs of your relatives and enforce this law.

Family Discord

DEAR MISS MANNERS:

Our family is a selfish, self-centered bunch. I feel we don't know how to go out or come in our home. It is a constant pattern of stress and conflict. I feel we don't know how to be civil. And I see this all as a repeat pattern from my own childhood. It seems whenever I enter the house, I start issuing orders. "Pick up . . . Put away . . . Do . . . Do . . . Do."

If the children ask a question and get an answer they don't like, they nag, whine, complain, even threaten disobedience. I know it is learned behavior. We too often give in. My husband and I are in competition almost all the time. We disagree about many things concerning the kids, and we often do this in front of the kids. All may stem from reacting rather than thinking and taking time to talk to each other first. The strange thing is we are a solid one-marriage family. Our kids are approaching college age—that is how long we have been married.

On one hand, I think it is too late to change so much (our table manners are awful); on the other, we can change anything if we want to, can't we? Can I? How can I learn new mannerly ways of behaving with a group of people who will resist? How can I practice and remember and keep from being sucked back into my old bad habits? I really want to change the very fabric of our chaotic life.

GENTLE READER:

Miss Manners would imagine that you do. Your household, as you describe it, cannot be a warm refuge from the vicissitudes of life, although she trusts that there are compensating pleasures you have omitted from this account.

Oddly enough, your own behavior, which prevented you from teaching them manners when they were small, could encourage them to learn with you now. An admission that you are all to blame, and you all also suffer from the resulting atmosphere, is the basis on which to suggest that you make a joint fresh start.

What will overcome their resistance is the anxiety you can stir up about the near future. Suppose their college roommates refuse to put up with them? Suppose they get on the nerves of the people with whom they fall in love? And suppose you and your husband are left alone in unrelieved disharmony?

The greatest incentive will be to outdo one another in the new behavior, and to catch one another's mistakes. Miss Manners therefore urges you to make your first household etiquette rule a polite and sportsmanlike way of pointing out violations of the other rules.

DEAR MISS MANNERS:

Do you believe it is proper for parents to fight—argue, shall we say—in front of their children? There is one theory that it is bad to burden them, and another that it's educational for them. Which do you think?

GENTLE READER:

Both. Parents should conduct their arguments in quiet, respectful tones, but in a foreign language. You'd be surprised what an inducement that is to the education of children.

DEAR MISS MANNERS:

When my father gets in a bad mood, he screams and shouts and carries on over the least little thing. This morning, it was the toaster. The toast wasn't the way he likes it, or at least that's what he said, and he yelled at the toaster. We think he was really mad at Mother, but he didn't say anything to her, just kept banging at the poor innocent toaster. He was completely out of control. Isn't that considered bad manners?

GENTLE READER:

No, and that is not considered being out of control, either. Everyone must shout once in a while, and it is both correct and disciplined to remember then that appliances are meant to be shouted at, but people are not.

FAMILY CRISES

Jealousy

As a motivating force for unassailably correct behavior, jealousy, Miss Manners has noticed, is not a conspicuous success. Why is that? Miss Manners should think that people who believe themselves to be on the losing side of romance would endeavor to make their behavior more attractive, not less, to their errant loved ones. And yet the usual procedure is for the person who suspects a waning of interest to adopt a mode of action so outrageous as to supply grounds for dismissal on that basis alone.

Miss Manners has always believed jealousy to be a waste of time. She has never known anyone to be the better off for having it. But if you must go in for it, she begs you to observe a few rules of decency. It is important to identify correctly the object of your ill will. Too many people make the mistake of directing this to the person who got the promotion rather than the employer who failed to give it out properly, or on the romantic replacement rather than on the person who did the displacing. It is, in Miss Manners' opinion, pathetic to see two women, for example, engage in a vituperative rivalry while the object of their dispute sits luxuriously on the sidelines, perhaps even urging each of them on in the fight. Disgraceful indeed.

The correct attitude of one lady to another in such a situation is calm, polite and somewhat distantly cheerful. And since Miss Manners was talking about motivations for politeness, she will add that such behavior is very worrisome to anyone with rivalrous intentions. Why is she so unruffled—is she really anxious to dump him on me?

As for behavior toward the cause of the trouble, that too must be within the bounds of propriety. Faithlessness in one person does not absolve another from ordinary rules of good conduct. Lawlessness, usually in the form of some sort of spying, is not allowable. Miss Manners would even go so far as to say that evidence obtained by such means as opening another person's mail, reading diaries, going through pockets or making disguised-voice phone calls is not admissible when arguing the original crime. It can only lead to a mistrial in the matter of infidelity, with a new issue, that of unethical snooping, the subject next taken up.

Then there are the modes of behavior that are not exactly unethical, but not exactly attractive either. This includes all material for four-page letters and midnight telephone calls. Ladies and gentlemen do not threaten each other, and they do not attempt to force themselves on each other when they do not seem to be welcome. If this is true in social intercourse, it is doubly true in—in romance.

Miss Manners wishes that she could guarantee that the patient observance of excellent manners under trying circumstances would reinspire errant lovers to know what treasures they are losing. She cannot. But she does promise that no one was ever inspired to fall back in love because of a campaign of unrelenting persistence, or because of a threat of suicide, murder or financial ruin.

~ *Flirting* ~

DEAR MISS MANNERS:

My husband and I, along with two other couples, went "out on the town" last night. All evening my husband made eyes at a pretty young lady (young enough to be his daughter) sitting directly across from our table. To make matters worse, the young lady enjoyed every minute of the same and reciprocated. This ruined my evening. I wanted to kick my husband and slap the girl's face, but instead I made jokes to my friends about my husband's flirtation.

Question: In the future, how can I handle a situation like this—in a classy way, without looking like an insanely jealous wife? Also, should I let the next young lady know I don't appreciate her participation, or only my husband? Please answer soon—I'm depressed, still!

GENTLE READER:

Please stop being depressed. Miss Manners can't bear it, and besides, you should feel proud of having done—as you say—the classy thing.

This does not mean that she does not sympathize with your position. Trying to look as if you are having a jolly time while the person with you manifests a romantic interest in a stranger is a severe strain on the facial muscles, to say the least. It does not matter whether this "interest" is wicked or innocent. Well, perhaps it matters to the wife. But from the standpoint of manners, it is just as embarrassing for the gentleman to pay a personal compliment to the waitress, under the mistaken impression that this is a form of tipping, as it is for him to send his office key and a bottle of champagne to the next table.

Nevertheless, Miss Manners would not advise you to teach manners to strange young ladies in night clubs. It will be enough if you can teach them to your husband. Please be careful not to discuss this so as to make it sound like jealousy—an unattractive emotion in a wife, as you have noticed—rather than etiquette. The age of the young lady has nothing to do with it, for example. You certainly do not want to get into such doomed questions as whether she was prettier than you, how he really feels about her, ditto about you, and so on. Merely say that you find such behavior rude and are afraid it makes him ridiculous in the eyes of your friends. Miss Manners trusts you to say this with tact, as well as firmness.

Perhaps he will change this behavior to oblige you. Perhaps he will change it when it is suggested that other people view it as ludicrous and pathetic, rather than dashing and charming. Perhaps not. In that case, Miss Manners suggests that you save yourself this embarrassment again by separating your social life from his. Let him wonder, when you go out to dinner alone with another couple, how the table gets evened out.

Snooping

DEAR MISS MANNERS:

I am heartbroken because I discovered that my husband has been receiving love letters from another woman, but he keeps changing the subject by saying I had no right to read his mail. Who is right?

GENTLE READER:

You are quite right to seek advice from an etiquette column, rather than a psychologically oriented one. Miss Manners believes that the true value in people is not what is in their murky psyches, which many keep in as shocking a state as their bureau drawers, but in how they treat one another. You are wrong, however, in your dispute with your husband. To be deceived is the natural human condition; to read another person's mail is despicable.

~ *Confessing* ~

DEAR MISS MANNERS:

Some time ago, I had a short, tempestuous affair with my wife's boss's wife. There was a lot of anguish involved, and I guess the most excitement I've ever had in my life, although it's hard for me to believe, now that it's over, how reckless we got. We thought we were in love. We even talked about running away together. All of this happened within six months. She broke it off—stopped taking my calls and completely avoided me. For a while, I could hardly get out of bed, let alone work. My wife was incredibly decent about it. She accepted the idea that I was having some sort of nonspecific, middle-aged depression, and was cheerful and supportive without pressing me about the meaning of it. It's thanks to her that I recovered fully.

I think that my wife deserves an explanation. I want to be in the clear with her, and I also am aware that some word of what happened could still get back to her from people who might have seen us together. This woman and I used to meet in a cheap midtown motel, where we often sat in the restaurant, figuring it was not the kind of place where anyone we knew would go. The truth is that we were so besotted that we figured we were invisible and actually held hands in the restaurant, even though we also had a room. At least once, I saw, on the way out from lunch, two women I couldn't place but who looked familiar and were probably friends of my wife.

The trouble is that my ex–great love hasn't told her husband and doesn't plan to. I might mention that my wife is a lousy actress. Whatever she thinks is written all over her face. I don't think she would tell him, if she knew, but he would know that there was something funny going on. God knows I don't want to make any more trouble for anyone, certainly not now. But it seems to me that my only responsibility now is to my own marriage, and that I no longer need consider the possible consequences to someone who, when you get right down to it, did not hesitate to sacrifice my feelings to save her own marriage. Don't you agree?

GENTLE READER:

No. The only person who would feel better after such a confession would be you, and you don't deserve it. Whatever she suspected, your wife does not deserve the pain caused by certainty and vividness.

Besides, a secret affair is, by its nature, a secret jointly held by two people. Although she has dissolved this union, you retain joint custody of the secret. That a gentleman may find himself participating in a dishonorable situation does not excuse him from the obligation to pursue the course of honor within that situation.

~ Counseling ~

DEAR MISS MANNERS:

My husband has just turned forty and I believe is experiencing a mid-life crisis. After an indecisive two years, he took off his wedding ring, said he didn't want to be married anymore, and moved into his own apartment. He further elaborated that a woman friend that he'd known for many years (lunch, etc.) and with whom he'd been having an affair for some time, said she had never loved anyone as much as she loved him. He said he wanted to investigate this relationship further and wanted to find himself, etc., etc., etc. After several weeks, we mutually agreed to see a marriage counselor (a psychologist) separately and then eventually together. We also see each other once a week with our child, age eleven.

The question: He wants to resume sexual relations without any commitment. He says he wants to continue the counseling on a weekly basis to negotiate a truce and he wants to try to make it together again.

What is correct? If my husband is having a sexual relationship with another woman or women, should I, as his legal wife, also have sexual relations with him? Separation—that is, a legal separation—has not occurred. My husband has implied that I'm being a prude by not having sexual relations with him, and am seeking an eye for an eye, etc. He says he wants to move back in with us (me and our daughter) after we have negotiated the truce. The counselor says the decision is up to me.

I feel we should be married again before we resume our sexual relations or before he moves in again. My husband has not said in so many words that he is sorry he caused me pain or that he has totally shut off all relations with the other woman. I feel he wants to have his cake and eat it, too. My husband has said he wants to try to make our relationship work and he doesn't want a divorce or a legal separation. Since we are not legally separated, I am not dating. How would you handle this situation—confusing as it is—correctly?

GENTLE READER:

You have come at last to the right person. It is kind of the marriage counselor to say that the decision is up to you, but who else should it be up to, pray? You have obviously been too long among people who use sympathetic terms for your husband's behavior and pejorative ones for yours, thus disguising the fact that (1) you were the injured party and (2) you are now in the position of strength.

Thus, when he cuts off intimacy with you, it is called experiencing a crisis and investigating a relationship, and when you cut off intimacy with him, it is called prudery and eye-for-an-eye revenge.

The only valid metaphor in use here is the one of a "truce." Let us look at this in terms of diplomacy. He deserted. He now wants to resume the privileges of citizenship. You have the right to readmit him or to refuse to do so, on the grounds that he has forfeited his rights. You can even assume his tactics, if you want, and declare your own midlife crisis, a state that he has defined as relieving one of duty to others.

What is up to you, therefore, is not only making the decision, but setting the terms under which you are willing to live. While Miss Manners does not ordinarily tell people when or when not to engage in lovemaking, she will say that no diplomat in his right mind would confer privileges before obtaining agreement on obligations.

⸺ Acknowledging ⸺

DEAR MISS MANNERS:

I'm not sure I seek etiquette advice, but maybe . . . Almost 30 years ago, I had an affair and a daughter was born. The lady and I parted, she married and her husband adopted the girl.

When the daughter came of age, I wrote to her. She responded with demands for money and much vituperation. I broke off relations. Now, in her late 20s, she has resumed writing and she seems very nice. She never asks for money. She does, however, often allude to my other children and she does ask for details about my life, which I have not given her.

My wife knows of her and, after some rough times, we are very comfortable together. My children do not know about her. I am afraid she might tell them. I'm sure my children would explode once and then repair the damage and we would be in good shape; still, I don't want it to happen. Is this an etiquette question? If so, any advice?

GENTLE READER:

Perhaps we should start with your explaining to Miss Manners what you would have considered proper etiquette on the part of a daughter in response to belated paternal overtures.

Not a financial claim. Nor an emotional claim. Nor a request for her family history.

And certainly not any attempt to know her half-siblings. So—why did you get in touch with her? Did you hope for a letter from camp: "I'm fine, having lots of fun, but I miss you, Daddy, love and kisses; P.S., the counselors make us write home before dinner"?

Now to your query, which is whether you have an etiquette problem. As you can hardly expect Miss Manners to assure you that you behaved like a perfect gentleman, you must be referring to the awkwardness of perhaps having to acknowledge a fact whose consequences you had successfully eluded for thirty years.

Miss Manners' guess is that this will not come up. Having been so thoroughly rejected by you, and put off even after you initiated contact, the young lady is not likely to feel that she is welcome in your home. Should it arise, you would best behave with extreme humility and graciousness. If you have no other incentive to do so, you may be assured that your legitimate children will be watching you to see how you might have treated them had they been born at an inconvenient time for you.

⁓ "Getting Over It" ⁓

DEAR MISS MANNERS:

Many years ago my sister ran off with my husband. Naturally, this has been a thorn in my side as I did not suspect a thing. (We had a daughter and I thought everything was going OK till he asked for a divorce. My sister had been staying with us and I considered her my best friend.) The real problem is that the rest of my family thinks I should "get over it" and act like we are a normal family (reunions, etc.). I am very uncomfortable with seeing them together as if nothing happened. I have not caused a scene but feel betrayed not only by my ex-husband but also by my siblings (there are eight of us). Am I being unreasonable?

GENTLE READER:

Time for a quick explanation of what is and what is not an etiquette problem, Miss Manners observes. There is an etiquette problem here, but many Gentle Readers would have an understandably hard time finding it among the glaring moral and psychological ones.

When a sister and brother-in-law run away together, it is a moral transgression, not an etiquette problem. How the wife or her relatives feel about it, and for how long, is a psychological reality, not an etiquette problem. But acts and feelings have the unpleasant habit of creating explosive social situations, and those are indeed etiquette problems. Here we have a whopper of one:

Is your family correct in treating the transgressing couple as normal members of the family, and in expecting you to do so? Or are you justified in continuing to avoid them and feeling that your family should do so?

In the last century, society went from one extreme to another in its treatment of people connected with scandal. At the century's beginning, everyone touched by such a situation would have become a permanent social outcast, even the wronged wife. "She must have done something to drive him to it," people would have murmured.

By the century's end, sympathy for the wife or condemnation of the husband and sister would be quickly replaced by intolerance for anyone who dwelt on the matter when it was no longer fresh. The aggrieved party would be at fault for not getting over it (as your family argues) and her supporters for being judgmental.

Miss Manners realizes that marital rifts have become so commonplace that if each one occasioned a full-fledged feud, there wouldn't be any peaceful society. She also believes that the children's interests are paramount and scenes on mandatory family occasions must be avoided. That holds.

But neither a child nor society is served by treating such a heinous double betrayal as a mere passing annoyance. Decent behavior cannot be taught or sustained if no judgment is passed on indecent behavior. Your relatives should beware of wishing you to "act normal" toward that couple, much less of drawing you into situations where you must confront them unnecessarily. Rather, they should be proud of you if you are able to stifle your normal impulses and act aloofly dignified when you cannot avoid contact with them.

Hedging

DEAR MISS MANNERS:

My niece, married several years with two children (one newborn), discovered that her husband is a serial cheater. He travels on business weekly and routinely uses the Internet to set up liaisons in destination cities. She's heartbroken, confused and unsure of her next move.

How do I handle the next meeting with this scoundrel, which is likely to be a family gathering in my sister's home? I know I can't kill or even seriously wound him, but neither can I be the hail-fellow-well-met uncle of the past. Should I greet him with a flat "Hello," and move away, leaving no doubt that I want no further conversation? Must I shake hands, which I would rather not? I don't want to embarrass my sister or my niece, but I can't pretend I'm glad to see the husband or even want to be in the same room with him even though we formerly were very friendly and have shared many happy times.

GENTLE READER:

Shunning scoundrels is one of society's duties, sadly neglected by those who refuse to pass judgment, and who may also have discovered that scoundrels sometimes make lively companions. Miss Manners is glad to see that you are ready to do your part.

As you have noticed, it is a complicated part. However much you may want to protect society in general from cads, it is your niece in particular whose betrayal arouses your indignation. And she—understandably, especially with a newborn baby—has not yet decided what she will do. She may reconcile with him, in which case cutting him will cut you off from her. Even if she divorces him, she is likely to maintain some sort of relationship in regard to their children, and this may occasion your meeting him in her house or your sister's. You are therefore not free to administer the worst snub, which is to refuse to shake his hand, hold any conversation with him, indeed, to recognize that he exists.

The setting you want, until you see what happens, is not freezing, but cool. The flat hello and turning away is fine, and if you turn away fast enough, you may be able to avoid shaking hands. In case of a divorce, you can lower this to cold, which precludes anything but a curt nod, yet if there is a reconciliation, you can turn it up to lukewarm, adding short neutral conversation.

～ Shunning ～

DEAR MISS MANNERS:

I do not know how to behave in a delicate but serious situation. My husband's adult sister told us that she had been sexually abused as a child by their uncle (by marriage). We believe her and want to be supportive of her.

However, she has not told other relatives nor confronted the uncle about the abuse. We do not wish to cause harm or distress to his sister or to other family members. Yet we see this uncle at Christmas, and have been repeatedly invited to visit his house. It is very difficult for us to be civil to a man we believe caused great harm to someone we care about. We have tried to avoid him, but because no one else in the family knows about the abuse most relatives keep inviting him to all the family gatherings. Avoiding him completely would entail missing Christmas with the extended family, something we would miss terribly. We live in another state and see many relatives only during the Christmas holidays.

How should we behave at a family gathering where he is present? Should we avoid these gatherings altogether? If we do avoid gatherings what, if anything, should we say to him or to other relatives as to why?

Gentle Reader:

Miss Manners is going to do you the courtesy of answering the question you asked, which is how you can reconcile your conviction that this person has put himself outside civilized humanity with your desire to participate in a pleasant gathering with people who are not aware of it.

She emphasizes this, because other Gentle Readers will demand to know why she did not answer the question of how to humiliate the uncle in front of everyone. Because you did not ask it.

To avoid involving others, the technique to use is a modified form of shunning. Rather than pointedly withdrawing your hand if he tries to shake it, you occupy it by patting your hair; rather than turn your back if he approaches you, you say "Excuse me" and turn to go elsewhere; rather than greeting any friendly overtures with silence, you respond only with a nod. Above all, you refuse to smile or to discuss "what's wrong." The punishments of etiquette may sound weak, but Miss Manners assures you that to be treated coldly with no opportunity to explain is frightening.

Visiting

THE CHARMING old custom of calling, or paying short regular visits to one's entire acquaintance to thank them for hospitality, mark the milestones of life and generally acknowledge their existence, has died out of general use simply because it was time consuming, boring and without content. Eventually, Miss Manners has noticed, it was replaced by television and computer games.

In its true form, calling was a lady's principal occupation. Each one chose a day of the week on which she declared herself at home to receive calls, and the rest of the week was spent out inflicting visits on others. Births, engagements, marriages, moves and deaths required that those who performed them, or their immediate relatives, be called upon. Every guest had to call on every hostess after every party. Then every call had to be returned with a call equal in length but opposite in direction.

It kept the ladies on the streets, rather than off, and rebellion arose. Dear Edith Wharton recalled her mother's day, when "the onerous and endless business of 'calling' took up every spare hour" and how "by the time I grew up the younger married women had emancipated themselves and simply drove from house to house depositing their cards, duly turned down in the upper left-hand corner [please see p. 599], to the indignation of stay-at-home hostesses, many of whom made their servants keep a list of the callers who 'did not ask,' so that these might be struck off the next season's invitation list—a punishment borne by the young and gay with perfect equanimity, as it was only the dull hostesses who inflicted it."

For a long time, the drama continued symbolically with the actors absent from the stage. Small strange niceties developed, such as a lady's being honor-bound to be present in her carriage while her footman took the cards—one each from each lady in her family for each lady in the called-upon family, and a card each from the gentlemen in the calling family for every person in the called-upon family—to the servant whose job it was to announce that the lady of his house was not at home.

The virtual disappearance of this crucial servant brought an end to the vestigial remains of calling, everywhere but in a few diplomatic communities where the civilized pleasure of sitting face to face for fifteen minutes with someone with whom you have little in common, perhaps not even a language, is still appreciated.

Otherwise, modern calling has been reduced to the following paltry rules:

- Real, old-fashioned, in-person calls are paid upon a birth and death and, if appropriate and welcome, on the occasion of an illness. Calling on new neighbors is charming but optional. In all of these cases, one must telephone to make an appointment, but new parents and the newly bereaved are supposed to make themselves available to receive these visits.
- Hospitality is generally considered sufficiently acknowledged by the offer of comparable return hospitality. The exception is the seated dinner, for which a letter or a telephone call (Miss Manners prefers the letter) is required. Other letters of thanks for hospitality are always appropriate, but not mandatory.
- Routine social calling is done by telephone or email. That is, one can call, in this fashion, nearly any time of day and expect, as the ladies plying the avenues in their carriage did, to be received unless there is a specific excuse offered. The facility with which people can be trapped by callers by telephone and flooded with email is, in Miss Manners' opinion, one of the serious drawbacks of modern life. She recommends leniency in accepting excuses by the called upon of not being able to respond immediately, and makes it a point of honor never to recognize the voice of a lady explaining that she is not at home.
- Dropping in does not exist in proper modern society. Those who practice it should be prepared not to recognize by sight ladies who are trying to establish that they are not at home.

~ *Unannounced Visits* ~

DEAR MISS MANNERS:

What are my obligations to people knocking on my door? Most are solicitors or religious proselytizers, neither of whom I wish to speak to. The only way to see who is there is by looking out the door's window.

If the person sees me, do I then have to answer the door? I don't like opening the door to strangers. I can see the street, so I know if a police car or fire truck is out there. If I do open the door, can I cut off their scripted speeches and say I'm not interested? Some are quite aggressive, even hostile. How polite must I be? Cutting someone off seems rude, but then so does their imposition on me.

Neighbors sometimes knock also, and I don't always answer. How does one tell neighbors not to stop by unannounced, without offending them, especially when they are stopping by with a small gift? I may have let the neighbor situation go on too long to correct it now. Am I obligated to tell anyone that sometimes I don't answer the door? Must I always answer the door if I want to remain a member of (somewhat) polite society?

GENTLE READER:

If Miss Manners says yes, it would mean that you would be rude in refusing to open the door when you saw a masked gunman. If she says no, it would mean that you would be polite in peering clearly at your neighbors, and then walking away, leaving them standing on your doorstep holding flowers from their gardens or pies from their ovens. Couldn't she get out of this by making you install side curtains and a peephole?

You don't have to answer the door at all if the caller does not see you and can therefore assume that you are either not home or occupied with something that prevents you from responding. You still don't have to answer the door for strangers, whether they are holding guns or Bibles or lottery winnings, and if they catch you looking or opening, you can cut them off by shaking your head and saying thank you.

Neighbors are different. "Dropping in" is an old, warm, friendly, neighborly custom which is properly despised by those on whom it is practiced. If they see you, you must open the door—but you need not let them cross the threshold. In the absence of a butler to say that you are not receiving, you must say it yourself, "I'm sorry, I can't receive you now," after which you may shut the door firmly. The unannounced visitor must learn to expect this sort of nonreception. The world would be a better place if we all had butlers again.

DEAR MISS MANNERS:

I mistakenly left my front door unlocked one Saturday afternoon when my older children were out for a few hours, the younger ones were napping, and my husband and I were enjoying some rare time alone with each other. I heard the doorbell ring and decided not to get it because our time was important. Imagine my horror when I heard a friend walk right into my house after about one minute on the porch and begin calling for me.

I ended up going downstairs to have a visit for about one hour until my children came home. My husband says I did the only thing I could do in this situation, but I find myself feeling very angry with my friend for her rudeness in walking right in and not calling first. I am also angry with myself for allowing her to ruin my precious time alone with my husband and allowing her to dictate my time, home and privacy.

Shy of coming down the stairs naked and flushed, how does one handle this without being equally as rude?

GENTLE READER:

Can't you tell these people that if you and your husband wanted to abandon all hope of privacy and have people wandering around your house whenever they like, you would have had children?

Oops, you do have children. A number of them, Miss Manners gathers. And went to a lot of trouble to get them properly occupied, only to have a nonresident grown-up making herself at home and clamoring for Mother to drop what she's doing and pay attention to her.

Politeness does not require you to comply. It was self-sacrificing (not to mention husband-sacrificing) of you to do so, but it sets a bad example. Having made your friend welcome as a drop-in guest, you had better make certain that you never again leave the door unlocked. What you could have done when caught was to call down in an alarmed voice, "Oh, it's you! I thought a stranger had broken into the house. What's wrong? Is it an emergency?" This makes the point that her visit constitutes housebreaking, and that the only excuse would have been to warn you that the house was on fire. You need not even have gone downstairs, garbed or ungarbed. A quick "Sorry, I'm busy—can you let yourself out and phone me later?" would be a proper response to an improper action.

Miss Manners is glad you resisted the temptation to embarrass the intruder by making clear what she had interrupted. When people are as cheeky as your visitor, you can't be sure that they wouldn't enjoy the drama and drop by again for another show.

⌒ Receiving While Watching Television ⌒

DEAR MISS MANNERS:

My husband and I had friends over for dinner and to visit and he insisted on having the TV on while we were chatting. They don't come to our house very often. I think it is rude and he says there is nothing wrong with it. What is the proper etiquette?

GENTLE READER:

To do what? To make it clear to people that you expect to be so bored by them that you have taken the precaution of supplying yourself with other entertainment in their presence? The only proper way to do this, Miss Manners is afraid, is to refrain from receiving visitors.

~ Receiving While Reclining ~

DEAR MISS MANNERS:

Are there any circumstances in which one can receive guests while in bed? I'm not kidding, and I'm not talking about sex, either. French kings used to hold court while they were in bed, you know. Obviously, a person in a hospital can receive friends while lying in bed. So why can't I, who spend most of my free time reading, working, or telephoning in bed, ask guests who drop by the house to come upstairs and visit me when I'm comfortably in bed? What's the difference?

GENTLE READER:

A general rule of hospitality is that the host does not enjoy anything that he does not also offer to his guest. The difference between you and a hospital patient is that the patient may safely assume that his visitor does not wish to be given whatever it was that landed him in bed.

~ Welcoming ~

DEAR MISS MANNERS:

Finally, finally, the dreadful people who lived next door have sold their house and moved away, taking their rotten children, their foul dog, and several of my electric appliances with them. There is very little turnover in this neighborhood, so this salvation is more than I had dared hope. It is generally a friendly area, however, and I would like to get off to a good start with the people who bought the house. The real estate agent says they are nice people; how can I be helpful without making them think that my house is an extension of their house?

GENTLE READER:

It is a charming old custom for the residents of a neighborhood to welcome newcomers. The reason it is so charming is that the established resident gets an early look at the impossible furniture and worse colors with which the newcomers are ruining a fine old house. When you perform this gesture, it is useful to be prepared to give out addresses and telephone numbers of shops and services for which the newcomer might ask. Otherwise, you might be tempted to offer to lend your things and "find out" whom to see about what.

It is also wise to refrain from providing the useful service of characterizing the people the newcomer is likely to meet. Tempting as it is to be in there first with the gossip, you should remember that the new person's loyalties are still to be developed. It would be a disservice to your established neighbors to make them feel they had to run *you* out of the neighborhood and call on the people who will replace you.

～ Inspecting ～

DEAR MISS MANNERS:

What excuse should one use when visiting a house in the neighborhood—open for sale—when one is not interested in buying but only interested in satisfying his curiosity as to price and furnishings?

GENTLE READER:

"Thank you, but I was hoping to find something with less closet space."

～ Shrieking ～

DEAR MISS MANNERS:

Some friends of mine have purchased an old town house at an insane price and are "doing it over" with skylights, hanging plants, exposed bricks—the works. They are extremely proud of it and gave a series of small parties after they moved in, to show it off. At the one I was invited to, they took us for a long tour, pointing out every feature. During this house tour, a mouse ran across the kitchen. Several people shrieked, and everybody was terribly embarrassed. The hosts didn't say anything, but it obviously spoiled the whole effect. I felt sorry for them, but what could I have done? Was there any way to cover up after all that screaming we all did?

GENTLE READER:

You could have said, "I'm sorry I yelled, but your gerbil startled me."

Houseguests

IT IS EASY to be the perfect houseguest. All you have to do is to remember everything you've learned in the last few years about being totally honest, in touch with your feelings, able to communicate your needs and committed to doing what makes you feel comfortable. And then forget it.

The perfect houseguest is often dishonest, in touch with others' feelings at the expense of his own, able to refrain from communicating his needs and cheerful about doing what bores him. Contrary to current popular belief, such behavior can be quite pleasurable to those who indulge in it, and leads to fulfillment, happiness and invitations to beach condominiums, shooting parties and yachts. However, it takes practice. For example, what do you suppose the perfect houseguest says when asked what time he generally gets up in the morning?

1. "Noon, and I like absolute quiet until then, if you don't mind"; or
2. "Oh, I'm up and around any time—just call me, why don't you, when you're having breakfast."

What do you suppose the perfect houseguest likes for breakfast?

1. "Fresh orange juice, buckwheat pancakes with real syrup, none of that synthetic stuff, croissants with butter and bitter marmalade, not the sweet kind, and good, rich coffee with heavy cream"; or
2. "Oh, anything. What are you having?"

What does a perfect houseguest like to do for recreation? That depends. If the host suggests family relay races, that is what he especially likes. If there are no suggestions, what does he say?

1. "Do you know any interesting people, anybody I might have heard of, you could ask over?" or
2. "Just to take it easy, if you don't mind. I brought a book I've been dying to get into."

And so on through the day, up until bedtime, which occurs when the perfect house-guest has observed that the hosts are looking sleepy. The only critical observation that perfect houseguests may allow themselves is to notice quietly what the household lacks in the way of material comforts—in order that they may purchase that item and send it as a way of thanking the hosts after their visit. What is the reward for all this selfless-ness? Why, to be invited back, of course, in order to do it all over again.

Long-term Houseguests

You have all heard what dear Benjamin Franklin said about what happens to guests and fish after three days. He was speaking from the point of view of the host. Miss Manners will now address the problem from the point of view of guests and fish.

Guests and fish tend to hang around where it is possible for them to swim. People who have beach houses or pools sometimes have bursts of generous hospital-ity, and it is in the interests of the recipients to ensure their not living to regret this. Anyone ought to be able to be a good houseguest for that three-day period, which is why God invented the weekend. One's time is more or less planned, and one's hosts are able to sustain an act of graciousness and calm, postponing weeping over the antique you broke or barking orders at their children, until the house is theirs again.

Long periods require greater variety of emotion, and the considerate long-term houseguest will assist in making his hosts feel at home. Otherwise, he will quickly find that he is. The most helpful way of doing this is to plan frequent absences from the house. These should be announced in advance so that there are no uncertainties about whether the guest is coming to dinner or other family events. If necessary, the guest should invent excuses and go off by himself, to give the family opportunities to cry, argue or relax in privacy. If, however, unscheduled eruptions take place while the guest is present, the guest should ignore them and disappear. Under no circum-stances should a guest take a side in family differences or offer suggestions for improving the family's way of living. All appeals for such help must be resisted. Ultimately, nobody wants a live-in family counselor, however sympathetic or fair.

It should be unnecessary to mention that the houseguest should create no addi-tional work for the family. It is his obligation to keep the guest room clean, whether he likes it that way himself or not. Even behind a closed door, a guest room with an unmade bed or newspaper-strewn floor acts as a reproach to the hosts. The guest must share the chores, but not by running about asking "Can I help?" and taking no for an answer. By simple observation, one should be able to notice what needs doing, and wheedle permission to do it. Preparing meals, cleaning up, baby-sitting and occasional grocery shopping—selecting what the family likes, and paying for it—are activities that make a guest seem worth keeping.

So do little presents, given at perhaps the rate of one a week. The best present a guest can make after he has left and written thanks is his silence. This must consist not only of the wonderful silence that pervades the house when he leaves, but of his own precious silence in refusing to divulge the family secrets to others.

⟶ Fish Footnote ⟵

DEAR MISS MANNERS:

Note a mistake. Samuel Johnson, not Benjamin Franklin, made the comment about fish and guests smelling after three days.

GENTLE READER:

Miss Manners begs your pardon. Dear Mr. Franklin not only made the remark, but at least two variations on it; but, then, so did nearly everyone else, except possibly dear Dr. Johnson. Miss Manners' usual haphazard research reveals that the witticism was first made by Plautus, in about 200 B.C., and was perfected by John Lyly in 1580, but it was also attributed to half a dozen others.

⟶ Impolite Houseguests ⟵

DEAR MISS MANNERS:

All summer long, we share our house on a lake with friends, most of whom come year after year to waterski, swim, kayak, play badminton, etc. Among them are a wonderful couple with three bright, happy, well behaved children—but they are not good guests.

I let guests know that I need everyone to pitch in with household tasks. This couple is reasonable as long as they are given some direction, but thoughtless when it comes to going beyond the directions. Other guests understand that when they leave, someone else is certain to be arriving, so they put clean sheets on the bed, lightly clean their bathroom sink and shower and empty their wastebaskets. This couple instead leaves their room as if they were leaving a hotel room, trash strewn around the room, not even always in the wastebasket, bathroom dirty, and so on, effectively making me their maid. They use the phone for social calls of up to an hour, in spite of my repeated hints that someone else is waiting to use the phone or that we might be expecting a call. Moreover, they have left us with phone bills exceeding $80 for the week.

I realized that they simply did not understand houseguest etiquette the time they said, "We thought we'd invite our friends, Lora and Schnora, to your house for the day. You could teach them water skiing. You'd really like them." Not being prone to suffer in silence, I explained that although I may spend two hours a day taking our guests and family waterskiing, teaching total strangers would be a time consuming and intensive affair and I would prefer to spend my free time working or being with my children. They were genuinely surprised.

Never in five years have these particular guests arrived with a gift. Frankly, I am not looking for gifts; a number of gifts that well intentioned guests have given us, we could do without. It is just one more indicator that this couple do not give consideration to being good guests. They do sometimes buy groceries and take my children with theirs to a fun activity like miniature golf, which allows me to get some work done. I want to continue our friendship with this couple, but given that they seemed to have missed proper instruction as children on being good guests, is it my job to instruct them year after year? Do I have no choice but not to invite them in the future?

GENTLE READER:

That is the solution to guests who have no redeeming qualities. However, you like these people enough, and have entertained them enough, to put them into a special category of guest: intimates of the household.

That is the way they seem to feel, when they assume such family privileges as inviting other guests and freely using the telephone. All you have to do is to respond in the same spirit. Intimates of the household (others in this category include visiting grown-up children of the house) know they are dearly welcomed, so they can take clear and polite instruction rather than hints:

"I'm so sorry you're leaving. Here are some clean sheets and a trash bag—I won't have time to straighten up for the next arrivals. I'd love to meet your friends some other time, but I can't deal with more guests now. You'd better bring your own telephone—we need to keep ours free."

~ *Bedroom Assignments* ~

DEAR MISS MANNERS:

My son, who is gay, will be visiting my wife and me for a weekend in the summer, and is bringing his boyfriend along. They have been together for two years, but have never visited before. When my daughter visits with her boyfriend, they share the same room.

I am unsure if the boys want to share a room, or if this arrangement will be uncomfortable to my wife. I don't want to raise an issue if there isn't one, so the solution I have come up with is to make up both guest rooms and let my son decide, and let my wife know that this should be our son's decision.

GENTLE READER:

No, you really don't want to raise the issue, as the example of your wife's not minding straight cohabitation is so close at hand. Even your solution goes a tad too far.

All you need do is to tell your wife that you have made up both bedrooms. Miss Manners trusts it will not be necessary to dissuade her from patrolling the halls at night. Attempting to direct the intimate activities of one's adult guests always leads to disaster, even when the hosts are the parents of the houseguests. The most we can do to houseguests is to regulate their social conduct. In other words, you can assign people separate rooms, but you cannot insist that they stay in them after dark.

~ *Timing* ~

DEAR MISS MANNERS:

I have some friends with a weekend place in the country. There's nothing much to do there, but it's restful, and I enjoy staying there when they invite me. The problem is that they are late risers, and I get up early. They tell me to make my own breakfast, which I would be happy to do, but the minute they hear me running the water for my coffee, one of them comes out—sort of grumpily—and makes breakfast for me. I've taken to staying in my room, reading and pretending I'm asleep. How should I time getting up so I don't inconvenience them?

GENTLE READER:

Time your emergence from your room with the first sound of running water in the bathroom. That way, you should inconvenience no one (except yourself, of course, because you will find the bathroom occupied).

Downtime

DEAR MISS MANNERS:

A house guest brought along her personal computer and spent much time online, receiving and sending email. I was taught that as a guest, one used the hosts' 'phone only for brief, necessary calls—not tie up someone's 'phone line for an hour at a time. I wonder what a guest would think if I sat down and wrote out five letters to friends in his or her presence? What are your thoughts on this?

GENTLE READER:

That writing letters used to be considered a major activity at house parties. You probably remember this too, as you indicate by use of an apostrophe that the word "phone" is the instrument's nickname.

As Miss Manners recalls, "I'm afraid I have some letters to write" was the euphemism guests used when they wanted to escape to their rooms. The one used by hosts when they wanted to escape from their guests was, "If you have letters to write, this would be a good time." Furthermore, the hosts were expected to provide the materials, which is to say paper, pen, ink and little desks in the guest rooms. Guests were expected not to abuse hospitality, for example by stockpiling these items for future use or writing letters when they should be at meals or other planned activities.

Let us now translate this into modern times:

Houseguests still need some private time, and are allowed to communicate with the outside world. But they should not allow this to cut into the sociability for which they presumably accepted the invitation. They should also understand that the telephone line was not put at their exclusive disposal, and use only a very modest share of it.

Laundry

DEAR MISS MANNERS:

We have recently had two different house guests and they removed their linens in different manners. My question is: Which is correct?

Guest One: Removed the linens (sheets and blankets), left them folded on top of the bed and then "made the bed" putting the bedspread and pillows in place.

Guest Two: Removed the sheets, put them on top of my washing machine, then "made the bed" as described above.

GENTLE READER:

The guests are both fine, having put their linens where you would find them and left the room looking neat. But Miss Manners is wondering whether it is quite polite of you to have two such considerate guests when some people haven't had any.

⌒ Bread-and-Butter Letters ⌒

DEAR MISS MANNERS:

Is there ever a point at which it is no longer necessary to write a thank you note after a brief visit? My beloved and I have visited his best friends six, seven times over the last year and a half, usually staying overnight since they live a few hours away. I always express many thanks during and at the end of the visit, and I am beginning to feel slightly stiff continuing to send a bread and butter note (signed only by me). I fear that I'm coming across a bit prim, though my notes have become more casually written, since I now consider this couple my friends, too.

If I asked him, I know my sweetheart would advise me to not write, since he speaks with them frequently and thanks them by phone for both of us. At what point, if ever, is that sufficient? (All parties are 30 years old, if that makes any difference.)

GENTLE READER:

The point you mention is known as Taking People for Granted.

In one sense it is comforting to be able to take people for granted. Miss Manners has never known why, for example, it is considered wrong to take one's spouse for granted. Is it more stimulating to wonder every night whether your spouse will be coming home?

But when people complain of this, as they do, they mean that they are being cut off from appreciation and other pleasant feedback that those who are presumably less important to you get to enjoy. When friends put themselves out for you, as hosts do for houseguests, they are not charmed with the idea that it is no more than you have come to expect.

⌒ Reciprocation ⌒

DEAR MISS MANNERS:

When our family was vacationing in California last year, cousins of mine invited me, my wife and our two daughters to spend a weekend with them. This summer they will be traveling not far from where we live, and I would like to reciprocate their hospitality. But we simply don't have the room for them that they had for us in their more spacious house. What can I do?

GENTLE READER:

Returning hospitality does not mean returning it in kind, but in spirit. Miss Manners is appalled at the number of people who fail to reciprocate because they cannot match the standard of their hosts.

So why don't you build an addition on your house?

No, no, Miss Manners is kidding. Tell your friends effusively how thrilled you are that they are coming and how sorry you are that you don't have room to have them stay over, but that you can recommend a comfortable hotel or bed and breakfast nearby and that you want them to take their meals with you.

⌖ Payment ⌖

DEAR MISS MANNERS:

I need to know if it is appropriate for a guest (especially family) to give money to help with food, bills, or what have you after they visit for a week-end or a couple of weeks. My mom always feels that you should give the home owners something to help make up for the extra electricity or food bills.

I don't agree. I have had sixteen family members at once in my house, and I don't expect them to buy anything. It is a once a year visit, and I just get prepared.

As a daughter visiting some weekends, should I pay? Even if I visit an aunt with my husband and our three children and help buy groceries because she is a single parent of two, should I leave her money when I leave?

GENTLE READER:

Of course you shouldn't be paying your mother, or any other hostess, to visit her. But Miss Manners is wondering whether you should be helping to support her.

Considerate guests, even if they are the hostess's children, have plenty to do without insulting their hosts by indicating that their precious gift of hospitality has a price tag on it. They should clean up after themselves, help with the additional chores, provide treats and, for extended stays, take over the responsibility for an occasional meal, either by taking their hosts out or by doing the shopping and cooking.

They must also reciprocate, preferably without checking to see whether the electricity their guests use is no greater an amount than they used at that person's house. However, if your relatives are in need, you should find a way to help them financially, without tying it to any visits you may make.

HOUSE-SITTING

Everybody knows how to behave in another person's house when the owner is looking, Miss Manners trusts. Now it is time to learn how to behave in someone else's house when the owner is not at home. This is not an etiquette lesson for housebreakers, although goodness knows they behave badly enough. Miss Manners is addressing this to house sitters.

House-sitting ought to be the ideal arrangement between the haves and the have nots. People with property usually lack the confidence to leave it unguarded. People without property usually lack property. The two groups seem made for each other. What prevents house-sitting from being one of our major solutions to social problems is the basic distrust that the landed have for the lacklands. People who are temporarily vacating their houses tend not to match themselves up with those who simultaneously are being evicted. They choose, instead, people who were born members of the propertied class, but are temporarily propertyless, through restlessness or youth.

This identification of class presents a difficulty. House sitters who are friends of the house owners, or offspring of such friends, confuse house-sitting with house-guesting. These are two different occupations, although the same person may perform both in the same house at different times. A houseguest is supposed to make his presence more desirable than his absence. A house sitter need only be more desirable than those whom his presence is intended to discourage.

However, he must keep the odds on his side. If you leave your house empty during your absence, it is possible that it will be undisturbed, and you will find it just as you left it. So the amount of breakage, disarray and snooping done by the house sitter should not exceed the amount likely to be done by housebreakers—after it is averaged in with the possibility of nobody's touching the house.

Neatness counts only when the owner is back to see the state of the house, and therefore house sitters do their straightening on the day before the announced return. They should bear in mind that travel plans do get changed and home owners are given to walking in without notice as if they owned the place. The rules of breakage are not the same as for a houseguest, who need only replace small items if the host fails to protest after the second offer. House sitters must always replace what they have broken, in kind or in money. What is more, they must confess.

Invasions of privacy must be confessed only if they are going to come out anyway. If you have ruined the house owner's reputation with his neighbors or the police, you might just as well tell your side of the story in the most favorable way. If he is likely to meet people you have entertained in the house, their names should be mentioned. The fact that you showed them all the private rooms need not be, as this can be classified as getting lost on the way to the bathroom. Under no circumstances should a house sitter confront a house owner with information gleaned from the house owner's diary.

Unpleasant Facts of Life

MAJOR AND MINOR ILLNESSES

~ Ignoring the Ill ~

OF ALL the qualities that ladies and gentlemen are most proud of cultivating, the very nastiest is squeamishness toward tragedy. It is a common and even natural reaction. People have an instinctive revulsion at seeing the ravages of illness or decay, probably from a terror of being infected, whether or not that is a realistic danger.

As one who will choose civilized behavior over natural instinct three times out of three, Miss Manners says that this feeling must be stamped out. It should certainly not be admitted, as people do when they confess, "I just can't bear to look at him," or, in a more advanced form, "I'm sure she wants us to remember her as she was," as if they were confessing to fastidious taste.

What they are really talking about is indulging a minor quirk of their own, in order to deny the deepest human claims of people they have cared about when they were strong. Base neglect of the dying cannot be interpreted as refined. This is the one area in which the natural human propensity to grow callous may be used to advantage. If people are not protected in childhood from ministering to their declining relatives, they grow used to the presence of human decay. Soon the unpleasantness is hardly noticed, and one learns that great lesson of valuing people for their positive attributes, rather than focusing on their disabilities.

Patience and compassion develop to take the place of squeamishness. Horror of the situation is replaced by pleasure in continuing to enjoy, as well as to serve, the human being. Self-satisfaction expands into the area that would otherwise have been occupied by guilt. "I did everything I could" is really a much finer feeling.

Coaching the Ill

"Get well soon!" is an odd exhortation to fling at the sick, when you come to think about it. It isn't as though people who feel rotten don't realize that they would feel better if they recovered.

In her right mind, Miss Manners does not indulge in examining the literal meanings of conventional niceties. There are enough people at this already and enough foolish suggestions about replacing innocuous pleasantries with statements that accurately convey the wishes of the speaker. So why does she suddenly feel funny when she hears that upbeat command "Get well!"?

It is because people are expanding upon it in ways that show that they do mean it literally as a command. They mean: Take responsibility for having been struck down as a result of the way you eat, the way you exercise, the way you work and your attitude toward life. They mean: Don't just do whatever your doctor tells you, but find out about your illness, look it up on the Internet, ask around, question your treatment. They mean: Talk about it, find yourself a support group of other people who've had this, bare your heart to your friends and relatives, let us know that you are facing your fears. They mean: Don't just lie there; do something!

But these people don't feel well. Miss Manners hopes they reply to these hearty exhortations by saying "Thank you" and perhaps, "Oh, dear, I'm afraid I'm supposed to be getting a nap now, but you were so nice to come by." She hopes they aren't voicing a peevish "No, I like it this way, leave me alone."

She is well aware that there are many people who do feel better when they change their habits, acquire some expertise about their health and talk about their condition and their worries with others who share them or care about them. Her objection is not in their doing so; it is in their being bullied to do so. There are so many aspects to illness that curtail the dignity and independence of being an adult, that they should not have to undergo superfluous bossing.

Quizzing the Ill

DEAR MISS MANNERS:

I suffer from several chronic illnesses. Neither illness is curable, but I have hope for the future.

I am in pain every day, and am quite fatigued. I have been made to quit so many of my hobbies and interests, as well as my job and volunteer work. My weeks are filled with visits to various physicians; I must take quite a lot of medications, and I require a lot of rest. Many days, I do not feel up to going out, but when I do, I take great care in my grooming and dress, so that I do not look haggard and sick. I am happy to stay close to home, but inevitably, some errand or social obligation will require me to go out.

How do I respond to people's demands to know what is wrong with me? I do not like to discuss my illness, so I tend to say as little as possible. Also, how do I respond to the shocking and awful things people say to me?

Some people demand to know what "they" are doing for me, why aren't I cured by now, and infer that my physicians are a bunch of charlatans. I have been accused of being a hypochondriac, needing a facial or a vacation, and told that if I would just have a baby or get a job, that I wouldn't have time to be sick. I have been told that my illness does not exist, and that I need mental health counseling. These outbursts are made by family members, "friends," and acquaintances of my husband.

When I am tired and in pain, these comments seem especially cruel. It would be easy to be snappish, or to remind these folks to mind their own business, but it is more painful to me to think that I have offended someone by my reply. How can I respond without alienating these folks?

GENTLE READER:

Like you, Miss Manners would very much not like to hear from people who believe the universal treatment is to talk about one's illnesses to whoever is brash enough to ask, and that the only reason for refusing to do so is a false shame that stands in the way of recovery. Furthermore, she thinks that people who practice medicine without licenses at least ought to observe the courtesy of not undermining the treatment of their legitimate colleagues.

As you say, it would be easy to be snappish back—but rude. It will be easier to be polite if you make it a practice to focus on their motivation—generously presuming it to be concern for you rather than nosiness—and to steadfastly ignore the rest.

Keep repeating "I appreciate your concern," to whatever they say. Any attempt to explain your disease or defend your treatment admits them to a discussion of your case for which they are not eligible, socially or professionally.

~ *Visiting the Ill* ~

What a satisfying act of charity it is to visit the sick. One need only pop unannounced into a hospital room, hand out a dripping bundle of flowers, reassure the patient that his or her bath, dinner, nap or whatever need not be interrupted during one's stay—just his privacy—and commiserate with some such conventional phrase as "Oh, you look awful!" One can also put things in perspective by reciting the history of one's own greater ills, and offer practical assistance by explaining treatments at variance with what the patient is undergoing that would be more beneficial.

There are those who so much enjoy performing this service that they faithfully visit hospitalized acquaintances with whom they are not moved to socialize during those people's bouts of good health. Such kindness is not always fully appreciated by those upon whom it is visited. No wonder sick people have an unfortunate reputation for being cranky.

One must humor them, however, so Miss Manners feels obliged to require the charitable to curtail their good offices somewhat to meet the whims of the unhealthy. The first rule is that one requests the invitation to make a hospital visit, and accepts no for an answer. Many people who are hospitalized do not feel up to enduring being cheered up. Those who have limitations on their energy or on the number of visitors or time for visiting may prefer to devote these resources to intimates of their own choice rather than the voluntary visitor.

Visits should last no more than half an hour, and twenty minutes is ten minutes better. The question "Am I tiring you?" is better not asked, as the likelihood of the answer's being both honest and polite is small. It is customary, but not obligatory, to bring a small present on a hospital visit. Living vegetation should be self-contained, which is to say that one brings potted plants or flowers in vases. Other presents that hospital patients have told Miss Manners they especially appreciated included bottles of champagne, books, games, body rub for massages, a liverwurst sandwich with a can of beer, and a bottle of gin. It is considered improper to bring anything that the doctor has declared likely to help kill the patient, however much the patient may appreciate it.

The difficulties of the patient, whether or not they are discussed, must be acknowledged to be the ranking current woes, and it is rude to attempt to top them with one's own or anyone else's tragedies, past or present. It is the patient who decrees whether the illness is to be discussed and who does any talking on the subject. The rule that it is bad manners to discuss one's operation, or anything else to do with physical well-being, applies later, but not to those still hospitalized. The visitor may either chuckle or cluck-cluck at the patient's description, depending on whether it is narrated with humor or with pathos, but opinions, anecdotes or advice offered by the visitor can only end in conversational disaster. It is of surprisingly little comfort to be told that one's sickness is considered by others to be either more serious or more trivial than one has oneself decided that it is. And if the visitor is reminded of her own operation or his once miraculous recovery, the patient may sink back on the pillow with closed eyes.

A hospital patient has no obligation to keep visitors entertained; on the contrary,

When visitors cease to be entertaining, the host may ask them to leave. Hospitalization confers the official status necessary to legitimize errant behavior, and a sick person with a healthy attitude will seize the chance.

∽ The Farewell Scene ∽

DEAR MISS MANNERS:

My husband and I have a very difficult and heart-wrenching problem. We only just learned of a dear friend's terminal illness, and he is not expected to live more than a few weeks. I would love to write to this gentleman and his wife and let them know how meaningful his friendship has been, but we don't want to intrude or be inappropriate. Also, in the interest of time, if we did send such a missive, would doing it via email be in poor taste? Your speedy reply would be much appreciated.

GENTLE READER:

Many times people do deliver accolades for the about-to-depart. Ill people sometimes develop a wryly cynical attitude about nice-knowing-you letters, especially from people who have not otherwise been in touch with them.

Miss Manners does not mention this to discourage you from writing. It is only to caution you that there are indeed taste problems to take into account. This is one of those rare instances in which casual is better, and so although this refers primarily to the tone, email would not be unsuitable. The idea is to avoid sounding funereal while your friend is alive. Saying that you are thinking of him, perhaps invoking some happy memories, is fine; summing up—whether you are summing up his life or the end value of the friendship—is not.

∽ The Death Watch ∽

DEAR MISS MANNERS:

My husband's 87-year-old father, a patient in a nursing home under Hospice care, has some dementia, but is lucid quite a bit of the time. We walked in on a conversation at the foot of his bed between my husband's younger sister, her husband and one of the staff nurses, who were discussing specific "time frames" in full voice as to his life expectancy.

We were shocked! I gently tapped the nurse on the shoulder, as her back was towards me and whispered, "Don't you think this should be discussed somewhere else?"

At that point, the brother-in-law said, again in full voice, "Oh, he knows."

Of course he "knows." Hospice has a compassionate & realistic approach when it comes to keeping patients apprised.

But we felt that this was an egregiously vulgar conversation to conduct within earshot of the patient.

My husband and I both began our college years in pre-med & later switched majors. In those days, we were always taught as a matter of dignity and respect to the patient to watch our conversation in the patient's presence. This universal dictum applied to patients who were in deep coma and hadn't responded to crude stimuli for years.

On a more mundane level, we feel this is a vulgar violation of everyday manners. This event has caused quite a rift in the family.

GENTLE READER:

There is nothing petty about the etiquette involved—and grossly violated—in this situation. It addresses the fundamental principle upon which the entire noble field of manners is based: respect for human beings, simply because they are human beings.

Yet paradoxically, it suspends the usual advantage that manners have over morals, namely that if you don't get caught, it doesn't count.

The violation is flaunting the belief that the person is incapable of understanding how rudely he is being treated. Never mind whether your father-in-law was aware of this conversation or of his situation. What your relatives did was the equivalent of thumbing their noses at a blind person.

The Deathbed Scene

DEAR MISS MANNERS:

Is it proper to invite one's family and close friends to the hospital, preoperation of course, in order to make one's bequests?

GENTLE READER:

The deathbed family gathering is a social event of such drama and excitement that Miss Manners cannot understand why it is so seldom staged in modern times. Perhaps potential hosts don't feel up to it, or perhaps they think of it too late. Miss Manners commends your effort to keep such a vital custom alive.

Here are some guidelines:

1. Be sure to invite friends and relatives who are incompatible, if not sworn enemies. This is no time to consider who will be comfortable with whom. The

thought of life's fragility, as demonstrated by you, should keep them from killing one another, and it should give you a sense of peace to watch them all trying to control their jealousy and greed.

2. It is not necessary, in fact it is unseemly, for you to provide any refreshment for your guests. You are feeding them hope, which is what people live on.

3. Keep your bequests vague. "I want to give you my most ancient and treasured possession" is better than "I'm leaving you my baseball card collection." You don't want your actual death to be an anticlimax.

4. Omit none of your guests from your speech. It is an ordinary social convention that no person should be left out, and it continues to apply in the deathbed scene. It is, after all, unforgivable to ask someone to make a special trip in order to be snubbed. In the spirit of vagueness described in (3), you may say, instead, "You, Cousin Atherton, may be assured that I have remembered everything you have done for me since we were children."

5. It is not necessary, after this type of social event, for the host to make a quick exit. You may be happy to hear that it is perfectly correct to recover from the operation and, when you have regained your strength, to have a relapse and stage the entire event again, provided you vary the details to keep everyone alert.

MESSY EMOTIONS AND MINOR EMOTIONAL DISTRESS

"You wouldn't want me to pretend to something I don't really feel, would you? You don't want me to have to put on an act when I'm feeling rotten, do you?"

Miss Manners is always puzzled by such questions. Her answer is, "Why, yes. Please." She spends the better part of her life (never mind how she spends the worse part) trying to persuade people to fake such feelings as delight upon receiving useless presents, curiosity about the welfare of the terminally boring, pleasure in the success of competitors and sincerity in the wish of prosperity for all people, even those who dress offensively. She also expects everyone to give a rousing imitation of having loved the school concert.

What the world needs is more false cheer. And less honest crabbiness. Miss Manners does not dispute your right to feel miserable, if that is what makes you happy. She has been known to get a bit tetchy herself on days when the air is thick with rudeness, and to have to retire with a cool compress on her fevered brow.

It is when misery starts issuing invitations for company that she objects. To have a dear friend who will occasionally listen to a recital of woes, in exchange for services in kind, is a blessing. To require this regularly, or to impose it upon those who have not volunteered for such tedious duty, is the sin of adding to the total of unhappiness on earth. The proper place for a person who is out of sorts is out of sight. If one does not feel up to putting on a good act, one should ring down the curtain. Or at least post the notice. Tersely polite warnings, such as "I wouldn't do that right now if I were you, dear," should be heeded.

For many people, however, out of sorts is a geographical location where they set up housekeeping. They may have had a genuine tragedy in their lives, or they may merely enjoy the universal conviction that no one suffers more from the unjustness of life than oneself. Whatever the cause, the air of grievance looks the same, once it has settled on the face. That is the time to put on a false face.

Please notice that Miss Manners is trying hard to refrain from pointing out that there are people who overcome adversity with courage, bravery and determination, who turn their attention resolutely away from their own dissatisfactions and toward bettering the lot of others. She has been told that this example is of no use to those who cannot manage that exemplary feat, so she is not demanding true cheerfulness.

Naturally, the more skillful the performance of false cheer, the more pleasing the effect is upon one's public and on that private audience to whom one owes even more. It is also true that the semblance of happiness eventually, by some alchemy of the spirit, turns genuine. But even the crudest effort is better than tossing one's problems to others, like an unexpected volleyball aimed at the stomach.

The answer to "How are you?" is not "Uhhh" or "How should I be?" It is not the answer that a gentleman of Miss Manners' acquaintance received when he posed the polite question to an elderly guest at his wedding, and was told, "Oh, not so good since Bill died." Bill had died eight years previously.

 Sharing

DEAR MISS MANNERS:

What do you do when you have been having a perfectly respectable conversation about airport security with your seatmate during a flight, but he begins to volunteer information about the way he was abused as a child out of the blue? How can one express sympathy without seeming to wish to hear more? I felt very uncomfortable listening to these confidences from a complete stranger.

GENTLE READER:

Then reply, "I'm very sorry to hear that. But to get back to what you were saying, don't you think there is any way they can speed things up without compromising security?"

You will note that this is minimal sympathy, second only perhaps to "You're kidding! But is that drinks cart ever going to get to us?" Perhaps you will accuse Miss Manners of callousness. However, if people are going to make small talk of their most personal confessions, they should expect to have these treated as small talk. Any serious show of sympathy would be acceptance of the serious job of confessor and consoler.

⌒ Sounding the Alarm ⌒

DEAR MISS MANNERS:

I have a small circle of loyal friends, and I think I am mature enough to understand how fortunate I am to be thus endowed. My problem is that they always call me when they are depressed, discouraged, angry, bored, or suicidal. My job is demanding, and my day is long. How do I handle their moody, frustrating (and basically selfish) ramblings without estranging them or sending myself over the edge?

GENTLE READER:

Loyal friends do respond in one another's hours of need, but if these happen every hour, the loyal friends have a right to become suspicious. If your friends cannot diagnose their minor ailments properly, you must learn to distinguish their whining spells from their emergencies. A friend who calls because he is out of sorts, at loose ends, at sixes and sevens or in any other states encountered during the normal ups and downs of life should simply be told that you are too busy to talk now. No apologies are necessary. If you occasionally allow him to gripe at you during your free time, you are more than fulfilling the requirements of friendship. You might try cultivating people of more cheerful dispositions. They make wonderful friends, especially when you feel blue.

⌒ A Phobia ⌒

DEAR MISS MANNERS:

My daughter and I share a severe strolling musicians phobia. I hope you can help us learn to cope with this problem gracefully.

When dining out and a strolling mariachi band inflicts themselves upon us in midmeal, what on earth is the proper etiquette for our response? They make us very uncomfortable, and we don't know whether to stop eating until they leave our table, letting our food get cold and soggy, or to continue eating, which seems extremely rude. Do we make eye contact and smile, or attempt to continue with our private conversations? Do we tip each of them or just the singer? Also, if you tip them, will they go away or will that just encourage them to stay and play longer?

We've tried it both ways and sometimes they seem to be determined to play until you tip them and, at other times, when we tip them, they want to play longer to give us our money's worth. As you can see, this can be a very delicate matter.

GENTLE READER:

Miss Manners seems to recall an indelicate song on the subject by Mr. Tom Lehrer. She feels it relieves her from any temptation to treat the subject with levity.

You could select a cuisine from a music-hating culture, of course. Or a restaurant whose musicians are sensitive enough to understand that a small shake of the head, accompanied by a regretful smile, means "Thank you, but we came here to talk."

Otherwise, your best chance is not to tip the musicians, but to tip the person in charge of the dining room with the instruction, "My daughter and I wish to be left alone, so please see to it that the band doesn't approach us." Miss Manners trusts that this person's stares, occasioned by his concluding either that this is not your daughter, or that you have come here to attempt to talk her out of marrying the town drunk, will bother you less than the music.

DISGUSTING HABITS

"Noises You Can Make," we'll call this problem. Miss Manners is referring, of course, to noises you can make inadvertently, and the proper responses which should be made advertently. There are three categories of such noises:

1. Sympathetic noises. These are noises that evoke sympathy, not noises that express sympathy, such as cluck-cluck, an unharmonious sound which is nevertheless made on purpose, in response to such statements as "My daughter's dropping out of college; she says she's going to major in Life." One sympathetic noise is the sneeze, and the correct response is, of course, "God bless you," or any foreign equivalent which might comfort the sneezer and which the sneezed-at feels comfortable pronouncing. Another is the repeated cough,

to which the proper response is "Are you all right?" The problem of answering is supposed to take the person's mind and throat off his cough. These responses are made only to adult sneezers or coughers. If a child sneezes, one says "Don't you have a handkerchief?" And if a child coughs, one says "Didn't I tell you not to go out without your knee warmers?"

2. Acceptable noises. These are noises such as burping or the sounds accompanying choking, to which the response should come from the noisemaker himself, provided that the choking was not complete, in which case he is absolved of all social responsibility except that of having left his papers in order. Society acknowledges that these noises are made from time to time, but does not dignify them with a response. The offender says "Excuse me," and the subject is considered closed.

3. Unacceptable noises. Miss Manners does not plan to mention them, chiefly because they are unmentionable, but you all know who you are. What they are. At any rate, these are noises that are acknowledged by neither the noisemaker nor the noise recipient, because socially they do not exist. The practice of staring hard at the person next to you when, for instance, your own stomach has given off a loud rumble, is therefore to be condemned on grounds of etiquette as well as morals.

You will notice that there is a noise left uncategorized, namely the hiccup. Technically, the hiccup is not socially unacceptable; nevertheless, people should try to ignore it. A person who is hiccupping has enough troubles, especially if he is foolishly pretending nothing is wrong and trying to prove it by talking soberly in between the hics, without a bunch of crazy people trying to pour water down his throat or clap a paper bag over his head.

⁓ Burping ⁓

DEAR MISS MANNERS:

I know that it is common courtesy to cover one's mouth when coughing or sneezing, but is it also necessary to do so when burping? My husband is irritated if I burp too loud without covering my mouth or trying to cover it up somehow. Is there a polite way to handle burps?

GENTLE READER:

Technically speaking, it is not polite to burp at all. It is strange, but nevertheless generally recognized, that some inevitable natural phenomena, such as coughing, are socially acceptable, and others, such as burping, are not. (Perhaps it is because society recognizes the necessity of breathing but ignores digestion as much as possible.) The correct thing to do, therefore, is to treat the burp as if it were a socially acceptable cough. In other words, cover it up by making your hand into a fist and placing the thumb side against your mouth.

~ Sneezing ~

DEAR MISS MANNERS:

Obviously, you should use a tissue if you sneeze. But what if you can't get it out of your pocket in time? Is there any way, short of carrying it around in your hand all the time just to be prepared in case you ever sneeze, to avoid having people look at you as if you were a slob because you sneeze without using a handkerchief? I'm not talking about messy sneezes, but small, neat ones that are over when they're over.

GENTLE READER:

As the sneeze comes on, you reach for the handkerchief, and then you get it out whether or not you have managed to outrace the sneeze. Holding a handkerchief in one's hand after a sneeze is the next best thing to holding it over one's nose during the sneeze. It indicates good faith.

~ Nose-Blowing ~

DEAR MISS MANNERS:

Is it acceptable to blow your nose in a restaurant? Using a napkin? My son says it's preferable to sitting at the table sniffling. I say, get up, go to the restroom, and do it right.

Do specific circumstances matter? For example, a paper napkin after too much salsa at Taco Bell? A linen napkin in the main dining room of the Queen Elizabeth 2?

GENTLE READER:

As opposed to the Grill Room of the QE2?

Never mind. Since you were asking so many of the wrong questions, Miss Manners thought she would ask one of her own. The right question is: Where is your son's handkerchief?

The handkerchief is no more out of date than the dripping nose. Every civilized person is supposed to carry one, so as not to have to insult napkins, sleeves, curtains and hapless onlookers. Miss Manners advises you to teach him to blow his nose without noise and without exhibiting any interest afterward in the success of your temporary cure. This may not be clear, but Miss Manners does not know how to put it more plainly without doing distracting things to her own appetite. Serious nose-blowing is done in restrooms, which also feature resources for the unprepared.

DEAR MISS MANNERS:

What do you do with tissues, after you have blown your nose in them, when you are out in public or at a friend's house?

GENTLE READER:

For such occasions, you employ a cloth tissue, a clever little invention which is a square of cotton or linen that may be conveniently carried in the pocket and reused throughout the day. One should never begin the day without a fresh one of these concealed about one's person. Consider, for example, the difference this would make if you should have occasion to weep in front of others. Weeping into paper is disgusting; weeping into fine linen is romantic drama.

Cleaning the Nose

DEAR MISS MANNERS:

At an informal business meeting in a local restaurant, my colleague and luncheon companion, a well-educated man with a Ph.D. from a prestigious university who heads the state branch of a well-known non-profit organization, frequently picked his nose and then ate the results of his efforts.

I was understandably shocked and perplexed. I chose to ignore this bizarre behavior, rather than embarrass him. What should I have done?

GENTLE READER:

Pretended not to notice, and frankly, Miss Manners wishes you hadn't.

Picking the Teeth

DEAR MISS MANNERS:

I know that picking the teeth is considered gauche in this country, but other cultures are more sensible about the discomfort of food stuck in the mouth. What do you think?

GENTLE READER:

Miss Manners realizes that dislodging food from the teeth is one of life's great sensual pleasures, and believes that great sensual pleasure should be enjoyed in private.

Perspiring

DEAR MISS MANNERS:

We are a couple of college girls new in town and are concerned with what we view as an imminent problem as summer fast approaches. How does a lady discreetly deal with perspiration?

GENTLE READER:

A lady does not perspire. When dear Orson Welles was married to Rita Hayworth, someone spoke of her as "sweating," and he replied coldly, "Horses sweat. People perspire. Miss Hayworth glows." There is nothing wrong with dewy college girls. Within reason, of course.

Scratching

DEAR MISS MANNERS:

Is it permissible to scratch in public if you have a bad itch?

GENTLE READER:

What would you do if Miss Manners said no?

Cracking Knuckles

DEAR MISS MANNERS:

What do you think of cracking knuckles in public? Do you think it's unlady-like or annoying? Please reply immediately, because it is a big issue in my house.

GENTLE READER:

Cracking knuckles is unladylike, ungentlemanlike, unchildlike and unpleasant. Please insist that everyone stop it this very minute.

~ *Chewing Gum* ~

DEAR MISS MANNERS:

Would you please give me the dos and don'ts about chewing and cracking gum in public?

GENTLE READER:

Don't.

~ *Removing Saliva* ~

DEAR MISS MANNERS:

Please list some tactful ways of removing a man's saliva from your face.

GENTLE READER:

Please list some decent ways of acquiring a man's saliva on your face. If the gentleman sprayed you inadvertently to accompany enthusiastic discourse, you may step back two paces, bring out your handkerchief and go through the motions of wiping your nose, while trailing the cloth along your face to pick up whatever needs mopping along the route. If, however, the substance was acquired as a result of enthusiasm of a more intimate nature, you may delicately retrieve it with a flick of your pink tongue.

Miss Manners can't believe she said that. Please disregard that, and use the more delicate method of resting your cheek momentarily on his shoulder, until his jacket absorbs the mess.

CITIZEN PARTICIPATION

Citizen participation is such a wonderful thing that Miss Manners always wants to do something in return for the well-being of people who voluntarily give up their free time to attend civic meetings. The best thing she can think of is to go around from meeting to meeting making motions for adjournment, so that these people can go home while they still have their sanity.

In theory, the best and fairest way to run any public project is for as many people as possible who will be affected by it to gather and freely express their opinions about how it should be done. It's only in practice that this is so dreadful.

In the interest of preserving this great democratic tradition, Miss Manners would like to make a few suggestions for controlling the unfettered self-expression of the people. She is not even going to mention such breaches of courtesy as "Perhaps the gentleman will be kind enough to tell us what his qualifications are for making such a patently ridiculous suggestion?" or "Well, who asked you to move here anyway?" She assumes that no good citizen would even consider them.

The transgressions she means involve the waste of good time. Here are some matters you might consider before exercising your inalienable right to make known your deepest feelings and convictions:

1. If people do not agree with you, it is not necessarily because they do not understand your position. The reason that the same few people use most of the time at any given meeting is that they entertain this erroneous assumption. Stating your position louder after each statement of opposition occasionally wears down a few of the weaker souls, who drift off down the block, but it does not win the hearts and votes of the majority.

2. Your personal experience is only relevant up to a point, however cleverly packaged in amusing anecdotes. A story beginning "Let me tell you how we used to deal with this problem in Winnetka" is passable, but only once. Extreme caution should be exercised before telling such stories. Anecdotes in which political insight is attributed to your taxi driver, the feelings of a race or ethnic population to your cleaning woman, or in which your child is the authority on matters of education, should never be told.

3. Group therapy traditions notwithstanding, a speech at a public meeting that opens with "I'm trying to figure out exactly how I feel about this" should not be given. A person who finds himself of two minds should consider that one has canceled out the other.

4. There is no disgrace attached to finding that one's thoughts have been adequately expressed by others. Unlike in school, you do not get separate marks for class participation.

If everyone were to keep these few rules in mind, we could all do our civic duty and be home by bedtime. But perhaps Miss Manners would then need to add one more:

5. A short meeting is not necessarily a sign of public apathy.

⌒ Civil Disobedience ⌒

DEAR MISS MANNERS:

What is the proper conduct of demonstrators at White House demonstrations, and of recipients (targets) of demonstrations?

GENTLE READER:

The first obligation of the demonstrator is to be legible. Miss Manners cannot sympathize with a cause whose signs she cannot make out even with her glasses on. The next rule of conduct is that demonstrators not vent their discontent on passersby, whom they should be impressing with their goodwill and reasonableness.

As for the recipients, the proper thing is to resist the temptation to look out of a White House window. Peeking is a mistake when one may wish to declare, the next day, that one was unaware of the demonstration.

⌒ Spontaneous Demonstrations ⌒

DEAR MISS MANNERS:

How should one comport oneself at a political convention during a so-called spontaneous demonstration (a) for one's own candidate, (b) for the opposition?

GENTLE READER:

The spontaneous demonstration has, as you recognize, a strict code of behavior. In the case of one's own candidate, the correct form is to jump up and down, waving one's arms and legs, releasing balloons and tossing straw hats in the air. The facial expression should be dazed delight, the dazed part of which is not difficult to achieve when one has been more than half an hour at a national political convention, and the delighted part of which is signified by an open-mouthed smile, which, if properly done, signifies a state of pleased idiocy not otherwise seen in this country from one four-year term to the next.

Opposition to the candidate is signified by removing the smile, but keeping the mouth open and limbs still. You would be surprised what a dampening effect this posture—which looks something like that of a person who has just been arrested for jaywalking and has not yet collected his thoughts enough to ask the arresting officer why he is not engaged instead in pursuing real criminals—conveys.

∼ *Spontaneous Outbursts* ∼

DEAR MISS MANNERS:

How does one respond to and stay cool in situations where people disagree and are very vocal? I have been in awkward situations where vegetarians have accused meat-eaters of being "animal killers" and "carnivores," students have accused people wearing certain brands of clothing as supporting the exploitation of child labor and underpaid factory workers in Third World countries, and non-white people dating white people have been accused of being "whitewashed" and of "selling out." Is there a general strategy that one can use in such situations?

GENTLE READER:

Uh, how many on each side? Is anybody armed?

Miss Manners hopes you are talking about nothing more life-threatening than the noisy forum in the streets and parks or the ruin of sociability by people who believe that their moral sensitivity entitles them to go around being rude and nasty. In neither case is a response required.

Any one of these positions might be something you would be willing to hear out or debate civilly. But this is impossible under the conditions of crude attack, as the atmosphere ensures that no one is open to anyone else's opinions. So if it happens in public, the answer is merely to walk on, and if it happens under social conditions, it is to refuse to discuss it.

4. *Rites de Passage*

Bar and Bat Mitzvahs, Communions and Confirmations

⤙ Bar and Bat Mitzvahs ⤚

SOMETHING STRANGE happens to children when they turn thirteen years of age, but Miss Manners is not sure she would call it adulthood. Nevertheless, the special celebration of the thirteenth birthday seems as right to her as having New Year's in the crisp, begin-again air of autumn, as the Jewish calendar does, instead of when the roads are already icy and dangerous.

The bar mitzvah, for Jewish boys, and the somewhat less traditional (but only fair) bat mitzvah, for girls, carry religious responsibility for the person who is coming of age. But no child should be considered to be legitimately approaching adulthood who has not also mastered some social responsibility. Celebrating a bar or bat mitzvah, whether by receiving the congratulations of the congregation in the synagogue or by being the guest of honor at a hotel dinner-dance for four hundred, is an excellent test of social skills.

No thirteen-year-old should be permitted to begin whining, "But I'm not a child anymore—you always treat me like a baby," let alone to call itself by the dignified title of adult, without having mastered the ability to:

- Accept the idea that no occasion, least of all a social event, is so important as to justify subordinating all claims to the pleasure of one person. While life is often a compromise, parties always are, and learning this early will spare the child enormous emotional grief on wedding days, inaugurations, retirement parties, and whatever other milestones are stepped upon.
- Realize that there is a relationship between the financial resources of the

Mr. and Mrs. Alexander Wise

request the honour of your presence

when their son

Guy Noah

will be called to the Torah as a Bar Mitzvah

on Saturday, the first of April

at half after ten o'clock

Brookdale Hebrew Congregation

Brookdale Connecticut

Luncheon following the services

Dinner dance

at half after seven o'clock

125 Primrose Path

Brookdale, Connecticut

The favour of a reply is requested

The invitation to a bar mitzvah (or to a daughter's bat mitzvah) with enclosed invitation card for evening. Divorced parents may issue the invitation alone, together using their current names or with other spouses, specifying "his" or "her" son. Note that an invitation to a religious service does not require a reply, as places of worship are in theory open to all, but that invitations to related social events, including the luncheon at the synagogue, do. For reply wording, see p. 538.

family and the amounts of money it can spend. It is difficult to understand that money spent on nonpleasurable items for a child, such as shoes and tuition, have a connection with the amount of money available to spend on things the child actually wants, such as live bands and ski trips.

- Analyze one's family and friends dispassionately in the interests of forming a proper guest list. For example, not being able to stand a certain relative counts for nothing; the only thing that counts is how closely the person is related. There can be a cutoff on the family part of the guest list, but it is made on the basis of how much blood there is in common, not how many interests. While it is true that friends tend to be people one likes, there are often more important considerations, such as how close one's parents are to their parents, or whether invitations were forthcoming to their parties.

- Accept a compliment, no matter how silly. The answer to "What does it feel like to be a (heh, heh) man, kid?" is a smile.

- Stand in a receiving line looking pleased to see everyone, no matter how detestable. Related to this is the discipline to circulate, in both talking and dancing, without distinguishing between the people one likes and the people one was forced to invite.

- Perform introductions, fully and correctly. No person who cannot introduce to his grandmother the chief troublemaker of the eighth grade, getting the proper sequence and the correct name of each, and entirely concealing terror of what one might carelessly say to the other, can be considered an adult.

- Behave as if age were not the single most distinguishing factor among human beings, and act as if it were perfectly natural to have a room full of people of different generations who are not even all related to one another.

- Write prompt thank-you letters, each with an opening other than "Thank you for the ———. "

Miss Manners wishes you to note that this is a minimum list. If, on top of these skills, you can pile some grace and sense, she will promise to consider you a full-fledged human being.

~ *Communion and Confirmation* ~

DEAR MISS MANNERS:

My sister married a Roman Catholic and agreed that the children would be brought up in that faith. My eldest niece is about to take first communion. Can you tell me what to expect, and what my wife and I should do? Do we give her a separate present from her birthday present? What about her confirmation?

GENTLE READER:

In both cases, you will probably be invited to attend services, with a small celebration—at church or in your sister's house or at a restaurant—marking the occasion. Yes, you should give the child a separate present, because the religious milestone is different from an ordinary birthday. The rule about having all such presents strictly religious in nature has been somewhat relaxed, but Miss Manners urges you to remember the nature of the occasion and not give her a doll in a silver jumpsuit who looks as if she would be in church to repent.

Graduations and Reunions

~ Graduations ~

GRADUATIONS ARE the perfect preparation for that laughable institution known on such occasions as Real Life or The World Out There. If you can sit quietly in the sun for two hours, listening to irrelevant platitudes with a respectful look on your face, and can survive with dignity the social mixture of your progenitors with your peers, life out there should hold no further terrors.

It is a mistake to think that graduations are held for the benefit of graduates, who therefore should be able to enjoy the celebrations as they choose or even boycott them. Graduations are held to mark the end of the sufferings of people who have been paying staggering tuition bills, nagging about homework until their own lives have no longer been worth living, or despairing that the efforts of their ancestors to achieve a modicum of civilization have been lost under their supervision.

The relief of these people on finding that one of society's most obvious goals has been achieved often borders on the hysterical. Otherwise sensible and reserved parents will attempt to involve their graduating children in odd forms of exhibitionist behavior, and encourage younger siblings to do the same. They will create havoc by shooting film at every possible moment, and when they are unable to accost strangers to find outlets for bragging, they will exchange such remarks with each other in unnaturally loud voices.

All this must be endured with grace by indulgent graduates. Not looking ashamed of one's parents, no matter what they demand to be shown, whom they insist on meeting and what they cannot be prevented from saying, is a rite de passage certifying the maturity of the graduate.

He or she is not, however, permitted any unconventional behavior. Blue jeans that can be seen below academic robes, protest demonstrations against the school or any of its invited speakers, or any behavior that distinguishes one graduate from

another—other than accepting prizes—cannot be tolerated. The graduation ceremony, in all its mesmerizing monotony, was carefully designed to fulfill the fantasies
of families, not to enable the graduate to express his independence. Even the
allegedly private aspects, the proms and the parties, carry their family obligations.
If you pose prettily beforehand and fabricate a comforting report afterward, it is
possible that you and your peers will be allowed a small amount of private pleasure
in between.

Satisfying one's family by going along with all their graduation expectations, no
matter how silly or embarrassing, is not the graduate's only obligation. He or she also
owes something to the educational institution, and that institution owes something
to its older alumni—or if it doesn't, it isn't from lack of trying. Alumni who are using
graduations as the setting for their reunions are not always raucous and drunk.
However, they are always caught in a mysterious time warp that leads to behavior
that can be just as offensive. Graduating seniors must listen with patient smiles to
the questions and comments of alumni who have discovered that the school no
longer has curfews, single-sex dormitories or four years of required Biblical studies.
That look will serve them well on job interviews and other such exasperating situations held Out There.

Graduation Invitations

DEAR MISS MANNERS:

I am a high school senior who was recently accepted to an Ivy League university.
Would it be terribly rude of me to include a copy of my acceptance letter with each
graduation invitation, simply to let people know which university I plan to attend in
the fall?

GENTLE READER:

Not only rude, but transparent. Besides, if they are not among your closest relatives whom your parents already told, they are not close enough to be invited. A
graduation is a tedious event for everyone whose eyes are not misted with pride.

Miss Manners trusts that you will soon be tutored—if not in modesty, at least in
reverse snobbery. It is customary, in the Ivy League, to spare outsiders the dazzling
effect produced by the actual name of one's college. Thus you must learn not only to
refrain from making announcements, but to respond to inquiries with only a geographical reference, such as "I go to school in New Haven" or "in the Boston area" or
better yet, "in the Northeast."

⌒ *Graduation Announcements* ⌒

DEAR MISS MANNERS:

I am a high school senior with several questions about announcements and thank-you notes. Who exactly do announcements go to? All relatives and friends, or just those who do not live nearby? Also, I was wondering how I could personalize thank-you notes? Perhaps with senior pictures?

GENTLE READER:

Miss Manners does not generally recommend applying logic to etiquette problems—so much of it is simply custom that it would be like studying history by working out what you think should have happened. However, logic would be useful here. You might ask yourself: What is the purpose of a graduation announcement?

The correct answer is: to inform people who would be pleased to hear about the graduation. Everybody who put down that the purpose is to inform people that a present is due gets a blank diploma.

Some of your relatives and friends already know of the event, so you need not announce it to them. Some people who do not know might be distant enough not to be especially interested, so you wouldn't want to announce it to them. By this process of elimination, the people to whom to send announcements would be those who you could reasonably assume would care but may not know, and perhaps some who already know but care so much that they would treasure your announcement as a souvenir of your achievement.

This is basic to what you call "personalizing"—tailoring what you send to the recipient, more than merely showcasing yourself to everyone whose address you happen to have. It is especially required in letters of thanks. By all means, send a picture of yourself to anyone you think would enjoy receiving one. But as these letters must be individually written, each geared to the addressee and expressing gratitude for the particular present that person sent, they cannot help being personalized.

DEAR MISS MANNERS:

What is an appropriate response to a college graduation announcement? We are planning to send them out soon, and our son has hopes of cash gifts to help him start out.

GENTLE READER:

Start out what? His career fund-raising in the private sector for his favorite beneficiary?

The proper response to a college graduation announcement is a letter of congratulations. People who are fond of your son may be moved to send him some token to commemorate this event, but if your decision to send out announcements was based on the hope that a more substantial return is mandatory, Miss Manners hopes that she has caught you in time to save you from wasting your stamps.

～ *Graduation Speeches* ～

The requirements for a graduation speech are that it be uplifting, interesting and short. If the distinguished speaker cannot manage more than two out of these three, the one to skip is interesting.

Miss Manners says this out of respect for ceremonies, not a desire to get them over with. As she takes the precaution of wearing a shade-bearing hat and is inclined to skip the beer-drinking marathon, her concern about moving things along is altruistic. But when someone on the stage makes reference to audience impatience with the ceremony, she squirms. Speakers are prone to doing this in the hope of establishing a humorous rapport:

"I don't remember a word of what my graduation speaker said, so I don't expect you to remember anything I say."

"Hey, you're almost there, this is the last lecture you'll have to listen to here."

"Okay, you can go to sleep now, just remember to wake up when they call your name."

Miss Manners does not dispute the idea that graduations, which tend to feature uncomfortable seating, numerous speeches and the calling out of names that are each of interest to only a handful of people in the audience, usually fail to meet the general standards of mass entertainment, such as they are. She only disputes that they are intended to do so.

A ceremony is not a show, and the emotion connected with it is supposed to be derived from participating in a known ritual, not from being diverted by jokes and surprises. The tendency to undercut ceremonies—which is being done frequently, not just at graduations but at weddings and even funerals—all but directs the participants and audience to be bored. And by the way, it is not itself amusing.

It is not as though the platform doesn't come with a choice of traditional topics practically etched into the lectern. Among them are:

"We expect you to make the world a better place."

"Use your education wisely."

"Your education is not finished, because you will be learning all your life."

"There is no goal you cannot achieve if you work hard enough."

"You have an obligation to help others less fortunate than yourselves."

"The field I am in is a worthy one and I want you to consider entering it."

"Do not be discouraged if you make mistakes along the way."

"Have a moral purpose to your life."

"I have a plan for rehabilitating war-torn Europe."

No, that last one was used at the 1947 Harvard graduation, where the significance of George Marshall's announcement apparently escaped much of the audience, which included professional journalists.

That leaves plenty of others to choose from, however. Miss Manners is all for significance, eloquence and wit on the part of speakers who are able to provide any of these qualities. She only maintains that these are luxuries, while dignity and moral purpose are essential. If people don't pay attention it is too bad, but it is still better than having them pay attention to the message that no occasion is worth taking seriously.

⌒ Graduation Presents ⌒

Here is a multiple-choice test Miss Manners suggests administering to new graduates, just when they think they are free of the pesky things:

1. *Relatives and friends sent you graduation presents or checks because:*

   (a) They owe you.
   (b) Giving gives them pleasure; it's how they get their kicks.
   (c) It is better to give than to receive.
   (d) They think it is better to give than to receive.
   (e) You were clever enough to put a list of what you wanted on your web site and to do a mass emailing asking for money to help you get launched.
   (f) You have a warm relationship with them, including the exchange of presents as a way of sharing one another's happy occasions.

2. *Now you owe them:*

   (a) Nothing, because you are young and your time and money are limited.
   (b) Nothing, because their reward was the pleasure of giving to you.
   (c) Nothing, because it is your parents' problem.

(d) An email saying "Thanks, folks" to the people who came across.

(e) A posting on your web site saying how close you got to your goal and reminding people that it's not too late to contribute.

(f) An individual letter thanking each person specifically, telling something of your plans and asking after them.

3. *The correct time to be in touch with them is:*

(a) After beach week.

(b) Just as soon as you can get to it.

(c) In the fall, when you have something more to tell them.

(d) When your birthday is coming up.

(e) Before Christmas.

(f) Yesterday.

4. *Failure to have thanked people already can be best explained as:*

(a) The need to recuperate from the draining effect of all those years of schooling.

(b) Being grown up and in charge of your own life.

(c) The inevitable reaction to nagging.

(d) The intention of doing something even nicer when the opportunity presents itself.

(e) An idealistic stand against the selfishness of people who don't give for the pure joy of giving.

(f) Rudeness.

DEAR MISS MANNERS:

When I received a note from my cousin which began, "Bill and I would like to thank you for the graduation gift you gave to Tom," I was beginning to wonder whether Tom had not been taught how to write.

My fears were allayed, however, when I received a canceled check endorsed "Tom Smith." The check had been made out to Thomas D. Smith, as I understood his full name to be from the graduation announcement. The check was cashed by the local liquor store. Perhaps Tom, only eighteen and unaccustomed, we hope, to strong drink, spent the entire sum of twenty-five dollars to sample some of the many varieties available, and as a result was temporarily unable to lift a pen. Am I being terribly old-fashioned to think it would have been more proper for the young man to express gratitude himself, whether or not he felt any?

As Miss Manners understands it, the phrase "being terribly old-fashioned" is the apologetic way in which people admit to a timid, hopeless desire to be treated with common decency by the young. It is interesting to observe how your cousins are attempting to live a double standard, acknowledging the propriety of your being thanked, but not imposing the necessity for doing so on their son. All this cravenness is, in Miss Manners' opinion, why there is a crisis of manners in the world today.

Of course the young man should have thanked you. (Actually, during a hangover is an excellent time for a nice, quiet activity such as writing thank-you notes, if one can stand the sound of the pen's scratching on the paper.) Generosity and gratitude should always travel together, and since the gratitude is absent, Miss Manners suggests you squelch the generosity.

(For more on presents and thank-you letters, please see pp. 606 and 614.)

⟶ The Reunion ⟵

Modesty is becoming in all endeavors, but it is essential for people attending college reunions. Miss Manners realizes that this seems to contradict the purpose of attending college reunions, which is to demonstrate that one has turned out better than anyone expected. Modesty is not intended to prevent this goal, but to prevent it from backfiring.

Bragging is not the only pleasure associated with returning to the scene of one's education, but it is the chief one. Others include walking through classroom buildings knowing that one has no papers overdue, and spending the night in a dormitory without wondering whether one will go through life unloved.

All of these joys derive from the knowledge that one is better off now than one was in college. Merely being in one's late teens is a state from which it is hardly possible not to improve. But colleges tend to be competitive, and improvements will be compared. The entries will be in three categories, Success, Happiness and Wisdom, as is obvious from the Class Report, which will consist of variations on the following essays:

SUCCESS

"Life as a designer of household paper products continues to be interesting, stimulating and challenging, with special opportunities for growth in the visual arts as well as in my special interest—people. Having been named Outstanding Promising Junior Citizen in my suburban area was an unexpected honor that I hope to live up to."

HAPPINESS

"The high point of this year was the birth of our sixth child, and watching the older ones prosper and grow thoughtful and strong, bubbling with life and learning. Gloria, still beautiful, sensitive, compassionate and talented, has made our reconverted chicken house into a veritable treasure store of needlepoint, and also finds fulfillment in the candle scenting that she does, for fun and profit, in her dining room office. All of us love to travel as a family and by next reunion we hope to have visited all of America's battlefields and civil disturbance areas."

WISDOM

"As we enter our mature years, we gain in self-discovery, awareness of the needs of others and of our purpose for being on this earth. I continue to be amazed and optimistic as I see our society examining its defects, agonizing over its mistakes and rising again to meet the challenges before us. On a personal level, I try to live one day at a time."

There will be a fourth type of entry, consisting only of the alumnus' address. That person will show up at the reunion, listening to others and saying nothing about himself. It will turn out, after everyone has gone home, that he has published a witty new translation of Sanskrit poetry, has just completed the leading role in a major movie, is married to a woman whose name is being mentioned for the Supreme Court and has a son who won the Moscow piano competition and a daughter who is the country's youngest mayor. There is one like that at every reunion. If you keep your mouth shut, people may suspect it is you.

Debuts and Dances

IT IS FASHIONABLE for a well-heeled young lady, upon reaching the age of eighteen, to signify her membership in adult society by announcing that she refuses to make a debut. This innovation has many advantages over the old debutante system, including being a lot cheaper. A girl who refuses to come out, like a groundhog under similar circumstances, creates a certain amount of interest, while girls and groundhogs who do come out as expected simply create expectations that they may not be able to fulfill.

The reason for this negativism on the part of Miss Manners, whose usual custom it is to fight fiercely for the preservation of outmoded rituals (so would you if you were the only person alive who knew how to make correct morning calls from a brougham), is that the surviving debutante tradition often makes a mockery of its original purpose. Bringing young women out presupposes keeping them in beforehand. But that has always been a more or less futile prospect, and it is not the cause of Miss Manners' objections. What distresses her is the atmosphere into which they are brought out.

The original intention was to introduce one's daughter to one's friends, and if they happened to have sons with good prospects, so much the better. In some private dances given by close relatives of debutantes, and in some church or civic groups, where cotillions are organized by members who know one another well, this idea still prevails.

Far more often, the cotillion is run by a competitive committee, more or less in business for the purpose, and it screens debutantes slightly more thoroughly than colleges screen their applicants. The debutante who is accepted is then allowed to bow, as they put it, to an artificial society composed of people brought together for that purpose alone. It is not uncommon to have an ambitious debutante presented to strangers in a strange city by parents who don't know anyone present and will probably never see them again.

In such a determinedly organized setting, the presence of young men is not left to nature and what she has chosen to supply in the normal course of events to the adult couples representing society. Each debutante is assigned to scout out what are euphemistically referred to as "escorts," by whatever means possible. In the interests of providing a shared "stag line" of extra men, debutantes are usually required to dredge up two or three escorts each. Remember that these are supposed to be innocent young girls making their first appearance in the world among eligible men, and then ask yourself how they are supposed to have already acquired—and be prepared to donate to their sister debutantes—several.

Standards are necessarily lowered for this dragnet, and the young men begin to understand that they are at a premium. So for the expense and the trouble of the modern debut, fond parents are able to attach a permanent date to their daughter's youth, have her scrutinized by strangers and arrange for her to meet a lot of young men who have come to believe that the world owes them free champagne. That is why Miss Manners will not be offended if you decide to skip this particular tradition.

⌒ Young Ladies' Responsibilities ⌒

To young ladies contemplating making debuts or *quinceañeras*, Miss Manners has an invaluable piece of general advice: Don't.

This need not at all be applied to the question of whether one should go ahead and bow to society, as we say, by which we mean enjoying a little season of having all sorts of people figuratively bowing to the wishes of teenaged girls. But it is applicable to practically every other question apt to flicker through the guest of honor's young head during that season and is especially appropriate to impromptu suggestions from contemporaries that begin with "I know! Why don't we?"

This is the time for loving parents to squelch any notions their daughters may have that no expense should be spared, that all arrangements should be dictated by their taste and pleasure, that they are to be forgiven any lapse of manners and indulged in any whim because of the specialness of their position and that everyone else should be subservient to them for the period of their glory. It will save the parents trouble when these ladies turn into brides.

The principle tends to be forgotten that such occasions are supposed to be presentations by the parents of their daughter to the society in which they move. It should therefore follow that it should be in their style of entertaining that the adult portion of the guest list is as important as the young people's and that a level of taste acceptable to the parents' notion of propriety be maintained.

Then how come there are so many rock bands, swaggering young men and

Mr. and Mrs. Geoffrey Lockwood Perfect

Miss Daffodil Louise Perfect

At Home
(line may be omitted)

Saturday, the first of April

at five o'clock

123 Primrose Path

Mrs. Plue Perfect

requests the pleasure of the company of

(space for guest's name to be handwritten)

at a small dance

on Saturday, the first of April

at half after ten o'clock

Society of Early Dames

Kindly send response to
127 Primrose Path

Invitations to a debut. The first is a tea given by the parents, although the word "tea" is not mentioned; the second is a grand ball given by another grown-up, but the word "ball" is never used. Even the debutante's name is not used, Mrs. Plue Perfect being extremely strict, but as this tends to make debutantes sulky, the words "in honour of" may be added after "small dance," with the debutante's full name on the next line.

abashed adults fading into the wallpaper? Why, because the parents want, as they say, "the young people to have a good time."

Miss Manners is not actually against that. She merely insists on the form of deference to that society to which the young lady is so prettily bending her knees. The responsibilities of those young people (and Miss Manners wishes to point out that assisting at a sister's party is a recognized rite de passage for young men, and a rigorous one too) include: presenting only known people as candidates for invitations; acknowledging all other invitations, flowers, presents; dressing properly (no promise that an extravagant dress will be later worn as the young lady's wedding dress is to be believed); engaging in as many duty dances as ones for pleasure, being hospitable to all guests, regardless of age; discouraging disruptive behavior in themselves and others; and keeping up the fiction that the parents are giving the party.

Young Gentlemen's Responsibilities

DEAR MISS MANNERS:
What are the responsibilities of a young man on the debutante circuit? If any.

GENTLE READER:
The first is to wipe that smirk off your face. The others are to answer all invitations immediately and correctly, to show up properly dressed when expected, to greet the hosts, even though they are not of the debutante generation, to dance with the debutantes, to avoid characterizing the relative merits of the debutantes within earshot, and to refrain from being sick on the premises.

Prom Invitations

DEAR MISS MANNERS:
If I ask a boy to my Junior Prom, should I pay for the dinner? Should I be the one to plan and make the dinner reservations also?

GENTLE READER:
Unless you can persuade your parents to do it. You are not likely to interest a corporate sponsor, and who else would be interested in picking up your hostessing bills?

Never mind answering that; Miss Manners knows whom you had in mind and is hoping to shame you out of suggesting it to him. To attempt to have it both ways—asserting equality of the genders in issuing invitations and inequality in paying the costs these invitations occur—is unseemly. Even when Miss Manners was a slip of a girl, busily luring innocent young gentlemen to female seminary festivities, it would have been unthinkable to shirk the duty of hostess when the bill arrived.

DEAR MISS MANNERS:

A person that I do not wish to attend our high school winter formal with has asked me, and I was so caught off guard that I said that I would go with him. What is the most polite way that I can turn him down, if there is one?

GENTLE READER:

Go with him. Unless prom night would be a convenient time to have your tonsils out, there is no polite way to break your word that would not involve enough intrigue and deceit to bring down a government.

As compensation for this unwelcome advice, Miss Manners would like to offer you some protection for the future. This is not just that you should learn to hedge, which is an indispensable skill in the adult world ("I'd love to, but let me just check with my assistant and my husband and get back to you"), although nearly impossible in high school, where everybody knows everybody else's business.

It is the warning that people change dramatically. The teenager you snub today can be miraculously transformed into tomorrow's rock star or tycoon—still smarting from your insult.

⟶ Prom Activities ⟵

As parents know, the choice of prom clothes is a crucial factor in human development. One small mistake and that's it. Nothing ahead but a lifetime of bitterness and therapy. Time and attention must therefore be properly devoted to this ritual. Here is what Miss Manners understands to be necessary:

1. Activity: choosing formal clothes. Time required for young ladies: senior year (although strict parents have been known to insist that a student finish her college application essays before devoting full time to this project). Time required for young gentlemen: week of intermittent interest scheduled to coordinate with closing times of rental shops.

2. Activity: posing for pictures before leaving for prom. Time: half an hour and up. Corresponds to patience level of the seniors, which is to say the graduating seniors, not their seniors.

3. Activity: wearing formal clothes while actually dining or dancing. Time: one hour and a quarter.

4: Activity: having problems with formal clothes, such as spills and tears, and making adjustments and repairs to them during dinner and prom time. Time: three and three-quarters hours (young gentlemen allotting nearly of all this time to inflicting problems on their clothes, young ladies allotting nearly all of this time to making adjustments to theirs).

5. Activity: partying on prom night, after having exchanged formal clothes for everyday ones. Time: six hours.

As most graduates and their parents accept this ritual without question, although perhaps not without exasperation, Miss Manners will address herself to those few who wonder—expressing it with varying degrees of humor—what this is all about.

In theory, it is about entering the adult world, with its understanding of the dignity and beauty of formality. But since the adult world long ago abandoned all that in the hope of breaking into the adolescent world, we have a problem. Brought up with moralistic devotion to The Casual Life, today's youth periodically explode from repressed lust for formality. A prom is usually the first opportunity, the successive ones being their successive weddings.

On all other occasions in their lives, up to and including their funerals, which Miss Manners supposes they wouldn't enjoy anyway, an inclination toward formality produces the sort of reaction—raised eyebrows, psychological explanations, resignation at being subjected to watching—once prompted by social drunkenness.

In the hope of softening the future, Miss Manners considers the prom to be a priceless opportunity to make some basic points about formality:

- Formal clothes are not costumes worn by plutocrats (heavens no; modern plutocrats are arrogantly defiant about refusing to dress up); they are not costumes at all. The idea is therefore not to be funny or outlandish, but to look dignified and attractive.
- Occasionally, nearly everyone enjoys a stylistic change, and dressing differently for special occasions is not a betrayal of one's "real" self or egalitarian beliefs. It is not necessary to pretend that one is only doing it to be funny.
- Modern formal dress is no less comfortable than most casual clothes, and a great deal more so than tight pants and miniskirts.

- All clothes are subject to being mussed when worn, and the possibility does not justifying messing up the evening.

Miss Manners does not expect prom-goers to have mastered these concepts before graduation. She only hopes that this knowledge, like the rest of their education, will be drawn upon later, when they need it.

DEAR MISS MANNERS:

Could you provide any information regarding what teenage girls/boys should and should not do during proms, dinners, etc. What wrist should girls wear their corsage on, the left or right? Where should a young man's boutonniere be worn? What forks would they use for specific foods at the dinner table etc.?

GENTLE READER:

Flowers are generally worn on the left, and forks are used from the outside of the place setting toward the plate itself. That part is easy.

But Miss Manners really doesn't want to give impressionable young people a list of things they should not do during proms and dinners, much less during the etc. part of the evening. It seems to her that they manage that quite well enough without her assistance.

⌒ Unauthorized Activities ⌒

DEAR MISS MANNERS:

I am senior class president at a local college, and our annual commencement ball, an extremely formal occasion, will be held in a few weeks. What should I do about inebriated guests who lose control? Is there a proper way to ask them to leave without causing an uproar? Finally, a question about what I anticipate will be our worst problem. Certain groups of students have taken to strange dances, which degenerate into overt love acts—right out on the dance floor. How can I politely request that such activities not occur at our commencement ball?

GENTLE READER:

Welcome to polite society, where the attempt to fit the chaos of human behavior into the patterns of civilization has always been a difficult, but noble, cause.

No form of nonviolent social life would ever have been possible without law enforcement. Traditionally, this task was divided between the generations. The only reason that guests at Victorian tea dances didn't copulate drunkenly on the dance floor with anything that moved was that they were afraid of (1) the dragons disguised as dowagers and (2) the young ladies who pretended to be terminally shocked and the young men who pretended to be mortally insulted.

You must recruit modern versions of these people. A few of the tougher faculty members should be invited, and a dance committee of students should be convened to decide what behavior will be considered unacceptable, with their decisions made known beforehand to other guests. When unacceptable behavior occurs, as it will, the offenders should be approached by these people of authority, possibly in cross-generational pairs, and escorted off the scene with determination but no fuss except that which the offenders themselves may unwisely make to call attention to their disgrace.

Courtship

THOSE DISILLUSIONED with the current practices of what may humorously be called courtship sometimes claim to yearn for the dating system of the mid-twentieth century. Back then, Miss Manners has heard the young maintain, the two sexes (there were officially only two) treated each other with respect.

Gentlemen gallantly entertained ladies without considering what they could expect in return in the way of bodily demonstrations of affection (or failing that, of enthusiasm). Ladies accepted or discouraged their attentions gracefully, without calculating the level of monetary investment at which they could afford to bestow their affections. Even very young gentlemen sent flowers and sincere valentines, while the young ladies knitted socks and sent coy valentines. Romance progressed in an orderly fashion, from telephone calls the next day to the exchange of class rings and sorority and fraternity pins to marriage. And the universality of the practice meant that no one need be lonely on a Saturday night. The only drawback was extreme sexual repression, which pretty much limited everyone to kisses and perspiration. Anything beyond that led immediately to forced marriages, from which there was no escape, ever.

The elders of those who believe all this should be ashamed of themselves. It is not nice to take advantage of the gullibility of the young to fool them like that.

As Miss Manners recalls, the people who were caught up in the dating system disliked it so intensely that they finally managed to destroy it. But not because they were as repressed as they led their parents (and later their children) to believe.

Dating was universal in theory, but not in practice, leaving plenty of people lonely, if not shamed, for lack of Saturday night alternatives. The presumption that a date was the only natural way in which the sexes could mix put a damper on non-romantic relationships that now provide a variety of other social activities. Far from encouraging respect, this fostered competition. Those seeking to break hearts were pitted against those striving to overcome inhibitions. The progression from courtship to marriage lacked a stage for the development of friendship.

But at least there was a pattern there, and everyone knew what it was. It is the chaotic situation today, where intimacy is tied to no stage and can disappear as quickly as it strikes, that is responsible for that uninformed nostalgia. The reformers who broke down the rules of dating wanted venues that would allow friendships, which might or might not proceed to courtship. They wanted both sexes to be able to orchestrate occasions from which a romance could develop, not to eliminate invitations and hosting. The idea was to add a stage for the development of romance, not to do away with courtship.

So if there are any reformers thinking about improving the current social patterns, Miss Manners hopes they will figure out how to combine the orderliness of the past with the easiness and egalitarianism that is supposed to characterize the present. And she warns them not to rely on anyone who claims to have experienced or discovered any period in history in which ladies and gentlemen always behaved themselves.

⁓ A Modern Substitute for Romance ⁓

DEAR MISS MANNERS:

I am almost embarrassed to ask this question. I expect you won't like it. It's just that a friend called me up yesterday to complain about it, and it's fresh on my mind.

Occasionally, when one is an adult single person in the big city, one has a, ah, liaison with a member of the opposite sex whom one does not know very well. It's customary in such things to exchange telephone numbers afterward, and it is here that the problem arises. My friend and I agree that it is the proper, well-brought-up thing to do to call the other person afterward, merely to query idly after their well-being and tie things up, as it were. A postcard would serve the same purpose. However, she has recently had a series of brief relationships where the gentlemen in question never called again, and in at least one case, never returned her call after she left a message.

Is my friend being totally unrealistic to expect these men to call her? Are they being boorish cads to give her a peck on the cheek in the morning and never show their faces (or voices) again? If one has a pleasant and enjoyable time at dinner, or some similar social function, a telephone call thanking the hostess is taken for granted. Why do so many people ignore it when the hospitality extends overnight? Or is this merely an antiquated convention, another way of expecting unrealistic behavior from innocent acquaintances? I am not asking for pronouncements on the morality of such interpersonal engagements, since I'm afraid they must be taken for granted in modern life, but rather for your opinion of proper conduct afterward.

GENTLE READER:

The social event to which you refer is, Miss Manners believes, known as a one-night stand. By its very nature, the night stand, whether it is of the one-, two-, or three- variety, does not require social continuity. You are confusing it with an entirely different social tradition called courtship. Miss Manners cannot find your young men remiss, provided that they met the basic requirements of the night-stand act, which apparently they did.

DEAR MISS MANNERS:

I'm a twenty year old college student who recently had the pleasure of meeting a very nice young lady via the internet. We talked a lot and finally met for a "date" of sorts. After returning to her place and talking, she asked me if I would sleep with her.

The problem arises in that I'm not the kind of guy who will hop right into bed with someone, regardless of what I think of her (and let me make it clear that I certainly did think a lot of this one). I did accept the invitation to sleep beside her, each of us enjoying the other's company (in a non-perverted way, mind you), but I later learned that she was actually hurt because I turned her down. Despite my attempts to set right her presumptions, the damage had been done.

While I don't at all think that I'm lucky enough to have similar situations arise often, I don't want to lose another potentially wonderful relationship. How can I say "no" without hurting the girl or giving her the wrong impression? Would my response need to be different if I meant "Not yet"?

GENTLE READER:

It strikes Miss Manners that the problem here is not with your manners, but with your morals. While declining to mate with strangers, which currently passes for high morality, you describe someone who does as "a potentially wonderful relationship." Her manners are no better either, as she has taken insult at your offering her only your company. You would be better off deciding, as many ladies do, not to pin any hopes on someone who won't bother with you if all you offer is your company.

DEAR MISS MANNERS:

What should a lady keep on hand for the comfort and convenience of a gentleman guest who may be spending the night unexpectedly? An extra toothbrush? Shaving equipment? Perhaps a comfortable bathrobe? Slippers? Should I keep them in different sizes (small, medium, and large)? I'm only interested in being a gracious hostess.

GENTLE READER:

Yes, Miss Manners can see that. But what are you running there? Or rather, as Miss Manners deals in manners, not morals, what do you want to appear to be running? Suppose you were overcome with passion while visiting and were then offered a wide choice of sizes and styles in nightgowns?

Even the most gracious hostess, and that is what you say you aspire to be, offers her houseguests nothing more than a fresh toothbrush, towel, soap and perhaps a good book to read if they get bored at bedtime. If you think your gentleman guest might be embarrassed to leave your house unshaven in the morning, you might keep a fresh throwaway razor designed for women on hand, and tell him it was a spare one of your own.

⟞ Romance Revisited ⟝

DEAR MISS MANNERS:

I have been enlightened by your august self as to the fact that one-night stands are not to be confused with courtship. I now know what to expect from a one-night stand, but the identifying characteristics of the latter still elude me. Does anyone still fall in love? If they postpone thinking about sex for two weeks or more, should one begin to worry about their psychic or hormonal tendencies?

GENTLE READER:

The stages of courtship were best described by dear Marie-Henri Beyle, who had an interesting career as a writer under the name of Stendhal, but whose primary occupation was falling in love. The succession of admiration, fantasy, hope, doubt and what he calls crystallization—in which a plain human being appears dazzling through the eyes of a lover, as a plain twig does when covered with crystals in the salt mines of Salzburg—was described in his little book *On Love*.

Neither Mr. Beyle nor Miss Manners pretends that tremendous periods of reflection are needed to run through these stages. On the contrary: Nothing is as inimical to passion as the slow, sensible weighing of practicalities. But the rapid calculation of practicalities is not conducive to falling in love either. The expediency of thinking "Well, why not? This will suit the needs of us both, and we needn't make an undue fuss about it" is equally chilling to romance whether it concerns an early-nineteenth-century arranged marriage in France or a twenty-first-century one-night stand in America.

The customs of courtship vary in time, place and class. But they are always based on the desire to secure the affections of a person one believes to be too perfect to be reasonably attainable, not a person whose most conspicuous characteristic is convenience.

⌒ *Young Stirrings* ⌒

Modern parents assume that their children are too sophisticated to require guidance about the dangers of romance. But even knowing more than their parents do about the physical technicalities fails to equip an unsuspecting child for the emotional aspect.

Dear child (each must be told), you are about to experience a stirring of feelings toward someone else that is universal and natural. What it is, is a desire to be looked down upon by someone whom you feel is better than you are, coupled with a more generalized desire to look down upon people whom you feel are worse off than you are.

This works as follows: Two or three children in your crowd exhibit, either from cleverness or accident, an air of self-confidence not normally linked to their age group. All the girls then fall promptly in love with the boy who has this air, and all of the boys fall in love with the girl who does. Just as automatically, they all decide that they despise all the other members of the loved one's sex, most especially those with the bad taste to admire their unworthy selves. (Many people go through life falling in love on this law, which by definition guarantees unhappiness, but everyone starts out that way. There is no such thing as a thirteen-year-old whose affections have been aroused by the charm of vulnerability.)

Dear child (you must continue), you cannot avoid these feelings, but you must learn to disguise them in order to avoid jeopardizing your present and future social life and therefore creating for yourself even more agony than is already built into the situation. If you indulge in your inclination to insult those who look soulfully up to you, it will come back to haunt you. The reason is that while it is extremely common for the desirability of a person to change radically after his early adolescence—sometimes during it, from one year to the next—everyone goes through life with a vivid memory of insults and kindnesses (if any) experienced when very young. The popular boy or girl for whom you lusted from afar may live to bore you silly, which is an excellent reason against early marriage, but the beautiful creature you slighted when she had pimples or he stuttered will be only too pleased to break your heart for you when it gets big. And that, dear children, is why we must learn to be polite to others.

⌒ Prolonged Adolescence ⌒

DEAR MISS MANNERS:

I am, according to friends and family, a very attractive, good looking man. I, too, like to think I am quite good-looking. This, however, is not the issue . . . but it is part of it. I, like most men, am attracted to gorgeous women. As such, I am holding out for the right woman to enter my life. I've made myself available to all the women who are and have been important to me. But the problem is this: they are either intimidated for no reason or they just get all possessive and just plain crazy . . . which, by the way, is a huge turnoff. I've been cheated on by girlfriends and alienated by the girls who've called me their friend. What do I do about this conundrum? Is it me?

GENTLE READER:

You and everyone else. Even if you are the best looking person you ever saw.

Miss Manners is obliged to inform you that there are only three possibilities in courtship:

1. You care for the other person more than she cares for you. You are welcome to call this being intimidated or, when she finds someone else, cheating.
2. The other person cares for you more than you care for her. Like you, everyone describes this as being possessive and crazy.
3. The caring is mutual. This is what you will call The Right Woman, for whom you say you are holding out while making yourself available to others.

⌒ Awaiting Maturity ⌒

Nice guys are the gentlemen who are unfailingly polite and dependable, and who grow even more useful and sympathetic when things go terribly wrong. They have the testimony of numerous attractive ladies who turned to them for comfort when they were badly treated by the cads they adore and needed a brotherly shoulder on which to cry before returning to the romantic fray.

Miss Manners happens to admire these gentlemen, who take care to follow her strictures about proper behavior. They listen as well as talk, and take into consideration other people's needs and preferences, along with their own. They honor their word, even if it drives them to the extreme of having to show up for an appointment they themselves contracted or accepted. They give thanks when it is due and have been known to produce something nice, such as flowers or candy, when it is not required. They even know how to dress, eat, speak and perform other ordinary human functions.

In theory, they are much beloved for all these good qualities. It is only when they try to have an actual romance that they run into trouble. So do the objects of their affections, but in that case, the trouble comes when the ladies in question try to explain to their hopeful parents why they are not interested.

Like those poor parents, Miss Manners has never understood what was so unappealing about gentlemen's roses and reliability, and so appealing about the shenanigans and sloppiness of their rude rivals. Or rather, she understands, but does not share, these tastes. Therefore, she feels obliged to warn those nice gentlemen that they are in for a wait.

Through their teenage-hood, most people are testing their desirability by aiming high, which they define as being someone who can afford to treat them badly. A few seem to be born with the maturity to realize what a dumb standard this is, some wise up after years of disillusionment and some never do, but the average person should catch on in early adulthood.

So what the nice gentlemen need to look for in a romantic partner is the fine qualities they themselves possess. But then, maybe they would find that comforting but dull, and can only find excitement in being scorned.

⌁ Meeting ⌁

Parents no longer have to warn their daughters about cads with evil intentions, or their sons about gold diggers with greedy designs. The young now warn themselves. They warn one another. They warn strangers, over the Internet.

And they warn the cads and gold diggers, even before candidates for these positions have had a chance to do anything caddish or gold-diggish (or perhaps golden-diggeryish). Reciting to innocent people a list of the sort of behavior to which one has been subjected by others in the past and the declaration of never putting up with it again has become one of the rites of early courtship.

Miss Manners isn't even sure she would know how to define a cad or a gold digger by today's standards. Once a cad was someone who enticed a lady into consummating a promised marriage before the ceremony had taken place. Now, perhaps, a cad is someone who tells the mother of his children that he's not ready to make such a serious commitment.

A gold digger may no longer be someone who strings gentlemen along while she works busily to get hold of their fortunes. She is more likely to be someone who strings gentlemen along because she is too busy for them while she is working to make her fortune.

The big change that Miss Manners sees here is in the identity of the person who is too wary to be fooled by the enticements of romance. This is a job that was traditionally performed by people who had long since found their own secure life partners, so they had the luxury of being cynical on behalf of the young.

The youthful cry of "Let me do it myself" has spread far beyond tying their own shoelaces and driving other people's cars. In romance, it covers everything.

Miss Manners is not saying that the young were wrong in demanding to choose their own marriage partners, although the success rate of marriages did not soar as promised. Nor has it been helped by the demand to conduct the courtship without chaperonage—for example, by the couple's renting an apartment of their own for that purpose.

It was obviously a mistake for them to do away with society's mechanisms for throwing single people together so they could meet on their own without the help of community activities, social dances and awkward dinners at which the only two eligible people found themselves sitting next to each other while everyone else smiled expectantly. They have figured out no better way to do it than to advertise themselves like dry goods to strangers.

So they have all the more reason to be wary. The trouble is that being constantly suspicious is as unattractive a state as—well, as being held under unprovoked suspicion. It is decidedly not conducive to romance. This is why it was useful to divide the job. Parents didn't mind being unattractive, while those they guarded could afford, under their protection, to be winningly trustful.

～ Matchmaking ～

DEAR MISS MANNERS:

I have a gay friend who I would love to introduce to a colleague who I suspect is gay. Ordinarily I would simply have them both to dinner, but the colleague lives several hours' drive away. If I were certain of his sexual preference, I would be straightforward and ask him if he'd like to meet my friend, but for professional reasons, I feel it would be indiscreet to try to discover this information by doing "undercover detective work." Do you have any suggestions?

GENTLE READER:

Before you fix up anyone, you are supposed to know something about both people. If mere availability were the only qualification necessary, matchmaking, such as you are kindly interested in offering, would be unnecessary because just about any-one would do.

Miss Manners suggests asking the colleague what sort of person happens to interest him. If you pay attention to the pronouns in his reply, you will have your answer, as well as the just-as-crucial information about his taste and availability.

~ Pickups ~

DEAR MISS MANNERS:

As a newly single male in my mid-thirties, I am somewhat confused by the proper etiquette, if there is one, in indicating to a woman with whom you are not acquainted, for example in a bank line, that you find her attractive and would like to make her acquaintance, say, over a glass of wine. Do you, Miss Manners, feel ill at ease when approached by a strange male in such situations? Is there a non-boorish way to accomplish this? I would appreciate it if you would respond forthwith and have decided not to go near a bank until I hear from you.

GENTLE READER:

Miss Manners dislikes being approached by strange men at cash machines, par-ticularly after she has withdrawn money. Even before this transaction, an overture made to a lady waiting in such a line does seem connected with the expectation of her coming into money soon.

What you are really asking is whether there is a proper way to make a pickup. Certainly. There is a proper way to do everything, and usually several improper ways.

Pickups, to seem respectable, must be contrived to seem accidental. No lady wants to meet a stranger whose object is to meet a strange lady, because such gentle-men tend to be rather—well, strange.

You must begin by choosing an unlikely place. A bar, for instance, or a beach, is a likely place; an unlikely place is one in which your emotions could be presumed to be engaged in the business in hand. Such as the fish market or traffic court. You begin by attempting to engage the lady in conversation on a relevant topic, on which you may reasonably expect to discover mutual sympathies. If the business ends before the conversation does, you may suggest continuing it nearby, again in the least romantic place possible. After that, what you do will be your own business.

⌒ *Put-Backs* ⌒

DEAR MISS MANNERS:

Scenarios: two parties connect via the internet through some cyber-dating service. A couple of social emails exchanged. Both parties prove to be highly educated, decent and kind people. Then comes the exchange of photos via the net. One party gets "visually disappointed" and does not wish to pursue the relationship, the other party is getting so excited. Please, no accusation of "being hung up on looks" because being visually inspired is an integral part of being in love, the question here is how to back out with grace?

GENTLE READER:

You needn't have the slightest worry that Miss Manners will ever use the expression "hung up"; set your mind to rest about that. No more than she would attempt to argue with you about what you find attractive, or urge you to meet a stranger about whom you have misgivings.

Her sole concern here is that you not insult someone whose attention you had sought. She hopes you realize that it is therefore out of the question that you supply him with the real reason. Not that you should supply another reason, which would not only be false but might offer him the opportunity to attempt changing your mind. The idea is to say something vague that will allow him to think it is something in your own life, totally unrelated to him, that has aborted the relationship. If there is any advantage to cyberspace society, it is that he doesn't really know anything about you—not even whether you are really the lady in the picture you sent—and can comfort himself with the notion that there are a lot of frauds and nuts out there.

⌒ *Dating* ⌒

DEAR MISS MANNERS:

I'm sure you're aware of the confusion of "male-female" roles in courtship these days. I, for one, am particularly confused. You see, I was rather a, uh, sexually free young lady, starting at fourteen.

The problem is that I don't know the "proper" way to act on a date because I have never before attempted to be "proper." What does one say? Can one get personal? Do you kiss and hug on the first date? How soon is it OK to ask a man over for dinner? Obviously, I don't know the etiquette and I am so tired of those shallow, quickly ended relationships. Actually, I'm a bit frightened of men—will this one and the next reject me, too? I have been told that I "try too hard" and "fall too fast," so I'm trying to restrain myself.

GENTLE READER:

Welcome to the world of propriety. We have more fun here than you may have been led to believe, just as the world of promiscuity, as you have discovered, offers less fun than you may have been led to believe. Like fast food, it tends to be of poor quality and may leave you with worse problems than the hunger it was intended to quell. Preparing something decent takes time and effort, but the preparation can be fun in itself and the results will be better.

No getting personal. No hugging and kissing. No come-over-to-my-place. In the proper world, romance is supposed to develop out of friendship. A gentleman and a lady both pretend that they are cultivating each other for common interests, shared humor or whatever—and then they both act surprised when passion strikes.

This shock is considered exciting by proper ladies and gentlemen, who regard instant mating, based on the idea that we all have standard parts that may be fitted together interchangeably, to be dull as well as distasteful. You will find that rejection by a friend who does not become a lover is less painful than rejection by a lover who does not want to go on to become a friend.

Now, are you willing to try? Can you act friendly to a man while being reserved enough to discourage either emotional or physical intimacies? Can you treat him as a pleasant enhancement to your life, and not the answer to your prayers? Miss Manners doesn't want to upset you by too quick a transition. But can you hold out until the second date?

⌐ *Paying for Dates* ¬

DEAR MISS MANNERS:

My boyfriend and I have been dating steadily for nearly two years now, and because we often spend time together, it becomes difficult for us to distinguish between actual dates and just normal time spent together, i.e., more mundane daily activities. Thus, there is not so much of the typical dating scenarios of the man paying for the woman (if anything, I am the one who pays for both of us, as to repay him for some sort of favor he has done for me, etc.).

This brings me to my question: am I just old fashioned or should there be some times where my boyfriend offers to pay for me anyway, regardless of the situation, just to be "boyfriendish"?

My mother has given me grief over this, saying he should pay for some things out of respect for me and as a "repayment" for my company, but this could just be (and seems to me) because she is old-fashioned and from the south.

I have a gut feeling that sometimes the boyfriend should pay, especially when we distinguish ourselves as going on "dates," however, I just wanted to know what is proper under these circumstances. Should I ask him to pay? Should he automatically offer? Are there special situations where he should or shouldn't (or where I should or shouldn't)?

GENTLE READER:

Your mother thinks you should be selling your company to your beau? And you think this makes her a nice, old-fashioned lady?

Miss Manners, who actually is one, needs her smelling salts.

It is true that a proper date is one in which one person is host, doing the inviting, the planning and the paying, but this is something you can do as well as he. An old-fashioned lady remembers that even when ladies did not pay bills, they always found ways of reciprocating gentlemen's hospitality—asking them to home-cooked meals, producing theater tickets they claimed had been given to them by relatives and serving them iced tea on the porch.

The current system, by which people often pay their own way, does not preclude occasions on which one person entertains the other. If you wish to initiate that, it would be more fitting for you to play hostess, as an example, than bill collector.

Nonexclusive Dating

DEAR MISS MANNERS:

In the past, while dating a potential suitor, I would not consider dating anyone else concurrently, and would politely rebuff others' advances.

Due to, shall we say, a convergence of the stars, I find myself dating two different gentlemen, whose company I find equally enjoyable. Granted, it has only been about two months, but both gentlemen have intimated that they enjoy my company and would like to continue to do so. While there have not been any problems yet, I feel slightly dishonest by not informing the beaux of each other's existence.

I fear they might, at some point in the future, feel slighted to learn that I am not dating them exclusively. The only reference I seem to be able to draw on is that of Scarlett O'Hara, with her multiple suitors, and this image does not comfort me.

I must say, though, that my unaccustomed situation has had the benefit of slow-ing the rate of becoming romantically involved with either gentleman. In the past, I have found myself swept up in the romance, and have offered my heart up too soon.

What is the etiquette of dating multiple people at the same time? Could you please give me some guidelines to prevent hurt feelings and wounded hearts?

GENTLE READER:

If Miss Manners correctly understands your allusion to restraint in offering your heart, then you are doing nothing wicked. She hopes this does not put a damper on the excitement, replacing the damper of your unnecessary uneasiness.

Excitement is what dating is supposed to provide, so that you could tell the difference when it no longer seemed as exciting as being exclusively with one person. When this custom was replaced by successions of temporary intimacies, they had to be exclusive so as not to be promiscuous. But a gentleman should not presume that he has exclusive access to a lady who is merely dating him unless they have agreed on such terms.

Miss Manners regrets to tell you, however, that there is no system of romance, and never has been, that eliminates the risk of hurt feelings and wounded hearts.

~ Declining Dates ~

The roles of the pursuer and the pursued are well known in society, and there is no excuse for those who have practiced one side to botch things and plead ignorance when playing the opposite part. Miss Manners has no objection to a lady's initiating a social engagement, provided she does so in the dignified, straightforward way that ladies have always appreciated in gentlemen. This means that one suggests a specific date and activity, and is gracious if it is declined. After three separate refusals, one stops asking. Gentlemen should realize that it is perfectly proper to refuse such an invitation politely if one is not interested, and that elaborate excuses need not be given.

Why is it, then, that a lady who knows what it is to be pestered with unwanted attentions does not know how to shrug and accept fate when her advances do not meet with success? Neither continued pursuit nor bitter behavior is gentlemanly, she should know. A gentleman, who knows what a rebuff is, will sometimes yield to the attentions of someone he doesn't really enjoy simply because he feels put on the spot at having been asked. He should know that it is a lady's prerogative to say no. They should both know that sexual attentions should never be demanded or given out of the disgusting notion that they are a return to the person who pays the entertainment bills.

∼ *Declaring Love* ∼

DEAR MISS MANNERS:

My boyfriend and I are having an argument about what the response should be when someone says "I love you." He once replied, "Thank you," and I said that one does not say "Thank you" when someone says "I love you." What can one say in response, besides, "I love you, too"?

GENTLE READER:

There is no doubt that "I love you too" is the only really acceptable reply to "I love you." Acceptable to the lover, that is.

However, making the other person feel good is not, as Miss Manners keeps telling you, always the object of etiquette. If you do not love the person making the original statement, replying kindly could lead to all sorts of dreadful complications, not the least of which is further and even more unfortunate questions, such as "But do you really love me?" or "More than you've ever loved anyone before?" or "How can I believe you?"

One needs, therefore, to make the lack of reciprocation clear while showing gratitude for the other person's good taste. Your boyfriend's suggestion is not bad, although Miss Manners prefers "You do me great honor." If, however, his object was merely to give variety to the conversation of happy lovers, "Thank you" is a little stiff, as it is firmly attached, in most people's minds, to "You're welcome," and that has a kind of finality that rounds off the conversation, rather than leading it to "Let's run off to Paris for the weekend."

If he doesn't want to keep saying "I love you too," let him offer one of the many restatements of this remark in every true lover's icky vocabulary. But Miss Manners has never understood why lovers can't keep saying the same thing over and over. They keep doing the same thing over and over, don't they?

∼ *Declaring Ultimatums* ∼

DEAR MISS MANNERS:

I have been dating a fellow for a year and one half, during which we only saw each other on weekends, due to the distance involved. During that time, we were both basically happy and he told me he loved me. Recently, during our one and only big argument, I brought up "commitments" and felt that our relationship should be more integrated after this period of time. His response was that he cared but that something tells him that he wants something different, which would include more freedom and the possibility of dating other women. He wants to be friends. We are still dating occasionally. I can tell that the feelings are still present, but neither one of us has discussed the outcome of our argument.

What do you do when you still care just as much as ever, but now are only seeing him occasionally, not knowing if in between times he is seeing others? I feel that if I give him an ultimatum and question him, he'll know it bothers me. The situation is driving me crazy and I'm just not sure how to handle it.

GENTLE READER:

Of course the situation is driving you crazy. The slow jilt is bad enough, but it is at least clear that one must not hang around waiting to get the last possible twitch of torture. When there is real hope that a slow courtship, rather than a slow jilt, is what is going on, the response is more difficult.

You are actually doing quite well. Miss Manners knows that it is fear, and not understanding, that keeps you from blurting out, "Why can't you make a commitment? Don't you love me? If you really loved me, you'd want to," and all those tedious remarks.

Whatever the motivation, the action required in this situation is no action. A commitment is made when both people want certainty. Pressing an unwilling person to make a commitment is giving that person the certainty without extracting it. It thereby removes his incentive of securing certainty by giving it freely.

Miss Manners apologizes if this sounds like the old keep-'em-guessing routine. She is well aware how exhausting, degrading and debilitating such antics are for the sure and loving heart. That is why God invented marriage: to give people a rest. Miss Manners wishes you the best and only asks that should you live through this courtship to marriage, you appreciate certainty and not start whining about how there is no more magic in your life.

~ *Declaring Intentions* ~

DEAR MISS MANNERS:

I am a twenty-eight-year-old male and have been seeing a twenty-three-year-old woman for almost one year. We work together and see no one else. My problem is that I am in love with her, but she is unable to verbalize any feelings at all for me. She has never had a relationship last for more than a few weeks and says she has never been in love. All of her friends and relatives like me and she is well liked by everyone I know. Many of her friends often say, "When are you two getting married?" She says she cares for me a great deal; but I feel I could very easily lose her. Every six weeks or so, I become depressed and get the feeling I am being used.

Is there a way for me to get her to express her true feelings? Even if they were negative, I would at least know how she felt and I would then have to deal with that.

GENTLE READER:

Yes, there is, but it is so simple that people lose sight of it while they are busy with such complicated things as feeling used, being unable to verbalize or getting depressed. Ask her: "Will you marry me?" If she says yes, it will mean that she cares for you as more than temporary companionship, and if she says no, it means that she doesn't.

～ Mysterious Declarations ～

DEAR MISS MANNERS:

I received a troublesome invitation last week, and I need your advice. Two former college friends sent a silk-screened card inviting me to "partake in a ritual celebrating the congruence of their lives." Knowing the couple makes me doubt very much that this is a wedding, yet I think it is something more than the exchange of friendship rings. Just what are my social duties in this case?

Do I congratulate them, and if so, on what? What sort of gift does one send for a congruence, and how should one dress for the occasion?

GENTLE READER:

Miss Manners had hoped that the plague of social originality among lovers had been stamped out, but here it is flaring up again. If it were Miss Manners who had been invited, she would go in a chiffon pastel dress and garden hat and send them a silver chafing dish. The other dignified approach is to play tourist and write, "I am afraid that I am not familiar with the customs of your faith. Would you be kind enough to explain to me exactly what you are doing?"

～ Displaying Affection ～

The birds are singing, the flowers are budding and it is time for Miss Manners to tell young lovers to stop necking in public.

It's not that Miss Manners is immune to romance. Miss Manners has been known to squeeze a gentleman's arm while being helped over a curb, and, in her wild youth, even to press a dainty slipper against a foot or two under the dinner table. Miss Manners also believes that the sight of people strolling hand in hand or arm in arm or arm in hand dresses up a city considerably more than the more familiar sight of people shaking umbrellas at one another. What Miss Manners objects to is the kind of activity that frightens the horses on the streets, although it is not the horses' sensibilities she is considering. It's the lovers and their future.

Heavy romances—we are speaking of the kind in which the participants can hardly keep their hands to themselves, not the kind in which they have nothing better to do with them—can progress in only two ways:

They can (1) end. In this case, if you have displayed the height of the romance publicly, the public will take pleasure in seeking you out in the depths. Just when you are being very careful not to move suddenly because you have your heart tied together only with bits of old string, it will spring at you and demand to know "Where's Rock? I thought you were inseparable?" or "How come I saw Hope out with three other guys last night?"

That is not the worst that can happen, however. Romances can also (2) not end. The participants can get married and live happily ever after. Then they are in trouble.

This is because one day they will stop behaving conspicuously. Then everyone will notice. The cause may not be that the romance will have gone out of the marriage, but that it will have a home to go to. With more opportunities to express affection, the couple no longer seizes the opportunity to do so on other people's sofas. The other people will then have a good snicker which, unlike the original snickers, cannot be passed off by the loving couple as jealousy. The Duchess of Windsor once said that she hated to have dinner in a restaurant alone with her husband because if they failed for one minute to chatter sparklingly at each other—taking, say, a moment to chew their food instead—everyone in the restaurant would be saying, "You see? That's what he gave up a throne for, and now look how bored they are."

∼ Broadcasting Affection ∼

DEAR MISS MANNERS:

I am 22 and have been in a relationship for three years now. My best friend, who is the same age, is also in a relationship, going on over a year, and she seems to feel the need to relay to me every single aspect of their romance, whether it's sexual, emotional, or even "Oh, guess what John said/emailed to me today!"

I don't mean to be callous; it's natural for a young lady to be excited about a relationship, but that tell-all feeling usually passes after the relationship has entered the long-term phase. I know I personally still don't feel the need to report to her every detail in the relationship between my boyfriend and me. It's getting more and more difficult to muster up enthusiasm or even interest in the minutiae of their courtship.

I've joked with her that "Thirty years from now, when you two are married, I might not listen anymore!" but she just laughed and carried on. Should I keep listening or is there a gentle way to say that maybe it's time she keeps all these details to herself? I'm happy for her but I'm ready for a new topic of conversation.

GENTLE READER:

As you understand, your friend is in the familiar shouting-it-from-the-housetops stage of romance, which, fortunately, does not last forever. The lady in question appears to have less discretion than most, but Miss Manners promises that even she will eventually stop.

In the meantime, best friends do have to endure some of this. From your remark that you don't "still" feel the need, Miss Manners gathers that at one time you must have cornered this lady, or other friends, with similar confidences. You can make a few protests, such as "You know I can't keep a secret," and "I'm never going to be able to look John in the eye," and "Stop, please, you're embarrassing me." Beyond that, Miss Manners recommends resigning yourself to using the time for a mental review of your grocery list.

⌒ Obtaining Approval ⌒

DEAR MISS MANNERS:

We are three brothers and a sister whose mother, having been married more than once, is now living, without marriage, with a man who we all feel is below her socially. He goes around the house in his undershirt—that kind of thing. How can we tell her tactfully?

GENTLE READER:

Tell her what? That her gentleman friend doesn't have a shirt on? She knows, she knows.

In the course of growing up, did you or your brothers or sister ever bring home a person you cared about who could perhaps not have seemed to your mother to be exactly what she might have wished for you as a partner? Did your mother ever indicate such a feeling? Probably not. If she did, you would have replied, with high indignation, "I don't care, she's my friend, and I'll choose my own friends, and I don't care about what you think of their clothes" or whatever. Perhaps your mother is old enough to choose her own friends.

~ Lukewarm Love ~

DEAR MISS MANNERS:

I am a senior citizen with a very nice Gentleman Friend who lives in another state. From time to time, he will call or write and say he would like to come to see me. I then respond giving him a specific week (allowing time for the airlines, two-weeks-advance-purchase). Then I wait—and wait. Eventually, he will write and say he is not sure about the dates etc., etc., and how about . . .

I keep a busy calendar, some things that could be changed but I would rather not. How do I courteously let him know that this habit (and it is a habit) upsets me? We do have a good time together, but to me, this is rude, even though I think it is unintentional.

GENTLE READER:

You wouldn't want to inject some warmth into this scheduling negotiation, would you? Miss Manners doesn't want to promote anything untoward, but you said this was a Gentleman Friend, and a nice one at that. So why does it sound as if you are complaining about waiting for the plumber?

The plumber would probably be more forthright in making the point that everyone has a busy schedule, lady, and not everyone is ready to jump when you name a time. If, instead, you said, "Oh, yes, please do come, I'm dying to see you," named several dates, and if none of these was convenient, still others, Miss Manners imagines he would come running. He might even bring the plumber with him.

DEAR MISS MANNERS:

I plan to visit a man that I met on the Internet. If things go as well as we think, we plan to become engaged. He has children in elementary school who will be with us part of the time. I asked about sleeping arrangements while they are there and he answered that they will not think anything of me sharing his bed. I refuse to do this while they're visiting. He thinks that I am too old fashioned. I say that I have too much respect for them to do this. I feel that we would not set a good example for them. He tells me that they understand that adults are allowed choices that children aren't. I say that right is right, no matter the year. What do you say?

GENTLE READER:

Unless Miss Manners missed the part about how you first arranged a meeting with this person on safe ground, then got to know him and then fell in love with him—you are talking about agreeing to consummate—not exactly a relationship, but an exchange of emails with a stranger.

Furthermore, this is a stranger who is dismissive of your opinion in a matter of high concern to yourself, as well as of the concept of setting a good example for his children. If this is what is meant by an adult choice, Miss Manners is afraid she wants no part of it.

LOVE PROBLEMS (FROM BAD TO WORSE)

~ Timing ~

DEAR MISS MANNERS:

I am hopelessly in love with a woman who is in love with another man. For some time, I thought my case was hopeless; however, this spring, I found out her boyfriend is moving away. At first I thought she would be heartbroken, but instead she has been very casual about the situation. What would be a proper waiting period before asking her out or demonstrating my interest in developing a closer friendship? Also, when I do get her to accompany me out, should I act only slightly interested and pretend not to be overwhelmed by her charm, or should I let her know how I feel about her?

GENTLE READER:

There is no formal waiting period observed by a lady who is bereaved because her boyfriend has moved away. In fact, there seems to be no such waiting period for any kind of bereavement any longer, although Miss Manners did think it in questionable taste when she heard of a proposal being made to a gentleman whose wife had almost, but not quite, completed the formality of dying. So let us abandon the pretense of talking etiquette, in this case, and talk strategy.

Strategically, it is best to be the next romance but one, when following a romance that has come to grief one way or another. It is an unfortunate fact of life that the generous soul who listens to outpourings of anguish, devises ways to distract the unhappy one, takes the midnight telephone calls and selflessly suppresses his or her own desires in order to devote full time to nursing the beloved back to emotional health—that person gets thanked and dumped when the recovered patient is ready to fall in love again. This is frightfully ungrateful, of course, but it happens all the time. The nurse is associated with the unpleasant atmosphere of the sickroom.

Nevertheless, Miss Manners understands that you, having waited out this gentleman, are not prepared to wait for a second to come along and then go along. Also, she knows that every once in a while someone marries the first candidate on the rebound, rather than the second, and that you would be perfectly furious at Miss Manners if this turned out to be one of those cases.

Her advice, then, is to step in now, but to be as little like a therapist as possible. Do not encourage this lady to talk about her woes, do not allow her to treat you sloppily on the grounds that she is not feeling her best, do not be excessively understanding, at the expense of your own comfort. Be a confident suitor, expecting the lady to behave well toward you, and acting cautiously and casually. Miss Manners is sorry to have to tell anyone to be less kind and unselfish than he would like to be, but surely you have heard about nice guys finishing last.

~ Nomenclature ~

DEAR MISS MANNERS:

I am a divorced woman who has been involved with a divorced man for almost six months. We are both in our 30s, have children and maintain separate homes. What is the proper way to refer to this man? "Boyfriend" sounds like we're teenagers.

GENTLE READER:

Respectable nomenclature for unmarried people who form a social unit is the Great Unsolved Etiquette Problem of our time, and as Miss Manners has been struggling with it for years, she was hoping someone would come up with a solution.

Not quite, but thanks for trying.

"Boyfriend" and "girlfriend" are, as you say, adolescent; "significant other" and "special friend" are too coy; "lover" and all other references to what they do in private are not coy enough. Over the years, countless other suggestions have been made, but none are quite to Miss Manners' satisfaction. Some are too vivid, some too obscure. Foreign words and manufactured words are too stilted. Common ones, such as "companion," "roommate" and "housemate," are too easily open to misinterpretation. Picky, picky, picky.

Tradition is no help here, because until recent decades, there was no need for such a term. You were either engaged or married or you weren't, and if you weren't, you didn't go around announcing it. Unmarried people who lived together let others assume they were married, and lovers who had separate residences because of such complications as concurrent spouses, described themselves as "great and good friends."

"Partner" when the couple lives together, and "friend" when they don't, remain the fall-back terms. Note, however, that the circumstances have reversed: Rather than needing to fudge the situation, the people involved now sometimes need to make their situation clear.

As you can imagine, Miss Manners is not countenancing their talking about the private aspects of their association. Discussing that will always be vulgar, no matter how many people insist upon doing so on airplanes and television, and the ban applies to the married as much as to the unmarried.

What has changed is that the unmarried couple is socially recognized. It is necessary to know who goes with whom for those who are issuing invitations, either to parties (in which case they need to know if there is someone who should always be invited with a particular person) or to closer relationships (in which case they need to know if someone is already spoken for).

In such cases, "friend" isn't going to help. Too many guests ask "May I bring a friend?" when they mean they are going looking for one so they won't have to depend on the company provided. Announcing that one has a friend doesn't convey the idea that it is a bar to acquiring another one. In the absence of a modern term, Miss Manners would rely on old ones: "This is my beau" in introductions, and "I'm keeping company with someone" by way of explanation. She understands, however, that most people would not be able to do this with a straight face. For them, saying "We're a couple" will have to do until someone comes up with something better.

DEAR MISS MANNERS:

How do you like this one: my daughter is twenty-six, and lives with a divorced man exactly my age and his twenty-two-year-old daughter who has an adorable eight-month-old baby girl. At this stage in my life, I can't think of anything I want more than a grandchild—I baby-sit this "semi-step-great-granddaughter" (or whatever she is besides being simply darling), but this isn't exactly what I've had in mind. And talk about making introductions when my daughter and I are out to lunch or shopping with the baby—whew! It's one of the few times I'm almost rendered speechless. Any suggestions?

GENTLE READER:

Whew! is right. If you attempt to explain this relationship to people you meet while out lunching or shopping, the baby will probably grow up and move away before you finish talking. Miss Manners suggests you curtail the introduction to merely "And this is Baby Snooks," or whatever. People will naturally assume that you have kidnapped this child for complex psychological reasons or hope of financial gain, or that she has selected you for her nursery Adopt-a-Grandparent work project. But so what? She will grow up learning that you can't explain everything to everyone, which is a valuable lesson in life.

⌒ Incompatibility ⌒

DEAR MISS MANNERS:

I am a material girl who appreciates many of the finer things in life. I was raised by wealthier parents who taught me to only have the best. Therefore, I wear designer clothes, attend the theater/symphony regularly, and only travel first class on airplanes.

When I started dating my boyfriend one year ago, I was informed that he had a very similar childhood. Our families were supposedly very much the same. He made a point of telling me repeatedly that he made a lot of money, and liked to have a good time with it. He wanted to spoil me.

My boyfriend and I are very much in love. We have a wonderful time together and have many of the same goals in life. The problem is that he is what I consider a "cheapskate." I bought him a very lavish Christmas gift. He purchased me a nice watch and a few other nice things. This may sound hideous but I totaled up the cost of my Christmas gifts. It was less than half of what I spent on him. I know that feelings cannot be "totaled up" with a monetary value. However, I feel like I may be signing myself away to a lifetime of coupon clipping and two-for-one dinners.

His cheap behavior is something that has been instilled in him from a very young age. For his birthday, his parents took us to dinner. It was him, me, his two brothers, and their significant others seated around a bowl of spaghetti and a pizza at a family-style restaurant. I did not dare order a drink or, ask for more food—even though I had to eat dinner when I returned home that night. I thanked his parents for a lovely evening and sent a thank you card for their generosity a couple of days later.

I would like to know how I approach the subject of his cheapness. Even if you advise me to wipe the tears I cry away with my Armani dress as I whine.

GENTLE READER:

Wipe away, because Miss Manners is sorry to inform you that this would be a most unsuitable marriage. Your backgrounds are far too different.

Love has been known to overcome vast differences of incomes. Even differences of goals may be rendered compatible. But not basic differences in manners. A marriage between someone brought up with a major sense of entitlement and someone who was brought up to the modest code of simplicity is doomed.

～ Irritability ～

DEAR MISS MANNERS:

My girlfriend and I have been seeing each other for two years and we generally cook for each other when at each other's homes. I also take her out once in a while, and when we do a project at the other's home, the visiting person gets taken to dinner or made dinner. At my house (and I've told her this) I have the position that whatever is in the fridge is open for her to indulge herself. Basically, whatever is mine is hers, and I've told her there's no reason to even ask, just take what you want.

In recent months, my girlfriend will call me out or make dinner and then accuse me of "sponging." On occasion, I've helped myself to juice and I'll get a comment like, "Just drink water." Am I overstepping my boundaries? She's intimated that she expects the man to pay for all outings. Is that fair? And with me being hospitable to her in my home? I just did my taxes (I keep all receipts), and I spent over $4000 just on entertainment, not to mention presents on Valentine's, birthdays, Christmas, etc.

I think it's just rude to ask someone out and then criticize them because they accept, or to tell me to drink water after I've extended the use of my beverages and food at my home.

GENTLE READER:

Miss Manners is sorry to tell you that it won't help you in the least to have her side with you. The lady in question is deeply miffed at you, and water and juice have nothing to do with it.

Whether or not the situation is terminal, Miss Manners cannot say. It is possible that the lady is irritated because she wants a bond that is not merely that of two friends trying to be fair—marriage being what comes to mind. It is also possible that what irritates her is the sight of you, and that what she wants is to put you out of her life as well as her refrigerator.

In neither case would it help to bring out all the receipts to show her how much you spent on her. This is one of those rare situations in which Miss Manners recommends what everyone else recommends for all situations, including those best left alone: Sit down with the lady and ask her gently what is really bothering her.

❧ *Impulsiveness* ❧

DEAR MISS MANNERS:

I made a blunder by going out with a friend, and as one thing leads to another, I ended up kissing and caressing her. I thought she was into it but then she suddenly got up and abruptly ended it all.

I apologized for what happened. But she said I have taken advantage of her. I said I wasn't. My only probable reason to her was I got carried away by the romantic notion of the encounter. I felt very bad for my actions and I could feel her cold and unenthusiastic response when I call her, unlike before. I want to make amends and hope we can be friends again. I am married with no children. Miss Manners, what would be your advice?

GENTLE READER:

Miss Manners' advice is for you to keep your hands off the telephone and everything else. Otherwise, the next advice you seek should be on the legal, rather than the etiquette, aspect of your behavior.

❧ *Repulsiveness* ❧

DEAR MISS MANNERS:

What is the correct response to the occasional drunken email from an ex-girlfriend, with whom I am on civil—if distant—terms?

It is embarrassing and tedious to read of her night's sexual conquest or even worse, her professed continuing love amid a cornucopia of typographical errors and misplaced punctuation. Is polite admonishment in order? Perhaps we need to legislate EUI (Emailing Under the Influence) and install breathalyzers on the workstations of habitual offenders.

GENTLE READER:

When someone you know is, as we delicately say, "not herself" the polite reaction is not to notice (or, in cases where it is necessary to confiscate keys or visit emergency rooms, not to remember having noticed). If Miss Manners is not mistaken, your computer has a key designed for that purpose.

⌒ *Disease* ⌒

DEAR MISS MANNERS:

I do not consider myself to be a promiscuous person, but recently, much to my dismay, I learned that I have contracted a social disease. The man from whom I received this dubious honor was a passive carrier, so he was unaware of his condition. Since he is not from the area, I called him to inform him of the problem. Is it wrong of me to expect some kind gesture from him? Maybe some get well flowers or even a note? I'm not sure how modern etiquette would deal with this situation, so I'll be eagerly awaiting your response.

GENTLE READER:

Modern etiquette does not have a specific rule to cover the social situation you mention, but it is Miss Manners' experience that traditional etiquette has a rule for everything. The one that applies here is that a note or flowers or both would be a charming way to apologize for having inadvertently caused another person discomfort.

⌒ *A Mental Lapse* ⌒

DEAR MISS MANNERS:

What can you do after accidentally calling your present lover by your former lover's name?

GENTLE READER:

Seek a future lover. Such a mistake is easy to do and impossible to undo. Why do you think the term "darling" was invented?

BREAKING UP

DEAR MISS MANNERS:

I am interested in knowing what is the proper method of breaking off a relationship. For the past several months, I have been exclusively dating a young lady whom I was extremely fond of. Everything seemed to be going great until about two months ago, when she suddenly seemed to lose interest in me. Every time I wanted to see her, she was busy, etc., until finally I just stopped calling her. I have not heard from her since. What do you think of breaking off a relationship in this manner, and how should it be handled?

Gentle Reader:

What you describe is your basic Kafka Romance Dissolver, and you handled it exactly correctly. Do not be offended if Miss Manners approves of the young lady's behavior as well.

Naturally, you were hurt and bewildered when your invitations were repeatedly rejected without explanation. Miss Manners would like to point out to you, however, that there is no possible way for one person to end a romance that the other person thought was going great without causing pain and bewilderment. The chief difference between the Kafka method and those more socially approved ones that come with explanations is that the latter engender humiliation, as well as pain and bewilderment. What, after all, can the explanation be?

"Sure I like you, but I met someone I'm really crazy about."

"I know you can't help it, but there are a lot of things about you that were beginning to get on my nerves."

"It was fun for a while, but lately I've found myself getting bored and restless."

And so on. Rarely, these days, does anyone break off an exciting, stimulating, fulfilling romance to lead a life of service or to save the family through an expedient alliance. Therefore, all explanations can be reduced to the fact that the other person would rather do something else—sometimes anything else—than continue the romance. Attempts to obfuscate, such as "I love you, but I need room to grow," don't fool anyone.

The patronizing sweeteners customarily added to these explanations are particularly galling. It is easier to bear being denounced as a villain by someone you still love than to be told that you are a "nice person but."

Perhaps you will object that the method without explanation took some time, because its comparative subtlety confused you about what was actually happening. Granted. Nevertheless, Miss Manners maintains that the period of suffering was, in the end, shorter. The early part, say the first two rejections, was annoyance, rather than devastation, because you did not yet believe it. Then you began to suspect and pay attention; you guessed; you tested the hypothesis by ending your calls; and then you had your proof. Indeed, that period must have hurt.

Consider what that time would have been like had you been spending it discussing the situation with the young lady. As the explanation method spuriously suggests reasons for the whims of the heart, the reaction of the rejected person is always to offer counterarguments. It would have taken just as long, and as the young lady would be forced to escalate her objections to overcome your arguments, the pain would have been more intense.

The true reward comes now. In your memory, you may set this young lady forever as a fool who didn't know how to appreciate you. You needn't carry around the certain knowledge of how little she appreciated you, nor the memory of your having made a fool of yourself trying to argue the matter with her.

DEAR MISS MANNERS:

I gave my girlfriend diamond earrings for Christmas and she dumped me a week ago. She admitted she was thinking about breaking up before Christmas. Should I expect them back?

GENTLE READER:

Not likely. Just a guess, but a lady who disobeys the etiquette rule against accepting valuable jewelry from a gentleman to whom she is not related—and to the extent of accepting this from a gentleman she is thinking of dropping—does not strike Miss Manners as devoted to the rule about returning love tokens from a defunct romance.

DEAR MISS MANNERS:

A few months ago, my partner of some years and I decided to end our relationship. The decision was cordial and mutual and there remains a bond of history and of love between us. The immediate cause of the break-up, however, was a relationship he had developed and concealed over the past year.

I am not 12 years old and I have read novels and so I am aware that this has happened before, but nonetheless, I decided to take the High Road (as there was no one else there competing for space) and say that our split was cordial and mutual. Only when asked did I mention where X had moved and then I answered, with a practiced poker face, who he was living with. If asked, "And are they friends or . . ." I always simply said, "You'll have to ask X about that."

So far, so good. But what about the several times when someone asked directly, "and are you sure that they are just friends?" (Believe me: it is their behavior over the last six months which prompted those questions.) Is "You'll have to ask X about that" still the preferred response, and if so, was I really awful in saying (again with a poker face), "I think you would get different answers from X and me to that question."

GENTLE READER:

Stop! You're looking in the wrong direction. That way will take you off the High Road. And you were marching along it so proudly. You have not yet fallen into the mud, Miss Manners acknowledges. But watch out. Your proposed statement is a road sign pointing your questioners toward the Low Road, and hinting that you can be enticed to guide them there.

DEAR MISS MANNERS:

I need advice, please, on the etiquette of dealing with a broken heart in the course of everyday business and social affairs. Having just lost a wonderful man, my world is naturally diminished. While I am handling the situation very well most of the time, I find that at times I am caught off-guard. I have burst into tears in public places, failed to complete work assignments, and lost the thread of conversations in mid-sentence.

What I need is a way to communicate my present state of withdrawal and vulnerability to friends and co-workers without baring my soul, offering excuses, or asking for sympathy. If I had a broken leg, most people would respond with uncommon decency and expect me to get better as soon as possible so that they could go back to treating me any way they felt like. Do you have any words, Miss Manners, which are as symbolic of a broken heart as a cast is for a broken leg?

GENTLE READER:

The symbol is the heart worn on the sleeve, but Miss Manners does not advise wearing it, as it is much less attractive than a leg cast. In fact, the comparison with the broken leg does not work at all, as you will realize if you think about the questions people address to those in leg casts: "How did you do that?" "Was it your fault?" "When are you going to be getting around again?" "Are you suing?"

You really do not wish to have such questions asked about your broken heart, do you? Perhaps we would be better off using an ailment as private in nature as the broken heart. If you had hemorrhoids, for example, you would excuse yourself when necessary merely by saying, "I haven't been feeling terribly well," and when pressed for details would add only, "Oh, it's nothing really, and I'd rather not discuss it."

5. *Marriage (for Beginners)*

Engagements

THE ENGAGEMENT, that sweet time before an emotional commitment is turned into a legal commitment, is, of course, a trial period. The reason it is such a trial is that a couple who can get through an engagement, with all its etiquette land mines, ought to find marriage a cinch. The failure of so many young marriages, however, leads Miss Manners to suspect that these people are not enduring sufficiently rigorous engagements and are doing their fighting after marriage, when it can take a nastier turn.

The popular belief that sex and money are the two subjects that couples split over is erroneous. People who love each other don't break up over such trifles. They must learn to handle the explosive subject of conflicting etiquette. For example, a situation where one marriage partner is feeling playfully amorous and the other is taking the bar examination in the morning is an etiquette problem of dangerous proportions.

Here, then, is a checklist of etiquette fights an engaged couple should have, so as to be ready and tired enough for a peaceful marriage. Miss Manners is presuming that the couple is well suited and in love, and that fortune and their families are smiling upon them.

SIX MONTHS BEFORE

- Fight over whether wedding is to be formal or informal.
- Fight over what is meant by "formal" and "informal."
- Fight over size of wedding.
- Fight over whether seventy-five people can be considered a small wedding.
- Fight over whether silver and china fit into your way of life.
- Fight over whether silver and china are a better investment than electronic equipment.

THREE MONTHS BEFORE

- Fight over whether anybody can really tell the difference between engraving and raised print.
- Fight over whether relatives who had bitter divorces should be invited, as well as their former spouses.
- Fight over whether their own former lovers should be invited.
- Fight over whether the mother of the bridegroom should be forced to wear a type of dress she dislikes in order to be visually paired with the mother of the bride, who finds that style flattering.

TWO MONTHS BEFORE

- Fight over the discovery that the bridegroom's family has not only exceeded its quota of guests, but has provided a list using initials instead of names and terms such as "and family" for children.
- Fight over whether guests' requests to bring their current love interests should be honored and who is going to tell people that their small children will not be welcome.
- Fight over slurs made toward relatives who sent cheap or tasteless presents.

ONE MONTH BEFORE

- Fight over whether it is the bride or the bride's mother who is at fault because elderly friends are beginning to complain that their presents have not yet been acknowledged.
- Fight over whether the seating arrangements should be done according to tradition or according to who is speaking to whom.

ONE WEEK BEFORE

- Fight over the failure of some guests from each side to answer invitations and about who is going to prod whom so as to provide accurate numbers to the caterer.
- Fight over how much luggage is to be taken on the wedding trip.
- Fight over the wisdom of marrying a person now discovered to be short-tempered, stylistically alien to one's own tradition and completely absorbed in petty details to the exclusion of any intellectual or romantic activity.

AT THE WEDDING

- Fight over whether the ceremonial kiss should demonstrate enthusiasm for the marriage or protect the bridal makeup.
- Fight over whether it is each other, the wedding guests or the videographer who deserves the bridal couple's chief attention during the reception.

This is only a minimum list, and every young couple should make additions. For example, there are people to whom a wedding reception means dainty tea sandwiches and champagne only, and others for whom no wedding is recognized by God unless everybody present is groaning audibly and able, through the bounty of the hosts, to go home sick. If the mothers' dresses fight appeals to you, you may expand it by attempting to force all grandmothers to match, which could stir up a great deal of irascible excitement.

The important thing to remember is that no one rule of etiquette is as essential as the general atmosphere of conflicting standards. People who have conscientiously fought out all such matters during the engagement will find themselves only too grateful to be living happily ever after.

Dear Miss Manners:

I was informed that engagements should not last longer than six months, ideally, or a year at the most, due to the strain it might cause. Has this ever been a rule of etiquette? My fiancé and I will not be married until after I get my doctorate, which may take four more years, and I don't think this will be more stressful than simply dating for that time.

Gentle Reader:

What about the strain on your relatives and friends? Do you think they can bear four years of listening to you talk about your wedding color scheme and which band you should hire? (That's a rule Miss Manners just made up, but she is happy to grant you an exception if you promise to show some exceptional bridal restraint.)

There have been times that society has encouraged short engagements, so that the couple would not have to exercise a different sort of restraint for a prolonged time, and other times in which it has encouraged long engagements so the couple could get to know each other better. We no longer presume either problem, and therefore leave the length of your engagement for you, your fiancé and your caterer to decide.

⟿ *The Proposal* ⟿

Now that weddings have become drama festivals, the marriage proposal has turned into a pageant that serves as the curtain raiser. Unlike the main events, this has a sole producer, the future bridegroom, and what he is supposed to produce is—a surprise.

Miss Manners can imagine that it is not easy to surprise a lady whose relatives have been asking her for years if the two of them were ever getting married, and who may even have been asking the question herself. However, valiant tries are made. Romantic trips provide the scenery, and a hidden ring (preferably not hidden in something the lady goes ahead and drinks) is the prop. If enough work is put into it, the gentleman will be exhausted enough not to mess with the wedding arrangements, thus enabling the bride to (1) have it all her way, and (2) complain that if he loved her, he would take more of an interest.

The truth is that surprise was never a successful element of the proposal. Ladies who blushed and protested that they had never thought of such a thing (but would start doing so right away) were merely meeting expectations. Here is the basic form for bridegrooms who can't figure out how to get the ring through airport security without the accompanying fiancée seeing it:

1. Arrange the lady on a sofa.
2. Kneel in front of her. That should put her into shock. If she is still able to talk and says something like, "What do you think you're doing?" simply smile mysteriously.
3. Pull out of your pocket a small velvet box with an engagement ring inside. That should put her back into shock, giving you the opportunity to perform the next step, while you are still holding the box.
4. Say "I can't live without you. Will you marry me?" Got that? Not "I think we might make a go of it," or "My mother says she's tired of her friends asking when we're getting married," or "I've talked to my tax consultant, and I think we can get married without getting hit too badly."
5. Open the box, take her hand and put the ring on her finger.
6. Congratulations. You are now engaged.

Miss Manners does not guarantee this. The lady may actually not want to marry you. But by this method, it may take her a while to recover and remember that.

DEAR MISS MANNERS:

Can a woman ask a man for his hand in marriage and if so, what is the protocol? I would like to ask my live-in boyfriend of 2-1/2 yrs. to marry me but am not sure how to do it. Is there a ring involved? Please answer soon, I would like to ask him on his birthday next month and would like to do it right.

GENTLE READER:

Whether it would scare your prospect for you to pop out at him brandishing a diamond ring, Miss Manners cannot say. But the idea certainly scares her.

Mind you, she believes it is as appropriate for the lady to propose to the gentleman as it is for a gentleman to propose to a lady. It is just that there is a difference between that and playing "Okay, you be the girl now and I'll be the boy."

She supposes that those contemplating marriage know what is acceptable to their particular sweethearts. But she happens to favor dignity. No one who is otherwise favorable was ever put off by being told "I love you, and I want to spend the rest of my life with you."

⌁ The Engagement Ring ⌁

DEAR MISS MANNERS:

I am contemplating proposing to my girlfriend, probably in two or three months. I would like to offer my future wife one of my grandmothers' rings. I am the oldest grandson on both sides of my family (I am not sure if that means anything or not); both grandmothers are alive, but widowed. Is it unusual for a living grandmother to give up her ring to a grandchild? I am uncomfortable asking anyone in my family about this until I know what the proper etiquette is.

GENTLE READER:

It is charming to offer one's fiancée a family ring if one is available. It is conceivable that a living grandmother might be willing to undergo the wrench of parting with the engagement ring given her by her own dear departed husband for the pleasure of knowing that it would live beyond her as the cherished symbol of her dear grandson's love.

But Miss Manners gathers that neither of your grandmothers has had any such thought. You can bubble on about your romance and hope for inspiration, but if your question is, "Is it proper to wrestle a grandmother to the ground to rip her ring off her finger and give it to your girlfriend?" the answer is no, dear, it isn't.

DEAR MISS MANNERS:

Is it necessary to buy my fiancée an engagement ring?

GENTLE READER:

No. Nowadays, it isn't even necessary to marry her. We do everything by the dictates of the heart these days, which accounts for the astounding divorce rate.

Examining the Engagement Ring

DEAR MISS MANNERS:

I have recently become engaged and my fiancé was very generous when purchasing my ring and it is lovely. I am curious as to the proper response when someone sees my ring and instead of just saying, "How pretty" their response is "It's huge!"

Do I just say, "thank you"? That sounds a little funny to me.

GENTLE READER:

It is more than a little funny, because these people actually believe they have delivered a compliment, as the situation demands, and are confidently expecting to be thanked for having sized up your ring rather than admired it. To thank them would not be conspicuous, but Miss Manners understands that it would be galling. Murmuring something bridal, such as "Well, he has a big heart," would do just as well.

The Bridegroom's Ring

DEAR MISS MANNERS:

Please help settle a disagreement between my husband and I. Though a friendly disagreement, it would be nice to find out who is correct!

Who should purchase the groom's wedding ring? I say the groom since it matches the bridal set, they are picked out together and the rings are a symbol not a gift to be exchanged. He says the bride; since he is getting her ring, she should purchase his.

GENTLE READER:

On the surface, this seems like a simple question. The bride purchases the bridegroom's ring, as she gives it to him (presents are always symbolic, by the way). It does not need to match her ring, but if that is what they both want, all the bride needs to do is to buy the bridegroom's ring wherever he bought her bridal rings.

Under the surface, however, this question is teeming with something Miss Manners would not describe as friendly. Where is the marital attitude that everything you have is shared, and yet, paradoxically, that one of your greatest pleasures is to be able to give to the other?

~ The Parental Meeting ~

DEAR MISS MANNERS:

When a young man asks a woman to marry him, what should his parents do? Should they call the future bride up and perhaps take the couple out to dinner to celebrate their engagement?

GENTLE READER:

What the bridegroom's parents have to do is comparatively easy; it is what they have to refrain from doing that is difficult. It is their duty to initiate the relationship between themselves and the bride and her parents. This is better done by inviting the bride and her parents to dinner in their home rather than taking them out, as they will be madly curious to see how the bridegroom has been brought up. They, in turn, will be deluged with information about the bride's family's taste and behavior as wedding plans are made. Refraining from offering critiques of this is the hard part of their job.

~ Clashing Manners ~

DEAR MISS MANNERS:

I am engaged to be married, but there are moments I think it will never work out—usually when I am with my fiancé's family. I have been brought up to expect certain things from people and it seems at times they have no manners at all. They think I am picky and stuck-up, with no warmth at all. Help!

GENTLE READER:

Please allow Miss Manners to wish you happiness by attempting to deflect you from the misery you are wishing on yourself.

Marriage, my dear, is the formation of a family from two existing families. The two are likely to have different styles of behavior, which can cause friction. When it is said that marriages are easier between people who come from "similar backgrounds," that is not a euphemism for money, religion or race, but an accurate warning about clashing manners. Generally, one family has a more formal style than the other. The more formal side refers to the less formal as having "no manners at all," and the less formal to the more formal as being "picky" or "stuck-up" or having "no warmth at all."

That there exist many different styles is not, in your case, the point. The point is how to create a harmonious marriage out of disparate elements. You cannot ask your fiancé's family to maintain your style, or your family to maintain his. He is your best guide to explaining his family's motivations and what they expect from you—you should be listening to him on this, and you evidently are not—as you are about yours. What you can expect of him is to reach a stylistic agreement with you for the new family—you, him and your future children.

Do not be shy about establishing compatibility in manners as a prerequisite of marriage. Many foolish young people think that if they can establish physical compatibility, the manners will follow easily, whereas it is more likely to work the other way around.

DEAR MISS MANNERS:

At a beautiful engagement party which we gave for our daughter and her fiancé, they went around telling all our friends that they never plan to have children. We were horrified. It isn't that we don't understand that they are young (twenty-two and twenty-three) and maybe shouldn't have children for quite a while; and it isn't that we're anxious for them to provide us with grandchildren. We just think their statement was in poor taste. If they do have children, those children are going to think they were unwanted. Also, what must our friends at the party have thought of such a declaration?

GENTLE READER:

It is never charming to announce your reproductive plans socially, but Miss Manners does not think that your friends will remember the statement with anything except amusement should the couple later change their minds. Didn't your daughter announce to you, a decade or two ago, that she was never going to get married because boys were so icky?

⌀ Engagement Presents ⌀

DEAR MISS MANNERS:

Am writing to ask you if it's necessary to give a gift when you're invited to an announcement of an engagement party? The wedding isn't to take place for another year.

GENTLE READER:

It depends on whom you ask.

There are those who believe that the chickens should turn for advice to the fox, and who therefore consult the restaurant and hotel industries about how much to tip restaurant and hotel employees. If you asked the engaged couple, you might hear that it is not only necessary on this oddly contrived occasion (doesn't announcing that you're going to announce something defeat its purpose?), but that you must give them something they have preselected.

However, you asked Miss Manners, who has no personal stake in the matter, only the mission to uphold propriety. She can tell you that the only traditional engagement present is the ring that the gentleman gives his fiancée. There is no proper basis for anyone's expecting engagement presents from other people, including those who will have ample opportunity to symbolize their affection by giving wedding presents when the time comes.

DEAR MISS MANNERS:

Our daughter has recently become engaged, and the young man's parents have given them a set of table linens as an engagement present. Is it necessary for us to give them an engagement present, too? We plan to present them with something nice as a wedding gift, but you know how easily engagements are broken. For instance, who would keep the linens if the wedding never comes off? Would it be better for us to give her a shower, with a smaller, shower-type gift?

GENTLE READER:

Nothing is certain in this world, least of all anything having to do with romance, and Miss Manners understands your caution. (One of these days, she is going to announce a new rule that couples must return all presents unless the marriage lasts a minimum of six months. She is still working on the details, such as what if the present is slightly used by then?)

Engagement presents are already safe, because they must be returned to the givers if the wedding does not take place. You cannot give your own daughter, or anyone related to you, a shower. There is nothing to stop you from giving her an eggbeater, or whatever you consider to be a shower-type present for an engagement present, but perhaps you will feel more generous now that Miss Manners has promised you that you will get it back.

⁓ Bridal Showers ⁓

DEAR MISS MANNERS:

I often have the chance to give bridal showers, and love doing so. A problem often arises with the invitations. My mother says that I should send them to friends and relatives who live out of town or state, just to be courteous. I feel that a shower is only for those who live near and that the others will give their gift at the wedding or send a congratulatory note, with a possible gift. Postage is so high, and invitations aren't cheap, either. What do you say?

GENTLE READER:

Miss Manners hates to go against the judgment of mothers who are pleading for courtesy, but she has to say that you are correct. Perhaps your mother is confusing the courtesy of inviting people to a wedding without presuming to anticipate whether they will be able to attend. One does not do that with lesser parties. A wedding is considered to be enough of an event to make a trip worthwhile, but a shower, however pleasant, is not.

DEAR MISS MANNERS:

Twice this year, co-workers in long-standing co-habitation arrangements have gotten engaged to their partners. Don't get me wrong: I approve of their getting married. It's the right thing to do. The thing that irks me is the attendant hoopla.

These girls are flashing gaudy diamonds, giggling like schoolgirls and planning lavish weddings, complete with white dresses. And the response of the girls in the office? "Oh, we must throw a shower!"

We must? I was under the impression a shower was to help the new bride set up her household. After living together for nearly a decade, having children and buying a home together, I think those households are pretty well set up. Besides which, a moral issue exists: If you stole a car off the lot, drove it around for five years and then brought it back and announced you were ready to pay for it, would you expect a ticker-tape parade in your honor? These couples have stolen the privileges of marriage for themselves. Isn't it incumbent on them to set matters right discreetly and humbly?

I would like to offer congratulations and sincere well-wishes, but I don't care to be a party to the party, if you get my drift. Nor do I wish to put these girls on the spot by explaining what I think. I've got a faint suspicion that no matter how I word it, it's going to seem rude. On the afternoon of the first shower, I discovered some suddenly urgent "personal business" to attend to, and unless you have an alternative, I will do the same this time.

GENTLE READER:

Miss Manners shares your reluctance to insult people and spoil their fun concerning an activity she finds morally distasteful. Only in her case, it isn't focused on wedding hoopla, as you put it. Overdue marriages need to be celebrated too, and she can't be bothered to keep track of couples' tardiness for the unpleasant purpose of deducting carats and discouraging giggles.

Miss Manners' distaste is for pseudosocial life at the office, because it is occasioned by proximity rather than affection. She believes we should all just work through, go home earlier and give showers for our own friends. So here is a gracious way of getting around both your scruples and hers. Go early and say to the honoree, "I'm so sorry I can't stay because I have work to do, but I want to wish you happiness."

Ceremonial Questions and Explanations

DEAR MISS MANNERS:

My daughter is getting married soon, in a big church wedding. We thought it was charming that her young man asked my husband's permission to have her hand, even though they have been living together for nearly two years. During the wedding festivities, his family will be staying with him at their apartment, and my daughter will move back into her old room at our house. The thought of her there, among her doll collection, old teddy bear, and childhood books (which I am saving for her children, the first of whom is expected in six months) touches me and I would like to hold the traditional mother-daughter talk with her about sex the night before the wedding. Do you think this would be superfluous?

GENTLE READER:

Oh, no. Surely you remember reading her those childhood books aloud. Was your mutual pleasure lessened just because you both knew how the story came out? Asking the father for his daughter's hand may have been superfluous—as a gentleman of Miss Manners' acquaintance replied in similar circumstances, "Why not? You've already had the rest of her"—but you nevertheless found it charming.

Ceremonial Drinks

DEAR MISS MANNERS:

My fiancée and I have been in one continuous whirl of parties practically since the day we got engaged. We are also having a large wedding, and there will be several parties before it. Mind you, we are not complaining. It's hectic, but it's fun.

My question has to do with being toasted. Someone is always proposing a toast to us, or sometimes just to me. People seem to think that champagne is the only fit drink for us now—and, again, I'm not complaining about that, either. But last night I got a little high, and started telling funny stories about the time I almost ran off and got married to a boy who got arrested, soon afterwards, for stealing cars. That is, I thought these stories were funny. Nobody else did. There were a few forced laughs, and my fiancée turned white. In short, I think I had better stop drinking so much at the pre-wedding parties, or there won't be any wedding party. Yet I know there is nothing more gauche than refusing to drink a toast. What shall I do?

GENTLE READER:

Fortunately for you, there is something more gauche than refusing to drink a toast, and that is drinking a toast to oneself. Since you are the object of all these liquid good wishes, all you have to do—in fact, all you should do—is to sit there, hands in lap, and smile demurely while everyone else drinks to you. You are supposed to be sufficiently drunk on happiness. If you can manage a blush, that is nice too. It is only after the toast is completed that you may join the guzzling, or not, as you see fit.

When England's Princess Margaret Rose was a child, she was said to have asked her father what he sang while everyone else was singing "God Save the King." The answer to your question is the same as the answer to hers: Try to look gratified and dignified, but under no circumstances should you join right in.

⁓ The Broken Engagement ⁓

The solemn rule that one must never break an engagement just because something better has come along does not, of course, apply to engagements to enter into holy matrimony. A person who would break an engagement to dine for reasons other than sudden death is a cad, but for an engagement to be married, the excuse "I don't know, I just don't feel like it" will do.

Miss Manners does not mean to suggest that breaking such engagements is not a serious, delicate matter. When doing so, one cannot be too careful of the tender feelings of those most concerned—the caterer, the bridesmaids and the mother of the bride.

Miss Manners would never advise anyone to marry someone they don't like just because the arrangements have been made. The social mortification of calling wedding guests, packing up the wedding presents to be returned and breaking the news to the prospective spouse must be endured, in preference to living unhappily ever after. Society may miss a good party, but it will not have to endure listening to the story of the divorce.

⌐∽ Announcing a Broken Engagement ∿⌐

DEAR MISS MANNERS:

My wedding invitations were mailed on Saturday morning, and on Saturday night I broke my engagement. It was to have been a large, formal wedding, so there will be lots of people receiving engraved invitations which must now be recalled. How shall I do this? May I use the envelopes from the announcements?

GENTLE READER:

Miss Manners wishes to congratulate you on your good fortune. This is not a reference to the departure of the bridegroom, with whom Miss Manners is unacquainted, but to the fact that you have the engraved announcements at your disposal. You can alter them with a pen to achieve the correct formal wording you would otherwise have had to engrave or handwrite:

> *Mr. and Mrs. Geoffrey Lockwood Perfect*
> *have the honour of announcing*
> *that the marriage of their daughter*
> *Daffodil Louise*
> *to*
> *Mr. Jonathan Rhinehart Awful, 3rd*
> *will not take place*

⌐∽ Recovering from a Broken Engagement ∿⌐

DEAR MISS MANNERS:

Our family recently experienced the breakup of our daughter's engagement. The future groom called the whole event off. Of course our daughter was devastated, his actions were cold and callous.

We're in disagreement with him right now because we feel that total reimbursement for all deposits should fall on his shoulders, most of which are nonrefundable or at the very best contingent on re-booking. His family has not one cent invested in the matter, and of course feel their son is correct in his opinion. Our daughter did give back the engagement ring, which he claims is his personal property, therefore we feel that he should also pay for the wedding dress in return. The material has been cut and full payment is due.

He tells us that it is nowhere written that he owes us anything. I feel he is in the wrong and would like to know if we are correct in our thoughts. He also feels that demanding reimbursement is our way of ruining his life. We just want to handle this properly. Please advise us since we just want to be fair.

GENTLE READER:

But you already have the best of the bargain. You got back your daughter's future.

Miss Manners understands that you would like some financial compensation as well, and supposes you might find a lawyer who would try to get it for you. The law did once offer compensation for breach of promise, and current feeling favors turning pain into cash. But etiquette takes the opposite view: that no self-respecting person would want to accept anything from a cad, and that a lady should not only return the engagement ring, but spurn any participation in obligations that her own family incurred.

Before you reject this no-doubt quixotic approach, Miss Manners suggests you calculate what repayment would cost your daughter in the way of public embarrassment and private humiliation. Rather than put her in the position of appearing both jilted and greedy, you should put her into that dress—dyed and refashioned to make a splendid ball dress—and allow her to plunge back into social life, unsullied by sordidness, to meet a genuine gentleman.

Families and Friends

SHOULD THE BRIDE's grandfather's live-in girlfriend be sent a corsage? Is the matron of honor allowed to be pregnant? Must the bridegroom's mother and step-mother sit in the same pew, and if so, does the father sit between them? Suppose the bride has twelve friends who want to be bridesmaids, and the bridegroom doesn't have enough male friends to supply as many ushers? Does the bridegroom's son sit at the bridal table or at the parents' table? After the bride has danced with the bride-groom, her father-in-law and her father, can she dance with her mother's husband, who helped rear her, before she dances with the best man?

This is a sampling of the kind of question Miss Manners gets. Being a good sport, she usually answers them. (Some sample answers are: Yes, no, why not, it depends on if they speak, and oh, go ahead.) There is a limit, however, and Miss Manners thinks she may have reached it. Such silliness has got to stop. The supposi-tion behind these questions is that a wedding is a set piece, with rigidly prescribed roles, that the wedding party must be ruthlessly cast to fit the parts, and, as is the way of the theater, too bad for those who won't do.

What is the historical precedent for this series of tableaux? Miss Manners, being a scholar, is aware that wedding customs are a jumble of evolving traditions, and that even the proper Victorian wedding was much more a part of the bride's family's own style of entertainment than an abstract law of correctness for all. In fact, the only wedding custom with a pretense to long tradition and universality, that of public checking up on the consummation of the marriage, seems to have been dropped. Miss Manners can't think why.

The pattern that so many modern brides apparently have in mind can be traced to Hollywood, California, circa 1948. According to this, the bridal couple are not allowed to have stepparents, children, more than one grandmother apiece or more than one grandfather between them. The small size of the family cast was compen-sated by the number of places available in the wedding party for friends, provided these friends were young, unmarried and of uniform height. This is a manageable group, and any director can arrange it into decorative patterns.

So what happens if you have more people than you need for some roles, such as mothers, and fewer for others? Dear brides, you rewrite the script to fit the company. You group your relatives as makes sense to you and them, in terms of their closeness to you and toleration for one another, and you arrange a wedding party that includes your friends, whatever their size, shape and number. If you complain that this is not correct or traditional, Miss Manners will come around and check up on you the next morning.

DEAR MISS MANNERS:

In this day of sequential marriages, I have an etiquette question for multiple parents of the groom. Jeff and I have been married two years and Jeff's son, Tyke, is planning to be married. Tyke has a mother and two stepmothers. He's been close to all three. He also has a grandfather, grandmother, and step grandfather on his mother's side. All will probably attend the wedding, and all are relatively simpatico except the grandparent trio. The wedding will involve expensive travel for all. My question regards seating arrangements at the wedding and rehearsal dinners. What arrangements are called for by proper etiquette?

GENTLE READER:

What do you mean by "proper etiquette"? Do you imagine that there exists, somewhere, a stone diagram indicating the correct placement of sequential spouses according to some staid tradition? How many people do you figure that such a chart will allow in each collection of parents or grandparents?

Or, as Miss Manners hopes, are you asking her what would be a sensible and gracious way of distributing these people at dinnertime, so that they are not likely to be insulted either by the arrangements or by one another? There are many families, nowadays, chock full of people who do not correspond to the little figures on wedding charts for receiving lines, pew assignments or dinners. Some people try to cut the families to fit the charts—Grandpa can't bring his fiancée, and Mother is told she can arrive with her third husband but may not invite the second one who did so much carpool duty on behalf of the bridegroom.

Miss Manners calls this the Procrustes School of Etiquette. He was the ancient Greek gentleman who, you will recall, stretched short guests on the rack or chopped off the feet of tall guests to make them fit his bed.

You may put parents and grandparents in front pews, you may have mothers and even fathers in receiving lines and you may have a parents' table at dinner, seating the clergyman or woman and spouse there, and the grandparents too if you wish. If they are amicable—and Miss Manners believes they have an obligation to seem so, on such an occasion, however they may really feel—put them all there. The bride's chief father acts as host, with the bridegroom's chief mother at his right; the hostess is the bride's chief mother, with the bridegroom's chief father at her right.

By "chief," Miss Manners generally means the original parents, whomever they may now be attached to. However, a stepparent with whom the bride or bridegroom has grown up would not, according to good sense and affection, be replaced by a parent who, say, disappeared at birth. Where there are hostile feelings, obviously you must separate antagonists. A simple and gracious solution at the dinner is to have several small tables, with one parent or grandparent, or one current couple, serving as hosts at each table.

THE BRIDE'S FAMILY

~ Four Parents ~

DEAR MISS MANNERS:

My parents are divorced and both are remarried. I would like to include them all, parents and stepparents, in my wedding equally. How do I do this, and in what order, without hurting anybody's feelings? What do I put on the invitations and announcements, and who walks down the aisle with me? My father is paying more of the cost, but my mother is contributing, too.

GENTLE READER:

Miss Manners is beginning to think that each member of a family should hire an agent before there is to be a wedding, so that questions of billing and roles may be worked out in a businesslike manner. Otherwise, you are bound to get not only hurt feelings but overcrowded casts. Perhaps you could do two performances of the wedding, with a different pair in the role of parents each time.

The sensible alternative is to choose one couple as hosts, who will have their names on invitations and announcements, and one father to walk you up the aisle. You might have one father and one mother do that. (It is a Jewish custom of particular charm to have both parents accompany the bride—and both of the bridegroom's parents accompany him—and it is beginning to spread to gentile weddings as a replacement for the anachronism of the father's "giving the bride away.")

For example, you might have your mother and her husband (or your father and his wife) issue the invitations, all four receiving guests after the ceremony, and your original father (and original mother, if you wish) accompany you up the aisle. Your emotional ties and the civility or lack of it among these people are legitimate considerations when you make your choices. Miss Manners urges you only not to offer these parts for sale on the basis of who contributes most to the wedding costs.

~ A Single Mother ~

DEAR MISS MANNERS:

My daughter is planning her wedding. She has asked me, her mother, to walk her down the aisle. I have raised her by myself since she was two years old. I got married four years ago to a wonderful man. He has been a good stepfather to my daughter. Her father hasn't been in her life much since the divorce—he is remarried and living about six hundred miles away—but my daughter loves him in spite of his absence and has decided to ask me to give her away, because she doesn't want to hurt either her father or stepfather by having one of them give her away. She said if I didn't give her away, she would prefer her stepfather, as he will be the one who pays for the wedding, and her dad would be third choice. She talked to the minister, and he said it would be all right. My second question is, if I do walk her down the aisle, what do I wear?

GENTLE READER:

Miss Manners thinks it is a charming idea for you to escort your daughter in positive acknowledgment of the fact that you were the sole parent who reared her. Obviously, you do not dress as the Father of the Bride; nor do you dress as a sort of senior bridesmaid, although you may want to choose a color that will not actively clash with the attendants' dresses. The usual Mother of the Bride dress is lace or chiffon, in beige, blue, yellow or pink, and makes the Mother of the Bride look fat. Miss Manners hopes you can find a pale, dressy dress that doesn't.

~ Two Mothers ~

DEAR MISS MANNERS:

My lesbian partner of 26 years and I will be helping our daughter with her straight wedding plans. We are out to our immediate family and friends, as well as the groom's immediate family. Our daughter is NOT asking her father to walk her down the aisle, but wants her mother to do so.

My questions are:

1. If mom walks our daughter down the aisle, how should I as mom #2 enter with the wedding party?
2. How should the invitations be worded to indicate that both of us, as well as the groom's parents (both his mom and dad have remarried after their divorce) are announcing the wedding of our respective children?

The bride and groom have no particular religious convictions, so the ceremony can be a bit unconventional and without pretense. We are, however, hoping to maintain as much of the traditional wedding etiquette as possible.

GENTLE READER:

Then you will have to accept Miss Manners' definition of traditional.

That is to regard wedding etiquette as a basis for symbolizing the families involved as they actually exist, and not to try to jam them into roles that may not fit.

Giving away a bride is already an anachronism, retained for its charm. People who are fixed on the idea that it must be a gentleman, and who hunt up a remote one in the absence of a father or stepfather, render it meaningless. The point is that it should be one or more parents, or someone such as a stepparent or guardian, who has served as such.

How you assigned yourself to be "mom #2" in this regard, you do not say, but if you feel that the other mother alone should give your daughter away, then you should enter last as hostess, and sit up front. But it might also be fitting for you both to give away the bride.

Invitations are usually issued by the bride's family alone because they traditionally acted as sole hosts. But if all of you parents are giving the wedding, all of your formal names with honorifics should appear at the top of the invitation, beginning with the parents of the bride, and using as many lines as it takes to request the pleasure of your guests' company at the marriage of your respective children.

~ *Two Fathers* ~

DEAR MISS MANNERS:

My stepdaughter wanted her father to walk her down the aisle at her wedding. Not until rehearsal night did she tell her Dad that he would share this event with her stepfather. She wanted them both to walk her down the aisle and give her away. My husband found this very uncomfortable and refused to do it. Was he wrong?

GENTLE READER:

At some point, willingly or unwillingly, your husband contributed to putting your stepdaughter in the position of having two fathers involved in her upbringing. It is possible that she found this position uncomfortable, but she seems to have accommodated herself to it graciously.

In contrast, Miss Manners finds your husband's truculence in refusing to allow this situation to be expressed symbolically to be decidedly ungracious. While it is true that the wedding convention is for the bride to be given away by her one father, it was equally conventional for her to have only one candidate for this position.

～ Three Fathers ～

DEAR MISS MANNERS:

Would you kindly inform me, my wife, and her daughter as to who should dance at the parents' dance at the daughter's wedding?

The daughter's real dad is divorced and is going with another woman. He left a lot of sore spots and hard feelings during the married years and very sore spots during the divorce proceedings, and left a real financial responsibility on my wife's shoulders. She does not want to have anything to do with him—much less to dance with him. The daughter stated she'd like her real dad to dance with her mother at the dance. Let me point out to you, Miss Manners, that the mother and I are married and I am the bride's stepdad. The mother and I agree that we should do the parents' dance at the wedding.

GENTLE READER:

Miss Manners quite agrees with you. If, considering all these various sore points, you and the mother manage to be polite and charming to the father during this family occasion, you will be making enough of an effort to please the bride. If she dances with all her fathers (Miss Manners is counting the new father-in-law, as well as the biological father and stepfather), she will be too busy to notice.

～ Other Relatives ～

DEAR MISS MANNERS:

I am twenty-two years old and about to be married. My father died when I was a child and my mother, who never remarried, died two years ago. Since her death, I have lived for the most part at college (I graduated last month) and have spent summers and holidays with my grandparents, my father's brother (he is my only uncle), and my two older brothers, both of whom are married. Ours is a close-knit family and all of its members have been important in bringing me up and in helping me—financially and emotionally—through the difficult times following my mother's death.

Because my family is so important to me, I want to be married "from the family"—in other words, I want to be "given away." But by whom? Does someone have a traditional claim to the right to do the honors? I would hate to have to choose among my brothers, uncle, and grandparents only on the basis of personal preference, because I would be miserable if my choice made someone unhappy. If there is a traditional preference, my problem will be solved.

GENTLE READER:

Miss Manners supposes it's of no use to tell you to choose whomever you feel closest to. You love them all, equally, don't you? That's why you are making Miss Manners choose, isn't it? There is no formal order in this case, but you might consider the question of who, in the old-fashioned sense, is the head of the family. It would be your grandfather, if you are thinking in terms of the clan, or your elder brother, if you want to have someone from your nuclear family.

THE BRIDEGROOM'S FAMILY

DEAR MISS MANNERS:

Our son is getting married at an informal lawn wedding. I believe there will be a picnic-type reception afterward. I would like to know the proper things to do on my husband's and my part. Immediately upon learning of our son's wedding, we gave a dinner in our home for the parents of the intended bride. What else is expected of us? Wouldn't a long dress for the mothers be wrong for an informal wedding? Who gives the bachelor party? Should there be a rehearsal dinner? If so, who gives it and who pays? Would it be wrong for us to offer to pay for anything, like the cake or the food?

GENTLE READER:

The chief duty of the bridegroom's family is to take orders from the bride's family. Some people find this a difficult task, but it is cheaper and less time consuming than the tasks assigned to the bride's family. Thus, the cake, other food and even the length of your dress come under their jurisdiction.

Your side may run three side events, one obligatory and two optional, that you have already properly identified. The social overture to the bride's family, which you have performed, is required. The bachelor's dinner is not necessary, but if it is given, it is given by the bachelor, a.k.a. the bridegroom. The rehearsal dinner has become a customary way of the bridegroom's family taking the responsibility, financial burden, and the wedding party away from the bride's family on the night before the wedding when they are apt to have as much, or more, than they can handle.

⌒ Giving the Rehearsal Dinner ⌒

DEAR MISS MANNERS:

My son is being married next week and his father and I are hosting a rehearsal dinner the night before the ceremony. I invited my nephew, since he is my son's best man. Now my sister is mad at me for not inviting her as well.

I've always thought rehearsal dinners followed wedding rehearsals and were given for those members of the wedding party (and their partners) who were taking part in the ceremony and had to rehearse their roles. Am I wrong?

GENTLE READER:

You would have been right, back in the days when weddings were shorter and marriages were longer. Until the invention of the marathon wedding, the rehearsal dinner was, as you suggest, merely a small supper for the wedding party following the rehearsal. It served the purpose of preventing those exuberant young folks from seeking their own nocturnal fun and rendering themselves ill-fit for their duties the next day.

However, Miss Manners notices that you are not strictly citing that model either, as you already take for granted some modern changes. Partners, for example. If you truly wanted to do things the old-fashioned way, you would invite people only with their spouses or formally intended spouses—pretending to think that "partners" must refer to their business associates—and thus turn the wedding into cultural warfare. Miss Manners does not advise this.

Under the old system, however, you would not even have had that problem. The astonishing discovery had not yet been made that weddings have bridegrooms, as well as brides, so rehearsal dinners were offered by the parents of the bride, who were solely responsible for wedding hospitality. (They were also in charge of seeing to it that the young couple left town during the wedding reception so there was no need to give a brunch the following day.)

Now the so-called rehearsal dinner has become the bridegroom's parents' chief opportunity to share the burden of entertaining, and, if they are so inclined, to stage a rival show hoping to make the wedding seem anticlimactic. Some invite all the wedding guests, some only out-of-towners who might otherwise be hanging around their hotels eyeing one another warily. You know your guests and Miss Manners does not, so you should have an idea whether they would be thrilled or exasperated to find that attending the wedding involved a prolonged commitment.

But you didn't know your sister's feelings. So perhaps Miss Manners needs to point out that relatives consider such occasions to be akin to family reunions, and therefore they, along with the wedding party and their, ah, partners, should be on the basic guest list for the dinner.

NEW FAMILY NOMENCLATURE

DEAR MISS MANNERS:

When I got married I kept my last name, and there are people who outright refuse to use it. I have even lost my first name entirely with these people and am now Mrs. John Doe, not even a Jane! Among others, my mother refuses to write both our names on envelopes because she says it takes too much time and socially I should use my husband's name. "It's just right!!!" she says. My grandmother refuses to acknowledge it altogether and even new people we meet and introduce ourselves to with our respective last names get all frustrated and say they will just remember our first names!

Why is this phenomenon so difficult for people? It is no different than if we were roommates and someone sent us a joint letter—they would not dare to put in an incorrect last name just to save time or tradition! My feeling is it is rude not to acknowledge us as individuals and to assume we are one person because we are married!

GENTLE READER:

There are several reasons that this is a particularly volatile question:

1. We do not now have a standard system for the use of wives' names. Even those who reject the traditional system disagree about what should replace it—whether surnames should be retained separately, hyphenated or otherwise combined, and whether to use honorifics at all, and if so, which ones.

2. There are reasonable arguments to be made for both the traditional system (that it is traditional, and has therefore acquired sentimental associations; that it was, until challenged, standard, and therefore did not require guessing

or analyzing; and that it identifies present family affiliations) and the newer systems (that they retain paternal and professional identities and omit the disorientation—which even the most traditional ladies always felt—of changing names as an adult).

3. There is no "fair" system possible, as one's entire heritage cannot be represented, even aside from the matter of also representing one's family of spouse and children.

4. Name usage is fraught with symbolism, so everybody on every side is busy interpreting what everybody else's choice means philosophically—and not generously. People on both sides each assume that theirs is the only legitimate system, and that those who think or practice otherwise are ignorant and vicious. And that's just for starters.

However, Miss Manners has also noticed that some are beginning to acknowledge that this is a time of choice and that people ought to be addressed as they wish to be addressed, but also conclude that it is nevertheless not worth making an issue over it with one's relatives. That is what enables Miss Manners to struggle on.

DEAR MISS MANNERS:

Recently, I had a discussion as to the proper and legal name when one married. Does a new bride retain her maiden name and discontinue the use of her middle name? Is either correct?

GENTLE READER:

Miss Manners would not even presume to call any of the combinations of maiden, married or hyphenated names one now sees "incorrect." However, if you ask what we staid, fastidious, super-proper ladies have traditionally preferred, it is to "change" the last name. In other words, one retains one's first and middle name, and changes the surname of the father for that of the husband.

DEAR MISS MANNERS:

My soon-to-be-married son refuses to call his fiancée's parents Mom and Dad. He claims they aren't his parents, which is true, of course. His future in-laws do not want to be called by their first names. Things are at an impasse, with my son avoiding the issue whenever possible by not calling them anything. When necessary, he uses Mr. and Mrs. with the surname. This doesn't seem friendly to me. Any suggestions?

GENTLE READER:

That impasse you describe runs across the country, and therefore a great many married people address their parents-in-law as "Um." The truth is there is no satisfactory solution. Those who use some variation on "Mom" and "Dad" are forever having to explain, to third parties such as their own spouses, whom they are talking about. Some people consider first names too familiar and "Mr." and "Mrs." too distant. Other unsatisfactory solutions your son might consider are combining the parental title with the given name or surname. Thus you get "Mother Agnes" or "Father Jones," which reek of parochial school.

The compromise Miss Manners prefers is to let the older generation choose, on the grounds that whatever discomfort your son feels about their preference he can make up for by some day imposing his on his unwilling son-in-law.

DEAR MISS MANNERS:

What do I call my husband?

GENTLE READER:

Probably "honey." How would Miss Manners know? Possibly you are asking what to call him when referring to him in conversations with other people. Use his name, or if you have trouble remembering names, refer to him as "my husband." What are to be avoided are terms that suggest you know him too little or too well, such as "Mr." or "lover."

THE ATTENDANTS

For decades now, Miss Manners has been telling people to stop putting such a ridiculous emphasis on gender in connection with forming wedding parties. For goodness' sake, she has always protested, you're supposed to be gathering people who are important to you, not casting roles in a play.

If brides are traditionally attended by bridesmaids and bridegrooms by groomsmen, it is because it used to be assumed that friendships only existed within the same genders—any mixing of the two being considered too exciting for simple friendship. The point was always the relationship, not the gender.

But things have changed. Childbirth deaths, which had left more single fathers than mothers, declined, while divorce and births outside marriage, which leave more single mothers than fathers, soared. The disappearance of chaperonage and parietal rules demonstrated that the young were not as indiscriminately stimulated as had been assumed, and that real friendships (as opposed to the courtship kiss-of-death known as "Let's just be friends") are indeed possible.

Yet even those who now recognize this in making up their wedding parties do so self-consciously, as if they were violating the rules. Miss Manners has been bombarded with silly etiquette questions: What should a gentleman who attended the bride as her friend, or the lady who attended the bridegroom as his friend, be called? How should they dress?

Oh, stop it, is her reply. Having recognized that gender is not the deciding factor, why would anyone then imagine that these people needed to cross-dress or assume laughably inaccurate nomenclature?

DEAR MISS MANNERS:

My husband's sister has chosen to have all of her siblings and their spouses as bridesmaids and groomsmen, except for my husband and myself. The reason (in their words): I am "too heavy" and they don't want anyone to be "embarrassed"; and it would be "rude" to include my husband and not me. The entire family knows why I am being excluded, and they've more than hinted that if I lose weight, I can be a bridesmaid.

I am still expected to help address invitations and put together favors, attend a shower, bachelorette party and the ceremony, and, of course, to bring gifts. They regale me with details of the wedding preparations every time I see them, and have asked if my son could be the ring-bearer.

I feel I've been publicly snubbed and it's very humiliating. I don't want to be rude, but I am so hurt I want nothing more to do with this wedding. Do I have to attend, or can I simply send my regrets and a gift? Am I obligated to help with the preparations as the other sisters are? I feel like such a hypocrite and a doormat helping someone who is so openly embarrassed to be seen with me and who obviously has no regard for my feelings at all.

GENTLE READER:

Miss Manners cannot think why you, your husband or your son would want to have anything to do with a family that treats you so unspeakably—except one: You are all in that family. As callous as they are, they don't even seem to be trying to drum you out of it. So what are they trying to do?

The heartless notion that bridesmaids are there to give the wedding a certain look, rather than to surround the bridal couple with people to whom they are especially close, is common enough, Miss Manners is afraid, and accounts for many a slight. But this isn't just a slight, it is wholesale insult on the part of the entire family.

This leads Miss Manners to suspect that they have some ghastly notion that they are doing this for your good; that by holding out the notion that you can have this family honor if you lose weight, they are providing you with an incentive to do so.

Far from excusing them, this provides you and your immediate family with a reasonable incentive for skipping the proceedings entirely. Sending your regrets and a present is a generous way of indicating that you are not looking for a family feud, but are merely removing your presence in reaction to their promptings. They will have to understand that their rudely misguided scheme has failed.

Nevertheless, divining their motivation also suggests an approach for at least trying to fix this. You can do nothing, but perhaps your husband could talk to someone—if not his sister, perhaps his parents—who could be made to understand the damage they have inflicted and the necessity for begging your forgiveness.

~ The Job Description ~

DEAR MISS MANNERS:

I am the maid of honor for a friend's wedding. She and her fiancé have asked me to contact all invitees, ask them for cash instead of gifts, and then plan their honeymoon. Is this usually requested of bridesmaids? What is?

GENTLE READER:

Oh, raising funds, issuing warnings and threats to anyone who doesn't pay up and performing whatever chores the bride doesn't feel like doing herself, such as cleaning up after her.

Not in polite society, Miss Manners hastens to add. There, the bridesmaids' only duties are to make a special fuss over the bride by gathering around her at the wedding and, in the weeks before, by pretending to be interested in all the wedding details. It is also nice, but not obligatory, for them to plan a girlishly informal gathering—a luncheon or a shower—for her beforehand.

But your friend seems to have different ideas. Miss Manners recommends informing her regretfully that you cannot possibly do what she asks, and that you would therefore gladly accept demotion to being a mere wedding guest who wishes her well.

⁓ Soliciting Services ⁓

DEAR MISS MANNERS:

Eight months ago, I wrote to my first cousin's wife, asking her to play the organ during my wedding. She replied that she would be happy to, and that she requests only a baby-sitter for her daughter. Now, four weeks before the wedding, she called stating how all the music was set, and that as usual, the service would be a wedding present. She said that my only cost would be to pay for her flight to the Midwest. If this cost was to be too expensive, and if I was able to find a less expensive organist, she would understand.

I responded with a letter, stating that I had never intended her as only a participant, but as a welcomed guest at the wedding. Furthermore, as the distance was so great, I would not have ever asked her for that sole purpose. Furthermore, I was able to contact a local organist, so if she wishes to come, to please come as a guest only. Also, I apologized for the misunderstanding. Was this the correct thing to do?

GENTLE READER:

Indeed it was, and Miss Manners trusts that you have learned from the experience never to ask your guests to donate their professional services. Now please tell your photographer friend just to come as a guest and have a good time, because you have hired someone to take the pictures.

⁓ The (Material) Compensation ⁓

DEAR MISS MANNERS:

What are the proper presents to give bridesmaids and my fiancée's ushers? Is something so untraditional as a good book—different books for each, of course, according to their tastes—all right instead of things like bracelets and cuff links they may never use?

GENTLE READER:

Are you trying to give these people something they might enjoy, or are you trying to do the proper thing by them? Books, at best, are only read, but useless, monogrammed silver objects that cannot be returned serve to remind one of the occasion of their presentation every time one sees them tarnishing away, unused. Cuff links and bracelets are all right, since everyone has too many of them, but silver golf tees or toothpaste tube squeezers are ideal.

Weddings

BRIDES ARE being callously deceived. Bridegrooms are being fed deliberate untruths. And not even necessarily by each other.

Armed with the true but dangerous knowledge that customs evolve with the times, amateur and professional wedding advisors have promulgated certain procedures as now being essential to a proper wedding. Often they try to claim these changes as "traditional," as if they had been given the august imprimatur of etiquette.

Miss Manners would be grateful for this unrequested assistance if the new procedures were, in fact, proper. Aware that the wedding pattern that is still followed in the twenty-first century stopped corresponding to reality by about 1917, she has sanctioned changes herself. Not wide-scale ones, as it remains charming and amusing to see headstrong veterans of the various sexual revolutions mince along, disguised as parent-dominated innocents. But certain adjustments have become necessary.

For example, weddings often involve travel, now that the only people who marry the boy or girl next door are those who became overly friendly as neighbors during their first marriages. The save-the-date letters that annoy some guests are designed to allow them to take advantage of airplane bargains requiring advance purchase. No commitment is involved—to the hosts, that is; people are more willing to commit to airlines—so when the actual wedding invitations arrive, the guests still have a chance to claim previous engagements.

Considering the time and trouble involved, it is no longer acceptable, as it once was, to invite some guests to the ceremony but not to the reception. Miss Manners never cared for that custom anyway.

But the innovations that are most widely followed, even by those who resent them, are vulgar, impractical or nonsensical—and almost always expensive. Here are some of those that Miss Manners refuses to sanction:

- That "wedding" is a collective noun referring to a long series of events minimally including an engagement party, numerous showers, bachelor and spinster (Miss Manners is incapable of saying "bachelorette") parties, a rehearsal

dinner, the ceremony, a dinner, a dance and the next day's brunch, until everyone concerned has been worn to a frazzle. And that they all require presents.
Only the ceremony and a celebration immediately after have the full sanction
of etiquette; the rest is only for those who have the stamina. A true engagement party is one at which the bride's father announces the engagement as a
surprise, and showers are solely at the discretion of friends.

- That the hosts are responsible for answering their own invitations as well as
for issuing them. If there are no preprinted responses—and sometimes even
if there are—guests claim to be stumped about what they are supposed to do.
If there are no stamps on the return envelopes, they turn indignant. It is as if
they never before had received an invitation ("Would you like to catch a
movie tonight?") without being handed the possible answers ("Now you're
supposed to tell me either yes or no").

- That hosts must allow anyone who is single to bring along that ubiquitous
person, And Guest. And Guest doesn't know the hosts or care about the wedding and, if left at home, would allow the person who was invited to meet
someone with a better attitude toward the occasion.

- That the wedding couple is not only entitled but obligated to think up their own
presents, and that guests are bound to buy them as directed. Worse, that guests
are supposed to bring goods equivalent in value to the cost of the food and drink
they receive. And that the couple has a year after the wedding in which to send
their thanks. Getting married does not endow people with the privilege of levy-
ing taxes or charging admission. It does give them the obligation of expressing
their gratitude in writing immediately, and to refrain from complaining what a
burden it is to be the recipient of many people's generosity. Presents are voluntary, and should be selected by the giver, but never brought along to the wedding,
where collecting them causes no end of trouble.

- That anyone who seeks to decrease the pace, the expenditure and the anticipated take, while increasing the amount of thoughtfulness required from and
on behalf of the guests, must have no sense of romance. Or be impossibly
romantic.

~ *The Wedding Date* ~

DEAR MISS MANNERS:
June used to be the traditional time for weddings, but customs are so different
now. Is there any preferred date for weddings in modern life?

GENTLE READER:

It is preferable to hold them after the divorce and before the birth of the baby.

~ *The Location* ~

DEAR MISS MANNERS:

My husband's sister is having her wedding ceremony and reception in Bermuda; she and her husband are not planning to have a separate reception afterward in the U.S. My husband and I are in a difficult position: She has offered to help us out with expenses, but we don't feel this is her responsibility. At the same time, we don't have the finances ourselves for such a weekend. We want to be with her on her wedding day, but this situation is causing us a lot of stress.

GENTLE READER:

You are not the only people for whom these new package vacation weddings are causing stress. It does not seem to have occurred to the couples who merrily plan them that friends and relatives who would like to attend their wedding may not be prepared to go on the honeymoon.

It is more than the cost, from the complaints that Miss Manners hears, although cost is an important deterrent. Often it is taking vacation time one might want to spend otherwise. Sometimes it is being committed to spending more time with someone else's relatives and friends than one might choose.

In any case, such an invitation cannot command the sort of attendance that one would normally expect for an important ceremonial event alone. Your sister-in-law is kind to offer financial help, but if she could not accept your not being there, she should have consulted you before the arrangements were made. Miss Manners' advice is to decline in favor of tossing your own party in honor of the couple at another time.

DEAR MISS MANNERS:

We are the parents of a groom who will wed his fiancée at a destination wedding. We would like to host the rehearsal dinner, but are confused about who should be invited to it. Everyone will be from out of town and to invite all of them just seems like the first of two weddings. We were planning a sit down dinner party for the dinner, but then does that exclude a daughter, grandfather, etc. Help!

GENTLE READER:

Too late. Miss Manners cannot rescue you from entertaining people whom you and yours have lured on a vacation trip—because that is what a destination wedding amounts to. She only wishes she could rescue those who have agreed to vacation with you under the impression that you wanted to spend several days with them.

⟋ The Wedding Budget ⟍

DEAR MISS MANNERS:

My 23-year-old son is engaged to be married next summer. His finance is planning a large wedding (400-plus). My son recently informed me that, according to her, it is "customary" for the groom's parents to pay for the liquor at the wedding reception and for a honeymoon to Hawaii (as this is where all young couples now go). The estimated cost of the reception's open bar is $12,000 and the Hawaiian honeymoon nearly $5,000.

It was my understanding that the bride's family was primarily responsible for the wedding and that the groom's family paid for the pre-nuptial meal and the groomsmen's gifts. Any other financial assistance from the groom's family was optional. We are not involved in planning this wedding and are certainly not of the financial means to cover such large expenses.

Can you provide some guidance? We want to fulfill our obligations and maintain cordial relations, but are not of a financial means to spend thousands of dollars to fulfill the bride's every wish.

GENTLE READER:

Fully half the letters Miss Manners receives about engagements and weddings put an extra "n" in the words "fiancée" or "fiancé," as you did. She used to think it was a typographical accident.

Apparently not. The state of being engaged is now interpreted as granting license to control other people's finances. Parents, wedding attendants and guests are told what they must allocate through contributions, sponsorship and purchase.

And what authority is there for granting this unprecedented ability to dictate expenditure regardless of the owners' thoughts or wishes? "Etiquette," claim the finances and financees. It is only proper that others fork it over, they declare.

Oh, no they don't. Miss Manners is not going to stand for etiquette's being portrayed as extortion, and she is surprised that anyone else submits to being victimized. Furthermore, the finances and financees always prove to be ignorant of what is "customary."

Customarily, the bride's family pays for all the wedding festivities, and the bridegroom pays for the groomsmen's presents, the entire wedding trip and any other expenses the couple may incur from then on. In recent years, this has been modified in the interest of fairness, so that the bridegroom's family may offer to give a dinner the evening before the wedding or otherwise share in the wedding expenses. However, all of this, including the bride's family's assumption of costs, is voluntary, and saddling people with bills that strain their means is as improper as it is cruel.

~ Perfection ~

You, out there in Brideland, you sweet thing: Are you planning your wedding so that it will be perfect in every detail? Do you expect it to be the happiest day of your life?

Miss Manners sincerely hopes not. Few of those who prattle about that "happiest day" seem to consider the dour expectations this suggests about the marriage from its second day on. They don't realize that a wedding reception is basically a large party, and is therefore not perfectable because there are too many variables, not to mention too many people who one thought would not accept. At any rate, someone whose idea of ultimate happiness is a day spent at a big party, even spent being the center of attention at a marvelous big party, is too young to get married.

This notion of a wedding persists, often working directly against the purpose of a wedding, which is to create a new family, and not to put cracks and strains in old ones. Miss Manners' advice to young brides is to plan weddings that will be pretty and festive, but not to attempt to make them grand on a scale unrelated to the rest of their lives, and not to expect them to be perfect. Many an otherwise lovely bride has turned ugly attempting to create a "dream" occasion and to make everyone else conform with her conception of their roles in it.

A warning that one has strayed too far afield is an excessive preoccupation with everything's being done "right." Weddings are rare events in most people's lives, and Miss Manners has no objection to the participants' seeking advice on correct form. She dispenses such advice herself, right and left. But if one needs professional direction—not just help or advice—in every aspect of the wedding, it may mean that one has wandered into completely foreign social territory and should think about heading home. One's wedding should be a heightened version of one's best social life, not an occasion for people to attempt to play grand and unfamiliar parts in a fantasy play.

Another warning about expecting a perfect day is that this carries a built-in potential for disappointment. (There are adults who go through life expecting other people to make their birthdays perfect for them; and if you ever meet one of these, watch out. Nothing will ever be enough for them.)

What Miss Manners wishes all brides is not the happiest days of their lives, but jolly gatherings of family and friends, in which they are the object of general admiration, but everyone has a good time. They will then have some happiness left over with which to live happily ever after.

~ *An Imperfectly Attentive Bridegroom* ~

DEAR MISS MANNERS:

My fiancé refuses to take an interest in the arrangements for our wedding. There will be about two hundred people, one hundred from his side and one hundred or slightly more from mine, with a reception in our families' country club. There is a lot of work to do, and I don't mind that so much, but it worries me that he is so bored by it. Is this a bad sign?

GENTLE READER:

No. While a bridegroom is not actually superfluous at a wedding—most states require one before issuing a license—he is all but superfluous, and need not be as enthralled by the preparations as the star. However, this tendency might bear watching. If his lack of interest interferes with his participation—in other words, if he doesn't attend the wedding—that would be a bad sign.

INVITATIONS AND RESPONSES

DEAR MISS MANNERS:

Is it acceptable to invite guests to a small wedding by writing each person or couple a nice (short) handwritten letter? Not a form, of course, but along the lines of "Dear Aunt Joyce, We are so happy to announce our engagement, and would love to have you at our wedding and reception, which will be held . . ."

The wedding is informal but is this too casual? We are trying to keep the wedding within our means, which are very limited.

GENTLE READER:

The simple answer to your apparently simple question is sure, go ahead, it's fine. To leave it at that, however, would deprive Miss Manners of the opportunity to shock you and outrage an entire industry. Here goes:

Handwriting is not a substitute for engraving. Engraving is a substitute for handwriting.

In a perfect world, people would handwrite all their formal invitations. But as we live in a world where people wish to marry before hundreds of their closest friends, and they claim to have more urgent tasks than copying out hundreds of invitations in their own dear handwriting, we substitute engraving.

Engraved or handwritten, the most formal wedding invitations are put in the third person, but for less formal weddings they should be written as exactly the sort of letter you suggest. Heaven forbid that this would make your wedding seem "casual." Weddings are a serious business, and the only casual ones Miss Manners can imagine are the kind where the spouses wonder the next morning what can have possessed them.

(For the correct wording of formal invitations, please see p. 537.)

DEAR MISS MANNERS:

It's not the money, but I think it's silly to have our wedding invitations really engraved. It is virtually impossible to tell the difference between engraving and good raised printing, and it seems a waste of money to pay for something extra that doesn't even show. My fiancée disagrees with me, but she can't give a valid reason. Can you?

GENTLE READER:

Yes. The world is full of nasty people who examine the backs of wedding invitations and run fingernails over the front in order to tell whether the thing was properly engraved. Miss Manners is one of them. Handwriting and engraving are equally correct; fake engraving and computer generated fonts are imposters.

Selling the Honors

DEAR MISS MANNERS:

My fiancé and I are selecting our wedding invitations, and we don't know how to word them. The bride's parents are paying for the catering. The groom's parents offered to pay for the rehearsal dinner. The bride's parents offered to invite the guests to their house after the mass. My fiancé and I are paying for the hall, cake, marriage, license, flowers, music, and drinks. Who gets the honour of inviting the guests on the invitations?

GENTLE READER:

You are making the common, and often justified, assumption that honors are always for sale. In this case, they are not. The bride's parents issue the invitations. However, the tradespeople issue their bills to those who have indicated a willingness to pay them.

Extending the Honors

DEAR MISS MANNERS:

My mother divorced my father fourteen years ago, and remarried. I came to love my stepfather very much. I never really saw my real dad, and that never bothered me, because I was quite content with my stepdad, who raised me since I was five years old.

My stepfather is even going to walk me down the aisle, because I asked him, and I wouldn't want anyone else to do it. But how do I go about filling out the invitations? I want my stepdad's name down, and my mother says it can't be done that way. My real father and stepmother are invited to the wedding also.

GENTLE READER:

Having been right once, in marrying such a nice man, your mother cannot expect to be always right. She and her husband can be named as hosts merely by substituting "her" before daughter, instead of "their."

Under other circumstances, both original parents' names can be used, sometimes with their present spouses, although when the list becomes too top-heavy, Miss Manners advises omitting them all and sinking back into the passive tense. (For that wording, please see illustration on p. 398.)

A trickier matter is the understandable desire of the bridegrooms' parents' to work in their names, which are omitted on the traditional form, not out of spite, as some seem to believe, but because they are not the traditional hosts. Various solutions have been used. They can be cited as co-hosts with the bride's parents, in which case the invitation is "to the marriage of their children . . ." Sometimes a line is added under the bridegroom's name, "son of Mr. and Mrs. . . ."

Although Miss Manners sympathizes with the desire to avoid puzzling the bridegroom's family's guests, she prefers the less radical solution of having them simply include their formal card with the invitation.

Honorifics

DEAR MISS MANNERS:

My daughter will be getting married in September. She has a Doctor of Veterinary Medicine degree, and is therefore "Dr." as is her husband-to-be.

My question is, do I use her title in inviting the guests to the marriage of my daughter (I am a widow) as Jan Lee, Dr. Jan Lee, or Jan Lee, D.V.M.? Also, how do I title Tom? It is very possible Jan will opt not to use her title on the invitation, but I would like to know the correct way if she decides to use it. Also, she is keeping her own name (what else is new?) and I don't know what to do about stationery for her. These should be our biggest problems.

GENTLE READER:

As luck would have it, the bride is usually the only person who does not use an honorific. This is because her surname is not used unless it differs from that of the people issuing the invitation, generally her parents. The bridegroom does need a title with his name, so you would use Dr. here instead of Mr. If she absolutely refuses to do without her "Dr.," it must be used with her full name. Do not—repeat not—use the initials, except on her business stationery. Please persuade her to omit any reference to her education on her social writing paper; this may be engraved with her maiden name, as she will continue to use it socially.

~ *The Double Wedding* ~

DEAR MISS MANNERS:

My two daughters became engaged to two young men within a week of each other, and they want to get married within the year. I have always promised the girls the kind of wedding they want (big), but I never thought they would want them at the same time. Is there any way I can marry them both off properly without taking out a second mortgage?

GENTLE READER:

The solution to your problem is the double wedding, one of the few cases in which tradition and practicality join forces. Issue one invitation, either with a normally worded invitation for each bride on either side of the inside of a double sheet or in the following form:

Mr. and Mrs. Geoffrey Lockwood Perfect
request the honour of your presence
at the marriage of their daughters
Viola Brentwood
to
Mr. Alexander Dashing

and
Daffodil Louise
to
Mr. Jonathan Rhinehart Awful, 3rd
& c

The ceremony itself proceeds either as two individual weddings with extra people hanging around (in which case each bride can be maid—or matron—of honor to the other, presuming they are still speaking to each other after doing all the double planning), or as one large ceremony with each part repeated twice. In the processional, the older sister (with retinue) comes down the aisle on her father's arm, followed by the younger sister (with retinue) escorted by her brother, uncle or other unoccupied male. If this precedence gives the unfortunate impression that the older bride is rushing down the aisle to beat her younger sister to the altar, don't blame Miss Manners. She does not make up these rules.

A Post-wedding Reception

DEAR MISS MANNERS:

My son is being married out of state. The bride's mother is having a lovely reception. She asked me not to invite more than eight guests, as she will be inviting eight also. My husband and I have many new friends and business acquaintances who should be invited. We therefore plan to have a large post-honeymoon reception, inviting two hundred guests, including the parents and family of the bride. Can you advise me about the invitations? Do we invite these people separately, or would it be proper to enclose an invitation along with the formal wedding invitation? Do we print announcements of the wedding and enclose our party invitation? I want to do the proper thing, but it is physically impossible to invite the large number of friends, relatives, etc., to the out-of-town wedding.

GENTLE READER:

Indeed, a delayed reception, such as you propose, is the correct and gracious solution to the bride's family's space limitation problem. But you must be careful not to seem to be passing this off as part of the original wedding festivities; it is, instead, a charming but different tradition, namely a reception in honor of a newly married couple.

Your invitations should not be sent with the wedding invitations or with wedding announcements, both of which are issued by the bride's parents. For a reception such as you describe, the form is:

In honor of
Mr. and Mrs. Jonathan Rhinehart Awful, 3rd
[or, less formally] Daffodil and Jonathan
Mr. and Mrs. Jonathan Awful, junior
request the pleasure of your company
on Saturday, the eighth of May
at eight o' clock
The Racket Club

～ Original Wording ～

DEAR MISS MANNERS:

I need your help in interpreting the wording of this invitation:

Mary Jane Doe
and Stephen Michael Roe
invite you to share the joy of the beginning of
their new life together
when on Saturday, the fifth of July
at three o'clock
they exchange marriage vows at
Union Methodist Church

The bride and groom invite you to join them in a buffet dinner reception
following their marriage.

I understood this to be an invitation to a reception only, and therefore did not attend the wedding ceremony. This led to an angry confrontation, and if I was wrong, I wish to apologize to the family members. To what was I invited?

GENTLE READER:

Heaven only knows. A wedding is a solemn, public ceremony, and Miss Manners hates to think what these people contemplated doing in church to create new life and joy, let alone to share it. This illustrates the reason for Miss Manners' fervent rejection of the "originally" worded pseudoformal announcement. It is vulgar in its assumption that this wedding is somehow more joyous than others, and it is open to severe misunderstanding. (It is also redundant, as is the silly phrase "buffet dinner reception.")

You owe no apology. In any case, a ceremony held in a church is theoretically open to the congregation and it is not therefore customary to reply that one is, or is not, attending; what requires an answer is only the invitation to the private social event following.

~ Response Cards ~

DEAR MISS MANNERS:

Is it correct to use response cards for certain cases? I realize it may be insulting to assume the recipient will not R.s.v.p. with a handwritten note, but, as is typical in the small town where I will marry, my parents are having a sit-down dinner and need a fairly accurate head count. At twenty dollars per head, it seems too risky to rely on good manners.

GENTLE READER:

Miss Manners loathes response cards, although they are indeed widely used. However, the users report that the problem of nonresponses remains, probably because someone too rude to answer by hand will probably also fail to take the trouble to mail the card. So there goes your stamp, as well as your head count. Nevertheless, Miss Manners sympathizes with your problem. The cumbersome but polite solution is to telephone the rudely missing people a week before the wedding and ask them whether you will have the pleasure of their company. If that doesn't shame them, nothing will. And sometimes nothing does.

~ Other Inserts ~

DEAR MISS MANNERS:

Please help me to correct my fiancée and her mother on a point of etiquette. I have generously refrained from interfering with their preparations for our wedding thus far. Regarding invitations, however, I dared to speak my piece: guests must be sent maps if they are to find the church. Aimless wandering about will not do. My fiancée and future mother-in-law, however, insist that the insertion of maps ruptures the formality of the invitation, sending our wedding into the depths of boorishness. Should I return to passive acceptance of the rampages of two women gone mad?

GENTLE READER:

It may reassure you to know that this particular form of madness—the abandonment of all common sense in the desire to conform to a concept of rigid correctness

Mr. and Mrs. Geoffrey Lockwood Perfect

request the honour of your presence

at the marriage of their daughter

Daffodil Louise

to

Mr. Jonathan Rhinehart Awful, 3rd

on Saturday, the first of April

at twelve o'clock noon

Our Lady of Propriety Church

Brookdale, Connecticut

Wedding Breakfast
immediately following the ceremony
123 Primrose Path
Brookdale, Connecticut

The favour of a reply is requested

An invitation to a wedding, with a card enclosed for the wedding breakfast. Divorced parents may issue the invitation alone, together using their current names, or with a current spouse, with "their daughter" corrected to read "his daughter," "her sister," "their niece" or whatever. The bride's last name is included if it differs from the host's.

The pleasure of your company

is requested at the wedding reception of

Stacey Awful

Vice Admiral, United States Navy

and

Trevor Nuisance

Major General, United States Army

on Saturday, the eleventh of November

at six o'clock

Fort McBoom Officers' Club

R.s.v.p.
General Nuisance
Cannonball Barracks

The honour of your presence

is requested at the marriage ceremony

at half after four o'clock

The Memorial Chapel

Fort McBoom

Invitation to a wedding reception, with ceremony card enclosed. The phrase "the honour of your presence" is used for religious ceremonies; for home weddings, those taking place in clubs or hotels, and for related social events, the proper phrase is "the pleasure of your company." The variations used here, such as the absence of hosts and the use of military titles, may of course be used when the main invitation is to the ceremony. This form is used for an intimate ceremony, followed by a large reception.

in matters on which there is, in fact, nothing at all written in stone—is nearly universal, but temporary. It is possible that if you lie low, you may find yourself ending up with a wife and mother-in-law as sane and reasonable as they were when you first suggested the relationship.

It is also possible that you will find yourself being married in an empty church. Miss Manners sees nothing wrong with including small, neat maps, but if that drives them madder still, you might suggest a separate mailing of maps—or just do one yourself.

You should, however, stand firm against the tendency to give wedding invitations the nuisance value of magazines that come stuffed with subscription cards. Two such cards—for example, a reception card and a map—are the limit.

~ *Stuffing Envelopes* ~

DEAR MISS MANNERS:

Please tell me what is the proper way to stuff wedding invitations? Etiquette books and local stationers have given me conflicting answers about whether it is correct to put all the enclosure cards (reception card and response card) inside the invitation itself, or simply on top of the invitation, before inserting into the inner envelope. Also, do I use the tissue paper provided, even though the reason for it is no longer valid? If so, where does it go? The invitation opens like a greeting card and is blank inside.

GENTLE READER:

Please listen carefully, because this is going to sound like instructions for making paper monkeys out of bubblegum wrappers, as translated from the Japanese.

Fold the double-sheeted wedding invitation in half again, engraved side in, and insert it into the inner envelope (the one without the glue), with the fold side at the bottom, and the top of the invitation facing the reader who has the flap of the envelope facing him or her. Put the extra cards, writing also toward the flap, in the center of the main invitation. If, however, the invitation is small and does not need folding, the cards go in front of it, which is to say, closer to the rear of the envelope.

Tissues are provided to prevent the engraving from smearing after the folding. You may include them, but you don't need them if the cards are in between. You don't need them if it's not real engraving, either, but in that case you may want them for motives Miss Manners will not mention.

"EVERMORE"
121 PRIMROSE PATH
BROOKDALE, CONNECTICUT

Mrs. Plue Perfect
accepts with pleasure
the kind invitation of
Mr. and Mrs. Perfect
for
Saturday, the first of April
at twelve o'clock noon

Acceptance of a wedding invitation on "house" paper, which may be used by anyone in the house, including the guests, for formal letters.

Mrs. Perfect used to copy out more of the invitation, putting, instead of that one lonely word "for," four extra lines reading "to the wedding breakfast of their daughter / Daffodil Louise / and / Mr. Jonathan Rhinehart Awful, 3rd," but she is now forced by her arthritis to use the modern form.

To decline the invitation, one would substitute "regrets that she is (they are) unable to accept" for the second line, and add the adverb "very" before the adjective "kind" in the third line.

～ Addressing Invitations ～

DEAR MISS MANNERS:

I heard someplace that I shouldn't put "and Family" or "and Guest" on my wedding invitation envelopes. Well, how else do I let them know everybody is invited? Also, why do I have to use two envelopes? It seems like a waste to me.

GENTLE READER:

Using "and Family" on your invitation carries its own punishment. You cannot then complain if your sister-in-law's dog disturbed the ceremony, and you didn't know where to seat your bridegroom's best friend's stepgrandfather's new friend. The word "family" can be very broadly construed where free champagne is involved, and those who use "and Guest" on their invitations are courting disaster in the way of unsentimental strangers.

If you care enough to invite people to your wedding, you will find out each one's name and use it. You need not send an invitation to every man, woman and child. You may send married (or otherwise cohabiting) couples a single invitation, and you may even include, beneath those of their parents, the names of daughters living at home, as in:

Mr. and Mrs. Jonathan Rhinehart Awful, junior
The Misses Awful
129 Primrose Path
Brookdale
Connecticut

Their brothers, "The Messrs. Awful," should be sent a separate invitation, even if they live at the same address. It is best not to include more than two adults in one invitation. It is a treat for children under about age thirteen—if you really want to invite them—to receive a separate invitation addressed "The Misses and Messrs. Awful."

The purpose of these two envelopes is to protect the invitation from the ravages of the modern postal service, now that invitations are no longer hand delivered by footmen. That they may also make the invitations too fat for modern letter-sorting equipment is beside the point.

Titles and full names are used on the outer envelope; the street address, city and state are written out in full, in black or blue-black ink, each on its own line (see example above). The inner envelope has the titles and surnames only.

There is, of course, a good reason for all of these rules: They make the writing of proper thank-you letters seem simple.

⟨ Mailing the Invitations ⟩

DEAR MISS MANNERS:

How many weeks or days in advance should you mail out wedding invitations or hand deliver them?

GENTLE READER:

Traditionally, wedding invitations were sent three or four weeks before the wedding was to take place. But although this was sufficient for giving people time to worry about what they were going to wear and how much they were expected to spend on a wedding present, it ran afoul of airline regulations. We have now moved the time to six to eight weeks ahead, in order to allow the guests to take advantage of bargain travel.

Even earlier warnings are now being issued, requesting guests to save a date long in advance. Miss Manners prefers that these be in the form of charming notes, rather than printed cards, lending them the air of especially wanting the individual guests, rather than advertising coming attractions.

⟨ Formal Responses ⟩

DEAR MISS MANNERS:

What is the correct way, these days, to answer a formal, engraved invitation?

GENTLE READER:

What do you mean, "these days"? Are you suggesting that just because modern life is chaotic, you can get away without a beautifully handwritten formal reply with all the lines neatly centered? Do you know how much it cost those people to have that invitation engraved? Do you think they want to hear your cheery voice on the telephone saying "sure, why not?"

Oh, all right. Miss Manners will shorten the task for you slightly, but not much. You may write that you accept with pleasure, or regret that you are unable to accept, your friends' kind invitation for whatever date it is—and you don't have to repeat in the reply the time, place or bride's name. You still have to write the thing out, though. And get those lines centered!

(Please see illustration, p. 400.)

⟜ *Responding to Response Cards* ⟝

DEAR MISS MANNERS:

When a wedding invitation comes with an answer card enclosed for me to fill in my name under "Will attend" or "Will not attend," does this take the place of a handwritten reply?

GENTLE READER:

Never. It is meant to, however.

Miss Manners finds such cards an abomination and invites you to help foul up the systems of people who try it. Use your own letter paper to write a conventional formal reply. This will be too big for the filing box in which the hosts are keeping track of who is coming and who isn't, and thus drive them crazy. Maybe then they will learn to behave better by the second wedding.

⟜ *Illicit Responses* ⟝

DEAR MISS MANNERS:

I'd just like to know how one is supposed to cope with responses that include uninvited guests. Children, in particular, were excluded from the invitation to my daughter's wedding. Two guests asked the bride about bringing the child ("Never before excluded from the parents' coming and going"). Another guest (single guests were invited to bring a friend/companion) added two friends to the number of dinner guests to expect.

I'm probably allowing my mind to distort this out of proportion—but am I wrong to resent this behavior? What is the best, mannerly way to handle such situations?

GENTLE READER:

If Miss Manners feels like weeping when she hears of how rudely people attempt to impose on those whose only crime is to invite them to a wedding—and Miss Manners isn't even in the emotionally wracking throes of putting on a wedding— how can she call your resentment wrong, or even out of proportion?

Do not listen to the pleas of parents claiming that umbilical cords have not yet been broken at any social event; these are the very parents who will permit their children to whine during the ceremony. Nor should you allow any guest to run his or her own party-within-the-party with a guest list not chosen by you. Even allowing single guests to bring their own friends is more than Miss Manners would do.

The answer to how to deal with these outrageous requests is: firmly. "I am so sorry—we are not having children," or "No, I'm afraid we're only inviting our own dear friends." Do not allow these people to blackmail you by threatening their own refusals. The answer to that is, "Well, I'm so sorry you won't be able to come. It would have meant a great deal to all of us to have you there."

DEAR MISS MANNERS:

I am a widower in my sixties and receive wedding invitations, some of which are marked with my name only, and others with my name "and guest." Both contain R.s.v.p. cards requesting "Number of persons attending —— ". Am I allowed to bring a guest if the invitation is marked with my name only?

GENTLE READER:

Certainly not. A wedding should not be treated as if it were a public institution, like a club, to which one can bring an anonymous date. If the hosts make it that, you may take advantage of it, but please don't institute this practice on your own. Besides, you might decide you like the maid of honor better than anyone you already know.

DEAR MISS MANNERS:

My daughter and her fiancé do not wish to invite anyone under sixteen to their wedding reception. Is there any polite way to express their feelings to family and friends without causing any hard feelings?

GENTLE READER:

There is no polite way to issue negative invitations. Neither is there a polite way to accept invitations that have not been issued. Address your invitations to the adults whom you wish to invite, without mentioning their children. If they inquire whether they may bring the children, explain your policy. Miss Manners hopes you appreciate the difference between committing a social error yourself and merely responding to someone else's error.

ANNOUNCEMENTS

DEAR MISS MANNERS:

As an immigrant to this country in my mid-20s, I am at a stage in my life where many of my friends are getting married. I have lived in the US for about 10 years now, and consider myself "assimilated." However, I am at a loss for words for one curious custom I have now encountered for the second time, and don't feel comfortable discussing it with any of my native-born friends, as I instinctively consider it rude, but if it is a socially-accepted norm, do not want to offend anyone.

Recently, a letter arrived in my mailbox from an older acquaintance. She had told me months ago that her daughter—who is my age—would be getting married, and I assumed that this letter was an invitation for said wedding. Imagine my surprise when I opened it to find that the wedding had already passed—the previous weekend.

Thinking that the folly was mine, I checked the postmark on the envelope, and saw that the letter had been mailed only two days earlier. Upon further investigation, I found it to be a "wedding announcement"—complete with the new couple's names and their new address. I am confused. Should I send a gift to the new couple? What is the purpose of this announcement, if not?

Where I come from, if someone gets married, they send invitations if they want you to attend. If they don't want you to attend, they are most probably simply acquaintances and do not mention it to you, assuming you will eventually hear about the wedding from a third party or from themselves at a later date—and of course no feelings are hurt in this situation because it is understood that the two of you are, after all, simply acquaintances and not dear old friends.

GENTLE READER:

You are assimilated all right, which makes you just as confused as everyone else in the society seems to be about wedding invitations and announcements.

Formal wedding announcements date from a time before American marriages occasioned the sort of extravaganza that is now common. One celebrated the actual event with family and close friends, not business contacts, acquaintances and the entire Christmas card list of people one wouldn't recognize if one fell on them.

Nevertheless, there were those among them who might be presumed to be interested in the news of the marriage, and they were sent announcements. These should be acknowledged, but nothing is required beyond congratulations.

At Home Cards

DEAR MISS MANNERS:

Do people still put "at home" cards in with wedding announcements? What is the purpose, and what is the correct wording?

GENTLE READER:

The traditional reason was to let people know where they could call upon the newly married couple after the wedding trip, and the traditional motivation was to let tardy present-givers know where to direct their offerings after the wedding.

Now there is a better reason, which is to let everyone know what the bride and bridegroom have decided to call themselves—his surname, hers, a combination or an invention. The old form was engraved on a heavy oversized visiting card (please see illustration on p. 407). A practical new one might be:

Ms. Alexandrina Awful
Mr. Ian Fright
After the 29th of February   127 Primrose Path

DEAR MISS MANNERS:

Are those paid newspaper announcements of weddings, engagements, etc. proper? I seem to recall something about a lady only having her name in the paper twice—when she was born and when she died.

GENTLE READER:

Thrice. Marriage, as well as birth and death—but only one of each—are the traditional occasions on which a lady is expected to undergo the pain of public scrutiny. Miss Manners, however, is in no position to criticize those who exceed their limits.

⌒ *Illicit Announcements* ⌒

DEAR MISS MANNERS:

We are eloping and sending out announcements after the fact. We live in a studio and cannot possibly fit any more "stuff" into it. Does anybody have a good way to request gifts of money? We are thinking about putting up a personal website about the wedding (with the URL on our "we're hitched" announcement) and maybe having a link to Paypal. Is this really offensive? Any ideas?

GENTLE READER:

You may be surprised to hear that Miss Manners is not in the extortion business, so she cannot advise you how to do this. But if she were, she might ask herself not only whether soliciting such funds is offensive (yes) but whether it is likely to be persuasive (doubtful).

Not that your plea of having too much stuff doesn't touch her heart, mind you.

Mr. and Mrs. Jonathan Rhinehart Awful, 3rd

have the honor of announcing

the marriage of their daughter

Alexandrina Grace

to

Mr. Ian Fright

on Saturday, the first of April

Two thousand and five

Our Lady of Propriety Church

Brookdale, Connecticut

Ms. Alexandrina Awful-Fright

Mr. Ian Fright-Awful

will be at home

after the fourth of July

127 primrose Path

Brookdale, Connecticut

Announcement of a wedding with enclosed at home card. At home cards traditionally omitted the name, but that was when people could figure out the bride's new name by adding Mrs. to her husband's name, as shown on the announcement.

But neither that nor the fact that someone has gotten married without requesting her presence moves her to charitable largesse.

The inoffensive thing is to ignore the issue of possible gain. You may even do better in the end by leaving this to the voluntary generosity of your family and friends and discreetly using the Internet to auction off the take.

DEAR MISS MANNERS:

Because we decided to only have our two witnesses present, none of our family and friends attended our wedding. We planned on having a casual summer reception to celebrate our marriage with our family and friends. However, after sitting down to discuss the costs of the reception, we discovered we really cannot afford even a casual reception at this time. My husband left his company last month to try starting his own business and we are currently in the process of rebuilding our home.

We feel like we would like to at least acknowledge the fact that we did get married, and thought it might be nice to send out a wedding announcement instead of having a reception. We did register before our wedding in case family and friends wanted to send gifts instead of money. However, now that we are not actually having a reception, do you think that it is appropriate to send out registry cards with our wedding announcement, or do you feel that that is inappropriate because we are not actually hosting a reception?

GENTLE READER:

Miss Manners' advice is not to supplement your marriage announcement with the suggestion that your willingness to dispense with the company of your relatives and friends does not mean that you would deny them the opportunity to buy you what you want. You may find yourself in the process of rebuilding your social life, along with everything else.

WEDDING CLOTHES

⟶ *The White Dress* ⟵

That brides now wear debutante dresses is symbolically baffling to Miss Manners. True, this is only one of many bridal choices that she finds incomprehensible, quite aside from the bridegrooms. Why do brides want to schedule so many hours, even days, of activities that their guests end up crying to go home? Why do they serve elaborate desserts right before everybody is obliged to eat wedding cake?

And why are they now wearing the sleeveless, often strapless, white ball dresses traditionally associated with ladies who are out looking for husbands rather than those who have found them?

Mind you, Miss Manners has always refrained from taking an unseemly interest in the symbolic interpretation of wedding clothes. The idea that white packaging advertises untouched goods has always struck her as being as vulgar as it is unlikely.

Because the white wedding dress was invented by Queen Victoria, it became associated with the circumstances of her marriage—an unhappy childhood, heavily supervised, which took a dramatic turn for the better with the appearance of a handsome prince and the discovery, with unbounded enthusiasm, of the very secret that the supervision had been designed to keep hidden. Miss Manners need hardly point out that life has changed considerably since then. For one thing, princes are not as handsome as they used to be. For another, wedding dresses are no longer worn as dinner dresses during the first year of marriage, so a practical consideration has arisen of finding something more reusable.

Yet for Miss Manners, as for anyone who doesn't have a heart of stone, the charm of the white wedding dress and veil remains. It is well to have something special to wear, since simply choosing one's "best clothes," which was the custom before that white costume appeared, is now likely to produce scary results. She is therefore quite willing to gloss over the details and consider bridal regalia symbolic of a young lady's leaving her single life to enter upon the state of matrimony.

All right, a not-so-young lady. Understanding the wisdom of attaining some degree of maturity before attempting such a venture, she is not going to quibble about a few years here or there. And all right, maybe even leaving behind a life rendered single by divorce. Although Miss Manners remains an advocate of the tasteful second wedding, in which the translation of tasteful is dressy-suit-with-hat, she can't bring herself to condemn excessive indulgence in frothy white fabric if it serves to remind a bride that this marriage counts.

Having admitted to such laxness, why is Miss Manners now balking at the bare-shouldered wedding dress? Because its symbolic message troubles her. She has discounted the symbolic associations with youth and innocence, but she is unwilling to let go of the symbolic evocation of solemnity.

A ball dress is a party dress, perfectly suitable for the celebrations that follow a wedding ceremony but not for a momentously important sacrament or ritual (and easily attainable, by means of removing a jacket). This is expressed by formality, a

Least Acceptable

Told mother if I can't wear strapless, I won't wear anything

Most Formal

Least Formal

garden Wedding

Afternoon

Mother ...sure of only one thing— she'll wear her pearls

Evening

Flower Girl

Bridesmaid —refuses to wear over-priced, over-done dress

Ladies' Wedding Clothes. The bride's style of dress is determined by the degree of formality of the wedding, rather than the time of day. Most formal is a high-necked, long-sleeved dress with train and long veil. A less formal wedding dress may have short sleeves, some or no train and be worn with a hat or flowers in the hair. At second and other informal weddings, a dress or suit is worn with a hat or flowers. The couple's mothers and the female guests should wear long dresses only at evening weddings of some formality, but the bridesmaids wear long dresses if the bride does and should try not to complain that they hate them.

fact which is almost universally recognized by the choice of clothes that are indeed formal but merry-making-formal, rather than ceremonial-formal.

The wedding ceremony, which is not "about" the couple, as many mistakenly proclaim, but about their assuming socially sanctioned duties and obligations, requires a certain amount of awed modesty. One is not showing oneself off to society at that point but entering into one of its most cherished states. Considering that half an hour later the bride will be appearing under peak show-off conditions, one would think she could wait.

DEAR MISS MANNERS:

My niece is getting married next month in a long white dress after living with the man three years and having two children. Do you think this is proper? One little girl will be flower girl. Having a reception afterwards, too.

GENTLE READER:

This event comes under a particular category of "Proper" known as "High Time." In this area, there is no time for quibbling over dresses or other accessories. Go and wish the couple joy. You cannot accuse them of rushing into matrimony without due consideration.

⟶ Wearing Glasses ⟶

DEAR MISS MANNERS:

Do I have to wear my glasses to my wedding? I can't see without them and have never been able to tolerate contact lenses, but I think I would look prettier without them, and they seem inappropriate with the wedding veil and cap I am planning to wear. Is it all right to look different for that one day?

GENTLE READER:

If your fiancé does not recognize you without your glasses and you cannot properly identify him without your glasses, it seems to Miss Manners that you are running a dangerous risk. If members of the bridal party promise to guide you properly through the ceremony, you might chance it. Miss Manners advises putting the glasses back on for the reception. It's one thing not to recognize one's new husband, but it would be rude not to be able to recognize one's old friends.

Morning dress

"Black Tie"

formal evening

formal day-time

"White Tie" most formal evening

business suit for less formal weddings

Page or ring boy

Father —would rather wear a business suit but must match the groom (not including jeans)

Least Acceptable

Gentlemen's Wedding Clothes. The bridegroom's clothes are dictated by the time of day and by the bride. The most formal, when the bride wears a dress with a train and veil, are morning dress for daytime weddings and white tie for evening. Black tie may be worn at an evening wedding, and a blue, black or gray business suit for an informal wedding at any time of day. The jeans are there only to show what no nice girl should marry.

The fathers and the groomsmen dress as the bridegroom does. It is a mistake to attempt to distinguish the bridegroom by his clothes. The bride can usually tell which one he is, and no one else much cares.

~~ *The Bridegroom* ~~

DEAR MISS MANNERS:

What are the proper clothes for a black-tie wedding? Of course, the ushers and the best man will be in black formal wear, but what about the bridegroom? Should he wear white tie to distinguish himself from the other men? And what about the guests? What do they—both men and women—wear? Suppose the wedding is in the afternoon?

GENTLE READER:

There is no question of that. Wearing black tie during daylight is no way to start a marriage. The cutaway with gray, striped trousers is formal daytime wear.

As for the black-tie evening wedding, all adult men at it, in whatever relationship, wear the same clothes, although guests can also get away with dark business suits. There is no need to distinguish the bridegroom; he is the one marrying the bride.

~~ *The Bridesmaids* ~~

DEAR MISS MANNERS:

I understand that when one agrees to be part of the wedding party, one agrees to whatever the bride decides. Since I live out of state, I purchased my dress over the phone and several months later received it.

To be blunt, the dress is utterly awful. It is a "special occasions prom dress" that is incredibly revealing. Like the other bridesmaids and the bride, an old college friend, I am in my late twenties. I usually wear a size 6, but feel like a whale and naked in this dress.

I finally decided that I would make the best of it and smile my best smile as I walked down the aisle. However, my friend has put me on the spot by asking what I think about the dress. I was content to just wear it without offering an opinion, but she has pressed me. How do I proceed? And how do I handle feeling that she completely disregarded what the bridesmaids might feel comfortable wearing and spending quite a bit of money on? Does the bride not have some responsibility to think of the bridesmaids when she makes this decision?

GENTLE READER:

She is your friend, not Miss Manners', and in spite of your plea for consideration, you both seem to subscribe to the unfortunate and mistaken idea that brides are endowed with the power of dictatorship.

At an earlier stage, you might reasonably have voiced polite and mild objections to the dress or, for that matter, to being a bridesmaid. To resolve to make the best of it all the way down the aisle, only to yield to the temptation to tell the bride that you will feel like a naked whale, is unconscionable. Surely you can manage an evasive answer, such as "Everything will be lovely, but you're going to look so beautiful and radiant that nobody's going to look at us no matter what we wear."

Dressing Up

DEAR MISS MANNERS:

I have accepted the honor of being a bridesmaid in a same-sex (female) wedding. We need advice on the appropriate dress for everyone involved.

Both women are young professionals who usually dress in what is now called "business casual." Neither of them likes the idea of getting married with both of them in wedding gowns, both in tuxedos, or one in each. No one else in the wedding party has come up with a good idea, and of course our dress will depend on theirs.

GENTLE READER:

You didn't ask Miss Manners to consult tradition here, but that is what she is going to do. And not recent tradition either.

They should dress up. This is not a casual event. But neither is it a costume party, and much of today's bridal regalia is dangerously close to resembling that. Traditionally, people simply wore their best clothes for the occasion, and did not concern themselves with dressing for roles. Suits are always suitable, and Miss Manners leaves it to them whether either or both suits should have trousers or skirts.

Wearing Black or White

DEAR MISS MANNERS:

My friend's daughter is getting married in a few months. I had heard that mothers of the bride and groom should not wear white or black to the wedding. But I thought that rule went out with "white signifies virginity." Anyway, the bride's family is all upset because the groom's mother is wearing white. I also had intentions of wearing white. My friends and I would like to know the restrictions, if any, on black and white worn by the mothers of the bride and groom. Also should guests follow the same rules?

GENTLE READER:

The mother of the bridegroom should not wear white to the wedding, whether she is a virgin or not. Neither should any of the guests. Nor should any of the mothers of guests wear black; this rule, too, is unrelated to physical characteristics that are none of anybody's business. Black signifies mourning. No woman should show up at a wedding at which she is neither the bride nor a mourner wearing white or black. Those in deep mourning should not attend weddings. Those in second mourning may wear beige, gray or lavender.

(Please see p. 806.)

∾ A Reasonable Excuse ∾

DEAR MISS MANNERS:

I have been invited to a wedding next month, when I will be seven and a half months pregnant. I have a black maternity party dress—is it proper to wear that?

GENTLE READER:

Marriage, childbirth—there is a whole cycle of life behind this question, isn't there? Miss Manners pictures you, in your charming dilemma. Having been a bride once yourself, you are sensitive to the dress violation of wearing black to a wedding, and thus lending a sort of bad witch appearance to an otherwise light event. At the same time, you have your child's future to consider. What sort of a heritage will a child have whose mother squanders her money on a party dress she will wear only once?

Miss Manners' feeling is that while it is incorrect to wear black to a wedding, it is insane to invest good money in another party maternity dress. Use the black as a background color, adding a light coat, shawl or scarf to disguise it, if not you.

∾ Unreasonable Interference ∾

DEAR MISS MANNERS:

My son's girlfriend, having never been to a wedding, asked me if the dress she intends to wear to my niece's wedding is suitable. While the dress is perfectly appropriate for a wedding, I think it will make her outshine the bride.

My niece is rather plain and her wedding dress is not as flattering as it could be. My son's girlfriend is an extremely attractive woman, and the dress, while modestly cut, is very flattering and makes her look stunning. The problem is, while I don't want my son's girlfriend to steal all the attention from the bride, this head-turning dress is the only one she owns that is suitable, and as a student she can't easily afford a new one. Should I ask her to get another dress, or would that be going to far?

GENTLE READER:

Goodness knows that Miss Manners is horrified by a lot of what is being worn to weddings—but you want her to object to a dress that you acknowledge is both appropriate to the occasion and modestly cut?

Is there something about it that you haven't told Miss Manners? Does it come with its own spotlight? There are lots of mind-boggling possibilities, but she can't think of any that would not be disqualified as both immodest and inappropriate.

If there were a rule forbidding wedding guests from being prettier than the bride, Miss Manners supposes that they, not the bride, would have to wear veils. Besides, attractiveness is in the eye of the beholder. If the bridegroom finds this lady more attractive than the bride, Miss Manners only hopes he finds out before the ceremony.

~ *Long Dresses* ~

DEAR MISS MANNERS:

May I wear a long dress to an afternoon wedding?

GENTLE READER:

Certainly, and best wishes to you, my dear, for your future happiness. (Miss Manners is assuming you are the bride. A wedding guest would of course not dream of wearing a long dress in the afternoon.)

WEDDING PROCEDURE

When is the correct time for a bride to get prenuptial jitters, who should be present, where should each person stand, what should they wear and does this event require a separate present? This is the only ingredient Miss Manners can imagine that has not yet been codified into the marathon of wedding events recommended by florists, photographers, social consultants and other such well-wishers.

Of course, the more subevents there are in a wedding, the more opportunities for squabbles between the two families and among their members over those two major issues—who controls the procedure and who pays for it—that Miss Manners has never succeeded in convincing anyone are unrelated.

Far be it from her to interfere with such a sacred tradition as the founding of family feuds, so here is a schedule of traditional activities from the arrival of the wedding party until the departure of the bridal couple.

TWO DAYS BEFORE THE WEDDING

1. Bachelor dinner, given by the bridegroom to provide his friends with an opportunity to disparage marriage in general, and to entice him to behave in such a way that the bride will call off the wedding.
2. Bride's luncheon (or tea or dinner), given by the bride to provide her friends with an opportunity to complain about the color of the bridesmaid dresses and the quality of the groomsmen.

ONE DAY BEFORE

1. Bridesmaids' and ushers' dinner, given after the rehearsal for all members of the wedding party, including clergy and, if possible, out-of-town guests. Traditionally given by the bride's parents or godparents or close family friends.
2. Rehearsal dinner, which takes the place of the bridesmaids' and ushers' dinner and is identical to it, except that the bridegroom's family pays for it, an increasingly popular custom, especially with the socially and financially exhausted parents of brides.

WEDDING DAY

1. Bride lives out all her royalty fantasies by acting spoiled at the expense of parents, sisters and friends as she gets dressed. Bridegroom, separately, endures pathetic jokes at his expense by his groomsmen, parents, other relatives and friends.
2. Wedding ceremony is performed, a necessary event although it allows for the least leeway, except to very young relatives who may use the opportunity to make innocent but loud remarks which are interpreted by the congregation as dirty. In the processional, the bridegroom and best man come in sideways, and down the aisle come, in order, the ushers, bridesmaids, ring bearer, flower girl

Processional

Altar

Recessional

Receiving Line

The Proper Order in Which a Bridal Party Arrives, Endures, and Recedes from the Wedding. (In the receiving line for the wedding reception, fathers are optional. To exercise the option, insert the father of the bridegroom between the mothers, and the father of the bride on the bride's right.)

and bride with father; or in a Jewish wedding, bridegroom flanked by his parents after the ushers, and bride, flanked by her parents, after the bridesmaids or flower girl. In the recessional, the bride goes on the arm of the bridegroom, followed by attendants, bridesmaids first, or paired off with male attendants.

3. Wedding breakfast (which is to say lunch) following morning wedding, or reception (which is to say tea) following afternoon wedding, or dinner (which is to say dinner) following evening wedding.

a. Receiving line so everyone can tell bride she looks beautiful and then mess up her makeup. In the receiving line, the hostess, who is the bride's mother, greets guests first, then the bridegroom's father, the bridegroom's mother, the bride's father, the bridal couple and the bridesmaids. The fathers may agree to get themselves drinks instead.

b. Eating, which may include a full meal. At a seated wedding breakfast or dinner, the bridal pair sit together with their attendants at one table, while the parents (again with bride's mother as hostess and bridegroom's father as ranking male guest) sit at another table with the officiate and his or her spouse, the grandparents and other close relatives. Toasts are made (to the bride by the best man and anybody else who wants to, including the bridegroom; unless the bride offers return toasts to the bridegroom and her parents, she will never get any champagne) and the bride and bridegroom cut the cake together and try to feed each other bits of the same piece without ruining their clothes.

c. Dancing, first by the bridal couple, then each with the opposite-sex in-law, then with their own parents, then with the best man and maid of honor, then with whoever asks.

d. Ancient and disgusting rituals, such as the bride's throwing the garter to the groomsmen, a custom from the days when the attendants helped the couple change out of their wedding clothes, so to speak; and throwing the bouquet to be caught by a bridesmaid who is already engaged, or tired of being asked when she is getting married.

e. The couple, having donned travel clothes, depart in a shower of fertilizing rice, rose petals or confetti, in an automobile which their friends have ruined with wedding graffiti.

DAY AFTER THE WEDDING

The couple sometimes shows up to continue the festivities. This must be discouraged, no matter how long they have lived together and how short a time they have off from work. Enough is enough.

⌒ *Jewish Customs* ⌒

DEAR MISS MANNERS:

I am being married at home, in a Reform Jewish ceremony, and I am somewhat uneasy about some modifications of traditions that my mother is suggesting. If they were really as common as she says, why is she always saying that it isn't necessary to bother the rabbi about them?

The first is, is it really all right to have the chupah made out of flowers? I have always seen cloth ones, but my mother and the florist say any canopy will do. The second question is about the ring. My engagement ring is part of a set, and the wedding ring is an odd shape to fit around it, and is set with diamonds. I know that only a plain, gold, unbroken circle is traditional for Jewish brides and wonder if the fancy one will seem frivolous. I know I should have thought of this earlier, but it bothers me. The last question is about breaking the glass. My mother tells me it is customary to substitute a light bulb, since it is wrapped in a napkin anyway and no one can see it, and that the bridegroom has less trouble crushing it under his heel to ensure good luck.

GENTLE READER:

What luck do you expect to have with a husband who can't be trusted to smash a glass? Please use a real glass. Do you think God can't see inside a napkin? Anyway, the gesture is said to symbolize the destruction of the temple at Jerusalem, not luck.

Miss Manners will approve the floral canopy if you ask for a plain gold ring to receive at the wedding, saving the diamond one for whenever you feel like wearing it instead. Not only is the symbolism of the plain ring beautiful, but it won't tear your stockings in everyday use.

(For the processional in a Jewish wedding, please see p. 419.)

⌒ *Wedding Hazards* ⌒

Perfectly charming people can plan perfectly charming weddings, only to have these events sabotaged by a variety of wedding-related outsiders who have their own ideas of what a wedding should be like and put them into action without asking.

In the interests of protecting innocent brides, here is Miss Manners' Wedding Booby Trap List of people and ideas that proper brides should make sure of disarming ahead of time.

1. Officiates, including clerics, who missed their real calling as talk-show hosts and use the ceremony to crack jokes (favorite subjects: the bride's father having to pay the bills, the bride's being more eager to marry than the bridegroom, everybody's expected antipathy toward in-laws), share their thoughts ("In my own marriage . . ."), recount the couple's courtship (including sly references to their having already lived together, in case there is a grandparent who was hitherto shielded from reality) and offer generic, mean-spirited psychological counseling ("There'll be times when you hate each other . . .").

2. A professional M.C.—or a bandleader or club events coordinator—with a microphone whose function it is to narrate the reception, and who not only cracks the same jokes featured in the ceremony while he was back fooling with the amplification system, but orders people around ("Now let's have the bride's parents dance together") and milks the wedding guests for applause ("How about a hand for the newlyweds?").

3. A photographer who sees the event as primarily a photo opportunity and keeps hauling the principals away to pose them.

4. A videographer who goes from table to table catching people eating and instructing them to recite their thoughts about the couple.

5. Bartenders, waiters and people who hand out towels in bathrooms—all of whom you paid, handsome gratuity included, in advance—who set out cups with dollar bills in them to hint that it would be nice if the guests tipped too, bills only, please.

6. Any commercial establishment that manages to get the guest list, and then targets the guests with advertising cards that appear to come from the couple, directing the guests what to buy them.

7. Stationers who claim it necessary to have response cards with "M———" (Monsieur?) and then a line for "number of guests attending," thus encouraging people to think about whom they would like to bring along, and other inserts ("Check choice of entrée") that make the invitation look like an advertisement for a resort or a corporate picnic.

8. Anybody remotely capable of playing a practical joke.

9. Professional advisers who recommend any product you would never dream of using, much less buying, in your normal life and right mind, such as monogrammed food, elongated cars, printed programs, monogrammed paper napkins, frilled toothpicks, party favors, white cars, amplified music, confetti, live centerpieces, drink-spouting fountains and ice sculpture.

10. Anybody who suggests anything at all by using the phrase "People will expect you to have . . ." or "What's very popular with this year's brides is . . ."

⌒ Homemade Hazards ⌒

All the world loves lovers except, of course, the people who were married to them when they fell in love. This does not mean that anyone wants to sit through a wedding ceremony that is a dramatic presentation of your own personal love story, beliefs and aspirations, told honestly and openly in your own words. Love is no excuse for inviting people to a popular pageant and treating them, instead, to amateur theatrics about sex and philosophy.

When people write their own wedding ceremonies, it is generally with the belief that the standard ones are boring or hypocritical (not to mention the peculiar idea that *The Prophet* is more beautiful than the Bible). This is a basic misunderstanding about the nature of ceremony.

Miss Manners has no objection to bridal couples doing some discreet editing of the standard ceremony, omitting details they find offensive, such as obeying and giving away. Certainly the innovation of including children from previous unions who will be underfoot in the new one is an important consideration. But they should bear in mind that symbols are intended to apply generally to the social function of the occasion, and are not clues to private behavior. The bride and bridegroom should not use the occasion to announce that they have considered themselves married already, belittling the social and legal sanction they are now receiving. It is rude to brag about your sex life at a public function.

Nor is it charming to air your cynicism. Traditional ceremonies, whether civil or religious, express hopes and ideals; they do not make realistic predictions. Statistically, it may be true that it is likely to be the bride and bridegroom's subsequent feelings, not death, which do them part. But that is no excuse for making lukewarm vows to stay together "as long as we both shall love." How would you like to hear a President of the United States take an inaugural vow to uphold the Constitution as long as it doesn't interfere with his political plans?

The long, droning parts of the ceremony do not, in fact, bore the wedding guests. These merely give them time to enjoy appropriate thoughts for the occasion, such as "What does she see in him?" and "What does he see in her?"

WEDDING RECEPTIONS

～ The Receiving Line ～

DEAR MISS MANNERS:

At the reception hall for my son's wedding, there was no receiving line for parents to greet the guests, just a lot of people in one room. Is it proper etiquette for the guests to then approach the parents and say hello/goodbye?

I tried to make the rounds and greet everyone, but with the number of people, it was difficult. I just felt slighted that some people I couldn't greet didn't come over to me.

GENTLE READER:

Is it proper for the guests to overlook the slight offered to them by hosts who fail to greet them, and take the job upon themselves? Yes, but let us not forget here who created the problem.

Miss Manners has heard a lot of nonsense about a receiving line being "too formal" for people who are entertaining dozens of people on—guess what?—formal occasions. So far, they have not come up with a substitute that would allow them to greet every guest upon arrival at a reception, and say goodbye to every guest who is departing. "Making the rounds," as you have discovered, does not do the job. Once the reception gets going, both hosts and guests find themselves waylaid in conversation and hesitant to interrupt other conversations. So they both feel slighted.

～ Good Wishes ～

DEAR MISS MANNERS:

I don't have an embarrassing story to accompany my question. I just want clarification of current proper etiquette as I don't want to be rude or perpetuate a rule if that is not a rule any more.

I am in my 30s and grew up in a conservative area. Boys asked girls out, not vice versa. Men asked women to marry them. However, the marriage ceremony did not say to honor and obey the husband or "Man and Wife."

I was always taught that when addressing a bride and groom, the appropriate things to say to each were the following:

To the Bride: "Best Wishes"

To the Groom: "Congratulations"

It was made clear to me that it was offensive to say "Congratulations" to the bride, as that conveyed "Congratulations—you found a guy." I have found over the years that I am about the only person that is aware of this element of proper etiquette. Was I instructed incorrectly as a child on this matter? Has etiquette changed? Should I continue to try and help people (my husband and child for example) understand the reasoning behind this form of best wishes/congratulations?

GENTLE READER:

What, no embarrassing story? Miss Manners is disappointed, but not surprised. Even though the rule is still in effect, most people break it, yet modern brides are highly unlikely to be insulted by being congratulated.

This is not because the courtship patterns have changed. Even if the lady proposes to the gentleman on bended knee, Miss Manners and other polite people should figure he is lucky to get her. Nor is it entirely because those who offer congratulations mean well but don't know the rule and it would be churlish to quibble.

It is because today's brides hear far worse. Those who are repeatedly told "It's about time!" and asked "Are you pregnant?" are only too happy to accept kind thoughts, however they are phrased.

∼ A Bad Question ∼

DEAR MISS MANNERS:

I am a single, twenty-five-year-old professional woman who will soon be participating in my younger sister's wedding, the family's first. Faced on this occasion with the inevitability of parrying personally objectionable inquiries about the duration of my single state, how might I respond without appearing needlessly rude? Also, may the bride's attendants wear wrist-length gloves at a morning summer wedding?

GENTLE READER:

Questions such as "And when are you getting married?" do not deserve to be answered. (Questions about wrist-length gloves do, and the answer is yes.) If you do not wish to be needlessly rude, a resolve Miss Manners admires, your reply should be a smile, the statement "Oh, I don't know" and a change of subject.

⌒ *Departing* ⌒

DEAR MISS MANNERS:

I need guidance as to whether an ancient rule of etiquette is still applicable in this day and age. Now, I know that your immediate response will be a resounding "Yes!"—but please hear me out.

I am referring to the rule that says that guests may not leave a wedding reception until the bride and groom cut the cake. I agree that this was a perfectly good rule when the bridal couple used to leave the wedding reception at a decent hour in order to commence their wedding trip.

It seems to me that now that brides and grooms no longer believe that marriage is a prerequisite to having what used to be called marital relations, they are much less eager to commence the wedding trip. They are remaining at the wedding reception for hours on end in order to enjoy the party for which they (or their parents) have paid dearly. The cake remains untouched into the very late hours of the evening.

Please, Miss Manners, may the rules of etiquette be adjusted to reflect that the guests may leave the reception after a reasonable period of time, say, after the food has been eaten, they've danced a dance or two, and they've gushed over the bridal couple—although the cake is not cut? I am begging for some relief here!

GENTLE READER:

Miss Manners resents the assumption that she will defend all ancient rules against reform. It is an essential part of her life's work to guide such change when it is warranted.

However, this does include resisting change that would merely constitute deterioration, such as the common bridal presumption that it is no longer necessary to thank one's benefactors. But your point is well taken.

In fact, it was not just the cake-cutting for which guests were supposed to wait, but the departure of the bridal couple—many of whom now stay around until breakfast. Miss Manners hereby releases guests who have stayed through the ceremony and the meal or reasonably long reception that follows, lest they begin to despair that they are in for witnessing the entire marriage.

DEAR MISS MANNERS:

Our daughter is being married soon in a formal ceremony, although she is, only too obviously, I am afraid, pregnant. It's a long story, and perhaps you will think her

father and I are wrong to allow such a public wedding when everyone knows the situation, but it is what she wants. Anyway, my concern is that people do not laugh at
us. She says it is nothing to her friends, but her father's and mine are still not used to
such things. For instance, wouldn't people think it ridiculous for us to throw rice at
the bridal couple, symbolizing fertility, when everyone will be able to see that that
has already been assured?

GENTLE READER:

You could throw minute rice, symbolizing that things are happening any minute
now. Miss Manners prefers the paella or pilaf approach: The more good things in
your symbolism the better, but don't examine it too closely.

Food and Drink

DEAR MISS MANNERS:

My son is getting married about two hundred miles from where we live. They
are sending out invitations to our family, relatives, and friends. If you invite people
to your wedding and it is two hundred miles away, shouldn't the reception consist of
more than cake and plain punch? After a little protesting, they finally agreed to have
turkey salad sandwich loaves. I even offered to help pay expenses, but that is all they
want. I say you shouldn't invite people to your wedding when they have to travel that
distance unless you are going to provide a meal.

GENTLE READER:

You have to realize that the food at a wedding is of such emotional significance
that practical considerations, such as feeding people who have been driving all day,
have nothing to do with it. Overstuffing is an important part of many people's idea
of a wedding. Unless people groan at the very sight of the buffet table at the reception, or at the approach of still another course at a wedding dinner; unless most of
the conversation consists of "No, no, I couldn't" and "Can you imagine what this
must have cost them a head?" and "I didn't even see the crab legs over there"; unless
a junior bridesmaid gets sick and a grandparent has to be led to a chair and fanned—
the wedding has not been a success. Others are of the cucumber sandwich and two
glasses of champagne persuasion.

Miss Manners does not favor one tradition over another, but advises against trying to win converts from such deep convictions. Take a hotel room in town, and

invite your side over to eat after the wedding. You will have a good time laughing among yourselves at the skimpiness of the bride's family.

DEAR MISS MANNERS:

I'm in a bind as to how I can suggest to the parents of my future son-in-law that if they want an open bar type of cocktail hour before dinner at the reception, they should spend for it. They are quite able to do this financially. My husband could pay for it, but we agree that we should not have to spend for something we don't like, especially since it is quite unnecessary. We do not drink, and neither does my family. I was thinking of serving a punch or beer.

GENTLE READER:

It is unfortunate that in weddings, as in divorces, money is often used as a weapon when hostilities have nothing to do with cost. In this case, you say there really is no financial problem in paying for the drinks. Why, then, do you wish to stick the other family for a bill for an occasion for which you are the hosts?

The answer is that you don't like having to entertain people who drink. This is clear when you say that there is no need for liquor because your family does not drink—as if you were not equally obliged to be hospitable to the family into which your daughter is marrying.

If your convictions prevented you from presiding at an event where liquor is served, Miss Manners would support you in explaining politely to the other set of parents that you could not violate this policy. However, you have made it clear, by bringing up the matter of money, that this is not the case. Miss Manners is afraid that it is too late to pretend that it is; you should have thought of this earlier. Allowing some of your guests to drink but refusing to pay for it cannot be passed off as a moral position.

~ *The Cash Bar* ~

DEAR MISS MANNERS:

Recently an acquaintance invited my husband and me to her wedding. This was quite a surprise, since I have heard that she was complaining about the cost of said wedding and the fact that she would have to spend two dollars to feed each person. She succeeded in getting this amount reduced to a dollar and fifty cents and has reportedly invited one hundred and fifty people. In addition, she has borrowed the wedding gown from the matron of honor, and has asked two guests to help, one to cut and serve the cake and one to pour and serve the punch. I have also been told that there will be a cash bar at the reception. What is your opinion of a person with such a limited budget inviting so many people? Is it proper to invite guests to your wedding and then ask them to serve as waiters and waitresses? Is it proper to expect your guests to buy their own libations?

GENTLE READER:

It may surprise you to hear that what you call serving as waiters and waitresses is, under the odd verb "to pour" (as in recruiting friends to pour tea at one's tea party), a traditional honor. Nor is there anything wrong with borrowing a wedding dress or inviting many people. However, you may be relieved to hear that selling drinks is disgusting. By serving them tea and homemade cake, she could be perfectly gracious within the limits of the budget.

⌁ The Wedding Cake ⌁

DEAR MISS MANNERS:

Most wedding cakes are so vulgar, with all the overly fancy trimming, and I would prefer to have a perfectly plain cake. My fiancée, who generally has very good taste, and who agrees with me about keeping the rest of the wedding simple, says that would look "cheap" and wants one of those several-tiered monstrosities. She has forgotten that she once told me a story about being a flower girl and looking up at her cousin's cake which had a bride and groom on the top, and probably that's what she really wants but is ashamed to admit it. This is such a dumb argument, but it makes me wonder what else she is keeping from me in the way of secret ickyness.

GENTLE READER:

Who are you, the Mies van der Rohe of the pastry shop? Wedding cakes are supposed to be vulgar. Go buy yourself a doughnut to satisfy your aesthetic sense, and let her have that wedding cake.

PHOTOGRAPHS

Memory, to the best of Miss Manners' dim recollection, used to be an interesting and original thing. It was eccentric in what it selected, skipping the obvious in favor of the curious. One's wedding was often a blur, while moments containing nothing more than the touching of fingertips may have been framed in gold. A child's first birthday may have disappeared, while a babyish look of trust may have gotten itself accidentally bronzed. An exotic trip may have faded, while the picture of a domestic moment continued to burn brightly.

Naturally, all of this was possible only before the widespread use of the camera. Now that every family has its official record maker, there is no room for wispy memories in the world of indisputable snapshots. Life is no longer something to remember. It has become, as we say in the media business, a photo opportunity. Baby is not allowed to take his first step when he first feels brave enough to attempt it: He must wait until his parents have loaded the video camera.

Here Miss Manners must step in. Miss Manners is the patron goddess of all social events, and a lot of family events as well. She is therefore in a position to tell all professional and amateur photographers that they may record such events only if they allow the events to take place. A wedding in which the bride and bridegroom are followed around by video, portrait and guest photographers, posing as they are standing with their wedding party, standing with their parents, cutting cake, eating cake, eating ice cream, standing with the out-of-town guests, drinking champagne, throwing bouquets and otherwise following an album-dictated schedule of expected events, is not a wedding.

Now, Miss Manners does not wish to incur the outrage of all camera enthusiasts, knowing, as she does, that they are armed. Therefore, she wishes to suggest a compromise by which photographers may save such activities for the albums, without having to destroy the activities in order to do so.

One way is the truly "candid" picture. A candid picture is not, as many people seem to believe, a photograph in which a bride has been instructed to feed cake to a bridegroom who, in turn, has been instructed to eat it. There is also the true photo opportunity. The old set-up photograph, done at a crucial moment between the bride's last hair appointment and the wedding ceremony, well served the true purpose of wedding photographs, which is to give the couple's descendants something to laugh at years later. Posed photograph sessions at weddings are so notoriously abused that Miss Manners would ban them entirely, relying for all the "formal" pictures on the advance sessions, and trusting to catch-as-catch-can for the rest. Otherwise, those who aspire to record life photographically must be made to realize that they must not interfere with the natural course of life and record things that would not have taken place otherwise. There is little enough improvisation left in life as it is.

⌒ Family Portraits ⌒

DEAR MISS MANNERS:

What is the correct way to picture the bride and groom and parents and grandparents when the parents have been divorced and have remarried, so that there are then three sets of parents? Is it improper to picture the bride's mother and father together, since they now have different spouses? Or does one take two sets of pictures?

GENTLE READER:

Miss Manners remembers when people got married because they wanted to. Then bridal couples started saying that they were getting married for the sake of their parents.

From what Miss Manners has been able to observe, weddings are now held for the convenience of photographers. Nevertheless, there is no correct, or incorrect, order for the taking of wedding photographs. Some divorced couples are friendly enough to climb into the same photograph together, and others are not. If you must have pictures posed in parallel groups, Miss Manners advises ascertaining the wishes of the bride's parents and respecting them.

⌒ Joint Portraits ⌒

DEAR MISS MANNERS:

Does a formal bridal portrait have to be just of the bride alone? I have seen many, with announcements and in people's houses, that show the couple in a formal pose—I'm not talking about the candids of her feeding him wedding cake, or anything like that—instead of just the bride in her wedding dress, and it seems to me that it makes much more sense. After all, they're both getting married, aren't they?

GENTLE READER:

It is true that many couples have the notion that the bridegroom is as essential an ingredient of the formal wedding as the bride. Miss Manners wouldn't mind this so much in matters such as photographs if she didn't know where that kind of thing leads. It leads to husbands thinking that they have as much right as wives to play starring roles in the delivery room—that's where it leads.

WEDDING PRESENTS
(AND OF COURSE THANK-YOU LETTERS)

When bridal couples invite those who are dearest to them to share the public solemnization of their happiness, they may be sure that all their cherished friends and relatives are having the same thoughts: Do we owe them a present? How much do you think we have to spend? Can't we get away with less? How much did they spend for us?

In a society that uses the terms "free gift" and "mandatory donation," it is not surprising that the exchange of presents is treated as an unpleasant commercial transaction, while impersonal fees are disguised as voluntarily given presents. Miss Manners once tried to step into the Metropolitan Museum of Art in New York after having discovered that there was no admission charge—only to be detained by an employee who admitted that one could enter "free," but explained that that could only be done after one made a voluntary donation to the museum. Miss Manners naturally inquired as to the meaning of such a voluntary donation.

"What do you want to give?" this person countered.

"A wing," replied Miss Manners, and was explaining that unfortunately she had not yet saved up the cash to carry out this wish, when she was interrupted with the information that intentions aside, she must give.

That is voluntary gift-giving in commercial life. In social life, however, there is no such thing as an obligatory present. You do not owe your friends anything just because they are getting married. Nevertheless, it is customary that when one values people enough to want to participate in occasions that are important to them, one is moved to express this emotion in some tangible form.

Get that? In other words, if you decline to attend a wedding to which you have been invited, or merely receive an announcement, you are considered involved only to the extent of a letter wishing them well. However, if you want to partake in the couple's bliss and also their champagne, you should feel moved to spring for something more tangible. The same principle may be applied to other occasions. You must care enough about people to want to gladden their hearts with a token of your esteem if you accept their overnight hospitality, celebrate Christmas, their birthdays or graduations with them or expect a large inheritance from them.

~ Owing Presents ~

DEAR MISS MANNERS:

My best friend believes that a wedding gift needs to match the quality/cost of the wedding. She feels if the invitation states "Reception at the Ritz," you would purchase a more expensive gift.

I believe a gift is supposed to come from the heart, and is based more on how close you are to the couple getting married. If my sister were to get married in the back yard, I would still give her the best gift I could afford. Would you please explain the proper wedding gift etiquette?

GENTLE READER:

Really, this is your best friend?

Miss Manners is amazed, considering how different are your respective approaches to personal relationships—of which presents that are exchanged are symbolic. Your idea seems to be that such ties should be governed by emotion, whereas your friend's sentiment is that to them that has should be given. You may love her anyway, but there is nothing proper about her position.

~ Bringing Presents ~

DEAR MISS MANNERS:

If I bring a wedding present to the reception, shouldn't the bride open it while I'm there? I have had presents pushed aside, which hurt me. I choose things carefully, and would like to see the pleasure on their faces.

GENTLE READER:

Please don't bring presents to weddings or wedding receptions. Please. Let us stamp out this unfortunate practice. For one thing, the bride and bridegroom cannot take the time from their guests to open presents. For another, they (or their parents) must then figure out how to get the present home, or carry it with them on their honeymoon. For still another, the pleasure on their faces, at, let us say, receiving their fourth Crock-Pot, is best enjoyed in privacy.

DEAR MISS MANNERS:

When my husband and I attended the wedding of my first cousin, we brought our wedding gift with us, and during the reception my husband retrieved the gift from our car and put it on the gift table. Several weeks after the wedding I was unloading items from the trunk of my car and found the wedding card that was to have accompanied the gift. Apparently it had fallen off the gift, and my husband failed to notice that it was missing.

Is there a tactful way to let the bride and groom know that we did indeed get them a gift, and which one it was? My cousin came to our wedding and gave us a very nice gift, and I don't want her to think I've forgotten her.

GENTLE READER:

You have a trifling etiquette problem here, but you hold the solution to a hideous one. For heaven's sake, call them immediately and tell them what happened. Miss Manners keeps hearing from frantic brides who are eager to do their solemn duty of writing thanks for presents, but prevented because cards were lost, or even because presents were stolen. This is why Miss Manners keeps telling people not to bring their presents to the wedding—to send them ahead or—since one Gentle Reader waxed indignant about the extra expense for postage—drop them off before the wedding at the bride's house.

Sending Presents

DEAR MISS MANNERS:

Please advise me on the proper way to address the name on a gift to be sent ahead of time to the home of the bride-to-be. Is it "Mr. and Mrs. Joe America" (name of the groom-to-be) or Jane Doe? Need an answer soon.

GENTLE READER:

The custom is to address all pre-wedding presents to the bride-to-be, and those sent after the marriage to the couple. Some people may take offense at this, as a sign of inequality. Some people will take offense at anything. However, sending people presents goes a long way toward mitigating any offense.

Soliciting Presents

DEAR MISS MANNERS:

I am soon getting married and will be sending wedding invitations to a lot of out-of-town relatives. Would it be proper to enclose a card stating my patterns that I have picked out in crystal, china, silver, etc.? If this is proper and not too aggressive, how can I word the card and not appear too forward?

GENTLE READER:

Unless you want to appear forward, not to mention greedy, you must go into reverse immediately. *Any* indication that you make a connection between wanting certain people at your wedding and expecting presents from them is improper.

⌒ *Soliciting Payments* ⌒

DEAR MISS MANNERS:

My fiancé and I have been cohabitating for over 2 years and have all the household things that we could need. Consequently we registered at a travel agency because a honeymoon is something we could really use and won't be able to afford after paying for the wedding ourselves. Call it extortion or not, I have every intention of including a card designating which agency. Any ideas how to delicately phrase "I don't want any cheesy frames or cheap crap like that so get me a travel voucher"?

GENTLE READER:

Miss Manners is afraid that that's as delicate as it is going to get. The fact is, it is a cheesy thought.

⌒ *Soliciting for Charity* ⌒

DEAR MISS MANNERS:

I will be getting married for the first time this April. The wedding and reception will be small. In lieu of gifts to us, we would like to have people contribute to a charity or similar organization.

I can think of a number of organizations that would not be controversial that people might like to contribute to. Is it acceptable to ask people to contribute to a charity of one's choosing? Should more than one charity be listed? Should people simply be asked to make a donation to a charity of their choice? How can we properly convey the name and address of the charity? Should we be registered someplace for people who don't want to make a charitable gift?

GENTLE READER:

Please allow Miss Manners to make two small corrections before she wishes you well in your marriage:

1. Adding "for the first time" to the statement that you are getting married is unduly cynical and ought to be worrisome to your fiancé.
2. The fact that other people's money is under their control is not suspended in the case of wedding guests, so that you cannot properly tell them how to dispose of it, even though you suspect they have set some aside for you, and even in a good cause.

Of the many letters Miss Manners receives from people who want to have some control over the selection of presents they expect, yours is only in the mildly offensive category. The severely offensive ones ask, "How can I let them know I want money instead of some crummy toaster?" or "Instead of giving us pieces of silver we won't use, why can't our friends get together and pay our mortgage?" Least offensive are the ones from people who either sympathize with their friends' problems of buying presents or profoundly distrust their taste, and want to say "No gifts, please" on their wedding invitations.

What Miss Manners must tell all of you, regardless of your motives, is that there is no tasteful way—not even any moderately decent way—of directing present-giving when you are on the receiving end. You must even seem pleasantly surprised when they give you something. To act as if it is such standard payment that you can acknowledge your expectations is rude-rude-rude.

Perhaps what has confused you is the business gimmick of the bridal registry, by which engaged couples inform stores of their tastes in the hope that their friends will come in, get this information and act on it. There is just enough distance between the giver and the receiver to make this a passable practice. The bride and bridegroom do not actually instruct their friends—they only tell their preferences to a neutral business establishment. And the present givers only receive the information if they ask for it.

Your wedding guests should not be asked to "memorialize" you with a charitable contribution in your name. If they want to remember you charitably, they can invite you for dinner.

A Charitable Solicitation

DEAR MISS MANNERS:

My fiancé and I are both in our forties and have never been married and so have nearly all of the things needed to form a household. In fact, we have more than a single house can hold since we both own our homes. The problem is how to tactfully say in the invitations that we prefer the Wishing Well Wedding since we really don't need or want a bunch of gifts.

GENTLE READER:

Some things don't lend themselves to being said gently. A prime example would be: "When you come to our wedding, we're planning to collect money from you."

Miss Manners has another unpleasant message she would like to put tactfully. Hers is: If you have more than you need, perhaps twice over, why aren't you thinking of giving things away to people who are in need, rather than wishing for more?

Thanking for Presents

DEAR MISS MANNERS:

Two months ago, I received three wedding invitations and purchased each a gift. I still haven't received a thank-you. Have any rules changed with regard to sending a thank-you note?

GENTLE READER:

No, the rules haven't changed, but neither, unfortunately, have the brides. Successful love creates an exaggerated feeling of worthiness, which leads all brides to believe that it is reasonable to expect everyone whom they, their parents and their parents-in-law know to spend large amounts of time, effort and money sending them presents, but that it is outrageous to assume that they can spare the three minutes each it would take to acknowledge these presents.

Therefore a little ritual has evolved, to teach brides that most valuable of life's lessons: that generosity should always be encouraged.

As the unacknowledged donor of wedding presents, you are in exactly the right position to get this training going. Telephone the bride's mother or, if your connection is to the bridegroom, his mother, and say gently, "I know how busy Alexandrina must be now, setting up housekeeping, and I don't like to trouble her, but I wonder if you could just make a discreet inquiry for me. I'm so afraid—you know how stores are these days, and I don't have to tell you about the postal service—I'm worried that my little package might have gotten lost. Could you just find out if she got the china service for twelve I sent two months ago? I don't want to make her think she has to take the time to write or anything—I just want to know if she got it, because otherwise I'll have to have it traced, so I can let the insurance company know it was lost."

As you can see, this speech, a traditional one, is designed to drive Alexandrina's mother crazy. She knows that you know that Alexandrina and Ian set up house together three years ago, and if there's any housekeeping done by either of them, nobody's seen any signs of it yet. By going to her, you have made it clear that you have traced the reason for Alexandrina's having no manners. Because you are voicing a practical concern and because you have placed yourself in the faultless position of a generous person who expects no return, she can't offer any defense.

So she murmurs that "the young people have been so pressed with all the festivities and settling down to their new life that I'm afraid they've been terribly remiss," and she promises to speak to Alexandrina about it.

Does she ever. You can probably hear the reverberations in your own living room. If it is the bridegroom's mother you have talked to, the scolding is administered in sweeter tones, or perhaps it is delivered through the bridegroom himself, who will be asked to "make her" write the letters. (This is a true no-win situation and the bridegroom, if he is clever, will then write the letters himself. However, this will only ensure that the recipients will refer to him and his wife from that moment on as "poor dear Ian and that woman.")

In any case, you will soon have a stilted letter thanking you for "the lovely present," but not informing you whether it was appreciated, exchanged or broken, or even whether they know that you were the one who gave them the china. Your satisfaction should come from knowing that you have participated in a significant romantic tradition.

⌒ *Frank Thanks* ⌒

DEAR MISS MANNERS:

I enclose herewith the text of a recently received thank-you note, and wonder what you think of the bride's forthright frankness. Do you consider this the *nouvelles mercies?*

Dear friends:

Thank you so much for the beautiful vase. Unfortunately, it was the seventh one we received, so we did want you to know—and we hope you won't mind that we exchanged it in order to complete our china pattern. We send our love to you, etc.

GENTLE READER:

It isn't the bride's frankness that worries Miss Manners—it's her brain. If one has seven vases, it should not be difficult to figure out how to exchange six of them, while letting the seventh represent, to each of the seven donors, the one that was kept. Miss Manners hopes that this couple is not planning to have children.

⁓ Emailed Thanks ⁓

DEAR MISS MANNERS:

After several people from various parts of the United States went to a foreign country for the wedding of a family member, I received an effusive email communication from his mother, thanking those who had gone, as well as asking if anyone had taken any wonderful pictures, of which she would very much appreciate copies. She addressed the mail to me and to my two daughters, with copies to ten other people.

I feel uncomfortable receiving what is in effect a mass thank you note. Perhaps I should be satisfied to have received a thank you note of any kind, since I did not expect one. But my feeling is that an individual thank you would be more appropriate, by means of email (although the technology of mail is such that she could have very easily have sent the same message individually to each person, but that is not the issue here), snail mail or preferably by a phone call.

Perhaps I am being a nitpicker and/or a curmudgeon. Since email is in its infancy as a mass method of communication, I don't know how much protocol has developed.

GENTLE READER:

You also have to learn to sort your email properly. Miss Manners is puzzled about what threw you off, because you were doing fine until you faltered in your conclusion.

As you suppose, it would be rude to send a mass-produced letter of thanks by email to fulfill the requirement for an individual, handwritten letter. But as you also mention, you did not expect a letter of thanks, presumably because you know that it is unnecessary for a hostess to write thanking her guests. (In the case of a wedding, it is not even customary for the guests to write such letters to their hosts, although it is charming to do so.)

You have only to realize that what you got was not a letter of thanks but a request for photographs. The part about appreciating the guests' attending was merely a polite opening. If you had written this lady to inquire whether anybody had found the scarf you left with your coat—another informal message that can properly be sent by email—Miss Manners hopes you would have opened with a statement about how much you enjoyed the beautiful wedding.

⌐ *Joint Thanks* ⌐

DEAR MISS MANNERS:

My daughter was recently married. Most of her gifts arrived after the marriage, and we have had notes engraved Mr. and Mrs. John Doe, which she had intended using to write her thank-you notes on. However, we now question whether she can correctly use stationery that is engraved with both their names. If it is acceptable, does she close with just her name or both their names? If joint stationery is not acceptable, what would be your suggestion?

GENTLE READER:

Miss Manners understands the temptation to use informal cards or notes for this occasion, because they have less space on them to fill, and to sign both names. However, this must be resisted. The letters should be written on letter paper which may be engraved with her married name. They should be signed only by the letter writer. Otherwise, the day will come when Mrs. Awful starts signing her letters "Love from Kimberly, Rhino, Lisa, Adam, Jason, Kristen and Fido," and at least one of them is not going to have authorized the sentiment. It is perfectly acceptable for her to write "Rhino loves the electric shrimp deveiner" without consulting Rhino.

DEAR MISS MANNERS:

Over the years, I have kept in communication with my granddaughter who lives about 1,000 miles from me, primarily on her birthday and at Christmas, and she has done the same with me. Two years ago, she visited me and I met her young man for the first time, and we got along fine.

I was, of course, invited to their wedding, and intended to go, but had to cancel shortly before because of health problems. A few weeks before, I mailed them wedding presents, which included a crystal set, and to each of them a check for $500.00. At about the same time, I sent the prospective groom four or five dozen golf balls, and several golf gadgets which I no longer had use for.

Shortly after the wedding, I received a thank you card from my granddaughter, but not a word from her husband. I admit to being old fashioned and confused by the values that are important to people in their age group. Am I correct in feeling hurt by not receiving a personal note of thanks from my grandson-in-law, or have what I consider common courtesies changed that much?

Dear Aunt Patience,

Rhino and I are thrilled with the magnificent silver sugar shaker you sent us. It adds not only beauty and dignity to our table, but amusement, too, as some of our friends who are both ignorant and daring have not waited for the berries to be served, but have shaken it over their meat. "This could only have come from your Aunt Patience," said one, and we were proud to say that it had.

Rhino joins me in thanking you for your kindness. We look forward to having you in our new home.

Love,
Daffodil

A letter from a bride, thanking the giver of a present. This monogrammed paper can be used for any private correspondence. It would be perfectly proper for the bridegroom to write such a letter on his monogrammed or initialed paper, but he refused.

GENTLE READER:

They are changing—not being eliminated—but your granddaughter and her husband are not keeping up. They are going by the old-fashioned custom of the wife's doing all the social correspondence for both, while you are expecting the modern modification of each doing his or her own.

True, your granddaughter forgot to mention the golf equipment when she thanked you for everything else. But Miss Manners would prefer to assume that she forgot about the extra package in her gratitude over your wedding presents, and that when she told her husband she had written you, he presumed that she had fully spoken for him as well. Miss Manners is happy to remove you from the Hurt Grandparent annals, which is overcrowded with people who haven't heard anything.

Preprinted Thanks

DEAR MISS MANNERS:

I recently got married and received between two hundred and fifty and three hundred gifts; two hundred and fifty or more were money, so I had pre-printed thank-you notes made, along with my invitations, and sent them out. A few family members felt that I should have written in each and everyone to thank them for exactly what was given. This meant that I was supposed to write thank you for X number of dollars. I felt that this was in poor taste. Who is right?

GENTLE READER:

Nobody. Everyone is wrong. You are wrong, because you should have written each person a letter. It's a lot of work, and might take you a while, but if someone has taken the trouble to write you a check, you can take the trouble to write that person a letter. Your family is wrong about having to mention the sum. The most gracious way is to do the present selection that the giver should have done in the first place, and then thank that person for the object. "Robin and I had been longing for a" (statue for the front lawn, Scotch tape dispenser or whatever would approximate the buying power of the cash) "and you made it possible for us to rush right out and buy it."

Admittedly, this taxes the imagination of the bride, especially if she is receiving several such presents. In that case, the person may be thanked for an "incredibly generous" (over $500), "extremely generous" ($100 to $500), "very generous" ($50 to $100), "kind" ($25 to $50) or "thoughtful" (under $25) present.

∽ *Printed Golden Thanks* ∽

DEAR MISS MANNERS:

How should thank-you cards—the good white ones that usually have "thank you" in gold script on the front—be properly used?

GENTLE READER:

Over Miss Manners' dead body. If you can't take the trouble to write out the words "thank you" yourself, you do not deserve to have anything for which to thank anyone.

∽ *Overdue Thanks* ∽

DEAR MISS MANNERS:

My husband and I had a wonderful wedding this month last year, but I haven't sent any thank you cards to anybody and I haven't bought anybody in the wedding anything. Now that the money situation is a little bit better, I would like to see if you have a suggestion how to make up for that. Is it necessary or is that tradition?

GENTLE READER:

Is it traditional to brush aside duties owed anyone else until it is convenient? And even then to ask if one really has to go through with it?

Neglect of wedding guests is not a tradition, except in the sense that shoplifting may be traditional among some teenagers, but it is certainly common. An increasing number of people believe that getting married entitles them to exact tributes from others without doing anything for them in return, not even expressing gratitude. The remedy for this appalling lapse is to write long, effusive letters accompanied by charmingly well chosen presents to tell these people how much you valued their participation in your wedding and appreciated their presents.

You might spare them your excuses, especially the one about money being tight. They saw what you spent for that wonderful wedding, so they realize that the decision was based on priorities. And just as you concluded that your resources were best devoted to yourselves, they may be thinking that the money they spent on you might have been better devoted to themselves.

⌒ *Returned with Thanks* ⌒

DEAR MISS MANNERS:

My daughter was married on a Saturday to a young man she'd known for many years and lived with for over a year. The marriage abruptly ended the following day. What do we do with the shower and wedding presents? Some presents have been opened and the boxes thrown away and possibly even used already. How do we write thank you cards? It is a very awkward situation and I am unclear as to how it is to be handled. Any advice would be greatly appreciated. Thank you.

GENTLE READER:

The most important advice is never again to mention that part about the marriage ending the day after the wedding. Naturally, Miss Manners is burning to know what happened, as would anyone else who heard this. It is not, however, in your daughter's interest to have everyone she knows affix this unfortunately dramatic scene (imagined or, worse, real, if she should be tempted to explain) to her reputation forever.

Technically, wedding presents need be returned only if the wedding does not take place, and this one did. However, it would be gracious of your daughter to return unused presents anyway, if only to head off unpleasant comments about her motivations should she marry again. The accompanying letters, which actually should go out to all the wedding guests, should thank them for their good wishes (and for their specific presents), noting only that the couple "soon came to the sad conclusion that the marriage had been a mistake."

⌒ *The Last Word on Thanking* ⌒

DEAR MISS MANNERS:

When is a written thank-you note for a wedding gift not necessary?

GENTLE READER:

When no wedding present has been received.

The Trousseau

SILVER

YOUNG COUPLES who think that silver is impractical should be told a few rough facts about what has happened to its price over the years before they attempt to discourage their relations and friends from giving them silver as wedding presents. Affordable presents are more likely now to be individual forks or spoons, rather than place settings, but there is still no opportunity like a wedding to get the basic pieces. In fact, it is the single most striking argument Miss Manners knows against the what-difference-does-a-piece-of-paper-make theory.

Miss Manners' idea of a basic place setting is slightly different from that of silver flatware manufacturers. Hers is the large knife, large fork, small fork, and oval tablespoon, with small knife as the choice if there is to be a fifth piece. Teaspoons are properly used only for coffee and tea, and those confining themselves to the basics are not likely to use their silver at family breakfast or to give tea parties. The tablespoon may be used for soup, as well as dessert. The small fork is used for salad, dessert (you run out and wash it during the cheese course) and luncheon, and may also fill in for the fish fork or the fruit fork before you acquire those luxuries. The

444

small knife is also used for luncheon and, of course, for courses other than the meat course, at which the large fork and knife are used.

After one has a service of place settings, Miss Manners advises getting the teaspoon, the butter knife and the fish knife and fish fork. Next in usefulness are the demitasse spoon (which certainly needn't match the table silver, as demitasse is served in the drawing room, but Miss Manners prefers those that do not say "Souvenir of Atlantic City"), the fruit knife and fork and, if you have leftover money and go in for that sort of thing, the oyster fork, the iced-tea spoon, the bouillon spoon, the grapefruit spoon or whatever else you can find.

In the time of great financial boom—Miss Manners is thinking of the Industrial Revolution—all kinds of strange implements were invented, and if you are rich and clever enough, you can set a table on which, as a lady of Miss Manners' acquaintance says of her inherited silver, it is not clear whether dinner is to be served or a hysterectomy performed.

Silver is marked with the three initials of the bride's maiden name. This is particularly practical these days, when silver lasts much longer than the average marriage.

A carving knife and fork, two large serving spoons, perhaps one of them slotted, another large fork and a small ladle are the basic serving implements, to which you can then add a soup ladle, a flat cake server which can also be used for quiches and such, asparagus tongs, grape scissors (nobody ever uses them, but Miss Manners adores them), large fish knife and fork and so on. Why some people think they need special forks for serving cold meats Miss Manners doesn't know, but then, not everyone understands why she needs asparagus servers.

As a secret tip, Miss Manners confides that sterling silver does not wear out. Therefore, buying it secondhand, whether it is modern or antique, makes a great deal of sense. There is nothing quite so grand as setting a table with the kind of old European silver which is engraved on the back, thus giving your guests a terrible shock when, not knowing that those pieces are correctly placed with the fork prongs and spoon bowls facing the tablecloth, they conclude that you have set the table upside down.

⟶ Tea and Coffee Sets ⟵

DEAR MISS MANNERS:

Can you help us resolve a lively debate about the proper use of the waste bowl in a coffee service? At a recent elegant dinner party, one guest was certain that it should be used to hold hot water that has been used to "preheat" the cups. Another was equally certain that the dregs of one cup of coffee are poured into it before the cup is refilled. Our hostess was very uncertain, and admitted that she does not use hers for fear of doing so improperly. This seemed to us like the waste of a good bowl.

GENTLE READER:

Quick! Stop! Please! Oh, good heavens, why didn't you call for help earlier? *You are using a tea set to serve coffee.*

Actually, Miss Manners can think of no good reason why you shouldn't. She just doesn't want to spoil that lovely party by siding with one friend against another. Surely if you are all equally wrong, no one can feel hurt.

It also explains why there is a waste bowl or, as it is sometimes so elegantly called, a slops bowl. This is for the dregs of tea. A coffee set consists of three pieces: a coffeepot, a sugar bowl and a cream jug. A tea set has five pieces: a teakettle for boiling water, a teapot for the tea, a milk pitcher, a sugar bowl and the waste bowl. (Miss Manners is not counting trays, tongs, caddies, strainers and such, any more than she is counting the teaspoons, until after the guests leave.) If you can subtract, you can figure out how your hostess can have a passable coffee set, free.

— *Iced-Tea Spoons* —

DEAR MISS MANNERS:

What am I supposed to do with an iced tea spoon after stirring my iced tea? Usually, there is no saucer to put it on, and I don't want to leave a spot on the tablecloth.

My husband insists that you said to leave the spoon in the glass while drinking, but, having a history of clumsy, unintentional, self-inflicted wounds, I am truly afraid of the damage I might do. (It's scary enough having to manage sharp objects like knives and forks; please don't make me hold a stick that close to my nose and eyes!)

The same messy spoon problem arises when I'm presented with a mug of tea, except then I also have a dripping teabag to deal with. Where is that supposed to go?

GENTLE READER:

Please inform your husband that Miss Manners said no such thing. If she had to choose between drinking with a spoon in the glass and ruining the tablecloth, the tablecloth would have to go. Those are more easily repaired than noses.

Your hosts should not have forced you to make that choice. Saucers—or small silver spoon rests, which were invented at the same time that putting ice into tea was—should be provided. In their absence, and the absence of any nearby plate or coaster, you may inquire of them where they would like you to park your spoon or (ugh) wet tea bag.

Demitasse Spoons

DEAR MISS MANNERS:

Are demitasse spoons useful?

GENTLE READER:

Does a duck swim? Miss Manners is not going to consider the possibility that you are serving full cups of coffee after dinner, or that you are asking people to stir their proper thimblefuls of coffee with great big old teaspoons. She is therefore left to believe that your question is whether tiny spoons have any function other than their primary one.

Some people collect them. Miss Manners is not sure what the thrill is in that, but sees no harm in it and acknowledges that it is a cheaper hobby than collecting Impressionist paintings.

If the spoons are not silver, they may be used as egg spoons. Silver does not go well with eggs, but the tiny spoon is more appropriate for eating boiled eggs from the shell than the ubiquitous teaspoon. This means that the demitasse spoons would be working both early-morning and late-night shifts, but you could give them alternative Thursdays off. Demitasse spoons are also good for eating yogurt when you are on a diet.

Runcible Spoons

DEAR MISS MANNERS:

What on earth is a "runcible spoon"?

GENTLE READER:

A runcible spoon is the instrument used by the Owl and the Pussycat to eat mince and slices of quince when they went to sea in a beautiful pea-green boat. It is a large, slotted spoon with three thick, modified fork prongs at the bowl's end, and a cutting edge on the side. According to Miss Manners' Aunt Grace, the spoon was fashioned after Mr. Edward Lear named this object for his poem. Miss Manners believes this with all her heart, but has trouble proving it, as neither dear Mr. Lear nor Aunt Grace is with us any longer.

∽ *Grape Scissors* ∽

DEAR MISS MANNERS:

Can you use grape scissors for any function other than cutting grapes?

GENTLE READER:

Not unless you pay overtime.

∽ *An Unidentified Silver Dish* ∽

DEAR MISS MANNERS:

How can you tell whether a small silver dish is meant to be used as an ashtray or as a candy dish?

GENTLE READER:

It was meant to be used as an ashtray, back when cigarettes in silver urns were part of the formal table service, but it is understandably ashamed to admit that now, and pretends to be a candy dish.

CHINA

DEAR MISS MANNERS:

The china pattern I selected has a bewildering variety of plates, ranging in diameter from five inches to ten and a half, and of course the saleslady tells me that no well-stocked household could do with less than ten of each. Maybe someday I'll get around to all that, but would you tell me, in the meantime, what each one is for, which are more useful than others, and whether it is better to start with, say, four complete place settings or eight incomplete ones?

GENTLE READER:

It depends on whom and what you like for dinner. Assuming that you would prefer simpler meals and more friends—although Miss Manners has no grounds for making such an audacious judgment—start with these basics:

Dinner plates. Those are the largest ones, and you will need one for every person you have to dinner.

Luncheon plates. Get the eight-inch ones, so that you may use them not only as the main plate at breakfast or lunch, but also as salad plates, dessert plates, tea plates and for serving first courses such as fish or pâtés. Of course, if you use them for fish, salad, and dessert at the same meal, you will spend on soap and kitchen help the amount of money saved on buying dishes.

Bread-and-butter plates. These are five or six inches, and may also be used for serving fruit or as underliners for bowls.

Two-handled bowls with saucers. These may be used for cereal, gooey desserts and all soups, provided you promise Miss Manners that you will put aside your first earnings to buy wide, rimmed soup plates for formal dinners and small bouillon cups for lunches.

Tea or coffee cups and demitasse, each with the appropriate saucer. Teacups are slightly smaller and thinner than coffee cups, but unless you serve both coffee and tea, your guests will never be able to compare the cups and accuse you of having the wrong ones. There is no use trying to pass off your regular coffee cups as demitasse, however, no matter how large you claim your breakfast cups are.

Glass salad plates and dessert plates may be used with china dinner plates, and serving dishes can be silver, pewter, stainless steel or a plain china.

You can cut down on the amount of china you need by entertaining only at formal dinners, where soup bowls, bread-and-butter plates and coffee cups are not properly used, the respective replacements being soup plates, the tablecloth and demitasse. If that leaves you eating your own breakfast and lunch straight from the refrigerator, don't tell anyone Miss Manners recommended it.

GLASS

Always wishing everyone the best, Miss Manners is usually quite generous with your money. She feels wise and good-hearted when she urges you to have silver flatware rather than stainless steel, and linen napkins instead of paper. Even cries of economic disaster do not deter her; she merely bolsters her position by saying that silver on the table is better than money in the bank, and linen napkins last longer than paper.

When it comes to glasses, however, her conscience begins to assert itself. Miss Manners is perfectly capable of rhapsodizing sincerely, not to say poetically, about the beauties of crystal. But if you ask her point blank to justify the cost of extensive and expensive glasses, she could only mumble, "They're pretty." They also either gather dust on the shelves because nobody drinks anything except white wine and soda, or they make troublesome fragments at the bottom of the dishwasher.

So, although Miss Manners finds it reassuring to see five glasses neatly arranged above her knife at a dinner table (for sherry with the soup, white wine with the fish, red wine with the meat, champagne with the dessert, and water so she won't slide off her chair), she admits that one can live decently on only one wine glass and one water glass each. A large, stemmed glass and a slightly smaller one will fill (and be filled with) these needs. If you have a second, still smaller, wine glass, you can use the larger for red and the smaller for white. (It is as cheap to impress your guests with two wines as with one of which they will drink twice as much.) A third, smallest, wine glass used for white allows you to serve the Burgundy in the largest and claret in the middle one, a situation not likely to come up.

Sherry glasses, you may be surprised to hear, are for sherry, although Miss Manners would not refuse a late-afternoon offer of the topaz liquid if it were served in the regular wine glass, rather than the Y-shaped one. Wide-rimmed champagne glasses are for whipped desserts and frozen daiquiris, as well as one's daily ration of champagne. Tulip-shaped champagne glasses are snazzier but not as versatile. One can also have fat-bowled glasses on short stems for brandy and teensy glasses on weensy stems for liqueurs. However, sticking one's face in the former and snorting, or tossing the content of the latter down one's gullet, are bad form.

Unstemmed glasses have all sorts of names for themselves. They insist that they are highball glasses or old-fashioned glasses or iced-tea glasses or fruit juice glasses. Don't believe them. They are either big glasses or small ones. The tall ones are used for mixed drinks, iced tea, low-calorie pop, high-calorie pop, the children's milk and the children's beer. The short ones are for straight liquor and the following morning's fruit juice.

It may aid you in saving money to know that having many types of glasses for complicated drinks shows an interest in bartending that is not quite nice. Miss Manners doesn't recommend stirring your guests' drinks with your fingers, but a bar full of liquor-connected tools and devices is vulgar.

You should also know that if your glasses are reasonably thin, hardly anyone can tell the best crystal from more durable crystal, or sometimes even from plain glass. At least, they can't by candlelight. When they get to the store the next day, to replace the fragile glass of yours they broke, they will find out the difference.

LINENS

DEAR MISS MANNERS:

When I was a little girl, my great-grandmother gave me her hope chest and now that I am thirty-four and all my relatives have given up hope, I am actually getting married. My great-grandmother is long since dead, and even my mother said she never thought she'd live to see the day. But anyway, my mother once promised to fill the chest with linens when I became engaged. I plan to hold her to this, although she claims that the decision, by me and the man I have been living with for six and a half years, that we might as well get married, is not her idea of a proper engagement. While we fight over that, would you mind settling the next issue, which is bound to be: What does a proper linen trousseau consist of?

GENTLE READER:

Do you mean to say that you are going to send Miss Manners out of the room to count the sheets and towels, while such an interesting fight as you are having now is taking place? Oh, all right. She's going, she's going.

The linen trousseau is subdivided into Bed, Bath, Kitchen and Table, of which Table (surprise!) is the most interesting.

TABLE LINENS

It is well known that no bride can enter matrimony with her head held high unless she has a damask tablecloth and twelve dinner napkins, each twenty-four inches square, to match. It is well known that the bride never uses these items until her silver wedding anniversary, and that someone then promptly justifies her caution by spilling red wine all over them. Nevertheless, the cloth should be monogrammed diagonally high on one corner, and each of the napkins on the part that will show when the sides are rolled under and it is centered on the service plate.

A linen luncheon set, consisting of a tablecloth and smaller napkins (about fifteen inches square), is also needed for those luncheons that every bride rushes home from work on weekdays to give for seven of her closest friends. Linen or cotton table mats and napkins may be used for breakfast. An endless supply of teeny-weeny hors d'oeuvre napkins are necessary, as guests always put them in their pockets.

What about the wipe-off mats, brightly colored cloths and napkins that don't show stains, imaginatively used designer sheets for the table and bridge-size cloths that the bride will actually use? The bride buys them herself, probably on sale; those are not part of the trousseau.

BED LINENS

Six sheets for every bed and three pillowcases for every head (meaning six for a double bed) are the minimum and naturally they should be monogrammed. Hemstitching, which rips off like perforated toilet paper, is nice too. Miss Manners allows only white sheets, and prefers that the monograms be in white as well.

Naturally, each bed needs a silk or muslin blanket cover, and a bedspread. Miss Manners likes blanket covers to be monogrammed, but never bedspreads. Don't ask her why.

Again, all that permanent press, jungle-patterned mix-and-match junk you use for sleeping in, and the fitted quilted things you use to avoid making the bed, are not properly part of the trousseau.

BATH LINENS

The most important items here are the linen face towels and linen hand towels, none of which are ever used, even by the guests. You are also allowed to have terry cloth bath towels and washcloths, which are used, although what a respectable person does with those small terry-cloth towels always sold to match, Miss Manners cannot imagine. Monogramming terry cloth strikes her as silly, unless you are a hotel with untrustworthy guests.

KITCHEN LINENS

Linen towels are needed to keep up the pretense that the bride will never put her fine china and crystal into the dishwasher. They have no other use. Rough towels and pot holders are quite useful, however, which is why they do not belong in a proper trousseau.

～ *Marking the Linens* ～

DEAR MISS MANNERS:

What monogram does an engaged girl use on her trousseau sheets and towels—the initials of her maiden name or her married name?

Gentle Reader:

The old-fashioned custom was to use the initials of her maiden name, and the modern bride will find that there is a lot of sense in this rule, as the trousseau will then see her through any number of marriages. Marriages don't tend to last as long as they used to, but, then, heaven knows that sheets don't either.

The Well-Appointed House

To keep a house in which every object, down to the smallest bibelot, is in perfect taste, is in shocking taste. No house can be truly tasteful unless it contains at least half a dozen atrocities of varying sizes and uses. This must not include the residents, however.

Such an apparent attack of madness on the part of Miss Good Taste herself is not to be confused with the unfortunate notion that a house should have the look of being "lived in," or, as Miss Manners terms it, "slovenly." If disorders were indeed sweet, we could solve the teenage summer loitering problem by leasing adolescents out as decorating consultants.

It is rather in the selection of furnishing that care must be exercised to include enough dreadful items to avoid the appearance of being mercenary, heartless and socially aggressive. The discriminating person always has on hand a few things that could not possibly have been chosen for their aesthetic value, thus emerging as a person of tradition and sentiment.

For those who find it difficult to commit taste errors, here is a small list of horrible things from which to choose. If one does not come by them naturally, it may be possible to purchase them at yard sales.

CHILD-MADE OBJECTS

No household, even one that is blessed with no children, should fail to have at least one item whose provenance is clearly Arts and Crafts Hour at a school or camp. Ceramic ashtrays, a favorite present from children who have never noticed that nobody ever smokes in the house, are good, as are yarn pot holders, because they are relatively permanent. Things made out of cardboard, straws and pipe cleaners tend to disintegrate, although not so quickly as one would like. Artwork must be rotated on the standard exhibit space (the refrigerator door), because it is found in such prodigious quantities.

HIDEOUS PRESENTS DONATED BY ADULTS

These should be displayed and cherished in proportion to the sacredness of the bond between giver and receiver, divided by the number of miles they live apart. Thus, wedding presents from friends may be quietly returned, but a spouse's poor choice should be tolerated unless you are willing to exchange the giver at the same time.

Inviolate are presents from one's servants. We are not all as fortunate as the lady whose faithful butler returned from a trip to his ancestral land of Egypt with an electrically lighted sphinx for his employer's living room, but we should all be as wise as that lady, who considered what her friends would think if she kept it, considered what the butler would think if she expelled it, and gave it a place of honor. One can always make new friends, but a good butler is not easy to find.

SOUVENIRS

This category includes sports trophies, wedding albums, framed awards, family photographs (as long as they do not include famous people) and items pertaining to happy vacations (as long as they are not of the sort that could only have been stolen from public accommodations). No member of the family should be allowed to contribute items from more than one of these categories to the general decor, and they must all be kept in places that indicate the owner's embarrassment for having them at all. The powder room walls are an excellent place for awards, the photographs go in the master bedroom and the trophies are used as doorstops in the guest room.

What Miss Manners does not want to see are awards hung in the library, children's artwork professionally framed and put in the drawing room, wedding albums on coffee tables, photographs of any member of the family shaking hands with the President hung anywhere at all, or any restaurant or hotel property, including matchbooks. The ostentatious display of bad taste is in extremely poor taste.

6. *Work*

Interviews, Recommendations and Raises

DEAR MISS MANNERS:

It's not as easy as you imagine to be polite while you have to scrounge for a living. You give me a surefire way of getting rich quick, and I promise to behave perfectly from that moment on.

GENTLE READER:

Very well. Think of a business that particularly caters to some legitimate need of single people. There must be nothing about it that suggests recreation—not even music playing in the background. The atmosphere should be no-nonsense, utilitarian and eminently respectable. Then devise some way of keeping all of your customers waiting. Service should be delayed just long enough to get people grumbling to one another, but not long enough to make them walk away in disgust. You should aim at having a good-sized group of unattached people standing together with a common practical purpose and nothing to do but to talk to one another while they wait. Miss Manners realizes that she has just described a laundromat, but perhaps you can think of something else.

~ *The Job Interview* ~

HAVING DEVOTED her life to extolling the virtues of modesty and quiet charm, Miss Manners feels bound to admit that these are not wildly successful qualities to exhibit in job interviews. Few employers are seeking models of self-effacing gentility to reward with responsibility and money.

In Miss Manners' day, there was no conflict between being ladylike or gentlemanlike and seeming competent and efficient, because ladies and gentlemen did not seek jobs. The respectable solution, for aristocrats short on cash, was marrying for money. Now honest labor is appallingly chic, and everyone needs a set of business manners, as well as social ones.

The best job applicant is one who is able to sing his or her own praises without embarrassment, confident enough to steer an interview away from inappropriate areas, and persistent. When you would demur, socially, with "Oh, it was nothing, really," you would, in business, say, "I graduated with honors, had the best sales record in my last job, and left because I felt the job wasn't really using my abilities." When you would tell a prospective host, "I would be simply delighted to be there," you tell a prospective employer, "I think I could contribute to your company in ways you would find beneficial." To a dinner partner, you might say, "Why, yes, my husband is the one over there with the blond mustache, and we have four beautiful children from three marriages"; to a personnel person, you say, "I don't think my personal life will have any bearing on my work." Crispness replaces flirtatiousness; showing that you know the other person's business is not nosy but intelligent; and stating one's capabilities is the mark of the able worker, not of the bragging bore.

There is one social skill that can serve as your strongest asset in a job interview. In private life, it makes people fall in love with you and seek you for purposes ranging from honored dinner guests to spouse; and in business, it helps more than any other single qualification, with the possible exception of being the owner's eldest child. That is enthusiasm. A look of vitality and happiness, an interest in the world and an eagerness to participate in life comprise what is called charm in the social milieu; but in the working world it is called competence. One may practice such a look. It is chiefly done with the eyes. If they can be made to shine radiantly, the rest of the face will automatically compose itself into the properly attractive expression. Practice staring into the mirror as if you have fallen madly in love. Most people have little difficulty with this when they have thought it over. Such a look, accompanied by short, to-the-point remarks about one's native abilities, one's invaluable experience—not only in previous jobs, but in volunteer work, education and hobbies—and one's deep interest in the work being done by the company to which one is applying, convinces an employer that what you can do for him is more important than what he can do for you.

It should make the face look so intelligent that it can see the wearer with dignity through such shabby interviewing tricks as being deliberately kept waiting while the employer takes a personal telephone call, or being badgered to take a drink when one knows one shouldn't. It should make refusals to disclose one's present salary or discuss how long one might stay on the job seem businesslike rather than weasly. It is also useful because you needn't change it when going from the office out to dinner.

∼ Dress and Demeanor for Interviews ∼

DEAR MISS MANNERS:

I'm preparing for a rather significant job interview with a company that has an extremely casual corporate environment. In my wardrobe, I own plenty of traditional corporate clothing (traditional suits in traditional colors, ties, braces, etc.). I also own plenty of less traditional snappy professional attire. The latter, I have never worn to a job interview before. I don't want to be seen as "stuffy" or archaic, yet I don't want my attire to convey the message that I think I already have the job. Which should I wear?

GENTLE READER:

The stuffy clothes. It may be the last chance you have to wear them. As soon as you are hired, those casual people will, just as you predict, jeer at you until you adopt their style. All the same, Miss Manners assures you that they, like everyone else, interpret clothing for symbolism. That is why the standard wisdom is to dress as if you already had the job.

However, this is a corporate job, and these people want more from you than simply fitting in with the crowd. The traditional clothing you describe symbolizes competence and dedication—no matter how they choose to dress themselves, secure in the belief that they are obviously competent and dedicated.

The same is true of your manners. You can always loosen up and become friendly as you work there. Employers don't want the job of tightening you up.

∼ Reserved Recommendations ∼

DEAR MISS MANNERS:

A friend wants a job at my company and asked if I'd give her an "in." While she's a great personal friend, I don't think she's qualified for the position, and she has a spotty employment history. I don't want to hurt her feelings. Do I turn her off the company or let her go through the interview process and let the company decide? If my employer asks for my opinion, I can't in good conscience give a positive one. If I brush my friend off with a vague excuse, I know she'll dig and dig.

GENTLE READER:

You certainly don't want to offer a frank excuse, which would be, "Don't even try, they only want top-notch people like me."

Miss Manners is aware that people often dig when they encounter vague excuses, but they have to stop digging when they hit rock. To your friend, you say, "I can introduce you if you want, but frankly, I think you'd be making a big mistake. I know you, and I know them, and even though it works for me, I know it's wrong for you, and they're not going to appreciate what you have to offer." To your employer, you say, "I can only tell you she's a great friend."

DEAR MISS MANNERS:

I am in the embarrassing position of having been asked to write a letter of recommendation for someone I can't honestly recommend. I don't want to be cruel and prevent his getting another job—what am I saying? I desperately want him to get another job. That would save me the trouble of firing him. But I don't know if it's right to stick the next person by misrepresenting his qualifications.

GENTLE READER:

Ah, the great moral conflict in life—honesty or kindness? Miss Manners tends to choose kindness, feeling that there is quite enough honesty in the world, but this is an occasion for compromise. Sometimes one can avoid writing a letter of reference, saying, "Perhaps you could find someone who would be able to write you a stronger letter than I could," or "I don't feel I know enough about your qualifications." Those take care of the troublesome student, or an acquaintance's nephew.

When failure to write any letter would be a blot on the person's career, something must be produced. The object is to suggest severe problems without zapping the person. The tone to take is: "He probably has talents that would come to light in a situation where skills such as alphabetizing correctly aren't needed."

~ *Internships* ~

DEAR MISS MANNERS:

I am interning this summer in a New York agency where, for lack of anything better to do, I read the paper and exchange emails with equally-bored interns. During my first weeks, I started every morning by finding my bosses, apprising them of the work I'd done, and asking if they had anything else I should attend to. These appearances were met with blank stares, and then apologies: "Oh, I'm sorry, there's nothing . . . we really can't think of anything for you to do right now."

Since these visits seemed more disruptive than helpful—my bosses, after all, have "work" to do—I no longer make special trips. Other than greeting them when they enter my office, or waving when I pass theirs, we don't have much contact. We go days without seeing each other, especially since I get to work before they do.

I've offered assistance to other interns, to their bosses, to our secretary; I feel rather fraudulent sitting here doing nothing on company time. Should I simply enjoy my freedom, having made it clear to all that I'm available by phone or email whenever they need me? It's silly to complain about being paid to do nothing.

There was a rigorous application process for this position and my bosses know both my qualifications and exactly how much they cost per diem. On the other hand, my bosses shouldn't have to track me down. Furthermore, the internship was taken to give me experience in the field, which I am not getting. I'd like to be useful, but I certainly don't want to be annoying. Has my boredom driven me to over-think this? It's hardly the responsibility of my bosses to keep me busy—or is it?

GENTLE READER:

Considering the number of full-time employees who spend their office hours exchanging personal emails and playing computer games, Miss Manners is amazed that your agency was not grateful to grab you to do the actual work. Or perhaps they are preparing you for that "work" they really do.

As a matter of conscience, she believes you are in the clear. You have repeatedly made yourself available to earn your salary, and it is the agency that has let you down by lack of planning.

But you wanted to spend the summer advancing your career. You can do this by noticing what humble tasks need to be done around the office—not poaching others' jobs but devising your own—and doing them without asking. Miss Manners would not recommend this to a permanent employee, who would then get a reputation for "liking" to do humble jobs. But this will keep you alert to how the office functions, and make everyone miss you when you leave. Just be sure to bargain for a better-defined job if you decide to come back.

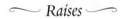 *Raises*

DEAR MISS MANNERS:

An accountant at my company accidentally forwarded an email that listed salaries of several of my peers. Even though I share the same title, responsibilities, and years experience as these peers, they are being compensated substantially more than I am. I'd like to bring this up with my manager but how should I handle it?

GENTLE READER:

It depends on what you want to bring up. Length of service, devotion to the company and faithfulness in performing one's duty are valid reasons for having one's salary gradually increased, but these dogged virtues rarely inspire employers to provide rewards. If you add to them proof of imagination and energy in the performance of your tasks, you are more apt to suggest that you would also have the imagination and energy to place yourself better if you were not satisfied. In the working world, as in teenaged romance, the person treated best is the one who might be lost, not the one whose feelings would be most hurt.

Now, if you tell your manager what you told Miss Manners, the topics you will bring up are: executive confidentiality, what's wrong with the accounting department, the ethics of reading mistakenly forwarded email and what's wrong with the general state of business ethics. Just about the only topic you will not bring up by this method is adjusting your salary.

Fortunately, you can benefit from the information without supplying material for such a filibuster. Miss Manners suggests that you simply ask for a raise, naming a figure that would bring your compensation in line with that of your peers and stating that this is commensurate with your title, responsibilities and years of experience. Should your manager claim that this leap would be out of line, you should say firmly, "No, I believe it is not only fair, but the going rate around here."

You must promise Miss Manners not to reveal how you know this, no matter how challenged or probed. Besides bringing on the filibuster and getting the accountant into trouble, this would ruin the impression that you have great inside sources and an eerie command of everything going on in the company.

～ Respect ～

It used to be the custom for ladies to gather in a corner of the drawing room to speak, in hushed tones, of the Servant Problem. Now that they can shout it from house to house without any danger of being overheard by servants, the fun is gone.

What pleasure there used to be in comparing the gaucheries and debaucheries of the lower orders, as observed at close range by those who could only stand and be waited upon. It was a fine time, too, for ladies of Miss Manners' profession, who wrote exquisite essays on the three daily costume changes required of the parlor maid, and sly, hypocritical reassurances to the hostess who attempted to feed eight people with only a cook and a waitress to help.

It wasn't that the Servant Problem went away, just that the servants did. The reason for this was that it had never really been a Servant Problem so much as an Employer Problem. Hushed tones or no, the servants found out from the employers' attitude, to say nothing of their wages, hours and responsibilities, that they could serve their own best interests elsewhere. One can say that the servants served the employers right. Human dignity is better served when each individual is able to be self-sufficient, which includes both earning one's bread and making the sandwich.

However, it is not practical for everyone to do each and every task of daily life. The hope remains that someone else will perform the services you cannot personally manage—for love or money. Fewer people are willing to do it for love these days. They found that they were running into the same problems as the servants: lack of appreciation, ready money, time off and job security.

Miss Manners would like to resolve this unfortunate situation, because she has always wanted to write about the correct attire for footmen. Her revolutionary suggestion is that service jobs be treated as being as important as we say they are when people perform them for themselves. A woman who keeps her own house clean is considered to be a model for others. A person who cooks for his or her friends is thought of as warm and creative. A father who spends time caring for his children is deemed a paragon. Why, then, are people who clean, cook or care for children professionally at the bottom of the vocational ladder?

Let Miss Manners review briefly for prospective employers of servants what a decent job is. It is, at most, a five-day, forty-hour week, with overtime pay for time over. It has vacations, sick leave and a pay scale providing increases for merit, experience and cost of living. One should also be able to earn respect, which means using one's own judgment about managing the assigned tasks, and not being accused of stealing every time something has been misplaced.

These principles apply to hiring a cleaning woman or a nanny for part-time every other week, as well as to running a household full of servants. It is the only way to solve the Employer Problem; and the only way Miss Manners will ever be able to plunge into that exciting argument about whether the butler should stand behind the host or the hostess at dinner.

~ Self-Respect ~

The idea has gotten around that there need be no hierarchy in the job structure. And since there obviously is—one need only check one's paycheck—people in the service jobs seek compensation by behaving with inefficiency and surliness to those whom they are supposed to serve. The worst offenders are not those who are stuck in such jobs, but the people—such as college students with temporary jobs—whose upward route seems clearly marked. The widespread use of first names, sports clothing, audio recreation and other attributes of "informality" in the work world has assisted in the illusion that no one really needs to perform a service for anyone else. The result is that badly paying jobs are badly done.

Miss Manners has not failed to catch the irony here. She is not unsympathetic with the ambitions of workers to be paid their worth; only with the determination to scale down the performance to worthlessness. People in service jobs—waiters, clerks, parking lot attendants, taxi drivers, whatever—do not prove, by being inefficient and rude, that they are meant for better things. They merely show that they can't properly handle the jobs they have, many of which can be done with cleverness and skill.

Workplace Etiquette

ARE FEMALE workers, especially executives, not behaving in a sufficiently ladylike manner on the job?

Posing such a question is like tossing a boomerang into the workplace. Even Miss Manners would be tempted to throw something back if she weren't so unbearably ladylike. Obviously, this is that nasty double standard which we keep thinking we have banished, only to see it repeatedly hauled out of retirement. When a man asserts himself, it is called confidence; if a woman does, it is called arrogance. If a man is considered forceful and commanding, a woman who uses the same tactics is called emotional and bitchy. So women are supposed to handicap themselves by holding back, because they'll be called names if they behave the same way men are admired for doing.

And what does being ladylike have to do with the tough world of work anyway? Are men expected to be gentlemanly?

Yet this charge is made, and not only by horrid old bigots for whom a fitting retirement present would be a big fat lawsuit. Not infrequently it comes from younger women, who managed to grow up never quite believing there was ever a real problem about working equality for women. (Their retroactive advice to senior feminists: "Well, then, why didn't you just say you wouldn't stand for it?") It has even been known to come from some of those senior feminists themselves who are shocked and not a little ashamed to think this of their female bosses.

Without withdrawing the countercharge, Miss Manners sees that there is a problem here. More than that—and more than the various people snapping at one another over this—she understands how it came about. When society was organized under the premise that women should confine themselves to the domestic and social spheres, they were naturally expected to have the appropriate ladylike manners. As this included offering hospitality and refraining from showing off, they were handicapped when they brought those manners to work, and because they found themselves expected to be quiet and fetch the coffee. Workplace manners are different, which is why women fought to change not only the situation but their own inhibitions. They adopted workplace manners, as exhibited by the men.

So far so good. Miss Manners used to wear herself out in those days, explaining that social manners were out of place at work. For example, it is vulgar to discuss money socially and impossible to do business without doing so. Miss Manners may be the only person who remembers and observes the social rule now, but it long operated to make women reluctant to ask for raises.

Women have learned since then. But here is what a lot of women missed: The social rules applied to gentlemen too, but there were also separate business manners for gentlemen, and a huge distinction was made professionally between gentlemen and cutthroats.

Here is what a lot of women didn't miss: Gentlemanliness in the working world became rarer and rarer as it came to be considered a sign of weakness. So many women patterned themselves on the cruder but more successful businessmen. Because they were fewer, they were more conspicuous.

Now here's what a lot of men continue to miss: As society tires of crude business techniques, good business manners become more expedient. When most people adapt the attack mode, its advantage is cancelled, while polite professionalism is as treasured as it is rare.

Gender should not be a factor in the workplace, and the manners of ladies and gentlemen in business should be as indistinguishable as are the lack of manners in both.

⟶ Harassment ⟵

DEAR MISS MANNERS:

I am one of three on-site female employees in an almost exclusively male company of about 28 employees. While I like many of my colleagues, I am increasingly reluctant to come to work because of the non-stop sexual innuendo, joking and outright comments that surround me all day long.

I am an attractive, young woman and it seems that the men I work with, including my two bosses, cannot resist turning any statement I say into some sort of sexual play on words. One of my bosses even reads to me the subject lines of the porn emails he receives. The other one openly assesses my figure every time he speaks to me. I am uncomfortable at work and have begun keeping my office door shut to ward off a co-worker who likes to "pretend" to pick the lint off my sweater.

I understand that what happens is up to me in that I have the choice to either find another job or make a formal complaint, neither of which I am prepared to do right now. And I feel partly responsible for not drawing the line when I was first employed here, four months ago, but I was worried about fitting in and keeping my job. Now I fear I have allowed my co-workers to assume I am receptive or at least amenable to all this "wink-wink, nudge-nudge" talk that goes on, when in fact it makes me very uncomfortable and is often personally offensive to me.

I am hopeful you can provide me with some polite but firm responses—things to say to help me establish boundaries and ward off these conversations before they start. And to hold me until I can make a decision about remaining here. It is very dispiriting to work with people who seem to have a juvenile fixation on sex and it is insulting to me that they don't consider me enough of a lady to spare the talk in my presence.

GENTLE READER:
First, Miss Manners must warn you that etiquette does not have a good record in discouraging this sort of thing. That is why the law had to step in, once society finally acknowledged the seriousness of the problem. Etiquette depends on the reluctance of most people to persist in annoying and angering others. So when we find polite ways to draw their behavior to their attention, they usually desist. However, it is the object of lewd behavior to annoy and anger those to whom it is directed. Your question is almost like asking for a polite way to let a flasher know that his trousers are open.

Miss Manners agrees that resorting to the law should be a last resort, but you should give everyone involved a gentle reminder that it is available to you. In as cool and unruffled a tone as possible—because the fun is in getting you hot and bothered— you should say that you suppose they have been used to a locker-room atmosphere, but they should know that it makes an offensive working environment for female employees. The wording should be vaguely legalistic, but not contain an accusation or a threat. And you should keep saying it up the chain of command until you get to someone who—regardless of his own feelings or behavior—has the sense to get frightened.

Affairs

DEAR MISS MANNERS:
I have been dating a woman in my office for several months. We've been quiet about it, but want to let more people in on our relationship. Our company has no policy against inter-office romance—except between bosses and their direct reports, which doesn't include us. Should we tell our coworkers and our bosses? How should we behave? Can we, for example, hold hands in the company cafeteria or kiss each other as we leave the building?

GENTLE READER:

What are the emotions you are hoping to arouse?

No, no, not in yourselves. Miss Manners doesn't want to know about those, and neither do your colleagues. It is their emotions she is inquiring about. Do you imagine that when they see you kiss and hold hands, they will think "Awww," as their hearts melt at the sight of true love?

Miss Manners doubts it. One of the sweet delusions of love is that it has the same softening effect on spectators as on participants. She is sorry to have to report that what love at work really inspires in colleagues are thoughts about favoritism and slacking off the job. Never mind whether or not these can be justified—the burden of proof will be on the lovers. The best defense is their retroactive surprise when you announce your engagement or, Miss Manners knows she needs to add, when the staff list shows that you have the same address. If they didn't notice you were courting, they can hardly claim that it gave either of you an unfair advantage.

~ *Proper Dress* ~

DEAR MISS MANNERS:

A colleague in my office has a fondness for hot pants, tight tops with plunging necklines, and bracelets that rattle together. While her outfits might be suitable for a tailgate party at the baseball game, I find them incredibly inappropriate for work. Whenever I invite clients to the office for meetings, I dread bumping into her in the hall. I don't want to hurt her feelings, but what's a good way of getting her to put on some more clothes?

GENTLE READER:

Why, the hussy! Running around like that while the rest of the business world is so meticulously dressed.

Miss Manners thought she would supply this reaction, because she is afraid that visiting clients will disappoint you by failing to do so. Only Miss Manners seems to have the stamina left to be shocked.

There are other reasons for dressing professionally than that it might shock clients. Businesses that spend fortunes on maintaining their professional images should discourage their employees from sabotaging it by looking as if they are goofing off or trolling for romance. That is not easy to mandate, however. Miss Manners suggests that you be grateful, as you go about your business, that it is not your responsibility to critique your colleagues.

⌒ Security ⌒

DEAR MISS MANNERS:

Like many office buildings, the one in which I work uses an access-card entry system. I keep my card in my wallet. Often, instead of taking out the wallet to run it by the sensor, I merely swivel my hip slightly to allow the card to be "read."

Is this hip move considered rude if (a) no one is in the vicinity? (b) if I believe no one is seeing this? (c) I'm only with close colleagues?

GENTLE READER:

Rude? Actually, it sounds exciting. Miss Manners lives in a city with hardly a building standing that doesn't require an access pass or at least a show of identification, and that has no folk dance. Would you care to come to Washington, D.C., and teach it to us?

⌒ Boundaries ⌒

DEAR MISS MANNERS:

I now work in a loft warehouse where I sit in a large open area with no private offices. I enjoy listening to music while I work and like to customize my computer to beep when I get new email, etc. But I also want to be respectful of my neighbors' space (especially since we all have so little of it). How do I set coworker-friendly boundaries?

GENTLE READER:

Lucky you, you have just joined the etiquette business. The drawback is that you don't get to make up the rules alone. You may be sure that nobody regrets this more than Miss Manners.

Any community that values peace sets rules restraining behavior that is legally permissible but likely to drive others crazy. In small groups, such as an office or a household, these rules can be whatever everyone agrees upon. So if all of your colleagues enjoy your music and look forward to your customized beeps punctuating their day, there should be no problem.

But merely asking "Do you mind?" is not enough to get a frank consensus. Someone who says no now, just to be agreeable, may strangle you when feeling less agreeable. Call an office meeting, solicit complaints—and politely issue yours—and obtain consent for office rules. At the very least, this will provide you with witnesses at the attempted murder trial to support your claim that the defendant failed to object to your beeper noise before it drove him over the brink.

DEAR MISS MANNERS:

I share a cubicle with a coworker that happens to be allergic to peanuts. I normally bring my lunch into work and eat at my desk. When I pack my lunch, I tend to forget about his allergy. I often pack peanut butter sandwiches and crackerjacks. I suppose I didn't quite understand his sensitivity to peanuts because he recently snapped at me for eating them at my desk and left to go take allergy medicine. My question is, should I be the one inconvenienced and have to find a new place to eat lunch?

GENTLE READER:

Yes. Miss Manners assures you that this is considerably less of an inconvenience to you than having to haul him off to the hospital when he has an allergic reaction.

~ Stealing Ideas ~

DEAR MISS MANNERS:

A colleague at my company has the annoying habit of appropriating others' ideas and presenting them to the boss as though they were his own. For instance, at lunch with a group of coworkers I recently mentioned that I thought a slogan on a direct mail campaign we were about to send out could be offensive to older people. My colleague took my idea for the rewording and presented it to our boss. The campaign wording was changed and our boss thanked my colleague for his clever catch at a public meeting the next day. When I confronted my annoying colleague about it, he said he did tell the boss that it was my idea too.

How can I tell our boss that the idea was mine without looking petty? And how can I get my colleague to stop stealing my ideas?

GENTLE READER:

Have lunch with your mother. Miss Manners doesn't care for what your colleague did, but he couldn't have done it without your help.

You could tell the boss how glad you are that he changed the wording because you had been worried about it enough to seek the advice of Mr. Snitch, who agreed with your suggestion. But Miss Manners advises letting it go and learning from the experience not to air your ideas before you submit them.

∽ *Planting Ideas* ∽

DEAR MISS MANNERS:

I'm a seasoned businessperson with many years' experience managing teams. A few years back, I made a career change and in my current job, I report to an individual who is a good 20 years younger than me. She does a fine job in many respects, works hard, and is intelligent, but I see her make obvious management mistakes. I don't want to appear disrespectful or create an awkward situation, but I'd like to offer her advice every now and then. Is there a tactful way to make suggestions, or should I keep my trap shut?

GENTLE READER:

There is no tactful way to suggest that you would be better at her job than she, however clearly you may have noticed this. Miss Manners therefore trusts that you are not inquiring how to do that, but how to avoid seeming to do so.

The intelligent boss appreciates good ideas, but nevertheless has to be careful not to undermine her authority by taking orders from subordinates. That is why the intelligent subordinate uses the weasly language of suggestion (such as "I wonder if it would be helpful to try . . ." and "Have you considered . . .") rather than the more satisfying directness of command (such as "Here's what you should do" and "The way I always handled this was . . .").

∽ *Pleasantries* ∽

DEAR MISS MANNERS:

Please tell me how to respond to people at work who ask me how my weekend was and then walk away. I find this worse than saying nothing.

GENTLE READER:

We seem to have a geographical problem here. Or are you asking what to shout at their backs as they retreat?

Even then, Miss Manners would have trouble understanding the problem. A colleague's "How was your weekend?" is a mere pleasantry, not an invitation to explain that you did the crossword puzzle in ink, washed the dog, googled an old flame, rented some movies and ate too much. So unless you fell off your balcony, in which case you probably would not be at work on Monday, the answer is "Great. Yours?" This should not take long enough to allow your retreating questioner to get far.

∽ Lunches ∽

DEAR MISS MANNERS:

Is it proper for a married woman to have lunch with one of her male co-workers?

GENTLE READER:

Yes, provided that he is not her husband. A woman who meets her husband for lunch in a restaurant is only inviting scandal. Everyone will assume they have met downtown for the purpose of visiting a lawyer.

DEAR MISS MANNERS:

As a businessman, how do I allow a businesswoman to pay for my lunch?

GENTLE READER:

With credit card or cash, as she prefers.

DEAR MISS MANNERS:

I am a woman and my assistant is a man. I enjoy taking him out to lunch sometimes to show my appreciation for him, and he seems to enjoy it, too. Sometimes the waitress makes a rude comment to him such as, "YOU should be buying HER lunch!" I know that it must embarrass him, and I always feel bad when it happens. I am married and he is gay, but people have told me that we look like a couple. Is there something tactful that I could say to save his embarrassment?

GENTLE READER:

The best way would be to select a restaurant where the staff does not presume to size up the relationships of the customers and offer them advice. As Miss Manners trusts you realize, you are not going to lessen the gentleman's embarrassment by saying, "Oh, we're not really a couple, he just works for me."

It is the waitress who needs to be embarrassed into realizing that she has made a mistake. Miss Manners forbids you to do this rudely, but you could say pointedly to him, "I'm sorry to have exposed you to this," and to her, "Please just give me the bill."

⌒ *Presents and Bonuses* ⌒

DEAR MISS MANNERS:

How is one supposed to respond when the company Christmas gift to its employees is a donation to a charity in "our" name?

This seems like a cheap shot to make the company look conscientious and generous in "our" name. Plus I was angry that they would donate to a charity of their choice in my name. How can I state my distaste for this act without losing my job?

GENTLE READER:

Miss Manners is afraid that there is no point in stating your distaste for this distasteful maneuver. Charities don't give refunds. What you want to do is to prevent its becoming a company tradition.

You and your co-workers should write a letter of thanks (oh, go ahead, it won't kill you) stating that you are glad the company recognizes its employees' interest in philanthropy, and—for that very reason—asking to be in on any meetings choosing beneficiaries. Or you could suggest a matching donation program, by which the company adds to any Christmas donations the employees choose to make.

Miss Manners warns you to be prepared to be told that this would make the process too cumbersome. And the answer you should prepare is: "In that case, we would prefer to go back to the traditional system, by which we each take our Christmas bonus from the company and decide how best to use it."

DEAR MISS MANNERS:

My boss' birthday is coming up, and for the life of me, I can't decide whether giving her a gift is appropriate or not. She always gives managers personal gifts for the holidays and birthdays. If I do buy a gift, how big should it be?

GENTLE READER:

The relationship between employee and boss is not an inherently social one, and it is certainly not one between equals. So if she wants to confer benefits on the employees in the form of presents—although Miss Manners has always thought that boss appreciation is better expressed with commendation and raises—you needn't match them. It would be kind to wish her happiness on holidays, and you could even make a token present, such as flowers or candy. Anything more would only throw out an unattractive challenge to your colleagues to compete with you for your boss's gratitude.

DEAR MISS MANNERS:

I am employed by a small firm that provides professional services. Consistent with the norm for my profession, a portion of my compensation arrives in the form of occasional bonuses, the existence, timing, and amount of which rest in the sole discretion of the firm's partners.

All of my colleagues at the firm understand that their base salaries are comparatively low to reflect the fact that they will participate, through bonuses, in the expected financial success of the firm.

I have just been chided by one of the firm's partners for my lapse in failing to thank him for a mid-year bonus. I certainly felt silent gratitude, but had been taught that an employee should not insult the dignity of service by thanking his employer for each compensation of office. To my understanding, this includes bonuses, which are fundamentally compensation, albeit contingent and arbitrary. Of course, one still must thank one's employer for courtesies beyond compensation, such as granting a vacation request for a particular date, or permitting one to leave early for errands.

I offered this rationale to my miffed employer. He warned me that I had relied upon "bad advice" in this regard, and if such a rule ever existed it is antiquated and no longer has any basis. Have I erred? I cannot bear to think so.

GENTLE READER:

Miss Manners cannot bear the notion that the grace notes of politeness should be ripped from the ordinary transactions of life that can be reasonably expected. By that reasoning, no one should ever praise you for a job well done, because that is what you are being paid to do. Absolutely, you should thank them when they grant the requests you list. What does it cost you?

Business Entertaining: Neither Businesslike nor Entertaining

BUSINESS ENTERTAINING is rather a curious term, Miss Manners has always thought. What is amusing, pray, about having to work overtime and to pretend that it is just the same as having a real social life with real friends?

Nor is she convinced that it makes the business world go around any faster. Miss Manners spent years of her life attending diplomatic parties, for reasons she has forgotten, and the only useful result she could see was to maintain modest citizens, such as Miss Manners herself and members of the international diplomatic community, in a style of nineteenth-century lavishness complete with eighteenth-century furniture, none of which even the richest can now afford.

That is a worthy cause, of course. If it were not for expense accounts of one kind or another, we would all have to live within our means and what would become of the champagne industry? But the common justifications—that business entertaining generates goodwill, makes informal exchanges possible and is necessary to keep up with one's rivals—merely mean that one must do it because it is done. It seems to Miss Manners that any sensible business can be conducted directly, that goodwill does not prevent bad business, and people can as easily blunder as ingratiate themselves in pseudosocial circumstances. It is Miss Manners' belief that most people make their professional decisions on the basis of their best judgment, unclouded by an ecstasy of gratitude brought on by the offer of a free drink. She also feels that disguising the business relationship as friendship produces more dangers than rewards. A person who behaves disgracefully at a party ought to lose his friends, perhaps, but not his livelihood.

Having said that, Miss Manners will now turn her attention conscientiously to the business of business entertainment. Lunch in a restaurant is by far the best way to do this, as many people resent carrying business over into hours usually devoted to families, friends or sitting in a hot bath with a good book. There is no excuse for being late to a business luncheon, short of having been run over on the way there. Everyone is "busy" and "rushed" in the middle of the day. The person who proposed the luncheon insists upon picking up the check; gender is not a factor, and any suggestion that it is should be cheerfully ignored.

For business dinners—unless they are held among people who are going back to work afterward, in which case they are treated as lunches—it is customary to invite the spouses or their equivalents as an acknowledgment that the event will be occupying private time. If these people have any sense, they won't go anyway. For that matter, the employees should be able to regard these activities as optional overtime.

Large-scale business luncheon or dinner parties will succeed in the proportion that they imitate real social events. Correct invitations, a prominent guest of honor or important occasion as an excuse, good food and drink and a decent amount of general conversation help to lull people into thinking that they are there because they want to be, not because they have to be for the sake of their careers.

The business cocktail party is a bastardization of an already unnatural form (or rather, natural, if one is to stay with the metaphor). People are at their most greedy and ungrateful when appraising cocktail parties, even when the hosts are friends. So the best chance for a business to impress them is to entertain on a scale not usually available to the guests—the food, the drink, the place where it is held. After all, this is, as Miss Manners said, the real attraction of organization-sponsored entertainment.

And the ideal office Christmas party starts before lunch, with an invitation issued by the boss. The exact wording of this invitation should be: "Why don't you take the rest of the day off?" It does not require engaging a caterer, and it does not leave the office littered with plastic cups and personnel problems. It costs nothing and delights everyone. Nevertheless, many people persist in the notion that office parties spread goodwill among co-workers.

Annual experiences to the contrary never seem to dislodge this often fatal error. The fraudulent attempt to pass off people of different ranks and degrees of power as a bunch of jolly equals can only lead to trouble. Take, for instance, the matter of "There's something I've always wanted to tell you." Such things, whether they involve how you feel about the shortcomings of a superior or how you feel about the personal attractions of an inferior, are always better left unsaid. That is why you didn't say them all year, isn't it? Remember?

Anyone who attempts to have fun at any of these events in the usual social way—overeating, overdrinking, heavy flirting—would be jeopardizing his or her career. So enjoy these occasions, but just don't have a good time. That is what friends are for.

The Friday Bash

DEAR MISS MANNERS:

Every Friday, my company has an all-staff beer bash. I don't drink and am uncomfortable at these events. But when I skip them, I get a lot of jibes about being "stuck up" and "not a team player." Not exactly the image I want to project. What's a polite "team player" way of getting out of these boozefests?

GENTLE READER:

With the demise of the social cocktail party, a valuable social skill has been lost. Back when sophisticated entertainment consisted of gathering a random assortment of people, packing them densely into an overheated space and depriving them of chairs and satisfying nourishment, people knew how to fulfill the obligation to attend a party without actually having to endure it.

The ploy of arriving late and/or leaving early is a simple one, and the tact is all in how you do it. The greatest practitioner Miss Manners ever knew was an ambassador whose technique was to arrive when a party was at its height, slither inside inconspicuously and immediately go through the receiving line backward (that is, beginning with the person deepest in the room and ending with the person nearest the door), exclaiming what a marvelous event it had been and what a delightful time he had had. Total time there: three to five minutes.

Let us adapt this for your situation, as even Miss Manners is aware that office booze parties do not have receiving lines. They are probably held right in the office, making it difficult to arrive late or to leave early without being noticed.

Difficult, but not impossible. The way to join the party late is to call out merrily, "I'll be right with you, just as soon as I finish this," and to keep on working. You might want to save tasks that require minimal concentration to do then. Eventually, you plunge in, saying "Great party" to everyone, and head out the door, telling anyone who notices how much you hate to leave. The point is the enthusiasm. Your colleagues won't mind your disappearance as long as they are sure they don't suspect it is accompanied by your disapproval.

～ *The Office Celebration* ～

DEAR MISS MANNERS:

What is proper etiquette in inviting co-workers to non-business related functions (weddings, showers, birthday parties, etc.). I don't want to invite my entire office, but I also don't want anyone to feel snubbed. What should you say to the uninvited who find out about the event?

GENTLE READER:

The rules are the same for both categories of people who get so excited over their birthdays that they can't get through the day without everyone's acknowledging them, namely kindergartners and office workers. If you celebrate where others are working (or crayoning), you must invite them all.

If, as Miss Manners trusts, you were not planning to hold your wedding at noon in the staff lunch room, then you should invite only your relatives and friends. No one who does not see you socially should feel snubbed at not being invited, but Miss Manners advises all brides to spend the entire engagement telling everyone that it will be a very small wedding.

This would be a good time to clarify the distinction between your professional life and your personal life. Getting married is presumably not a work assignment, and therefore your wedding belongs to your personal life and is not the occasion to perform that oxymoron known as business entertaining. If you have made genuine friendships at work, those are the ones who should be invited. If you are not sure, ask yourself whether, if a particular person was fired, you would keep up the tie—which is not the same as keeping on saying, "We must have lunch some time."

～ *The Boss's Party* ～

DEAR MISS MANNERS:

Every December, the twelve people in my office receive invitations from our supervisor to attend her annual holiday party at her home. The time is always during a week-end, spouses and children are invited, and we are asked to bring a dish of some kind. Our supervisor provides liquid refreshments and serving ware.

My wife and I have attended this annual party for the last seven years and I no longer feel obligated or inclined to attend. We are not "party people," much preferring the prospect of a quiet evening together at home. This year, I wrote my supervisor a note in which I thanked her for the invitation, adding that we would not be able to attend.

Now, I have been confronted by colleagues who either hint or state directly that my office "spirit" is lacking, that I'm lucky to have a supervisor who seeks to entertain her staff, or that I'm just plain ungrateful! One colleague, assuming incorrectly that my wife and I have a conflicting engagement, offered to suggest to our supervisor that she change the date of the party to accommodate us!

I don't feel that I should be apologetic about not attending, but my colleagues are making me feel angry and resentful, as well as guilty. I resent feeling obligated to attend a work-related social event that does not take place during regular work hours; and I resent my colleagues who are making me feel guilty and meddling in what I consider my right to decline an invitation. Am I over-reacting? I have tried politely to decline the invitation, and I have not sought to offend anyone.

GENTLE READER:

Compulsory parties! On unpaid overtime! Another feature of the friendly workplace.

Miss Manners is even more vehemently opposed than you to such goings-on. You just want a peaceful evening at home; she wants to abolish these altogether. Not out of pure meanness, however. Far from wanting to discourage either office friendships or management generosity, she has better ideas for accomplishing them. Friendships are better formed when they are freely chosen, and they are better nourished free from the observation of bosses, however generous they may be. You would be luckier to have a boss who recognizes this and channels her generosity into holiday bonuses or time off, rather than drinks and cooking assignments.

In the meantime, it might be more tactful to tell your bullying colleagues that you have family responsibilities. Surely your responsibility to yourself should count as such.

Business Communications

IT IS NOT in the nature of Miss Manners' business to have sudden emergencies. When she steps out for some innocent amusement, she need not carry technology in her beaded bag to be reachable in case she should be wanted by someone at another dinner needing to know if it would be proper to ask for thirds.

Oddly, she seems to be the only person left who is willing to slack off. Ever new and improved toys have put everyone else voluntarily on call all the time, and the air about her is crackling with the great game of business communication. The more difficult it is—if the recipient is, say, on vacation and in the shower and also taking another call, email, fax and instant message at the time—the greater the triumph. People seem to enjoy this pastime more than working.

Miss Manners will confine herself, then, to issuing two reminders:

The newer means of communication do not oblige us to forgo the old ones. We have more means at our disposal, but the newest and fastest is not always the best. There is still a place in this world for the letter.

No form of communication has or will be invented that is free of etiquette rules.

BUSINESS LETTERS

⁓ Salutations ⁓

DEAR MISS MANNERS:

With the problem of "political correctness," I don't want to be doing something wrong. I am sure there are many, many others that would like this question answered.

Years ago, I was taught that when writing a business letter in which you don't know the name of the person to whom the letter is going, you address it as "Dear Sir" or "Gentlemen." I certainly don't want to say "Dear Sir or Madam" or "To

Whom It May Concern." That is just too much. So what do I say to recognize the fact that the CEO may be female?

GENTLE READER:

You are quite right: There are many others who would like this question answered, and Miss Manners has not covered this matter since, oh, maybe last week.

The answer is that you should get over whatever makes you think that "Sir" and "Gentlemen" are respectful titles but the female equivalents, "Madam" and "Ladies," are ridiculous. If you can't manage to say "Dear Madam or Sir," you may say "Ladies and Gentlemen."

DEAR MISS MANNERS:

My sweet bride and I see no reason for you to be ashamed because, in a brief lapse, you could offer nothing better than "Dear Madam or Sir" to those who wish not to offend the unknown recipient of their letter. May we suggest "Dear Friends"? We assume that there are enough nice people about that the chances are reasonably good that, if we met, we might be. At any rate, the "Dear Friends" signals good fellowship and sets a proper tone.

We remain perplexed when forced into correspondence on ugly matters; "Dear Knucklehead" or "Hey, ratface," seem in poor taste, and may well be counterproductive.

GENTLE READER:

Miss Manners is perplexed when you call it setting a proper tone to anticipate friendship with an unknown person. One might just as well go the whole way and imagine falling passionately in love with one's unnamed bank representative, for example, and therefore address that person as "My Own Darling."

As for insulting a person in the salutation—why, that takes the fun out of the letter proper, does it not?

Miss Manners' solution to adjusting the conventional salutation is to use "Mesdames" or "Dear Madam," under the assumption that a well-run business is run by women. If she sends a letter of complaint, she uses "Gentlemen" or "Dear Sir."

 Closings

DEAR MISS MANNERS:

I write occasional business letters. What is the proper complimentary closing? Many are to people whom I do not necessarily respect; that lets out "respectfully."

"Yours" is obviously out; I am most certainly not. While I hope I am almost always sincere, "Sincerely" seems to be out of place in a business letter. So does "love," whether agape or filial. How about just "very" or how about nothing?

GENTLE READER:

How about "Yr. most humble and obedient servant"? How about not being so literal? Miss Manners signs herself "Very truly yours" to business people and "Sincerely yours" to acquaintances—believing that "Sincerely" alone is as close to nothing as "Very" alone—and has not yet been required to surrender herself to any of them.

～ Folding a Real Letter ～

DEAR MISS MANNERS:

I have come across an interesting problem regarding how to properly fold business letters. Should they be folded so that the name of the addressee shows immediately upon opening the letter, or folded so that the name is on the inside, and only the blank reverse-side shows upon opening it? This question has generated much discussion in my office.

GENTLE READER:

Folded? Are you talking about paper? And when you refer to putting it inside, do you mean that your plan is to put this piece of paper into a paper envelope? Miss Manners considers this a wonderful idea, but she is not surprised that your colleagues are confused. It is getting to be a lost art.

All right, that's enough nostalgic wandering. A business letter is folded in thirds, the bottom third toward the middle, and the top third down over it. Thus the blank, reverse side of the top part of the letter is what is seen when the envelope is opening from the back, but the letter itself then can be unfolded right side up.

TELEPHONES

DEAR MISS MANNERS:

I frequently get put on speakerphone by callers—including salespeople, administrative assistants, and even senior executives. Unless I'm on a group conference call,

I don't like the idea that my voice is being broadcast to everyone within earshot. Is it rude to insist that I be taken off speakerphone?

GENTLE READER:

Probably, or Miss Manners suspects that you would not have proposed starting out with the third step, which is to "insist," rather than the first step, which is to "ask." Politely, as in "I'm afraid I have trouble with speakerphones, so would you be kind enough to pick up the receiver?"

The second step, should your callers deny your request, is to keep saying "What? What?" until they are driven crazy. (See? Miss Manners is not against solving the problem, only against doing so rudely.) This should make insisting unnecessary, but the polite way to do that is to say, "I'm sorry, but I really can't deal with this. Would you be kind enough to email me instead?"

DEAR MISS MANNERS:

Aside from loud gum chewers, my biggest pet peeve is people who see that I am on the telephone, but approach my desk anyway and stand in front of me until I end my call—which I do, prematurely, because of the intrusion. Sometimes the approachers have the gall to talk at me while I am in the midst of conversing. Despite the frequency of such occurrences, I have not mastered the technique of designating an ear to each person.

I cannot understand why people do not come back when I am not indisposed. Perhaps I am unreasonable and they do have the right to camp out at my desk. Please enlighten me and suggest how I may best handle these annoying situations.

GENTLE READER:

Without disputing that this is annoying, Miss Manners would like to point out that it is no worse than call waiting, which many people pay to have done to them.

At any rate, the international gesture for "Go away, I'm busy" is to look sadly at the intruder and shake your head as if in exasperation that the call is long and uninterruptable. Having done that, you may swing around to face away from the intruder, who you may assume has given up.

DEAR MISS MANNERS:

My cell phone inadvertently re-dialed the last number I called, so the receiver overheard a private conversation in which I revealed sensitive—okay, blistering—information about recent company layoffs, including those of a few of her friends. I have since been reprimanded for the breach, but I feel as if no one in the office trusts me now. Any advice on smoothing ruffled feathers?

GENTLE READER:

While Miss Manners was quite aware that cellular telephones are fully capable of such treachery, she had never actually taken the time to pause and review every call she had ever made, while vividly imagining the results of those conversations being overheard by the wrong people. Thanks so much.

Actually, we should be grateful to receive yet another warning that the devices we use to gossip about others feel no loyalty to their owners. Even without this strange form of involuntary conference calling, cellular telephone conversations, like email, should never be considered secure.

Miss Manners regrets to say that there is no quick way to regain trust after delivering clear evidence that you indulge in mean-spirited gossip. (Had it not been overheard, she would be willing to call it crisp business sense.) Your only hope is the insanity plea ("I don't know what got into me—that isn't even really the way I feel") and time.

Ending the Call

DEAR MISS MANNERS:

When a person returns my business call to them, which one of us is to initiate the closing? Do I, since I was originally calling them or do they since they are only returning a call that I initiated?

I have consulted business etiquette books and called business professors at a local university. No one seems to know the answer to this often uncomfortable and clumsy position.

GENTLE READER:

In these brusque and hurried times, Miss Manners is charmed to hear of business people's hanging on to telephone calls long after the reason that prompted them is concluded for fear of seeming abrupt. Nevertheless, she can't have commerce grinding to a halt. The person who initiated the transaction is responsible for bringing it to a close. Those who fail to do so in a reasonable amount of time may be asked politely if there is anything more that needs to be settled.

DEAR MISS MANNERS:

I was recently excoriated by an outraged business acquaintance for a deal that fell through. I tried calming him down, but he seemed carried away by his agitated state and he became more and more abusive. Is it excusable that I hung up on him?

GENTLE READER:

Once Miss Manners might have reassured you that your acquaintance is hardly likely to accuse anyone of bad manners. Now the rude feel as entitled as anyone else to cite etiquette violations. Yes, hanging up on someone is one. But first replying, "I'm not listening to any more of this" would have gotten you off the hook, as it were.

EMAIL

DEAR MISS MANNERS:

Help me; I work at a high profile TV network and made the mistake of sending an email to everyone in my address book, including a cousin, warning them of a new computer virus which could wipe out their system. My cousin was thrilled to see all the email addresses of network executives and sent them emails promoting a book he's writing on his extra-sensory experiences with the spirit of his dead lover. What's worse, he used my name to introduce himself. He sees nothing wrong with this, while I'd like to see him join his dead lover; I feel he certainly owes me an apology. Do I in turn need to apologize to all my coworkers?

GENTLE READER:

Unless you want your employers to think that your idea for a hit series would be the extrasensory adventures of a man communing with the spirit of his dead lover. (And what does Miss Manners know about television? Maybe it would be.) Fortunately, everybody is familiar with both junk email and embarrassing relatives. You need only send around a message that suggests people delete any future messages from him, as he made unauthorized use of your name and mailing list, for which you apologize.

Whether you can extract an apology from your cousin, Miss Manners cannot say. For one thing, he sounds too preoccupied, and for another, he does not seem to have a highly developed sense of etiquette. Perhaps your request to desist from communicating with your bosses, after having embarrassed you with them, will inspire one.

DEAR MISS MANNERS:

I sent a colleague an email critiquing a recent company business decision. Without my permission, she forwarded my message on to several peers and a supervisor. She says she did so because she thought my note contained some "really good points." But I didn't write the note with the intention of broadcasting it and think some people in my company might be offended by it. Am I right to be mad at this woman? What's the best way of handling this situation.

GENTLE READER:

You have already chosen what is evidently not only the best way of learning that email is not private, but the only way. No matter how many times Miss Manners and others issue warnings not to use email to send messages you don't want others to see—and most especially not to use office email to criticize others on the same system—people only seem to learn after they suffer the consequences.

It is not necessary to thank your colleague for teaching you this lesson. But blaming her is rather like blabbing your secrets to others, and then blaming them for being so loose-lipped as to tell others what you could not keep to yourself. People do that all the time too.

NOTEBOOKS AND LAPTOPS

DEAR MISS MANNERS:

In many business meetings recently, people will answer email and send messages using electronic notebooks. While someone else is talking, they'll be busy typing messages under the table. How can I politely ask them to stop?

GENTLE READER:

Are you running the meeting? In that case, you could say, "Please don't take notes. I'd rather have your full attention. If there's anything you feel you've missed, we can go over it afterward."

If you are not running the meeting, you can still object, but you should be aware that you will be annoying your colleagues. For example, Miss Manners does not recommend leaning over, peering into someone's lap and saying, "Wow, I don't have that game, it looks like fun" or "Amazing that they can't find a way to make this sort of thing illegal."

The least offensive method would be to bring your own notebook to the meeting and ask the person running the meeting, publicly and politely, if he or she would prefer that you all not use them.

DEAR MISS MANNERS:

Giving a laptop presentation to a group of my peers and bosses, I accidentally launched a gag application that a work friend had sent me. The application contained some bawdy humor. I quickly closed the program and went on with my presentation. But I feel I should explain the inappropriate software to my superiors. What should I say?

GENTLE READER:

There is something that you could have said at the time. You would have had ample opportunity to say it during that silence when everyone else's jaw was hanging down (which was just before the jaws came back up to produce all those smirks).

It would have been: "All right, who's the joker?"

Now, when you go to your superiors, it should be with more of an apology than an explanation. Miss Manners is as gullible as they come, but even she has trouble with that story about the friend.

"I'm sorry about that embarrassing incident," you could honestly say; "it's obviously somebody's idea of a joke. I have a fairly good idea of who it is, but I don't want to say. I'll make sure it doesn't happen again."

Customer Service

~ *Misplaced Arrogance* ~

DOCTORS HAVE so much in the way of the world's riches that it is not necessary for them to have manners as well, many people believe. These people tend to be doctors.

Miss Manners does not mean to say that the world is not full of charming doctors. Those who specialize in social events often have lovely manners. But the ordinary rules of the profession are set up in a way that enables, one may say compels, the doctor to treat his patients rudely as a matter of routine.

Patients are exasperating people, Miss Manners is aware. They inevitably have some complaint or other, they want to talk about themselves, which is always a bore, and they show up when they're not feeling well, which might make them cranky. Not the sort of people you would think of to enliven a dinner table. Nevertheless, many doctors are forced to deal with these people, and could do much to make the encounters less jarring. To do this will require two adjustments in the way the medical profession is regarded, in comparison to other professions.

First, there must be recognition that there are other services offered in the world that are of comparable value, and that some of these are actually performed by patients when they are not occupying medical facilities. Second, there must be an acknowledgment that doctors are not entitled to the adulation, presumed omnipotence and, consequently, the arrogance of automobile mechanics. A doctor who remembers that his patient has his own mantle of dignity—which is admittedly not easy to think about a naked person clutching a sheet and wearing an alarmed expression—will not be patronizing in his form of address. He will not call patients by their first names while expecting to have his own title used, and he will not object to explaining what he means when it is not clear to someone whose education has been in a different field. He will do his best not to keep these people waiting for his services, because he will understand that their time is, to those whom they serve, as valuable as his. If there is inevitable waiting, he will warn the patient, at least as well as an airline might do, of how long the delay is likely to be. He will not keep music playing in his waiting room, knowing that patients may be people who have work or thinking to do in times of enforced idleness. (You will notice that Miss Manners has used the pronoun "he" about offending doctors. This is because she has observed women doctors who behave better. That may be a statistical error.)

Doctors and automobile mechanics have in common the necessity of dealing with complicated and unpredictable machines whose owners have little idea of how to care for them or what has gone wrong when the things won't work properly. The mechanic is justified in refusing to share with the owner any information about what he will do, when he will have it done and how much he plans to charge. The client can, after all, jolly well walk until he is given his car back.

Not so, in the case of the doctor's patient. By necessity, the patient must be present when all the tinkering is done, and cannot get by on other equipment during the servicing period. It is incumbent upon the service person to tell him—without giving away the entire contents of an expensive medical education—how the repair job will be handled.

~ A Misguided Maxim ~

DEAR MISS MANNERS:

What is the proper etiquette for dealing with unreasonable, offensive and rude customers? As a customer service representative, I interact with hundreds of people via email or the telephone every day. Although the majority of problems are due to a customer's misunderstanding or error, I always sympathize, empathize and respond kindly. I do like to educate customers so the mistake won't be repeated, but I do not place blame; I only explain and find positive solutions.

My problem lies with unreasonable customers. What is a polite way of telling them that they are completely out of line? The company I work for is overly generous when it comes to customers, but some of the demands are not only unreasonable, they're absolutely impossible. These people also tend to be rude and belligerent.

Without disputing their feelings of disappointment or anger, how can I say no to their irrational demands, or respond to vicious words of attack, which have even turned personal on occasion?

I do hope you can help me. Much as I want to assist customers, I would like an appropriately polite defense for myself when necessary. Thank you for your advice.

GENTLE READER:

Whoever came up with that slogan about the customer always being right meant well, but did the commercial world a disservice. It is unhelpful not only in placating customers who are clearly wrong, but it is clearly an unjust affront to people who have to deal with the public.

Goodness knows, as Miss Manners certainly does, that people who work in the customer service business are driven close enough to the brink by customers who berate and threaten them. Next to them at the brink, if not already over it, are the customers. They have been driven there by having their problems met with recordings saying "Your call is important to us" while their calls are being ignored.

In this explosive situation, we have a Gentle Reader who politely asks how to do a better job with unreasonable and unruly customers. Repeating that the customer is always right only suggests that it is the customer representative who must therefore be in the wrong. Yet suggesting retaliating with complaints, rudeness or the refusal to deal with the situation only validates the customer's rudeness.

Passing on the problem to a supervisor does not answer the question; it passes it on. It also demonstrates to the supervisor that anyone unable to cope with problem customers is in the wrong job. (If supervisors succeed because only they have the power to make concessions that work, the frontline people should point out that it would benefit the business if that power were also granted to them. Employees who don't just think in terms of divesting themselves of problems, but are interested in improving efficiency, are the ones who get ahead.)

The job is to soothe the customer back into some sort of reasonable state. This is done by beating him at his own game, which is to say meeting complaints, no matter how offensively worded, with apologies and expressions of indignation at what he has suffered and to repeat this as often as necessary. Eventually it becomes impossible to keep berating someone who is being sympathetic, and a steady stream of "Oh, I'm so sorry" and "How awful!" will eventually wear him out to the point where you can meet impossible suggestions with "No, I'm afraid that wouldn't work, but here's what we can do."

Why is this simple policy so difficult to carry out?

Because, as the Gentle Reader points out, many customers have no sense of decency and turn to attacking them personally. That rattles them, they admit, and tempts them to behave like the customers.

But it is based on a false premise. These are not personal attacks—no, not even the ones like "You're an idiot." The customers don't know them personally and don't care who they are—they are attacking them as representatives of the company. The customer service person should no more take these ravings personally and leave the detached professionalism of the job than should the nurse in the psycho ward.

Miss Manners has a new motto for you to repeat to yourself in times of stress: The customer may be horrid, but I am here to help.

If that doesn't work, add "even though he doesn't deserve it" and "he doesn't know where I live."

⟶ *Misplaced Friendliness* ⟵

Have you been directed to chat up the customers? Offer some small talk to make them feel at ease, and at home?

Personally, Miss Manners doesn't see the need for chatter in commercial establishments beyond a simple greeting and a pleasantly informative discussion of the business at hand. When she wants to feel at home, she doesn't go out. She takes her ease more easily when she doesn't have to field inquires about where we folks are from. However, she realizes that quiet mutual respect is not one of the current choices. Harmless conversation is admittedly preferable to the only available alternative, sullen silence.

In many businesses, employees who deal with the public are supposed to make sociable conversation with them. So although she is sympathetic with the waiter who is working on memorizing his lines or the bartender who is working out the plot to her novel, Miss Manners is perfectly willing to reveal to the geographically curious where she is from.

But not all such talk is as harmless as well-meaning employers or workers suppose and intend. There is a good reason that cautious people are so interested in whether others agree with them about the niceness of the day or what a shame it is that it is raining.

Miss Manners presumes that bellhops no longer tease young couples who are checking into hotels by asking them if they've been married long. Probably too many have replied, "Hey, we're thinking about it, okay? You're not our parents." Or perhaps "Oh, yes, but we're not married to each other."

The disaster-prone habit of teasing perfect strangers nevertheless persists. Someone who walks in with a lot of packages is asked "What'd you do, buy the place out?" It is possible that she is celebrating a promotion with a splurge or is buying her trousseau and is delighted to have the opening to discuss these happy circumstances. It is also possible that she is replacing her wardrobe because her house burned down or her husband trashed her closet before he left.

How, after all, could a stranger know? But everyone should be expected to know that nobody is pleased to be branded a spendthrift, especially by someone with whom she is unacquainted, and even more especially if it occurs in front of someone with whom she is acquainted. Piggy isn't a popular label either, which is why it is not a good idea to comment on how fast or how much people eat. Waiters who can't pick up an empty plate without saying humorously "I guess you didn't like that" do not greatly amuse their customers. The situation requires no comment at all, not even the neutral but uncharming alternative, "You still working on that?"

So what is there left to say that would indicate a cheerful interest in the customer without the risk of being offensive? Miss Manners recommends those welcome words—"May I help you?"

DEAR MISS MANNERS:

In earlier times, when I was shopping, a salesperson would ask "May I help you?", a question easily answered with "Yes, please," or "No, thank you." Perhaps management felt this question was too direct or pushy, as the refrain everywhere now is "Are you finding everything okay?" Not only is this question grammatically annoying, but I don't even know what they are asking: Am I finding what I am looking for? Do I think everything I see is okay?

Perhaps I am being too literal-minded, but how do I answer this question? If I say "No," that doesn't mean I need assistance, I'm just answering the question, but then I feel I'm being rude. And what if I'm not looking for anything in particular, just shopping—I'm not finding anything (okay or otherwise) because I'm not looking for anything. I'm sure the question was not intended to send me into such a flurry of confusion, but those of us who take words literally would appreciate a little assistance on how to respond.

GENTLE READER:

Those of you who take conventional expressions literally are always going to have problems. Miss Manners is surprised you haven't been stymied for years by that question, "May I help you?"

Help you with what? Looking? Finding? Making the payments? Is there a hidden insult in this? Does the question imply that you look helpless?

That opening, too, is just an expression, as is the perhaps less graceful replacement. And you know perfectly well that what is meant is whether you have found what you want, and that the answer—if it is not "Where do you keep the gym socks?"—is "Thank you, I'm just looking."

DEAR MISS MANNERS:

We dine frequently with another couple at a favorite restaurant where we usually ask to be seated in a certain waiter's section because he has been courteous, friendly and efficient to us. Recently we were there before he came on duty and thought it very nice of him to stop by our table to greet us. It was early and there were few people in the restaurant.

However, he chatted endlessly. When our food was brought, we were hesitant to eat with him standing there, except the food was getting cold. Finally we just began to pick at our food and he continued to tell us about a sports injury.

Afterwards none of us knew what we should have done. We did not want to be rude to the young man. The table was for four, but should we have offered to buy him a cup of coffee and squeeze in?

GENTLE READER:

If you wish to be friends with this young man, you should arrange to dine with him in another restaurant. In this particular restaurant, he is on duty.

Sadly, he probably thought he was performing this duty in entertaining you. Miss Manners agrees that you should spare his feelings, but that is not the same thing as giving up your enjoyment of your food or of your evening with your friends. A social friend of yours who happened to be in the restaurant would be equally rude to hang around your table in such a manner.

Just because you are sitting down doesn't mean you can't excuse yourself. "I'm afraid our dinner has arrived," you could have said. "Thank you for stopping by."

⟶ Misguided Acquiescence ⟶

DEAR MISS MANNERS:

I am a cleaning lady, and I also clean my church. My problem is that when I go to someone's home for a social occasion where I'm invited as a guest, I'm expected to help serve and clean up.

I had one lady hand me a dish towel when I came in, and was told to wipe off glasses and fix the drinks while she visited with her guests. I don't mind helping, but I think if you are an invited guest, you shouldn't be expected to serve. How can I tell them nicely I would like to be treated like the others?

GENTLE READER:

It is true that Miss Manners is in the business of putting sticky statements nicely, but suddenly she doesn't feel so nice.

What these people are doing is outrageous. This is not helping a friend, as a guest may volunteer—but not be conscripted—to do. This is using a social pretext to get your professional services free.

Miss Manners has three suggestions for you, all of them polite but firm statements to deliver in a pleasant manner. Frankly, she is hoping you will choose the third.

1. "Oh, my goodness, I misunderstood; I didn't realize you wanted to hire me for the evening. Let me tell you what I charge."
2. "I'm afraid you had better ask one of the other guests to help. I do this for a living, as you know, and so when I accept an invitation to go out, it's only to relax."
3. "You know, I've been doing this sort of thing all week, and suddenly I find that I'm tired. You will excuse me, but I think I will go home now to rest. Here's your dish towel. Have a pleasant evening."

~ Misplaced Appeals ~

Homeowners are familiar with the Pity Story as a method of explaining why a contracted service has not been performed. Their indignation dissolves into embarrassment when the response to an angry and anguished complaint ("It's been three weeks since you promised you would be here to fix it!") is not an apology or a renewed promise, but a reciprocal dose of anguish.

It seems that the person being importuned, whom they know only as the representative of a business that has failed to live up to its obligations, has a seriously ill child or is mourning a parent. Who would not be ashamed to be carrying on about some mere commercial service in the face of stark human tragedy?

Miss Manners can tell you who: the customer who has heard similar stories too often, perhaps even from the same source.

After a while, even emotional pushovers find their hearts hardening. One does not have to be so cynical as to assume that anyone whose work commitments are perpetually thwarted by life's cruelty might be less than completely honest. One can simply reflect that the constant victim of unforeseen circumstances is never going to fix your sink, so you might as well contract the work to someone who is on better terms with the fates.

Clearly, something new was needed. The Pity Story was ceasing to work.

Miss Manners is able to report a triumph of business ingenuity. A new version of the Pity Story has been developed to replace the worn-out one.

Furthermore, the distribution method is amazingly efficient. When she first heard it, she thought it was a brilliant improvisation on the part of the person who used it on her. But all she had to do was to mention it, in order to hear reports from others who had had the same technique used on them by different businesses. Here is how it works:

Customer: "Six weeks ago, you replaced one of my fan units for $1800, and one of your people stepped on two of our air ducts and flattened them, and you still haven't been out to fix them, and we've been calling and calling."

Manager: "I know about it, but I don't have someone to send yet."

Customer: "But we want it fixed before it gets hot."

Manager: "Lady, you've got most of your air-conditioning working. Some people don't have any. Don't you think they should come first?"

Customer: "But we have a service contract. And it was your people who caused the damage."

Manager: "I've got a pregnant lady whose air-conditioning is completely out. You want her to be sweltering in the heat?"

What impresses Miss Manners is how skillfully the line of argument is switched. Having sold the customer a regular service contract, the business is now portraying itself as a rescue agency handling humanitarian emergencies.

Indeed, in hospitals and during times of widespread disaster, decent people sacrifice their own needs to those with more acute problems. So the fact that an ordinary business is admitting to being unable to meet its regular obligations to all its customers is lost, while one customer is being asked to judge which of them should get the service for which they have all paid. With any luck, the customer will be too cowed to mention that it wasn't even hot out yet when the exchange was taking place.

Ever an admirer of rhetorical skill, Miss Manners was disappointed to hear that this performance was old by the time she heard it. If business consultants are teaching it, it is time for them to stop, she is afraid. Word has gotten around.

⌐ *Misguided Manners* ⌐

DEAR MISS MANNERS:

We are having a lot of work done in the house, and I feel funny sitting there eating meals while the painters and electricians are working nearby. I'm not saying that I'm willing to cook for them, and anyway, the ones that are there all day bring their own lunch pails. But I can be having my lunch, sometimes with a friend who's stopped by, and we're at the table while the men who are doing over the kitchen are standing around, and I feel as if I ought to ask them to sit down and at least have a cup of coffee. I don't really want to, as lunchtime is when I do my reading if I'm alone and if I have a visitor I'd rather talk to her, but doesn't it seem snobbish not to ask them to join us?

GENTLE READER:

It would be snobbish to ask them to join you. Such an invitation presumes that you believe that you, whose walls are peeling and whose wiring is a mess, who don't even have a functional kitchen, are the social equal of honest laborers.

DEAR MISS MANNERS:

House painters, window installers, roofers and the like have asked to use my bathroom. I could hardly say no, but I wanted to. Is it all right to refuse them, or is it in poor taste?

I am a woman alone with a one-bathroom house. I consider it an invasion, and feel that they should drive to the nearest gas station or have a portable potty in their truck.

GENTLE READER:

Having work done on your house is already an invasion. Don't tell Miss Manners that while you are getting your roof fixed or your kitchen painted, your house would be all nice and neat and quiet if it weren't for the workmen using the bathroom.

She suggests that you put away your dainty lace towels and be gracious until the work is finished. Not just good taste, but human decency (not to mention good sense) requires that you allow people on your premises to use your bathroom.

WHEN THINGS GO WRONG

The mental health industry in this country, also known as the Feel Good Business, has put a massive effort into reducing the Gross National Guilt. But in so doing, it has only increased the distressing amount of unresolved blame that is going around.

Nobody is taking any blame for anything any longer. The new battle cry is "It's not my fault." Perhaps it's not. But Miss Manners, who believes that collective civilization is more important to the public happiness than a lot of little satisfied psyches bumping up against one another, does not like the result. She believes that if each one of us were to accept graciously a small portion of blame, it wouldn't all be hanging there, clogging up the air.

Example: Mrs. Ipswich receives, in her department store bill, an offer she cannot refuse for a bottle of hair goo, "free" with the purchase of a related product. She duly fills in the form that will avail her of this unprecedented commercial opportunity. Some time later, a package arrives, containing the free product, but also a bottle of shampoo for redheads, when Mrs. Ipswich had clearly ordered the shampoo for blue-headed ladies. There is a delivery charge that Mrs. Ipswich had not noticed. Attempts to reach the department store by telephone fail, a fact that puzzles Mrs. Ipswich as she is always being deserted at store counters by salespeople who prefer to answer the telephone. Mrs. Ipswich packs up all the hair products and goes to the store. The shampoo counter is part of a vast cosmetic department divided by brands and populated by idle salespeople, all of whom refuse to have anything to do with Mrs. Ipswich's problems because these come under the jurisdiction of the one occupied salesperson on the entire floor.

Mrs. Ipswich grows increasingly fidgety as she waits to be waited upon. When her turn comes, she recounts, in her soft voice that is the delight of six grandchildren, two elderly beaux and the staff and patients of the hospital where she pushes a book-mobile, the ills that have been perpetrated on her. The salesclerk maintains an unpleasant silence. She then informs Mrs. Ipswich that she cannot read the sales slip pasted on the package, so she must assume that Mrs. Ipswich was charged for the red shampoo, which is cheaper, and now must pay extra for the blue. Mrs. Ipswich requests that the delivery charge now be removed, as she was forced to make a trip to the store to complete the purchase. The clerk refuses to do this.

Mrs. Ipswich cracks. After sixty-seven years in which she has never said anything harsher than telling the fat pigeons in the park to allow the thin ones to share the bread crumbs she brings, Mrs. Ipswich goes bananas. At this point, the salesclerk decides to give Mrs. Ipswich a lecture on etiquette, of which the theme is that the ills recited are "Not My Fault." Whatever has been done to Mrs. Ipswich—by the person who packed the wrong product, those who should have answered the telephone, those who make the rules about delivery charges and about territorial division of the cosmetics department—has not been done by this particular clerk. "Don't yell at me, lady," she says coldly. "It's not my fault."

Perhaps not, as Miss Manners acknowledged earlier. But there is a greater human issue here, which is that Mrs. Ipswich has to vent to someone. It would not hurt the clerk nearly so much to take the blame as it would Mrs. Ipswich to swallow her indignation. Miss Manners believes it is the salesclerk's duty to identify with her offending employer, asking "What can we do to resolve this to your satisfaction?" as many times as necessary for Mrs. Ipswich to recover.

So Miss Manners' advice is: Take some of the blame. If you are the fifth wrong number at City Hall whom a person has been connected with, say, "I'm so terribly sorry." If you are the driver of a bus, apologize for the bus that passed by the person for whom you are stopping. If everyone takes a little blame, there will be less of it going around.

DEAR MISS MANNERS:

People seem to be apologizing for things that are not their fault. For example: I visited an ATM in one of my local supermarkets. I discovered I had left my card at home. Although there was someone staffing the banking center, he apologized because he didn't have cash on hand to allow me to complete my transaction. It wasn't his fault that I forgot my ATM card.

GENTLE READER:

You are shopping at the wrong store, Miss Manners is afraid. You should have no trouble finding one in which the correct answer to your problem, and indeed all customer needs, is "Hey, lady, what do you expect me to do about it?"

Your finding one of these businesses would have the beneficial effect of shortening the line at this one for the rest of us, who would be only too pleased to deal with the employee whose politeness offended you.

DEAR MISS MANNERS:

I have worked for over 18 years in a pretty high stress customer service position. I'm finding that people are becoming much harsher, more demanding of immediate resolutions, that sometimes are simply not possible. When I try to explain to someone that I am working on their problem, but that it is going to require some time, I get the inevitable "that's just not acceptable."

I then try to explain that there are processes that have to be followed, and I am sorry, but unable to make things happen instantly. They continue to be belligerent; mind you, this is not a life or death situation: ever. I know that I can't turn the situation around, and I know (from your wisdom) that rudeness does not respond to rudeness, but I want to be able to . . . well, get them off my back. Once they've irritated me, it's definitely going to take longer to get this resolved.

GENTLE READER:

Indeed, customers get irritable, which makes customer service people irritable, which makes customers more irritable, and so on. As you have learned, helping this cycle along does not make the world go around faster, let alone more pleasantly.

Therefore, Miss Manners recommends taking the opposite approach. In the most charming manner you can manage, as if you were delighted to encounter someone eager to appreciate what it is you do, say, "Please let me explain to you what is involved." If possible, offer the customer a seat. If he protests he hasn't the time, murmur reluctantly, "All right, I'll go back to work on this, if you insist. But really, I'd be glad to explain. It saves time in the long run if the customer understands why we do things in what we have found is the most efficient way."

COMMON COMPLAINTS

~ *Taking Calls* ~

DEAR MISS MANNERS:

What do you think of a store clerk who leaves you right in the middle of writing up a purchase, in order to answer the telephone and take an order for someone who isn't even there?

GENTLE READER:

Miss Manners thinks that is the same clerk who puts the telephone on hold, when you are the one calling, in order to pretend to take the order of someone who is in the store. Between the two systems, a clever clerk is able to avoid the hurly-burly of the marketplace entirely.

DEAR MISS MANNERS:

When you are actively assisting a customer and they take/receive a phone call on their cell phone, does one excuse themselves to assist other customers in their zone, or does one stand there looking foolish while they talk? Can one depart to help the other customers when the person on the phone has grabbed them by the elbow while they talk?

GENTLE READER:

When you talk about standing foolishly by, do you mean to say that the transaction has come to a halt because it requires the full attention of the customer?

Miss Manners is just checking to make sure that the problem is that the customer with the telephone is wasting your time and that of the other customers. If your customer is able to talk and hand over a credit card at the same time, it is not a violation.

If not, your desire to continue doing business, rather than remaining transfixed while your customer tends to other business, is as reasonable as it is courteous to other customers. And, for that matter, to the rude customer. You need only accompany shaking your elbow loose with a regretfully understanding look that telegraphs that you are sympathetic with his need to telephone and will occupy yourself with others, rather than hovering over him, until he is finished.

∽ *Using First Names* ∽

DEAR MISS MANNERS:

Please chastise presumptuous medical assistants who address patients by their given name. Perhaps the physicians are simply poor administrators or lack the time properly to instruct their employees. Perhaps the employees are simply dense or densely simple. My example ("Thank you, Miss Crimp") and cold looks availed me nothing. I feel it inappropriate to go further, exceed the bounds of good form, and chide the offenders, especially as they have power over my body. Miss Manners, rescue us all from that sad deterioration in standards. It may be that the transgressors are not too far lost to civilities to learn the gravity of this offense and mend their ways.

GENTLE READER:

The trouble is that we have here two deteriorations, or at least two low points. One is the increasing use of first names in situations that are not social, and the other is the insufferable old habit many medical workers have of calling patients by their first names while themselves expecting to be addressed with their titles. Fortunately, the cure in both cases is the same. If Miss Crimp, or Dr. Botchitt, says, "How are we today, Hortense?" one replies, "Why, just fine, Millie; *and you?*" Those being rude for medical reasons will then stiffen up and understand. Those without a medical excuse may never understand.

DEAR MISS MANNERS:

I am an elderly woman. I clean house for several families. The people for whom I work pay me well. They treat me well. They all tell me I do a fabulous job. So why am I writing to you? Just one thing mars all this for me! They all call me (unasked to do so) by my first name. How do you think I like being introduced to their relatives and friends—"Mrs. Ryan, this is my housekeeper, Hilda"? Their children also call me by my first name.

I have been told by others (younger than I) that they, too, resent this first name business. My children were brought up to use surnames unless asked otherwise. I like to think of doing housework as a reputable profession. I really like my employers and try to be trustworthy and do a good job. I am older than any for whom I work. Please write about the etiquette of this.

GENTLE READER:

It is an oddity of tradition that occupations that are of real use in the world, such as yours, have been accorded less respect than many that are of no perceptible use whatever. Miss Manners is in full sympathy with your desire to be addressed by title and surname, as befits your age and business relationship with your employers.

Miss Manners advises household employers to ask their employees, when hiring them, what they prefer to be called. But you must make your wishes known. You can put it something like this:

"Mrs. Awful, there is something I have been wanting to tell you."

"Yes, what is it, Hilda?"

"Well—that's what it is. I have never felt right about your calling me 'Hilda.' I'm not a young girl, you know, and I feel entitled to the respect of my age and my occupation." (Then you put in the rest about how you try to do a good job, and generally feel that your employers treat and pay you well. Say everything that you put into your letter.)

Mrs. Awful will then be covered with embarrassment. She will protest wildly, "Oh, Hilda, I never meant any disrespect," and then she will realize what she just said and get even more embarrassed. She may even suggest you call her Daffodil. But eventually, she will learn. And you will have performed a service, not only for yourself, but for all working women.

DEAR MISS MANNERS:

My mother had to spend the final year of her life in a nursing home. My sister and I spent most of our hours for the first week at her bedside, helping her through a difficult loss—of her preferred autonomous life at home. A couple of months later, I journeyed to that city to pay her another visit, and I went into the nursing home, a good one with liberal visiting hours. The staff were always kind and helpful, and considerate in many ways of all the patients. My mother had been known always to her friends and neighbors of her age as "Mrs. Jackson," and to her relatives and intimates as "Ellen," her middle name. I was aghast to find that twenty-two-year-old aides would invariably come in and say to my eighty-year-old mother, "How are we feeling today, Margaret?" using her first name, which she had never used.

What to do? I was concerned that if I said, "My mother's name is Mrs. Jackson," they, or some of them, would just take it out on her when my sister or I were not present. I said nothing, because I saw it as a no-win situation. Was there a way to win?

GENTLE READER:

Miss Manners is determined to find a way, having no intention of spending her old age being cheekily patronized by those who recognize no gradations of intimacy or respect. What makes the battle difficult, as you recognize, is that the intentions are probably good, although the effect is dreadful. Those who believe in instant and universal informality generally mean well, although they will never understand the joy of real warmth that is allowed to develop naturally and therefore slowly.

In this case, you should simply have explained to the offenders that your mother was used to being addressed as Mrs. Jackson and preferred it. They would put it down to hopeless old-fashionedness, but so be it. Miss Manners cannot believe that otherwise kind, helpful and considerate professionals would hold it against an old lady to prefer old ways, much less retaliate against a patient for any reason.

⁓ . . . and an Uncommon Complaint ⁓

DEAR MISS MANNERS:

When I was hit by a drunk driver a few years ago, it was a chaotic day, and I forgot to call my hair stylist to cancel my appointment. That evening, she called and yelled at me that no one misses her appointments, and that being hit by a drunk driver was no excuse to miss my appointment.

I finally hung up on her. Miss Manners, that stylist not only lost my business, but the business of the rest of my family. Rudeness (on either side) is unacceptable.

GENTLE READER:

Whew. Miss Manners thought she was tough, with her dictum that it is unforgivable to break a dinner engagement unless—got that "unless"?—you are run over by a truck.

Your decision to break off business relations strikes Miss Manners as wise. One should never offer one's head to a rude person wielding sharp instruments.

The Job Ends

IN THE DAYS before callous commercialism, when the true holiday spirit was upon everyone, it was a legendary custom in the American business world to schedule firings for Christmas Eve. The employee would be called in on December 24th, just as everyone was engaged in joyous leave-taking, told that it wouldn't be necessary to return after the holiday and wished a Merry Christmas.

It made for a pleasanter Christmas. The boss could enjoy the holiday free of an unpleasant chore, and the company would have a fresh start for the New Year. The employee had more time off than anticipated, a great deal more as a matter of fact, plus something new to talk over with the family during the holiday gathering. Other employees were spared having to deal with their erstwhile colleague's situation because it would be over when they returned.

Miss Manners is hedging with the term "legendary" because she did not actually know anyone to whom this happened. She heard numerous vivid accounts of its being done, even in her own profession, journalism, renowned for its sense of compassion, but these were always secondhand and set in the past.

A lot has happened in the working world since then to protect the worker. People are still fired, often ruthlessly, but it is not so easily a matter of the boss's whim. Legal responses are more common, and the bosses know it. There are cases in which employees are told to clean their desks out and be gone within the hour, but an awareness of morale problems among remaining employees, not to mention armed responses from those who depart disgruntled, have inspired such humanitarian institutions as post-firing counseling and job-hunting assistance.

The old ruthlessness has given way to a form that has the advantage of being more subtle, more drawn out and, in keeping with the spirit of our time, more psychologically oriented. It leaves the employee just as fired, but with only himself to blame.

This technique involves planting and nurturing the idea that the employee is an embarrassment to himself. Through carelessly disparaging remarks, downgraded assignments and downgraded working conditions, the employee's confidence is shaken until the point when an offer to leave with a shred of dignity still intact seems generous.

That this may be an accurate assessment of a particular employee's worth does not make Miss Manners consider it any the less appallingly rude. Furthermore, it has been found to be so effective a strategy in persuading the employee to slink away without protest that it gets used in cases of general downsizing, rather than dissatisfaction with individuals. When mandatory age retirement became illegal, it began to be used on perfectly satisfactory employees, to speed them on their way.

Miss Manners is not under the illusion that there is any painless way to fire an employee. But there are uncivilized ones, and they ought not to be used. As a token of farewell, humiliation is not an adequate replacement for a gold watch.

⟋ Firing ⟍

DEAR MISS MANNERS:

Help! I need to lay off 50 members of my staff. I'm a young manager and have never fired anyone before. Some of these employees are much older than me and have families to support. Can you give me a primer on how to fire someone?

GENTLE READER:

You are not too young to have broken off a romance, Miss Manners supposes, nor to have been on the receiving end of such a break.

She is far from suggesting that you should therefore know how to sever a connection painlessly. If you were so heartless as to find those experiences painless, you would not be interested in acquiring more finesse than it takes to say "Yeah, yeah—skip the sob story, just take your stuff and be out of here by five."

What she expects you to have learned, and to be able to transfer to this situation, is that there is no such thing as a painless dismissal. Nobody likes being fired, not even those who were planning to quit anyway. The kindest method is therefore not to worry about justifying your action more than is legally necessary, but to allow the other person to retain some dignity.

Paradoxically, this means making the firing impersonal, although gently so. Ending a person's job, like ending a romance, is not the time for recriminations: That turns the target either antagonistic or falsely optimistic. Rather you should blame circumstances (vague references to "the climate" or "restructuring" being the professional equivalent of vague declarations of needing to find oneself), set out the best terms within your power and accept as inevitable that you will be resented.

∼ Consoling the Fired ∼

DEAR MISS MANNERS:

Last week, half of my company was laid off. I fortunately still have a job, but have found it awkward to communicate with my friends and others who were let go. What's appropriate behavior in these circumstances? What should I say to them?

GENTLE READER:

Here are a few things not to say:

"Found anything yet?"

"You're lucky—those of us who are left have to do all the work now."

"Well, they had a lot of dead wood to get rid of."

"You always said you wanted to spend more time with your family."

"We're real busy right now, but I'll call you for lunch."

What you should say is "How about lunch"—but only if you name a specific day. Job leads would be helpful, but it is essential to show that you are not embarrassed to continue the association.

∼ Quitting ∼

DEAR MISS MANNERS:

I work in a small department. I am, in fact, planning to leave the job in a few months. My boss and my co-workers have no knowledge of my plans as of yet. I have not communicated much to them recently, because I realized that when I try to talk to them, they either can barely mask their boredom or proceed to tell me how I am young and therefore ignorant of the ways of the working world. This, of course, does not inspire my confidence in or loyalty to them.

Now, my problem: When it does become time to break my news, I know that they are going to feel betrayed and hurt because I have not confided in them all along or asked for their guidance and counsel. How do I manage to defend myself without breaking the rules of civility, against the inevitable onslaught of their attempts to make me feel guilty for keeping my own counsel?

GENTLE READER:

Miss Manners cannot understand why you would want to leave a job where everybody is trying so hard to make you feel incompetent, ignorant, sneaky, and guilty. However, you do not need to tell her the reason, and you need not tell one to these people either. The reason for not announcing a new job until it is time to give proper notice of leaving the old one is always that it had not yet become "definite."

DEAR MISS MANNERS:

I recently accepted a position at a new firm and have been working there for a couple of weeks. To my dismay, I am slowly learning that I may not be the ideal fit that I once thought I would be. However, I do not want to leave immediately, as I view that as very unprofessional (I was at my previous firm for over 5 years). What is a recommended minimum length of stay for an employee before I could leave on good terms and how can I phrase it to my employer so I don't seem like I'm a quitter?

GENTLE READER:

Miss Manners supposes she should be flattered at the amount of faith in etiquette that your question demonstrates. All she has to do is to devise some polite phrasing that will enable you to quit without appearing to be a quitter.

Suppose it works. What would your boss think when he didn't see you around any longer? That if he waited long enough, you'd come out of the restroom?

All right, all right, Miss Manners will give it a try. Let's see—how about some pungent phrases that will make your employer fire you?

No? Then let's work with your own words, throwing in a few nice ones of Miss Manners' devising: "I'm in a peculiar position here. It's a great place to work, but I realize that I'm not the ideal fit for this job. In fairness to us both, I've decided to leave sooner rather than later. It's a shame, because I've enjoyed it, but I've given it a lot of thought, and I know it's the right thing to do." The time to leave is before the employer starts wondering how he should phrase the idea.

⁓ Retiring ⁓

DEAR MISS MANNERS:

A friend who will be retiring soon has worked thirty years for this major company. The company will be giving a retirement celebration for him. Is it ethical for his wife and daughter-in-law also to give a retirement party? I have never heard of individuals giving retirement parties. Normally it is the company that gives the party.

We live several thousand miles from them and will not be able to attend either event. Other than sending a nice card should we also include a gift?

GENTLE READER:

Ethical? Unless there were threats used in a shakedown to suggest that sending a present would be prudent, Miss Manners sees nothing unethical about a family party celebrating retirement. Many companies have skipped doing this, and colleagues or relatives have marked the occasion so that a worker doesn't simply slip out unnoticed.

Even in this case, where there is also a company event, she doesn't object to a private celebration, although it is odd to endow it with such importance as to assume that guests would be willing to travel to attend. A parting gift for faithful service is, however, the sole responsibility of the employer. You need send only your congratulations.

7. *Intermediate Civilization*

Social Forms, Some Stunning and Others Ghastly

THE IMPULSE of expansive hospitality is such a charming one that Miss Manners would like to encourage it by showing how one can make hospitality somewhat less expansive. Ah, er, cheaper.

For while it is true that no form of social entertainment is quite so enjoyable as the "little" dinner party of ten people, five courses and three wines (unless it is the private Aegean cruise, which is also a pleasant way to see one's friends), this kind of thing now runs into a considerable amount of grocery money. Nor does Miss Manners quite believe all those articles about clever, thrifty cooks who make perfect soufflés Grand Marnier out of discarded orange crates.

A simpler solution, it seems to her, is to invite people to visit you when they are not hungry. One cannot say, "Do come by some time when you're stuffed"; but one can learn to socialize at times other than the dinner hour. Six to eight o'clock at night is exactly when most people are getting ravenous, which is why the cocktail party has had to turn into a buffet dinner, and why you will find, after a "wine and cheese party," that all the paper doilies under the cheese have been eaten.

Four o'clock is much better. Bread and butter, cucumber sandwiches, cookies and tea will satisfy most people at that hour, and if they are also given an iced cake, one inch square, and a thimbleful of sherry, they will consider themselves to have been treated lavishly. (For more extensive directions for tea parties, please see p. 520.)

There are other times, morning, noon and night to be exact, when most people actually prefer eggs, breads and salads to higher-priced staples. There ought to be more weekend breakfasts and luncheons given anyway. Dinners represent a greater effort on the part of the guest, as well as on that of the host. One feeds the children first, dresses up, turns the children over to another keeper and goes out, committed for three hours or more. But a breakfast or luncheon invitation can be a welcome short break in an otherwise busy day, and children should be encouraged to come along (and then encouraged to "go out and play").

Light food also looks luxurious late at night, because even the greediest people know they are not really entitled to a midnight supper. The way to get people to your house for a midnight supper is to invite them to something beginning at nine-thirty or ten—dancing, for example, or an amateur concert given by friends who are good enough to be bearable but not so good as to become unbearable. Or one can invite them to supper after a movie or play that they and you are attending.

For a really chic and cheap party, suppose you find out which of your friends have opera tickets the same night as you do and invite them to come home with you afterwards, adding "We'll dress," which means that you are dictating the importance of an event for which they have paid. You then allow them to kick off their evening shoes and feast on scrambled eggs and chilled wine. The least they can do in return is to invite you to vacation with them in the Aegean.

"Potluck"

DEAR MISS MANNERS:

Friends of ours have made it a habit to entertain often and ask particular guests to bring dishes for usually 16–18 people. I am often simply left a voice message telling me to come with a specific dish.

As I am known for my cooking, the dishes requested can be very elaborate and time-consuming. At the most recent event, two guests of the eight couples invited were asked to bring a dish for dinner. As I was unwrapping mine, the hostess asked that I mix it together with the other dish, which had been purchased at the supermarket. My reply was that I had been asked by her to bring the dish and had spent quite some time preparing it, and that I would rather not mix them. The hostess did not seem pleased with me.

I'm thinking of accepting future invitations with the statement that I would like to contribute to the party in some way, and that we would be happy to bring some wine. Any other ideas? Please don't advise that we not accept dinner invitations from this family—they are my husband's oldest friends, and our husbands do business together. This couple is wealthy; they could afford to cater these events.

GENTLE READER:

They are having their parties catered. For free. "Potluck," which used to mean that an unexpected guest would be served whatever the hosts happened to have on hand as there was no opportunity to provide more elaborate fare, now means that the guests do the work. Unlike cooperative parties, which are announced in advance and where no one is really a host (although someone does the organizing and someone provides the venue), those who give them want full credit for entertaining.

This is part of a general breakdown of social contract between guest and host that Miss Manners considers to have made a mockery out of hospitality.

"Why should I have to grovel with gratitude, just because someone feels like giving a party?" the guests started saying, when taxed with failure to perform such basic guest duties as answering invitations, showing up when expected, thanking their hosts and reciprocating invitations. "They like to entertain but I don't. Anyway, how do I know I'll even feel like going when the time comes?"

"Why should we have to do all the work?" the hosts were meanwhile reflecting. "They're glad enough to come over here and eat and drink at our expense, but what do they ever contribute?"

Mind you, these are all friends talking about friends.

As a grudging compromise, guests started handing over a door fee in the form of a bottle of wine or an offering of food, which they believed compensated for their other omissions, and which the hosts found to be no help at all. One bottle of wine doesn't go far when you're having a party, and the food was not likely to fit in with the rest of the menu. Not knowing what—or how much—to expect, hosts still had to plan a full set of refreshments.

So the hosts started issuing orders: You bring the dessert, you bring the salad. Some began to get the idea that they could farm out more and more of the chores that way. After all, they were contributing the venue, and would be the ones who had to vacuum afterward. Thought of that way, mixing the dishes is not such a leap. If this should be a two-way street, someone needs to direct traffic.

But thought of in terms of what hospitality is all about, this is a sacrilege and so is all that thinking on the part of both hosts and guests that led up to it. Miss Manners is not using that term lightly: Many religions have stories in which a test of character is willingness to share what one has (with a god in disguise), and typically the begrudging rich are punished for a disgraceful showing, while the poor who have shared their last crumb are rewarded.

She is therefore glad to report that etiquette requires a lower standard of behavior than sainthood. If this Gentle Reader is in the habit of entertaining her hosts with her well-reputed cooking, she need have no compunction about saying politely that she is unable to provide food for their parties. If she attends these frequent parties without reciprocating, she can still decline this inhospitable request, but only if she proposes an occasion at which she would have the privilege of entertaining her hosts without their doing any work.

⸺ The Party Pitch ⸺

DEAR MISS MANNERS:

I am receiving an increasing amount of invitations to so-called sales "parties" for everything from expensive baskets to cookware to craft items. This reader kindly asks Miss Manners to address the protocol of these parties. If one accepts an invitation to a party such as this, is it implied in the acceptance that one will make a purchase? Or can one attend without being obliged to purchase anything? While I have bought items on one or two occasions, I generally find the "guilt" of not purchasing anything takes away from the social pleasure of attending these parties.

GENTLE READER:

Considering how bombarded everyone is with commercial pressure, Miss Manners is relieved to find that few people are fooled by the deceptive guises it takes. The Gentle Readers who worry her are those who identify themselves as professionally connected with such ventures. Poor things, they are so out of touch or bored with human society as to believe that it is actually stimulated and enlivened by the addition of sales pitches.

Most Gentle Readers see this situation for what it is. Friends may shop together, friends may also do business together. But to lure friends by offering them hospitality—the defining characteristic of which is generosity—when one is collecting money for their presence and their buying power is a scam.

Yet Miss Manners is not convinced that her clear-sighted Gentle Readers would be as free from embarrassment in practice as they are in theory. The fact that it is more difficult to refuse a pitch from an acquaintance or a colleague than a frank sales person accounts for vast numbers of purchases, donations and even business decisions that would not otherwise be made.

If this increased susceptibility came of being charmed or persuaded, Miss Manners would not object. Sales parties may attract people who are flattered to be invited, people who find it a delightful way to shop and people who accept sales pitches as an inoffensive part of all aspects of life, and she wishes them all a good time.

But the form contains deliberately contrived embarrassment for those not so inclined. These people worry, bless their hearts, that they are violating manners or hurting feelings by not participating. They feel funny about turning down the apparently hospitable overtures of a neighbor or friend, time after time. They feel funny about rejecting items that are displayed in a friend's house, because this almost seems like rejecting her personal taste. They feel funny about being the only person there who isn't joining a group shopping spree.

Even though Miss Manners thoroughly agrees with the position that none of these apparent social duties is legitimate under such circumstances, she cannot remain untouched by these twinges of politeness. Yes, one can certainly attend such a party without buying anything, just as anyone can listen to any other sales pitch without succumbing. But anyone sensitive to the pressure of having been invited as a potential customer would be better advised to decline.

∽ The Surprise Party ∽

DEAR MISS MANNERS:

Would you please explain to your readers, in your well-reasoned and irrefutable way, why people should not inflict surprise parties on their friends? I just discovered accidentally that a surprise bridal shower was in the works for a date and time that would have been disastrous for me. If I hadn't discovered this and persuaded the host to reschedule, one of two things would have happened: either I would have reacted very ungraciously, thereby alienating my friends and relations; or I would have grinned and borne it but resented them forever for throwing off my plans for the day (which couldn't have been reconstructed at any other time).

Why can't people manage a simple "I'd like to organize a shower for you, would the 20th at 11:00 a.m. work, or is something else preferable?" Such an approach would elicit the feeling of happiness that someone going to the effort of planning a party on another's behalf surely hopes for, and would ensure that when the event arrived, the guest of honor was prepared—physically, mentally and cosmetically—to enjoy his or her own party.

Please say Miss Manners agrees with me; it's all I've ever hoped for in life.

GENTLE READER:

After that declaration, Miss Manners would probably agree to anything. But she agrees that you have deftly pointed out the problem with surprise parties. They take the guest of honor by surprise.

Her idea of a successful surprise party is one at which the guests, having had their fun popping out and shouting "Surprise!" spend the rest of the evening asking the perfectly groomed and relaxed guest of honor, "You mean you really had no inkling?"

The BYOB Party

DEAR MISS MANNERS:

At a Bring Your Own Bottle (BYOB), who drinks what? Can you taste anything on the table, or must you stick with your own bottle? Who provides the mixers? Who gets to keep the leftovers?

GENTLE READER:

Miss Manners has the feeling she would not be very good at a Bring Your Own Bottle party. She would probably wander about as if she were at a picnic, saying, "Won't you have a drop of my port?" and "Do have some of my rye," generating a jolly spirit of sharing that would have everyone pie-eyed in no time. The selfishness of everyone's being glued to his own bottle would be too much for her. One solution to the problem, which Miss Manners assumes is a financial one, is for the hosts to provide inexpensive wine instead of providing the mixers. Another is for all the bottles to be parked without private ownership, and the resulting collection to be used as if it were the hosts' bar.

The conventional BYOB arrangement is that guests take their own bottles home with them, having shared their liquor with the hosts, whose contribution is the mixers, the premises and food. However, Miss Manners is beginning to get upset at squabbles at cooperative parties. The reason such events exist is to allow sociability among people who cannot, for reasons of time or money, entirely sponsor parties individually. If you are going to fight over the scraps of food and the dregs of liquor, Miss Manners is going to confine each of you to your own home and there will be no more parties until everyone is in a better mood.

The Housewarming Party

DEAR MISS MANNERS:

I am 35 years old, I've been living on my own for three years now along with my eleven year old son. I am in this program to become a homeowner. I don't have any close girlfriends. Would it be inappropriate for me to throw my own house warming party? I would like to invite people from my church, job and old acquaintances.

GENTLE READER:

You may be surprised to hear that it is customary to give one's own housewarming party. That is because the idea is to welcome people to your new quarters, not, as many now seem to believe, to coerce them into furnishing it.

Miss Manners is not saying that you cannot benefit from the likelihood that people will bring you presents. But you must appear to be surprised and grateful if they do so, when your only apparent intention was to offer your hospitality. And yes, this does rule out drawing up a shopping list and tucking it in with your invitations.

DEAR MISS MANNERS:

Is it proper for parents of new house owners to lay the plans, extend the invitations, serve as hosts, or express appreciation for any gifts given for the occasion?

GENTLE READER:

It is not. If you aren't old enough to warm your own house, you aren't old enough to have one.

DEAR MISS MANNERS:

What is the time frame in which a house warming party can be given? I read somewhere that a house warming party should be given within a year after purchasing the house, but that after a year a housewarming party would not be appropriate because the house would no longer be considered new. I know that most warranties for new homes are for a year but would this translate into the appropriate period for a house warming party?

GENTLE READER:

The warranty has nothing to do with it, Miss Manners is afraid. And the house doesn't even have to be new.

The test is whether it is newly enough in the possession of the present owners that their friends can still have a wonderful time wandering around saying, "I wonder if they know that that's dry rot?" and "That must be the undercoat—no one would choose that as the final color." If they have already had the opportunity to do that, there is no point in giving the party.

⌒ The Wine and Cheese Party ⌒

DEAR MISS MANNERS:

I would like to have a wine-and-cheese party, but since I have never attended one, I'm unsure of the proper procedure. How many different wines and cheeses are served, and are they cut into cubes or slices? Also, I cannot justify buying twenty-four wine glasses for the occasion, so would the plastic champagne variety, that can be purchased in a liquor store, be acceptable?

GENTLE READER:

Never attempt to slice wine, which is about as unacceptable as . . . as forcing innocent people to drink from plastic glasses, particularly silly hollow-stemmed ones that think they are hot stuff. At the simplest wine and cheese party (as opposed to the so-called wine tasting, which is usually a disaster), you need serve only one kind each of red wine, white wine, sharp cheese and mild cheese. You needn't even cut the cheese if you provide boards and knives for each, and biscuits on which to dump the shreds. Cheap glasses are, in the long run, cheaper than plastic, the long run being your second wine and cheese party.

⌒ Afternoon Tea and High Tea ⌒

DEAR MISS MANNERS:

I should like to begin having tea on a daily schedule with friends stopping in, with or without invitations. At what time is "teatime," and should coffee be offered or placed on the table?

GENTLE READER:

Miss Manners commends you for attempting to revive another venerable tradition, that of being "at home" to friends in the afternoon. There are few more charming ways to spend an afternoon than to sit, surrounded by fine china and friends, wolfing down scones and bringing up epigrams. But she must caution you that even the most accomplished hostesses of Miss Manners' day did not attempt it more than once a week.

If you wish to test the water before jumping in even on a weekly basis—and water for tea should always be boiling—invite people for a specific day, writing:

Tea
Tuesday the seventeenth
four to six o'clock

in the lower left corner of your visiting cards. Later it may be "Tuesdays, four to six o'clock."

Tea is made by the hostess, in full view of the guests, symbolizing her hands-on care for her guests, even if everything else she offers them comes from the cook or the carryout. The proper method is this:

Place on a tray a large silver or copper kettle over an alcohol burner, and a tea caddy, with the teapot, cups (which have been warmed with boiling water), teaspoons, a slops bowl (for the dregs when giving a second cup), a tea strainer, a milk pitcher (cream would be horrifying), a bowl of lump sugar, little plates, and napkins.

Rinse the teapot with boiling water. Give your teaspoons a chance to do the job for which they were trained (instead of sneaking out for dessert) by putting in one teaspoon of loose tea (tea is claustrophobic and hates being stuffed into little bags) for each tea drinker, plus one. Now pour on the rapidly boiling water from the kettle (with more always ready in the kitchen). When the tea has steeped for about four minutes, ask your guest of honor how she takes it. Using the strainer, pour straight from the pot for strong tea, and dilute it from the kettle for weak. Then add sugar (the reason for using lump sugar is so you may ask the traditional "One lump or two?") and milk, according to her taste. (According to dear Evelyn Waugh, "All nannies and many governesses . . . put the milk in first," which gave rise to the disparaging remark, "She's rather milk-in-first, darling.")

When this ritual is performed, the guest takes her tea from the hostess, or if there is a gentleman present he takes it to her. She then takes a plate, napkin and a modest selection from your platters of hot breads, tiny sandwiches, cookies and cake.

If you become addicted to this form of entertaining, you may need to move on to stronger doses, such as the reception, which is tea served in the dining room. The tea service is placed at one end of the table, and the teacups, napkins, plates, forks if needed and a larger supply of tea food (at least two of each kind mentioned above) go in the middle. At the other end stands an urn of chocolate, bouillon or, more often lately, to Miss Manners' dismay, coffee. You may ask friends "to pour," that is, to serve the tea and chocolate for you, as you move among your guests. Being asked to pour is an honor just short of knighthood.

However much this may sound to the contrary, a tea is an informal party, and your guests may wear whatever they normally wear when out in the afternoon. To Miss Manners "informal" means the flowered dress, pearls, gloves and picture hat one wears between lunch and dinner; others may be in the habit of wearing street clothes. The hostess unfortunately may not wear a hat, another advantage to being a guest now and then.

The traditional time for tea is four o'clock, which is perfect if you have your afternoons free. However, coffee is only one of the sad things that has happened to tea over the years. Some people have the idea that there is something more important to do in the afternoon than sip tea and eat buttered bread—such as earning a living.

If you have friends who work, Miss Manners suggests that you schedule your tea on a weekend or at a time convenient to them on their way home, when you could give them yet another variation, high tea, so as to replace, rather than interfere with, their supper. High tea is more substantial in all matters of food and drink than afternoon tea. It could include a whiskey and soda tray. Along with the dainty foods traditional to afternoon tea, there are soft-boiled eggs, sausages, sardines on toast, kippers, chicken livers and such. While some unscrupulous restaurants try to make afternoon tea sound more "high society" by calling it high tea, the word "high" is actually related to "It's high time we had something to eat." As social events go, high tea is lower on the scale than afternoon tea, because the chances of being fed dinner are small on a day you are given high tea. In that respect, it is like the "cocktail buffet," than which there are few lower social events.

(For a description of a tea service, please see p. 445.)

DEAR MISS MANNERS:

What is the proper position of the little finger when holding a tea cup? Raised? I had tea with a local dowager, and she clearly, but not pretentiously, raised the little finger on the hand that was holding her tea cup. I know that this is not a question of world-shattering importance, but it is serious, and I am sure that many people would like to know the proper form for holding the tea cup.

GENTLE READER:

It depends on how old the local dowager is. In the seventeenth century, when tea was introduced into Europe from China, it was drunk in dainty, handle-less cups, and anyone with any sense kept as few fingers as possible on the (yeow!) hot cup.

When some genius invented the handled cup, this was no longer necessary, and Miss Manners finds it astonishing that the gesture has stuck in public memory all these years. Your dowager happens to be the only one who remembers it seriously. Because imported tea had been frightfully expensive, the gesture has lived on for centuries as an affectation of the rich and pretentious.

∽ The Television Party ∼

If Miss Manners tells you how to give a television-watching party during Presidential elections and the Super Bowl, will you promise always to snap off the television set when you have guests on ordinary days?

This is a good time not to invite one's friends who have a predilection for violence. Highly excitable people who prefer red wine to white are also to be avoided by hosts with white velvet sofas. Mild range of opinion can be interesting, if it is kept in bounds. What is even better than an articulate but tolerant person with the ability to explain his views reasonably is a guest who is physically capable, for short periods of time throughout a long evening, of watching without eating. Otherwise, a host could easily serve the equivalent of four suppers during a hotly contested election.

Television food needs to be safe, manageable and digestible. Any nursery school teacher's aide who is in charge of snack time can give you the general idea, although that drink menu probably needs to be supplemented. It's just that people who consume nothing but beer and the contents of cellophane bags until the polls close in Hawaii are not happy people when the election is called, no matter who wins.

The key is to have more than one center of interest. The television set and the food table are two, and a second set, perhaps turned to a different channel, would be a third. The point of this is to get people moving before their limbs petrify, and to separate the lecturers from the commentators. (Miss Manners is not suggesting that any provision be made for those who want to watch in silence. They should stay home.) Talking back to a television set is an acceptable exercise, and all that some people get. But two forms of conversation are possible, and those who practice one are apt to be annoyed at the intrusion of the other. At one set, you should aim for a discussion group on the material being watched—how the election is going in relation to one's own predictions, or how one would oneself have played the game. The other is on how it is being televised—the commentary, personalities of announcers and such. If no permanent damage has been done to anyone's digestion or friendship at the end of many hours of television watching, the event can be counted as a success.

∽ The Cocktail Party ∼

Anyone who could remember the heyday of the cocktail party probably doesn't. That would have been the only person who was having a good time, in ways that we now find pitiful and didn't much care for then. As Miss Manners recalls, proper behavior for respectable people was to stand around cocktail parties telling one another how much they hated cocktail parties.

You can see why this ritual lasted for many decades, and hangs on even now in somewhat disguised forms. There is nothing to bring people together like a common grievance accompanied by refreshments. For this reason, the cocktail party has been eagerly seized upon by the commercial world, which generates goodwill by luring people who feel obligated to go there for the purpose of planning their escape.

Miss Manners is only afraid of its coming back socially. Martinis are already back, and the next thing you know it will be tiny napkins with comic roosters on them. To sound the alarm before it is too late, Miss Manners will explain to the young what was so awful about cocktail parties:

- The guest lists were not made up with any thought for charm or compatibility, but to throw in together everyone whom the hosts owed, so as to get all their social obligations over at once. Knowing this, people did not feel particularly flattered at being invited, and tended to be lax in meeting such obligations as answering the invitation, showing up, helping make the party a success and reciprocating.

- There was no set form to the event, so people were left to mill around on their own, with those who were aggressive conducting brisk interviews to find out who was worth talking to, and those who were retiring being left mortifyingly isolated.

- Food was available, but it could only be obtained by hunting and gathering, which has never been a secure way to be nourished. Nor is it decorous. Guests would gather around a table, mowing down everything within reach so that stragglers would have to lean over to pluck the remains from the middle, or they would be on the alert for trays being passed by waiters, whose sport it was to be gone before shells, picks and other debris could be returned to them.

- Drink being the featured attraction, the quality of the cocktails was supposed to be a point of pride with the hosts. But with a huge variety of recipes and preferences, there were endless discussions and wrangling over what was good and what wasn't. Alcohol should not bear the full responsibility of having made people pass out: The arguments about how to make a martini could do this on their own before anyone tasted a drop.

A great deal of social progress has been made since the era of the cocktail party, Miss Manners has noticed. The concept of the obligation-free guest has spread to all social events, even the most structured, such as weddings, and has overtaken the hosts, who no longer feel they are responsible for providing the guests' refreshment or enjoyment. Grazing has become the normal eating style, and pickiness about cocktails has spread to pickiness about food and water.

We therefore do not need to revive the social cocktail party.

DEAR MISS MANNERS:

Am I obliged to serve huge amounts of food when I invite people to a six to eight evening cocktail party?

GENTLE READER:

You have an obligation not to take up your guests' dinner hours without feeding them.

⌒ The Charity Ball ⌒

The charity ball ranks second only to the cocktail party as an event that people who attend regularly profess to dislike. And yet there are those who believe that the rich know nothing of the rigors of self-sacrifice!

Miss Manners does not indulge in the popular vulgarity of comparing the menus, clothes and social practices present at charity balls with those customarily enjoyed by the objects of the charity. A good benefit is beneficial both to the benefactor and to the beneficiary. It not only raises money for the unfortunate but, by roping off the bountiful in their ballrooms, protects the poor from the misfortune of being visited by them, as was once the custom, and getting money diluted with advice. Ballgoers are enriched, not only with the satisfaction of having done a good deed with photographers present, but by being allowed to participate in an obsolescent ritual.

The private ball, in its day, was a fine work of anthropology. Miss Manners cannot understand why it is that so few people these days choose to maintain private ballrooms in their homes, which they can open to their four hundred closest friends once a year. A warm heart, two orchestras, enough food, champagne and footmen to keep continuous service open until three in the morning, and an awning and carpet for the street are really all that is needed to give people several hours of pleasure and the opportunity to end and begin romances with their entire social circle watching. The public ball is just not the same thing, no matter how hard well-meaning committee members try to reproduce the spirit of the grand hostesses of yesteryear by saying, "Let's make sure those dreadful Piffles don't get an invitation."

Nevertheless, it is the only opportunity the average person with the above-average income will have to wear full evening regalia, including whatever grand jewels remain after those whom they encounter on the sidewalk while going in to the ball have had their pick. It is therefore incumbent on ball organizers, Miss Manners believes, to simulate a pleasant social event for the benefit of the ticket buyers.

Instead, she has found, most public balls combine the crushing, noise and surly service of a club with the self-congratulations, entertainment level, and commercial breaks of a televised awards show. Rather than thanking one another for having worked so hard while requiring the guests to listen and even applaud, the committee members might spend the time doing the duty of hosts—greeting those whom they know at the door, introducing people, rescuing those who get stranded and so on. They might see to it that there is room to dance, a place to take a flirtatious walk or to make good an escape from an unwanted partner, music that everyone can dance to, and which even allows the human voice to be heard by a nearby human ear. (You don't want it to be possible for the human voice to carry to a third person; no sensible person tries to have a sensible conversation at a ball.) They might refrain from bragging about getting favors, prizes, decorations or whatever free. The rule ought to be that if the donor requires oral acknowledgment, not just a discreet program note, his donation is not free, nor worth accepting.

In fact, all the time should be devoted to amusing the guests—which can best be done by allowing them to dance, mix, chat, sit down, walk around, and eat in peace. To give a good time to people who pay dearly to attend—now that would indeed be an act of charity.

⌒ The Voice of Experience ⌒

DEAR MISS MANNERS:
If you had to give a single piece of advice to a couple who want to break into society, what would it be?

GENTLE READER:
"Don't bother."

⌒ *Party Favors* ⌒

The inflated expectation and proliferation of party favors and souvenirs has led to some ugly behavior. One need only linger at the door as the late crowd departs from a swish charity event.

Inevitably, the little shopping bags of free perfume and gadgets that are considered as essential to the festivity as drinks will have run out before all the charitable guests do. The tickets for these fund-raisers may be hundreds or even thousands of dollars, and the ticket holders may have many times that in the way of dry goods on their own persons. Yet this deprivation arouses an unseemly display of righteous and unseemly indignation.

Thus the sweet gesture of giving guests party favors, adapted—as so much modern behavior is—from the model of the children's birthday party, has developed into an entitlement and a disappointment.

At that, the behavior of the disgruntled, also patterned on that at children's birthday parties, is likely to be a step above that of some of the earlier-departing ticket holders. They are the prime suspects in causing the shortage by swiping more than one bag of party favors apiece.

Invitations and Replies

MISS MANNERS provides a sympathetic shoulder for those who have come to be known as People Who Still Entertain. Many of their guests think of them as a subdivision of People Who Still Wear Spats—eccentrics who are pleasant company, but whom no one in his right mind would think of imitating.

What is it that these genial folk do that is so strange? They invite friends home instead of meeting them at restaurants. They mark special occasions, theirs and other people's, with parties. They give dinner parties for no reason other than getting people together whose company they enjoy and think would enjoy one another's, undertaking all the planning and work themselves.

What do they get in return? Lots of happy times, pleasant memories and the satisfaction of knowing that their hospitality has been a source of delight for others.

That, along with the odd bottle of wine handed over at the door, ought to be enough, their guests believe. That hosts should also expect definitive replies to their invitations and honored commitments strikes the people from whom they expect this as excessive.

Indeed, anyone who has not quit entertaining altogether has already scaled down his or her expectations, forfeiting most traditional hostly privileges. Guests have long since ceased to allow their hosts to control such things as time of arrival or departure, guest list, menu or dress code, and instead routinely announce that they are arriving late, going on to another party, bringing someone extra, eating selectively and not dressing up.

But People Who Still Entertain do cherish the hope that some day they too will be invited to cross the thresholds of some of their guests. They do occasionally get reciprocal invitations, but these tend to be to meet people in restaurants, attend fund-raisers or otherwise tag along and entertain themselves at what their sort-of hosts are planning to do anyway.

Then there is what one Gentle Reader calls the half-invitation. "Our acquaintances don't seem to be able to actually fully invite us do things. Instead we get emails or phone messages such as: 'We really enjoyed going to the emu races with you last Saturday. We should get together again sometime soon. Give us a call some-time. Thanks, Pat & Pat.' I believe they are sincere, just indecisive or wanting others to take charge. We don't mind being the instigators, it's just that sometimes we'd like to let others take charge and let us relax and enjoy the company."

⌒ *"Hold the Date"* ⌒

DEAR MISS MANNERS:

Fully two years before the actual event, some friends sent us a "Hold-The-Date" notice for their son's Bar Mitzvah. The actual invitation arrived about five weeks before the Bar Mitzvah.

Five or six months before the Bar Mitzvah, my wife found out it was the date of her college's 25th reunion (she realized that it was her 25th reunion year, but she didn't know the precise date until the college announced it), which she was very much looking forward to attending.

Following the rule of "first come, first served," I argued that we were obligated to go to the Bar Mitzvah, since its date had been made known to us first. My wife argued that the actual invitation to the Bar Mitzvah arrived after she had read about the 25th reunion date in the Alumni Bulletin. So the date was already "taken," so to speak, and we should have declined the Bar Mitzvah invitation when it arrived.

We ended up going to the Bar Mitzvah.

In my opinion, our friends had sent the "Hold-The-Date" card precisely for the reason of pre-empting any other plans for that date, so it would be socially awkward to claim a prior invitation. Very likely, they believe that they were doing the prospec-tive guests a favor by allowing them to plan their calendars far in advance. My wife thinks "Hold-The-Date" notices are tacky, and that only the genuine invitation "counts" in determining whether we accept. We would both be interested in your views, especially since we have just received another "Hold-The-Date" card from different people.

GENTLE READER:

And you see control of your life disappearing as this catches on and people start booking your future without your consent.

No, no, calm down. The "hold the date" card is not a summons, only a warning.

Miss Manners cannot agree with your wife that it is tacky to warn people when their company will be requested, but she acknowledges that receiving such notice does not constitute an acceptance. Legal arrangements may be binding forever (or they may not be, depending on the quality of the lawyer retained by the person who wants out), but social arrangements far into the future lapse if they are not confirmed.

The only problem is that no one quite agrees on when this is. If you agree to go to dinner in two weeks, you had better show up; if you agree to go to dinner next winter, you had better confirm before you do. If you accept an invitation to go skiing at someone's chalet next winter, you had better show up; if you accept an invitation to go shopping at the mall in two weeks, you had better confirm before you do.

Miss Manners regrets that she cannot produce an exact formula, but the matters to be weighed are the importance of the occasion and the importance of the social tie. Now a bar mitzvah is an extremely important occasion, but, then, two years is an extremely long time socially. A person engaged to be married in two years would be prudent to confirm the commitment sometime during those two years rather than simply appear at the altar when they are up.

If you are close with these friends, you will consider their ceremonial occasions a high priority, and be grateful that they have given you ample time to decline lesser invitations, as well as to make any necessary travel arrangements. If you are not, you are at liberty to decline (without an excuse, although in this case, you could have pleaded a commitment to attend the reunion whatever its date) when the actual invitation arrives. However, if you accept the actual invitation, no other appointment—unless with a surgeon or an undertaker—can take precedence.

In other words, you may well consider yourselves bound to attend the bar mitzvah before receiving the invitation, but it would be the friendship that bound you, not the advance notice.

～ The Belligerent Invitation ～

As Miss Manners recalls, offers of hospitality used to be written in a charmingly suppliant tone. Would-be hosts didn't simply invite people, they begged, pleaded and cajoled:

"Please come . . . we would be so happy if you would join us . . . it would be such fun to have you here . . . I would be thrilled . . . We were hoping . . ." Even the most formal invitations emphasize what a pleasure the guests' company would be or what an honor their presence.

Some of this ingratiating wording is retained through habit, but Miss Manners fears that the spirit is lost. The modern invitation soon turns to snarling:

"Reply by December 16."

"Dress creatively."

"Female guests should not wear black, red, white or orange."

"Adults only."

"By invitation only."

"No smoking."

"Promptness requested."

"Send in an original poem for our memory book."

"Submit a square for our quilt."

"Bring a dish that serves eight."

"Bring a food donation for the cause."

"Bring your checkbook."

"Cash bar."

"Currency only."

"Monetary gifts preferred."

And a new one on Miss Manners to which a Gentle Reader reports being subjected: "Leftover food and drink welcome."

She recognizes that part of this bossiness—the part that isn't screaming greed—is the guests' own fault. If they behaved themselves, it wouldn't be necessary to bark orders at them. But the solution of making so-called guests pay their own way is a crass one.

There is a certain amount of direction that hosts must legitimately provide. They set the date, time, place and style of the event, and get extra credit if they throw in how to get there and where to park. And as a sad commentary on human behavior, requesting a reply has crept into the language of both formal and informal invitations. It used to be obvious that if someone asked you over, you had to reply, yes ("I'd love to") or no ("Oh, I'm so sorry, that's the day I wash my beard").

Additional orders, especially any concerned with money or presents, are rude. Miss Manners lives in hope that guests will tire of hearing them and just go ahead and do their duty. Wouldn't it be worth it to be spared all that nagging?

Secondhand Invitations

DEAR MISS MANNERS:

I have been alone for a number of years, and on some occasions have been invited to attend various affairs. However, the invitations come through the third persons not the hostess. They tell me that so and so is giving a shower or the like, and to bring me along too. If for some reason I'm unable to attend, I'm told to call the hostess so she will not prepare the extra place setting.

The latest is a wedding where a relative told me that I am invited. I do not feel bound to respond if I do not receive a direct wedding invitation, and I hope you agree.

GENTLE READER:

People who forge etiquette rules should try harder to make them sound plausible. How likely is it that there is a rule stating "Secondhand invitations must always be answered firsthand"?

Miss Manners recognizes no such thing as the secondhand invitation, for any but the most informal, drop-by of occasions, and even then, the person a firsthand guest has been asked to bring should have the invitation confirmed by the hosts. Considering that your own relative did this to you, Miss Manners can only suspect that you are being treated shabbily because you are single, an unspeakable practice but a common one.

Of course you needn't get in touch with hosts who have not gotten in touch with you, and of course you shouldn't go. But Miss Manners doesn't want you staying home all the time either. She suggests you make a point of sending gracious invitations of your own to any of these people you consider worth seeing in spite of this appalling lapse. Not only will this demonstrate that you are willing to socialize with them, but it will show them how this is properly done.

Impulsive Invitations

The ancient Greek laws of hospitality are the ones to which Miss Manners still subscribes. A host's duties to anyone under his roof are sacred, no matter how anxious he may be to polish him off, for reasons related or unrelated to the visit. However, if the Greeks had followed Miss Manners' rules of preventive hospitality, they would not, she suspects, have had to give their guests such expensive hints as fully manned ships.

Some people are naturally careful about the invitations they issue, and others enjoy promiscuous socializing. But a surprising number of people are subject to hysterical fits of hospitality, in which they issue invitations ruinous to their every comfort, with mad insistences that these be accepted.

"Let's all go over to my house!" they cry, just as the fatigue of an evening's round of merriment hits them.

"Come on—I won't hear of your going home this early. I'm right near by, and I'll whip up something delicious in a jiffy."

"Don't be silly—you're not going to stay in a hotel," they declare to acquaintances who speak of coming to their town to look for jobs and houses, however long that might take. "I have all this room, and it won't be any trouble at all. I'll hardly know you're here."

"Why, we've been talking about going to Mexico too!" they scream brightly to people who are part of the ties they had been scheming for months to get away from for a complete rest. "Let's rent a van and all go together."

To anybody who will listen, they say, "Come by any time—any time at all, we'd love it," when they had planned to get some work done at home.

These are the people who go to pieces when their privacy is invaded. If you think they look bad, you should see their spouses. Miss Manners' attitude is that it is better to bar the door to unwanted guests than to back them out through it. She therefore believes in strong measures to break the invitation habit: Never issue invitations on the spot to people you have just met. Instead, find out where to reach them, which is just as flattering, and do not call with a specific invitation until you have slept on it.

No invitations to spend more than three hours under one's roof should be issued without the consent of all of those who dwell under it, if they are to be responsible for entertaining the guests. If one spouse cannot think why the Awful family should not be asked to spend their spring vacation in the guest room, the other ought to be able to. And if neither of them can, the children, who have met the Awful children, may have some information to contribute.

It is not more gracious to issue open-ended invitations than timed ones, and besides, it is insane. "Please stay with us till Thursday" and "We're free Sunday between four and six, and would love to see you" are perfectly respectable offers of limited hospitality. They do not result in the hosts' sneaking off to write Miss Manners desperate letters begging her to tell them how to get their guests to leave.

⌒ Invitations to Pay ⌒

DEAR MISS MANNERS:

My mother's 80th birthday is next weekend. We, her two sons and their spouses and a daughter, are taking her out to a very nice restaurant. We will be paying for and supplying the pre drinks, cakes, present, a commemorative 80th engraved gift and Mom's dinner and of course our dinners. We invited some of my mother's friends and relatives to the restaurant for her party. My Mother is upset that we expect her friends to pay for their own dinners. We are not rich and with Christmas just around the corner we are really feeling the bite. Who pays for what?

GENTLE READER:

Ah, yes, Miss Manners keeps hearing that so-called guests should be able to understand that they are not being invited to partake in hospitality, but are expected to purchase the opportunity to attend other people's personal social events. What she fails to hear is that so-called hosts might understand that if they cannot afford to entertain in a certain style, they must entertain in a style that they can afford.

Hosts pay for guests. Miss Manners is afraid that you are not breaking her heart with your filial devotion and Christmas obligations. Nice children think it more important to do what their mother feels is right than to embarrass her with an outing that they cannot afford.

DEAR MISS MANNERS:

Ladies today often receive invitations to formal events that require that tickets be purchased. If the lady wants to invite a gentleman with whom she does not share an intimate relationship, is it appropriate for the lady to ask the gentleman to pay for the tickets, or is it the responsibility of the lady to purchase tickets and invite the gentleman?

My friends and I have been puzzled about this for several years. We are divorced, and of an age at which attending benefits are a regular part of our social lives.

GENTLE READER:

Miss Manners is afraid that there is no age or condition in which it is proper for one person to issue an invitation and then tell the person who is invited to pay the bill. Nobody likes it, and only deposed royalty can get away with it.

~ *Invitations Not to Donate* ~

DEAR MISS MANNERS:

We're giving a party a few months from now, celebrating my sixtieth and my mother's ninetieth birthday, which fall about a week apart. I don't want the invited guests to feel obligated to give gifts. My mother, especially, doesn't want gifts. What is the most tactful and effective way of handling this:

1. Don't say anything on the invitations about its being a birthday party.
2. If the invitations say it is a birthday party, put "no gifts" in some form on the invitation.
3. Enclose a separate note with the invitation conveying the no-gift message.

GENTLE READER:

Although Miss Manners sympathizes with your motivation, she is opposed to conveying the message "No gifts" on an invitation in any form, as it is not up to the hosts to expect presents, even if they wish to head them off. Therefore, Miss

Manners chooses your first solution. It will be all the more fun to announce the birthdays at the party.

⌒ *Reciprocal Invitations* ⌒

DEAR MISS MANNERS:

Some people whom I don't like finally lured me to their home by inviting a couple whom I had always wanted to meet. Now that I know this couple socially, I would like to include them at my next dinner party. Frankly, the people who introduced me to them wouldn't fit in. I seem to recall that there was an old rule about not inviting new people unless you also invite the people through whom you met them, but I don't know why or whether this is still in effect?

GENTLE READER:

Yes, it is, but you need invite them only once. The purpose is to clothe the art of social climbing with some decency, so that the act of acquiring new friends is not directly linked with the related act of dropping old ones.

DEAR MISS MANNERS:

If the Browns invite the Smiths for dinner for a particular evening without suggesting a date that is mutually convenient, is it up to the Smiths to do the inviting in the near future? Does this let the Browns off the hook, so to speak?

GENTLE READER:

Having made one social overture, the Browns have established their desire to offer hospitality to the Smiths. They may do so once more. If the Smiths wish to establish social contact, they may issue an invitation after refusing the first, or after the second. If, as your comment about "the hook" suggests, these people do not really care for one another, they may all forget the whole thing right now with no one's feelings being legitimately hurt.

⌒ *Failing to Reciprocate* ⌒

DEAR MISS MANNERS:

If you visit people several times and they do not repay calls; you write letters and get no answers—I say the people are giving you a message. My family disagrees. Will you please advise the proper etiquette?

GENTLE READER:

Look at it this way: If such people really want to maintain a relationship, there are many things they can do. They can explain that something has prevented them from seeing you but that they truly want to, they can also extend invitations, they can call and protest that their neglect should not be counted as a lack of interest. If they don't want to have anything to do with you, what more can they do to show this than exactly what they have done? Miss Manners believes that it is essential to proper, dignified behavior to know how to accept a snub graciously.

RESPONDING

"R.s.v.p."

DEAR MISS MANNERS:

Please solve this debate. R.S.V.P. is French for Reserve Seating Via Phone. Is this correct, or the letters have no significant meaning?

GENTLE READER:

Evidently they signify nothing to most people, because everyone who offers hospitality suffers from the ignorance of people who refuse to either take it or leave it.

Your translation is a new one on Miss Manners, who would be amused if she weren't horrified by the implication that hosts should be treated like airlines, in that the only obligation to them is to secure oneself a place if one wants one. At that, it is a step up from ignoring their overtures altogether.

The French abbreviation R.s.v.p. (Miss Manners prefers the upper- and lower-case version) stands for "Repondez, s'il vous plait," which means "Respond, please." The fact that the French phrase for "please" is literally "if you please" should not imply that there is an option here.

Accepting

DEAR MISS MANNERS:

Would Miss Manners please tell me, once and for all, what is the correct way to answer a formal invitation?

GENTLE READER:

All right, Miss Manners will tell you, but she is under no illusion that it will be once and for all. Now pay attention:

Mr. and Mrs. Perfect
accept with pleasure
the kind invitation of
Mr. and Mrs. Hoping
For Saturday, the twenty-third of November

These gracious words are handwritten, and each line is centered on plain white or ecru paper. You will notice that Miss Manners does not consider it necessary to repeat, in the answer, every gruesome detail of the invitation, such as the fact that there will be dancing, that it will take place in a club because their house isn't grand enough, or that they have palmed off their daughter Lucretia Marie. This is called modern, streamlined living.

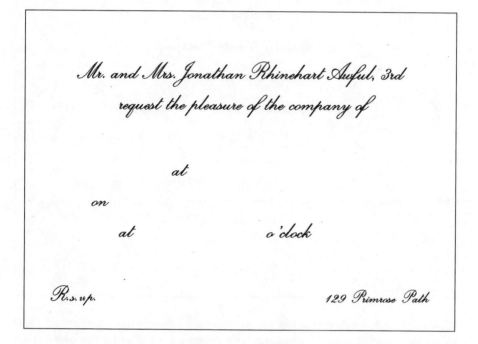

An all-purpose invitation on which one fills in the name of the guest, the type of event (dinner, tea, reception), the date and the time. The "R.s.v.p." may be crossed out and replaced with "To remind" for a second round.

Vice Admiral Stacy Awful-Nuisance

accepts with pleasure

Mr. and Mrs. Awful's

kind invitation for

Saturday, the Third of February

at eight o'clock

General Trevor Nuisance

regrets exceedingly

that he will be unable to accept

Reply to a formal invitation to dinner, tea, reception, small dance, whatever. The answer may specify the occasion ("to dine," "to a dance" with the modest "small" of the host omitted) but need not. This is a partial acceptance, with the husband declining. The paper is that of the wife, because she is writing; a general's wife would not use his flag.

DEAR MISS MANNERS:

What is the best way to handle a "stall" when I offer an invitation to either a friend or a man I am dating to join me for an evening or a day out? In my experience it is very rare that a friend who says they'll get back to me is courteous enough to actually call me at all. I make every effort to be polite and thoughtful of my friends and dates when offering invitations. If one person does not want to go, although they will be missed, I want to know right away so that I can ask another person. I do not want to be put in the position of being stalled but I would like to offer invitations. Is there a polite phrase I can use to tell someone I want an answer at the time I offer the invitation?

GENTLE READER:

"Oh, I'm so sorry, you must be terribly busy, I'll try you another time."

Miss Manners is suggesting that you treat a stall as if it were a definite no. Ordinarily, one would allow a day for friends to discover that they had failed to consult their office calendars or spouses or children, all of whom had already booked their time. But those who do not get right back should no longer be entitled to such a courtesy. Any attempt to explain that they are undecided, rather than declining, should be brushed aside with the explanation that although you need to plan now, you understand that they are not in a position to accept and you wouldn't dream of pushing them.

DEAR MISS MANNERS:

When invited to a party, I always like to know who else is invited, so I can be mentally prepared to meet them. Is it improper to ask the hostess who else will be there?

GENTLE READER:

This would depend on whether you ask before or after you accept the invitation. Discovering a previous engagement after you hear that the hostess is asking her high school sorority sisters whom she hasn't seen in years is decidedly bad form. To announce heartily, "Oh, won't that be fun!" and then add offhandedly, "Who else are you asking?" seems to Miss Manners to be within the bounds of politeness. The only problem that a prospective guest might have in taking the initiative in this is that the guest list might not yet be complete. The response, if the hostess doesn't seem to know yet who else will be there, is to be flattered that she took care to secure you first.

⟨⟨ Failing to Respond ⟩⟩

DEAR MISS MANNERS:

What would you do if you received minimal "R. S. V. P.'s" to an upcoming party you were hosting? It seems pretty rude to not even respond to an invite, but do you track everyone down?

GENTLE READER:

Unfortunately, you have to, unless you want a lot of leftovers or a lot of hungry guests. If it were Miss Manners, she would hang on to the list of people who needed prodding. It will serve as an invaluable reminder, for the next party, of whom not to invite.

⟨⟨ Accepting but Not Attending ⟩⟩

DEAR MISS MANNERS:

Over the years, I have read several letters from writers who have complained about guests invited to catered functions not showing up, and the related costs for the "no-shows." These writers need to keep in mind that a caterer does not charge extra for a "no-show," just the same amount as a guest who did show up. They are paying the same amount whether that guest showed up or not (after responding that they would show).

What they are missing is the pleasure of that person's company. After all, the hosts cared enough (hopefully) about that person to include them in a significant event in their lives. Maybe they could keep the issue in perspective and not take it as a financial affront to them.

GENTLE READER:

They know that. They just think it is more respectable to admit to caring about money than to admit to caring whether their friends are polite to them.

THE SOCIAL UNIT

If Judgment Day were scheduled for tomorrow, the question most people would be worrying about today would be "Can I bring a date?"

The kaleidoscopic state of love these days has left everyone uncertain about who goes with whom, including, sometimes, the parties concerned. As always, it is the innocent who suffer most from these couplings and uncouplings. Miss Manners is referring, of course, to hosts and hostesses. If you invite an impossible person for the sake of getting his marvelous spouse, you will be informed that he will come, but not she. If you have finally captured the perfect mate for a lonely friend, that friend will insist that she bring someone of her own choice along. There are roommates who hate being invited together, because it should be obvious that they are trying to lead their own lives, and roommates who are furious about being invited individually, because it should be obvious that they are inseparable.

Let us try to salvage a semblance of order by defining what is a social unit of two and what is not. The most likely couple is the one that is engaged—that is, engaged in the sense of having decided to get married, not just using the term to confer respectability on their children. Engaged couples must be invited together, but the reward is that they nearly always appear together. (For the application of this rule to wedding guests, please see p. 401.)

Less certain is the married couple. While they must be invited together, they must, if necessary, be accepted singly. It is considered offensive, for instance, not to urge a wife to attend by herself just because her husband is out of town. One also may find that the couple has separated or divorced since last seen the previous week. In that case, the one who answers the invitation is the one who is urged to attend alone.

Unmarried couples, whatever their genders, are generally offended if not invited together. However, it is up to them to make themselves known as a social unit, as in, "Oh, Perry and I always go out as a couple."

The most grateful of all to be invited to the same gathering are adulterous lovers, and the more dangerous the situation, the more thrilled they are to be treated conventionally. You may not want to countenance such relationships, but if you do so, even perhaps providing a cover excuse, they will cherish you as do no other guests.

The least grateful are the single people involved only in transitory alliances, who nevertheless will not trust your ability to provide entertaining company, but insist on bringing their own dates. This practice should be discouraged. With all the couples one has to allow for, the least single people can do is to appear singly. Otherwise, they will have no one but themselves to blame when they come around whining that they have such a hard time meeting anyone new.

~ Going Along ~

DEAR MISS MANNERS:

My mom and dad were given an invite to a Christmas party. On the envelope it reads Mr. and Mrs. My mom says I can go!

I say no because my name was not put on the guest list. If the envelope reads Mr. and Mrs. and Family or if the invite is for my mom and dad and me, only then I can go along.

I say I am right. My mom says she is right. Please help me out.

GENTLE READER:

Help you? Miss Manners wants to grab you and put you in the etiquette business. Without parental guidance—even in the face of misguidance—you were able to figure out something which has mystified much of the adult population—namely, that there is a relationship between the people who are being invited to a function and the names of the people who receive invitations. No well-bred person assumes that anyone whose name is not written on the invitation is invited.

~ Going Alone ~

DEAR MISS MANNERS:

My husband is not interested in meeting and socializing with other people. I'm involving myself in church and have met wonderful people. I find myself receiving and refusing invitations to include my husband for dinners, seasonal parties, quiet get-togethers, etc. He feels as if I'm imposing on him people of whom he has no need.

Where do I stand socially? Should I resign myself to nursery school mothers and women's church groups? Have you any suggestions on how to encourage some socializing with adults from time to time as a couple? Should I go it alone as if I were single, not dating other men, obviously, but attending parties alone?

GENTLE READER:

Miss Manners attributes the high divorce rate to the custom of considering married couples to be socially inseparable. This is an excellent reason for conducting your own social life, independent of your husband, but if you need another reason, it is that this gives you lots of interesting material with which to entertain your husband privately afterward. However, if you reciprocate invitations with dinner parties, your husband should not absent himself.

∽ "And Guest" ∽

DEAR MISS MANNERS:

If I receive an invitation that says, "and guest," am I obliged to bring a guest, or can I go alone (having indicated beforehand that I will be unaccompanied)?

Also, could I take a female friend, or does it have to be a date? As an unattached 29-year-old woman, I would rather attend some events, like weddings, alone or with a girlfriend instead of dragging along some poor fellow who will be bored stiff while I spend the night explaining to assorted people who he is and whether or not we are "serious." Can I attend such events alone or with a friend, or should I just decline invitations addressed to me, "and guest"?

GENTLE READER:

Miss Manners has been waiting for people to catch on that one of the most useful functions of a wedding is to inspire other weddings. Now, more than ever, when the traditional respectable venues for eligible people to meet have all but disappeared, an event at which they get to meet all of the relatives and friends of people they already like should be considered a godsend.

The silly habit of "and guest" kills that possibility. It also ropes strangers to the hosts into a wedding or other grand occasion in which they have no emotional investment. Miss Manners heartily encourages you to attend such events alone. You will be able to flirt with all the eligible gentlemen while their dates aren't looking and the other ladies are occupied looking after theirs.

∽ Unknown Guests ∽

DEAR MISS MANNERS:

When my wife and I planned a dinner party for younger couples in my office, we discovered that many of the married couples use different names. For example, it was not Mr. and Mrs. John Smith; it was Mr. John Smith and Ms. Lydia Brown. The problem was how to address the invitations.

We solved the problem in the case of each of the female office members by addressing the envelope only to her, and stating on the invitation, "We hope that you and your husband will be able to join us for dinner," etc. In the case of each of the male office members, we addressed the envelope only to him, and included a similar message in the invitation. We would like to know whether this was an appropriate way of handling the situation. Or should we have addressed the envelope to Mr. John Smith and Ms. Lydia Brown?

GENTLE READER:

Either is correct, but your solution is particularly good because it emphasizes your wanting the office worker, whether or not the spouse can attend. In fact, it's so clever, Miss Manners wishes she had thought of it herself.

⟨ Estranged Couples ⟩

DEAR MISS MANNERS:

Will you please advise me how to address invitations to a couple who are separated, when you wish to invite both, each with a friend or escort? They are living at different addresses.

GENTLE READER:

It should be an exciting party. Write to each separately, at each separate address, and state your invitation and the fact that it includes the opportunity for each to bring a guest. It is, of course, common courtesy to inform these people that they will be confronted with—and exposing their accompanying guests to—their estranged spouses, but Miss Manners understands that doing so may ruin the fun you have planned for the evening.

⟨ Inviting by Gender ⟩

DEAR MISS MANNERS:

Do you have to invite the same number of men as women, or does it matter if you have more of one sex or the other?

GENTLE READER:

It depends on what sort of activity you are inviting them to engage in. If the activity is to be conversation, it doesn't matter.

(For seating at a formal dinner, please see p. 576.)

BREAKING SOCIAL ENGAGEMENTS

There are social engagements that may be broken, and those that may not. For example, a time-honored method of indicating that you do not wish to fulfill an engagement to be married is to fail to show up at the altar. It is a dramatic and effective way to indicate that your ability or disposition to go on has changed. It is quite another thing to fail to show up at the altar if you have promised to be a maid of honor or a best man. That would be truly unforgivable.

In the matter of dinner engagements, the following may not be broken under any circumstances short of sudden death: seated dinners for ten people or fewer, dinners at which you have been requested by the hosts to help entertain a difficult guest, and restaurant meals when you have promised to meet one other person and cannot notify him or her that you will not be there, leaving that person to sit there playing with the napkin for everyone to see. As for theater engagements, it depends on how hard it was to get tickets.

DEAR MISS MANNERS:

I know you're not supposed to break one date when a better one comes along. I went by this rule when I was dating because my mother drummed it into me, and I think I missed out on some terrific opportunities while I dutifully entertained the drips. Virtue isn't always rewarded. Anyway, now I'm married, and my husband and I love to go out. We don't feel bad about breaking a date to go out to eat with another couple if someone else invites us to a dinner party, because that seems to be a different level of engagement, if you know what I mean. But what about canceling one dinner party to go to another? Is there any socially impeccable way of doing this?

GENTLE READER:

Only one. The correct wording is:

> *Mr. and Mrs. Alexander Dashing*
> *regret extremely*
> *that an invitation to the White House*
> *prevents their keeping*
> *their previous engagement for*
> *Saturday, the seventh of March*

(For refusing to go, at the proper refusal time, please see p. 703 [excuses].)

Social Procedure

~ *Timing* ~

DEAR MISS MANNERS:

Is "five-ish" socially correct form? If so, until what o'clock does "ish" embrace?

GENTLE READER:

"Ish" has come to be acceptable for spoken, although not written, invitations. It is extremely tricky, however, because the meaning varies with the hour and the nature of the invitation, so perhaps Miss Manners had better set out a timetable.

Five-ish for tea means five twenty P.M., while five-ish for drinks means between five thirty and six fifteen.

Six-ish for drinks means six forty-five, but six-ish for "an early supper" means one should arrive at seven and will be fed at seven thirty.

Seven-ish for "a drink" means seven ten, but seven-ish for dinner means one should arrive at seven thirty and will be fed at nine.

Eight-ish for dinner means one should arrive at eight fifteen and will be fed at nine. There is no nine-ish.

People who expect their guests to show up at specific hours should not ish.

DEAR MISS MANNERS:

For parties at which guests need not show up at a precise hour (e.g., cocktails, tea, at home), the first couple to arrive feels awkward about having arrived first. Furthermore, it is the fear of this awkwardness that causes guests to arrive at some random interval after the invitation time, and, in turn, causes hosts to second-guess their guests when choosing that invitation time in the first place.

My wife and I, therefore, invite a particular couple to serve as the designated first couple for the event. This couple, usually flattered to have been made an official part of the proceedings, agrees to show up exactly on time, and of course feels no awkwardness at arriving first. No other guest ever does arrive first.

While we cannot be sure that this custom of ours is responsible, we have found that, over time, guests are arriving nearer to parties' invitation times. If you like the idea of a designated first couple, please feel free to share it.

GENTLE READER:

Indeed, Miss Manners would be delighted, provided you will allow her the privilege of reciprocating.

Her contribution is sort of the bookend to yours. This is the designated first person to go home—the dear friend who, at a glance from the host, gets up and says, "My goodness, I had no idea what time it was!" Even after a wonderful evening, it serves to relieve guests who mistakenly believe that there is something rude about going home, as well as hosts who are beginning to believe they never will.

DEAR MISS MANNERS:

When you are having a party, dinner or whatever the occasion and you state a time that it starts, what do you do when a guest comes unexpectedly an hour early? What is the proper etiquette on handling guests arriving to a party before the start time of the event?

GENTLE READER:

First you reassure the embarrassed guest that he need not be embarrassed, by saying "I'm so glad to have a chance for a real visit with you before the others get here." Then you leave him sitting alone with his embarrassment while you finish getting dressed.

～ Entry Offerings ～

DEAR MISS MANNERS:

When a guest brings a package to a party I have normally thanked the person and then put the gift off to the side inconspicuously. I did not want others who did not bring something to feel like this was a required "entry fee."

However, last year one present was food; I only discovered later that this was a dish meant to be served that night. I am sure the giver must have thought I did not approve of the dish or the food since it never made it to the table. What is the best way to handle this situation?

Finally, when these types of gifts are received, I normally send thank-you notes. If this is correct, what is the difference between a regular present and a food gift in terms of thank-you notes? I have been told the host does not need to do this, that the partygoer should send me a thank-you note.

GENTLE READER:

Everyone has to be thanked. You have to thank the guests for their presents. They have to thank you for the hospitality. So the question Miss Manners is left with is whether this should be done in writing, or by word of mouth, or by chewing of mouth.

If possible, you should thank anyone who arrives with a present, grabbing a quick look at it, perhaps on a trip to the kitchen. You need not serve any food that is brought, because you presumably have a meal planned, and can assume you will enjoy this later. The guests are obligated to write their thanks to you, but you need write only if you have not managed to thank them on the spot, or if the present is an extraordinary one beyond the category of hostess present. A whole ox, perhaps.

DEAR MISS MANNERS:

It is common practice for dinner guests nowadays to bring gifts of wine. The wine may or may not be appropriate for the hosts' menu, and may or may not be any good. Does courtesy require that the host offer to serve wine given in this fashion at the meal to which the donor has been invited?

GENTLE READER:

Only presents of boxed wine brought to the spaghetti dinner parties of impoverished graduate students need be consumed when and with whom they appear. Otherwise, it is presumed that the host will provide all the goodies and that the guest's reward is emptying the host's larder and cellar. All one has to say, when accepting the wine, is "Why, how lovely. We'll think of you when we enjoy this." The fact that one plans to enjoy it in one's salad, with plenty of olive oil to counteract the taste, need not be mentioned.

DEAR MISS MANNERS:

I entertain often, in a formal way, and am justifiably known for my cooking, beautiful table settings, and so on. I do not think I overlook any detail for my guests' comfort and enjoyment. However, I cannot always say that the reverse is true.

The thing that annoys me most is people showing up on my doorstep with bunches of loose flowers that they just hand to me in a soggy mess. I am then expected to leave the front door, where I should be available to greet other guests, go into the pantry, find the right vase, fill it with water, arrange the flowers, find a place for the flowers in the living room—and you may be sure that I have already arranged the living room perfectly, with flowers where they are needed.

It seems to me that this is very inconsiderate of my time and of the duties I should be performing for my other guests during this time-consuming period. Isn't it proper to send flowers to a hostess either in the afternoon, before the party, or the next day to express appreciation? And don't you think it's more thoughtful to send arranged flowers in a vase, rather than a box of cut flowers or, worse, a bunch bought on a street corner?

GENTLE READER:

When Miss Manners entered the advice business, she knew that some day it would break her heart. As dear Nathanael West warned in his *Miss Lonelyhearts*, mass exposure to the insoluble suffering of this world can drive one to despair.

Now you've done it. Miss Manners doesn't know if she can bear to go on living in a world where people such as you—for surely, no problem is unique—are plagued with the untimely floral offerings of their friends. What to do? Miss Manners, although she is herself groping for the strength to go on, will offer one last timid, faltering suggestion to help you in your time of need: Why don't you just keep a filled vase in the pantry on party nights and dump whatever you get into it?

Two Social Skills

DEAR MISS MANNERS:

What is the proper reply when someone says "Excuse me"?

GENTLE READER:

A weak smile. The way to perform a weak smile is to raise the corners of the mouth without moving the center part of the lips, which remain closed. The length of the weak smile depends on the magnitude of the act for which the excuse was requested. For example, if a person has asked to be excused for burping, the weak smile in response should last only a fleeting moment, as did the burp, one hopes. If he is asking to be excused for breaking a porcelain vase that your great-grandfather brought back from China, the weak smile becomes fixed. This is to distract attention from the expression in your eyes as you stare at the fragment of china on the floor.

DEAR MISS MANNERS:

Now that I have mastered a "weak smile," I find that I have need for a "hollow laugh." Can you please tell me how to do it?

GENTLE READER:

Ah, the hollow laugh. Yes, indeed, it is a most useful social skill indispensable for responding to tasteless jokes, excessive kidding and other unacceptable forms of behavior. Miss Manners will be glad to teach it to you.

For the hollow laugh, you first smile with the lips wide open, displaying all of the forward teeth, while the rest of your face registers a puzzled look. You then force up from the throat a noise that does not resemble a genuine laugh, but rather imitates the words "Ha ha" or "Huh huh" that writers use to transcribe the sound of a laugh. When these words have been emitted, leave the open smile hanging there for a moment, as if you had forgotten about it, and then abruptly close the mouth into a solemn expression.

~ Background Music ~

The adage "Silence is golden" has never been more true, in Miss Manners' opinion. Its value is rising astonishingly every day, and it is getting correspondingly harder for most people to have any.

By silence, Miss Manners means something you can hear a bird tweet in. As if the hum of the mechanical world and the blather of the human world were not enough, individuals and industries have combined to produce a constant stream of nasty noise masquerading everywhere under the inappropriate name of music. Restaurants, hotel lobbies and shops are wired for sound. Hand-carried radios take care of the streets and buses. In private houses, the choice is usually between the informal, or lower-class, sound of unattended television sets or the fancy sound of mild classical music used as a "background."

(It has been objected that many fine pieces of music were written for the purpose of providing a background for the activities of patron-hosts and their guests. If Mr. Handel does not mind making *Water Music* while your guests are slurping their wine, Miss Manners will reluctantly permit it.)

Miss Manners is not even going to tell you what the medical consequences probably are to steadily assaulted ears. The fact is that all this noise is rude. It is rude to the captured audience of half-listeners, and what is more, it is rude to the music.

Music worth listening to is worth listening to, which is why symphony concerts provide the world's dullest "visuals," a huddle of people in black and white, sawing and blowing away. If you want something to look at while you listen, you can go to the opera and watch people stab one another, or go to a rock concert and watch them stab themselves with their instruments.

What you cannot do is put conversation or thought in the foreground and music in the background. Noise-producing industries have studies to prove that "background music" soothes (as on airplanes before takeoff or other antics) and stimulates (as in factories and hen houses). Whichever it is, it is an impertinence for public services or private hosts to attempt to manipulate the feelings of their customers or friends.

If you really want to soothe and stimulate a guest, what is wrong with sherry? The chief results of piped-in noise, as far as Miss Manners can see, are self-absorbed salesclerks who don't attend to their customers and half-shouted conversations that ought to be nearly whispered. We have gotten so used to it that silence has come to be considered somewhat frightening—an admission of social failure, or the world's being empty. It is now possible to make anyone confess anything—not by torture, but by looking at them in silence for so long that they will tell all, just to break it.

Here are some suggestions of other things to throw into silences while you are (please) tapering off noise:

A naughty smile.

A satisfied look around the room, pausing at each face.

A thoughtful expression.

An appreciation of the sound of ice clinking in glasses, crackling fireplaces or rustling leaves.

Words, produced by a mind that has had the quiet in which to think.

⌁ Checking Out the Background ⌁

DEAR MISS MANNERS:

Our living room has two large built-in bookcases, filled with some of our favorite books. (Still others fill up our study.) The first guests to arrive at our parties will occasionally stand near the bookcases and scan the book titles without taking any book from the shelf.

My wife regards such behavior as rude, and insists that such persons are probing too deeply into our personal interests. I, on the other hand, figure that the books are visible in the room; we aren't hiding them. For a guest to casually look at the spines of the books is a far cry from probing into someone's bathroom cabinet to see what cosmetics or medications are there.

GENTLE READER:

Accustomed as Miss Manners is to denouncing snoops, she is much too atwitter with curiosity to manage doing it here. What on earth are you people reading?

Swinging with Dick and Jane?

Recognizing the Rodents in Your Kitchen?

And if so, why don't you tuck them behind Stephen Hawking's *The Theory of Everything* where no one will ever find them?

People are supposed to talk about books. This is respectable conversation. It is actually fun. Miss Manners knows people who chase around their hapless friends, desperate to make them read their own favorites, and are chased by them in turn. (All right, she is referring to herself.) The loathsome term "conversation piece" is applied to books that are left around expressly for the purpose of getting a good conversation going.

(Free anecdote: Once when Miss Manners' Aunt Helen was trying to be hospitable to a neighbor, conversation was lagging for lack of an interest in common. Valiantly, the neighbor looked about for a possible topic and her eye landed on Aunt Helen's poetry collection. "Oh," she said, "I notice you are interested in anthology.")

No, examining books on your hosts' shelf is not like looking into their medicine cabinet. It is like looking at the pictures on their walls. Miss Manners notices that you are interested in sunflowers, if your wife doesn't find that too personal an insight.

～ The Kitchen ～

DEAR MISS MANNERS:

I have several friends who are gourmet cooks, and I enjoy eating at their homes. But I never know what to do when the host goes into the kitchen. Should I follow him to be sociable? Or stay in the living room doing—what? One friend of mine got really irritated, it seemed to me, when I went into his kitchen to continue our conversation; another friend just kept shouting at me while she was in the kitchen and I was in the front room, until I felt I should go in there so she could converse without going hoarse. What would you do?

GENTLE READER:

Ask. By all means, you may ask Miss Manners, since Miss Manners knows everything, but you might also ask the individual cook if you should go into the kitchen or not. Some people enjoy entertaining in their kitchens, while others prefer that their guests not observe them sticking their fingers into the food, licking the stirring spoons, and other such maneuvers that good cooks perform.

⌒ *The Bathroom* ⌒

DEAR MISS MANNERS:

My partner, a person of genuine taste, has me confused, because she insists it is proper for the top of the lid of the toilet to remain raised, a sign of hospitality. This strikes me as a bit distasteful. I've always thought closing the top lid of the toilet was the better part of discretion.

GENTLE READER:

A sign of hospitality? You mean, like a welcome mat?

Miss Manners doesn't know what your partner is thinking, but hopes she will stop. That guests sometimes have to excuse themselves is a fact of life. We have no evidence that they derive comfort from believing that their hosts are pleased to recognize this fact.

⌒ *The Guest Towels* ⌒

DEAR MISS MANNERS:

Since there's no longer a His towel (as in those His & Hers sets that were popular several decades past) how can I make it clear that the towels on the rack are Mine?

My place is small, hence the one bathroom must serve for both me and my guests. Though space is limited, I do have a basket of hand towels always available for their use. I wish some of my friends would do the same. There have been times I've dried my hands on my petticoat rather than the much used My towel hanging in their bathrooms.

Rather than insult them by labeling the basket For Guests (and some friends and family do not consider themselves "guests"), what can I do? Short of standing guard and directing them to use the guest towels, (which isn't practical when I am busy elsewhere with other "guests"), or simply removing all but the guest towels from that room (which also is not practical as I often have—and do heartily welcome—drop-in guests), HOW do I inform them that the towels in the basket are for their use?

Some of my family and friends are aware of the protocol and do use guest towels without being offended, but then another dilemma occurs: What to do with the used guest towel?? In my instance, there is enough space on the vanity top to leave the used/damp towels, but is there a better solution for those of us who practice good hygiene along with hospitality? When I am elsewhere and they do provide guest towels but there just isn't an empty spot to place it, what do I do with the used towel?

GENTLE READER:

Could someone please explain to Miss Manners how the guest towel got to be the great totem of modern times? She can't wait to hear the part about why people think it is more polite to allow their hosts to realize, when they clean up after the visit, how many hands they have shaken that were apparently never washed after use.

It strikes her that if people were to exercise only one form of self-restraint out of consideration for others, they might pick something better. Such as not scooting into parking spaces that other people are already positioned to back into.

Use the guest towels, folks. That's why they're called guest towels. And leave them crumpled on the rack or sink or basket, so the host can put them in the wash when you have left after a hygienic embrace.

Efforts to cure guests of this inhibition have been pitiful. Some hosts put out small terry-cloth towels in the hope that guests will think they use them for quick baths of their own, and that therefore anyone is free to grab them. Or paper ones, with the idea that the guests will figure they can destroy the evidence of their transgression, although not, one hopes, by making these disappear into the plumbing.

There are even hosts who have gone over the brink themselves and go in for a horror they call a "decorator towel," put out to tantalize guests who are not expected to use it.

Miss Manners is afraid the taboo may be too powerful. She suggests removing your bath towel when you have warning and, when you don't, issuing your own warning by calling out, "I'm afraid I've left my bath towel there—but there are towels for you in the basket."

～ The Buffet Table ～

DEAR MISS MANNERS:

As a general rule, does one proceed to the left or the right when approaching a buffet or tea table?

GENTLE READER:

The general rule that Miss Manners finds in effect is that everyone hangs back until the hosts are in despair, and then all rush forward at once, hovering defensively over whatever access to the table has been achieved, and then moving in either direction or both, bumping into one another and reaching across other people's plates.

This is not proper, and it isn't pretty either. The correct method is to start where the plates are, and to quit when you hear the people in line ahead of you saying, "That looks like that mousse again." You will find that the usual pattern requires you to go clockwise, although large buffet tables are set out in a mirror image fashion, so that one may pick either side and march in the direction of one's choice, still coming out with the same results as those who chose a different path. If one is really hungry, one may nibble discreetly as one goes along, thus clearing the plate at the same time one is refilling it, which may be kept up indefinitely or until the hosts wise up.

⌒ *The Departure* ⌒

If hospitality is a divine obligation, it certainly has an immediate earthly reward. Miss Manners is referring to that sublime moment when one's guests all go home. If they ever do.

Anyone who has prepared a meal for others and has set out clean implements with which it can be eaten, who has performed the feat of looking around his or her own living room at his dearest friends while managing to recite their names correctly, and who has spent an evening encouraging others to tell their best stories which he already knows by heart, deserves a treat. The treat is to remove his shoes and eat the leftovers.

This can be done only if the guests depart. It is nearly impossible to manage both giving guests a good time and getting them to budge promptly. No thoughtful host should be without his own resources for speeding the departing guest.

According to books drawn from the *Analects* of Confucius, as summarized by dear Harold Nicolson, an ancient Chinese guest was amply provided by his host with clues on when to leave. "When visiting a superior, it is permissible to ask leave to retire when the host either yawns, stretches himself, looks at his watch, or begins to eat leeks or garlic as a cure for sleepiness," Sir Harold noted in *Good Behaviour*.

Unfortunately, yawning and stretching are considered unsubtle in our society. Watch looking is borderline; watch shaking is out. Now that last suggestion—there is a wonderful idea. Miss Manners also admires Mr. Max Warburg, the Hamburg banker who is reputed to have concluded his entertainments by looking at a clock and declaring, "Why, you naughty clock, you're driving my guests away!"

For simple, modern good manners, Miss Manners recommends that the host merely arise at the proper time and, with a grateful smile and outstretched hand, say, "You were so very, very kind to have visited me." The key part is the stance. Few guests can remain planted in their chairs while a host or hostess is standing in front of them, beaming with smiles.

DEAR MISS MANNERS:

I like to think I'm a good guest, but sometimes, I wind up at parties that are uncomfortably crowded, or are held in basement apartments with uncomfortably low ceilings. (I'm over 6 feet tall, so this is an issue.) Under such circumstances, how long should I stay—30 minutes? an hour?—and keep up a sociable facade before ducking out politely, pleading another engagement (even if it's only on my own couch)?

GENTLE READER:

By ducking out, Miss Manners trusts that you, being an exemplary guest, could not possibly mean slipping out the door while the host's back is turned. That would be unthinkable.

The polite thing to do is to threaten to do so. You run up to the host when he is obviously engaged in talking to others and say, "I don't want to interrupt the party, but unfortunately, I have to tear myself away." Then you blubber about what a wonderful time you had, how you hate to leave, you wouldn't dream of letting him see you out and so on, all said heartily, while you back up toward the door. The leave-taking should add only about five minutes to the half hour minimum you must stay.

DEAR MISS MANNERS:

Is it true that the guest of honor must leave a party first because no one else is supposed to depart before that? It seems unfair. When a party is in your honor, you are likely to be having a better time.

GENTLE READER:

This is exactly why one must allow the others to go home. Being honored is enjoyment enough for one evening.

SOCIAL DISASTERS

DEAR MISS MANNERS:

This may sound silly, but I'm serious. When someone suffers a particularly embarrassing accident in front of you and many others, what is the socially appropriate response? My husband and I got into an argument about this. We recently visited Boston, and while we were there, we attended a large party where everyone was elegantly dressed. At the party, a lady in a low-cut gown tripped, stumbled, lurched across a table, falling face first into a bowl of guacamole dip, and in the process "popped out" of her top. After an initial stunned silence, practically everyone in the room burst out laughing, even though it was obvious that the lady was terribly embarrassed. Then the hostess rushed over to help her and ushered her upstairs.

After we left the party, I criticized my husband for laughing and told him I thought it was very bad manners. But he said that it was not impolite for people to laugh at something like that as long as they meant no harm and didn't "overdo" it. I said it was inconsiderate of the person's feelings to laugh at all. He said it's the social custom. Could you settle the argument?

GENTLE READER:

What do you mean "something like that"? Miss Manners doubts that there is anything in the world like an elegantly dressed Bostonian lurching across the room and diving face first into a bowl of guacamole dip while simultaneously disengaging her bodice from her bosom. Therefore, Miss Manners has a wee bit of trouble preparing a general rule for dealing with this eventuality. Nor, if she were your husband, would she attempt to justify a reaction on grounds other than direct cause and effect.

One might try to ignore a less spectacular accident. If, say, it were avocado dip, rather than guacamole, and the lady had merely trailed her sleeve in it, one could pretend not to have noticed. To pretend not to notice a performance such as you have described—even if it were humanly possible—would be to suggest that the lady did it all the time and her friends have gotten used to it. It is far better to comfort her later by telling stories of your own about hilariously embarrassing accidents you have survived.

～ Medical Emergencies ～

DEAR MISS MANNERS:

Please tell me the proper behavior for host, hostess, and guest when one or the other suffers a heart attack, stroke, or has a miscarriage during a party. I assume the correct thing would depend to some extent on the size of the gathering. Should house guests who are not relatives or close friends leave (or be thrown out)? Should guests at a large barbecue stay and eat? On what grounds can one cancel a party at the last minute? I would rather not go to the house of someone whose kid has the flu.

GENTLE READER:

Acute nausea, heart attacks and miscarriages are all acceptable reasons for canceling large parties. If they should occur when such a party is already under way, you are right in assuming that the party is over.

One small point of etiquette that you neglected to inquire about is how to treat the victim of sudden disaster. Allow Miss Manners to suggest that it is quite proper to take such a person to the nearest hospital, however much this may dampen the festive spirits of the other guests. These people may then, if they wish, hang around under the guise of "waiting to hear how she is" and may quietly consume the remaining barbecued ox while doing so. If, however, there is a medical reason against moving the ill guest, healthy guests are expected to remove themselves from the immediate scene unless they can be of some genuine practical assistance. Houseguests need not leave the premises entirely unless their rooms are needed.

What you think the size of the gathering has to do with anything, Miss Manners cannot imagine. It is as improper for seven carefully chosen dinner guests in formal clothes to watch the eighth one having a miscarriage as it is for a cocktail party comprising a year's worth of social obligations.

⟿ Bodily Injuries ⟿

DEAR MISS MANNERS:

Is it possible to be guilty of being rude when you absolutely can't help it? Everybody treated me as if I had made some terrible error, but I only reacted naturally. It was at a party, and I was sitting in a steel and leather chair. The arms were steel; this is important.

A woman I'd been talking to took the seat next to me, in another chair just like mine. In order to continue our conversation, she drew the chair up exactly next to mine, pinning my arm, which had been dangling over the arm of my chair, between the two steel beams. It hurt like crazy, and I screamed. She then said, stupidly, "Did I hurt you?"—and of course I said yes. Even if I hadn't, it was plain from the red mark on my arm that she had done considerable damage.

How it got to seem like my fault, I don't know, but I saw people glaring at me and shooting her sympathetic looks as I rubbed my arm. I can tell you other examples, but they are all pretty much the same. Each time, I have cried out in pain before I even thought about it. As often as not, the person who does it doesn't even apologize, so I'm not sorry that I let them know, in this perfectly natural way, that they did something wrong. What should I have done? After all, I didn't decide to yell; I just did.

GENTLE READER:

Natural instinct only excuses you so much in polite society. Etiquette, after all, is the imposition of civilized behavior over the chaos of instinct.

In society, we occasionally consider the motive. What might be an obvious insult—a direct blow, than which one can hardly deliver more of an affront—is not taken as such if no offense was truly intended. Granted that you could not help crying out, you must then reply to the stupid question by saying, "Oh, no, no, I'll be all right. I was just startled." The red mark will belie this, of course, but that only makes you seem the more saintly in your forgiveness. Miss Manners does acknowledge that the scream is helpful in obtaining the necessary apology. This apology is what should bring forth your denial. If none is forthcoming, you may leave the scream as your final remark.

⌒ Missing Property ⌒

DEAR MISS MANNERS:

Early this spring, we sat on the front veranda with a couple of dinner guests. It became cool, and I lent a new white sweater to the better half. I think she inadvertently wore the sweater home. She has an almost identical sweater. How can I ask her to check her closet without seeming to accuse?

GENTLE READER:

There are two matters here on which Miss Manners is not quite clear. (1) Did she have "an almost identical sweater" before you lent her yours, or is that what she has now? And (2) What is it you are trying to avoid "seeming to accuse" her of doing?

Miss Manners is puzzled because she suspects you of stating the problem in social euphemisms. Miss Manners adores euphemisms, and if you want to practice them on her before using them on your friend, that is fine. But Miss Manners needs to know—and you can be quite frank with Miss Manners, who never breathes a word of anything to anyone—whether your problem actually is: I lent a friend my sweater and she stole it from me and wears it now as if it were hers.

You see, if you really believed that she had inadvertently kept it, all you would have to do is to say, "Do you still have that sweater I lent you? I could use it if you don't need it," and she would return it. There's no rudeness involved in "seeming to accuse" someone of having been forgetful. Do that anyway, even if you think it wasn't inadvertent, because that would accomplish the same purpose, while saving face for her. That is what euphemisms are for.

DEAR MISS MANNERS:

Recently I borrowed seven sheep from a dear friend. They were to have mowed my lower lawn, but somehow they went out into the lane in the woods. When my dear friend came to collect them, there were only six sheep. My problem is, how do I compensate him for his lost sheep? I offered to pay him, but he refused. Then I sent him a gift certificate for one hundred dollars, but he returned it. I feel awkward about this large loss, for which I am responsible. What do you suggest?

GENTLE READER:

A leg of mutton? Or how about offering to baby-sit for his children? That ought to do it.

～ Spills ～

DEAR MISS MANNERS:

While engaged in animated conversation at a dinner party recently and holding my coffee cup momentarily motionless in an elevated position, I did not notice that I was holding it tipped at an angle, until shouts of alarm from several other guests made me aware that the cup was dripping rapidly (but fortunately, directly above its saucer). Feeling embarrassed at this faux pas, I meticulously picked up the saucer with my other hand, and carefully began pouring its contents back into my coffee cup, at the same time resuming my conversation. Almost immediately, however, I was startled by a cry from my hostess, and discovered to my astonishment that while I was still pouring, I had again inadvertently allowed the cup to tip, and now both the cup and the saucer were dripping directly onto the table.

My hostess was very angry, and I was understandably quite upset by this situation, considering that my intentions were only the best. Miss Manners, do you think that I deserved a public rebuke? Or, in a time when good conversation is so rare a commodity, do you not think that my hostess was unseemingly rude about this unfortunate incident? Also, what should I reply to wags who are now telling me that I can't handle drinking and talking at the same time, and should consider entering national politics?

GENTLE READER:

Why not enter national politics? You seem to take naturally to mistaking a well-meant warning against pursuing a course of disaster for a personal rebuke, and to feel that being a good talker and meaning well excuse you for making a mess of things.

DEAR MISS MANNERS:

At a formal embassy dinner, I was gesturing to make a point and accidentally knocked the meat tray from the waiter's hand, splattering an entire line of guests, including my dinner partner, who was wearing white. I feel terrible. Is there anything I can do to make amends?

GENTLE READER:
Renounce your social ambitions. You might just as well, under the circumstances.

~ *Falling Asleep* ~

DEAR MISS MANNERS:
From time to time, I give small dinner parties in which we talk about politics, art, theater, or other people, and they are anything but boring. I have a very dear friend who now and then falls asleep after dinner, in the middle of my party. Should I give her coffee, instead of the decaf she always requests? She is not old. I have talked to her about this problem, and I know she feels bad.

GENTLE READER:
Nearly everyone has, at one time or another, fallen asleep at a public or social event or watched someone else do so. But while it is common, natural and blameless, it nevertheless cannot be tolerated. It cannot fail to suggest boredom, even though that seldom is its cause, which could be medical. It also falls into the spinach-in-the-teeth category of actions, which cause more humiliation in the doer if he or she is uncorrected, than if it is pointed out at the time. (Please see p. 126.)

You must wake up your friend. Perhaps not with substituting coffee for decaffeinated liquids without her knowledge—Miss Manners is against administering stimulants to the unsuspecting—but with a word or an elbow. If no one else has observed your friend's mental departure from the party, you could grab her arm or nudge her, under the pretext of passing her a mint or brandy. If you cannot get near her without causing a disruption, call out her name and then draw her into the conversation, as in, "Marabelle! We were just saying how many wonderful candidates there are to choose from this year. What do you think?" Vague questions are best, you see, because even an alert person can be excused for replying, "Well, uh, I don't rightly know."

DEAR MISS MANNERS:
My leg fell asleep at a dinner party. I didn't want to make a fuss, and so I just sat there pinching it, but that didn't help, and I was in agony. Would there have been a polite way to handle this problem?

GENTLE READER:

Some medical emergencies take precedence over the ordinary rules of polite behavior. It depends not on the seriousness of the illness, but on how socially acceptable it is. Nothing would excuse your head's falling asleep, but the leg might squeak through. You could have waited for a pause in the conversation, announced calmly to the hostess, "I'm afraid my leg seems to have gone off again," and, with her permission, amused the guests by stamping around the dining room table until you had effected a cure. A more subtle solution would be to rub the back of the knee (yours, not your dinner partner's) to get the blood moving again.

APOLOGIES

A social nightmare:

You have wronged a friend, perhaps inadvertently, but apparently unforgivably. Apologies were proffered, and may even have been accepted, but things are not the same.

It becomes difficult to reach your friend, and impossible to secure a time when he or she is not too busy to see you. Further attempts at explaining are rejected as unnecessary, closing off any chance at obtaining forgiveness, which is not forthcoming.

Compounding the sadness of losing a friend is the misery of knowing that you brought the rift upon yourself. Loneliness and guilt—those unbeatable modern afflictions, all in one package.

Miss Manners is not without mercy, and often pleads on behalf of transgressors. Etiquette doesn't overlook social wrongdoing, but it has a lot of forgiveness built into it—if for no other reason, to put mercy in the bank in case one might need it oneself. Yet here is a worse version of that nightmare:

The avoidance and coldness are identical, but you cannot imagine what you did to deserve it. There must have been something, because a friendship that gave all signs of being mutually satisfying suddenly ceased with no explanation.

So now we have free-form guilt—the kind that doesn't dwell on one awful incident, but chases around mercilessly through one's past looking for that hidden cause. Only it may be a bum rap. The transgression could actually have been committed by the person who preempted the victim's opportunity to be offended (or, as Miss Manners would prefer to think of it, that person's opportunity to be graciously forgiving) by also doing the cutting.

These double crimes are often reported to Miss Manners by the perpetrators themselves. They admit that they neglected a social duty, such as appearing after accepting an invitation or offering thanks or condolences, and report themselves as "too embarrassed to face" their neglected friends.

Miss Manners is not charmed by this implication of self-effacement and remorse. What they are delineating is a plan to neglect the second social duty, namely that of apologizing for omitting the first one.

"But it's too late now," they wail at her.

This is a generally popular excuse. Procrastinators figure if they wait it out, whatever duty they were supposed to perform will be wiped off the record. But in this particular type of situation, the guilty party figures he has settled the record by administering his own punishment. He has sentenced himself to banishment.

That, too, fails to engage Miss Manners' sympathies. When it is too late for a simple apology, what is required is some full-scale groveling. Far from disappearing, the requirement has accrued additional penalties for being late.

Especially among friends, a good groveler can break down the grovelee in no time. As with consumer complaints, one person carries on about how dreadful this was and the other person is forced to argue that it's not all that important; the person who goes first gets to choose which role he plays, and the other one has to take the part that is left. Ordinary crimes of forgetfulness—as the dinner engagement

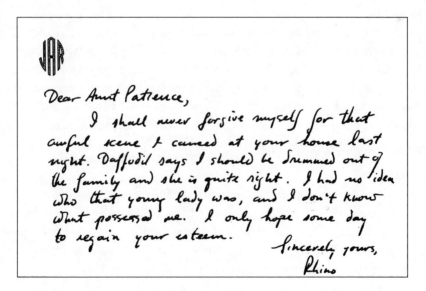

Dear Aunt Patience,

I shall never forgive myself for that awful scene I caused at your house last night. Daffodil says I should be drummed out of the family and she is quite right. I had no idea who that young lady was, and I don't know what possessed me. I only hope some day to regain your esteem.

Sincerely yours,
Rhino

A note of apology. This is a man's informal, monogrammed card, for short, informal letters.

might have been if it had been a large party, or served from the buffet, and if the absent guests had not been guests of honor—should be redeemed by an excess of thoughtfulness. One bombards the offended person with abject words, spoken and written, and with flowers until that person is exhausted enough to soften. The only excuse, as in so many acts better left uncommitted, is temporary insanity. To say "I was terribly busy" is another insult, meaning "I had more important things to do than to take time or effort to think of you." "That was such a dreadful, hectic time that I went out of my mind and neglected the very things that mattered to me most" is more like it.

The best apology for material damage is material. But "Can I pay for it?" is no help, said, as it is, with the knowledge that it will bring a protest, however insincere. "Who does your reupholstering?" or "What is your crystal pattern?" or "Who is your antiques dealer?" is infinitely more reassuring. In these cases, the bother, as well as the cost, should be assumed by the wrongdoer.

Silence, in contrast, transfers the blame, by default. That is a third social crime, right there.

⌒ *The Hungover Apology* ⌒

DEAR MISS MANNERS:

What do you say to a hostess the next day when you don't really remember how you behaved at her party? Maybe you were perfectly all right, in which case you don't need to apologize, and in fact, doing so would only call attention to something you got away with concealing, if you know what I mean. But maybe you weren't OK, in which case you ought to say something if you want to be forgiven and invited back some day. How about just "I had a wonderful time"? Is that neutral enough to be grateful-sounding without going into details?

GENTLE READER:

Well, no. She may be already aware, perhaps more aware than you, of how wonderful a time you had. The apology, if indeed you owe one, is likely to be needed in connection with the effect your wonderful time had on the rest of the party. How about saying to her, "You were magnificent"? That covers anything from her simply being a good hostess to her having tolerated your bad behavior.

⟶ *Accepting an Apology* ⟵

DEAR MISS MANNERS:

I am genuinely confused about what it means to forgive someone. Does it ultimately mean that, no matter what another person does to me, I must pretend to the best of my ability that nothing ever happened?

What is my responsibility when the offending party either refuses to apologize and accept responsibility for their actions or simply does not believe in apologizing, such as saying "love means never having to say you're sorry"? Is it ever correct for the forgiver to work out an agreement of forgiveness with the offender? Are there degrees/kinds of forgiveness depending upon whether the offender is friend, relative, coworker, soldier, criminal, stranger, institution, etc.?

I don't like it, but it seems to me that forgiveness boils down to the fact that no matter what another person does or says to me, I am the one who judged them to be wrong and who "let" them hurt me or make me angry. In essence, I am the weak one and a grudge holder; and forgiveness becomes my apology to the offender.

I can't change human nature—people will always do things to offend others. So, when an offense occurs, apparently I must abandon my sense of right and wrong just to keep peace? I must learn to not "let" people offend me, to swallow all pride, and to resign myself to living out my life as a doormat and perpetual forgiver. Is this what "forgive and forget" is all about?

GENTLE READER:

Well, no. Then we would just need "forget." There are two concepts there, and you can do either without the other.

Miss Manners has been known to forget offenses she would not forgive, simply because she doesn't want to carry around a lot of nasty stuff, but she does not wish to pass off as tolerance what is merely absent-mindedness.

Literary treacle aside—and Miss Manners advises against extracting your morality from romance novels—forgiveness is a response to an apology. Even accidents, obviously devoid of ill will on the part of the offender, require an apology.

Dinner Parties

IT IS POSSIBLE to consume an entire meal at home, sitting down at a real table as if one were dining out. Some have thought of using this as a way to entertain friends.

Naturally, this is confusing to people who have come to believe that restaurant manners are the last word in sophistication but never bothered with how to eat at home, let alone at someone else's. Whatever grace and dexterity they learned in order to elicit favorable judgments from the hired help at restaurants would be wasted on their families, they figured.

Restaurant manners are actually a spin-off from those that are supposed to be used privately, not the other way around, Miss Manners is afraid, and it is the private ones that are of a higher standard. No restaurant, no matter how fancy, can get away from the compromises that must be made because of the unpredictable and commercial nature of the business.

Miss Manners is prepared to help people make the transition by addressing some of the most common problems for those who are asked to go to their friends' houses to eat, rather than to meet them somewhere.

Q: How do I make a reservation, or is that necessary?

A: It is necessary, and you can't. You have to wait for them to call you.

Q: That's awfully exclusive, isn't it? But what if I don't know how many will be in my party?

A: It isn't your party. Only people who are asked by name can attend.

Q: How late can I cancel without a penalty?

A: Once you accept, you can never cancel.

Q: What do you mean, never? Suppose I change my mind? Suppose I get run over by a truck?

A: If you change your mind after accepting, you still have to go. It's true that you can arrange to be excused by being run over by a truck, but then you have to send a letter of apology, preferably accompanied by flowers.

Q: Is there a dress code?

A: Yes, and no one will tell you what it is. Inquiries will bring such non-guidance as "Oh, it doesn't matter" or "Just be comfortable," and the word "casual" has as many possible meanings as the number of people who so casually toss it in for every occasion.

Q: If I show up on time, will I be seated right away, or might I be told to get a drink until my table is ready?

A: You must show up on time, but you will still be given a drink elsewhere before being taken to the table.

Q: Is it all right to let them know after I arrive what I want to eat, or is it necessary to order in advance?

A: There is a fixed menu, no substitutes and no choices.

Q: Suppose I don't like it?

A: Okay, there is a choice: Take it or leave it.

Q: I'm very particular about wine. Can I bring my own?

A: You can bring it and hand it over, but you may never see it again. It will be considered a present, and is not likely to be served unless it happens to go with the menu and you have brought enough for everyone.

Q: How do I settle the bill?

A: By being charming and grateful and issuing a return invitation.

Q: Except for that, it's free?

A: Not of the need to be polite.

DEAR MISS MANNERS:

I understand that almost nobody sits down and writes out traditional, formal invitations to parties, dinners, dances, and the like—the kind of invitation that most people associate with weddings and embassy balls, but written out by hand rather than engraved or printed. Having said that, my wife and I are hosting a dinner, and we would like to send formal invitations to our friends. Please tell me how I might word such an invitation to our home.

Should I use titles even though these are good friends? (Mr. and Mrs. George Washington request the pleasure of Mr. and Mrs. John Adams' company for dinner . . .) Or would our full names suffice? (George and Martha Washington request the pleasure of John and Abigail Adams' company for dinner . . .)

Is it necessary to include the year, when it's obvious that one would never be inviting someone for dinner 13 months in advance? May we say "for dinner" and let everyone infer that they'll get cocktails and chat, too? Or should we say "for cocktails and dinner" so that they don't pack their own bottle of wine?

GENTLE READER:

Even though Miss Manners considers the formal dinner party just about the finest recreational activity we have (not counting the afternoon nap, with which it combines perfectly), you worry her.

Are you, in fact, giving a formal dinner? If so, are you inviting people you assume would enjoy this, whether because of their experience or their openness to new experience? If not, it would be pretentious and silly to attempt it.

The beauty of this form is that it is a set piece, its formal details—invitations, timing, clothes, food, service—intended as a flattering frame for the participants. You don't mess with those details to make it seem—well, less formal. Honorifics are always used, and the request is for the guests' company "at dinner" (not "for" dinner; the roast is for dinner, as old-fashioned wags were wont to say). "Dinner" is understood to include drinks, talk and, for that matter, bathroom privileges, so you need not spell these out. Telephone numbers and email addresses are not included, as the guests are expected to reply in writing. They are also expected to be smart enough to take the year for granted.

There should be a seating chart in the hallway, so that guests may study them before having to face the assemblage; cards with each lady's name put into a little envelope bearing the name of the gentleman who is to be her dinner partner; and place cards on the table. This gives the guests a sporting chance to fake remembering one another, avoid their dinner partners before dinner and, for the unscrupulous, to sneak into the dining room before dinner and improve their lot. And there should be handwritten menu cards on the table so the guests can pace their eating to leave room for dessert.

The table should be set with a white or off-white tablecloth in damask or lace, rather than the now-traditional flowered bedsheets or place mats. People who give formal dinner parties have no business being clever and creative. The centerpiece should be flowers flanked by candles, with small dishes of candy and fruit placed strategically and symmetrically. People who attend formal dinners should not require conversation pieces.

The guests should be announced as they first arrive, wives before husbands. Miss Manners is aware that this is reversed when the man has an official title, but has never liked that. She believes the two systems could be reconciled by giving all such titles to women. She expects the guests to arrive by eight minutes after the appointed time, and be allowed another twenty minutes for a drink before the butler announces, "Dinner is served." (Actually, Miss Manners prefers his saying to the hostess, "Madam is served.") Too bad for anyone who isn't there. People who give formal dinner parties should have learned ruthlessness.

She expects there to be identical platters and footmen (even if it is hard to find identical footmen these days) for each four to six guests. This is the only way to have proper Russian service, explained on p. 587. She does not want to see coffee at the table, or filled coffee cups, as the coffee should be poured in the drawing room when the liqueurs are offered.

However, she no longer cares to see ladies and gentlemen separate after dinner. There is no sense in being a slave to tradition.

If this has overwhelmed you, and you are simply giving a decorous dinner party, not one of high formality, a less formal invitation, but no less charming, should be issued. This is written in the first person: "We would be delighted if you could come to dinner . . ." with your names, minus honorifics, at the bottom.

THE GUEST LIST

The public sport of ruining people's lives by discovering their diaries or introducing their love letters into court is gone. Few people write such things anymore other than in emails sent to their entire address books, and as it has become the custom to deliver such information about oneself orally and voluntarily at social events, one could easily suppose that there are no written personal secrets in existence.

This is not the case. The most fastidious people still record information that would, if discovered, cut them off from decent society. Miss Manners is referring to the party book, in which one keeps the names of one's friends under the classifications one has given them as guests. Such a record is as useful as it is dangerous. In it may be noted guests' violent allergies, to food or to specific people, but the heart of it is a system that enables one to put together an interesting party. Risking ostracism, Miss Manners will explain her system, not only to show off how magnificently organized she is, but to illustrate what makes a good combination of guests.

You may have heard of "A" lists and "B" lists. All experienced hosts classify their friends this way, but only the clumsy ones allow their guests to know, from looking about a room, which they are on. (A gentleman of Miss Manners' acquaintance has the misfortune to live next door to a good friend who frequently entertains in her patio and has—through long, careful, window observation—discovered that, much as he enjoys the parties to which she invites him, they are not her first rank ones. He has chosen the wise course of ignoring this information.)

The A list should consist of what Mrs. Perfect calls "sparklies." These are people who, through their private status or their talented efforts, can "make" a party. The greatest artist of the day could fill this position silently, for instance, or a nonentity could do it with consistently brilliant conversation.

The B list, like the ideal middle class, should consist of solid citizens with a strong sense of duty. The duty is to listen to the sparklies and to be able to carry a reasonable amount of good conversation.

Then there is a C list which, like poverty, one is always trying to eliminate but can't. These are the social obligations—incurred through sloppy acceptance of their hospitality, ancient friendship from which the interest has disappeared, or the pleas of A- or B-listed friends—who do not earn their dinner. Miss Manners then cross-files these lists by occupation and level of achievement. One's friends tend to be from a limited number of fields. The question of achievement level is not snobbery, but the fact that people who are striving for advancement—a category that naturally includes almost all young people and even some people who ought to be enjoying their high status but can't stop striving—rarely give themselves over wholeheartedly to theoretical and disinterested conversation.

In the well-planned dinner for ten, there should be (taking out the host and hostess): two sparklies from different fields, four solid listeners and contributors from assorted professions, one charity case and one mystery guest whose classification will not be clear until after being auditioned at this dinner. Laurel-resters should, on the whole, be kept separate from ladder-climbers, unless the latter show extraordinary talent as listeners. All sparklies make as dull a party as all audience. Unless occupations are mixed, you will hear nothing but shop talk. Since a good party is such a mix, your best friends will never know what you consider them. Provided, of course, you keep your jaw and your desk locked.

Filling In

DEAR MISS MANNERS:

I must be the last person in the world who still gives seated dinner parties for eight people at which I expect my guests to come on time, in the couples that I invited—no last minute dropouts or additions on the plea of sudden divorce or falling in love—and I still seat them man, woman, man, woman around the table. It's not easy these days, as you know, but I'm in there trying. People do say they enjoy my parties very much, so they must feel it's worthwhile to cooperate with my rules.

Occasionally, however, people have iron-clad excuses for dropping out at the last minute—I mean like extreme illness, or a death in the family. I try not to hold it against them. My question, though, is what to do about getting others to fill in at the table for them. I find that six people is not as good for conversation as eight, and anyway, by that time, I have already cooked for eight and it seems a waste to have empty places. If I invite people the day before the party, or even the day of the party, do I have to pretend that it's a last-minute party and that I'm inviting everyone at that time? I'm afraid if I do, they will assume that it's casual and informal, which it's not.

GENTLE READER:

This is one of those rare social situations when a more or less honest confession is actually more flattering than a hollow lie. The correct last-minute invitation is worded as follows: "If you weren't such a dear friend, I wouldn't be able to ask you a very great favor. I have a rather difficult dinner tonight, and some people I was hoping were going to make it sparkle have just been called off on an emergency—would you be an angel and fill in? It would make all the difference."

If accepted, this invitation is followed, within the month, by an invitation to the filler-in, in which you offer a choice of dates for a dinner that you plan to build around him or her.

AT TABLE

~ Family Silver ~

DEAR MISS MANNERS:

My husband inherited some silver for the table from his family. It's a service for ten, very old and rather pretty (although hard to clean). The monogram belonged to his great-grandmother, and has no initials in common with ours. Also, it's marked on the wrong side. That is, the letters are engraved on the backs of the forks and spoons, instead of on the fronts. Why would that be? Should I have my own put on the front, where they can be seen, or what? I'd like to show it off to best advantage.

GENTLE READER:

You are headed smack in the wrong direction by attempting to pass off your inherited silver as new. Miss Manners does not suggest you go so far as to adopt the English insult, "The sort of people who buy their silver," but notifies you that such an expression exists in the hope of making you appreciate what you have.

Fortunately for you, everyone will notice this when you learn to set your table as this silver was intended to be placed—with the fork prongs and spoon bowls facing down, so that the initials may be seen. Because this is rarely done in this country, you will undoubtedly be asked questions by those who wish to point out that you have set your table backward. That will give you the opportunity to explain that you have old family silver. For this purpose, you must learn what each initial stands for, and a sweet anecdote or two about the original owner. Your only danger, in this triumph of status, is that some people will lump you with the sort of people who buy old silver and make up names to go with the initials.

⌒ *Silver Goblets* ⌒

DEAR MISS MANNERS:

We have received six silver wine glasses for our last wedding anniversary. Would it be proper to use them when serving wine at a formal dinner, or are they really just for show?

GENTLE READER:

Miss Manners does not believe in keeping useful objects from their use unless they have, as in the case, say, of an Etruscan vase, outlived their usefulness and may be put on a shelf to be respected in old age. Metal and wine are not, however, the happiest of combinations. The silver could lend an undesirable flavor to your wine; it also conducts temperature and could, if filled with chilled wine, give your guests quite a shock. Your glasses could be given a new use in which they could also be prettily shown off. You might put trailing flowers in them and use them at intervals along the dining room table for decoration.

⌒ *Service Plates* ⌒

DEAR MISS MANNERS:

What is the purpose of chargers? Very pretty ones are displayed for sale in department stores. For many years, I thought these over-sized plates were to remain on the table during the meal. Now I see hostesses remove them before the meal or after the salad course or, apparently, whenever they choose.

GENTLE READER:

Oh, good, now we have china guest towels. Household items that serve no purpose except that of being dangled in front of guests who are not allowed to use them.

Miss Manners assures you that chargers, a.k.a. service plates or place plates, do have a function in life. They work the first half of the dinner shift—not only greeting the diners, but serving as repositories for olive pits, soup plates or fish plates—before yielding their place to the dinner plates.

It is true that the dinner plates can manage without them, working the early shift and the main course as well, but service plates are decorative.

They should not presume on this, however. It's nice to have pretty dinner partners, too, but one expects them to contribute more than their looks to the evening.

~ The Napkin ~

DEAR MISS MANNERS:

Would you please tell me the correct side, when setting a table, to place the table napkin? Years ago, when I worked as a servant, I was taught to place the table napkin on the left side, but I have now been told that this is incorrect.

GENTLE READER:

In formal service, the napkin is centered on the service plate before the first course is placed on the table, with the hope that each person will remove his or hers before the soup plate lands on top of it. In modern practice, however, the first course may well be on the table when people come to the table, so that no one in a servantless household has to make that extra scoot around as the conversation is starting. In that case, the napkin is placed to the left, next to the forks, as centering it in the soup would be impractical.

DEAR MISS MANNERS:

I have, if I may say so, a talent for folding napkins into interesting shapes, such as fans and flowers. I have seen this done at restaurants, but never in anybody's house. Is there anything wrong with this for dinner parties? I feel it makes the table look more festive. Someone told me that it was an old-fashioned custom not only to do this, but to put bread—a roll, I guess—into the folds of the napkin. Would you approve of this?

GENTLE READER:

Would Miss Manners discourage a talent like that? Yes, making napkins stand up is an ancient art, lost in the hurly-burly of modern living—or so Miss Manners had thought. They certainly used to have buns hidden in them. Perhaps you should be cautious about that little surprise nowadays, however. People would not expect it and are apt to be dropping them, like marbles, from all sides of the table.

~ Knife Rests ~

DEAR MISS MANNERS:

I received as a gift what appear to be 8 little crystal dumbbells. I am told they are knife rests. Where and when would one use such a thing? Why would one use a knife rest? Shouldn't the knife be placed across the plate once it is used?

GENTLE READER:

They are, indeed, knife rests, and one would use them to rest one's knives if those were exhausted. Yours are not likely to be.

Miss Manners is not criticizing your table manners. On the contrary, modern ones are better than those used when knife rests were invented. That was when people brought their own knives to the table and used them to spear everything within reach. Now that we have dishwashers, there is no need to reuse knives rather than replace them as needed.

~ Soup Plates and Spoons ~

DEAR MISS MANNERS:

When eating soup from a bowl on a plate, where is the proper place to set the spoon between spoonfuls and again when finished? Is it the bowl or the plate?

GENTLE READER:

Miss Manners is going to drive you crazy on this one. You want a simple answer so you can eat your soup in peace and propriety, and she is about to douse you with technical terms.

Soup may be served in bowls or cups with small plates under them, in which case the spoon is always parked on the underlying plate, whether you are finished or just resting up for the next spoonful. That would be a simple answer if this were all there were to it, but there is more.

At more or less formal dinners, soup is served in a so-called soup plate, which doesn't look like a plate because it is a rimmed and wide, shallow bowl, but it is called a plate anyway. It goes on top of the service plate, and they are removed together when replaced with the plate for the fish or meat course.

When a soup plate is used, the spoon is parked in it, not in the flat plate below the soup plate. This is a shock to people who only learned soup bowl etiquette, and will think you don't know any better, but it is the correct method.

You can achieve an even greater shock with two-handled soup cups, where it is not strictly necessary to use a spoon at all, but permissible to drink from the lifted cup. However, Miss Manners does not consider herself responsible for the consequences of Fun with Soup.

∼ The Finger Bowl ∼

DEAR MISS MANNERS:

Please explain the finger bowl. I have not used any, but I am considering it, because I often serve messy foods, and it sounds like a sensible, practical idea.

GENTLE READER:

Actually, it is not. Correctly used, the finger bowl is a charming touch of no practical use whatsoever. When service is of a degree of formality to require finger bowls, the food is never messy enough to require them. If you want to clean off your guests before dessert at an informal meal, offer them warm, damp, small terry-cloth towels, served with tongs from a wooden tray.

Miss Manners must not get unpleasantly practical herself and forget that what you asked her to do was to explain the finger bowl. Very well. It is a small, individual bowl, usually glass but sometimes silver with a glass lining, half-filled with water in which small flowers or flower petals are floating. No lemons, please. It arrives on the dessert plate. For formal dinners, dessert service paradoxically consists of a lot of different things all stacked up together, just the way you told the children not to clear the table. On the plate from which dessert is to be eaten are a dainty cloth doily, the finger bowl and, on each side, the dessert fork and spoon. The guest is then expected to set the table properly, placing the finger bowl and doily to the left, and the fork and spoon on either side of the remaining plate, before taking dessert.

What the guest does not do is use the finger bowl as a sink. At the most, one can dab one fingertip in it, but many people consider even that vulgar. Finger bowls are not for people who cannot tolerate anachronisms.

(For correct table setting for a formal dinner, please see p. 155.)

ADDING THE GUESTS

DEAR MISS MANNERS:

I pride myself on my cooking and love to give elaborate dinner parties at which the timing of the food is very important. It drives me crazy that people just won't leave their drinks and come to the dining room when I tell them to. Last weekend, I had a fish soufflé as a first course, and by the time people finished their drinks and conversation, it was a mess. Not ruined completely, and they all pretended to marvel at it, but, believe me, it didn't look the way it would have if they had come into the dining room when I told them to. I was seething, but my husband says that people are more important than food, and if they were having a good time, I shouldn't have even tried to interrupt them.

GENTLE READER:

Like all generalizations, the idea that "People are more important than food" all depends. Many people are more important than fruit cup, for instance, but very few, in Miss Manners' opinion, are more important than fish soufflé.

In any case, it is not the guests who decide what time dinner is to be served; it is first, the cook, and second, the hostess or host. As you are both, you must take command. Instead of timidly standing in the doorway and begging people to "Come in to dinner, please," you must announce this in a tone that means business. If there is no general move in your direction, march into the room, grab the guest who is to sit on your right, and march him into the dining room with you. If there is still no response, go and get the guest who is to sit at your left. If no one else follows, the three of you may eat all their fish soufflé.

～ *The Seating Plan* ～

"Oh, just sit anywhere." That is the seating plan for the modern dinner party.

Here's how it works: Everybody stands around the table sheepishly, not wanting to make the first move, while the hosts keep repeating this non-instruction with increasing desperation. Finally, someone who is paradoxically both starving and fed up (everybody is, but some are more emboldened by that state than others) picks a chair, and the spouse of that person plops loyally down in the next seat.

For a few dreadful moments, this couple sits at the table alone. The other guests are pretending to be too engrossed in conversation to notice. They don't wish to appear greedy, as if they hadn't been scarfing hors d'oeuvres and looking at their watches for the last two hours.

Suddenly, it's Musical Chairs—everyone moves forward at once, and scrambles to grab any seat that doesn't already have someone's hand firmly on the back. When they are secure enough to look around, many make the appalling discovery of having landed back with the person whose conversational resources they had exhausted during drinks, a rival in the school board election, or an ex–brother-in-law who carries a grudge. With sinking hearts, the hosts note that except for the married couples, the gentlemen are pretty much lined up on one side and the ladies on the other.

Miss Manners is not surprised when this is the seating system used at dinners where the guest list was "Spread the word," the dress instructions were "Don't bother" and the menu was "Bring something." These hosts cannot be expected to attend to such details as they are run ragged before they entertain, busily hiding away everything fragile or valuable. But even at conventional dinner parties, where the hosts actually use all that luxury equipment they were so eager to get as wedding presents, many simply wave their guests toward the carefully set table and expect them to fend for themselves. "Oh, it doesn't matter," they declare airily.

Doesn't it? Dinner can take a long time. It can take forever, if you are sitting next to someone who bores or angers you. Or if you are sitting next to someone whom you adore and with whom you have everything in common, but feel inhibited from saying what you really want to say, such as "Did you bring home the software I asked you for?" or "What time can we decently leave?"

Meanwhile, the person the hosts said they especially want you to meet is tantalizingly out of reach. Having brought the situation that far, why don't the hosts provide direction? Their answer is that the concept is old-fashioned, and people should be free to sit where they want.

Miss Manners is not (entirely) opposed to freedom, although this may not be the particular freedom for which she would lay down her life. And she notices that those most avidly interested in the art of seating people are such old-fashioned sorts as fashion designers planning their openings and headwaiters ranking their customers.

It is true that customs change, and the seating formula no longer requires the factors of seniority and gender to overrule that of compatibility. Indeed, Miss Manners hopes the Noah's Ark dinner party has been left high and dry.

Guest lists in which the genders are exactly matched in order to alternate ladies and gentlemen at table are deemed unnecessary, as the custom penalized single ladies and spoiled single gentlemen.

⌒ *Two Protests* ⌒

DEAR MISS MANNERS:

Why must married people be separated at dinner parties? I enjoy sitting next to my wife.

GENTLE READER:

Oh, good for you. You can put your dining room table against the wall and sit together in the privacy of your home, if your wife agrees. It is delightful for a married couple to want to sit together during dinner, but, like some other marital pleasures, this one should be enjoyed in private. At dinner parties, married couples must be separated because they tell the same stories, and they tell them differently.

DEAR MISS MANNERS:

Recently I was invited to the home of a good friend of mine for dinner. The food was delicious, the table setting elegant, but the guest list consisted of three couples and me. I am a single woman, never married, and have broken up with my most recent romantic entanglement only a few weeks ago. Eating dinner with all those happy people sitting next to their loved ones affected me rather badly, but being a mannerly sort of person myself, I waited until I got home before becoming horribly depressed.

The question arising from this situation is twofold: namely, did she act properly in inviting me at all when she knew the situation, even though we are good friends; and how do I explain to her that although I value her company and appreciate the invitation, I'd rather not attend under such circumstances? I don't necessarily want her to fix me up with some dinner partner, but the inclusion of at least one other single person, whether male or female, in the party would have avoided my discomfort. Would I be wrong to bring it up to her as a confidence, or what?

GENTLE READER:

How can you call this woman a good friend, when she was so dreadfully insensitive as to invite you to an elegant dinner party with delicious food and cheerful people? Why didn't she fill her house with other depressed and lonely souls, so that you can find yourself a new liaison, or, at the least, commiserate over the dinner table with others who feel as sad as yourself?

In Miss Manners' opinion your friend's mistake is believing that you valued her friendship. (She should also not have seated couples adjacently at the dinner table, but that is a technicality that pales before your more glaring problem.)

Your mistake is in believing that the way to romance lies in pursuing it single-mindedly. Ironically, it is the people who most enjoy a variety of social relationships whom others are always wanting to introduce to their eligible friends and relatives. Miss Manners is at least glad that you had the discipline to conceal your depression at the dinner party. There is nothing quite so unattractive as a morose whiner. Happy couples and fascinating single people tend to react the same way to such behavior.

~ Two Tables ~

DEAR MISS MANNERS:

I am having a dinner party, strictly for couples, and there are eighteen people invited. My question is, how do I set up the seating arrangements? We will have two tables. One consists of five couples, and the other will have four couples. It is a buffet-style dinner, but I wish to have assigned seats. Do I sit at the larger table across from my escort, or does he sit next to me, or what?

GENTLE READER:

You sit at the head of the larger table, and he sits at the head of the smaller table. The idea when arranging more than one table is to prevent the guests from having any suspicion that there is an A table and a B table. There is, of course, but you must do everything you can to avoid letting the guests find proof.

You will naturally want to seat the gentlemen whom you consider most important next to you, and you may do so, provided you put their wives (or mates—Miss Manners is not sure what you mean by "strictly") at the other table. You put the ladies you consider most important next to your escort, and their husbands or mates at your table. That way, when couples try to talk on the way home about the "better table" at which they failed to be placed, they will either be contradicted or convinced that the prestige of the family, at any rate, has been recognized.

~ Turning the Table ~

DEAR MISS MANNERS:

What does the term "turning the table" mean, and how is it done? Is it, in fact, still a social custom, or is it archaic?

GENTLE READER:

Turning the table is one of those marvelously civilized customs invented by our ancestors who knew, in their wisdom, that no one person should be forced to endure the conversation of the same individual for an entire dinner party. Conscientious hostesses still practice it, although they must pretend they do not, because now we are all supposed to believe that spontaneity is best and that anyone is fascinating providing you get to know him well enough.

Whereas in the old days a hostess could perfectly well confide to Mr. Crawbeard on her right that she was now planning to talk to Mr. Fiddlediddy on her left, she must now be more subtle. Say Mr. Crawbeard has been explaining to her, from the soup course until halfway through the roast mutton, the troubles he has been having with his automobile. She should then turn to Mr. Fiddlediddy, who hasn't heard a word of this because he has been busy making plans for slipping away after the dinner with Mrs. Boltenbrook on his left, and says in a loud voice, "Don't you agree, Simon?" If he has any sense of propriety, he will agree, after which he and his hostess may begin a conversation on any subject they choose, while Mr. Crawbeard asks the lady on his right how many gallons she gets per mile, and Mrs. Boltenbrook begins sizing up the gentleman on her left.

⌒ Turning the Conversation ⌒

DEAR MISS MANNERS:

As the captain of a dinner party, how do I avoid ramming an iceberg when one of my guests suddenly startles everyone by making racist opinions? Naturally, I would prefer as few casualties as possible. (Well, maybe one.)

GENTLE READER:

Miss Manners is afraid that it is the obligation of such a captain to provide life preservers for all, regardless of whether he thinks them worthy to survive.

In this case, the life preserver to be tossed is: "I don't think you realize how that sounds. I can't imagine that you really believe that, but in any case, let's talk about something else." If the offending guest does not grab this and paddle madly back to safety, you may firmly move the ship on in another direction.

THE MENU

DEAR MISS MANNERS:

I am, if I may say so, a superb cook and an even more advanced eater, as are many of my friends. I would like to give an old-fashioned dinner party, with lots and lots of food. I know that eight- or ten-course meals used to be served at formal parties, but I don't know what all the courses were. If you will list them for me in order, I will promise to prepare, serve, and eat them all, correctly.

GENTLE READER:

Miss Manners is taking you at your word. Typically, there were fourteen courses.

1. Oysters or clams on the half shell. Fruit or caviar may be served instead.
2. Soup, giving each guest a choice of clear or thick.
3. Radishes, celery, olives and salted almonds.
4. Fish, served with fancifully shaped potatoes and cucumbers with oil and vinegar.
5. Sweetbreads or mushrooms.
6. Artichokes, asparagus or spinach in pastry.
7. A roast or joint, as we say, with a green vegetable.
8. Frozen Roman punch, to clear the palate and stimulate you to go on.
9. Game, such as wild duck or little birdies, served with salad.
10. Heavy pudding or another creamed sweet.
11. A frozen sweet. It is a nice touch to have tiny crisp cakes with this.
12. Cheeses, with biscuits and butter. Or you may serve a hot savory of cheese, which is more filling.
13. Fresh, crystallized and stuffed dried fruits, served with bonbons.
14. Coffee, liqueurs and sparkling waters.

Miss Manners offers this only as a basic list; you needn't consider yourself limited to it.

(For complete service *à la Russe*, please see p. 587.)

The Salad Course

DEAR MISS MANNERS:

Why, in all my travels through Scandinavia and France as a youth, was I served the salad after the entrée was eaten, while here in the United States, it is served and eaten before the entrée?

GENTLE READER:

The Europeans were following the conventional order for dinner courses, one that Miss Manners still prefers. (And they knew that an "entrée" is not the main course but the course before the main course, didn't they?) However, one more usually has salad served first in America for one or all of three reasons:

1. Some people believe it is better for the digestion or for the figure to fill up on salad first.
2. In California, which always has to do everything differently from normal people, salad is served first.
3. Restaurants serve salad first in order to give people something to eat besides bread while they are cooking dinner. Many people copy this because they believe that restaurants epitomize correct service. This is an error.

Bread

DEAR MISS MANNERS:

What is the reason bread and butter is not served at formal dinners?

GENTLE READER:

Like other happy couples, bread and butter must be separated at the dinner table, and their happy home, the bread and butter plate, razed. Butter is never directly invited to the formal dinner table, although it sometimes slithers in, having cozied up to the asparagus in the kitchen. The bereft bread, if it meets a more chic partner such as caviar or anchovy sauce, may appear in the canapés before dinner. If it is willing to be toasted and cut into bits, it may show up on the surface of the soup. The bolder ones just walk in, naked and dry, at this time. Tiny slices may sometimes slip onto the fish platter if they hide under tomato or cucumber slices. During the cheese course, a time at which the guests are on their third or fourth wine and not paying careful attention, it may stride in, in the form of biscuits, and sometimes it even sneaks the butter on its back.

(For more on bread at less formal meals, please see p. 181.)

The Hazardous Dinner

DEAR MISS MANNERS:

Why don't people put warnings out when they serve spicy food? Personally, I hate it, and I don't think it's fair to dish out some fiery concoction to an unsuspecting person who doesn't know what hit him until the taste buds have been burned off his tongue.

GENTLE READER:

The warning should come with the invitation. Miss Manners feels that all unusual, let alone cruel, forms of entertainment should be so labeled in advance.

⌒ The Ruined Dinner ⌒

DEAR MISS MANNERS:

When my mother and father had a small dinner party for friends they had not seen in quite some time, my mother, to her horror, accidentally set the oven setting too high and burned the veal beyond recognition. She served the burned veal along with the other side dishes and pretended nothing was amiss.

I personally feel that this was the wrong decision (not that I told my mother this, since the incident had already passed). If in the future, this happens to me, what is the correct way to proceed?

1. Explain what happened and take everyone out to dinner?
2. Explain what happened and order in Chinese?
3. Explain what happened and only serve the side dishes?
4. Serve the burned food and pretend it's Cajun?

GENTLE READER:

You are a remarkably self-possessed family, Miss Manners must say. Your mother is able to preside over a meal of charred remains without batting an eye, and you are able to restrain yourself from saying, "Ma! What were you thinking?"

You also share the same motivation, which is to spare your mother embarrassment. Miss Manners is afraid that acting upon this is kindlier in your case than in your mother's. You sacrificed your own pleasure (presuming you enjoy the normal pleasure of triumphing over a parent) for her sake; she sacrificed her guests' dinner and comfort for her own.

To spare the guests from pretending not to notice what is wrong with dinner, perhaps even to the extent of eating it, the hostess should confess her fault and yet make light of it so they don't feel they have to reassure her, perhaps even to the extent of eating it.

What your mother owed her guests was (1) dinner (2) an absence of fuss and

(3) an apology accompanied by the pretense that she found her own ineptitude hilarious and was counting on them to do so as well. Miss Manners also recommends (4) a can of tuna fish.

CORRECT SERVICE

∽ *With One "Servant"* ∽

It is of no use for Miss Manners to indulge herself by describing how to serve a dinner when there is a ratio of one footman to every two guests. The fact is that many people don't have any footmen at all these days, because, among other reasons, fine, strapping young men no longer seem to aspire to such a position. If one does have them, they probably came packaged with their own instructions, and have their own squadron leader, a.k.a. the butler, the last person in the world besides Miss Manners who takes a lively interest in arguing such questions as whether to remove finished plates gradually or when everyone has concluded a course.

If one does not have supporting troops, either in the household or rented for the evening, one is generally advised to pretend to be utterly crazy about informality, and give lots of picnics, pasta suppers and children's birthday parties. You are not supposed to be allowed to expect your guests to shower and change before arriving in return for a fine meal, served in comfort, at which they will have an opportunity to talk to their hosts without following them to the kitchen.

However, it is possible to serve such a dinner with what we can either call one servant or admit it is the cleaning woman coming in for an extra evening at time-and-a-half, or an indentured teenaged member of the family. This can be accomplished with a minimum of training, say one fifteen-minute rehearsal, plus kindly worded promptings from the table. It assumes that the host and hostess will perform the advance labor and graceful tasks that may be done among their guests, and that nobody is expecting perfect, silent and rapid service.

The host serves drinks from a tray in the drawing room, discouraging smart-alecky requests by saying something like "Will you have whiskey, gin or tomato juice?" instead of "What would you like?" The hostess uses the maneuver of passing a tray of canapés to regroup people according to her ideas of compatibility.

While the guests are seating themselves in the dining room, the helper makes a first, furtive appearance—in the drawing room, where he or she quickly removes all the dirty glasses, including the one under the sofa.

A four-course dinner is possible if the food has been planned for easy service. The first course should be soup, oysters, or fish in ramekins—something that may be properly portioned in the kitchen and brought in individually. Next is the main course, a meat or fowl that has been carved and arranged on a platter with potatoes or rice and, if there is room, a vegetable. Otherwise, to avoid a special trip for serving the vegetable, it may be served in another course, as a broccoli soup, say, or a green bean salad. The third course is the salad, and possibly also cheese. The fourth, dessert, is something that looks pretty on a serving dish and may be passed, such as a mousse. All this has been prepared beforehand, and only courses one and two need be kept hot. All the helper needs to know is how to arrange the food on platters, and how to serve.

Food is always served to the left of each guest, unless the guest announces left-handedness and asks to be served from the right. The first person served is the lady at the host's right, and then the service may either go clockwise, skipping the host and taking each person in turn, regardless of sex or place of residence (in other words, getting the hostess on the way around), with the host last; or counterclockwise, ending at the host. There are two schools of thought about the side from which plates are removed, both schools sparsely attended. Miss Manners prefers removing dishes from the right.

If the table has been set with place plates, which may be any large dish differing in material or pattern from the dinner plates, the helper has only to bring in the individually served first course dishes and put them on top. It may be done two dishes at a time, if Miss Manners isn't looking.

Upon hearing the signal of the hostess, a bell or a foot buzzer on which she has been careful not to place the leg of her chair, the helper appears carrying one dinner plate, preferably a warm one. He or she removes the first-course dish and place plate of the first guest and substitutes the dinner plate. It takes a while to do this eight or ten times, but the guests may chat among themselves to pass the time, and the conversation is likely to be friendlier than if two at a time had been attempted and guests are dipping their napkins in their water glasses to remove the soup stains from their clothes. The meat platter is then offered to each guest. Sauces that are served separately may be passed from guest to guest. Wine may be poured by the host, who, according to this plan, isn't going to get any food for a while anyway.

As the individual dinner plates are removed, a fresh plate is substituted for the salad, and the salad platter (not bowl) then presented to each guest. However, the salad plates are removed before any dessert plates appear. This is the time for a general clearing up of salt and pepper, forks people forgot to use and the larger crumbs. As we are not attempting finely tuned service, "crumbing" with napkin or scoop is not necessary if the helper will remove any conspicuous bits of garbage, such as cubes of beef Stroganoff.

Then we come to the tricky part, which is the dessert. (We are not attempting finger bowls. The helper has carried in the filled soup bowls without disaster, but let us not push our luck.) A dessert fork and spoon are already on the table, above the plate, or placed on each dessert plate and the combination put in front of the guest. The helper then passes the dessert. If the guest is unfamiliar with the nicety of placing the dessert silver on the plate—the host and hostess should, of course, set a good example—the helper will have to glare at the guest before the guest does the proper thing of putting his fork at his left and his spoon at his right.

At the conclusion of this meal, the hostess, who has not yet had to leave her guests, is given the coffee tray in the drawing room by the helper, who is then free to go upstairs to do his homework. It is, of course, a nice touch if the helper then washes all the dishes and silently puts them away, so that the hosts find an immaculate house as they close the door on the last guest and remove their shoes. However, we are trying to deal in reality.

⁓ Gang-pressing the Guests ⁓

DEAR MISS MANNERS:

At a dinner party a friend attended, there were about fifty guests and various round tables with place cards and numbers at each place setting. At the beginning of the meal, the hostess explained her rules of the house:

Everyone who had a number with a certain digit would be responsible for clearing the table after the first course and carrying out the second course. The second course had another number assigned to it and the lucky people with this number would be responsible for clearing off the second course and carrying out the third— and so on, throughout the dinner.

My friend was aghast, and wanted to know if you had ever heard of this extraordinary custom. The hostess is a wealthy woman and had two paid helpers in the kitchen. Does she need therapy or a book on manners?

GENTLE READER:

She needs to be taught fair labor practices.

To suggest to friends that you all get together and have dinner, sharing the work, is fair, as long as you don't think of it as your giving a dinner party. To accept voluntary offers of help from guests is fair if you don't overdo it. But to invite people to dinner and then conscript them as servers is not. Miss Manners suggests that this lady's putative guests enlighten themselves by talking over the job situation with those two employees in the kitchen. She has a hunch these people do not work merely for food.

The Hostess Alone

DEAR MISS MANNERS:

I do not have a maid. When I cook dinner for my guests, is it proper to leave the room repeatedly while checking the food in the kitchen? I feel uncomfortable doing this, as well as serving at table, such as bringing the soup in bowls, yet I don't see how else it could be done. Unless the answer is that all hosts should have partners. But there must be a way to conduct little parties if one is alone.

GENTLE READER:

You are certainly correct that, as there are two essential functions for a hostess to perform, feeding and talking, it is easier to have two people to perform them. If you have a child in the house old enough to walk, grab that. The quality of their talk is unreliable, but they make adequate servants and can often be persuaded to work merely for the opportunity to eavesdrop.

It is, however, possible to provide good meal service alone. Presuming that you have already figured out that you cannot serve food that requires a great deal of last-minute attention, "family style" service will keep your absences during dinner to a minimum. This means that the filling of plates is done by the hostess in full view and speaking distance of everyone, from the table itself or a nearby service table or tea cart. This should be viewed cheerfully as the only opportunity one has to show off to one's friends one's soup tureen or one's ability, or lack of, at carving.

Service à la Russe

It is a dreary convention of the modern etiquette business that the arbiter of manners assumes that her followers are so modest in ambition or means as not to employ servants, at least not of proper training or in sufficient numbers. Miss Manners is fed up with all this timidity and egalitarianism. Wouldn't you like to know how a dinner is properly served, whether or not you live to eat it that way? Miss Manners would like to tell you.

The place setting for each guest is called a cover, and it consists of a service plate (silver or china will do), all the necessary flatware except that for dessert, and stemmed glasses for water, and two or three wines, with the champagne. On the service plate is the rolled napkin, with the place card on top; and above the plate is an individual saltcellar, nut dish and the handwritten menu.

To the right of the plate, from outside in, are the oyster fork nesting in the bowl of the soup spoon, the fish knife, the meat knife and the salad knife or the fruit knife; to the left, also from outside in, are the fish fork, meat fork and salad or fruit fork. But, you protest, can't I eat both fruit and salad courses? Yes, yes, of course, but it is considered bad form to have more than three knives or forks on the table, so the salad or the fruit equipment is brought in on a tray when that course is served.

After the guest has been seated and removed the napkin, the oyster plate is put on top of the service plate; and when that is cleared, the soup plate is put on the service plate. The latter two are then removed together, with a heated plate put at the place. The rule is that a filled plate is always replaced by an empty one, and no place is without a plate until just before dessert. (Don't you love this already? Aren't you ready to head for the employment office to recruit the personnel? Ask for some-one who understands service *à la Russe*.)

As a filled plate is never put before a guest, the fish and meat courses must be served from platters. It is up to each guest to take notice of how many people each platter is expected to serve (one footman starts at one side of the table, while another starts opposite, with identical platters) and estimate his or her portion. No seconds, folks.

Before the dessert, everything is removed from the table except the wine and water glasses. (No, not the tablecloth and menus. No wonder it's so hard to get help nowadays. Who wants to work for a smarty?) The table is then discreetly swept clear of all crumbs, except, of course, those who are invited guests.

Dessert (which may be subdivided into ices, sweets and fruit, but never mind because the most you will ever see is the sweet, which may or may not be ice cream) comes next, followed by a fruit and cheese course—as Miss Manners was saying, the dessert plate is brought in with a doily on top, a finger bowl on top of that, a fork balanced on the left side of the plate and a spoon on the right.

The guest removes the doily and finger bowl, parks it to the left of the plate and places the fork and spoon on either side of the plate before dessert is served. That, Miss Manners supposes, was the beginning of self-service. And as that brings us around full circle, you will excuse Miss Manners, who is going into the drawing room for coffee.

(For the menu for a formal dinner, please see p. 581.)

⟨ *Waiting to Begin* ⟩

DEAR MISS MANNERS:

I was brought up to wait for the hostess to begin before I started eating. Occasionally now, I am told by a hostess who has not yet been served herself, "Oh, please go ahead before it gets cold." I recognize that as a legitimate suspension of the rules, and even do it myself, sometimes, when I have guests.

But what I can't handle is having my own guests just go ahead and start eating the minute they are served, without being asked by me to do so, because some of them do and others just sit there politely. If I don't start eating, even though some of the male guests might not yet have their food, I seem to be rebuking those who did; but if I do, I feel rude on behalf of those who have waited or who haven't been served yet. What is the polite way of doing this?

GENTLE READER:

The polite way of rebuking guests who have begun to eat without authorization is to say to them, "Oh, please go ahead," etc., while their mouths are full. The polite way to hedge, without rebuking anybody, is for the hostess to pick up her fork and hold it poised without putting it into her food. (Please note that at parties with individual tables, someone must take the lead or nobody will be able to touch anything.)

⟨ *The Polite Nondrinker* ⟩

DEAR MISS MANNERS:

I was always told that it was rude to cover your wine glass to stop wine you didn't want from being poured, but I saw a museum exhibit on manners that says this rule is as wasteful as "spraying a pig with Chanel No. 5." Was the rule just a way to show off, and should it be abandoned?

GENTLE READER:

Indeed, it was not wasteful, as the unspoken part of the rule was that all wine left untouched on the table belonged to the butler. You see that this is the opposite of piggishness. Dear Douglas Sutherland, in his book *The English Gentleman's Child*, offers his father's counterattack, which was to instruct the butler to "pour the wine over the offender's hand until it was removed."

～ *The Polite Vegetarian* ～

DEAR MISS MANNERS:

My husband is a vegetarian; I am not. When we are invited to dine at the home of friends, I maintain that my husband should inform our hosts-to-be that he does not eat meat. I know that when I entertain, I am always disappointed to learn that a guest cannot eat what I have prepared when it is too late to do anything about it. My husband, on the other hand, is perfectly happy to eat salad, bread, and any vegetable, and does not like to have people feel that they need to go out of their way to alter the menu on his behalf; he feels that if he tells them that he is a vegetarian, they will feel obliged to accommodate him. What is the socially correct thing to do?

GENTLE READER:

The socially correct thing for a guest to do is to be perfectly happy eating salad, bread and any vegetable; the socially correct thing for a host to do is to refrain from being disappointed when a guest does not, for any reason, consume everything that is offered.

Suppose the other guests call too, and announce themselves as being on the latest diet, kosher, allergic to seafood, and on the grapefruit diet. Is their hostess expected to be a short-order cook?

～ *The Impolite Enthusiast* ～

DEAR MISS MANNERS:

It is a matter of pride to me that food looks as good as it tastes, and I certainly enjoy being told that an aspic or, especially, one of my fancy desserts, looks spectacular. But the way people put it, usually, is "Oh, I'm not going to spoil this—it looks too good." I know they mean well, but I'm standing there, holding a platter out to them, and they don't do anything until I've said, "Go ahead" over and over until I lose my patience. It's heavy, after all, and I have to go around the whole table with it. How do I convey the idea to the first person that I made it to be eaten?

GENTLE READER:

By saying, "Well, I hope you'll change your mind," and moving on to the next person. By the time you get back to the first person, after everyone else has been served, the problem, if not the dessert, will have disappeared.

Social Correspondence

THE FORM

TECHNOLOGY HAS ALWAYS been popular with the bottom of the class.

Calculators! We don't have to learn arithmetic!

Spell-checking programs! It's a waste of time to learn to spell!

Search engines! We can skip doing research in dusty old books and they'll never know!

As Miss Manners recalls, one of the most successful campaigns to avoid learning was conducted more than a century ago by wretched, ink-stained children who hated the penmanship instruction that used to be required.

Heralding the invention of the typewriter, they made the case that the ability to write legibly was no longer a necessary skill.

Eventually, they prevailed. Penmanship was dropped from the curriculum and they were allowed to sail through life writing illegible letters, memos, prescriptions and checks. Resistance to penmanship became so pervasive that having an illegible signature became a point of pride.

But the schools got even. They instituted typing class.

The pupils struck back, of course, but it was years at the keyboards before the argument that typing was a trade skill for low-level workers, not a fit subject for academic study, led to the demise of typing class. It vanished just in time to leave the high-level types stranded when the arrival of the computer put them in front of unfamiliar keyboards.

Miss Manners admits to some unbecoming satisfaction at the dismay of gentlemen she recalls having bragged that they had no need to type because they had secretaries, and the advantage enjoyed by the ladies who had been told that typing was the only entry into the job market that they could expect.

Furthermore, the necessity for putting thoughts into writing has reappeared, thanks to technology. The bottom of the class, bewildered about how to convey tone and emotion into words, has had to resort to icons and acronyms to be understood in email, but Miss Manners cherishes the hope that they will catch up.

But they will still have to learn penmanship. Handwriting makes the most conventional statement, which would look dopey if printed, seem dignified. This is especially useful, as life's most important occasions are expressed in conventional phrases. Nobody ever felt cheered by the warmth of a card with "My Sympathy" printed in silver scrolls, or traced a typed "I love you" with a trembling finger.

～ *Writing Paper* ～

A "stationery wardrobe" is something Miss Manners has been dearly longing to have, ever since she first heard the term. She thought it meant dresses that didn't play the trick of looking too short one year and too long the next and that didn't capriciously change their fit through the years.

If poor Miss Manners were able to spell, she would not have made such an embarrassing mistake. It turns out that a "stationery wardrobe" is the commercial term for what ladies and gentlemen refer to as "writing paper." By that definition, Miss Manners has an ample wardrobe:

- Cards, in the proper ladies' size, engraved with her name; fold-over "informal" cards with her name engraved on the front and little lined envelopes; flat cards, once known as "the new informals," with her name engraved on the upper center and her address above it on the right, also with little lined envelopes.
- White double-sheeted paper with her monogram engraved in gray, to be used for serious letters written in black ink; cream double-sheeted paper with her monogram engraved in brown, to be used for frivolous letters written in brown ink; unmarked double white sheets for very grave letters indeed.
- Large single sheets with her engraved address for business letters and the use of anyone in the house including guests; unmarked sheets for the second pages of such letters.
- Red-bordered paper for Christmas letters; black-bordered paper for mourning (a leftover, rather than anticipatory, item); and unbordered paper for lists and memoranda.

Perhaps you begin to see, as Miss Manners suddenly does, why all this is called a wardrobe. It is because it is full of expensive things one never uses because they are impractical, have gone out of fashion or the occasion for using them will never arrive.

ANDREA DORIA

Dear Daffodil,
    You seem to have forgotten,
or perhaps you just don't
care, that today is my
birthday. Separated or not,
I am still your husband,
although I suppose you have
forgotten that, too. I don't
think you ever realized
that I am a person, as
much as you. I have
feelings, too, you know, and

A letter that should not have been written, on paper that should not have been used once the passenger was no longer on shipboard.

There is, for example, little modern justification for personal cards, more's the pity. (Miss Manners agrees with dear Nancy Mitford in refusing to call them "visiting cards" or "calling cards" on the grounds that those are what a dog leaves. On the grounds.) When people call on one another nowadays, the card sent in to see if they will be received is Caller ID.

The unmarked sheets for second pages of business letters are useless because only crazy people write business letters of more than one page. The way to get unmarked paper for writing notes to yourself is to cut off the back of a double sheet after you have ruined the front sheet with an ink blot.

Miss Manners does not approve of gimmicky printed "memo" pads, writing letters from home on office or hotel paper, or filling in your own name on printed or partially engraved invitation or reminder cards. Here is what she recommends as a basic, tasteful wardrobe for all occasions:

Necessary. A large single sheet, unmarked or with an address, for the personal and business letters of everyone in the house.

Optional. A double sheet, plain or with a monogram, for a lady's personal letters of various degrees of formality; a single sheet with a gentleman's full name and address if he wants it.

Useful. A postal-card-sized, thick card, with a lady's or couple's name and address, that can be used by itself for quick notes or in an envelope for invitations or notes with presents.

Smashing. A formal invitation card and matching reminder card, engraved with one's name and address, if one gives formal parties. Other written invitations may be issued in letters or on the cards.

There, now. Look at all that money Miss Manners has saved you. As a return favor, please invest it in the quality of the paper and of the engraving—or printing, if it is clear, frank printing. Engraving costs more initially, but subsequent orders, once one has the die, are much cheaper. Don't think Miss Manners can't tell the difference. She may not be able to spell, but she has a very sensitive fingertip.

⌒ *Appropriating Paper* ⌒

DEAR MISS MANNERS:

When you talk about proper stationery, I think you are putting your readers to an unnecessary, and sometimes actually counterproductive, expense. My law firm, for example, has beautiful letterhead paper, properly engraved in a way of which even you would approve. I find it does for almost all my needs; that, in fact, people pay more attention to such letters than they would to the complaints, for example, of an ordinary person on paper with just a name or street address. Hotels also provide impressive stationery, and using that—good hotels give you a generous supply you can take home with you—is beneficial to them, because of the advertising, as well as to the person who saves himself needless bother and expense. Why don't you advise your readers of this?

GENTLE READER:

Oh, that isn't necessary. You should see Miss Manners' mail. At first glance, you would think that she is constantly carrying on important legal business or being thought of by people in the midst of the most luxurious trips. The misappropriation of writing paper to give a false impression has caught on very well, without any help from Miss Manners.

She thoroughly disapproves of the practice. Using your professional letterhead paper to conduct personal business suggests, fraudulently, that the full weight of your employer is behind your every private transaction. When you try to create the impression that the ire of your law firm will be felt if the vacuum cleaner part you ordered is not delivered soon, any simpleton can see that it is a bluff.

As for hotel paper, Miss Manners believes that it, like the soap, towels and bed-spreads, was meant to be used in transit by people who do not have their own such articles with them. A person who writes from his hometown on paper from a distant hotel gives the recipient a vivid picture of his thriftily packing away in his suitcase whatever he thinks he can carry out of the hotel without being arrested. Miss Manners' favorite vision is created by a woman who has been for years using the paper of a famous ocean liner on which she once traveled. The ship is no longer in service, and when Miss Manners sees its name on a letter, she has a charming picture of the writer diligently keeping up her correspondence from the bottom of the sea.

 Appropriating Stamps

DEAR MISS MANNERS:

On occasion, I have been known to take personal letters I have written to the office, where I can mail them more conveniently. When I run out of postage stamps, I sometimes use the office postage meter (after paying for the postage, of course). I have been told that it is rude to use a postage meter on personal mail, but I've never been able to find any rule to that effect. Can you enlighten me?

GENTLE READER:

It is not the meter itself that violates etiquette, but the embarrassing impression you leave on the recipients that you violated office ethics. Miss Manners would consider it harder to figure out how to indicate that you reimbursed your employer than to lay in a supply of stamps.

⁓ Cards ⁓

The best card game in town has been busted up. Miss Manners has been left with some terrific cards in her hand, and no opportunity to play them.

Such cards are of bristol board and have engraved on them one's name and, in the case of a lady or unmarried gentleman, one's address. The game was to run about town, leaving them on everyone, for purposes of welcoming, congratulating, condoling, thanking, taking leave of or any other excuse for ringing other people's doorbells. Formal calling, when properly done, was a social form combining the maximum of effort with the minimum of communication. In its way, this was the perfect social event. Strange that it should have died out. The last known use was in the diplomatic corps, where the necessity of acknowledging one's colleagues, at posts where there may be well over a hundred missions, is believed to promote world peace, in that it keeps the diplomats from engaging in more active diplomacy.

For private individuals, the card may still be used to enclose with flowers or presents, or to bear little messages, such as "Looking forward to Saturday," or to mark one's place in a book. There are those who say that the corners are excellent for dislodging luncheon remains from the teeth, but Miss Manners wouldn't know.

Naturally, only the very best engraved cards will do for any of these purposes. Ladies' cards should be 3-1/8 inches by 2-1/2 inches, give or take an eighth of an inch; and gentlemen's, oh, say 3-1/4 by 1-5/8. Names and social titles are used, so that the sender can look ingratiatingly insouciant by crossing out the title in ink when the card is used.

Initials are never used on cards, and suffixes, such as junior, are spelled out in full. The card of a married lady or couple uses his name, so that one can't stare at "Mrs. Hendrik Thinglebottom" without realizing that behind it lies Sally Wretzle, the software tycoon.

In other words, these cards are uninformative, expensive and useless. Miss Manners is extremely fond of them. Her honest advice to anyone tempted to order them is to invest, instead, in the comparatively new invention of the oversized card, a nonfolding version of what used to be called an "informal" card. The size should

Mrs. Geoffrey Lockwood Perfect

A woman's card. This is engraved with her formal name, which may be her husband's, or her own name in full with the title of Miss, Ms., or her medical, military or noble title. There may also be an address engraved in the lower right corner.

Mr. Geoffrey Lockwood Perfect

A man's card. No address is used, unless he moves into his club, in which case its name is engraved in the lower left corner.

GEOFFREY LOCKWOOD PERFECT

PERFECT PRODUCTS
18 COMMERCE STREET
BROOKDALE, CONNECTICUT
(203) 555-1212

A business card. No title is used before the name, although the person's position, such as "President," may appear below his name. The name of the company, its address and telephone number or email may be given, but its motto, web site address, and six branch office addresses should be discreetly omitted.

*Perfect Pious
Ambassador of the
United States of America*

A diplomat's card.

For the art of turning the corners of cards to convey secret messages, see p. 599.

depend on the latest postal regulations, as the postal service hates little cards and keeps making rules demanding larger and larger mail. This card is engraved with the name or joint name in the top center and the address in smaller letters in the upper right corner. It has room on it for notes, invitations or replies to these.

Smaller cards have become the tool of business people who want to give their names to new associates in a more formal way than a lapel button reading "HELLO! I'm Gerry, your waiter." However, most businesspeople mistake the card for the résumé, and try to cram on it such details as email address, web site address, cellular telephone, fax number, telephone numbers of four branch offices and the company's motto and logo. The proper business card contains only the person's name, title, company name, one address and one telephone number or email address. This is quite as much as anyone needs to know about a stranger before deciding whether to extend the relationship. Besides, cards with too much engraving all over them make messy bookmarks.

~ *Presenting the Card* ~

DEAR MISS MANNERS:

What is the etiquette for social calling cards? I'm in the habit of exchanging business cards, but there are occasions when I'm sure they are not appropriate. Besides there are times when I'd like to give someone my card without either telling them (bragging about) what I do for a living, my position/rank, or feeling like I'm soliciting their business.

I'm vaguely aware that one leaves a calling card (usually there's a place for them by the door) when paying a social call on the first occasion. Does one leave a card upon leaving or present it upon arrival? Does it just provide a pre-printed name, or is a telephone number, email address and street address acceptable also? Or does one write these in by hand?

What is the convention for giving/exchanging social calling cards on other occasions, such as at a club, party, church social? Does one only exchange a social calling card on such an occasion if one is not formally introduced? If a formal introduction is made, would it not be appropriate to give a social calling card, or would the party making the introduction be the conduit for the exchange of the card?

GENTLE READER:

What a lovely question. Not only does it show a proper devotion to form and a laudable interest in keeping your social life untainted by pursuit of gain, but it allows Miss Manners to show off. Her extensive knowledge on the subject of social cards has been languishing unrequested for years, while those who lose no opportunity to angle for career advantage pass out tiny pasteboard copies of their dossiers.

A social card contains only one's formal name, complete with honorific ("Ms. Emmeline Bubbles Whitherspoon") and street address. If you wish to grant the person to whom you give it more immediate access, you can perform the charming gesture of writing the additional information just before you present the card.

However, it is also becoming to maintain some reticence in assuming that the other person wants to keep in touch. We do not automatically exchange cards upon being introduced as in some societies. Rather it follows on an indication that you or the other person wishes to continue the acquaintance.

(Meanwhile, Miss Manners hopes this one will continue with your asking about the etiquette of folding different corners of the card.)

~ Turning the Card ~

DEAR MISS MANNERS:

Okay, what does it mean when you fold the different corners of the card, and does it matter the direction in which you fold them; i.e.: in or out?

GENTLE READER:

Having shamelessly hinted that she was dying to show off this charming bit of arcane knowledge if only someone would ask, Miss Manners thanks you. Please excuse her as she hastily switches to a modest look and the pretense that she is only trying to be helpful.

Social cards were the voice mail of their day. That is, leaving them on friends indicated that you had attempted to deliver your message directly even if you had timed the delivery so as to avoid doing so. The code system of corners bent saved you (and those nice white kid gloves you wore when you went calling) from having to write out the message.

A card with its upper left corner bent forward means "I was here, and sorry not to find you in."

A bent upper right corner means "Congratulations."

A bent lower right corner means "Condolences."

And a bent lower left corner means "I'm leaving town, so good-bye."

If you promise to revive this custom, Miss Manners will permit you to get funny with it by, say, turning both bottom corners for "Too bad, I'm leaving you" or both right corners for "Congratulations on your loss."

~ Cards for Children ~

DEAR MISS MANNERS:

I have encountered a problem which other mothers may be facing and I do believe your expert opinion would be much appreciated. The situation is as follows: My young son, Elliott, age three, attends a lovely, very proper, private preschool. At the end of the school term, he wanted, as most generous youths do, to give his teacher a remembrance. We purchased a small but appropriate gift, and Elliott and I enjoyed the wrapping and making of a delightful construction paper note with his name drawn in his own dear hand.

However, Miss Manners, when little Elliott returned home, he was most distressed. It seems most of the other children had their own engraved cards to include in their gifts. Little Elliott had only his hand-drawn token. My question is—should I have little Elliott's cards engraved for him to include in future gifts? I do want to spare him every embarrassment. I need your answer as soon as possible, as little Elliott is invited to a small afternoon birthday party requiring a gift, and the question of the appropriate enclosure will again arise.

GENTLE READER:

For heaven's sake, do you realize there are children in the world starving who don't even have printed cards of their own, let alone engraved? Little Elliott has obviously fallen into bad company, although his own instinct for bribery indicates that he was a rotten apple to begin with. Save your anguish on his behalf. You will need it later.

~ The Informal Card ~

DEAR MISS MANNERS:

Please tell me about the size, paper, printing (or engraving) of proper informals today, since the size of envelopes that can be mailed has changed. What is the choice of paper, color, and printing versus engraving? As one of the old school who had calling cards and informals engraved, we kept the metal form for using again. I see much printing now. What is correct?

GENTLE READER:

You said the magic word: "proper." Miss Manners trusts that you do not make the mistake of writing full letters on informal cards. Brides often have the curious idea that they are suitable for their formal letters of thanks. They are called "informals," and they are meant to be used for informal invitations ("Bridge on Thursday?") and short messages ("So sorry about last night").

Many designs are neither proper nor improper. One can, for instance, have large cards in some pale color with one's name and address printed on them, and use them as postal cards or insert them in envelopes. These can be attractive and practical. Or not.

A proper informal card, however, is engraved in black ink on white rag paper. An improper one is a close variation of this—printing instead of engraving, or different colored ink or paper.

The fold-over card, with one's name on the outside, is funny looking in a large size, suitable for mailing, so it is more usual now to have a single card with one's engraved name centered at the top. In the fold-over version, one's address, in smaller lettering, was in the lower-right corner. On the single card, one's address is engraved on the upper right-hand corner, and one's name centered, slightly below that line. They must be at least three and a half inches by five inches.

In using your metal plate, the old address can be waxed out and a new one put in. Engraving is an example of a principle of old school thrift: The initial expense of having the plate made is justified by its long usefulness.

Ink

DEAR MISS MANNERS:
I am feeling very incorrect because I do not have black or blue-black ink, nor white letter paper. I have only green ink. Please tell me what I can do.

GENTLE READER:
Save up all your letters all year long and answer them at Christmastime.

Addressing Couples

DEAR MISS MANNERS:
Please clarify how to address the following:
Widows
Couples with different last names
Single women.
Perhaps I'm the only one confused as to the proper manner to address envelopes but I doubt it.

GENTLE READER:

Miss Manners doubts it too. Statistically, you have a greater chance of being the only one to get it right if you follow her instructions.

Not that Miss Manners blames people for being confused. There has been so much playing around with names and honorifics in the last few decades—and so much tiresome commentary bolstering each choice—that a great many people have given up trying and just slap the bald name on an envelope. Bless you for making the (retroactive) effort to get it right.

A widow is addressed exactly as she was when her husband was alive. That is to say, if she used his name, she is still Mrs. Eliot Hubbleside, not, as many unkind and incorrect people try to tell her, Mrs. Emmaline Hubbleside.

People with different surnames who live at the same address get a line for each name no matter what their relationship—marriage, blood ties, roommates or what we used to call Great and Good Friends. In contrast to the Mr. and Mrs. construction, the ladies go first with whatever honorific they use:

Dr. Emmaline Thrushbottom
Mr. Eliot Hubbleside.

Single women may be addressed as Miss or Ms., whichever they prefer. The problem, of course, is that you probably don't know which they prefer. Neither does Miss Manners, so take a guess and hope for the best.

∼ Doctors and Doctorates ∼

DEAR MISS MANNERS:

Several women doctors I know are extremely sensitive about being addressed socially as "Doctor." One of them is married to a "Mr." and another to a Ph.D. I created a furor by sending them cards addressed to Dr. and Mr. What is the correct way to do it?

GENTLE READER:

Illicit love has given us, if nothing else, the two-line method of address, which may also be applied to married couples with different titles or names. The doctor and mister may be addressed as:

Dr. Dahlia Healer
Mr. Byron Healer

and the doctor and academician, if he uses his title socially, which not all holders of doctorates do, as:

Dr. Dahlia Healer

Dr. Byron Healer
or as:
The Doctors Healer
or as:
The Doctors Byron and Dahlia Healer.

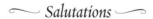

Salutations

DEAR MISS MANNERS:

My father states it is proper etiquette to have the husband's name listed first on a return address label. My feeling is that there is no right or wrong and that it is up to the couple to decide.

GENTLE READER:

That gentlemen appear first in the traditional designation of a married couple, Mr. and Mrs., should not be allowed to go to their heads. Given the choice whenever other forms are used, including the salutations, the lady's name appears first.

Your father's error notwithstanding, Miss Manners congratulates him on ordering his labels, rather than fishing them out of his junk mail like everyone else.

Closings

DEAR MISS MANNERS:

I am seeing a young man—how shall I say?—intimately, but not yet necessarily seriously. I would not be sorry if it turned out to develop into something permanent, but we are not at that stage at the moment.

At any rate, he has now had me twice to visit his parents, who have been very lovely to me. I am fond of them quite aside from my relationship with their son, and am grateful for their warm hospitality. In writing them thank-you notes, I would like to express my affection, but I am afraid that if I signed my letters "affectionately" or "love," they might get the idea that I am presuming on the relationship—that I, in other words, have expectations of coming into the family. This would not be a good idea to plant at this time. How about "cordially"?

GENTLE READER:

Please, no. "Cordially" in a letter closing is a word that Miss Manners, and other authorities before her, particularly dislike. Conventions were invented specifically to allow a person to retreat from having to make choices in situations open to misinterpretation. "Sincerely yours" is a perfectly good closing, neither cold nor warm. Miss Manners quite agrees that this is not the time to suggest that you feel like a daughter to these people. It is a general rule to err on the side of formality rather than of intimacy.

DEAR MISS MANNERS:

We are in our late 60's, a widower and a widow who just got married and both have married children and grandchildren. Please address Blended Family Signatures on cards to blended family members. Now what is the proper way to sign cards for the married children and grandchildren each of us have? Love Mom and Dad?? Love Grandma and Grandpa??

GENTLE READER:

Miss Manners has the impression that you care more that your titles match each other than that they match what your various relatives call you. She puts this down to your being newlyweds, and considers it all very sweet.

However, it might startle middle-aged people who had not thought of the newcomer as "Mom" or "Dad," however pleased they may have been at the marriage. And it might puzzle grandchildren who have a hard enough time as it is distinguishing one pair of grandparents from the other. If such is the case, you should sign "Love, Mom and Terence," or "Love, Grandpa and Grandma-Jenny."

THE CONTENT

⁓ *Letters That Should Not Be Written* ⁓

"Persons without a sense of humor always write long letters," observed dear Sir Herbert Beerbohm Tree, the great actor, "and I have noticed, too, that all madmen write letters of more than four pages. I will not venture to assert that all persons who write more than four-paged letters are mad. Still, the symptom should be watched."

As Miss Manners recalls, when dear Sir Herbert spoke of madmen without humor, he was referring to dear George Bernard Shaw. Personalities aside, it has always seemed to her an observation of remarkable truth. We are all quite mad and humorless upon occasion, and we all seize those occasions to fire off letters of four pages or more. The symptom should indeed be watched.

Miss Manners encourages, even begs, people to write letters. She spends much of her life urging you to write business letters instead of arranging oral duels between your assistant and somebody else's about who is going to get on the telephone when; to write charming little notes to bolster the generous impulses of those who have offered presents, hospitality and favors; to pen such simple sentiments as "congratulations" or "I love you" rather than waste time looking for commercial greeting cards to express them for you; and to conduct the interesting transactions of your life in such a way as to leave plenty of material for your biographer, perhaps even enough for a separate volume of letters, rather than a collection of little pink telephone message slips and a hard disk.

She recognizes, however, that there are some letters that ought never to be written. Most of them happen to be four pages long.

All letters that begin "Never in my life have I been subjected to such . . ." fit into the category of letters that ought not to be written. So do all letters that begin "You may not be aware of it, but I have feelings too." (Miss Manners would go so far as to say that all people announcing "I'm a person, too," should be strictly avoided until they have managed to pull themselves together.)

Letters explaining God's feelings, how they happen to coincide with the letter writer's, and what God plans to do to the receiver of the letter should not be written. These carry double violations, as they are traditionally nine pages long and have extra writing up the margins of the lined yellow paper on which they are written.

Threats in general, name-calling and other insults are not worth writing, because their effect tends to be humorous rather than frightening. Letters correcting the information and grammar of others should probably not be written, but at any rate should not be written in high sarcasm, because they are bound to contain errors of their own.

It is not a good idea to write letters that make clear the existence of a relationship that the receiver has not confided to other people at the same mailing address, such as her parents or his wife.

Miss Manners would be remiss if she did not pass on to you a suggestion about what to do if you find yourself seized with the desire to write one of these letters. She turns again to dear Sir Herbert, who said, "One of the most alarming signs of insanity, it has often seemed to me, is that of writing to the newspapers (invariably more than four pages) to prove that Hamlet was mad, and that Bacon wrote Shakespeare . . . I am satisfied that many of the learned commentators have only been kept out of lunatic asylums by the energy which they have expended in the harmless occupation of discussing these two kindred subjects in print. In many cases it has proved a most valuable safety-valve."

⌒ *Letters That Should Not Be Kept* ⌒

DEAR MISS MANNERS:

Where is a safe place to keep love letters? I don't want a moral lecture, just an answer. The relationship is over, but the letters are very beautiful and mean a lot to me. I can't keep them at home for obvious reasons, and I can't continue to keep them at the office, either, because he still works for the company (he was transferred out of town) and there are a lot of snoopy people here.

GENTLE READER:

The only safe place to keep damaging letters is in the fireplace, between burning logs. Miss Manners does not expect you to follow her advice in this matter; no one ever does. That is what used to make divorce cases so interesting. Now that no-fault divorce is routine—its place in sensationalism having been taken by no-marriage divorce— you may at least be comforted that your letters will go no further than the discoverer and everyone he can manage to tell by word of mouth.

⌒ *Letters That Must Be Written* ⌒

Pitifully enough, it strikes Miss Manners as progress that people are carping about the quality of the thank-you letters they are sent. This suggests that they are actually receiving more for their generosity than silence, a signature on a receipt or check and, if they push it, a lot of lip about how selfish they are for imposing on other people's busy schedules and for failing to achieve perfect satisfaction through the pleasure of giving alone.

Not a whole lot more, though. Gentle Readers have been reporting the appearance of the Generic Thank-You Letter. At best, it says in its entirety "Thank you for the wedding gift," perhaps with the optional extra: "We appreciate it." At worst, which is not far away, it is a mass printing that says "We thank family and friends for all the lovely baby gifts." Sometimes these are sent by email, to the entire guest list, including those who didn't make the final cut.

Another system making the rounds is one that Miss Manners would call Go Thank Yourself (but only if everyone promised her never to pronounce it carelessly).

At the event marking the occasion for which the presents are given guests are told to write their names and addresses on envelopes; in one case, the explanation was that these would be used in a drawing for a prize. The envelope may later be stuffed with the Generic Thank-You Letter, if the hosts are willing to spring for a stamp, or there may already be such a form letter at each place so that the guests can consider themselves thanked on the spot.

This is strangely akin to a method employed by some of the un-thanked. They too have come up with printed letters of thanks, or forms to be filled in, to be sent to themselves. Some are enclosing these with presents to be sarcastic, but some profess that if the form is mailed back, they will consider themselves adequately thanked, even though they had to do it themselves.

Nevertheless, Miss Manners will make the generous assumption that the writers of rote and form letters of thanks mean well but do not know what a proper letter of thanks contains.

It opens with a burst of enthusiasm: "What a delightful surprise," or "We were thrilled to receive," or "How kind of you to send . . ." and never with the words "Thank you for . . ."

It names the present with a flattering adjective: "the charming booties," "the beautiful lamp," "the generous check."

It contains a reference to the relationship: "You've always been so kind to me," "We were so pleased you attended," "We hope you will visit us."

Most importantly, it is written by the person who received the present, not the one who sent it.

⌁ . . . and Must Be Written Now! ⌁

DEAR MISS MANNERS:

What is the length of time a person can take to send a thank you for a birthday gift, Christmas gift, or any gift for that matter?

GENTLE READER:

Before the first enthusiasm for the present subsides, or just after the first disappointment does. However, Miss Manners sets the time limit at twenty minutes.

⌁ Thoughts That Must Be Omitted ⌁

DEAR MISS MANNERS:

I am always very good about sending letters of thanks for all occasions. However, recently, we attended a gathering at a friend's house and it wasn't too great. The association was awful, even offensive at times; the food was mediocre; we had to wait outside of the gated community for someone to let us in; all in all a bad experience. My question is: I always send such warm, heartfelt thank-you notes, however, I don't want to lie. It was awful. There was nothing good about the night, except our departure. Is it rude to just send a note that says "Thanks" and then sign it?

GENTLE READER:

Was nothing good? Not even the intentions of your friend?

It is not because Miss Manners doubts that you had a horrid evening or lacks sympathy over what you endured that she is prompting you to see this in a better light. She only lacks sympathy for your letting the host know, through your curtness, what a flop he produced.

What do you have in mind here? You could stick to the truth, the standard for which is not the same in a letter of thanks as in sworn courtroom testimony, by finding something to praise, if only his kindness in inviting you. If it is to imply "Don't you ever do that to me again," forget it. Your privilege is not to warn the host, but to decline his next invitation.

── *Feelings That Must Be Included* ──

DEAR MISS MANNERS:

A close friend of our 33 yr. old son just completed testing to be a kidney donor for him. He is not a candidate for the gift. Would it be proper, as parents, to show our gratitude for his ultimate gift offer, to send him and his wife a gift certificate for a dinner out or is a note of thanks all that would be in order? My husband says a gift "cheapens" it.

GENTLE READER:

He offered your son a kidney, and you are debating whether to offer him a steak? If you have a son in need of a kidney, you should not need Miss Manners to explain to you that this offer was priceless beyond compare. A "note," as opposed to an emotional letter pouring out your gratitude, and a restaurant gift certificate, as opposed to welcoming him to the bosom of your family, would both be ludicrously inadequate.

In regard to teaching children to offer thanks, Miss Manners has always argued that gratitude is not a natural reaction to generosity, so that the connection between the two—and the forms for acknowledging indebtedness—must be taught. But in your particular case, she really thought gratitude of a magnitude to match the generosity might have spontaneously overwhelmed you.

If not, you must show it anyway. As this gentlemen is not actually able to be the donor, you need not look after him in the hospital as well as you do your son, which is the way you should treat the person chosen. But in addition to pouring out your thanks and offering your eternal friendship, you should be endeavoring to discover anything serious that you might do for him.

GREETING CARDS AND CHRISTMAS LETTERS

~ Christmas Cards ~

DEAR MISS MANNERS:

The tradition of Christmas cards is slipping away: We have no time to write them, it costs too much to send them, and they are ultimately thrown into a landfill. Somebody has suggested a telephone call to everyone on the Christmas card list, observing "people will enjoy it more" and the money would be put to use elsewhere.

All true, as far as it goes, but a couple of points in favor of an old-fashioned, pretty card:

One of the joys my brothers and I share when we visit our parents during the holidays is a leisurely browse through the holiday cards they receive. A phone call would be nice—but the card touches more than the person who answers the phone. Many old family friends and even relatives don't stay in regular touch with the extended family—but Mom and Dad will get cards from out-of-town great-aunts, etc., who we rarely hear from except at Christmastime. Even the much-derided "mass letter" is a treat (I think the derision comes from cynics who don't want to write them, more than folks who don't want to read them).

On the other hand, folks who only send cards to people who send THEM cards should probably stop sending any cards at all. If holiday greetings are meted out as rewards for good behavior—they're a little insincere, aren't they? Or am I just lost in Irving Berlin Land?

GENTLE READER:

You were fine until you got to the part about it being insincere to stop pouring greetings into a void. Miss Manners, who practices charity toward all, assumes that one can be sincere and even jolly spirited without feeling the urge to spread greetings to people who never greet back. Even those people might be sincere, jolly-spirited folk who are racking their brains to remember who their greeters are.

The custom of taking time at the end of the year to keep in touch with those whom one does not ordinarily see or write to is a charming one. However, signing one's name to printed inanities, or mass producing a composition about one's petty triumphs over the year, is not keeping in touch. Keeping in touch means writing one's sentiments with one's very own hand. This may be a full letter, or only the words "Merry Christmas" added to a picture card, but one must write it oneself.

At Christmastime, there are many different types of paper and cards that may be used for this purpose. Miss Manners, who is ordinarily strict about the colors of papers and inks, gets giddy enough at Christmas to enjoy the use of red or green, in inks, borders of cards and lining of envelopes. She would even allow pictures in good taste, which may sometimes include those of one's own family. To those who feel that the Hi-There Greeting Card Co. has perfectly captured their feelings in one of its limericks, Miss Manners will only add the requirement that they nevertheless write out a message, however brief, between the poesy and the signature.

Now comes the question of to whom these cards should be sent. Miss Manners considers it superfluous to mail holiday wishes to those whom one offers such wishes to face to face, although one certainly may. At the other end of the list, she suggests crossing off people whom one would no longer recognize if they fell over one on the street.

This leaves the people one actually knows and likes, but cannot see or write to often during the year because of problems of time or distance. It might help to consider the extent of such people's interest. In some cases, they might find it sufficiently pleasant just to know that they are remembered. In others, there may be an eager audience for family news. It is unlikely, however, that anyone's interests extend to electronic diaries and photograph albums. Furthermore, such Christmas letters are usually highly biased bits of reporting, rarely containing the sort of juicy news that is of real general interest. They tend to run to the children's soccer scores, rather than to Mommy's new lover.

The final word Miss Manners offers on the subject of dignity in Christmas cards is the plea that they be properly addressed and properly signed. This rules out the use of such catchalls as "and family"; if you can't address people by their proper names, then you address the card to those whose names you know, asking to be remembered also to "the children" or "your father."

When signing a card, please, Miss Manners begs you, err on the side of more information rather than less. This means including your surname to nearly everyone but close blood relatives, and even making it clear which names belong to the parents and which to the children. You'd be surprised how many people stare blankly at such signatures as "Lisa, Adam, Kimberly and John" without knowing which of these people, if any, is a dear pal. The signature form Miss Manners prefers is:

Jonathan and Kimberly Awful
Lisa and Adam

The parents are the ones with the surname. The man's name is written first if the woman has done the signing and therefore would put herself second. If the man has signed for both, his name should be second. Children are listed by seniority. The family pet is not listed at all. He is expected to handle his own social responsibilities.

There should also be a return address. The only excuse for forcing your friends to play guessing games is the hope that the mystery will encourage them to drop you from their list before you drop them from yours.

~ Christmas Letters ~

DEAR MISS MANNERS:

Could you comment on the rising trend of writing Christmas letters—all the time?

I write lengthy letters which, I hope, enlighten, educate and entertain. Recently I've received such letters—without any personal touch. These writers discuss activities, lives and the future, but never mention personal views relating to the recipient and never answer questions nor issues raised in past letters to them. Letters I receive, you could receive. The impact would be the same.

It is not a one-time thing. One young writer has sent five such—four pages each, informative, insightful, incisive, but with zero "sharing" and/or a sense of one-on-one communication. This may help high track movers fulfill their social responsibilities to communicate with others, but to the recipients it becomes another sample of Christmas letter indifference and laziness.

GENTLE READER:

Before the miracle of email, these people would not have been able to do this. In those days, it took them all year to get the purple smudge off their fingers after mimeographing their Christmas letters.

But then, before the miracle of email, Miss Manners didn't have a succinct word to describe what they are doing. Sending out lots of material to a long list of people who have not shown a particular interest in receiving it is known as spamming. Not only does this not fulfill the duty of keeping in touch, but it constitutes an additional offense.

～ A Reply ～

DEAR MISS MANNERS:

OK—what is really wrong with Christmas letters? I know a lot of people make disparaging remarks about them, but suppose you have a lot of friends and can't possibly sit down and write each one a separate letter? Isn't the newsletter once a year actually a good way of informing people about your activities? I would find it helpful if, instead of looking down on this, you set some rules about how to write them. Our Christmas list has more than one hundred names on it, and I don't know any other practical way of letting our friends know what has happened to us—about our month at the beach house, Junior's new braces, my husband's promotion, and so on.

GENTLE READER:

Far be it from Miss Manners to look down on anyone so fortunate as to have more than a hundred friends so close as to be awaiting the news about your son's teeth. You will forgive her if she suggests that so high a degree of intimacy is not often maintained on the basis of a mass mailing once a year.

In other words, the trouble with form letters is that they are almost inevitably inconsistent with the relationship between writer and recipient. Friends and relatives who have a genuine interest in the details of your family life deserve some personal attention. If they can get through the year without wondering where you spent the summer, the chances are they are not burning to know now. And to bombard casual acquaintances with full accounts of your lives is to satisfy curiosity they may not feel.

So much for why Miss Manners dislikes the idea. Now to answer your question about how to do it.

First, keep it a reasonable length, and if you are emailing it, refrain from including items that take time to be downloaded.

Next, refrain from bragging. You wouldn't stand up at a party and shout "Lauren was made cheerleading captain!" or "We bought a boat!" or "We went to Maine last summer!" or "I got a raise!" Confine your "news" to more or less public matters—"We've moved to Colorado," "I've finally finished law school," "Annabelle has joined the Army"—and state them neutrally. The exception is that births, engagements and marriages include mention of the family's pleasure in them—although, come to think of it, why haven't these close friends of yours been notified of such important events at the time that they occurred?

Finally, refrain from offering your philosophy, politics or general wisdom gleaned from life: If the urge overwhelms you, it is better to write leaflets and hand them out to strangers on the street than to offend your friends by giving them unsolicited advice.

⁓ Chanukah Cards ⁓

DEAR MISS MANNERS:

Please help my husband and me settle an etiquette dilemma. During the holiday season, we send Christmas cards to our friends and relatives. I also like to send Chanukah cards to our Jewish friends. My husband feels this is inappropriate because it seems to imply that Chanukah is a Jewish version of Christmas and in some way signals a separate category for our Jewish friends. He would prefer a happy holiday card or no card at all.

I think he's quite silly, that thinking of someone and remembering one's special holiday is always correct. Naturally, convinced as we both are that your opinion will mirror each of ours, we have agreed to let Miss Manners be the final arbiter on this matter.

GENTLE READER:

Whether or not your husband is quite silly, Miss Manners cannot say, and if so, she hopes you have a weakness for silly gentlemen. But he is right in this instance. It is always nice to remember your friends, but do you also remember each of your Jewish friend's attitudes toward Chanukah and toward Christmas? They could celebrate a secular Christmas or a Christmas-like Chanukah or neither or both.

If you don't know, you are risking causing great offense by making presumptions about their religious practices. Of course, inquiring closely into other people's religious practices is also offensive. Why can't you sidestep the issue by sending secular cards?

Presents

IT'S NOT JUST less blessed to receive, a sizable minority of Miss Manners' Gentle Readers claim. It's a downright nuisance. While she is kept busy chastising the greedy for their blatant demands, the background hums with G.R. grumbles:

"My home has slowly become totally cluttered and overrun with a vast array of crafty, cutesy, tasteless decorative items and accessories given as gifts. I am running out of room, I no longer enjoy the way my home looks, and gift-giving season is upon us."

"For years now, my aunt has persisted in giving me bath oils and salts, chocolates and new age music. I am allergic to chocolates and perfumes, and I find nature recordings and new age music generally irritating."

"My husband and I boycott items manufactured in a certain country, because these places are notorious for the ill use of their workers, many of whom are under-age. We also try to instill in our daughter that Christmas is about love and family and charity and kindness by doing volunteer work and making donations. But every year, we end up at my husband's parents' house and his family gives her far more gifts than she needs, many of them from the precise country we boycott."

"My brother decided to present to all his siblings, a contribution in their name to a certain charity, unfortunately selecting a charitable organization that my wife and I do not support. Indeed, we oppose its mission and goals, and greatly suspect its management of incompetence, at the very least. My brother knows, as well as he knows his own name, how my wife and I feel about this organization."

"We live in a small apartment and have two garbage bags full of stuffed animals already. I have tried to get it across to both sides of the family that the children don't need any more—I have even suggested storage units as gifts—and only one person got the hint."

"My brother is a minister. Our religious views differ sharply. Each holiday season, he gives my two young children numerous gifts such as books, videos and puzzles, with overly religious messages, which I perceive as an attempt to influence the religious views of my children. I don't want my brother to give them any more such items."

As all of these people swear that they accept graciously whatever they are handed, trying not to look crestfallen, Miss Manners is slightly abashed. The gift registry, the gift certificate and gifts of cash, all of which she loathes, would also solve their problems as much as those of the ungraciously greedy.

Yet no one has a right to expect presents, and attempts to choose them—manipulating others into buying for you things that you want to buy for yourself—are inappropriate on any occasion. Miss Manners does not waver in her opposition to the solution of eliminating the elements of thought, symbolism and surprise from presents, and having people simply pay one another for getting through the holidays. There would be no point left in the custom, and we could each just do our own shopping.

But she is feeling responsible for the consequences. What about all that awful, unwanted stuff?

Here is the polite procedure for minimizing the damage:

Hints are in order in advance ("Check out my web site" is not a hint), as are mutually negotiated deals, such as "There are so many of us now, why don't we agree to get presents just for the children?"

When those fail, as Gentle Readers testify they so often do, the polite recipient protects the donor from knowing the present was a failure. Thanks, and no complaints. To refuse a present is a high insult, and that includes asking the donor to go exchange it.

However—here comes the relief—the donor is equally bound to silence, which means that the present does not have to be used or displayed. (Exceptions are wise when the donor is beloved and close at hand, but these are voluntary.)

This leaves room for returning, donating to charity and re-gifting, none of which is rude if the rule is strictly observed about protecting the donor from knowing. This requires fresh wrappings and logs of who gave what, and a ban on yard sales and re-gifting anywhere near the donor. You cannot moan over the loss of money involved, which could have been applied to something else.

And most of all, resigning oneself to not making a profit out of holidays.

That brings Miss Manners to her final word on the subject of budgeting presents. One spends a reasonable amount in terms of one's own resources—not the resources or hopes of the recipients—to get as nice a present as one can. What does "nice" mean? It means that you never give anything below your own taste level—something you wouldn't want, but suppose is good enough for others. It means that the present must be thoughtful, whether you made it for free or spent a lot; that it was chosen to please that particular person. The one rule about money is that you not overwhelm someone by giving something so valuable as to be inappropriate to the relationship or occasion. But, then, a well-bred person, not being aware of cost, wouldn't notice it if you did.

The following ideas should also be rejected:

1. The present that exactly reflects the interest of the person to whom it is given, such as giving a bug collector the latest book on comparative feelers, or a jogger the new designer bag for collecting sweat.
2. The present of a promise of service: twenty nights of baby-sitting with your ménage, or eleven certificates for pruning your hedge.

Miss Manners' reasoning on the first is as follows: The person who has a specialized interest knows more about it than the present giver. Having already cast his or her eye on all the bug books or jogging equipment, he has already, from superior knowledge, approved some things and rejected others. If your choice is something he has wanted, the chances are he has also acquired it, even if it meant mortgaging the children, your true expert being something of a fanatic. If he has not done so, it is probably because he has considered the object and scorned it.

As for those certificates for services to be rendered during the year, they are indeed charming and cheap to give. The reason they are cheap is that both the donor and the recipient know perfectly well that they are not collectable. Just wait until that muggy day when your dear friend lets you know that his hedge needs trimming.

Having delivered herself of these dampening options, Miss Manners might be expected to announce that one should give money or "gift certificates." Wrong again. Miss Manners objects to money as a present on the grounds that the recipient knows exactly what you paid for it. The charming equivalent of giving money is to give something that is easily returnable, and not to seem to stare at your friend's mantelpiece on New Year's Day, as if you were wondering where it was.

A more positive approach is to select something among those things of which one cannot ever have enough. In this case, you are paying attention not to the expertise of the receiver, but to his or her style. What falls into this category? Bottles of wine, diamonds and homemade cookies.

⌒ Reacting to Presents ⌒

Accepting a present graciously is not much of a problem when the present turns out to be tickets for an Aegean vacation. In that case, Miss Manners trusts you to emit the proper cries of surprise and joy, to place your hands over your face in the classic posture of one who is overwhelmed, to place your arms around the donor in another classic posture and to confuse, in your expressions of gratitude, the attractions of the gift with those of the giver.

What if the surprise is not of the pleasant variety? Can Miss Manners trust you to behave properly when given a present that disappoints you?

From greediest childhood, we build up so many expectations about presents that the chances of being let down are statistically higher than those of feeling unworthy of the bounty showered upon us. You can guess, of course, that Miss Manners' general rule in such instances is to fake the reaction she has described for you in detail. The ability to look delighted when not—now that is truly a gift.

You should modify this until it is plausible. But Miss Manners will also allow a form of, shall we say, constrained delight, to be used in cases where it is possible to warn the giver, without outright hurting of feelings, that more care another time might produce a better result. This reaction consists of a wide smile made with closed lips, and accompanied by a bright-eyed but sober look. The words are "Why, how nice!" Promise Miss Manners that you will not employ this to encourage more expensive presents—only more appropriate ones.

Another sort of inappropriate present—a car from someone one doesn't know very well, which naturally must be refused—calls for a different reaction. This calls for a third response. The mouth curves in a half-smile of regret before and after the protest, but the eyes shine.

⌒ Training Children to React Properly ⌒

DEAR MISS MANNERS:

Can you give me some suggestions for gifts for children? My husband and I spend the winter in Florida or the Caribbean every year, and shopping for the grandchildren there has gotten to be a pain. If we bring them back clothes, either they don't fit or they don't like them because they're not what all the other children are wearing. (Of course not—if they were, they wouldn't be souvenirs of a trip to a different place.) If we get toys, they already have them. If we buy curios or decorative items, such as weavings or pictures, they're not interested in them. Whatever we bring, they are disappointed with. And yet the first thing they always say when we walk in the door is, "What did you bring me?" There are four of them, ranging in age from three to nine and a half.

GENTLE READER:

Why, pray, do you wish to bring presents to these children? Surely not to see the childish delight break on their merry little faces. Your duty, as a grandmother, is not to feed their insatiable and ungrateful appetites, but to cure them from the multiple rudeness of "What did you bring me?" which combines greed with insensitivity.

The ways in which grandparents can teach manners to children, when the parents do not, are limited. You cannot train them to behave well in general, but you can insist on their doing so to you, which will not only make your life more pleasant, but inform them that there are higher standards of behavior than those with which they are familiar at home. If you have your grandchildren as houseguests, or perhaps take an older one on a trip with you, you can insist that your preference in manners be observed. Miss Manners considers this of sufficient importance to suggest that you think of ways to include these young people in your life under such circumstances.

When you are visiting them, you cannot impose rules different from those permitted by their parents. But you can, and should, refuse to cater to the attitude suggested by their demand. Children should learn that they must pretend not to expect presents, to the extent that they must look surprised at the regular birthday and Christmas offerings, and even more so at such less traditional occasions, such as the return from a trip. They must also learn to look pleased with whatever they get. And finally, they must treat the giver as if what pleases them most about the present is the thoughtfulness of the giver, because however much they love things, they love people more.

This is a difficult order for a small child, and no less important because it is not true. If they learn to behave as if it were, the better sentiment will gradually merge with the basic lust for possessions, and make finer persons.

Therefore, Miss Manners is going to answer your question by recommending the toughest present you can give, although it has the advantage of being cheap: nothing. Brave their disappointment by ignoring it, until it becomes clear to them that the valuable thing you have brought them is the presence of their grandparents.

When they have been shocked into understanding this, give them the present of an excursion with you, or a visit. Then, when they have learned to control themselves and at least to fake an interest in you, you can resume, on an irregular basis, bringing them presents. By that time, you should have gotten to know them as well, and therefore you will be better able than Miss Manners to judge what would please them.

DEAR MISS MANNERS:

Just when do you stop sending gifts for children's birthdays, whether they are monetary or otherwise? We are talking about children that are not your own, perhaps children of friends or maybe even nieces and nephews. It has been many of our opinions that when a child turns 18, that child is considered to be an adult, and the gifts should be no more. Cards, perhaps, would be continued to be sent.

GENTLE READER:

Here is how you can tell when it is time to stop sending children presents, and it doesn't even require remembering how old they are:

When they fail to thank you.

When they fail to have any relationship with you other than thanking you for sending them presents.

Miss Manners does not believe in cutting off a symbolic show of affection on the grounds of age. But she does consider that childhood is sufficient time for gratitude and reciprocal affection to develop if it is ever going to do so.

◁── *Personal Presents* ──▷

DEAR MISS MANNERS:

I am dating a wonderful man who is very kind, generous, and loving. In addition to being considerate and affectionate, he often does things for me (mowing my lawn, redoing the screens in my house, etc.), and he has given me several lovely gifts.

Recently, he bought me jewelry (a necklace and earring set). It is lovely, but definitely not my style. I never want to hurt him or to seem ungrateful for his thoughtfulness and generosity, but I also don't want to pretend with him. So far, I've managed to be very honest about who I am and what I want, as has he.

What should I do in this situation? Is it acceptable to explain to him that while I appreciate his thoughtfulness in giving me this gift, it is a style that I would probably not wear?

GENTLE READER:

And miss the opportunity to say, "How wonderful you are to me, but I couldn't possibly accept jewelry from a gentleman to whom I am not related"?

This is such an endearingly high-minded thing to say that Miss Manners regrets that so many ladies have been discouraged from uttering it by the fact that it requires relinquishing the loot. In your case, this would be no loss. Should the relationship blossom into something properly involving jewelry, you will have a better occasion to acquaint him with your taste.

DEAR MISS MANNERS:

I often perceive in your guidelines unresolved and potentially explosive issues that have been swept under the rug by today's gentry, or paraded in the guise of etiquette. Trusting your expertise to be upright and right-on at the same time, I direct my question to you. I will know, by your response, whether I am to be considered militantly feminist, outrageously gauche, or simply inexperienced if I carry out my plan.

Mother always warned me that gifts bestowed by a beau should never refer to the bedroom or related activities thereof. This includes such articles as: negligees, lingerie, bathrobes. By the same token, I have found a lovely satin bathrobe/smoking jacket which I would like to give my beloved. My dilemma is: Would I be flagrantly ignoring a hard-and-fast rule, or am I wandering onto the rocky road of changing social morals?

GENTLE READER:

Miss Manners never, ever sweeps dirt under the rug; she prefers to gather it up and plant flowers in it. In your case no such effort is necessary. This is one of these rare occasions in which tradition, conscience and personal preference all agree. The choice of whether to be militantly feminist, outrageously gauche or simply inexperienced (Miss Manners would choose one and three with an extra plate of egg rolls) may be avoided.

Your mother said you should never accept articles related to the bedroom. You should listen to your mother, and listen carefully. She never said you shouldn't give such presents, did she? Anyway, your beloved should not be smoking in bed. Tell him that Miss Manners said it is dangerous, and that he should wear his smoking jacket in the smoking room.

The Price

DEAR MISS MANNERS:

Whenever a friend receives a gift bought on-line, she goes to the site to see how much the giver spent on the item. While there's nothing wrong with being curious, I find this habit obnoxious and told her so. What do you think?

GENTLE READER:

About which obnoxious habit? Checking on the prices of presents? Bragging about checking on the prices of presents? Informing friends that they are obnoxious? Miss Manners isn't crazy about any of them.

She would, however, find it useful to know that a friend puts no value on presents other than their list price. She would be inspired to leave that friend alone to do her own shopping (with her own money).

DEAR MISS MANNERS:

What is your opinion of people who purposely leave the price tag on gifts in order for the giftee to be aware of the generosity of the giftor?

GENTLE READER:

That the least they can do is to scream as the person is opening the present, lean over and pull the price tag off and drop it into a nearby wastebasket, where it can be left, to be examined later at leisure by everyone.

⁓ The Thought ⁓

DEAR MISS MANNERS:

If it's the thought that counts in gift giving, how do you respond to a gift that obviously involved no thought at all? I have a sister-in-law who I swear does all of her holiday shopping in five minutes at the nearest discount drugstore. You wouldn't believe the cheap stuff she gives as gifts. It's not that she's poor or has bad taste. She's better off than I am and buys lovely things for herself. She just doesn't seem to believe in spending time or money on gifts. Frankly, I'd rather she gave me no gift. Can I tell her that?

GENTLE READER:

Kind thoughts and generosity do count, Miss Manners agrees, perhaps doubly at holiday time, so of course you will want to exhibit these qualities yourself. It would be generous to assume that your sister-in-law means well, thank her for whatever you get and kindly give her equally token presents so as to avoid embarrassing her.

Decent Dress
for Ladies and Gentlemen

DON'T EVER allow yourself to be put on the committee in charge of formulating the dress code. Serve on the Clean-up Committee, serve on the Suggestions & Complaints Committee, but keep away from the Dress Code Committee if you value your sanity.

Miss Manners is offering this advice against her own interests, which is to say against the greater interests of the society. (She has a hard time telling these apart.) The job needs to be done. In the absence of dress codes—generally understood ones for the society at large, and specific, often explicitly formulated, ones for particular places and activities—we do not enjoy the happy freedom of comfort and individuality that opponents of dress codes would have us believe. Here's what we enjoy instead:

People insulting one another unintentionally, because they are not familiar with the symbolic meanings they are conveying, and therefore wear baseball caps indoors or casual clothes to dressy events, unaware that others are interpreting their very presence as a show of disrespect.

People insulting one another purposely, either by defying expectations or employing shock tactics, and getting away with it by feigning ignorance if caught.

People allowing the fashion industry to take over the job of regulating clothing, although its aim is understandably to cause confusion and expense rather than order and relief.

If all that weren't enough burden on the civilized life, consider that when all of life is a costume party, costume parties are no longer possible. (Perhaps Miss Manners should be counting that one as a plus.)

When one or another of these situations leads to a crisis, the solution proposed is to promulgate a dress code. "This way, there will be no misunderstandings," declares some innocent person who does not understand what is to come.

Preliminary discussions are harmonious. Everyone agrees that the code must be simple and commonsensical. It should not cause anyone extra expense. It must not be substantively different for men and women, and it should allow exceptions for items of clothing pertaining to the wearer's nationality or religion. There will be no attempt to stifle anyone's individuality of expression (except that of the person whose startling appearance led to the clamor for a dress code).

A few bland examples are given: business attire to be worn on certain occasions, perhaps a ban on jeans and tank or halter tops, and a requirement that proper shoes be worn. This is quickly followed by the promise that every effort will be made to interpret particular cases reasonably.

As it turns out, that last declaration apparently applies only to the committee. Everybody else is busy applying that threatened creativity to interpreting the rules.

A gentleman notes that the rules are not supposed to be sexist and then demands that ladies be required to wear neckties. A lady retorts that gentlemen should have to wear panty hose. Someone whose foot is in a cast will note bitterly that wearing a proper shoe on it is not possible.

Business attire is challenged with the declaration that casual Monday-through-Friday is the modern business standard, and with illustrations from businesses that require bathing suits, paint-splattered overalls or tutus. Scornful questions are put about what is meant by jeans (does that include a three-piece denim suit?) and halter tops (then why not ban ball dresses at dances, because they are more revealing?).

You could take away the right of the citizens to vote and arouse less outrage. So the committee retreats into withdrawing the guidelines and recommending that people use their individual judgment, which returns the situation to its original state when it was agreed that something needed to be done.

Miss Manners agrees that reasonable people need to agree on the broad outlines of acceptability in appearance, and to be reasonable about interpreting what qualifies. What makes it difficult is that there is no strict requirement for reasonable people.

All the same, we seem to have arrived at a basic standard uniform for everyone, regardless of age, gender or financial resources: blue jeans, T-shirts, sneakers and baseball caps. In summer, the jeans are cut off to appear as shorts, and in winter, sweatshirts and parkas are added. There is still room for expressing one's individuality by the choice of slogans printed on the clothes by the manufacturer.

The suggestion that schoolchildren abandon this uniform in favor of a more distinctive one pops up now and then, but it generally pops down again, as it is thought to interfere with self-expression.

On festive occasions, everyone must wear black. Gentlemen have the option of adding a touch of red, which they oddly believe to be a comical commentary on traditional formal dress. They succeed better in amusing traditionalists by the mixture of traditional formal styles that gentlemen wear at their weddings.

Brides wear strapless white dresses, but on other highly festive occasions, all ladies wear black dresses held up by narrow straps. Black is not worn at funerals, because these are now considered to be casual occasions.

Miss Manners trusts that no one mistakes this for her dress code, much less her taste. It is simply what she observes around her. She admits that it simplifies dressing and eliminates the question of inherent quality in competition, as this no longer seems to be related to price.

Furthermore, the basic designs exhibit a certain utilitarian dignity. Blue jeans surely represent the pinnacle of design in working clothes, and ladies are surely entitled to the practicality of the black evening uniform from which gentlemen have long benefited.

Miss Manners is not going to remark that all this seems a bit drab, or that it reminds her of the way depressed and tyrannized populations looked before they discovered freedom and fashion. She has seen too much of what can be done by those who have free rein to express themselves in decorating their persons to encourage them.

She does note that it would be enormously helpful to society to be able to tell at a glance who is at work and who is at leisure and which occasions are considered to be of dignified importance and which less so. Furthermore, she believes that high school proms would not look nearly so peculiar if the young had ever experienced formality before.

And she would like to put in a plea for tolerating clothing eccentrics. She says nothing of herself, with her penchant for daytime dress in the daytime and evening dress in the evening, not to mention the accompanying gloves. But she has been asked to make the world safe for gentlemen of her acquaintance who would like to be allowed to go about freely without everyone's demanding that they remove their jackets and ties.

DEAR MISS MANNERS:

Would you comment on the decline of elegance? The fashions today look like rejects from a garage sale.

GENTLE READER:

Elegance in fashion didn't decline: It stopped short the day Worth stopped providing wardrobes to the heroines of Henry James' novels, who traveled seasonally to Paris for this purpose.

DRESSING FOR THE OCCASION

"What shall I wear?" is society's second most frequently asked question. The first is, "Do you really love me?" No matter what one replies to either one, it is never accepted as settling the issue.

The only sensible answer to the clothes question is one that Miss Manners learned long ago, when she was confined to the dormitory of a female college, an educational experience if ever there was one. In that establishment, everyone asked "What shall I wear?" every Friday, Saturday and Sunday so that, once dressed, they could go out and ask the other question.

"Wear your yellow silk, dear," a wise student used to reply each time the question was asked. It spared her a great deal of idiotic conversation about other people's wardrobes and how they felt about each item.

However, Miss Manners is willing to discuss categories of dress. The terms in current use are Formal, Informal, Semiformal, Don't Dress and Optional. None of them means anything.

Once, some of them did have meaning. Informal meant black tie, or what some people now call Formal, and Don't Dress meant dark suits, or what other people now call Formal. True formal dress was white tie, a style now kept alive chiefly by magicians and pianists. What Semiformal is, Miss Manners has never discovered, although it gives her a vivid picture of someone in tails with jeans, probably attending the Academy Awards ceremony. Optional is, of course, the same as saying nothing at all, but trying to make it sound organized.

You will notice that Miss Manners always explains the specifics in terms of gentlemen's clothes. This is because the difference between a lady's most formal dress and her second most formal dress is whatever she wishes to make it, while the difference between a gentleman's is down there in black and white, even before he gets the statement from the rental agency. For that reason, invitations that mean white tie or black tie come right out and say so. No improvised designations should appear on invitation cards, because they will only confuse the issue.

Ah, you say, but then, what do I wear? Miss Manners knew you were going to ask that. You have been invited to a dinner that has one of the above meaningless designations on the card, or no instructions at all, and your yellow silk is at the cleaners. The general rule here is custom. In many communities, everyone knows that "Just wear anything" means anything from the designer salon, or else anything from the floor of your closet, and "We're going to dress up" means either that we're all going to look smashing, or else we're all going to comb our hair.

It is with inexplicable pride that people describe themselves, their homes and their dinner parties as "casual" or "informal." From the tone of voice in which just about everyone says "Oh, of course, it's to be *terribly* informal" or "We're *always* casual," you would think that America now is like the court of Louis XIV, and that they, alone, have introduced some spontaneity.

When Miss Manners longs for a bit of style in daily living, she is by no means thinking only of styles that were associated with the rich. Until recent times, both rich and poor people distinguished between their work clothes and "Sunday best," between meals on the run and company dinner, between the family room in the back and the front parlor. This distinction was not an affectation, but a special effort made out of respect for an occasion, or aesthetics difficult to maintain daily. Miss Manners was once asked whether dress at her own dinner party was to be "Formal or comfortable," and, given such a choice, replied "Informal but uncomfortable." Informality does not necessarily produce comfort, and comfort is not necessarily desirable, as any wearer of high heels can attest.

When it is truly a matter of acute discomfort, Miss Manners is not opposed to the entire society's agreeing to make certain changes in conventional dress or furnishings. For example, Miss Manners always thought the stocking or panty stocking a fetching garment for springtime, autumn or heated ballrooms, but a menace in really cold or hot weather, and she is delighted at the spread of the "city sandal," which may be worn barefoot in summer, and the leather boot, which may be worn with heavy knee socks in winter. She would even be willing to listen to arguments in favor of replacing the necktie—if another formal daytime standard were universally adopted.

What she opposes is defying prevailing standards. Once the society has agreed what is proper—as in the cases of the boots and sandals, but not yet the neckties— Miss Manners expects people to observe this in public places.

～ *The Courtroom* ～

DEAR MISS MANNERS:

I have been summoned for jury service. What would be an appropriate dress code for the selection day? If selected, what is recommended for a female juror to wear while in court?

GENTLE READER:

There is no shortage of popular role models whose fashion examples in ordinary life may be questionable, but who are impeccable when it comes to dressing for court.

Captains of industry may be confused about the difference between work clothes and sports clothes, and stars of rock and screen may be confused about what it means to get dressed at all, but you can rely on their good taste when they show up in court. To a defendant, they all agree that proper courtroom dress consists of suits with ties for gentlemen, and with knee-length skirts for ladies, and little jewelry, none of it attached to unusual parts of the body.

True, citizens who are in court because they have been summoned for jury duty do not generally maintain such a strict standard of propriety. Regrettably, they often appear in the minimum their local courts will allow, and even more regrettably, some courts allow a minimum just this side of decency.

As you have asked Miss Manners, however, she must declare her agreement with the conservative element, which is to say the celebrity defendants. She believes you should show symbolic respect for our court system, even if your life or liberty does not depend on it.

The Porch

DEAR MISS MANNERS:

Is it necessary to dress to go out on the porch in the morning and pick up the paper?

GENTLE READER:

It depends on what you mean by dress. Hat and gloves are no longer considered necessary for such an excursion, but it is customary to be covered in such a way as to be able to pick up the newspaper without oneself making news in the neighborhood.

The City Streets

DEAR MISS MANNERS:

I am a middle-aged male who enjoys wearing women's clothing. I have always restricted this behavior to the privacy of my apartment, but now I have a wonderful opportunity to venture out in public while cross-dressed.

A sympathetic female friend has graciously invited me to dress as a woman and accompany her to New York City for a weekend of museum visits, theater-going, gourmet dining and shopping. She believes my appearance and demeanor are sufficiently ladylike to avoid ticklish situations. I have selected a subdued wardrobe characterized by modest hemlines, medium heels and demure makeup. I have no desire to draw attention to myself and I will endeavor to be as inconspicuous as possible.

Despite these precautions, some people may discern that I am a male in women's clothing. While I am prepared to accept any opprobrium that may ensue, I am worried that it may be impolite to impose—however tastefully—my uncommon sartorial tastes on an unwitting public. Please be so kind as to benefit me with your thoughts on this matter.

GENTLE READER:

Miss Manners has more faith than you do in the sophistication of New Yorkers. While it may be true that they have rarely observed anyone of ladylike appearance and demeanor, whose sartorial taste runs to the subdued, modest and demure, she believes they can be trusted to absorb the shock. She wishes you a pleasant holiday.

~ *The Workplace* ~

As the art of predicting trends consists of (1) claiming that things will keep going in the current direction until they reach the ludicrous limits of current imagination, and (2) hoping that no one will dig up your predictions at the time you set for them to come true, Miss Manners is not asking for credit. But you may be kind enough to recall that the very first time anyone used the term Casual Friday, she predicted that the rest of the week, not to mention general confusion, would soon follow. Rather than being a prelude to the weekend, Casual would spread throughout the work week, creating extra work.

Such has come to pass; one business institution after another allowed play clothes at work. And although this change is known as "relaxing the dress code," it required a new workforce of consultants, shopping guides, advisers and rule-makers whose function it was to draw up a new code to replace the older one, only with more detailed rules, and to teach people how to implement it in order to achieve casualness.

It seems that although people will fight for their right to wear casual dress to work, nobody knows what it is. Does it include jeans, athletic shoes and tank tops? Does it cover, or rather uncover, undergarments, tattoos and navels?

And what's this about its being comfortable? Does that mean a ban on tight pants and minimal skirts? Are exemptions made for people who are uncomfortable if they're not dressing for work the way they are used to doing?

As you can imagine, Miss Manners' sympathies are with that last sort. But unlike those who taunt them with being stuffy (and Miss Manners has to keep reminding herself that this is intended as an insult), she is broad-minded enough to look beneath the surface. Of the issue, she hastens to add, not of the clothing. That would be indecent.

It would also be naive. We still have the old form of naïveté, which says that people should judge everyone on what's inside, not what they're wearing, but forgets to tell us how we can sort through lots of people quickly, not to mention how we obtain a peek into their true selves. Now we also have an odd form of naïveté, on the part of dressing-down consultants who claim that dispensing with formalities increases the rate of information exchange.

A dress code is a way of exchanging information. Unlike race or gender, it can be chosen for symbolic meaning. People can read clothing instantly to see when you are on duty as well as whether that includes being crisply professional, when you are at leisure and when you are partying. If you match costume to role arbitrarily, you risk being misread, attracting advances when you want to attract business and vice versa.

But (here comes the broad-minded part) fashions change and so does the language of symbolism. People are already adjusting to the idea of billionaires appropriating working-class clothing, and to reading what used to look like a boss (in suit and tie) and stockroom boy (in jeans and T-shirt) as, instead, an employee and an owner.

So all right, we can change all the symbols and it will work just as well, as long as everybody learns how to read them. Miss Manners doesn't own stock in the stocking industry, and her fortunes are not tied to ties. Go ahead and decree that respectable citizens will be known by their orange jumpsuits and suspicious characters by their devotion to pinstriped suits.

⌒ A Business Reception ⌒

DEAR MISS MANNERS:

I'm a college student about to embark into the business world and I was wondering if you could please clear up the appropriate attire on cocktail parties before I make a faux pas. I thought a cocktail dress fell above the knee, but my roommate insists it can be any length, as long as it is sans sequins or other decoration. Could you please advise?

GENTLE READER:

Miss Manners doesn't suppose she could advise you to embark upon a business in which the first thing you need to know is not how to dress for drinks?

All right, then. In any decent line of work, people wear their business clothes to office parties, ladies adding whatever festive touches they can add in the ladies' room. You might want to be less decent when you go out socially, when cocktail dresses can be any length except floor length.

~ A Diplomatic Reception ~

DEAR MISS MANNERS:

I received a formal invitation from the Secretary General of the Organization of American States to a reception, and it says, in the lower right-hand corner, "Dark business suit/Long dress." As a matter of fact, I was planning to wear a business suit anyway. What did they think I would wear to a diplomatic reception—my jogging suit? It looks peculiar to me, if not insulting. I've seen "Black Tie" and "Informal" written on this type of card, but never "Dark business suit." What are they afraid of?

GENTLE READER:

Men in white silk suits and Panama hats with evil political intentions.

~ When the House Is on Fire ~

DEAR MISS MANNERS:

For several years now, I have occupied a succession of high-rise apartments, and in each of them this problem of mine has come up. Specifically, what is the correct attire for those little impromptu social hours under the lobby chandeliers during a fire in the trash chute? These occasions invariably occur well after midnight, so that one leaps from one's bed to attend the festive gathering.

My feeling is that one's dress should be adequately covering but informal. I generally wear a navy blue nylon pajama and matching coat, and tennis shoes. Last time, I spent an agreeable hour chatting with (1) a young man clad in running trunks and running shoes; (2) an executive type in a business suit with vest, carrying a briefcase; (3) a young lady in a scarlet caftan, her head swathed in a brilliant yellow towel. Her accessory was a brown grocery bag that contained a live cat.

GENTLE READER:

Your instincts are correct, but, then, so are everyone else's, as fires are classified socially with come-as-you-are parties. However, Miss Manners' instinct would be to avoid the man in the three-piece suit. A person carrying a briefcase at midnight is up to no good.

CONTROVERSIAL CLOTHING

~ Ladies' Trouser Suits ~

At the highest levels of government, for work and on daytime ceremonial occasions, American ladies in official positions are now routinely wearing trouser suits. (Well, at least senators, representatives and the ranking ladies who live or work in the White House are. You can never tell about those stylish justices.)

Miss Manners considers this an overdue triumph for decorum. The gentlemen are no longer subject to becoming overexcited by catching a glimpse of exposed ankle.

It is not often that she finds a sensible trend in the world of feminine fashion. Other such news—heralding the return of what Miss Manners actually wears, such as hats, gloves and evening dresses with trains, rather than what she countenances in others, as she does the trouser suit—amounts to nothing more than regularly repeated false alarms.

When the female equivalent of the male suit first began to be widely worn, it provoked outrage. Restaurateurs with fancy establishments declared that they would bar the door to ladies with the audacity to show up wearing pants. And that was in the first miniskirt era, when the same people had managed to accept the rapid retreat of skirts—apparently only with the proviso that these would not be replaced.

At the time, Miss Manners refused to become aghast. The prescience of denouncing ladies' tailored trouser suits struck her as an invitation to join members of the French Academy who barred the Impressionists, and the first-night audience at Stravinsky's *Rite of Spring* whose musical sensitivity led them to tear up the theater. One does not recover from such reputations. And surely there is enough nasty business around to keep the discriminating busy without having to scorn what will soon come to be considered conventional, if not classic.

The grand restaurateurs' understanding of the gender factor in fashion did not improve after this defeat. When the law forced them to abandon their policy of hiring only males to wait on table (on the notion that waitresses were better suited to simpler restaurants, where they could carry heavier trays for lighter tips), they dressed their waitresses in male formal dress, complete with bow ties.

What this says symbolically is: We still have male service, but some of it is done by male impersonators.

The difference between that and the female business suit, whether that has a skirt or trousers, is that it is an adaptation rather than an imitation. While benefiting from such advantages as freedom from worry of exposing various parts of the body to view and criticism and compatibility with low-heeled shoes, the suit retains feminine access to the full color spectrum and (with the addition of jewelry and scarves, and the addition or total subtraction of blouses) individualization.

More significantly, it provides that recognizably professional look that gentlemen have always been able to summon. In contrast, ladies were presumed to be present on official occasions only in a social capacity, and their prescribed wardrobes—floaty dresses with whimsical hats for the most formal daytime occasions—reflected that. Even now, there is an oddly reactionary tendency among young ladies to wear clothes to work that are amazingly, ah, social in original intent. The trouser suit, in contrast, symbolizes seriousness. So do the skirted suit and the coatdress, if they are of decent length, and Miss Manners will personally stick with them—despite that pesky problem of the provocatively exposed ankles.

⌒ Undergarments ⌒

DEAR MISS MANNERS:

We noticed that when men wear an open-collared shirt as "business casual," it exposes the collar of the undershirt. We feel it is sloppy, and there are V-neck undershirts available for a neat look. For a man, exposing the undershirt is comparable to a woman exposing her bra straps while in "business casual" dress.

GENTLE READER:

As opposed to exposing her bra straps in social dress? Or just going out on the town in her slip?

It is not to disagree with you that Miss Manners mentions such things, but only to expose the extent of the problem. A society where formal dress for ladies consists of what they used to wear before they got dressed is going to have a hard time explaining to gentlemen why they should be embarrassed to have their undershirt collars out. Yet they should be.

～ Adjustments ～

DEAR MISS MANNERS:

I have an embarrassing problem with my clothes that I also see other women having. My shoulders are fairly narrow, and my bra straps keep slipping down my arms. It isn't too obvious under most clothes, but it is very annoying. Is it ever proper to discreetly adjust your straps while in public? I see some women pull their straps up even in the office, while others just tolerate it until they get to a private place. What do you think?

GENTLE READER:

Some clothing emergencies are attractive and others are not. Tightening an earring, for example, can be a lovely gesture, but reaching inside one's front and giving a yank to an errant brassiere strap cannot. At sewing shops, you can buy tiny grosgrain ribbons with snaps on them to sew inside your clothing and hold the straps in place. This will leave your hands free to adjust your stockings.

～ Fur Coats ～

DEAR MISS MANNERS:

I bought a fur coat this year. It's not a terribly expensive coat, as fur coats go, and I got it on sale. I feel it is a better investment than buying a new cloth coat every two or three years, as this should last me quite a while. But I am really tired of people kidding me or worse about wearing a fur coat. What can I say in reply to cracks about how much it must have cost, it's making me such a grand lady, and so on?

GENTLE READER:

A lady always explains a fur coat by saying that she suffers terribly from the cold. This shifts the focus from her presumably bulging bank account, which is vulgar, to her presumably aristocratic frailty, which is not.

～ Gentlemen's Dinner Suits ～

How many of you gentlemen are engaged in righteous protests, fueled by outrage that it is your own closest relatives and friends who are pressuring you to betray your principles? Miss Manners finds it amazing how worked up gentlemen can get when they are asked to dress up. Those simple words, "black tie," make them see red.

Not all of them, of course. Some who see red are willing to don evening clothes if only they can turn the outfit into something more sprightly. So they add red ties and cummerbunds, or pink ones, or if they stick to black ties, ones that come in funny configurations. This is a whimsical, although curiously unamusing, form of protest. Diehards will refuse to wear any semblance of evening clothes, preferring either to defy their hosts or to stay home and sulk.

Miss Manners has never succeeded in finding out what this was really all about— but not for lack of hearing gentlemen's laments. The chief complaint is that evening clothes are uncomfortable—the same lament that those who are not invited out in the evening say about wearing ties at all. Mind you, we are not talking about white tie, with its stiff shirt, waistcoats and tails—the getup in which orchestra conductors habitually jump up and down and flail their arms about. Most formal events now require only the dinner jacket, which is cut like any ordinary suit, with which a soft shirt may be worn, so if it is less comfortable than other suits, complaints should be directed at one's tailor, not one's hosts. Especially if they come from people wearing tight jeans.

A distaste for conformity is a big issue to those for whom casual is law. But Miss Manners is afraid that any credibility this argument might have is undermined by those who make it. They have the impertinent habit of hectoring gentlemen who don't conform to their dress code of jeans or khakis and T-shirts, ordering them to take off their jackets and ties.

Another professed objection is based on the antique notion that evening clothes are the costume of comic strip plutocrats who smoke cigars and hang on to lampposts for balance. Americans used to pity and be amused at countries where the citizens all wore drab work clothes and the leaders were belligerently under-dressed for state occasions; now those people have discovered fashion, and we wear drab work clothes and are suspicious of formality.

Miss Manners suspects that what it really signifies is the reluctance of anyone over drinking age to be taken for an adult. While very young gentlemen are dressing like hardened thugs, their elders are trying not to look grown up. (The gentlemen, that is. As pubescent girls affect the jaded hussy look, their elders feel safe in doing so too.)

This seems a particularly bad bargain. If forfeiting stylistic variety and glamour could purchase eternal youth, Miss Manners (who was born old and marches happily on from there) supposes it might be worthwhile. But it has become just another compensation—along with precedence and other forms of respect—that adults have given up, for which they have gotten nothing in return.

CONFUSING CLOTHING

~ *Gloves* ~

DEAR MISS MANNERS:

What are "eighteen-button gloves"?

GENTLE READER:

These are white gloves that come above the elbow and make a riveting show when the wearer slowly peels them off before she can take a drink. They are called "eighteen-button" because they have three pearl buttons at each wrist.

DEAR MISS MANNERS:

No doubt this is a stupid question, and I am demonstrating my unfitness for respectable society, but *why* doesn't a pair of eighteen-button gloves have eighteen buttons on it, or even eighteen buttons a glove, for a grand total of thirty-six?

GENTLE READER:

Yes, indeed, this is a silly question, because everybody knows that there are buttons and buttons, and while eighteen-button gloves have three small pearl buttons each at the musketeer (which everyone knows is the opening at the wrist), there are, indeed, eighteen buttons on each in length. That button is a standard of measurement of approximately one inch. The approximate part is because it is a French standard of measurement.

If you begin measuring at the base of the thumb, you will find that four-button gloves end about the wrist, eight-button below the elbow, ten-button above the elbow, and twenty-six button, the longest, up to the armpit. Naturally, this system only comes out right on French arms.

DEAR MISS MANNERS:

I will be happy to carry on your crusade to increase formality in dressing by wearing gloves, once you fill me in. I know the basic rules, such as no eating, drinking or smoking with gloves on, that a lady keeps gloves on while shaking hands and that little white cotton gloves are worn only in summer, but I'm fuzzy about the rest.

What kind of white gloves are worn properly throughout the rest of the year? What are the acceptable ones made of, and on what occasions are different lengths of glove worn? When should gloves be carried? Is it improper to wear them to din-

INTERMEDIATE CIVILIZATION

ner or cocktail parties, where they must be removed to participate in the main event? If not, where are the gloves placed after removal and exactly how are eighteen-button gloves peeled off?

Is it proper to wear eighteen-button gloves in any color other than white? What other kinds of gloves may be worn in non-white colors? In the daytime, should certain kinds of gloves only be worn when one is wearing a hat? Are gloves removed upon entering people's homes or in certain buildings?

GENTLE READER:

Miss Manners congratulates you on taking up an activity so fraught with exciting symbolism. Those who believe the wearing of little white gloves to have been symbolic of female repression make her long for the days when a glove itself could be used to challenge such insulting nonsense.

Fun with gloves consists of pulling them on and peeling them off, as ladies and strippers both know. (It certainly isn't in trying to find someone nowadays who knows how to clean them properly.) So they should be taken everywhere; a lady does not leave her house without gloves, even if she is so rash as to dash out during the day without a hat.

Other than in summer, proper gloves are made of leather, and the only white ones a lady in private life wears are doeskin or glace kidskin with evening clothes. The idea is to establish a relationship between the sleeve and the glove—the longest gloves with ball dresses that leave the arm bare, gloves to the elbow with elbow-length sleeves and short gloves with long sleeves.

Temporary fashion insanity might result in the shorter gloves being of a color other than white, but white eighteen-button gloves must be white or whitish. For ladies, that is. For strippers, black mesh is probably better, and black mesh with appliquéd sequins even better.

Daytime gloves are also leather, but in reasonable colors (such as buff, navy, brown or black; fuchsia is not a reasonable color) to match or complement the clothing. These are removed when one goes indoors, and may be carried or stuffed into the coat pocket, purse, muff or nearest gentleman's pocket. Gentlemen remove their gloves when shaking hands; ladies do not. Please do not expect Miss Manners to justify this discrepancy on any basis of logic, morality or equal opportunity.

Evening gloves are kept on for dancing, but when they are removed to eat or drink, they are carried. If one needs both hands, for instance to eat dinner, they are put on the lap, where the safest way to retain them is to make a soft package by folding the napkin on top and around them.

The answer to how they are peeled off is—with slow drama. One tugs gently at the fingers of one with the other hand, and then softly pushes the glove along the arm, first from the wrist, then below the elbow (being careful not to catch it on jewelry, as any rings or bracelets are of course worn strictly inside the glove). Properly done, this should hypnotize every gentleman at the table—as ladies and strippers both know.

~ *Hats* ~

DEAR MISS MANNERS:

Where does one wear a hat these days?

GENTLE READER:

Same as always: on the head. (Whoops. You'll have to pardon Miss Manners, who occasionally gets giddy after a full day of this sort of thing.) The proper answer is that the occasions for wearing hats, for both men and women, are the same as always, but the purpose is the opposite. One used to wear a hat with daytime clothes to be conservative; it is now done to be shocking.

DEAR MISS MANNERS:

Everyone knows the proper thing for a man to do during the playing of our national anthem is to remove his hat or baseball cap. Are women also expected to remove their hats or caps?

GENTLE READER:

At the risk of making more trouble, Miss Manners suggests thinking of this in terms of the hat, rather than its bearer. Gentlemen's hats and caps are removed as a sign of respect, but ladies' hats are not.

When the rule was made, ladies did not wear baseball caps; if they choose to do so, they must abide by the rules that go with them. Miss Manners would appreciate no one's taking this argument to its logical conclusion in regard to gentlemen wearing ladies' hats.

DEAR MISS MANNERS:

I have recently purchased a charming chapeau that I dearly love, and I want to know when and where it is proper to wear them. Can I wear my hat indoors at a luncheon or dinner? Obviously, I wouldn't wear it at the theater, but is it correct at other social events? Can I wear it to church?

GENTLE READER:

The reason Miss Manners adores hats is that they have so much to say; you bear this out by describing yours as "charming." In order to decide where to wear it, you must listen to just what it is that your hat is saying so charmingly. There are charming little hats that say "When God created me, He did a fine job, and I am grateful for that," and these hats may be worn to church. Charming little hats that say "Why, hello there" are better left for later in the day. The general rule is that if the hat looks as if you had it built, it may properly go to daytime functions; if it looks as if it just landed in your hair (tiny bits of feathers, sequins or whatever), it is called a cocktail hat, and goes out at night.

A lady certainly may wear a hat inside church, a restaurant or anywhere else during the daytime. The exception is a function in her own house, where hat wearing would suggest that she had some place better to go, unlike her guests. It is gentlemen who must take their hats off indoors, although they are finding it difficult these days, because they don't have any hats either.

DEAR MISS MANNERS:

What would be appropriate attire for a gentleman accompanying a lady to theater, assuming she has chosen to wear something simple and classic topped off with a small, black, veiled hat?

GENTLE READER:

A cocktail hat is sufficient decoration for any two people, and therefore the gentleman should think of himself as background material and dress accordingly. If he does not wish to wear wallpaper, a dark suit will do.

DEAR MISS MANNERS:

What is the difference between a gentleman's top hat and an opera hat?

GENTLE READER:

The opera hat, like some gentlemen Miss Manners has observed at the opera, collapses.

~ *Shoes* ~

DEAR MISS MANNERS:

What is the proper way to walk in high-heeled shoes?

GENTLE READER:

Left, right, left, right, left, right.

⌒ White Shoes ⌒

DEAR MISS MANNERS:

I think some in our family don't know dress etiquette. I told my family members that one should not wear white when there is an R in the month. They doubt my knowledge. Do you?

GENTLE READER:

For a moment there she did, Miss Manners must confess.

"Oysters!" she felt like calling out. "You poor soul, you've mistaken your shoes for oysters."

This apparently nonsensical lament refers to the instruction (not issued from the realm of etiquette) that oysters should be eaten only in months that have the letter R in their names, namely September through April. The season for the ban on wearing white shoes (not on anything white; for example, it does not apply to shirts or teeth) is Memorial Day through Labor Day. She soon realized, however, that the two formulae are pretty close. We're talking about less than a month's difference. If Miss Manners were one to compromise, she would suggest splitting the difference, but unfortunately, she is not.

⌒ A Reply ⌒

DEAR MISS MANNERS:

I read with some concern your ultimatum about not wearing white shoes before Memorial Day, since I have been wearing cream-colored shoes on slightly formal occasions (church, theater, concerts) since spring began. You'll be gratified to know that on these occasions, I also wear a dress and spring blazer. I've noticed that most other women have adhered to wearing their brown and black winter shoes. Now that you have been so wonderful as to dictate when to and not to wear white shoes, would you please clarify this matter of when to wear cream-colored shoes?

GENTLE READER:

Nothing is ever black and white, except the rule that white shoes may be worn only between Memorial Day and Labor Day. Nevertheless, there are some gray areas, which include everything cream-colored.

If you can call your off-white shoes cream, bone, beige or taupe, you may wear them whenever you like. However, if they are merely dirty white shoes, clean them and put them away until Memorial Day. If you are being married in a white dress, you may wear white shoes. In fact, you may not wear any other color shoe, not even sensible brown-and-white spectator pumps. A white satin bridal slipper should not be open-toed in case the bridegroom is seized with the desire to drink champagne out of it. This is a messy way to start a marriage.

~ Handkerchiefs ~

DEAR MISS MANNERS:

Can the handkerchief in a gentleman's breast pocket ever be used?

GENTLE READER:

The handkerchief is in the breast pocket, where everyone can see how clean it is, to indicate that (1) the gentleman owns one; and (2) the gentleman does not sneeze. In the case of true gentlemen, Miss Manners takes the first for granted and does not believe the second. Therefore, she prefers that the handkerchief be kept in the trouser pocket and taken out when needed. A truly fastidious gentleman may wish to take it out three seconds in advance of need. It is always gentlemanly to offer something to dry any tears the gentleman has caused.

~ T-Shirts ~

DEAR MISS MANNERS:

Is there a proper way to ask someone to stand still long enough for someone else to read their T-shirt? I have seen many interesting looking ones, but don't feel socially correct in stopping someone because of their choice in clothing. Any hints?

GENTLE READER:

If people insist upon making billboards of themselves, Miss Manners can only imagine that they wish to attract readers. Surely it is reasonable to assume that they intend to waive the rule against staring at people's chests.

However, this is often not the case. This connection between writing and reading may have eluded them. One must therefore exercise caution and read discreetly. Exclaiming "Hold still—can't you see I'm reading?" or "Your arm is in my way" is not polite. The most Miss Manners will permit is "What an interesting shirt—do you mind if I see what it says?"

⌀ *Trains* ⌀

Nobody is more pleased than Miss Manners to see trains back on holiday skirts and dresses. She has always thought that ladies should occupy as much space as possible, symbolically and otherwise. But the rule—"Don't board the train while it's in motion, or, for that matter, while it is stationary"—is easier in theory than in practice.

When conducting a train, a lady should be on the alert for other traffic. In crowds, others have the right of way, so the lady should be prepared to clear the track (holding the train by a ribboned handle, a metal skirt lifter—expect that Miss Manners is the only one who seems to have one of these objects, once so useful for protecting a lady's wardrobe from the dirt and worse on the streets—or her own dainty hand). When standing in a crowded area, she can subtly rotate herself until the train is gathered into a neat circle around her feet.

Nevertheless, a prudent gentleman should also be on constant alert, walking ever so slightly ahead of any trained lady he is accompanying and keeping a lookout ahead for those he is not.

CHILDREN'S DRESS

DEAR MISS MANNERS:

When do children dress up these days, and what are children's dress-up clothes now? I want to send my goddaughter a dress, but I've never seen her wear one.

GENTLE READER:

Children have two styles of dress these days. One, which consists of velvet dresses for girls and velvet suits for boys, is worn only to performances of *The Nutcracker*. The other, which consists of rags, is worn for everything else life has to offer. Miss Manners does not condone this, but that was not your question.

⌀ *Uniforms* ⌀

DEAR MISS MANNERS:

We attend a small, coeducational, private school. We bear the awesome impediment of wearing the same clothes to school every day. (We do change the articles themselves. The "style," or rather lack thereof, is, however, constant.) We would like your opinion of such a uniform. If you could also address the question whether we should have a "non-uniform" day, when students dress formally but not in adherence to the uniform regulations—our gratitude would be abysmal.

GENTLE READER:

Miss Manners believes that doing away with rules for the young takes all the fun out of life for those in the rebellious years. She feels that even one free day violates this. Besides, students who are not required to wear uniforms all look so drearily identical in their T-shirts, jeans and sneakers. At least in uniform, your teachers can tell you abysmal students apart.

~ *Bathing Costumes* ~

DEAR MISS MANNERS:

We are vacationing in Florida this winter, and my seven-year-old daughter wants a bikini. Many of her friends wear two-piece suits, but I think it's in poor taste at their age. Would you settle this for us?

GENTLE READER:

Poor taste is displaying one's bosom. Displaying one's lack of it is poor judgment.

JEWELRY AND OTHER ADORNMENTS

Because it is vulgar to adorn oneself with too many valuables, there has long been a rule cautioning ladies to protect themselves against the danger of looking flashy. Miss Manners learned it from her dear mother: "When you believe you are perfectly dressed, and are quite satisfied with your appearance, before you go out, remove one piece of jewelry."

So that she would never forget, Miss Manners copied this rule onto the back of a photograph of Queen Alexandra, who is demurely pictured wearing five different diamond necklaces stacked as chokers, diamond drop earrings, two snake bracelets, nine brooches, five jeweled orders and a crown. At least that is all that is visible in this particular pose, which is only a three-quarter view, and shows her turned slightly to the side. Presumably the jewels nestling on one shoulder are matched on the other, and there seems to be something glittery peeking out from under the arm in which she is carrying a jeweled fan. Miss Manners has always wondered what it was that the dear lady removed.

The rule is just as good today as it was then, and probably just as faithfully followed. When today's ladies are dressed to face the world, they should check their appearance and remove one valuable object. But—what will it be?

The security identification on a chain around the neck? The telephone hitched onto the belt? The personal organizer sticking out of the jacket pocket?

Something's got to go, and the one earring that was taken off in order to answer the telephone doesn't count.

Miss Manners is not so much worried about ladies looking flashy as she is about their being overburdened. It seems that the more convenient and miniaturized a lady's necessaries become, the more things she has to pin or chain to her clothes. In addition to the likelihood of resembling an electronic bulletin board, there is the danger of pitching forward from the weight. If shoulder bags and backpacks weren't required for everything a lady must haul but can't actually hang or pin on herself, they would still be needed for ballast.

Ladies didn't used to need security tags. But of course that was in days long past. However, they had even more utilitarian objects to hang on themselves or their clothing: Before the invention of the wristwatch, watches were worn on the lapel, hanging from little matching brooches, or as rings for the fingers. Eyeglasses might be attached to an elastic to hang on their own brooch, or worn on a chain around the neck.

Also to be worn on the fingers were rings with tiny chains attached to clasps, to hold handkerchiefs, or to larger mesh circlets to hold gloves, or to tussy-mussies for holding nosegays. Coin purses and key rings were made with short chains and hooks to fit on the belt. So were skirt lifters (for lifting the long skirt slightly above the ground when the street was messy—what did you think?).

Then there was the chatelaine, the wide brooch from which all sorts of miniaturized but useful things might dangle on chains: scissors, pencils, notebooks, stamp holders, needle cases, thimbles, pin holders, button hooks, pen knives, spoons, pill boxes, mirrors, perfume bottles, vinagrettes, nutmeg graters and boxes to hold beauty marks. Presumably, a fastidious lady did not wear them all at the same time. Before she went out, she might have removed the stamp holder.

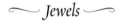 *Jewels*

DEAR MISS MANNERS:

I was taught that ladies do not wear jewelry made with precious stones, particularly those that sparkle, until after five o'clock in the evening. The background for this is that precious stones (except for one's engagement and wedding rings) are for formal dress, which was a nightly event in homes where the financial status made the ownership of such jewelry possible.

Has that changed since the advent of well-paying jobs for women, along with credit cards, has made it possible for women of any age to purchase such jewelry themselves, as well as being the recipients of such jewelry from persons who may not have had the advantage of being taught the old rules?

I often see diamond earrings, bracelets and pendants being worn around the clock and would appreciate knowing if this is an acceptable practice in correct society. Has correct society gone the way of the chaperone?

What is your feeling about the wearing of rings on every finger, even the thumbs, of both hands, again, around the clock or at any time?

GENTLE READER:

Miss Manners' feeling is that she would rather not shake hands with such a person. This has less to do with her disapproval of ostentation than with her fear of being crushed by all those minerals.

However, she does disapprove of the incongruity of fancy jewelry with daytime clothes, and the rule remains in place. How many people flout it to flaunt it is as irrelevant as who pays for it. And the magic hour is six, not five, unless you are counting transportation or going to a Wagnerian opera.

⤙ Pearls ⤚

DEAR MISS MANNERS:

When did it become against the "law" to wear pearls in the daytime? Is it OK to wear pearls to a big fancy luncheon?

GENTLE READER:

Wearing pearls day or night was illegal under periodic sumptuary laws in Venice and Florence between the sixteenth and eighteenth centuries, but Miss Manners understands that these have since been repealed.

Pearls are now properly worn at any hour, which is the endearing thing about pearls. They adore being worn and are said to react, in gratitude for this attention, by picking up the skin tones of their owner. For this reason, ladies sometimes wear their best pearls tucked into their nightgowns. It would be easier for Miss Manners to tell you when pearls are not appropriate than when they are. Never wear pearls with your bathing suit.

DEAR MISS MANNERS:

My fiancé gave me a double-strand pearl necklace as an engagement present. I would be much happier having the pearls in one long necklace, opera-length. What do you think about the delicate question of my having the pearls restrung?

GENTLE READER:

What Miss Manners thinks is that pearl necklaces must have odd numbers of strands—one, three, five and so on, depending on how long your neck and deep your purse. Having learned this rule in Japan or some place, she makes it a firm tenet of her life. Therefore, Miss Manners thinks that restringing the two strands into one is not only permissible but imperative. Perhaps, however, what you are really interested in is what your fiancé will think when he sees you have tampered with his jewels. In that case, why don't you ask him?

⁓ Watches ⁓

DEAR MISS MANNERS:

Help! My fiancé has asked me to select a watch for him to give me as an engagement present. (I am never on time, and this is a sweet way of reminding me.) He is quite, in fact very, well off (and nice, too!) so I have no need to think about cost.

In fact, the ones I am considering cost thousands of dollars, but I am afraid that some, which have faces in different jewel colors, might strike his friends as nouveau riche. (I was his secretary, so I have to be careful.) I thought I would get diamonds, because my engagement ring is a diamond cluster, and I will be wearing it with a diamond wedding ring. I have seen some where the face is surrounded by diamonds, and some where the face is made of pavé diamonds. Which do you think is in better taste?

GENTLE READER:

Nothing is in more exquisite taste, in a woman of modest circumstances who is marrying a rich man, than the protestation that she does not care much for jewels and would prefer something simple in gold with his initials and the wedding date engraved on the back.

This does not strike Miss Manners as being your style. However, allow her to urge it anyway, in the case of a watch. A watch case that is heavily encrusted with jewels is never appropriate. It is too elaborate for daytime wear, and an obvious watch of any kind is not worn in the evening, when people are supposed to pretend they are not keeping track of the time.

Also, with all the diamonds you plan to be wearing on your finger, a diamond watch would make your hand look as if you had left it outdoors and it had frozen over. Do not be inhibited by the idea that expressing a preference for simple things will be held against you later. The charming tastes of an impecunious fiancée are unrelated to the standards of a rich married lady.

DEAR MISS MANNERS:

My grandfather used to say that a gentleman never wore a watch with evening clothes. Is that true—or was it ever? I certainly see men looking at their watches at formal occasions, such as charity balls.

GENTLE READER:

The charity ball certainly inspires watch-watching. Your grandfather, however, would have understood that there is watch-watching and watch-watching. He told you—you were only half listening, weren't you?—that a gentleman never wore a wristwatch with evening clothes. The act of looking at a wristwatch denotes businesslike impatience, unsuitable for social functions.

In contrast, the act of looking at a pocket watch is a graceful gesture denoting respect for the night as a time in which sooner or later every civilized person ends his revels and goes to bed. It is an act of which your grandfather would have approved.

⸻ Medals ⸻

Strictly speaking, and with a few esoteric exceptions, medals should be worn only upon request, with the most formal clothes (which means white tie for evening, not black tie) and uniforms. However, as white tie has become a rarity and Miss Manners hates to deprive heroes, she is wavering on the question of allowing invitations that specify "decorations" with dinner jackets.

⸻ Tiaras ⸻

Tiaras also belong to special, full evening dress occasions. This would bar them to beauty queens, who are not likely to part with them without a nasty struggle. Even for mildly festive occasions, the hair was supposed to be "dressed"—the original meaning of hairdressing—with something. Hats not being permissible in the evening, jewels, flowers or feathers may be worn and, oh all right, perhaps discreet tiaras that could pass for ambitious headbands.

⌒ *Bracelets below the Waist* ⌒

DEAR MISS MANNERS:

Should an ankle bracelet be worn inside hosiery or outside? Is one or the other correct, or a matter of personal preference?

GENTLE READER:

An ankle bracelet should be worn on the arm, where it should call itself a bracelet. If it insists on leading a lower life, it should do so on the beach, where it can do no harm to stockings from within or without.

8. *Ever After*

Divorce

D IVORCE CEREMONIES! What fun! Honey, what do you think? If it doesn't work out, we can always get together again.

There really are divorce ceremonies being held, and not just in the spirit of mockery by one of the parting partners among intimate friends. These involve both divorcing parties standing together in front of invited guests, often with the sanction of clergy, sometimes at their instigation. Vows are made, rings are exchanged (back to their original donors) and blessings bestowed, for what God has presumably put asunder.

Miss Manners has listened carefully to the rationales for inventing such a thing and investing it with solemnity:

1. Ritual. We have rituals to ease us through other emotion-laden milestones in life—birth, marriage, coming of age, death—and divorce, which is also unquestionably emotion-laden, has become just about as common. Well, perhaps not quite as common as birth and death, but it sure does seem to be gaining statistically on marriage.

   Miss Manners is a great believer in the ability of ritual to provide the spiritual and social reassurance of knowing that one is part of a life cycle that has been going on from time immemorial. Never mind that most modern versions turn this upside down by "personalizing" ceremonies, so that they showcase the individuals, rather than emphasize that these people, like millions before them and untold millions to come, are entering into the rituals of their society and/or religion. The idea is still supposed to be to become part of a larger tradition, not to cut an existing one down to size for a cozy personal fit.

2. The Civilizing Influence. Goodness knows that Miss Manners is in favor of encouraging divorced couples to behave themselves, even to each other, and even around each other's later choices. Unless these ceremonies turn into melees, which is a clear danger, considering how many divorced parents do

this to their children's graduation and wedding ceremonies, it would provide a pattern of restrained behavior.

3. For the Sake of the Children. The idea has been jettisoned that parents should stay together for the sake of their children on the theory that children prefer to be the ones who sacrifice their immediate comfort for the sake of their parents' romantic fulfillment. But here they could do so just long enough to vow to remain bound to their children.

Miss Manners can even think of a fourth reason:

4. Party-Party. Couples who have spent months, even years, planning elaborate weddings have acquired a great deal of expertise, not to mention a taste for being the center of attraction, so naturally they want to do it again. Still-married couples have come up with a repeat wedding to renew their vows, and this is a way for divorced people to have another celebration.

With all those reasons favoring approving the divorce ceremony, how could Miss Manners object to it?

Because it's in rotten taste, that's why.

These people already had a solemn ritual in which they took the opposite vows. That they may have had good reason for breaking them is no reason to confer blessings on undermining the wedding ritual, stretching society's credulity and sanctioning abandonment in front of their children.

If they want ceremony, they need only take advantage of court proceedings. The legal ceremony should be attended by as few people as possible, but afterward it might be desirable to share a drink with each other or get together with supportive relatives and intimate friends. Dress should be conservative—suits for both ladies and gentlemen at their divorces, and conventional party clothes for the social events. The principals may radiate quiet happiness, but that all-out triumphant air is vulgar.

Children are naturally deeply involved in the occasion, both emotionally and logistically, but should not be present at any events. In private sessions, they are told what is about to happen, never asked or consulted as to whether it should (as nobody listens to their decisions anyway, they should feel innocent of any responsibility); and they are kept entirely apart from the public part of it.

In compensation for this restraint, Miss Manners is, you remember, suspending the stricter rules for subsequent weddings (please see p. 669). Thus, those who cannot wait for full-scale celebrating need only move to the next milestone.

ANNOUNCEMENTS AND DEMEANOR

DEAR MISS MANNERS:

How many times have I sat at my breakfast table while some woman friend my age (forty-seven) has wept and said, "I never thought it would happen to me." And all the while I would be thinking, "Yes, but it really won't happen to me!"

Of course it has. My husband of twenty-five happy (I thought) years has left, maybe to come back when he's had his fill of "freedom," maybe not. I can't stop him from making a fool of himself. But I want to know how to avoid behaving foolishly myself.

You see, while I've tried to be helpful to those women who've been crying at my table, and I always started out sympathetic, I found that after a while I began to resent them. I suppose this will come home to roost now, and people will treat me the way I'm sorry to say I have treated others—first pledging support, and then gradually dropping them. I can't tell you why, or exactly what it is. One friend of mine took to the bottle. I've had close friends who became different, somehow, after their marriages broke up. I don't want this to happen to me. I haven't done anything wrong, and there is no reason I should lose my friends.

My sister-in-law (who thinks her brother has behaved disgracefully) counsels me to take the opportunity to think more of myself, have a good time, maybe even "have a fling." She says I've been devoting myself to others all my life, and now's the time for me "to be selfish." I'm willing to try, but I don't know how to go about it. How can a woman who is gray-haired, a little stout, and used to being a reliable helpmate, compete in this modern world?

GENTLE READER:

Easily. The world is crammed with people who do know how to be selfish, who have no trouble thinking of themselves all the time, and who are eagerly in search of good times and flings. How can they hope to compete with someone who has a lifelong habit of being kind and unselfish?

Here are some things not to do. Perhaps you will recognize some of them as common symptoms of divorce, which, exhibited by your friends, contributed to your decrease of interest and sympathy in them:

Do not overdraw on the amount of sympathy to which one is entitled at a difficult period of life. Even with a close friend, try to limit your complaints and be sure to accompany them with a semblance of true interest in the vicissitudes of the other person's life.

Beware not only of the bottle, but of the telephone, which many people reach for with the same desperation, and overuse with the same self-indulgence and sloppiness.

Do not bristle with eagerness to have that fling. The glitter in the eye that advertises sudden availability is not attractive.

Do not dye your hair. This is the first gesture of the newly unattached middle-aged woman and, like the ditto of the male, which is buying a red sports car, it does not have the dashing effect that is intended.

What should you do? Continue to be a warm and cheerful person (even if you have to fake it for a while), making your interest and experience available to a widening circle of acquaintance, without dwelling on immediate benefits to yourself. This should make you quite a rarity nowadays, and there will be those who will appreciate it.

~ The Announcement ~

DEAR MISS MANNERS:

What is the correct way of announcing that I am divorced? Do I send out cards (and if so, how are they properly worded)? Can I give a party? Hire a billboard? Shout it from the housetops? I don't want to do anything in poor taste, but I am delighted with my new freedom and want to let people know about it.

GENTLE READER:

This will come as a shock, but society's laws about which events one may rejoice over and which one may not do not necessarily correspond to the true feelings of the participant. For example, if your nasty, crotchety, quarrelsome, critical old great-uncle dies and leaves you a fortune, you must try to look solemn, if not actually grieved. If your fourteen-year-old daughter is having a baby, you are supposed to act delighted.

You may call this hypocrisy. As a matter of fact, Miss Manners calls it hypocrisy too. The difference is probably that you don't consider hypocrisy one of the social graces, and she does. In any case, one does not brag about a divorce, however much personal satisfaction it may bring one. There is no formal announcement. Anything along the lines of hiring an airplane to write it in the sky is considered to be in poor taste.

You can write notes announcing a change of name or address and explain in them that it is a result of your recent divorce; that is a solution. You may even give a party, provided that the excuse is not the divorce itself, but a result of it, such as a party to show off your newly redecorated house, even if the redecoration is only the fact that you have put your clothes in both bedroom closets after emptying one of them of someone else's clothes.

Failing such pretexts, you must be alert for opportunities of working the news into conversation. This is not difficult. If someone says, "Tell me, how have you been?" You may answer, "Well, I think everything is settled down now, since the divorce." Miss Manners urges you, for the sake of propriety, to keep a straight face.

The Response

DEAR MISS MANNERS:

What is the correct thing to say to someone who has just told you of his impending divorce?

GENTLE READER:

Miss Manners used to say, "Oh, I am so sorry," until a lady replied, "If I'm happy and he's happy, what are you so sorry about?" Miss Manners was forced to acknowledge that a quiet "I wish you the best" is more appropriate.

Informing Relations

DEAR MISS MANNERS:

My one-and-a-half-year marriage ended in divorce. My relatives passed the word around, but I think not everybody knows. I got distant from them because there is "no divorce in the family." Eight months after, I got married again; but never told anybody, afraid of what they would think. Now, I just became a mother. How can I straighten things up?

GENTLE READER:

Well, you could keep going the way you are, and let them read the basic facts of your life in your obituary. Or you could just burst in with an important current announcement, presuming that they are already in possession of the previous ones, but providing recaps on request. For example, you can write everyone that you and Lester have just produced a baby girl, and then, when someone says, "I thought your husband's name was Hiram," you reply, "Oh, heavens no, Hiram and I were divorced ages ago and I was remarried the following year—I thought you knew." What is to be avoided is making direct announcements of marriage and birth at the same time—"Just wanted to tell you that Lester and I got married and we have a darling baby girl."

⌒ *Family Loyalty* ⌒

Is there family loyalty after divorce? Yes, there is. But before you ask Miss Manners indignantly if she realizes all the terrible things your former spouse did to you, let us talk about the reasons for family loyalty so that we can consider whether it should still apply. (Even then, Miss Manners doesn't want to hear what that awful person did to you. Dear Count Tolstoy notwithstanding, it is Miss Manners' experience that all unhappy families are alike.)

Loyalty to members of one's family before outsiders is a matter of decency, morality and principle, the principle being that one should never snitch on those who have too much personal information about one. Suppose, instead of former spouses, we were talking about siblings. Siblings do not even have the responsibility of having once chosen each other and may never have been tied by bonds of affection, even for an instant. So why must they be loyal to one another?

First, because one must tell one's secrets somewhere, or one will burst. If the family is, by definition, a safe place, one will be less tempted to go around proposing idiotic deals such as "Let me tell you something—but you must promise never to breathe it to another soul."

Also, many family secrets are right there for the observing, on the telephone, bathroom shelf or elsewhere, and without the protection of loyalty, there is no privacy. Obviously, reciprocity is a motivation for keeping one's mouth shut. The other reason is that bad-mouthing one's relatives is an exceedingly unattractive characteristic, making one's own mouth look worse than one's relative.

Both of these motives apply to divorced people. Saying disloyal things about one's former marriage partner is not only dangerous, in that it invites retaliation from one who is bound to have lots of ammunition, but it makes the speaker sound embittered. Must one then forgo the pleasure of revenge? Not entirely. In insisting that you say only kind and loyal things about a person to whom you were once married, Miss Manners is not excluding the possibility of ruining that person's reputation with a few well-chosen and kind words.

For example: "Good heavens, it certainly wasn't his fault. He was trying the best he could; you have to give him credit for that, even if it didn't work."

"She's such a nice woman, you know. I kept telling myself that that ought to be enough."

~ Taking Sides ~

DEAR MISS MANNERS:

My sister and I are close. Our husbands have become friends over the past twenty years. Now my sister and her husband are experiencing a long and unhappy, but not yet legal, separation. Although my brother-in-law has lived with his girl friend throughout the separation, he and my sister still profess a desire for reconciliation. How do my husband and I conduct ourselves without offending my husband's right to friendship, my sister's wounded feelings, and my loyalty?

GENTLE READER:

If your brother-in-law and his wife make their separation legal, you and your husband may certainly entertain them separately with whatever partners they may have. There are too many such disruptions now for anyone to expect others to take sides in their separations. If, however, you pursue this fair-minded policy now, during the trial period, and there is a successful reconciliation, they could easily, in their new harmony, transfer residual feelings of ill will to you. Worse, you could get stuck with the friendship of the now-deserted girlfriend. At that rate, you would always have at least one weepy person in the house. It seems to Miss Manners that a temporary policy of blood over friendship would be practical.

~ The Rings ~

DEAR MISS MANNERS:

I am a divorced woman—mother of five—married twenty-six years. I have a lovely diamond wedding ring and engagement ring. Is it ever proper to wear these after divorce?

GENTLE READER:

What you have on your finger falls into two categories: jewelry and symbolism. Confusing the two leads to foolish acts, such as tossing perfectly good gold into a river because the giver turned out not to be so good.

If you continue to wear the rings in the conventional way, you will retain the symbolism of marriage. Many widows want to do this and it is conceivable that a divorcee, divorced against her wishes or principles, may also. It is discouraging to prospective suitors, which you may or may not want to be.

Retaining the jewelry without the symbolism is another matter. The engagement ring may be worn as is on the right hand and reclassified as a dinner ring, and the wedding ring may be worn on the right hand, perhaps with other bands, as a guard ring. You could also have both rings reset.

DEAR MISS MANNERS:

My brother was married to his ex-wife for six years, and the last four she treated him extremely poorly. Without going into details, she was an absent wife and mother, consumed by money and power.

Our mother died in a tragic accident during the last year of their marriage. A month or so after that, while we were sorting through her precious possessions, my father generously gave each of his sons a ring which belonged to my mother, so that he could see the rings being worn in memory of my mother. Even though this daughter-in-law showed little respect for my mother and my mother was not fond of her, she received one. A few months after the ring was given to her, she left my brother, never to return, and put him through a horrible divorce and custody battle. She had been planning to leave even before my mother's death and before the ring was given to her.

It is now, after three years, when my brother has found a new wife and a wonderful soul mate who will treat him with respect and love, that he realized he never dealt with the ring during the divorce. He would like it back in our family and wants his wife to have it on her finger for my father to see. My father is very upset as well that our family is not seeing the precious heirloom. My brother asked for it back but his first wife will not return it. In fact, she is appalled that he asked her for it. Legally, it does not appear it will be easy to get back.

Please give us your thoughts as to whether we are wrong to want her to give it back or not and whether she is wrong to have accepted it and to keep it. We are grateful for any light you can shed on the appropriateness of our feelings.

GENTLE READER:

Whew. For a moment there, Miss Manners was afraid your lawyer had said, "I can't get it back for you, but why don't you find someone really tough who can?"

Rather you are asking a question that she especially welcomes: Why should you feel that something you know is legal is nevertheless wrong?

Because the legal system does not, and cannot, do the full job of keeping people from behaving badly to one another. It does its best to curb dangerous acts, and leaves the niceties to its companion system, manners.

Thus, your former sister-in-law has not violated the law; she has not even violated the etiquette rule that requires a lady who breaks off her engagement to return the ring and any family treasures she may have been given in anticipation of the wedding. But she has violated the spirit of manners, which should have precluded her accepting—and should now prompt her to return—a ring obviously intended to stay in the family when she was already trying to get out of it.

DEAR MISS MANNERS:

My husband and I were going through some old stuff last night and came upon his wedding band from his first marriage. He wants to throw it away but that seems like a waste. Is there something specific people are supposed to do with them?

GENTLE READER:

Got any cavities?

～ The Divorcée's Honorific ～

DEAR MISS MANNERS:

I have recently been divorced. I am very uncertain as to my title for mail, credit cards, etc. I was taught that "Mrs." means "the wife of," and so it seems wrong to use Mrs. with my first name. Of course, we know there is Ms., but I have mixed feelings on that. I am a woman in business and also a mother.

GENTLE READER:

If we know there is Ms., why don't we use it? Why is it that the people for whom this is the best solution—the only solution, in fact, as in spite of widespread usage, Mrs. is indeed incorrect with a woman's first name—have mixed feelings about it instead of unmixed relief?

The truly correct style is to combine Mrs. with your maiden and last names (Daffodil Perfect who married and divorced Mr. Awful becomes Mrs. Perfect Awful), but few people use it nowadays.

～ Former Relations ～

Why so many nuclear families explode is not anything Miss Manners cares to study. There are too many people in the field already, and Miss Manners has noticed that anyone who stands too close is likely to find something flying into his or her eye.

What Miss Manners prefers to do is to wait until the dust settles and then to study the new elements that have been formed, and their relationships. It isn't easy. Miss Manners has been asked the following questions:

- My son's ex-wife has remarried, and of course she is no longer my daughter-in- law. But I often see her because she has custody of my grandchildren. How do I introduce her to my friends?
- I grew up with the daughters of my mother's second husband. My mother and their father are no longer married, but we are still on affectionate terms. They introduce me as their "brother," and I have been introducing them as my "ex-stepsisters." Are they exaggerating, or am I being too precise and cold? We all have a half-sister in common, and we all call her our "sister."
- I often have dealings with my wife's ex-husband, because he is the father of the children I live with. How do I refer to him when we make travel arrangements and so on? We get along fine, and I want a pleasant term.

All of these people are trying to avoid the harshness of saying "ex." "Ex" is so final, and these relationships are obviously continuing, or there wouldn't be any problem. The other prefix they don't like is "step." This was given a bad name by the publicity attached to the unfortunate home life of Cinderella, although dear Edith Wharton refers charmingly to "the steps" resulting from various marriages of her characters in *The Children*, that marvelous jet-set novel written before such people had ever set foot in a jet.

Miss Manners believes in recycling old words and rescuing them, if possible, from bad associations they don't deserve. Many kind people who devote their lives to children they didn't foist upon the world resent the name of stepmother or stepfather, which suggests that they hand out poisoned apples.

In some cases, the relationship can simply be briefly described: "The mother of my grandchildren," "the father of my stepchildren." In others, it is not necessary to define the relationship exactly, and unless those so designated object, there is no reason why the terms "brother" and "sister" cannot be used for the variations on this relationship. Provided the whole thing doesn't get out of hand and we all wander around sounding like a vast revival meeting.

Or other terms could be invented, provided they are affectionate. One could refer to "the children's bio-daddy" or, even more sweetly, "the father of my children" as gentlemen of Miss Manners' acquaintance have suggested. Another gentleman of Miss Manners' acquaintance calls his younger stepbrother and stepsisters collectively, "my father's second litter," and a lady refers to "my sisters once removed."

DEAR MISS MANNERS:

How does one respond when being given a compliment for "your husband," when that person is no longer my husband? Also, how does one respond when people ask about his well being? "How is your husband?"

GENTLE READER:

The compliment: "Yes, isn't he? But he is no longer my husband."

The inquiry about his health: "Very well, I hope, but he is no longer my husband."

Miss Manners has no idea whether you are on peaceful terms, or any terms at all, with your former husband, but her replies would be the same in any case. To use a mere pleasantry to unload unpleasantries is unpleasant enough to make people sympathize with the target.

∼ Subsequent Relationships ∼

DEAR MISS MANNERS:

My husband and I have recently separated, and divorce is imminent. We have established separate households and share parenting obligations for our children.

The gentleman has recently moved in with his girlfriend of a few years, having recently revealed the clandestine relationship.

When I have encountered this person, dear Miss Manners, I am polite. I have not maligned her, either to my children or to the public. However, as you can imagine, I do not wish to associate with her in any way. The problem is that this person is attempting to be friendly and apparently trying to establish our former relationship. We were casual acquaintances prior to, and during, her affair with my soon-to-be-ex-spouse.

While I acknowledge the need to associate with her occasionally for the sake of the children, how can I handle this situation correctly, yet convey my unwillingness to be around this "person"?

GENTLE READER:

The setting you are looking for is Cool. Cold and Hot (whether the latter describes anger or passion) are out of place at family gatherings, because they demand partisanship on the part of others, a demand you have been courteous enough to avoid.

Cool behavior consists of doing everything socially required in a correct but abbreviated fashion. You greet the person with a short smile indicated by the turning up of the corners of the mouth but no accompanying sign of pleasure in the eyes. You answer any questions in few, neutral words ("Thank you, I'm fine"), avoid asking of your own ("I trust you are well" can substitute for "How are you?") and seize the first opportunity to say "Excuse me" and turn away.

Should this fail—should your former friend attempt, for example, to hug you—Miss Manners gives you permission to turn it up to Frosty. At that setting, "Excuse me" immediately follows the greeting.

DEAR MISS MANNERS:

My ex-husband has made advances towards me since we separated. I am having problems with how to deal with these advances. He is currently engaged to and living with the woman he left me for. I want to tell his fiancée about the advances but I don't think that she would believe me.

GENTLE READER:

Miss Manners understands perfectly why you want your former husband to stop annoying you, but she is less clear about why you want to tell his fiancée. Because you think she'll be a good influence on him?

How you protect yourself depends on the circumstances in which these advances are made. You may be in a position to cut off contact with him, but if not, you may need outside assistance, and should talk to your lawyer or even the police.

You cannot, however, protect his fiancée. However good-hearted your intentions, Miss Manners suggests you give up the thought of trying.

DEAR MISS MANNERS:

My son is divorced after a short, stormy marriage. He and my former daughter-in-law have a young child. Each year, she and her side of the family and my son and his side of the family get together to celebrate my grandson's birthday. This year, her boyfriend came to the celebration. She and her boyfriend together presented my grandson a gift.

After the party, I told my husband that I was surprised that the boyfriend would attend, and that his attending was in poor taste. My husband saw nothing wrong with the boyfriend being present. What do you think? I am considered to be an old-fashioned thinker.

GENTLE READER:

Miss Manners has that reputation herself, and cannot fathom why it is not considered a compliment. Yet she cannot quite follow your argument of its being poor taste for a divorced lady's suitor to show an interest in her child.

Perhaps it is the suitor himself who is in poor taste, or other liberties he is allowed. That, however, you cannot hope to control. To attempt to do so using the pretext of his presence at the child's birthday party is likely to antagonize both your grandchild's mother—never a good idea, however tempting—and the disappointed grandchild, which would render it impolitic as well as futile.

THE CHILDREN

Whatever else divorce may be for children, it is a severe etiquette problem. Miss Manners is always hearing grown-ups wail about the difficulties of maintaining social relations with mere friends when they are partners in a divorce. She thinks at least equal consideration should be given to the diplomacy problems of the descendants of such people. Whether they are big or small, residents or visitors in their parents' homes, these children have to consider such problems as:

1. How much can I cater to one parent's curiosity without betraying the privacy of the other?
2. How much free rein can I give to my natural discussion of what I see, hear and think without getting myself involved in my parents' feelings about each other?
3. How do I take part in special occasions, such as my birthday, graduation or wedding, with both parents present and not have the event taken over by their drama, rather than mine?
4. How can I play off one of them against the other to my own advantage?

Most children have a natural instinct for number 4 in this list, and Miss Manners is not going to abet them. But in numbers 1 through 3, they need all the help they can get.

You may expect Miss Manners to come out in favor of discretion, as she normally does. Indeed, she would suggest to the grown-up offspring of unhappily divorced people that details about money, sex or any other possible area of irritation—and in a rousing divorce, anything can qualify—be withheld when possible. But it is not always possible for grown-ups, and never really possible for minors. One cannot maintain a semblance of normal family life while constantly trying to censor one's conversation. Nor should children of any age be expected to curtail the great events of their own lives to pander to the sensitivities of their parents. Not having succeeded in one's own marriage is no excuse for spoiling the wedding of one's child.

Naturally, Miss Manners expects all parents to realize this, and control their own behavior accordingly. Naturally, Miss Manners realizes that they often will not and sometimes cannot. What can the children do to encourage them to be civilized? They can do nothing. If one parent seems to be abusing the other, a child who stares stonily back and does nothing will serve to remind an adult not to risk a good relationship by dwelling on a bad one.

⁓ Not Choosing ⁓

DEAR MISS MANNERS:

I am feeling incorrect. What am I supposed to do if my mother and father get a divorce? How are my brother and sister and I supposed to react? Do we have to pick a parent to live with? If we don't get or pick the other parent, do we get to see that parent a certain day or many days a week? If one parent asks us to do one thing and another parent another thing, which one do we listen to and why? Why does my brother, age six, hate my father so much? Please give me the answers because I can't figure them out for myself and I need the advice.

GENTLE READER:

There is no reason for you to feel incorrect, now or in any confusion that may arise from your new situation. It is a common mistake for those who have been put in an awkward situation by others to take upon themselves the responsibility for the awkwardness. Perhaps your brother's hatred is a feeling of resentment against the disruption of family life. Justified or not, it is likely to pass.

The fact is that all three of you children still have two parents. Whichever one you live with most, you will still be the children of the other. It is unlikely that you will have much say about when you will live where (but if you are consulted, Miss Manners urges you to go against your natural inclination and pick the one who makes irksome rules for you, not the one who lets you do whatever you want).

Your duty is to treat both of them with respect, and to obey the house rules of the one whose house you are in at any given moment. Miss Manners is sorry to spoil the game of But Daddy Lets Me Do Homework with the Television On or But Mommy Lets Me Eat Whatever I Want, but that constitutes incorrect behavior.

Not Stooping

DEAR MISS MANNERS:

My ex-husband is coming to our daughter's wedding and, as a matter of fact giving the bride away. Fine. My daughter wants it that way, and I have no objection. But he wants to bring that bimbo he calls his new wife, who is not much older than our daughter.

The divorce was very difficult. She is the one who took him away from me. I held on for a long time, thinking he would get over it. My friends and pastor had explained to me that it is natural for a middle-aged man to panic and have a little fling—but this one went on for three years, and I couldn't take it any longer. I have seen him once or twice since, and have managed to be dignified, but do I really have to see her? My daughter, although she sided with me, seems to be friendly with them, and thinks she should come. If so, do I have to be polite to her?

GENTLE READER:

As a point of etiquette, one cannot exclude a spouse from a wedding invitation or any invitation for which people are invited in couples. A marriage is a marriage and creates a social unit, regardless of whether it was achieved through kidnapping, as your account suggests. The wife's bimbohood is irrelevant.

However, Miss Manners cannot help noticing a flaw in your perception of who has injured you by dissolving your marriage. It is an old and ugly trick of society to pit the women against one another in a difficult situation and excuse the men even if, as seems to be the fact in your case, the women don't even know each other. Miss Manners thinks it would be helpful to consider this so that you may be in more of a frame of mind to work on your real question, which is: How can I triumph over my successor in front of all my friends and relations?

By acting triumphant. How does one act triumphant? Not by being haughty, as is your inclination, but by being generous. There is nothing like the full gratification of one's wishes to convince one that the world is a delightful place and all the people in it just as adorable as they can be.

Suppose it had been your fondest wish to unload your husband so that you could pursue a clandestine relationship with a man so important that his identity must remain secret, or to exercise your genius as a scriptwriter, or whatever. But because of your kindheartedness and your realization of how incompetent he is to fend for himself and how difficult for a woman to tolerate, you despaired of ever ridding yourself of his tiresome presence.

Along comes a woman eager for the job. But your conscience will not let you jump at the chance. She is too young to know what she is doing. How can you use her ignorance to stick her with this burden? Yet she insists. Well, you have tried your best to save her. Now it is your turn to live. Such a lady would greet her ex-husband's new wife with charm and care, just managing to suppress an air of triumph that would reveal the happiness and relief she has in her postmarital life. It is not an easy role to play. However, one is on stage, like it or not, at an event such as a wedding, and the alternative is to play an embittered woman who has lost what she wanted.

DEAR MISS MANNERS:

My husband-to-be's ex-wife frequently calls demanding me to give her "her husband." They have a five-year-old, and I have a five-year-old, both girls from the previous marriages. I get these calls early mornings. And since I'm not really the confrontational or jealous type, I say, "just a sec."

So, how do I handle these phone calls in such a fashion that common courtesy in conjunction with warranted respect is achieved?? Am I to request some sort of pleasantry on behalf of my husband-to-be and the girls, or am I simply to withstand such rudeness?? Of course, I do not wish to create an all-out war, especially with such young children within earshot; however, I do want to convey some subtle message that I do not wish to be treated as a mistress.

GENTLE READER:

Without bothering to cover the speaker of your telephone, just call out "Honey! It's your wife!" Miss Manners trusts that the lady in question will not have to hear the muffled giggles or jokes that follow in order to reconsider her approach.

~ Not Auditioning ~

DEAR MISS MANNERS:

Childless women who date divorced fathers would all agree, I suppose, that children should not have to meet and greet their dad's Flavor of the Week. The couple should wait until the relationship stabilizes. My problem is trying to keep a distance from these kids during the non-serious era, without rudeness.

Situations often arise where the kids and I will be thrown together unless someone moves away. My dad-dates appear offended by my doing so, as if I am rejecting their kids, or perhaps them by extension. And I certainly get offended by orders to back off, as if given half a chance I'd sneak in and audition for the role of stepmother.

Whether I say, "I don't think I should be meeting them yet," or he says it, someone will feel hurt. Should I just try to flee the situation without saying why?

Frankly, I think it is kinder for me to offer to absent myself than for him to tell me to get lost—but I am trying to focus on people other than the grown-ups and their self-protective measures.

GENTLE READER:

Somewhere around here, Miss Manners must still have the manners for meeting the parents of one's, ah, honey. If she changes "honey" to "flavor," will those do?

She supposes not. The circumstances are too different. People actually give some weight to the opinions their children form about their romantic prospects. Miss Manners is glad that you do too, and urges you to assume that so do the fathers—who are in a better position to know what is best for these particular children at this particular time than a lady who has never met them.

If they are in the stage of fearing that every lady their father meets is going to take him away from them, his reluctance would be understandable and you should not take it personally. Nor should you over-interpret a suggestion that you should meet. Perhaps the children are more afraid of a mystery lady and would feel reassured to meet her.

Miss Manners agrees that children should not be involved in a parent's romance until it is likely to affect their daily lives, but she believes they should get to know their parents' friends. And a friend is what you are (Miss Manners prefers to skip the ice-cream category), and should insist on appearing to be, in front of the children. True, children are no fools, but you need not provide evidence to the contrary.

Not Acting Normal

DEAR MISS MANNERS:

I am a divorced non-custodial father of a six-year-old boy. My ex-wife (and my son's mother) and I get along very well, and often the three of us will attend community events together. Frequently, we will engage in conversation with another couple who have children around our son's age. At some point in the conversation, we will be asked how long we have been married and other questions that couples have a tendency to ask one another.

Usually we respond that we are divorced, but are still good friends, and then try to steer the conversation away from us and toward the children. This does not always seem to be enough to prevent the other couple from feeling uncomfortable. Do you have any suggestions about how we could respond to these types of questions in a way that does not create an awkward moment for the couple we are talking with?

GENTLE READER:

No doubt these people would feel relieved to see you at each other's throats, the way they expect normal, divorced couples to behave. Miss Manners sees no reason to oblige.

Marriage Two (Prerequisite: Marriage for Beginners)

IT IS BECOMING the custom now for people who are already grown up to get married. Yet wedding etiquette has always been based on an assumption of youth and innocence on the part of the chief participants, and this is what gives traditional weddings their peculiarly bittersweet appeal. Grown-ups were not expected to get married, or at least to have any fun doing so.

Miss Manners doesn't see why not. Weddings between people who are well acquainted not only with life but with each other should be fascinating occasions. They should be equally festive, but different.

Grown-ups usually have children, toasters, grown-up friends, flatware and formed tastes. Grown-ups usually do not have friends who will dye shoes to match or wear colored bow ties and cummerbunds, the sense of permanence required to have towels monogrammed and parents who say, "Oh, what the hell, go ahead. We want this to be something you'll remember all your life."

It is stretching the imagination far enough to suggest that the father of a young girl has had any hand in disposing of her hand, but the pretense that a wedding means that a fledgling is leaving the nest is even less plausible than it is for youthful marriages. As that is the form for the traditional formal invitation, Miss Manners prefers skipping that approach altogether and writing real letters (please see p. 390).

If the couple simply cannot stay away from the engravers', they should issue invitations to the wedding reception as they would to another formal party (please see p. 671).

The effort of writing out the invitations is compensated by the reduced necessity of writing letters after the wedding to thank someone for the lovely electric wall ornament.

No one has to fork over more than one major present, so it is not necessary to give them for multiple marriages. Grown-ups getting married not only don't need electric hot plates and linen towels, but are likely to be in dispute over which of them should throw away his or her set. Only intimates, who know what might be useful and pleasing, and who take pleasure in the idea of making these people presents, need bother.

~ The Snicker Factor ~

DEAR MISS MANNERS:

 Is it proper to have a large wedding your second time around? I was married for a short time. My ex and I had a very small wedding. My fiancé has never been married before, and I don't think it would be fair to him if we couldn't have a large wedding. I wish the first marriage had never happened. Also, can I wear a white dress and invite my relatives who were at my first wedding? I see no reason why I cannot! Please advise. I have been divorced two years.

GENTLE READER:

 Miss Manners recognizes three general categories of weddings in which the bride is either not at her first wedding, or not in her first youth, or both. They are:

1. The Snicker-Proof Wedding. If you marry in a small chapel or judge's chamber, wearing a navy blue suit with a flower pinned on the lapel, have no one but your and his parents present, and celebrate afterward with a luncheon that nobody else in the restaurant can tell is bridal, you will violate no one's standards of propriety.

2. The This-Time-We-Know-What's-What Wedding. This can be small or large, but it is distinguished in its festivity by less formality and more sophistication than the veil-covered, if naked-shouldered, bride conveys. It does not mimic a first wedding, but replaces some of its fixtures with advanced good taste. The bride does not wear a standard wedding dress, but something more party-ish in a flattering color; she is not attended by a girl chorus, but by a real friend or surrounded by her own children; she does not have her parents send engraved cards, but herself writes a charming letter inviting each guest.

3. The I-Got-Cheated-Last-Time Wedding. This is the wedding in which the bride says the heck with what people say—I've always wanted a dream wedding with all the trimmings, and by God, this time I'm going to have it. If you want to do this—and Miss Manners takes it that such is your inclination—then simply follow the directions for a first wedding.

DR. TRACY TREMOR
12 ALTERNATE WAY
BROOKDALE, CONNECTICUT

Dear Alexandrina:

Brian Botchitt and I are being married here at the house on Saturday, the twenty-ninth of February, at four o'clock. We very much hope that you and Ian will be with us for the ceremony and a small reception afterwards.

Affectionately yours,
Aunt Tracy

An invitation to a second wedding. Really, this should be written on the bride's monogrammed paper or her formal house paper, but this bride prefers the modern custom of having one paper for private and professional use. Such a paper could have used the title "Miss" or "Ms."

⸺ *Telling the Children* ⸺

DEAR MISS MANNERS:

Could you give some advice on throwing a family engagement party? We are going to put together a his-hers-theirs family—my fiancé has custody of one of his three children, I have both of mine, and we are going to have at least one child of our own before we get too old to cope—and feel that this is the time to start.

It frankly hasn't been easy. His son refuses to accept me as a permanent fixture, and keeps pretending that I am just passing through Daddy's life so there is no need to get my name right; my daughter can't stay off his lap, and my son alternates between vying for my fiancé's affections with his own son, and ignoring all of us. And then there are the two children who live with their mother and will be with us on holidays—I never know whether they are going to be sweet as pie with me, or hostile.

We haven't told any of them that we have definitely decided to get married, because we want to do it all at once and make a festive occasion of it. This family is going to need some sense of tradition to keep it together, and this could be one of these times. I thought we would make our surprise announcement first, and then let everybody say how they feel about it. But we thought we could have a fancy cake and sparkling grape juice in wine glasses. Do you have any suggestions for this new type of engagement party?

GENTLE READER:

Yes. Plan a different form of entertainment. The cake and the grape juice sound fine, but for heaven's sake, don't ask all these various children to tell you how they feel about your engagement. They might do so.

Surprise engagement announcements should be made to people who will act delighted and can afford to do so because the new arrangements will not affect their lives. (Surprises can also be pulled on those whose discomfort will increase your pleasure, such as former spouses and sweethearts.)

The parents and the children of newly engaged couples have the right to be informed of the news in private, so that they can air their uglier feelings about the situation and the individuals before having to work themselves up into some expression of festivity. Each of you should tell your own blood relatives separately, taking care not to make the common mistake of putting the matter as a question that their inclinations could help decide.

Then have the party, each warning your own relatives to behave as if they were delighted for the sake of the others. If everyone at the party is pretending to be pleased, you should be able to enjoy your sparkling grape juice and cake, and will have set the proper tone for future ceremonial occasions.

⌁ *The Wedding Dress* ⌁

DEAR MISS MANNERS:

My daughter, aged twenty-eight, is marrying for the second time and she wants to have a church wedding this time. Would you please tell me what the differences are between a first and a second wedding? Should she wear a veil and have her father give her away? What color dress should she wear?

GENTLE READER:

The chief difference is in the amount of judgment the bride is assumed to have about what she is doing. It is not customary to have her given away as new, and therefore she is not gift-wrapped in white dress or veil. Miss Manners is not hysterical about the enforcement of this somewhat tasteless symbolism, as some people are, but the conventional bridal dress for a second (or fifth) wedding is a pastel dress or suit with a hat.

⌁ *Paying for the Wedding* ⌁

DEAR MISS MANNERS:

I have a problem. Our divorced daughter is marrying a divorced man. They are planning on having a meal after the church ceremony and a week later is the reception. What are our responsibilities in regard to footing the bills for the meals? Do we offer to pay for both, or neither?

GENTLE READER:

Miss Manners hopes you did not neglect, on the occasion of your daughter's first wedding, the ceremony of saying, "OK, kid, that's it. From now on you're on your own." It is a practical tradition these days. No, you are not responsible for paying for festivities related to a second wedding, although it is charming to do so if you wish. For that matter, the same is true of a first wedding. These decisions are usually based on the desirability of the bridegroom, as assessed by the bride's parents.

∼ Wedding Presents ∼

DEAR MISS MANNERS:

Is it proper to register for gifts at department stores for a second wedding? Both of us were married over 20 years ago the first time and everything is worn out! What do you suggest?

GENTLE READER:

These days, lots of people seem to be worn out by the time they get married. Miss Manners suggests that they save themselves the wear and tear of worrying how to get their guests to do their shopping for them, and leave the question of presents to the discretion of those who might be spontaneously moved to give them. Presents need not be sent for second or third weddings.

∼ Stepchildren in the Wedding Party ∼

DEAR MISS MANNERS:

I am writing on behalf of our daughter, who has two daughters by a previous marriage (ages seven and eight and a half years). This is the second marriage for the man she plans to wed, and he has no children. What role, if any, would her daughters play? It will be performed in church, with the reception in the church basement. They will have one couple as attendants.

GENTLE READER:

The etiquette rule barring children from their parents' subsequent weddings has now been largely abandoned. (This is not to be taken as general license for throwing strict old rules to the winds. If each person used his or her own common sense about every rule of etiquette, the world would be a sloppy place to live in, and how would Miss Manners earn her bread?) The children should play as large a part as they wish, which also means that a wish not to participate should be respected. Such a wedding is, after all, the beginning of a new life for them, as well as for the bride and bridegroom.

Although second weddings do not usually include great troupes of wedding attendants, however many children there are should be added to the basic two—maid of honor and best man—or be allowed to fill those parts. Your two young granddaughters could be flower girls, or one could be a flower girl and the other a ring bearer. If they don't want to be that deeply involved—and there are sometimes peculiar feelings among children in these cases that go against the natural instinct for glamour—they could simply stand with their mother at the altar, or they could sit in the front pew with you. Even if there were twelve children from six previous marriages, Miss Manners' would still recommend inviting them to be in the picture.

DEAR MISS MANNERS:

Until now, the distance between my home and my ex-husband's has been an asset, as it is a two-hour drive and keeps him from becoming overly involved in my life. My nine-year-old daughter has been asked to be a junior bridesmaid in his wedding. I know that the bride and groom will be too busy to drive four hours on a trip to pick up my daughter and another four after the wedding, bringing her home. When I expressed this concern to my ex, he explained that my husband and I will be invited to the ceremony, thus solving the transportation dilemma.

We are the parents of three young children, one a nursing infant. A trip out of town for a weekend will be a major project for us, as well as a considerable expense. This occasion is very important to our daughter, however, and she is looking forward to it. I would certainly enjoy seeing her in a wedding, although I did not hold the groom in particularly high regard and do not relish the thought of going to his wedding with all the inconveniences it will involve. Do you have any suggestions on how I can handle the situation gracefully and provide my oldest child with the pleasure of this occasion?

GENTLE READER:

What is the fun of divorce and remarriage if it does not provide you with many extra relatives to perform family tasks? Your ex-in-laws fall into this category (as will the new bride). One way of using them on this occasion would be to ask a grandparent, aunt, uncle or cousin of your child's on her father's side to provide her transportation. Another is to call your child's future stepmother and ask her to suggest other transportation. Miss Manners is sure that if you explain to her that you would adore to go to her wedding, that you would find it an absolute scream to watch your former husband being married again, she would assist in saving you the inconvenience of the trip.

Name Changes

DEAR MISS MANNERS:

I've been happily married to my third husband for 11 years, but I've felt sensitive about my son from my second marriage not having the same last name as me. It's as if belonging to each other is a constant explanation.

I am always addressed by his school, friends and parents using his last name. I also feel like having to prove I'm his mother because we have different last names.

After my divorces, I went back to using my maiden name as my middle name. Should I have kept my son's last name as my middle name or hyphenated his and my last name? Please enlighten me to the correct usage of names, especially where children are involved.

GENTLE READER:

Miss Manners wishes that ladies would face the fact that there is no way of having a surname that reflects one's family of origin, not forgetting the maternal line; one's current husband; one's former husband during whose time one established one's professional career; and each of one's children from a succession of fathers.

Any system you devise is going to leave out not just someone, but nearly everyone. Yet the idea is not only to satisfy yourself but to avoid hurting others.

Marriage and divorce are recognized as compelling reasons to change one's name, which parents almost always understand and children sometimes do. There may also be compelling reasons not to change, such as keeping one's parents' or child's surname, or one's professional name, and most people understand that as well.

But what you propose is only too likely to cause offense to your husband. Had you made the case for keeping your child's surname to your husband when you married him, that might have been different. But to drop his name after eleven years of marriage is a symbolic blow. Any argument you make about wanting to be identified with your child will only suggest that you no longer care about being identified with him.

Anniversaries

Awww. Look at them! They're still in love, after all those years of marriage. They just can't get enough of each other. You'd think they were newlyweds.

What else does this scene tell us? Probably that the couple in question is behaving tastelessly. And certainly that they want people to notice.

Miss Manners considers herself a soft touch for love and marriage, and the combination of the two. But she is beginning to appreciate an advantage of illicit romance: It requires discretion. Since the demise of the hotel detective, nobody is forced to watch.

Licit love, in contrast, has gone wild. Grown-up married couples are flaunting their respectability shamelessly. They keep their hands so firmly clasped that you have to wonder how they manage to eat. Perhaps in tandem, because they make a fuss when they go out socially if they are not seated next to each other. If momentarily separated, they blow kisses and mouth "I love you." They plant kisses too, carrying on as if they don't care who is watching. They tell everyone how they have hardly spent a night apart since the day they were married. They don't just celebrate anniversaries and declare they'd marry each other all over again—they actually do restage the wedding all over again.

What are these people up to? You would imagine that even if they don't care what other people think of them, they would be responsible enough to set a good example for the young.

Oh. That's what they think they are doing.

In a world of unstable romances and short marriages, they are demonstrating that love can last forever. So although they are breaking several etiquette rules—against showing off, against conducting romance in public, against ignoring social duties to focus on each other—are they entitled to exemptions on the grounds that they are performing a public service?

Miss Manners might consider granting that if they were doing a better job.

One problem is that so many of them turn out to be frauds. Misleading outsiders is a sadly understandable motive for attempting to make a bad marriage look good in public, Miss Manners acknowledges. It is certainly preferable to exposing others to whatever bad behavior might be a more accurate representation of what goes on privately. Eventually, however, such shows often betray their falseness, so they hardly set an example of marital happiness. Numerous ones have been the prelude to such spectacular revelations of unhappiness that tightly clasped hands have come to be a tip-off that the couple is in the last stages of being able to hang on.

But what of those who really are happily married? Isn't it useful for them to set an example? Not this one. It plays into the very idea that is disillusioning people about marriage: the seductive (or maybe tiresome, but at any rate implausible) idea that love, if it is the real thing, operates at a perpetual fever pitch. This belief has persuaded countless romantics to decide that relationships that eventually calm down have thereby proven themselves not to have been true love. Better then to cut one's losses and search again for the real thing.

Being unable to keep one's hands off one's beloved, even in public, is indicative of the relative novelty of the romance, not of its depth. This is why society smiles on the kittenish behavior of newlyweds, provided it doesn't get graphic or go on forever.

But that is not what a happily enduring marriage looks like in public. With all those married couples on display, you may not notice those who go out to socialize, and whose public communication with each other is therefore limited to understanding looks, mutually agreeable bantering and helpful prompting. But those are the ones who will stay together even after they get home.

DEAR MISS MANNERS:

Every year on our wedding anniversary, my husband likes to wear some strange outfit to dinner to remind me that my "real husband is not so strange at all." One year he was Mickey Mouse; another year, he was Sinbad the Sailor. It's funny, sure, but I think it should be a time for romance and tenderness. It's especially embarrassing when we celebrate with another couple. Is his "act" ill-mannered when we invite someone else over? How can I tell him without hurting his feelings? What should I do?

GENTLE READER:

Miss Manners hesitates to suggest "doing" anything that would interfere with such an exciting marriage. If there were any husband a woman would have to decide to love uncritically or to leave immediately, it would be a husband who dresses up as Mickey Mouse. If you have any desire to celebrate one more anniversary with this man, Miss Manners recommends that you declare it a costume party and wear a polka-dot skirt, white gloves and black ears.

∽ Anniversary Presents ∽

DEAR MISS MANNERS:

What are the proper gifts for different anniversaries? I mean like the paper anniversary, wood, silver, and so on. I've seen various lists, but they often disagree.

GENTLE READER:

A couple married for twenty-five years (to each other) may celebrate a silver anniversary and give or be given silver presents. At fifty years, they may celebrate a golden anniversary. A lady who has occupied the same throne for sixty years may celebrate a diamond jubilee and sell souvenirs, such as china plates with her profile painted on them.

Miss Manners regards any such designations for lesser milestones as being silly. If you wish to accept the dictums (or dicta) of various self-serving industries and believe that the eighteen-month anniversary means new back tires for the car while rotating the others, go right ahead.

∽ The Anniversary Ring ∽

DEAR MISS MANNERS:

I received an anniversary ring from my husband of ten years. I am in somewhat of a quandary, however, as to what to do with my engagement ring and wedding band. I wear an heirloom ring on my right hand, so that only leaves my left hand on which to distribute my engagement, wedding and anniversary rings. I would rather not wear all of these rings at once for fear that I may be inclined to start calling people "daahhling" and ordering them about.

Is it considered improper to wear my anniversary ring in lieu of my wedding band? The gentlemen for whom I work (both are attorneys) are appalled (go figure) that I would forsake the wedding band that had been blessed during my wedding ceremony. They also feel that an anniversary ring does not clearly earmark one as being married. My husband, however, does not mind my wearing only the anniversary ring on my left hand.

GENTLE READER:

It strikes Miss Manners that these gentlemen are far too interested in the extent to which you are committed to your marriage. If lawyers assume that a lady wearing engagement and anniversary rings is either unmarried or rejecting the symbols and vows of her marriage, they are sadly deficient in the ability to assess circumstantial evidence.

You have, however, done something improper. A lady should not be consulting other gentlemen about matters that concern only herself and her husband.

⌒ *The Anniversary Dress* ⌒

DEAR MISS MANNERS:

After all these years, my wedding dress still fits! Do you think it's all right if I wear it to my golden wedding anniversary party? I haven't yet tried it out for my husband.

GENTLE READER:

It depends on how well both of you have worn over the years. The desired effect is that of a lady of your age, whatever it is, in a becoming dress with sentimental attachments. Check with your mirror, but not your husband. If he advises against it, it will only set you thinking that the romance has gone out of the marriage.

⌒ *Toasts* ⌒

DEAR MISS MANNERS:

We are giving a surprise thirtieth wedding anniversary party to my brother-in-law and his wife. I must make the toast. Is it proper to thank everyone for attending, and can you give me an appropriate toast for the occasion?

GENTLE READER:

Toasting the guests for having made the effort to attend a party is Miss Manners' idea of excessive humility. She believes in having as few toasts as possible, and hold the butter. The best toast for a wedding anniversary is still "To Esmeralda and Gideon!"

⌒ *Renewing Wedding Vows* ⌒

DEAR MISS MANNERS:

My niece and her husband were married nearly a year ago in a small civil ceremony with only the immediate family present. They were expecting a baby, so the couple and their parents decided that a quick and simple ceremony would be best.

My sister recently informed me that the couple is planning to renew their vows in church followed by a reception for 50 people at a banquet hall. My niece will wear a traditional wedding gown with a veil and the couple will each have three attendants. My brother-in-law will walk my niece down the aisle and will give his daughter away.

Given the fact that the couple will have been married for a year and that they have a child, does this type of ceremony seem appropriate to you?

Because of the circumstances, my husband and I were not invited to my niece's wedding, but we did send them a wedding gift at the time of their marriage. Should we give another gift to recognize the wedding vow renewal ceremony? I have never been invited to such an occasion (except as part of a couple's 25th or 50th anniversary celebration) so I am at a loss as to how to proceed.

GENTLE READER:

Appropriate—compared to what? Miss Manners supposes that it is more appropriate to renew vows than to break them, just as it is more appropriate for people who are expecting a baby to get married than not to get married. But she hopes you don't think these are fine old social customs in which you are obliged to participate.

Your obligation was to recognize your niece's marriage, which you graciously did when she was married. Whether or not you attend this or any subsequent restagings, they are parties, not ceremonies. Additional wedding presents are just as superfluous.

DEAR MISS MANNERS:

Next year, we will celebrate twenty-five years of marriage. I am thinking of renewing our vows, but I'm at a loss to know all the procedures. Our children are twelve and fourteen years, so they are too young to give a party for us. Please send information on church etiquette and everything.

GENTLE READER:

Although Miss Manners has reservations about these events—those vows were supposed to be permanent, and renewing them implies an option not to renew—she supposes that the pledges of a couple who have been married for twenty-five years are more convincing than those of people who don't know what they are getting into.

The chief thing to bear in mind when planning such a ceremony is that it marks a continuation of your marriage, rather than a reenactment of its beginning. While you should invite the same people there who witnessed the wedding, you should not attempt to look or act like the couple you were twenty-five years ago. You may ask the same clergyman to perform the ceremony, or your present one to repeat the original service. And you should have the original wedding party there.

But you are now a grown-up couple with children. Include them in the wedding party. Dress festively but appropriately to your age. And entertain your friends afterward as grown-ups do, by giving a party in your own house.

∽ Begging Contributions ∽

DEAR MISS MANNERS:

My siblings and I are planning a 30th-anniversary party for my parents. We'd like to include all of their friends and extended family, but none of us has much money. Both parents have six siblings, so it'd be impossible to keep the guest list short without lots of hurt feelings. My sister suggested sending a letter to guests and asking for donations. I'm uneasy about this. Is there a good way to word such a request?

GENTLE READER:

How about a nice family photograph, showing all of you, and saying "Please donate to the needy"?

DEAR MISS MANNERS:

My husband's oldest brother and his wife recently celebrated their golden wedding anniversary. Prior to the actual date, my husband's niece forwarded an announcement of the anniversary with the information that there was to be a "money tree" to which we were free to contribute.

My husband and I discussed, at great length, the proper thing to do, and we decided to send a check for ten dollars. A few weeks later, we received a thank-you note from my husband's sister-in-law in which she thanked us for our ten dollars but indicated that many had sent gifts of twenty-five dollars and fifty dollars. We are totally at a loss whether we erred in sending any amount, or perhaps should have sent more than we did, or just what is the proper thing to do.

GENTLE READER:

If there is anything in worse taste than a "money tree," it is a shakedown, such as you describe. The improprieties are many here, but you have not committed them. Your sister-in-law never should have known the amount you contributed, as it should have been presented to her and her husband as one lump sum with the names of all contributors but not the amounts they gave, or better yet because it should have been used to buy a present larger than individuals might have given. In any case, a thank-you letter does not properly contain the information that your present compares unfavorably with others.

DEAR MISS MANNERS:

We are planning a party for our twenty-fifth wedding anniversary. Friends and relatives will expect to bring gifts to the party, but we don't want or need the usual assortment of bric-a-brac which is given for anniversary gifts. We really need our sofa recovered! How can we properly and nicely say on our invitations, "Please no little gifts. There will be a bank at the door for coins for a new sofa cover and an anniversary card for you to sign"?

GENTLE READER:

Miss Manners is horrified. She wishes she had caught you twenty-five years ago, when you needed to be told, as many brides do, that it is greedy and vulgar to manipulate the anticipated generosity of your relatives and friends. While it is true that people who attend weddings and anniversary parties usually give presents, it is not true that such donations are tickets of entrance to the event. They are (in theory) a purely voluntary expression of goodwill and affection from those who share your happiness, and are chosen by their taste and sense of what you might like, in consultation with their bank statements.

Any suggestions from you, unless specifically requested by an individual guest, are improper. This includes a ban on stating "No gifts" because, although less greedy than the attempt to pick one's own present, this also assumes that some sort of payment is taken for granted. If you did not learn as a bride to look surprised and delighted at all manner of horrible bric-a-brac, it is high time you did.

~ *Discouraging Presents* ~

DEAR MISS MANNERS:

Our children are planning to give us a twenty-fifth anniversary party. Is there a nice way to make an invitation asking them not to bring silver pieces? We really wouldn't use most of it, and I'm not crazy about it, anyway. We would much rather take a trip.

GENTLE READER:

As Miss Manners has often observed, there is no nice way to suggest that you do not want presents, as it always comes off sounding like "Don't try to kiss me because

I won't let you." In this particular case, the price of silver being what it is today, Miss Manners suspects you may have less of a problem than you anticipate. If you do get silver, however, do not complain. You can go a long way on it these days.

DEAR MISS MANNERS:

We understand your point about not putting "No gifts please" on our fiftieth wedding anniversary invitation. But if some of our guests do bring gifts, what is proper? Do we open them at once, later on in the evening before all the guests, or the next day in private? We don't want to embarrass the guests who don't bring gifts.

GENTLE READER:

This is precisely why bringing presents to parties, unless they are children's birthday parties or bridal or baby showers, where opening them is part of the entertainment, is a terrible idea. Any other presents should be sent, so that a person who is trying to give a party or get married or whatever can have her hands free. If people bring things anyway, thank them and put the packages aside while you are greeting other guests. If you are very busy, open them after the party and write a note. If there is a moment in which you can open such presents inconspicuously, do so and thank the giver quietly. And *then* write the note.

～ *The Posthumous Anniversary* ～

DEAR MISS MANNERS:

My father died a few years ago. I don't know if I should send Mom an anniversary card. It is still the date that my parents got married, but Dad is not here any more. What is the proper protocol?

GENTLE READER:

Anniversary cards usually say "Happy Anniversary." This does not sound likely under the circumstances.

Miss Manners has no doubt that you could track down some sort of modernized card that hedges on what must be a rather major point to your mother. But in less time, you could write or call her that day, and tell her that your thoughts are with her and your father and everything they mean to you. Don't you think she would prefer that?

9. *Advanced Civilization*

$\mathcal{P}$rotocol

IN THEIR infinite wisdom, our forebears decided to save Miss Manners a great deal of trouble by declaring that the American way would be that of dignified but strict simplicity. Thus there are no elaborate court rituals to be taught, nor subtle gradations in postures of humility. The only instruction Miss Manners has for Americans who bow or curtsy is "Get up" (unless they are performing artists, in which case it is "Get up before you hear the rattle of car keys").

She can teach you in minutes the basics of addressing all of our high public officials.

High American officials are addressed by their job titles, and the only trick is to know which titles are used alone (Governor, General, Judge) and which are preceded by "Mr." or "Madam" (President, Vice President, Secretary, Under Secretary, Speaker, Ambassador, Mayor). The Supreme Court, an equal opportunity employer, dropped its "Madam" or "Mr." some years ago, making the title simply "Justice Wise," although Miss Manners does not understand why "Madam Justice" would not do.

In many cases, one needn't know an official's name to address him or her with utmost respect, a convenience under a system where glory is fleeting. Surnames are, however, used with the title of Senator, and may be with Governor or Mayor; and when there are numerous holders of a title, such as United States Representatives or Assistant Cabinet Secretaries, they are addressed by surnames with social titles only (Mr., Ms., Dr., etc.). In writing to all of these people (except the President, Vice President, or Chief or Associate Justice), it is safe to use three lines: The Honorable/Full Name/Job Title.

There are no consort titles in America—no, not even First Lady, a term lacking in official recognition, in addition to sounding about as silly as you can get. The only difference between addressing officials' wives and private female citizens is that they use only a surname, not the husband's given name, with the title of "Mrs." Officials' husbands, never having used their wives' given names, retain their own.

See how easy it all is? Now let's take a turn around the room and say hello to everyone: "Good evening, Mr. President. Hello, Mr. Vice President, everything all right? Why, Mr. Justice—whoops, I mean Justice Fairminded. Madam Secretary, how

PERFECT PRODUCTS
18 COMMERCE STREET
BROOKDALE, CONNECTICUT

IAN FRIGHT
VICE PRESIDENT-PRODUCT DEVELOPMENT

The Honorable
Marjorie Stately
Governor of Connecticut
Hartford, Connecticut

Dear Governor Stately,

    I really must protest the outrageous

GEOFFREY LOCKWOOD PERFECT
SUITE 16, CRUMBLES BUILDING
TOWN SQUARE
BROOKDALE, CONNECTICUT

The President
The White House
Washington, D.C.

Dear Mr. President,

    I really must protest the outrageous

Letters to dignitaries, written on different but correct types of business paper.

BRIAN BOTCHITT, M.D.
324 MEDICAL BUILDING
BROOKDALE, CONNECTICUT
———
(203) 555-1212

The Honorable
Janet Elizabeth Tuff
Mayor of Brookdale
Brookdale, Connecticut

Dear Mayor Tuff:

    I really must protest the outrageous

BANK OF BROOKDALE

BROOKDALE, CONNECTICUT

GREGORY AWFUL
HEAD TELLER

The Honorable
Perfect Pious
House of Representatives
Washington, D.C.

Dear Mr. Pious,

    I really must protest the outrageous

nice to see you. Mr. Speaker, nothing new I hope? Madam Ambassador, how are you? Senator Aegis, I've been hearing interesting things about you lately. Governor, you're looking great. Mr. Mayor, everything all right?"

Over there? Why, that's Mr. Smith, Mrs. Jones and Mr. Brown. He's an assistant cabinet secretary, she's a member of Congress and he's a spouse.

What's that? You want to know how to introduce all these people to one another and in what order? Oh, don't worry about that. It's easy; they already know one another. And those who don't, fake it.

⌒ Foreign Titles ⌒

DEAR MISS MANNERS:

As an American corresponding with my husband's cousin, must I address the envelope "Lord Geoffrey and Lady Margaret"?

I am sure they prefer it, but it annoys me to call her "Lady." I don't mind addressing him "Lord" as he has earned the title bestowed upon him. I know British protocol calls for the title, but do I have to do so?

GENTLE READER:

It is not just that you, as a proper American, have an antipathy toward aristocratic titles. (Miss Manners knows that a great many American simply adore titles, and would curtsey to a kingfish if they had a chance, but this is not a proper American attitude.) It is your assumption that a title is better if the person who bears it has earned it.

Bless your heart, that is not the way the class system works, and it goes a long way toward explaining why America chose not to have one. The further away the title holder is from earning his distinction, the more distinguished he is considered. It may be all very well to be given a peerage for merit, presumably these days a life peerage, but it is far grander to be the inheritor of a title given to a remote ancestor for pulling a hapless king out of a ditch or some metaphorical mess.

Now let us get to the yes and no. Yes, you should address people as they wish to be addressed. Using someone's title is not a show of obeisance, the way bending the knee to a foreign sovereign would be. It is a violation even of good old American etiquette to annoy people on purpose.

But no, you don't have to address the envelope to Lord Geoffrey and Lady Margaret, because this would be incorrect. The full title is used on the envelope: The Duke and Duchess (or The Marquess and Marchioness, or The Earl and Countess) of Middlehamptonshirington; or The Viscount and Viscountess Twinkledee. Only the lowest ranking peers, barons, receive mail styled Lord and Lady, and then not with their given names—The Lord and Lady Hemhaw.

In speech, "Lord" or "Lady" before a given name means that the bearer has inherited the title (and it is only a courtesy title, because under primogeniture, only the eldest son is ennobled, and his siblings are commoners) as the child of a duke, a marquess or the daughter of an earl (earls' younger sons being styled Honourable, as are the children of viscounts and barons).

So unless Cousin Margaret is one of those, marrying up would not make her Lady Margaret, only Margaret, Duchess of Whoopdeedoo. And Cousin Geoffrey wouldn't be Lord Geoffrey if he earned his peerage, unless it was by putting up with his irascible father.

Yes, yes, Miss Manners admits that she knows more about this sort of thing than a proper American should. There is even more—grace notes that are added to the title when it is business correspondence, the importance of "The" when giving the title, ways to address knights and baronets and on and on. Fortunately, you are not addressing the entire peerage, only two cousins, and they ought to be able to tell you how they came to be called whatever it is they are called.

~ *Honoring the Defeated* ~

DEAR MISS MANNERS:

An acquaintance of mine was running for re-election in our county. Unfortunately, he was defeated. What is the best way to handle this situation? A phone call? Card? Or is it best to just say nothing?

GENTLE READER:

Politicians have an odd way of thinking that people who are not for them are against them. Your acquaintance is likely to count you as against if you seem indifferent to his outrageous fall from public favor. So unless you are tempted to say "I suppose the best man won," you should say or write something. But not "They stole the election."

Miss Manners advises, "I hope you will still play a part in public life, because you are very much needed." This has the virtue of covering all the territory between defeating the usurper at the next election to doing voluntary good works.

⌒ *Dishonoring Incumbents* ⌒

DEAR MISS MANNERS:

I was told that when addressing a piece of correspondence to an elected official such as a Governor, it should read "The Honorable John Smith, Governor." Just because somebody was elected, does not necessarily mean that they are honorable. In fact, some politicians and elected officials are anything but honorable.

Can I refuse to address a dishonorable person as "Honorable"? How does such an established mannerism such as this ever become changed?

GENTLE READER:

We're talking tradition here, for heaven's sake. Not literary analysis. Do you consider "Good morning" to be a weather report?

Of course you can address a governor using only the title of Governor; people will just assume that you are unaware of traditional usage. You might feel better knowing that this is how such traditions change—people forget to use them. Just please promise Miss Manners that you won't go around assigning our public figures adjectives that attempt to describe their actual characters. She is aware that that, too, is an American tradition. But isn't public discourse vulgar enough for you as it is?

⌒ *Curtsying, Bowing and Kowtowing* ⌒

Royal personages are like any other personages, only more regal. Their prerogatives include being called charming when they are civil, witty when they are pleasant, handsome when they are presentable, and astute when they are informed. They are entitled, by heredity and custom, if not by divine right, to have all their weddings referred to internationally as storybook romances, and all public meals in which they participate as feasts fit for a king.

However, they do not have the right to receive physical obeisance from American citizens. Miss Manners has had to issue the decree many times now that American ladies should not curtsy to royalty, and still there are those who do so at every available opportunity. They are in error, not only in the matter of world etiquette, but of geography, physics and ancient and modern history.

Miss Manners will now graciously explain the matter once more, after which there will be no further disobedience from her subjects.

Bending the knee is the traditional gesture of an inferior to a superior. We bend our knees to God, or whatever it is that we worship—debutantes traditionally curtsy

The Proper Way to Address Dignitaries. Note that it is often not necessary to know the names of high-ranking people in order to address them correctly. One can greet a president ("Mr. President"), a queen ("Your Majesty") or a pope ("Your Holiness") without the bore of learning which is Bloody Mary and which Good Queen Anne.

to society, for example. The curtsy is but one form of the gesture of adoring a sovereign. Other kingdoms have their subjects touch their foreheads to the ground or kiss the ground as royalty passes.

Thus, those who believe that curtsying demonstrates their own high social rank or breeding are mistaken. Their geography is faulty if they think that bending down will elevate them; the notion that there is a law of physics stating that what goes down must come up is erroneous.

As for history, Miss Manners considers that the matter was settled by the philosopher Callisthenes, who disabused Alexander the Great of the notion that the Persian custom of groveling to royalty could be established in Macedonia and Greece. According to an occasionally broken chain of information (Callisthenes' clerk, Stroebus, told Aristotle, who told Plutarch, who told Miss Manners), Callisthenes "stoutly stood against kneeling to the king, and said that openly, which the noblest and ancientest men among the Macedonians durst but whisper one in another's ear, though they did all utterly mislike it: where he did yet deliver Greece from open shame, and Alexander from a greater, bringing him from that manner of adoration of his person." (Miss Manners does not want to hear from scholars pointing out that Plutarch also characterized Callisthenes as grave, sour and not very pleasant. He was, nevertheless, right on this issue.)

If you require more recent history, there is that matter of the war that we Americans fought to free ourselves of subjugation to the British Crown. And for absolutely up-to-date history, by Miss Manners' standard, she has a report from a Gentle Reader of an encounter between that lady's mother and dear Queen Victoria after which, the American not having been instructed on what to do, the sovereign kindly informed her, "You need not curtsy, but turn and walk out."

How, then, do we Americans properly treat royalty? With the dignity and respect we naturally show to heads of state and other foreign officials. Our traditional form of greeting is to shake the hand. This gesture is not interchangeable with that of the curtsy, as the State Department once tried to suggest when obfuscating the matter, claiming that the word "curtsy" being derived from "courtesy," it signified no more. Your government should not have to inform you that the word "courtesy" derives from behavior in the courts of royalty, which is no business of ours.

 Kissing

Physical contact between common people and their ruler dates from the reign of Edward the Confessor, when the touch of the king was said to be empowered with the ability to cure disease. This was known as Touching for the King's Evil, and continued to be a practice long after, although the cure rate was never verified by medical statistics. (Dear Dr. Johnson was the last person to be so touched.) Nowadays you see people, notably at airports, making great efforts to be touched by the President, apparently feeling that there is some magical power in it. These people were not necessarily ill beforehand, but they exhibit strange behavior afterward, such as grabbing their right wrist with their left hand and saying, "He shook my hand! He shook my hand!"

Kissing among the rulers of the world is another matter. This is connected to a convention that all the sovereigns of the earth are of one family. Sometimes in history, when you have had a particularly family-conscious monarch who has set about finding thrones for all of his or her unemployed relatives—Napoleon, for example, or Queen Victoria—this has been pretty nearly true. But it is meant spiritually rather than literally. The correct salutation on a routine business letter from a king of one country to a queen of another and hers to him would be "Madam My Sister" and "Sir My Brother." (You may not have occasion to use this within the week, but Miss Manners thought you might like to know.) If they are actually blood relatives, this is indicated separately, as in "Madam My Sister and Cousin." When the president treats other heads of government as if they were family, he is acting within that tradition. Miss Manners' preference is for the American tradition known as Keep Your Hands and Mouth to Yourself.

⌒ *Letting Go* ⌒

DEAR MISS MANNERS:

I work in an office where we deal with guest lists, nametags and titles (both elected and appointed officials).

After an official is no longer holding elected or appointed office, what happens to their title? I know in some cases they retain their titles. Do the elected officials retain the titles, but not the appointed officials? Do some of the elected retain their titles and some do not, depending on the level of the office (example: A governor would retain his but not a school board member)?

GENTLE READER:

Alas, it is not as simple as whether the office holder was elected or appointed: A hodge-podge of historic custom makes some titles last a lifetime, while others disappear when the job does. Roughly, the job has to be high ranking, such as governor, colonel or judge, and yet not unique, such as President of the United States.

It is even less simple to get the former officials to let go of their titles when the time comes. Miss Manners has noticed that all former presidents now seem to retain the title, although she prefers to believe that they merely refrain politely from correcting people who wrongly address them.

The Flag

The best way to display the flag of the United States is in one's motorcade, with siren-flashing automobiles containing police and other security escorts placed just to the front and the rear of one's car. This shows that not only do you respect your country, but that the feeling is mutual. However, there are also ways in which the ordinary citizen can use the flag to display his love for his country.

Flag etiquette is extremely complex, and the first rule is to avoid international offenses in the use of the flag that could lead to war or other unpleasant reactions. For example, it is correct to burn a flag that has become tattered beyond repair, but it is wise to choose the circumstances of this ritual carefully and to know in advance the political positions of any chance witnesses. Although it is widely believed that the flag may not be flown after sunset, this is not strictly true. Like its citizens, the flag can flap about freely during daylight, but should stick to well-lighted areas if venturing out at night.

Emotions about the flag should not be flown higher than the flag itself. For example, people who feel that a flag that has touched the ground must be destroyed, or that there is a question about whether a flag may be washed or dry-cleaned (it depends on the material—to shrink the flag is an unfortunate sign, especially for the person in charge of the laundry), are violating what the flag stands for. It stands for, among other things, good old American common sense. Nor is it respectful to use the flag to imply that others are less fully American than one is oneself. Miss Manners does not approve of using the United States flag as personal adornment, whether in the lapel or the seat of the pants, if the intention is to provoke an attack from one's fellow citizens. It is one thing to fight for the flag and quite another to use it in order to start a fight.

The National Anthem

DEAR MISS MANNERS:
At a number of children's athletic events as well as at the dedication of a building with the President in attendance, I was confused over what to do during the

playing of the National Anthem. I was always taught to stand up straight and keep your arms at your side, but many people place their hand over their heart, like we do for the Pledge of Allegiance. What is the correct procedure?

GENTLE READER:

What you are supposed to do during the National Anthem, besides standing up straight, is to sing. But that presumes that (1) you are an American, (2) you know the words, and (3) Jessye Norman is not singing, because if she is, you should shut up and listen.

What you are not supposed to do is to applaud afterward, although nobody but Miss Manners seems to know that. As the National Anthem is not mere entertainment played for people's amusement, applauding is actually disrespectful. The hand position is right hand over the heart for civilians; military people in uniform should salute. The exception is gentlemen with hats, who must remove them and hold them in the hand-over-heart position. And yes, baseball caps count.

～ Public Meetings ～

Those masterful etiquetteers, Mr. Robert of *Robert's Rules of Order* and such colleagues of his as the Mssrs. Riddick and Reed and Mr. Jefferson himself, have done a superb job setting out the rules for meetings.

Where Miss Manners might propose a simple "Excuse me" (as opposed to a giddier "Whoopsadaisy!"), they have points of order and tabling and referring to committee and "Do I hear a motion to adjourn?" That our public discourse is not entirely conducted by means of name-calling and fisticuffs is something for which we should thank these gentlemen. Thus overcome with admiration, Miss Manners has felt that she could safely skip the whole business. (Not that she would ever skip out of a meeting at which she was expected. Not unless she thought she could tiptoe away without anyone's noticing.)

No good citizen can hope to sneak through life without at some time attending meetings. Probably a great many meetings. It is in doing her duty that Miss Manners became aware that even meetings run by strict parliamentary rules can profit from the addition of rules of ordinary etiquette.

Such as no snoring. And no enjoying listening to people unknowingly embarrassing themselves by snoring when a judicious elbow could rescue them.

Doodling has long been an approved method of passing the time in meetings, having been defined for the occasion as the respectable habit of taking notes, so Miss

Manners supposes she has to allow electronic doodling. As it is considered rude to peek at anyone else's paper or screen, there is no evidence that the activity is anything other than taking down the important thoughts that one hears uttered at any such gathering.

It is harder to batten down people who are able to make nuisances of themselves without technical assistance. Yet no meeting is considered to have a proper quorum unless there is one person present who always proposes, under New Business, a topic that has just been decided after a lengthy debate, and one who persists in whispering running commentary and jokes to a neighbor who is trying to listen.

Unfortunately, the most troublesome behavior comes from those who are paying attention and are obeying the rules. Every organization has someone who proposes that each issue being discussed be tabled or referred to a new subcommittee; someone who says that taking any proposed action will attract lawsuits; someone who opposes everything on the grounds that there is no precedent; and someone who opposes everything on the grounds that it has been tried before and didn't work.

Among them, the worst, Miss Manners is afraid, is the person who knows the rules cold, and uses them to impede the business at hand. Not just parliamentary etiquette, but the entire field suffers from people who use rules designed to make life work for the opposite purpose. With this in mind, Miss Manners proposes an addition to the work of her esteemed colleagues: No person attending an assembly can unreasonably interfere with the privilege of other members of going home when it becomes obvious that no useful work is being done.

The White House

ETIQUETTE BOOKS, including Miss Manners' very own, usually have a snazzy section tucked in the back on How To Behave If You Are Invited to the White House. You are now in it.

We do this for several reasons:

1. We figure that even people who never expect to set foot in the place, barring an unsolicited and overpowering write-in vote on the part of their unknown admirers, might nevertheless be amused to find out what it would be like if they did.
2. We need relief from the staple of this supposedly genteel profession, which turns out to be requests for help in being greedy ("How can I politely tell the guests at the birthday party I'm giving myself that they should bring all the food and liquor, and give me cash gifts?") and insolent ("Give me a smart retort to demolish people whose behavior I don't like").
3. Someone might need to know. People who have accepted the hospitality of presidents of the United States have not always behaved with the decorum one (the President, for example) might have wished.

The idea that an American president should be socially accessible to his people began with the founding of the Republic. "The social status of the President was as crude and illy understood or appreciated as was his Executive capacity and administrative authority," wrote one of Miss Manners' predecessors, De B. Randolph Keim. "The people generally were unaccustomed to the conventionalities of high official station, and often waived all ceremony in pursuit of their personal ends.

"It is said that the President's House was thronged at all hours of the day and night, and that frequently the crowd pressed into the private apartments of Mrs. Washington before she had arranged her toilette, and on several occasions, the President himself complained, before she had arisen from her bed."

This at least sets a standard of public behavior that it would be hard to fall beneath.

The tradition of entertaining the public at levees, drawing rooms or New Year's receptions, continued, nevertheless, well into the twentieth century. Occasionally, a president (notably Mr. Jefferson and General Jackson) went beyond the mere admittance of those who had demonstrated the minimal graces of dressing conventionally and leaving cards, inviting anyone who wished to come in and destroy the upholstery, and thousands did.

We don't really want to do that, though, do we? We might not get invited back. It was after a fracas in which the public celebrated his inaugural by tearing up the Blue Room that Mr. Van Buren decided to cut off the refreshments.

That was the beginning of the end for mere citizens who wanted to visit the President without waiting to be invited by name. By 1925, you had to get a card from your congressman to be admitted to a White House party. And then it wasn't too long before dropping in was discouraged altogether.

Unfortunately, it is not a good idea to emulate the behavior that has become common among those who have been invited individually to attend official receptions and dinners at the White House. Dressing for attention, souvenir-hunting (the relatively honest limiting themselves to paper goods) and attempting to interview fellow guests are popular sports among White House guests.

Miss Manners thinks the public at large capable of a higher standard of manners. She hopes that they would not need to be told to stay out of the Presidential family bedrooms, at least while the family is occupying them.

Here are some things you would need to know about attending a White House dinner, but that other advisers are afraid to tell you for fear of sounding disrespectful:

- Dress as you would for a dance at a conservative country club: black tie (white tie is making a comeback on certain occasions) and non-adventurous long dress. Anything unusually magnificent or chic will make you look as if you are trying too hard to be noticed. Unfortunately the Secret Service no longer checks whether the proper length gloves are being worn.

- You needn't rent a long fancy car and driver if you don't happen to have one lying around the garage. Many people drive their own, and parking space is made available.

- Don't forget the enclosed admittance card, which will be tested by machine to see if it is a forgery. Of course your face is your passport—until you try to travel on it.

- You will be told by an aide that the husband should precede the wife in the receiving line but this is only if he is the reason for the couple being invited. If the wife is the office holder, she should go first. However much the President

The president and Mrs. Eagle
request the pleasure of the company of
Mr. and Mrs. Awful
at dinner
on Wednesday, December 7, 2005
at 7:30 o'clock

Black Tie

On the occasion of the visit of

His Majesty

Handsome V.

King of Magicland

An invitation to the White House with surprise follow-up. The names of the guests, which are in the same style as the engraving, are handwritten.

and his wife express delight at seeing you, they are not eager to talk to you during the receiving line. Say "Good evening" and move on.

• Don't worry about minor points of etiquette, because the staff (many of whom have been hired for the night) and social aides are accustomed to steering people through. If a social aide asks you to dance after dinner, it is not because you are popular.

Please send response to

The Social Secretary
The White House

at your earliest convenience

Mr. and Mrs. Jonathan R. Awful, III

will please present this card at
THE SOUTHWEST GATE
The White House
December 7, 2005
at 7:30 o'clock

NOT TRANSFERABLE

MR AND MRS JONATHAN R AWFUL, II
129 PRIMROSE PATH
BROOKDALE, CONNECTICUT

THE PRESIDENT AND MRS. EAGLE REGRET THAT HIS
MAJESTY HANDSOME V WILL BE UNABLE TO VISIT
THE UNITED STATES AT THIS TIME BECAUSE OF THE
REVOLUTIONARY CIRCUMSTANCES NOW EXISTING IN
MAGICLAND. THEREFORE THE DINNER IN HIS HONOR
AT THE WHITE HOUSE ON WEDNESDAY, DECEMBER 7,
2005, HAS BEEN CANCELLED.

THE SOCIAL SECRETARY THE WHITE HOUSE

- It is not only gauche but useless to try to have a substantive conversation with someone you might not otherwise meet. Anyone that much more important than you will relentlessly return penetrating questions with comments on the weather, dinner and entertainment.
- It is not true that no one may leave before the President retires. Many a president who loves to dance all night has been left there—first by crotchety Supreme Court justices, then by a tolerant First Lady, and finally by everyone else except the three least important but best-looking women at the dinner.
- If your invitation is for ten o'clock, eat a good dinner secretly in your kitchen. You have been invited as a secondary guest, to the after-dinner entertainment only. But you needn't mention that detail when describing to friends later what a glittering and glamorous dinner it was.

∼ Declining the Honor ∼

The value of a White House invitation, among those who occasionally receive them, is not in the expectation of seeing magnificent clothes and jewels or hearing the political secrets and sparkling conversation of the country's most interesting citizens. The people you are likely to meet are distinguished by the size of their political contributions, and the only state secret you will hear is that the President feels a deep and personal friendship for whoever happens to be that week's guest of honor.

The value of the invitation is that one can cancel one's previous engagement by saying, "I'm afraid I must go to the White House that night." If necessary, one must make a previous engagement hastily for the purpose of doing this. (For the proper form of this perfectly correct snub, please see p. 545.)

The correct form for declining an invitation to the White House if one doesn't feel up to it because one is secretly planning to endorse a rival candidate publicly is:

Mr. and Mrs. Benjamin Mobile
regret that owing to the very grave illness
of Mr. Mobile
they will be unable to accept
the very kind invitation of
The President and Mrs. Eagle
to dinner
on Wednesday, the fifth of November

Mr. and Mrs. Jonathan Rhinehart Awful, 3rd
have the honour of accepting
the kind invitation of
The President and Mrs. Eagle
to dine on
Wednesday, the seventh of December
at seven thirty o'clock

A reply to an invitation from the White House. (For declining such an invitation, see p. 703.) Heraldic devices are rarely used on American writing paper, and this crest (without the full coat of arms) has been questionably assumed by the Awfuls.

However, it is no longer the practice that only extreme illness or death prevents otherwise well-bred citizens from accepting a White House invitation. Any important event or geographical distance is considered a sufficient excuse. One need only substitute "distance from the city" or "wedding of their daughter" for the illness in the above example. What is rude is to refuse and then to brag that it was really disapproval of the President's stand on some issue that motivated you. This only points out that you didn't take this stand publicly before, or the President would not have invited you.

Inaugurations

DEAR MISS MANNERS:

What does Miss Manners consider the proper behavior for Inaugural festivities, especially the Inaugural Ball? Correct and formal? Friendly and equalitarian? Gracious but aloof? Restrained but enthusiastic?

GENTLE READER:

Defensive, actually. Welcome to Washington. This must be your first Inauguration.

Inaugurations are jolly events and Miss Manners loves them, but they do not lend themselves to any of the gradations of behavior you mention. You are thinking coronation, when you should be thinking football weekend. If you can be cheerful about messy weather, failed transportation, spectator events you can't see, social events composed mostly of elbows, drinks acquired after massive physical exertion only to be spilled on one's best clothes, and the realization that one will never find those whom one had hoped or planned to see, then you have nothing to worry about. Provided you are not the person being inaugurated, of course.

Calling on the President

DEAR MISS MANNERS:

I am invited to a White House dinner, and I heard that it is proper to leave cards for the president and the First Lady the next day. Is this true?

GENTLE READER:

That was once, indeed, the charming custom. Unfortunately guards are now instructed to transfer to a psychiatrist anybody who approaches the White House exhibiting what they consider bizarre behavior.

～ A Visit from the President ～

DEAR MISS MANNERS:

You know how presidents sometimes go around visiting "average citizens" every once in a while, to get their opinions? Well, this may sound silly, but I keep wondering what would be the proper thing to do if the president came to visit me. I don't mean what opinions to give—I have plenty of those. What worries me is the protocol of it. Let me explain. I don't want to be disrespectful, but I don't think any president should be either, and I think that's what it is to go around calling people "average!" Maybe you would think I am average—I work hard, have a decent job, have a wife and two children, live in the suburbs and keep up with what's going on. I have trouble making ends meet like everyone else, but have never been in trouble. And yet I think of myself as an individual, something special, not "average." If the president visited me, how could I make that point without being disrespectful?

GENTLE READER:

By saying, "Mr. President, it is a great pleasure for me to meet an average president."

～ Maintaining Dignity ～

DEAR MISS MANNERS:

Some time ago, a lady was dancing with her male friend at the White House and her underslip dropped off on the dance floor, and the lady just kept dancing as if nothing had happened. Was this the proper thing for the lady to do?

GENTLE READER:

Actually, such events have happened several times to several ladies in Miss Manners' memory, which gives rise to the suspicion that the White House inspires a desire to "make history," or that the elastic industry is in deep trouble. As to your question of the proper response when one loses an undergarment at the White House or another respectable establishment, yes, the thing to do is to ignore it. A general rule of etiquette is that one apologizes for the unfortunate occurrence, but the unthinkable is unmentionable.

~ *Maintaining Standards* ~

DEAR MISS MANNERS:

A very dear friend of mine has just been named as ambassador to a fairly fly-specked post. It is his first ambassadorship and he is thrilled. Unfortunately, I will not accompany him.

He is a darling, thoughtful, attractive person, but has terrible table manners. I have gently informed him of his more egregious problem, but have never worried too much. Now I don't know what to do. I have found that the State Department provides no training in this area. Do I become bossy and didactic in the national interest, or do I let him become a darling, thoughtful, attractive ambassador with terrible table manners?

GENTLE READER:

Are you asking Miss Manners to suspend the rule against freelance etiquette-correcting by invoking national security?

All right. As you seem to be both diplomatically inclined and fond of the gentleman, she will trust you. Although Miss Manners can hardly expect the State Department to teach such basics of civilization as table manners and toilet training, the lack of them can indeed handicap an otherwise able diplomat. If he argues that table manners are unimportant, inquire whether he plans to make light of the customs, including the eating customs, of the country to which he is assigned.

But even if he respects foreign customs more than his own, he cannot be unaware that people all over the world are familiar with American manners, which are more or less the standard of international diplomacy. Does your friend really want to risk suggesting symbolically that the United States has sent them an ambassador who isn't up to American standards—who is, dare Miss Manners say, what you might call fly-specked?

The Large Household

SUPPOSE YOU had a whole staff of servants to wait upon you? Who would wait upon them, pray?

You would, of course, presuming that you are well behaved. Not necessarily by bringing them breakfast trays, although it might come to that in cases of illness, but by tending to their needs and wants as human beings. You would be responsible for seeing to it that they had safe, pleasant and dignified working conditions and enough pay, time off and security to enjoy private lives of their own. Even if this meant that after hours, you had to change the channel on your television set yourself.

Miss Manners regrets that she is professionally required to disabuse people of their fantasies of ever moving beyond having to be considerate of others. To be waited on hand and foot, with no reciprocal duties, it is not enough to attain riches and position. The requirement is that you must be too young or too sick to enjoy it.

At least she is not demanding that people with servants follow the tradition of domestic employers before them. This is a case where tradition was rude. It was based on the premise that the serving classes shared neither the wholesome desire for their own family lives nor the charming weakness for luxury enjoyed by their employers. It was therefore a kindness to give them the pleasure of participating vicariously in the family they served, and to keep them at it around the clock so as to shield them from mischief.

These insights into the serving person's psyche were passed around among those who suffered from having to put up with their ministrations. They did not find it necessary to check such information with their sources.

That sort of thing doesn't go over any longer. Miss Manners remembers the last of the grand old ladies in town confiding, in a state of exasperated fatigue, that she had been forced to fire her butler because he got the cook pregnant. The sympathy she expected to garner about the suffering she had endured on this account did not turn out to be satisfactory. Even among her own friends, there were those who thought that the butler had a right to get the cook pregnant, in view of the fact that he was married to her.

Yet the concept lives on that the only human emotion appropriate to domestic help is loyalty. And perhaps an overzealous devotion to cleanliness, if this does not involve throwing out the papers before the family is finished with them.

To foster this illusion, companies that train or place people to become what might be termed show-off "help," in contrast to the alternative of cursory help, go in for the job titles of the bad old days. (Morally bad, that is. Whether the situation was otherwise bad depended on whether you employed one of these people or were one.) You can now hire not only a nanny or butler, but a lady's maid, a gentleman's gentleman, a houseman, an upstairs maid or an estate manager. The implication is not that what is being offered is not just competence, but a robotic selflessness unknown in nature. But it would still be a human being, who required being treated as such.

～ Competitive Compensation ～

DEAR MISS MANNERS:

I have recently engaged a private chef and, needless to say, I entertain a great deal more. On one occasion, one of my guests, after enjoying one of his spectacular dinners, went into the kitchen to congratulate him, which I think is thoughtful and proper—but then offered him a tip.

Both my chef and I are confused as to whether he should accept this and, if not, how to decline politely. Is this a proper custom in a private home—to tip a private chef for a well done dinner? What if the dinner was catered? My mother could have answered, but unfortunately she has recently passed away at the age of 89.

GENTLE READER:

Your mother would have said, "Don't let your guests go into the kitchen," but not because she grudged the chef the compliment and tip. She would have added "and give that spectacular chef of yours a raise" before your friend hires him away.

～ A Full Staff ～

Many a householder performs the functions of a full staff. For purposes of self-pity, or on the off chance someone can afford to hire such a staff, here is what it comprises:

PANTRY DEPARTMENT

- The butler, who supervises this department and sees to it that meals are properly served, flowers arranged, silver polished, wine treated with respect and the downstairs halls, including the door and the telephone, properly covered. In poor households, he must serve the meat and the wine at dinner, but in more favorable circumstances he need only stand behind the chair of the lady of the house, waiting to receive orders for the troops. The butler is addressed by his surname, with or without the title of Mr.
- The footmen, who actually perform the duties of serving, answering telephones and cleaning up. In equal employment opportunity households, this work may be performed by waitresses. Traditionally, they are addressed by first names.
- Parlormaids, who are responsible for the drawing room, the library and delivering breakfast trays to ladies in dishabille. A Gentle Reader (and letter writer) recalls that in Victorian days "housemaids and parlormaids had to have appropriate names, for example: Jane, Sarah, or Alice; but names like Violet, Priscilla, and Katherine were definitely not used and were substituted with one of the suitable names. Parlormaids in a higher position were called by their surnames—they valet the gentlemen, too, so were considered more masculine." In equal employment opportunity households, this work may be performed by parlormen.

KITCHEN DEPARTMENT

- The cook, who cooks. The cook may be addressed as "Cook."
- The kitchen maids, who do the dirty work of the kitchen. In EEOHs—oh, never mind.

UPSTAIRS DEPARTMENT

- The lady's maid, who keeps the clothes and hair of the lady of the house in order, dresses her, draws her bath, listens to her cry when the master is behaving badly yet again, and delivers her love letters directly to the person for whom they were intended. She has a surname only.
- The valet, who does the same for the gentleman of the house. He has a surname only.
- Chambermaids, or housemaids (or men), who keep the upstairs clean, orderly and appropriate to the hour—that is, they draw the shades and turn down the

beds at night, and undraw them and turn them up again (in the better households they take the beds apart completely in the morning). See parlormaids.

LAUNDRY DEPARTMENT

- Laundress(es) (launderers), who are responsible for the cleanliness of all clothes not immediately occupied by their owners. That is, if the lady spills soup on her bosom, the lady's maid mops up, but if the lady takes the blouse off, the laundress gets it.

OUTDOOR DEPARTMENT

- A chauffeur, who drives the car, keeps it clean and repaired and keeps out of trouble with the law, especially when he is in the car alone and pretending that it is his. It is best to have two chauffeurs, one for day and one for night.
- The gardeners, who, under the supervision of the head gardener, keep the outdoor property in order and provide flowers for the house and vegetables for table.
- The gamekeeper, who—never mind what the gamekeeper does.

MISCELLANEOUS

- The housekeeper, who battles for control of the household with the butler and the cook. She is addressed by her surname, usually with the title of Mrs., whether or not she is married.
- Companions, governesses, tutors, nannies and nurses, who occupy positions above the servants but below the family members, which means that they tend to be lonely. Fortunately, someone always falls madly and inappropriately in love with them, except for the nanny. She may be addressed as "Nanny." The eligible ones are addressed as "Miss" or "Mr."
- The people who perform all of the above tasks on Sunday afternoon—the lady and gentleman of the household. Servants must arrange among themselves to let these people do the work occasionally. Otherwise, they get spoiled.

⁓ *Bodyguards* ⁓

DEAR MISS MANNERS:

I invited a very prominent person for dinner—I prefer not to say who. The person arrived with two bodyguards. My question is whether I am expected to feed the bodyguards, and if so, where? In the kitchen or in the dining room? I am afraid this is a very new etiquette problem.

GENTLE READER:

Nothing is new to Miss Manners, who has seen it all. This problem previously existed in the form of personal maids and valets who might accompany guests on house visits. At a good-sized country house, the servants' dining room could always accommodate more, but it was considered polite to inform one's hosts how many people one was bringing along.

Bodyguards, if announced in advance, should be provided supper in any convenient place away from the main party; if not announced, they may be offered whatever refreshment is available in the kitchen. This is perfectly proper, and need not cause you embarrassment when the bodyguard reappears, at your next social function, in the role of fiancé of the lady he was guarding. At that time, one simply moves his place into the dining room.

Celebrity and Publicity

APPARENTLY, when strangers scream with pleasure at the mere sight of you and vie to buy your nail clippings on the Internet, you get a funny view of reality. You develop a sense of entitlement and invulnerability based on an inflated idea of yourself that is fed by the adulatory way you are treated by others. You think you are something extra special, and everybody else seems to confirm this.

This resembles what educators have been hoping to achieve with programs to develop self-esteem in children regardless of their actual achievements. But it is thought to be a phenomenon of our celebrity-crazed society.

Even so, Miss Manners' favorite delineation of it appears in *Royal Highness*, Thomas Mann's novel about the personable and eligible heir-presumptive to a small principality whose job it is to perform its ceremonial functions. He has never in his life entered a train station that wasn't festooned with bunting, or looked into a face that does not have a foolish expression on it:

"There was nothing really every day, nor was there anything really actual, about his life; it consisted of a succession of moments of enthusiasm. Wherever he went, there was holiday, there the people were transfigured and glorified, there the grey work-a-day world cleaned up and became poetry. The starveling became a sleek man, the hovel a homely cottage, dirty gutter-children changed into chaste little maidens and boys in Sunday clothes, their hair plastered with water, a poem on their lips, and the perspiring citizen in frock-coat and top-hat was moved to emotion by the consciousness of his own worth.

"But not only he, Klaus Heinrich, saw the world in this light, but it saw itself, too, as long as his presence lasted. A strange unreality and speciousness prevailed in places where he exercised his calling; a symmetrical transitory window-dressing, an artificial and inspiring disguising of the reality by pasteboard and gilded wood, by garlands, lamps, draperies and bunting, was conjured up for one fair hour, and he himself stood in the center of the show on a carpet, which covered the bare ground, between masts painted in two colors, round which garlands twined—stood with heels together in the odour of varnish and fir-branches, and smiled with his left hand planted on his hip."

The prince finds his job strenuous, but undertakes it when his brother, the reigning Grand Duke, pleads that he has too much shame to undertake it: "You must allow that I do not despise the 'Hi's' of the crowd from arrogance, but from a propensity to humanity and goodness. Human Highness is a pitiable thing, and I'm convinced that mankind ought to see that everyone behaves like a man, and a good man, to his neighbour and does not humiliate him or cause him shame. A man must have a thick skin to be able to carry off all the flummery of Highness without any feeling of shame."

As our celebrities are not born into the calling but achieve it through some combination of work or chance, Miss Manners would think it worth their while to learn this royal cure for this affliction, which is the cause of painful disillusionment for them as well as rudeness by them. It is the knowledge that however enthusiastically others play the crowd scenes, they recognize it as flummery, so however enthusiastically the celebrity plays the part, it is unwise to be the only person who believes it is real.

⟿ The Entourage ⟿

DEAR MISS MANNERS:

It seems that anyone who is anyone has an entourage, and I feel that I would like to have one, but I am somewhat concerned about its composition. I do not, for example, need a dog handler, or a dietician; and I have no need of a publicist. I would, therefore, appreciate your advice on what you would consider the essential composition of a modest entourage. I am a single, heterosexual male in his sixties, and while I am willing to spend the necessary money, I do not want to appear crass or arriviste.

GENTLE READER:

Then Miss Manners considers it unfair of you to take on an entourage, thus depriving one of the many who does.

⟿ The Groupie ⟿

DEAR MISS MANNERS:

What do you think of people who display photographs of themselves with famous people? Is it too show-offy? I had my picture taken with our senator, and I don't know what to do with it. I have seen clusters of such photographs in people's living rooms or, more often, in offices. You know—signed pictures of celebrities, or pictures of the host shaking hands with some famous person. Should I put this one out where people can see it? If so, where?

GENTLE READER:

Miss Manners considers such displays unfortunate on several grounds. (1) It suggests that you have established a category—for which celebrities, but not friends, qualify—of those whom you consider worthy of having their likenesses contribute to your decor. (2) It shows the extent of your acquaintanceship with people in that category. (3) In the case of people who do have a large collection of such pictures, it requires some shifting about, as the subjects of the pictures go in and out of office or fashion, and that invites unpleasant comment. Therefore, Miss Manners suggests that you not display the photograph of you and your senator, unless he is equally likely to display the photograph of you. The exception to all of the above rules is an autographed portrait of the late Queen Mary, which always looks appropriate on a piano.

～ Pulling Rank ～

In a democracy such as ours, any ordinary citizen can cherish the hope of someday reaching the point where he or she will not have to endure being treated as the equal of an ordinary citizen. Our principles do not grant privilege with rank, but our nasty little hearts crave it. Being able to ignore traffic or other laws, never having to wait in line, always getting the best table, not having to pay for many goods and services—these are deemed the rewards of success, and not just by our ruling class of politicians and talk-show hosts.

This isn't democracy, but it isn't noblesse oblige either. Miss Manners knows of no more aristocratic statement than "Oh, please, don't do anything special for me— I just want to be treated like everyone else." Compare the ring of it with "Do you know who I am?"—an unfortunate question that suggests its own answer.

Miss Manners brings this up not for the fun of lecturing her betters (her *what?*), but because the practice has sifted down through the society until there is hardly anyone who can't pull rank on someone, and also because for sheer offensiveness, having an airplane held or claiming kinship with a friend of the mayor's beats coughing in the soup any time. Those of lower status resent those who pull rank; people of equal status who don't, resent those who do; and those who do, resent those who could but don't, on the grounds that it is ostentatious to pass up a chance to elude the ordinary annoyances of life. You see what a mess this makes. Wouldn't it be better if we all agreed to abide by the rules and confined our ambitions to achieving wealth and immortality?

Miss Manners doesn't usually offer incentives for good behavior, beyond that of choking with the sense of one's own goodness, but there is an advantage in refusing perquisites or, more precisely, a disadvantage in accepting them. This is the Nya-Nya Factor.

Each of those little conveniences is achieved at the inconvenience of people of lesser rank. Because of the nature of the privilege, they are not achieved anonymously. People demand to know why that individual is allowed to go to the head of the line, or they take a good look at the license plate of the car that is allowed to park illegally day after day. They then wait until the position that engenders this status disappears. In the case of politicians and entertainers, they may even have an opportunity to help this natural process along. Even absolute rulers are abruptly subject to these reversals, as recent history has shown us. Then comes the most terrific and satisfying nya-nya.

That is why it is a good, not to say becoming, idea for the people of rank to emphasize their obligations rather than their privileges. It is one attribute of success that everyone has unlimited opportunities to practice in advance.

⌁ Pulling Back ⌁

DEAR MISS MANNERS:

My husband is a very popular local public figure. We are often invited to spend the evening with people whom we do not like and with whom we do not want to spend time, but whom we don't want to offend.

These are people we know slightly, but have never invited to our house and never will, and they often live more than an hour's drive away. They call and mention several suggested dates up to two months in the future and we say we are "already busy" for all of those dates, explaining that my husband must go out for business reasons almost every night (hint! hint!). They then say, "So when are you available during the next year? You name the date."

How do we decline these invitations without offending them? Or, if there's no way other than to offend them, what's the least offensive way?

My husband wants to "get sick" at the last minute, but the one time we did that they cancelled the entire dinner and immediately made the same offer for the next calendar year. We can't say "we don't go out in the evening" because they know we do.

What we want to do is stay home alone together in our jammies and slippers with a takeout pizza without having to smile and remember names and make small talk. Help!

Gentle Reader:

George Washington's solution to this problem was to declare that being President made him so much in demand socially that he was granting himself and his successors an exemption from the general obligation of paying visits.

No one else is likely to get away with admitting to being so popular, and as Miss Manners recalls, there was quite a bit of grumbling at the time about just who did President Washington think he was. Canceling after accepting and skittering around about finding dates are only going to raise that question about your husband.

But if it is unseemly to confess that you cannot satisfy the social hopes of all your admirers, it can be endearing to confess that you share most people's difficulty in performing all your more personal social duties. Your answer to when you will be available should be "You're so kind to invite us, and we wish we could name a date, but it will have to be after we figure out how to manage seeing relatives and friends whom we feel we have neglected."

Accepting an Award

The job of a loser, at the Academy Awards or any other lottery, is simple. (Not easy: simple.) You need only smile radiantly while saying that you honestly feel that the winner deserved it more, and then smile shyly while saying that you are sufficiently thrilled with the honor of having been nominated. If you can manage both of these convincingly, you deserve an Academy Award.

Accepting an honor is more complicated. Many people can't even accept a compliment without making the giver deeply regret ever having uttered it. The formula for both begins with "Thank you." These are easily pronounced words, not difficult to memorize. And yet they are often omitted while the flustered recipient makes a colossal mess out of the optional second part of the response. The second part can be either (1) humility or (2) explanation. A small dose of one will do, but certainly not both. If there is any doubt, it is better to omit this section entirely.

An example of reasonable humility is "Thank you—my mother made it," and of a reasonable explanation is "Thank you—actually what I did was to transpose the violin part for trumpet." Anything along the lines of "Oh, this is nothing; I can do much better" or "The idea goes back to when I was a little boy and we all used to get together and make up stories . . ." is not.

The odd fact is that praise and awards always look bigger to the person receiving them than they do even to those bestowing them, let alone those looking on and wondering at the choice. Owing to some perverse quirk in human nature, too much gratitude gets people to thinking that something that overwhelming to the winner was probably not quite deserved.

Here are some guidelines for those who find that their chores include accepting an Academy Award:

1. Look pleased and grateful, but not hysterically so. The person who bursts into tears and sobs that this is the greatest moment of his or her entire life is over-doing it.
2. Thank two or three key individuals and perhaps a supportive group, but not your extended family, grade school teachers, and everyone else who has ever touched your life. That suggests that you are crediting those people with having created something magnificent (you).
3. Understand that you are being honored for one ability and not for being a general national treasure, and therefore keep any uttering of wisdom to your profession, instead of sharing your politics or philosophy of life.

If you can't manage all this, you might want to consider losing instead.

∽ Honoring Oneself ∽

DEAR MISS MANNERS:

I would like to endow a scholarship at my alma mater. I also have an idea for a non-profit agency that I would like to start, after reading an inspirational story about a local man who did the same.

Is it considered a breach of etiquette, or at least conceited, to name the scholarship or the non-profit after myself? It is, after all, my money, but I don't want to seem gauche.

GENTLE READER:

That chap Anonymous is always putting his name down for charity, and Miss Manners thinks the world of him. She also finds it becoming when people memorialize others by naming charitable contributions in their honor. All other named endowments, she finds—well, generous, and she does not like to quibble with generosity.

So no, Miss Manners doesn't think anyone seeing a scholarship or nonprofit agency named after you will think you are gauche. Just dead.

⌒ *Public Exposure* ⌒

The old rule about publicity was that a lady should allow her name to appear in the newspapers only three times: when she is born, when she marries and when she dies. This is no longer workable. Miss Manners herself may have already exceeded her quota, and she hasn't yet used up all her events.

A modern rule might be: A lady never gets married, gives birth or, if possible, dies on television—even if she is offered a million dollars for doing so. Nor does she train a webcam on herself.

The principle of ladies and gentlemen not conducting their lives in full public view is especially important in an era when fame has replaced fortune as every schoolchild's goal. Do they want to be tycoons, that respectable old American dream? No, they want to be celebrities. There is some confusion between the two, as it has been perceived that fame leads directly to such fortune-making opportunities as book contracts, lecture fees and photograph sessions in which the subject can keep the jewelry.

Nevertheless, the lust for notoriety now goes far beyond such considerations. Almost anyone will, if asked, publicly discuss his or her depressions and adjustments and give away sexual details and family recipes. If you think that's bad, look at the people who aren't asked. Surely a major cause of antisocial acts these days is the hope of being widely recorded.

This, in turn, has led to the bizarre notion that publicity, as our most valuable commodity, ought to be distributed as a reward and withheld as a punishment. ("Why do we have to keep hearing about that teenager who murdered his family, when there are so many good teenagers who haven't done anything?")

Miss Manners supposes that this indecent interest in exposure has something to do with a general feeling of anonymity in the world. If one's neighbors don't know one by sight, perhaps it drives one to seek recognition elsewhere. Isn't it strange, then, that we all agree that publicity does not bring happiness? Nor does the public truly admire that creature we call a "personality"—a personality being something less than a person, blown up to look like more. The highest compliment we can give to such a figure is to assert that it is actually very "real" or "human."

How much easier, and more ladylike and gentlemanlike, it would be if people did not work so hard to puff themselves up so that they then have to work themselves back down to human size. That energy is, among gentlefolk, supposed to be used to win recognition from those who really have a chance to see and judge one's relatives, friends, colleagues and acquaintances. It is a matter of working not on one's image, but on what modestly used to be called one's reputation. It lasts longer.

⌒ *Confiding in Journalists* ⌒

DEAR MISS MANNERS:

My husband has taken quite an important new job, and I was the subject of a lengthy interview about our so-called life-style. I assure you that I will never do that again. I have never been so embarrassed in my life, nor felt so betrayed. A nice young woman came to my house, and I gave her tea and then, because it grew late, sherry and some beautiful little sandwiches and cakes (from a party we'd had the night before). We chatted about many things, including her boyfriend, and got quite friendly. I thought of including her at our next party, because we have some quite interesting people, and it might make another story for her. You can imagine my horror when I saw that she had violated the spirit of the visit by printing every little thing I said, even little things about our new friends in high places, which look insulting in print.

It is true, as she said when I complained to her boss, that I had not specified that anything was "off the record." I didn't think I needed to, because I assumed that she had the good sense to know what was proper for her article and what not. I was not, after all, holding a press conference: I was acting as hostess in my own drawing room.

I wish you would say something about this particular form of rudeness. Personally, I plan to reply to any press question in the future, no matter what the circumstances, with "No comment." I may sound abrupt myself then, but at least I'll be safe.

GENTLE READER:

Not necessarily. Miss Manners remembers another lady in your position making just such a resolve, the result of which was that after she had danced with the President of the United States at the Inaugural Ball, a reporter asked how she had enjoyed the dance and she replied, "No comment."

Miss Manners feels you would be better advised to learn the difference between friends and working people. It is true that the same people can be both at different times, and also that a great deal of money and effort is put into blurring the distinction to gain professional advantage. Your safety, as you call it, would be in learning to see clearly through that blur.

Your interview was not a social occasion. You tried to make it seem so, with your tea and leftovers, in the hope that you would inhibit your visitor with the restriction people have when they visit their friends socially, to speak well of them afterward. The interviewer added to the social air, to the extent of chatting about her own life, in the hope that you would feel the conversational freedom of a hostess among friends. The evidence shows that you were taken in by her ruse, but she was not taken in by yours.

Miss Manners cannot condemn her for not having the good sense to censor the remarks you did not have the good sense to refrain from making. The ability to distinguish between business being conducted in social settings and a true social life among real friends will be of enormous value to you, not only now, but later in life. Have a good time, with your "new friends in high places," but learn which ones turn into real friends and which ones you see because of mutual professional advantage. This will save you the trouble, when your husband no longer holds his position, of moaning about the fickleness of those whom you value only because of their professional positions.

Being on Television

DEAR MISS MANNERS:

Because I have been active in certain community projects, I have been asked to appear on a television talk show along with some people who have long opposed what I am doing. There is one man in particular who has attacked me violently, and I rather dread being on television with him. He can be amazingly suave and almost convincing when he states his case. I know it's full of errors and sophistry, but it sounds so reasonable when he talks.

How can I argue with him on television without seeming rude? He has a kind of exaggerated old world courtesy when he deals with me face to face, and I don't want to look uncivilized. On the other hand, I sure don't want to look as if I have the weaker case. Because mine is the humanitarian view, I ought, by all rights, to be more sympathetic. I'm afraid of forfeiting that by getting angry.

Also, this will be my first time on television, and I'm nervous in general—quite without the dislike of meeting my chief adversary—probably because I don't know what to expect. How early should I get there? Will they make up my face? What clothes should I wear? Should I prepare a statement and memorize it? Will I get a chance to rebut inaccurate statements made by others? Should I be prepared to roll off statistics to support what I say? There must be some sort of etiquette that has developed rules for what to do and what not to do on television.

GENTLE READER:

The rule, Miss Manners regrets to say, is that good manners make bad television and vice versa. If you forget everything you know about restrained behavior, substantiated conversation and deferring to others, you will be a great success. Perhaps you will forgive Miss Manners for not watching this exhibition, however.

When the television people instruct you to be "lively," "spontaneous," "controversial" and full of "energy," what they mean is that you should feel free to ridicule others, interrupt, toss off opinions from the top of your head, argue with cleverness rather than evidence, and display intolerance for any opinion but your own. The person who tries to make a complicated point or to prove something with statistics or prepared examples, is, in the simple vocabulary of television people, "boring."

Bragging about your achievements, touting your latest venture and telling self-aggrandizing anecdotes are classified as "humor," and outrageously insincere flattery —telling everyone "You're the greatest"—is called "charm." Mock courtesy, in a tone of satirical derision, is very effective. All this pains Miss Manners, but she would not be doing her duty if she did not tell you these dreadful facts.

Now, there are a few techniques of polite society that *will* be useful to you. These she can relate in less sadness:

Arrive on time. But bring a book, because the time given will be much too early.

Dress simply. Black or white will not do, but something very plain in a bright color is effective. Don't try to make your clothes interesting: That job should be done by your face.

Powder your face so it will not shine, but do not otherwise attempt to change it much from your normal appearance. Television cameras are subtler than they used to be, and most local programs do not bother to make up the "guests."

Whenever possible, look at the camera, not at the person to whom you are talking. It represents the person to whom you are really talking: the viewer. Look at it with liquid loving eyes and passionate intensity. This is where a background of disciplined social politeness really pays off. You wouldn't think it difficult to look at a black box with breathless admiration and interest if you had trained by directing such a look at the faces of some of the dinner partners Miss Manners has had at formal dinner parties.

Being Interviewed

DEAR MISS MANNERS:

What is the etiquette for staff members of agencies such as the Department of Human Resources, hospitals, reformatories, etc., when interviewed for an exposé?

GENTLE READER:

The conventional procedure is to tell everything one knows at the time of the interview, and then to say afterward that one was quoted out of context.

Interviewing

DEAR MISS MANNERS:

I would appreciate your thoughts on the manners of reporters. My quandary comes from the dilemma of being polite, on the one hand, and asking the probing questions necessary to developing a good story, on the other.

GENTLE READER:

Miss Manners does not consider any profession to be an excuse for rudeness, even journalism. It is Miss Manners' experience that asking questions in a sweet and simple way, with a sympathetic expression on the face, is a good way to elicit startling information from people who feel they must spell things out for people who look dumb.

Attacking

DEAR MISS MANNERS:

Do you have any words of wisdom for those of us caught up in the culture of attack politics, "gotcha" journalism, in-your-face social behavior and general incivility that is all the rage these days? (Pun intended.)

I don't like what it is doing to me—just because there's much to be outraged about doesn't mean that constant outrage is a constructive thing. Indeed, I find it erodes my sense of well being and my own civility. There are those individuals who help me keep a sort of balance and I am most grateful for them. But the world is too much with us all. Help!

GENTLE READER:

Well, yes, it is with us, isn't it? But it strikes Miss Manners that rudeness can win only if people imitate it or vote for it.

DEAR MISS MANNERS:

Don't you think it's rude the way the press gathers around a house where there has been a gruesome murder? How do you think the family feels?

GENTLE READER:

That is what the members of the press are trying to find out for you.

CULTURE

INSTANCES of rowdy behavior in popular public gathering places are multiplying. People have simply got to learn to behave themselves if we are to continue to assemble peaceably. Habitués will, of course, recognize that one such place is the opera house.

A gentleman of Miss Manners' acquaintance was assaulted on the head by an elderly party wielding a rolled-up program. This vicious attack was explained by the perpetrator as punishment for the gentleman's having stood during a standing ovation, thus blocking his attacker's view of the curtain calls. The same gentleman was once chastised by a person holding a season ticket next to his because his "clap has too sharp a sting."

Another gentleman and a lady of Miss Manners' vast acquaintance got into a nasty tangle during *The Magic Flute* with a chronic whisperer who later attempted to justify her behavior by explaining that she was narrating the stage events to a blind musicologist. Whether the musicologist's enjoyment of the event was enhanced by being told that a man dressed in green feathers and a bird cage had just walked on stage is an open question, but in any case, that of the people nearby was not. Miss Manners herself was once glared at, if you can believe it, for laughing at comic lines and business during *The Barber of Seville*.

So it is high time for us to agree on the rules. Miss Manners is prepared to issue them:

No talking, eating, rustling of papers or prolonged coughing during an opera. Those who feel obliged to perform one of these actions must leave the auditorium.

However, one is permitted to enjoy the opera, particularly at those prices. Enthusiastic clapping and laughter at appropriate times are acceptable. At curtain calls, standing ovations are permitted, as are booing or shouting in Italian (and not "Bravo!" when one means "Brava!" or "Bravi!").

Let us all understand this. Miss Manners remembers when many cities had no opera house, and does not wish to see them taken away because we don't know how to use them properly.

⸺ *The Overture* ⸺

DEAR MISS MANNERS:

When one is arriving slightly late to a performance and is admitted during the overture, and then has to travel to seats in the center of a row, is it less rude to whisper apologies to each person one passes, which takes longer and makes more noise, or simply to move as quickly as possible to minimize the disruption and hope that one's body-language conveys apology?

Also, because I was admitted at the rear doors and after the lights went down, I was granted my own light-wielding usher, who held his free arm out to me. I felt that I did, indeed, have some need for a guiding arm, so I took it—whereupon he dropped my arm as if it were a wet codfish and seemed badly startled. Did I presume, or did he err?

I am, of course, aware that ideally one should not be late to the ballet. That is my new main goal in life.

GENTLE READER:

And a noble goal it is, too. Should you falter, Miss Manners would suggest watching from the back of the theater until the overture is finished and there is often a pause for latecomers. Overtures are not played to provide those who are tardy with incidental music by which to find their seats. She heartily endorses the strict rules that some halls and theaters have against seating latecomers until there is a natural break in the program.

This is for the sake not only of other patrons and your oddly flustered usher, but your own. As you should not whisper during the music and you should face away from those seated when passing them, Miss Manners cannot imagine what it would take to convey your apologies through body language in the dark. Ballet itself is a simple skill in comparison.

DEAR MISS MANNERS:

How does someone who cares about manners, but also about music, behave when already seated while others traipse in at their leisure? You're not going to tell me I should stand up to let them pass, are you? I feel I'm doing more than is humanly possible when I just refrain from giving them a good smack on the backside as they pass.

GENTLE READER:

Stabbing violators in the backside under cover of darkness only adds to the distractions it seeks to eliminate. You must put your case to the management, but in the meantime, you must put your knees to one side of your seat to let these people pass.

⌒ Exchanging Seats ⌒

DEAR MISS MANNERS:

My fiancé and I went to a movie and, arriving a bit late but before the main feature began, we discovered that there were only a few single seats available. After noticing an empty seat on each side of a couple, I asked them if they would mind moving over one seat so that my fiancé and I could sit together. They reluctantly accommodated us. My fiancé says that I was rude in asking the couple to move. Do you agree?

GENTLE READER:

Miss Manners would need to hear how you delivered your line. If you barked "Move over, will you?" and implied that it was your due to rearrange the seating, and annoyed all those people who find trailers more exciting than movies, it was rude. If you whispered "May we please ask you to move over one?" you have a different problem. You must decide whether you want a husband who would rather criticize your behavior than sit next to you.

⌒ Coming and Going ⌒

DEAR MISS MANNERS:

When I have soft drinks at the movies, I often have to get up about halfway through the picture and excuse myself. The people in my row seem annoyed when I go past them, first in leaving and then in returning. I only block their view for a minute. Is this inconsiderate of me, really?

GENTLE READER:

Perhaps. But then so is the alternative.

⌒ Shh-ing ⌒

DEAR MISS MANNERS:

I have been dismayed by the rude and boisterous behavior of people while visiting museums and art exhibits. Just this week, I asked a group of three young women who were speaking loudly and laughing if they would be kind enough to lower their voices. The exhibit was crowded and there were many people quietly looking at the paintings and reading the descriptive material.

Unfortunately, one of the women took umbrage and continued to act however she pleased. I have asked the museum to consider making small signs to remind visitors to keep their voices low and respect each others' viewing space.

I have also noticed that there are those people who will be instructing the person accompanying them about the merits of the painter, the period, etc. These folks, too, could be reminded that not everyone may want to share in the art history lesson and using a soft and quiet voice would be much appreciated by those close by.

GENTLE READER:

Without countenancing boisterous behavior, Miss Manners has to say that discussing the art in a museum is not high on her list of activities that must be brought under control if we are to lead civilized lives. Would you settle for a ban on saying "That's the one I want to take home" and "They call *that* art?"

Or perhaps we could require people who attend blockbuster shows in such numbers as to make them crowded and noisy to show proof of having first visited the museum's permanent collection.

Conversational tones are permitted in museums. Unless the person is actually shouting—in which case, guards will probably remove him before he spray-paints the pictures—you should move to another room and return when quiet prevails.

DEAR MISS MANNERS:

I believe in shushing people who talk during concerts. I didn't pay to hear them blabbering. Yet a friend who went with me told me I was being rude in telling people to shut up. It seems to me that what rudeness is, is talking during music.

GENTLE READER:

Both are rude. The polite thing would be to say to the noisy person, "I beg your pardon, but I can't hear the music. I wonder if you would mind talking more softly?" By the time you have said all this, a third party will utter a loud shush, thereby accomplishing your purpose without sacrificing your manners.

~ Audience Participation ~

DEAR MISS MANNERS:

I have enjoyed music all my life. I like to listen to it and I like to dance to it. Because I have also wanted to enjoy symphonic music, I recently bought season tickets to our city's concert series.

Is it rude to tap one's toes at the Symphony or even move in any slight way? I'm amazed that no one seems moved to move, but I've discreetly looked around and NO ONE is moving, not so much as a toe. Is there a rule that governs this sort of thing? If so, no wonder everyone there is over sixty.

GENTLE READER:

Maybe, but they can move when they're provoked. Miss Manners would not advise this.

The etiquette of symphony concerts is that the only muscles that may be moved are the ones needed for turning to glare at those who dare to breathe too loudly. What is done to toe-tappers is too horrible to mention.

DEAR MISS MANNERS:

I should like to bring to your attention a matter which I believe deserves your censure. I refer to couples who are so "close" that they totally obstruct the view of the person who sits behind them. I am far from the enemy of romance. And I have only sympathy for those so enfeebled that they need to lean upon each other, although in that case, one can think of institutions more appropriate to the circumstances. I don't like to spend my money to look at the back of someone's head.

GENTLE READER:

Romance and getting a clear view of what is going on are opposite experiences, but should not be irreconcilable. Perhaps you could suggest a compromise, such as, "Excuse me, but I wonder if you two would mind holding hands instead?"

⌒ Audience Indoctrination ⌒

DEAR MISS MANNERS:

Last Sunday, my wife and I attended a concert where our enjoyment was considerably marred by the family with two small boys sitting directly behind us.

Despite their parents' almost constant hushing, the boys whined, talked loudly, sang, and drummed their feet against the back of my wife's chair until their father mercifully removed them, midway through a Bach cantata. I think that it is a fine thing for parents to want to expose their children to cultural experiences, but must this ruin these same experiences for others? Do you have any suggestions or guidelines for parents who want to take their children to concerts, plays, and movies?

GENTLE READER:

Miss Manners is grateful that you phrased the question as you did, rather than demand, as many people would, that children be kept away from civilized entertainment and be condemned to watch cats chase mice across the screens of popcorn-infested shopping mall theaters until they are of a proper age to watch bloodletting.

It is her opinion, after some experiments in the field, that children do not have innately rotten taste, but put up with children's entertainment only because they have never been allowed to view anything more interesting. If you put together all the ingredients that naturally attract children—sex, violence, revenge, spectacle and vigorous noise—what you have is grand opera.

You are quite right that children must be properly prepared for such treats. This must be done in several stages:

1. Making them feel left out. Mama and Papa should get dressed up and giggly as they prepare to leave their children home with a cold television set and dash off to fun at the concert hall. Requests to come along should never be snapped up. The proper answer is:

    "Don't be silly. You wouldn't understand it, and you'd just spoil it for us. There probably won't be any other children there. Anyway, you know what tickets cost these days? It would be a big fat waste of good money for something you wouldn't appreciate. Now, you be good little children. We'll be home in a couple of hours—unless we decide to get a bite afterward some place. Now, don't whine. This kind of music is really sophisticated, and it's for adults only." If this is said with a mixture of condescension and obvious anticipated pleasure, the children should be begging to go. When you get them to their knees, lean heavily on the objection that they are not familiar with the music, or whatever the cultural treat is to be. They will then agree to cooperate in the next step:

2. Making them familiar with the program. The best way to teach them a piece of music that is to be played is to let them call up the local good music station and make a request. This is more fun than buying CDs, not to say cheaper, and will especially make an impression if the station mentions the child's name. Of course, the station may begin to tire of playing Bach cantatas, and then you can switch to recordings or picking it out on whatever instrument you or the child plays, or humming it. Plots of operas or of classical plays should be told as bedtime stories. Being able to recognize a tune or a theme will make the event comfortably familiar, rather than chillingly alien.

3. Teaching them cultural-center etiquette. You must include the tedious

reminders not to kick or comment, but these may be hidden among the finer and more interesting points of behavior: not clapping between movements, the mechanics of standing ovations, claques, encores, fan antics and so on. If a child feels privileged to go, understands what is being done and knows how to behave—even knows enough to catch misbehavior in others—he or she will be hooked on high culture for life.

Audience Appreciation

DEAR MISS MANNERS:

I am terribly upset about some people's deplorable conduct at the conclusion of a recent opera. Barely had the final curtain touched the stage, the opera stars not yet gone forward to take their bows, and throngs of what I consider extremely rude patrons started a fast exit up the aisles, supposedly to beat the crowds to the doors, parking lots, or after-theater suppers.

My being able to rise and applaud the players on stage is as much a part of an enjoyable evening at the opera as the actual performance, but when six people push their way past me to make their exits, and a near platoon is en route from the front rows, I am personally angered and goodness knows what the performers must think seeing a sea of backs.

I cannot believe that this is proper conduct, but I am at a loss on how either to halt this exodus or to appease my anger. Would you please help?

GENTLE READER:

Well, actually, no. Miss Manners prefers to make things worse. Courteous as it is of you to feel that your appreciation is as important a part of the evening as the opera itself, Miss Manners cannot believe that most opera lovers share your opinion that clapping must be accorded the same respect as music.

In fact, as a violent opera lover herself, Miss Manners (who just loves violent operas) endorses the lively school of audience reaction, rather than the genteel one that you represent. Uniformly respectful applause is the result of ritualizing the experience of attending an opera to the point that no real expression of opinion is permitted.

This codification is more prevalent when opera-going is treated as a tedious civic or social duty than among people who find opera exciting. Miss Manners is far too shy to shout "boo" or "bravo" (with the proper endings, depending on gender and number of singers being addressed), but she recognizes that you cannot permit one without the other, and that both are sanctified by operatic tradition.

Perhaps the answer to the booing problem is to recommend the Italian equivalent of "You stank!" (also with proper endings).

A less conspicuous method is to applaud when pleased and to withhold applause when displeased, or to leave the theater when unable to applaud. If Miss Manners were an opera singer (and she has all the qualifications but voice), she would prefer the occasional excesses of enthusiasm when ecstatic fans pulled her carriage through the streets (even if it also meant occasional obviously misguided disapproval) to hearing the same tepid politeness for both her triumphs and her failures.

Miss Manners would like to ask what you do after a truly terrible opera. She has sometimes sat enthralled through five-hour performances and stayed, tapping her little hands until the last person has left the theater, but she has also gone staggering out after an hour and a half that seemed a lifetime of torture.

In any case, the opera is over when the curtain comes down. It is not rude to leave the opera house then, and there may be many reasons for doing so, even aside from terminal ennui. One may have a train to catch, a baby-sitter to let off duty or a rendezvous backstage with the tenor. Therefore you will never succeed in halting the exodus. But there is no reason you cannot stand and show your appreciation while others leave. If you are the only one remaining to do so, it will be even more appreciated.

⌒ *Overdoing It* ⌒

DEAR MISS MANNERS:

At the end of every performance I have attended over the last few years, the performers have always been honored with a standing ovation. Do you think that the quality of these performances has greatly improved over the last twenty years or the ability of the audience to discriminate between mediocre and great has been lost?

GENTLE READER:

Miss Manners suspects that the audience is having difficulty discriminating between the robust tradition of judging a performance and the sweet but less thrilling inclination to reward the performers simply for having gotten through it. Unaware that audience response is supposed to render artistic judgment, people now speak of "thanking the performers."

Miss Manners doesn't like to discourage generosity. Nevertheless, she is sorry that this approach has changed the standing ovation from a rare and valued tribute into the equivalent of the tip awarded the taxi driver simply for having completed the trip.

SPORTS

Are football fans mature enough to be allowed to go wild?

Perhaps you have trouble believing that Miss Manners would be acquainted with the appeal of being in the midst of an exuberant and opinionated crowd that is expressing itself with uninhibited fury one minute and unrestrained glee the next. Perhaps you have never been to the opera.

As a survivor of many an opera house fracas, where cast substitutions, scores with the effrontery to be younger than the patrons and a mixture of fans with divided loyalties have been known to whip audiences into frenzies, she could teach the football crowd a thing or two.

Somebody should. They are not behaving at all well. Imagine throwing plastic beer bottles onto the field just because they disagreed with a decision! You don't find opera buffs throwing their plastic champagne glasses onto the stage just because they disagree with an interpretation, do you? Of course not. Opera house management is smart enough to take these away from them before they enter the auditorium. Football management is apparently more easily intimidated.

What none of them, fans or management, apparently realizes is that while some venues and occasions appear to allow a great deal of leeway in tolerating manners that would be unacceptable elsewhere—which naturally serves as a tremendous attraction—there can be no so thing as a totally etiquette-free zone. Football has its strict rules, as do all sports, or they wouldn't be recognizable as sports. Music has its rules, sometimes more apparent in the audience than in the performance; anyone who has had the nerve to cough soon discovers that. Even warfare has its rules, deeming certain tactics, weapons and forms of carnage to be beyond its limits.

These do not exist for their own sake, but to allow the activity to continue—as sports could not if the players freely bashed one another or the fans littered the field, and performances could not if they could not be heard. That the lack of rules might put an end to warfare is not exactly threatening, Miss Manners acknowledges, although it is in the case of bans on nuclear weapons.

The difficulty, naturally, is in enforcement. Policing can only do so much, especially in large, volatile crowds. It is also necessary for the participants themselves to accept the fact that manners can operate at different levels for different occasions, rather than being either on or off. There is no off button.

So—how does one do that? Historically and presently, music manners have been forcibly taught to audiences by highly respected, even venerated, musicians who made clear their contempt for out-of-bounds behavior and refused to play for badly behaved audiences. It's called using role models. Does the sports world, populated by nothing but role models, think the only people their role models can impress are little kids?

⌒ Self-Admiration ⌒

DEAR MISS MANNERS:

I was shocked to see a young Olympic contender applauding after her performance on the ice rink. Of late I have also seen the wives of politicians applaud their husbands' speeches, actors applauding on stage during a curtain call and actors applauding at awards ceremonies.

I dismissed my discomfort as being a spoil-sport until coincidentally, the next day, I watched a biography of President John F. Kennedy on television, and noticed that his wife did not applaud during his inaugural address, during his memorable "Ask not what your country can do for you" line.

Mrs. Kennedy's behavior is what I was taught as a child—that it is not permissible to applaud for oneself, nor for any close member of one's family.

Have I got it wrong? Or have times changed? And what about if one's spouse or child wins an award, or if they are participating in a sporting event?

GENTLE READER:

Speaking of spoilsports, what you observed may have been an example of the "Hooray for me!" ethic that has replaced sportsmanship. However, it could also have been just a thoughtless example of the general applause inflation that has everyone batting hands together all the time, like so many seals.

That times have indeed changed in these respects does not, however, move Miss Manners to declare public self-congratulation to be correct. Applause is a gesture by which outsiders demonstrate their approval. It should not be used to display one's own conceit, family pride or, in the case of those performing together, mutual admiration.

The proper response, when one receives an award, is modesty. Lowered eyes and a bashful smile will do it in most cases. Blowing kisses back to the spectators is not recommended unless you are certain they have gone wild with joy. In the case of family and fellow performers, supporters should beam a look of pride toward the winner.

∽ *Tuning Out (to Tune In)* ∼

DEAR MISS MANNERS:

Is it rude to wear headphones and listen to a baseball game while attending the game with others? Often it is helpful and informative to hear the radio announcers describe what I am watching. But my husband feels it is rude to listen and not engage in conversation with him during the game.

GENTLE READER:

Spectatorship can properly be an individual or a team sport, but not both at the same time. If your husband's sociability interferes with your enjoyment of the game, Miss Manners suggests that you attend alone and that he find more compatible companions with whom to attend.

∽ *Walking Out (to Tune In)* ∼

DEAR MISS MANNERS:

A wedding, which had, of course, been planned long in advance, turned out to be on the same day as the final playoff day of the hockey championship. About 120 of the guests left the reception early to watch the game on TV in the hotel lobby.

There were 175 guests total, so the exodus of two thirds was certainly noticed. The bride tried to coax them back to the reception, but they wouldn't budge. Only after the game did a few of them wander back.

After the honeymoon, the bride and groom talked to their friends about how they felt, and while some apologized, many people felt they were wrong to get upset and the maid of honor, who'd also left to watch, isn't speaking to them.

Was the guests' behavior as horrid as it looks, or is it somehow ok to leave a reception early for something so frivolous? What on earth could the couple have done? Should they have (God forbid) set up a TV in the reception hall? Or just given up on those people and enjoyed the company of those who stayed?

After the fact, what could they have done? Is there any polite way to tell people that one's feelings are hurt? Or should they just break off with those people and find a better sort of friends? How can one respond to this kind of social catastrophe?

GENTLE READER:

Wait a minute, Miss Manners just wants to hear the score, then she'll attend to your question.

As you have discovered, watching sports is considered to take precedence over every other human activity. You would be wise to make sure you don't die just before a big game if you want to believe that your friends would be moved to pay their respects.

What can people do when their so-called friends use the occasion of their wedding to demonstrate that this is less important to them than watching a game—and even watching it in real time, as opposed to recording it and seeing it later? Nothing. Leave. The ceremony was over, and there was no point in staying around to celebrate it when their guests had left. But surely the couple must have something better to do now than to associate with such people. Isn't there a game on somewhere?

Participatory Sports

⌒ Swimming ⌒

People who have swimming pools cherish the hope that they may be loved for themselves alone. Therefore it is a mistake to omit saying hello to them on your way from their front door to their patio.

It is, in fact, rude to omit any of the social amenities, in the belief that these people don't need them because they are blessed with swimming pools. You should not drop in on them unannounced, with an expectant smile on your face and an inflatable sea horse tucked under your arm. Nor should you drop in on them announced. You must wait for them to invite you, and if you can't wait that long to see them, why, you just invite them over to your house. In other words, you treat them just as you would if they were high and dry.

If they do invite you, it might be a good idea to behave well so that they will invite you back. Start by bringing the proper equipment. This is tricky, because if you are not specifically invited over "to swim," you are supposed to pretend that you are coming in order to enjoy the hosts' company. But since they may mention swimming after you arrive, and you do not wish to put them to the burden of supplying you, what you do is to bring the gear along, but hide it. Leave it in the car or in an oversized handbag. This means a bathing suit, bathing cap (to avoid clogging the pool with hair), sandals (to avoid tracking footprints on the floors) and whatever lifesaving devices or toys you may require when wet.

Pool owners are reconciled to having to provide towels, but it is a nice touch to bring them, too.

There are also things to be omitted because they are bad for the water or the filtering system: suntan oil, insect repellent, bandages. You also have an obligation to keep yourself well on the premises, so that the host is not left feeling uncomfortable because you broke your neck doing fancy dives or drowned in his pool. For this reason, one does not show off in a friend's pool, endanger others or learn to swim or dive there.

One does not engage in potentially offensive behavior there, such as merrily pushing others in the pool or stripping without the hosts' permission; and one monitors the behavior of one's offensive dependents, keeping the dog from swimming at all, and the children from shouting or splashing. Especially, one does not stand still in the pool, with a vague, abstracted expression on one's face. One puts on those sandals and goes into the house for that.

～ Jogging ～

When ladies and gentlemen were in the habit of taking afternoon strolls, they did not bump into one another and shout rude remarks to warn others to get out of the way. Miss Manners realizes that the world has sped up considerably in the last few years, but expects people to maintain this civility when jogging.

Miss Manners does not herself jog. She would not know how to manage her parasol while out jogging in summer, nor her muff in winter. She is willing to allow the right of others to jog themselves silly, but only if they, in turn, respect the rights of those who choose other methods of mobility.

Recreational and utilitarian transportation in cities includes the automobile, the motorcycle, the horse, the bicycle, the roller blade, the skate board, the jogging foot and the walking foot. While there are specialized areas for these pursuits, such as streets, sidewalks, horse paths and bicycle paths, many of these places must be shared, and none of them belongs exclusively to the jogger.

Two traffic rules should prevail. First, that the slower mover keep to the right and the faster pass on the left, and second, that the stronger yield to the weaker. For example, a jogger pulls over to the right to let a bicyclist pass on the left. An automobile yields to a pedestrian, but so does a jogger, who should be stronger than the walker or else the jogger has poured out an awful lot of sweat for nothing.

An exception is when the stronger method of transportation is likely to go out of control if startled. Miss Manners would not advise joggers to scare the horses on the horse paths. Even though joggers are weaker than horses, they tend to be brighter. Nor is there a reason for joggers to do their jogging in places likely to frighten people. It is a poor idea to do one's jogging in crowded streets, and if one does so, one must remember to yield to pedestrians. Joggers who do not wish to break their activity must jog in place until pedestrians have been allowed to pass. If there should still be conflicts, the correct warning is, in a normal tone of voice, "Excuse me, please." Not "GET OUT OF MY WAY!"

The correct clothing for a jogger is a sports costume that clearly looks like a sports costume. No city can keep its self-respect if its streets are filled with citizens who appear to be running around in their underwear.

DEAR MISS MANNERS:

If a gentleman walking along a narrow, cleared path through deep snow encounters a lady jogger coming around the bend at full tilt, who should yield and step into the deep snow?

GENTLE READER:

In all traffic situations, the first to yield should be the first who has realized that there is about to be a collision.

Tennis

The accident of two people being available at the same time, the physical stirrings that accompany pleasant weather, an attractive look, a well-turned remark—even, Miss Manners blushes to say, the fact that one person has a convenient place to go: These are the reasons for which people commit themselves. When they later discover each other's inadequacies, it is too late to dissolve the relationship without complications and hurt feelings. That is how people find themselves committed to playing tennis with partners who make them miserable.

Miss Manners is not, herself, a tennis player. Although warned by her dear mother, when she was a slip of a girl, that "all nice men play tennis," she soon figured out that it did not necessarily follow that all nice men were seeking nice young ladies who played tennis. Nevertheless, Miss Manners is scrupulous about not limiting herself to giving advice in matters about which she happens to know something.

She does know that tennis players sometimes mistakenly feel that social rules prevail on the court when those of exercise or sports should apply. There is such a thing as purely social tennis, but this means, as in any other social activity such as conversation, that one person does not seek to demolish the other, but both endeavor to keep the ball going back and forth. It is best, in such cases, not to keep score if one person is markedly superior to another.

Tennis for exercise is better if inequalities between the players are minimized; in tennis for sport, equality is essential. All social modesty and flattery should then be cast aside as people supply enough true information about their skills to enable them to find the right opponents. If, as often happens in life, reality does not measure up to advance notice, the arrangements may be dissolved without hurt feelings, as never happens in life.

DEAR MISS MANNERS:

I am frankly a very good tennis player, and would enjoy meeting new partners I can play with. But I am always being asked to play by people who turn out to be much worse than I am, which makes the game no fun for me. When potential partners ask me how I play, I don't want to sound conceited, but I say, "OK" or "Not bad," and they say they are, too, and I end up wasting a lot of time, in addition, often, to court costs. How closely can I quiz people about their ability, and how frank should I be about mine?

GENTLE READER:

You may be quite blunt about both. In one-to-one sports, each person has an obligation to represent his degree of skill and experience as honestly as he can in order to avoid catastrophic mismatching. This rule does not apply to lovemaking.

~ *Cards* ~

DEAR MISS MANNERS:

I and my partner play bridge in what is called marathon bridge. Every month we meet a different couple in a large group. Our scores are sent in to our chairman and at the end of the year we have a big bridge party at which the winners and their prizes are announced.

This month we played with someone I will call Mary. She is noted for being a poor loser. The two previous rounds my partner and I played we did not get good cards and were beaten roundly. I happened to know that in the two previous rounds Mary and her partner had played, they made big scores.

Well we were getting good cards for a change. When we were about halfway through, our hostess, Mary, said "I am going to change cards so the scores will be more even." I asked her if she also did that when she was winning. She dodged that question.

Frankly, I was incensed at what I felt was very poor sportsmanship and actually rude. I am wondering if this was ethical for her to do this. After we played a couple of rounds with the new cards, my partner asked her if it was time to change cards again. We did beat them anyway. What do you think of this?

GENTLE READER:

Miss Manners was wrestling with an ethical problem herself—whether she was obliged to remind you of old-fashioned behavior toward people who cheat at cards, which ensures that they are unable to do this again—when she realized something peculiar.

These people changed the deck under suspicious circumstances—but then you beat them. With the deck they chose.

While it is easier to protest cheating—in a time of changing moral values, when sympathy is expected to be the proper response to unsocial behavior, cheating at cards is about the only clear-cut, unforgivable crime left—being a poor sport is a violation of social rules. You could tell the chairman confidentially that you find Mary to be a poor sport, provided you do not expect her to be expelled on the spot. Miss Manners trusts that you will be a good sport about waiting discreetly until your charge is supported enough to justify protecting the integrity of the group.

DEAR MISS MANNERS:

My brother is very rude. When I play solitaire, he either leans over me and says things like, "Why don't you put the red eight on the black nine, stupid?" or he just grabs the cards away and does it himself.

GENTLE READER:

Playing solitaire in front of another person is in itself an effrontery, if not legally what is termed an "attractive nuisance." Solitaire must be played in solitude. Brothers count as people.

~ *Monopoly* ~

DEAR MISS MANNERS:

My mother and my sister and I were playing Monopoly. My sister was going broke, and I offered to trade her a hundred dollars and the Water Works for Ventnor Avenue, which I needed to get a set, so I could start building. The rest of the property was bought up, so that nobody else had a set, except Mediterranean and Baltic, which don't charge much. Anyway, my sister was about to trade when my mother said to her, "Don't do it, he'll murder us both." Was that fair?

GENTLE READER:

As you play Monopoly, it should be unnecessary for Miss Manners to remind you that life is not fair. Is it fair for a person to bankrupt his dear mother and sister, just because they happen to find themselves staying in a hotel they can't afford? You will find, however, that it is in the selfish interest of the rich to keep the poor marginally alive, in order to have customers for their marketplace. Therefore, Miss Manners finds it advantageous to you, as well as fair, that your sister be taught basic survival.

~ Competitions ~

DEAR MISS MANNERS:

Our daughter, Cynthia, has always been a good girl, and her father and I are very proud of her. But now she has thrown something at us that has me so upset I don't know what to do. My husband, who is a classics professor, refuses to get involved with it, and I don't know what to do.

Cynthia is a beautiful girl, and it's not just her mother who says so. Her boyfriends are all very nice young men. She has a B to B-plus average in nursing school, and has always wanted to work with children. She is also musical. She plays the cornet and the trombone and has recently started taking the flute. Now she thinks maybe she would like to have a career in music before going into nursing, or instead of, if it turned out to be a success.

The problem is that she thinks she can get started by entering a beauty pageant. Just the idea of my Cynthia parading around in a bathing suit before judges makes me sick. But she says that beauty isn't part of it anymore, it's personality and talent that is judged, and also that southern girls from the very best families enter these contests. I don't know about that. My New England forebears would be horrified at what Cynthia suggests, but she considers herself a southerner. I suppose I have no right to inflict other standards on her—as I said, she has always been a good girl—but she can't name me any other girl she knows who has competed in such a contest. Tell me, please—is she right? Are such things really considered proper behavior in the best southern families?

GENTLE READER:

Cynthia is right that Southerners from all levels of society, like people elsewhere, relish competition. However, in the best families it is customary to show horses or dogs, rather than daughters. As for the object of such pageants, ask Cynthia whether she has ever observed a talented fat girl in one, or a girl who has a charming personality and a bad complexion.

Happily, however, the country is full of competitions for musicians, in which they need not submit their bust measurements, nor have their legs scrutinized. You might investigate these and steer her to auditioning for a music school, orchestra or band. As for your husband, the classics professor, tell him that Miss Manners knows why he refuses to get involved. He knows that the ancient deities themselves once got into a beauty pageant, and while Cynthia, a.k.a. Artemis, didn't compete, Cytherea, a.k.a. Aphrodite, did, and won. You might remind him, however, that this caused nothing but trouble, a.k.a. the Trojan War. Also, if respectable people adopted the standards of the classical gods, there would be no decency left in the world.

CLUBS

⟶ Proposing Members—or Not ⟵

DEAR MISS MANNERS:

I belong to a very good club which is, although strictly a social club, not disadvantageous, shall we say, to the best businessmen in this city. I am a relatively new member, but am already thinking about proposing other members. In fact, I have been asked to put someone up, but it is someone I don't want to have in the club, although I don't want to alienate him permanently either. Can you tell me the appropriate way to (1) propose someone (2) propose someone without suggesting that I am putting my full influence behind his getting in.

GENTLE READER:

In the first, you write to the membership committee, "I would like to propose for membership Theobold Worthy, whom I know well and who I believe would be an addition to the club," followed by some information about his education, profession and family. In the second, you introduce the same information by writing, "I am proposing for membership Earl Pushing, who seems anxious to join this club."

⟶ Resigning ⟵

DEAR MISS MANNERS:

Is there a correct form for resigning from a club?

GENTLE READER:

Yes, but it is only useful when one is resigning for some simple reason, such as moving out of town or realizing how much the one lunch a season one eats at the club is actually costing when the annual dues are figured into the bill. This letter of resignation, addressed to the club's secretary, expresses the member's regret at finding it necessary to resign and merely asks that this information be conveyed to the club's board.

However, there is another reason for resigning from a club, which must be handled differently. Suppose you are resigning in high indignation because you have just discovered, as you are organizing your life in preparation for taking public office, that a club to which you have belonged for twenty years is not the affable community of like-minded spirits you had always assumed, but a hotbed of prejudice against blacks, Jews, Roman Catholics, women and people with Hispanic surnames. You must then make your disillusionment known publicly, so that others will not be similarly deceived. It is wise to do so before the matter is brought to your attention—publicly by others.

DEAR MISS MANNERS:

I am in a book club and a happy marriage. Book clubbers often spend a good part of the evening complaining about the men in their lives and the men in the books we've read. They often generalize about how horribly men behave toward them now, and how badly men have treated women in the historical past.

I am uncomfortable with these discussions. Does this mean my consciousness needs to be raised about my own situation, or that I should speak up about their sexism? Or, as common sense dictates, does it mean that I should just quit this club?

GENTLE READER:

So you are happy with your marriage, and unhappy with your book club. And your problem is—which one should you change?

Miss Manners is occasionally asked whether she has ever come across a problem that stumped her. Hitherto, she has not responded, because she wants to be truthful, but does not want to appear immodest. Would you be kind enough to consent to her citing yours?

~ Observing Privacy ~

DEAR MISS MANNERS:

I am dating a wonderful man who is a member of a very elite city club in Washington DC. I am from a smaller town in Colorado where we do not have much "society." My boyfriend wants to take me to this place, and I am a nervous wreck! I know I have good manners, but I am afraid of this place! I was told that this is the same place where our president eats dinner frequently. Can you give me any pointers on things I should and should not do?

GENTLE READER:

As a native Washingtonian, Miss Manners is wildly flattered that you think so highly of people here, even including those whom you voters have sent us. Such is not always the assessment we hear.

She can assure you that your good hometown manners will stand you in perfectly good stead in the Nation's Capital. The only additional rule you need to know is that however much the dining room or library may look like public space, a club offers privacy, even to public figures. Should you encounter a public servant, you should by all means discreetly nudge your friend, but you should not take the opportunity to approach that person as you might in public, even to give him a favorable job review.

ALCOHOL, TOBACCO AND OTHER STIMULANTS

Why do people keep asking Miss Manners what to say, in a social situation, when they are offered drugs? What ever happened to "Yes, please" and "No, thank you"?

What happened was that the interesting combination of being both widespread and illegal has given the use of drugs an air that tends to cloud the social judgment of users and nonusers. The refusal of an offer is therefore often seized upon by the refuser, or by the refused, as an opportunity to belittle a person of different habits and beliefs, a motive that, however gratifying, is in direct conflict with the purpose of civilized society.

An offer to partake of any possibly pleasurable extra at a social event, whether it is a Campari and soda with lime, a third helping of peach pie or a walk outside to see the stars, is only an offer, not a test and not a command. One accepts or refuses it simply, according to one's wishes, and one accepts a refusal as simply as an acceptance.

When the activity is one that is illegal (in addition to the disadvantages one might find in the above temptations), the person offering it has some special obligations. Everyone invited to a social event where there will be drugs should be notified of this in advance.

A host must never attempt to cut his entertainment expenses by offering any kind of refreshment to some guests and not to others. The drug party-within-a-party violates not only the law of the land, but the sacred laws of hospitality. The guest who chooses to participate has the normal obligations of curbing greediness and knowing his own limits, as well as one to remember that stimulants that make him more fascinating to himself do not have that effect on others. He should refrain as much as possible from describing his sensations. The one who chooses not to take drugs while others are doing so should try to refrain from supplementing his refusal with an excuse ("I work at the White House") or a boast ("I'm high on life").

DEAR MISS MANNERS:

I do not care to drink. When I'm asked out to dinner, the first question is "What do you care to drink? What wine, etc.?" How can I properly say no to a predinner drink?

GENTLE READER:

The phrase is "No, thank you." Learn it. Otherwise, you will find yourself with drinks, second helpings, desserts and heaven only knows what else that you do not want. Do not make any excuses, such as "I'm on a diet" or "I don't like the taste of liquor" or "I can't handle cocktails." This only leads to discussion of the matter. The only other proper answer to the query of "What do you want to drink?" is "Water, please." For those who wish to dress up this reply, it is now possible in restaurants to order water that is just as expensive as liquor or wine.

~ *Smoking* ~

DEAR MISS MANNERS:

Although my workplace prohibits smoking inside our buildings, people are allowed to smoke outside, including in the parking garage. I'm allergic to cigarette and cigar smoke, and every time I park in the garage, I have to fight my way through what looks like Los Angeles in August because the smokers insist on being as close as possible to the door when they light up. Besides loud coughing and flailing my arms in the air, what's the polite way to ask these carcinogenarians to move (far) away?

GENTLE READER:

Do you mean allergic, as in you turn funny blotchy colors and pass out; or allergic, as in you disapprove of smokers and have appropriated a medical term to bolster your desire to punish them?

Miss Manners suspects the latter. But in either case, you have a problem, because garages are full of nasty air anyway. They contain cars.

You would be best off explaining your allergy to your boss (preferably with the support of your doctor, your boss probably also being aware that the term is often used loosely) and requesting a special parking space that will allow you to avoid the problem. And in answer to your next questions: No, Miss Manners doesn't smoke, and yes, she does believe that smoking (like playing the radio) should be done where it does not disturb others. She just doesn't believe in righteously hounding people whose habits, however unfortunate, you do not happen to share.

DEAR MISS MANNERS:

I am almost at the point where I don't want to have people as friends if they smoke. It must be the most inconsiderate habit in the world, in terms of other people's health and convenience, and surely it is the ugliest. If I see people puffing away at parties, I steer clear of them. But sometimes the occasional smokers fool me. They're not smoking when I meet them, but when I invite them over—my husband and I enjoy doing a lot of entertaining, and like to mix in new people—they light up in my own house, which I hate. How can I stop this? I know it isn't nice to start giving guests orders, but, honestly, is there any reason to want to keep these people as friends?

GENTLE READER:

Actually, smokers make excellent friends at present-giving time, because they can always be given pretty lighters and ashtrays, and, if you are in love with one, although Miss Manners gathers you are not, an engraved silver cigarette case makes a marvelous present. However, that does not seem to cover your chief question. The answer to that is that when you invite them, you may say regretfully, "I hope you don't smoke, because we don't have smoking in the house."

DEAR MISS MANNERS:

My beau and I have been asked to be weekend guests by his friends in another town. These friends do not smoke, nor does my beau. His friends do not permit smoking in their house. I am a smoker and have refused to go because of these circumstances. If the invitation had been for dinner only, I could oblige by not smoking, but a weekend is impossible. Do you think my behavior stubborn or justified?

GENTLE READER:

Both. An honest person cannot accept hospitality with the intention of disobeying the house rules, and yet you have been startlingly honest with your beau about what your greatest pleasure is. A little less honesty—whatever happened to sneaking out at night?—would have been more tactful.

~ Drinking ~

Wine can do evil things to people. Otherwise gentle and mannerly souls turn arrogant and belligerent. The most retiring types will not hesitate to make public spectacles of themselves. Those who are imbued with the graces of modesty and toleration are transformed into show-offs and bullies. And that's before anyone has had a chance to drink the wine.

Miss Manners is the last person to question propriety and ritual, but she is getting dangerously close to believing that anyone demonstrating an excessive interest in his automobile, sound-reproducing equipment or wine is not a gentleman. (Horses and land are the traditional subjects on which gentlemen are permitted to lavish more care than on their families.) There are so many expertoholics about these days that it has become rather charming for a host to enlist help. Asking the lady to order the wine or entirely leaving the choice to a trusted sommelier or wine steward is, in Miss Manners' opinion, more gentlemanly than reeling off names and adjectives.

The general rule is that the host selects the wine to complement the food, and the general beliefs are that chilled white wines are better with light food, such as fish, poultry and veal; that full red wines are served at room temperature with game and heavy meat; that sweet wines are served with dessert; and that champagne goes with everything. Miss Manners holds to the last opinion very strongly. But these rules are not engraved in stone or, shall we say, stained on white damask. A host who is sure of himself may try some more daring combination at home, or he may do so in a restaurant with the advice and consent of his guests.

At one's own dinner table, the name of the wine may be made known upon request, but it is never written on the menu or otherwise used as a designer T-shirt to puff up the chest. The exception is a dinner among friends who are known to share a special interest in wine, and who may be especially invited to share a treat.

At home or in restaurants, it is the job of the host to be sure that the wine is in good condition. This is the point at which many people become hysterical with the awesomeness of the duty. One can occasionally be served a bad wine, just as one can occasionally be served food that has gone bad, and no one expects either to be consumed. It is, in fact, a favor to draw such a mistake to the attention of the responsible person.

But these days one does not enter suspiciously into a prolonged trial, any more than one generally employs a taster, to sample the food and certify that one's friends or, more likely, one's own household is attempting to poison one, unless it is proven otherwise. The normal precautions are to smell the cork, checking to find if it has gone musty, and to pour a sip into one's own glass and sample it. This has the advantage of making the host, rather than the guests, choke on the bits of cork he has clumsily splintered into the bottle.

Please note that it does not include pushing the cork up the nose, lowering the face into the glass, swirling the wine about on the tongue or discussing whether it has lived up to one's expectations. The best rule is that if you cannot tell whether or not a wine has gone bad, you might just as well drink it.

(For more on wine in restaurants, please see p. 754.)

 Cocktails

DEAR MISS MANNERS:

When cocktails are served before dinner in a restaurant, those guests who order martinis find their olives neatly speared on a plastic skewer, so that they may snap their olives without seeming to anticipate dessert by using their drinks as finger bowls. But can you advise those of us who prefer old-fashioneds or whiskey sours, which provide both cherries and citrus slices but without a deft handle?

GENTLE READER:

In the case of nourishment served in a cocktail, you may, of course, finish the drink and then tip the glass toward you so that the wet orange slice falls smack onto your nose. Miss Manners suggests, however, using the nearest fork, plastic stirring gizmo or spoon.

DEAR MISS MANNERS:

When served a margarita with salt and a straw, how do you get to the salt? I love the straw, but when I'm out, I remove it rather than lick the glass, then take a sip from the straw. Do you understand the dilemma?

GENTLE READER:

No. People who love to drink out of straws are not old enough to drink alcohol. Miss Manners believes it to be quite enough excitement for them to drive their parents crazy by blowing bubbles in their milk.

~ Champagne ~

DEAR MISS MANNERS:

Is it true that it's considered more elegant to open a bottle of champagne without getting the popping sound from the cork? I always associate that sound with special occasions, and think it's fun to let people know what's coming.

GENTLE READER:

It is not always fun for the person who finds out what is coming by getting a flying cork in the eye. Putting out champagne glasses is a more subtle announcement, and if that is too subtle, you can say in a hearty voice, "Well, let's have some champagne."

~ Toasting ~

DEAR MISS MANNERS:

When offering toasts, when do you clink glasses, and when do you smash glasses? I have heard of people throwing their glasses at the fireplace, but I'd hate to be the one to start it at a time when it turned out not to be the thing to do.

My wife doesn't drink, and is always embarrassed during toasts, not knowing what to do. She says she doesn't want to insult anyone, but if it's a choice between insulting and drinking, she'll do the insulting. Now, I do drink, but I don't know how many people at a dinner table I'm supposed to clink glasses with before I can take a sip. What if someone drinks to my health?

GENTLE READER:

For some reason, there are a great many more legends and customs associated with drinking than with, for example, the taking of vitamins. One story about the clinking of glasses is that the purpose is to spill each person's wine into the glass of the other, for assurance that nobody is being poisoned (or everyone is).

Another story is that the custom of clinking glasses originated in the Middle Ages, when any alcoholic drink was thought to contain actual "spirits," such as the demons in "demon rum," who, when imbibed, inhabited the host's body, causing the imbiber to do things that he would not ordinarily do. Since bells and other sounds were thought to drive spirits away (to this day, churches ring bells to drive the "demons" away from the sanctuary before worship begins), the clinking of glasses was thought to make it safe to drink.

Nowadays, it is better to touch the glasses of those next to you, and even better merely to raise your glass. Your wife should raise her glass too, even if it is empty, and then put it down without drinking. One never, ever drinks to oneself, but babies being toasted at their christenings are among the few people to know this.

On the subject of smashing glasses in the fireplace, remember that until the late 1800s, glassware for most people was a very high-priced luxury; the symbolism of smashing glasses in the fireplace meant either that the host (while refraining from toasting himself, he must give his approval by tossing the first glass) wanted to show his true affluence, or that he considered the toast to be of such importance that the glasses would never be used for a less worthy drink.

Miss Manners advises against tossing glasses into a fireplace with a live fire in it. That makes an awful mess when the glass melts and sticks to the brickwork, and is nearly impossible to remove. Break the stems instead.

Watering the Drinks

DEAR MISS MANNERS:

Is it acceptable or not to dip ice from my water glass with my spoon and put ice into my wine glass at my evening meal? I have seen this done. Is it okay or rude?

GENTLE READER:

You must have met the gentleman who told Miss Manners his secret for drinking champagne all day without getting drunk—an ice cube in each glass. He wasn't what you would call sober when he explained this, but then it was already ten o'clock in the morning, and she probably should have caught him earlier.

As a matter of etiquette, the practice doesn't stand up much better under scrutiny, but Miss Manners wouldn't actually call it rude if it is done inconspicuously.

Skewering the Drinkers

DEAR MISS MANNERS:

I went to a bar last night with a group of friends who are "social drinkers." (I don't drink.) Well, these social drinkers made complete fools of themselves last night. My question is, is it proper for me to remind them of their behavior (and subsequently) to laugh uproariously?

Gentle Reader:

No and yes. That is, have a good laugh, but do not share it with them. They had enough fun last night, and now it's your turn. It is, moreover, a bad precedent to tell people that they have made fools of themselves. Once that kind of honest criticism gets loose in the world, it is very difficult to control.

RESTAURANTS

It must not be easy to be a snob and a slob at the same time. Looking down on oneself cannot be gymnastically comfortable, and Miss Manners doesn't even want to think about it as a psychological position.

Yet people manage. Miss Manners hears from them when they are well into adulthood without having thought it worth their while to learn to eat in an aesthetically inoffensive way. That's the slob part.

The snob part is not that they now want to learn. In itself, that would be admirable. Miss Manners believes in the redemption of the rude, and would be sympathetic, helpful and reassuring, which she can manage all at once without the least strain. (Contrary to the panic they produce, table manners are quite simple. Please see p. 154.) Penitents only lose Miss Manners' goodwill when they take pains to explain why they need table manners now, but didn't up until now:

They are dining out in expensive restaurants, and are afraid that the waiter, the sommelier and that most feared and respected figure of all, the headwaiter, might find them unworthy of the privilege of buying food on their premises. No such problem had existed before, as the only people they might have offended then were their own family and friends.

Nice. And it's not as if Miss Manners had inquired. She accepts candidates for remedial eating without grilling them. All they had to do was to keep their mouths shut—incidentally another aspect of table manners.

It will astonish restaurant employees and patrons alike to hear this, but even the best restaurants are commercial establishments where people pay to be served meals, and not temples of social behavior where they submit themselves to be judged. Restaurant staffs are not all that interested, let alone expert, in critiquing table manners. The manners that interest them have to do with honoring reservations, refraining from making scenes and tipping lavishly.

Good restaurant service may be pleasant and smooth, but it does not represent

the highest standard of dining room service. As you are paying for your meal in a restaurant, it is perfectly proper to:

- Request a table in an area you prefer, say, near a window or away from musicians. For a customer to accept the employees' or owners' idea of "good" tables and "bad" tables and compete to be favored with their choices is childish.
- Sit next to whomever you want among those in your group. Unless one is giving a party in a restaurant, the social rules about seating do not apply. If couples want to sit next to each other rather than across, or with the gentleman against the wall rather than the lady, Miss Manners cannot see why they should not be permitted to do so.
- Know what is being offered, in the way of food and drink, and its price. If a list of "specials of the day" is recited, it is sensible to ask how much a dish will cost.
- Expect to be supplied with correct flatware, and resupplied, discreetly and tactfully, with replacements for dropped or misused implements.
- Talk only with those with whom one is dining. If strolling musicians, itinerant fashion models or sociable waiters or other service people present themselves, they may be dismissed with a pleasant but abstracted nod.
- Remain ignorant of the personnel hierarchy of the restaurant. If a restaurant employs an army of captains, waiters, headwaiters, priests of wine, busboys and hostesses, that is its privilege. But the customer should not be expected to recognize and treat according to rank the entire service. He may address any request to whoever presents himself with the expectation that that person, if not designated to perform the task, will find the person who is. Unless some special favor is given, the client should have to leave only one tip, to be divided by those involved according to their own standards.
- Enjoy his dinner, free of worries about the help critiquing his manners. Only Miss Manners is allowed to do that. But she is not sorry if restaurants' reputation for nannyhood spares both her and their families unpleasant sights.

Checking Coats

DEAR MISS MANNERS:

Does a woman have to check her coat at a restaurant? Some restaurants insist on it, and some won't even accept women's coats. If I keep it, what do I do with it—ask for another chair to put it on, or sit on it?

GENTLE READER:

It is true that the old-fashioned rule is that a lady does not check her coat, but Miss Manners fears that restaurants that do not accept women's coats are not thinking of correctness. They are thinking of their own skins or, as in the case of fur coats, their customers' skins. Safety and etiquette are thus making a rare appearance together. The coat is gently peeled back from the shoulders and hangs nonchalantly over the back of the chair.

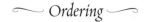

Seating Ladies

DEAR MISS MANNERS:

If a gentleman and his wife, together with a friend of approximately the same age, eat at a restaurant where guests are shown their table but not seated by the hostess, should the gentleman seat his wife or the "friend"? The "friend" is a widow who dines out frequently (on her own as to paying her check) with the couple.

GENTLE READER:

The gentleman should first help the friend to her seat, and then his wife. The wife should not consider it a discourtesy to follow the ordinary procedure of deferring to a guest before a relative, other things being equal. The letter-writer should stop putting the word "friend" in quotation marks.

DEAR MISS MANNERS:

Where should I put my purse in a restaurant?

GENTLE READER:

Where you can keep an eye on it.

Ordering

DEAR MISS MANNERS:

I understand there once existed a quaint, rather sexist custom of presenting menus with no prices to ladies dining at restaurants (presumably only those dining with gentlemen). These were called "ladies' menus," or so I have been told; I have never personally encountered one.

Do these menus still exist? Presumably restaurants would not today be foolish enough to assume that the lady is not the one planning to pick up the check, but it does seem like they might offer them to guests on the request of the host, regardless of gender. If these menus still exist, what are they called, and how would one request them when making the reservation?

The flip side of this question, of course, is what the polite thing is to do when one is handed a menu without prices. My parents taught me that when one is taken out to a restaurant, the polite thing to do is to order from the middle of the menu, unless the host has ordered the most expensive item, in which case it is permissible for the guest to do likewise.

The entire purpose of a menu without prices seems to be to thwart this inclination. On the other hand, it's not hard to guess that the linguine alfredo is probably less expensive than the lobster thermidore.

Should the guest try to guess which menu items are less expensive? Or should he accept that the entire purpose of this arrangement is to allow him to order the lobster, if that's what he's in the mood for, even if his host is ordering the linguine alfredo? After all, a generous host might be perfectly happy to pay for the lobster thermidore, but not much care for lobster herself, and a menu without prices is a more emphatic way to state this than merely saying "Oh, please do order whatever you'd like," an instruction that my parents always told me to disregard.

The reason we'd like to know what they're called is that we'd like to take my husband's parents out to a nice restaurant sometime, and we think they would probably enjoy the meal more if they didn't know how much it cost.

GENTLE READER:
Yes, they were called "ladies' menus," but this merely reflected the social pattern by which ladies were more apt to be the guests when eating out, and more likely to be hostesses for entertaining done at home.

And yes, these still exist, although they are rare. Miss Manners has encountered them at clubs, where menus with prices are called Members' Menus, and those without, Guest Menus. She also agrees that they are useful, in just such instances as yours with your parents-in-law.

But surely your own parents gave you enough instruction on how to navigate them to ignore the host's invitation to order the most lavish item unless he orders it himself. Which are the expensive items are not usually hard to figure out, as you have noticed. In addition, the standard phrase of instruction "Order from the middle of the menu" should remind you of the usual order of menus, where the dishes in different categories are arranged pretty much in order of price.

∽ Ordering Wine ∼

DEAR MISS MANNERS:

When wine is ordered "by the glass" and I have not emptied the glass when another is served, what do I do? Pour my leftover wine in the new glass and ask the waiter to remove the first glass? Let it sit unused? Or quickly drink what's left?

GENTLE READER:

Have you thought of not ordering a second glass until you have finished the first?

Miss Manners understands your fear that you may never again see a waiter, but considers it no reason to take up gulping. Simply respond to the request by asking the waiter to return shortly because you will decide whether to have another drink.

∽ Pouring Beer ∼

DEAR MISS MANNERS:

Should a gentleman pour his dinner partner's beer for her? My favorite companion and I often dine in exotic restaurants and she likes to drink beer with highly spiced food. The waiters usually pour out one glass and leave the bottle on the table near her. Am I responsible for refilling her glass myself, should I ask the waiter to do so, or is she on her own? I know that I am expected to see that her wine is refilled, by myself or, in more formal restaurants, by the waiter. Does this same rule apply to beer?

My own instinct is to refill her glass for her, but that may be less natural chivalry than an ingrained belief in Dorothy Parker's law of seduction: "Candy is dandy, but liquor is quicker."

GENTLE READER:

Miss Manners is under the impression that what beer does quickly is not what you have in mind. She is also under the impression that your Dorothy Parker quotation is a poem by Ogden Nash. You are probably under the impression that Miss Manners is never going to stop showing off and answer your question.

Pour the beer. You know perfectly well that the waiter is not going to get around to it, and fastidious ladies do not pour from bottles at table when there are gentlemen present to do it for them.

~ *Splitting the Check* ~

DEAR MISS MANNERS:

My husband and I suggested going out to dinner with another couple and introduced them to a restaurant we like. When the check came, they seemed to assume we were paying for dinner, because they thanked us and made no move to pick up the check. Not knowing what to say, my husband just paid for everyone. What else could he have done?

GENTLE READER:

It's not just your husband, if that's any comfort. Nobody knows what to say in this situation or how to interpret whatever is said. The confusion stems from the merging of two separate forms of socializing—entertaining and going out together—which are using practically the same wording. The difference between "We'd like to take you out for dinner" and "Let's have dinner out together" is easily lost in the telling or the hearing.

Miss Manners recalls when all entertaining was done at home or at one's club, so that going to restaurants with others assumed separate bills, because although someone was the instigator, no one was the host. Now there are many people who never invite others home to dinner, which sure makes you wonder why they registered for ten place settings, but who do all their entertaining in restaurants.

When the bill just sat there, your husband could have asked the other gentleman "Shall we just split this?" as if the choice were between that and itemizing the bill according to who ate what. But Miss Manners thinks he made the better choice in eating the bill, since it could easily have been an honest mistake on the part of your guests (as they turned out to be).

After all, if that was the case, they will have to invite you back, so you will come out even in the end. If they do not, you'll know not to invite them again without spelling things out carefully: "We were thinking of having dinner next week at a nice restaurant we know. If you'd like to try it too, why don't we go the same night?"

DEAR MISS MANNERS:

When our friends join us at any restaurant on a social evening, I find it awkward when they request separate checks. If we are close enough friends, why is this necessary? Seems to me it evens out over time, one more, or one less. Any clarification would be appealing.

GENTLE READER:

Not necessarily. Miss Manners has heard tell of some truly unappealing clarifications taking place among friends who are close enough to go together for dinner at a restaurant.

Such as "But you had two desserts."

And "Don't you think twenty percent is a bit excessive?"

And "But you drank twice as much."

And "Don't you think ten percent is a bit stingy?"

And "I want it all on my card because I need the frequent flyer points."

And "I want it on mine, because I'm going to claim it as a deduction."

In contrast, she feels that "Let's put this on separate checks" is downright friendly.

DEAR MISS MANNERS:

What do you do if a waitress tells you it's not "restaurant policy" to issue separate checks to two couples dining together?

GENTLE READER:

Separate yourself from the restaurant before ordering dinner. If there are enough crumpled napkins left behind by people who depart from the restaurant when this is announced, there will be a change of policy.

⌒ *Splitting the Dinner* ⌒

DEAR MISS MANNERS:

Some people wield satanic forks. Without even asking permission, they stab their used ones into my dish for a taste. Or into a serving dish for another bite. Or the latest throw theirs onto my plate when mine disappears. My appetite dies. And so do the relationships.

My daughter says I should have asked for a clean fork rather than say I was suddenly ill and had to go home. But when I tried to tell my ex-husband that he ruined the rest of the food in the serving dishes, he just laughed and kept doing it. Rather than try to reform the clueless, I keep looking for more sensitive friends. But I'm beginning to wonder if there are any out there. How would you handle these situations?

GENTLE READER:

Not as harshly as you, even if you had other causes for divorcing your husband. Fleeing the scene and leaving others to pay your bill also strikes Miss Manners as excessive. Such people are impolite, but if they were satanic you should be reaching for the garlic.

Instead, she suggests you reach for your bread plate. Cut off the area to which the offending fork has been applied, and pass it to the person. If it constitutes more than a fraction of your meal, you could say, "Here, you have this, it's good, isn't it? Just please order me another."

Rejecting the Food

DEAR MISS MANNERS:

When we went out to a fine restaurant, I tasted my entree and was unable to eat the dish because I just couldn't bear the taste. While the food was not spoiled in any way, it just didn't taste good to me. Would it have been acceptable to send back the dish simply because I didn't like it?

GENTLE READER:

If the food wasn't spoiled, what was wrong? The cooking? Surely, if the food is overdone and dried out, for example, any restaurant that considers itself "fine" would appreciate the chance to do better, although Miss Manners wouldn't suggesting trying this at your favorite rest stop.

But could it have been that something was wrong with the way you ordered? That you didn't remember what lapin was in English and weren't willing to ask? True, there are restaurants that are fastidious enough to take back a dish for the sake of placating spoiled clients. But the polite person quietly absorbs a loss based on his or her own mistake or whim.

Disposing of Trash

DEAR MISS MANNERS:

What does one do with butter, cracker/breadstick, and sugar wrappers at the table? At most private dinners, this is a rare problem, but at catered or restaurant affairs it is not uncommon. Does one place the wrapper in an ashtray, on the side of the bread plate, in a pocket?

GENTLE READER:

Ladies and gentlemen are only required to know how to respond to table service that, however complicated and artificial now, grew out of the natural causes. Serving food in commercial packages is the invention of overzealous health departments or lazy restaurants. The recipient of such practices need not pocket the evidence. If packaged food is served at the table, one need only crumple up the trash and leave it on the table.

⁓ *Overhearing Adults* ⁓

DEAR MISS MANNERS:

While I was dining with a friend at a small table in a rather posh restaurant, a single male took the small table about a foot away from us. To our astonishment, in between courses he placed a laptop computer on the table and proceeded to type away.

While this did not strike me as an invasion of MY privacy, my dining partner blew up with anger and could not stop talking about how offended he was by this kind of behavior in a restaurant. He eventually complained to the manager of the restaurant about this guy with his laptop and urged the manager to add laptop computers to his ban on cell-phones.

Actually, what the lone diner did was, in my view, in the worst possible taste, but I did not feel that he was "invading my space." Apparently, my dinner partner felt otherwise. Should laptop computers join cell-phones on the list of electronic devices that should be banned in restaurants?

GENTLE READER:

Surely another diner would not have to put his feet on your table to meet your definition of invading your space. It should be enough to spoil the general atmosphere for him to put his feet on his own table.

Miss Manners chose this horrid example to show you that your "worst possible taste" was an exaggeration. Nevertheless, the laptop was out of place. Its place would be a cybercafé, not a restaurant you describe as posh.

DEAR MISS MANNERS:

Is it polite to eavesdrop? I was at lunch at a famous restaurant where there were a lot of celebrities and was fascinated to hear what was going on, but my mother, who was with me, said it was very rude. Surely these people expected to be noticed, or they wouldn't eat there.

GENTLE READER:

Miss Manners deals in manners, rather than morals, and the answer is that it is highly impolite to be observed to eavesdrop. This is rude not only to the people whose conversation you are overhearing, but especially to your own companion, in this case your mother, whose conversation is thus pegged as being less interesting than that at other tables.

As for listening to what is going on, that, of course, is what such restaurants are for. Until you learn to smile and nod at your mother while picking up gossip from three tables away, you do not deserve to be taken there.

⌐ Overhearing Children ⌐

DEAR MISS MANNERS:

At dinner in a fine restaurant, several children ran around the room making a ruckus, shouting and banging on things. Just as my companions and I were served our seared ahi tuna platters, a dirty-faced little gremlin appeared at our table and began playing with my lady friend's silverware. During all this, never once did I see a parent ask their child to pipe down or sit still. I find more and more atrociously behaved children in "adult" public places these days. What should be done?

GENTLE READER:

You mean to safeguard our future from a generation of savages? Or to get through a meal in peace?

The first requires parents to teach their children manners and refrain from placing them in situations they cannot handle. The second requires you to refrain from telling them so. Miss Manners is not also requiring you to fight with gremlins for possession of your fork. It is the unpleasant duty of the restaurant management to ensure your ability to enjoy your meal undisturbed once you discreetly bring the problem to its attention.

DEAR MISS MANNERS:

What are the rules of etiquette in the little coffee shops that are usually found in one of the large bookstores? Are they libraries, or are they restaurants?

While huddled over a technical manual at one of these stores, I usually get distracted by the screaming children, chatty customers and incessant cell-phones. Usually, when I do feel disturbed, I try to throw dirty looks at the culprits, which are usually ignored. I am forced to leave my seat and find a quieter place within the store. Will it be disrespectful of me to ask them to "zip-up"??

What about the area outside the coffee shop, where the books are kept? Are those areas also considered libraries or are they considered malls where customers can bring in children that haven't been taught to keep quiet? There are specially marked "kids sections," which are cleverly placed far enough from the general seating areas, so as not to disturb the adult patrons.

GENTLE READER:

If they were libraries, people should be throwing you dirty looks for drinking coffee, and perhaps also for eating. If they were restaurants, you should expect people to be lively. If they were malls, you would be arrested for walking out of the bookstore without paying for the books.

These bookstore-cafés are a hybrid, allowing comfortable browsing along with shopping and socializing. No doubt people who can concentrate anywhere get a lot of free reading done, but this is not supposed to cancel the other activities. Should you want to study intensively, Miss Manners imagines that the bookstore might even be willing to sell you the book.

Having disposed of your similes, Miss Manners gets to examine the actual conflicts involved and make up new rules.

Chatting is improper in libraries, no matter how laxly the rule has been treated in recent years. It is, however, proper in both bookstores and cafés. Allowing children to scream freely rather than being hauled off and lectured is not proper any place where innocent people (as opposed to parents) are forced to listen. The same goes for screaming into cellular telephones, although they may be used with a normal tone of voice in stores and informal eating places.

However, telling people to "zip up" is never proper unless they are exposing themselves.

⌒ Clearing the Table ⌒

DEAR MISS MANNERS:

My husband works at a nice restaurant. He is a professional waiter who does a very good job. Last week, an older woman gave him grief because he tried to take away her empty plate. She scolded him for trying to take it before everyone else at the table was finished. Have you ever heard of this?

GENTLE READER:

Of scolding? Or of removing plates before everyone at the table is finished? Miss Manners has heard of both, and doesn't care for either one.

DEAR MISS MANNERS:

My boyfriend and I have a disagreement about whether it's proper when we finish eating at a restaurant for him to stack up the dishes. I have told him it's the waitress' responsibility. Who's right?

GENTLE READER:

Neither of you. It is the waitress' job to clear the table properly, and a good one would be just as horrified as Miss Manners at dishes being stacked.

⟿ Checking the Bill ⟿

DEAR MISS MANNERS:

My husband has taken to using his pocket calculator for adding up the bills in restaurants. I don't mind his quietly checking the waiter's figures—he has caught mistakes many times, and never in our favor, either—but this seems a bit much. He says he does it because his arithmetic is bad, and this is the quickest, most accurate way of doing it. I hate the little clicking noises it makes. People always turn around and look.

GENTLE READER:

Isn't that preferable to their turning around to hear him say "four and carry the two, plus seven, is fourteen?"

⟿ Checking the Make-up ⟿

DEAR MISS MANNERS:

My mother says putting lipstick on at the table in a restaurant is poor manners. I say if you have a beautiful holder or compact and don't take all evening, this is accepted today. Who is right—her (old school) or me (new school)?

GENTLE READER:

The new school is right. But wait—before you rush off to triumph over your mother, Miss Manners must point out that it is your mother who represents the new school in this dispute.

Before the first World War, ladies did not put on makeup in public for the sensible reason that they were pretending that they never wore any. After the war, some of them inaugurated the modern era of fashion by wearing little else.

Thus the really beautiful compacts, which it soon came to be permissible to flash at the table, date from the 1920s and 1930s. These often matched elaborate cigarette holders, as smoking at table was also permitted.

In recent times, onlookers revolted against both smoking and grooming at the table, on the grounds that they found those practices unappetizing. They have therefore been banned by the new school.

Tipping

Gouging for tips is getting ever more aggressive. Even the generous among Miss Manners' Gentle Readers complain of feeling hounded. Tip jars and saucers have appeared everywhere, from counters where prewrapped fast food is handed directly to customers, to private events where hosts who are paying the hired staff a service charge and tips on top of it little suspect that their guests will be targeted as well.

People on the receiving end are franker about stating the size they expect those tips to be and using embarrassment to pressure tippers into giving more. A particularly insidious technique in vogue now is to refrain from offering change and then loudly asking whether the customer "wants" it, as if taking it would be a breach of manners. One Gentle Reader reports being asked if he wanted change after submitting a $100 bill for a $40 meal.

Those in positions that were never associated with tipping, notably the owners of establishments such as restaurants and hairdressing salons, are letting it be known that they would be far from offended by being treated like their employees when it comes to tipping. Holiday collections are initiated by the would-be recipients, who are often not shy about announcing what is expected. Those who used to be tipped annually, such as newspaper deliverers, have added a line for tips on their monthly bills as well.

"I'm at my wit's end with the number of people expecting tips," writes one G.R. "I know they deliberately underpay waiters and waitresses, so I don't mind leaving 15% (though I do mind that the standard, I've recently been informed, has become 20%). I don't like it—why don't their employers just raise the prices that much and actually PAY them, so at least customers could make a reasonable budgeting decision upon ordering?—but I don't object.

"But on deliveries, I'm already being charged an extra fee. Why am I tipping on top of it? Maintenance workers are paid as well as I am, but I'm told that the reason my previous apartment was always in disrepair was that clearly I wasn't tipping the company's workers and it was revenge. Isn't that why I was paying a ridiculous rent in the first place?

"Hairdressers? Please! They already overcharge, given that I usually just want a shampoo and a very basic trim. Bell boys? Cabbies? Homeless men who decide to employ themselves opening doors without being asked? (I always say 'Thank you, sir,' of course, but I don't expect a doorman at 7-11 and am not going to pay for one.)

"The situation is totally out of control. I can't seem to budget for a day out because I never know how many people are going to expect a handout along the way. I was chastised for being 'Un-American' because I'm not willing to give people money for doing their jobs, but it was always my understanding that paying an agreed upon fee was paying for services rendered.

"It's not as if the services are cheap, or I'm a member of some idly rich class that can afford to just throw money around to show my largess. Is there any way at all to stop this trend? Or should I just put a tip jar out on my desk at work to cover the tips I'm supposed to be giving everyone else?"

Miss Manners can comfort you only by reporting that it is the custom of tipping that is historically un-American, as American workers at all levels of employment used to consider themselves too dignified to accept tips. Alas, the custom is now built into the pay scale of many jobs, and ignoring it would cut into the wages of those who can least afford it. For the others—those who have simply decided to trade their dignity for handouts—Miss Manners gives you full leave to refuse to succumb.

She dearly hopes that the day will come when the price of running such an establishment as a hotel, restaurant or topless go-go palace will be figured with the full salaries of all the employees, and the customers will not be left to guess how much of it they must make up out of their pockets after they have paid the bills. This does not mean an extra "service charge," as is often added abroad, but a clearly stated all-inclusive price, as overhead and salaries of clerks are included in the prices charged by shops.

There will then be those who ask Miss Manners how they may deliver critiques of the performance of service people. With smiles, letters to employers and the pressure with which you slam the taxicab door.

DEAR MISS MANNERS:

It's all very well to say that fifteen percent is a good standard tip for a restaurant meal, with up to twenty percent for a fancy restaurant, but life is no longer that simple. What about buffet restaurants, where the customer does all the work of getting the food, and the waiter only brings the rolls and water? What about dinner theaters, where some of the bill is for the entertainment, not the food? And suppose the actors do the waiting on table before the show—do they still get tipped? How about all those captains and hostesses and people that restaurants have?

GENTLE READER:

Miss Manners would dearly love to help you save a buck, which is no doubt what you have in mind, but not by telling you that waiters and actors don't need the money. Tip those people as you would the help in an ordinary restaurant, although you can count only the value of the food in a dinner theater.

If it is so much work for you to fill your dinner plate yourself, why do you go back and do it so often? Miss Manners saw you. However, you may save by not asking the captains or hostesses for favors, such as special tables. They should get bribes for such attentions, but do not get ordinary tips.

∽ *Tipping the Owner* ∽

DEAR MISS MANNERS:

A friend has recently opened a very small restaurant in her home. She does all the shopping, cooking, and all the serving alone. I am planning on taking a few friends to dinner soon in her new establishment. Is it proper to tip her, as proprietor, under the circumstances?

GENTLE READER:

Rule one: Friends are remunerated, in a business situation, to the same extent as are strangers who perform the same services.

Rule two: The owner of a restaurant or other business establishment is not tipped. The rationale is that it would offend the owner's pride, no matter how many of them tell Miss Manners that they don't have any.

Rule three: It is gracious to express one's appreciation in words to the owner of a restaurant if one has received her personal attention.

Rule four: It is gracious to acknowledge a friendship with someone who is performing a business service to you.

Conclusion: Introduce your friend to your guests, thank her and save the tip.

TRAVEL

The Vulgar American Tourist is a character who looms large in the refined American imagination. Half a century ago, Europeans did such a good job of ridiculing Americans for admiring their history and art that many have been tiptoeing through the world apologetically ever since.

Meanwhile, Miss Manners notices that Europeans have moved on to ridiculing one another in almost the identical terms. Depending on which country you visit, you will hear complaints about Swedish tourists, English tourists, German tourists, French tourists, and all varieties of Eastern European tourists. When they really get going, they also throw in Japanese tourists, Australian tourists and Argentinean tourists.

Natives of whatever country is being visited, oblivious to the fact that the same things are being said about them when they travel, will tell you in detail how awful the people are from whatever country they most attract:

They are loud; they are lewd. They don't know how to dress; they don't know how to eat. They don't speak the language; they don't understand the customs. They want to eat only the food to which they are accustomed at home; they only want to buy things that are made expressly for the tourist market.

Most damning of all, they have no interest whatsoever in whatever it is they have come to see. They don't know history; they don't like art.

These accusations have always puzzled Miss Manners. First of all, there aren't any tourists. People traveling abroad, seeing the sights and wearing clothes they washed themselves in hotel bathroom sinks all turn out to be "travelers" whose motivation for travel is "to avoid the tourists."

Secondly, although fussy, ignorant and arrogant people undoubtedly exist, and if you put together all these complaints, perhaps exist all over the globe, why would they be traveling?

The affronted locals have an answer: status. Tourists spend their vacation time and money doing what they hate so that they can brag about it to their friends back home. That is their theory anyway. Obviously, they have never traveled.

Anyone who has knows that "impressed" is not the right word for the way people back home react to travel stories. "Terrorized" would be more like it. The only way even intimate friends will agree to hear about some sublime discovery or wonderful little place where none of the tourists go is if they have just returned from a trip and will be allowed to retaliate.

This brings Miss Manners back to the question of tourist etiquette, which isn't all that hard. Visitors are not required to mimic the natives, only to be respectful to them and theirs, in terms that are internationally understood and practiced. This means dressing with equivalent formality to the place being visited, memorizing basic polite words and offering an apologetic admission if one does not speak the language, and expressing appreciation for the prevailing culture.

None of this should be a problem for Americans in Europe, where the natives wear blue jeans, use as many English words as they can squeeze into their vocabularies and indulge a taste for American movies, television and popular music.

~ Airlines ~

Many people argue, on their own behalf or in general, that stress inevitably produces rudeness. Miss Manners advises against boarding airplanes with such people.

Besides seeking to justify horrid behavior, this argument is spurious. Stress may produce crankiness, unpleasant-vocabulary recall and the desire to smack that silly expression off the nearest face, but such feelings are what etiquette exists to control. Alone against all other personal-behavior wisdom of the era, etiquette shouts "Don't express it! Never mind if you'll feel better if you let it all out—what about the rest of us? Keep it bottled up! It won't kill you. Be a hypocrite! Act as if it doesn't matter!"

All right, etiquette doesn't shout. It can't, if it hopes to keep everyone else from shouting. That is the very principle that belies the stress excuse: If stress were a legitimate excuse for behaving badly, it would have to excuse everyone under stress, and everybody in sight claims to be under stress, including those lying on the beach with their eyes closed. Yet if everybody behaved badly, there would be chaos, each person flailing away for himself. And this would cause everyone more stress.

Understanding this is what makes etiquette so prominent in activities that specialize in stress. Warfare, of the battlefield, legal and athletic field varieties, is characterized not only by grand rules having to do with honor, but by detailed ones in respect to dress, speech and gesture. And that brings us back to those people who have to travel by air. Only this time it is not to belittle their stress in comparison to that of people who face illness, death and poverty. It is to admit that yes, those are infinitely worse, but why does air travel have to be so awful?

Miss Manners doesn't really want an answer. We've all heard enough about demanding and granting rights to passengers, and we all know what to expect:

A choice between carrying on baggage that is still wider than the aisles and thus apt to bump those who are seated, or checking it and waiting, sometimes for days or forever, to get it back.

A choice between pinning your arms to your side or depriving the neighboring passenger of the armrest.

A choice between sitting in a cramped position or leaning back into the equally small space allotted to the passenger sitting behind.

A choice between taking a chance on food or bringing your own and risking tantalizing or disgusting your neighbor with your preference.

Notice that there are no right choices here. Miss Manners is not asking for total self-sacrifice, only weighing these choices with consideration to others, as well as to yourself. It is also necessary to understand that others' choices, however inconvenient for oneself, were probably not intended as acts of aggression.

A great deal of understanding and cooperation may be required to make circumstances bearable, laced with pleading ("Excuse me, but I wonder if you could raise your seat just a little so that I could get out to use the bathroom") and apologies ("I'm so sorry, I had no idea that was your lap I was resting on"). But not excuses.

∽ *Freeing One's Feet* ∽

DEAR MISS MANNERS:

Is it proper to remove one's shoes in an airplane?

GENTLE READER:

Yes, but it is highly improper not to be able to get them on again when one has arrived at one's destination.

∽ *Sharing Space* ∽

DEAR MISS MANNERS:

Who gets the shared armrest? Whenever I am stuck in the middle seat, it is inevitable that the people on either side of me, if men, will snag the armrests for themselves. Other women tend to either not use the shared armrest, only their own on the aisle or window.

When I am in an aisle or window seat, I only use my own armrest and allow the middle passenger to use the shared armrest. When in the middle, I have found myself placing my elbows on the armrests in advance of the other passengers' arrival. Once, when an aisle seat passenger hogged it the first two hours of a 5-hour flight, I waited until their drink arrived and snagged it when they lifted their arm to take the drink from the flight attendant. This of course, made me feel uncomfortable and rude. What is the proper thing to do?

GENTLE READER:

Above American territory, everyone leans to the right, forearm against his or her right armrest, but if this five-hour flight is to London, everyone must shift in mid-ocean and thereafter lean to the left. It is considered bad form to pretend to sleep through the announcement to change, but selfishness being rampant now, people do.

Wait. Miss Manners only wishes there were a rule that simple, although while she is wishing, she might as well wish for elbow room in coach.

Two people cannot share an armrest unless they are in love, so there is no system other than snagging. Like everything else, this is supposed to be tempered by consideration for others, and Miss Manners has no need to mention that she is not kidding about that being in short supply. Not everyone wants to use the armrest, so the first person who wants it snags it, and a second person who wants it awaits his or her chance, when a gesture or bathroom visit leaves the armrest vacant. Each is supposed to accept the other person's possession philosophically.

So while you were uncomfortable (naturally—you were occupying the middle seat in coach), you were not rude. The only other thing you could have done was to say politely and pathetically to one of your seatmates, "I'm so sorry, but I wonder if you could lean the other way for a while and let me use this armrest—just until I get the cramp out of my arm." Although it is possible that person would stand on squatters' rights, Miss Manners believes it more likely to arouse empathy with your discomfort.

∽ Sharing Food ∽

DEAR MISS MANNERS:

My partner and I were flying returning from a trip on our favorite airline, which is very highly regarded by its passengers but recently ended its meal service—china, linen and all. Passengers are now invited to purchase a meal during the flight if they are so inclined.

Is it appropriate to purchase a meal and eat it in the close confines of the aircraft with no idea whether the person next you is also going to eat? My partner thinks that the old rules about eating and drinking in public have been relaxed. Since everyone on board has the opportunity to purchase a meal, there is no problem here and I can tuck in without regard to those around me.

I still feel awkward about the situation. If the person in the seat next to me is not eating, should I ignore them? Should I excuse myself for eating in front of them? Or should I just avoid any chance of offence and go hungry?

GENTLE READER:

What old rules are there that you think might or might not have been relaxed?

The ones that say that nobody in the restaurant can start eating until the entire dining room is served, and apologies must be offered to any passersby on the sidewalk who might spot you chomping away when they are not?

There are indeed rules about not eating without waiting for others or offering them food, and Miss Manners is glad that you want to be careful to follow them. They are as good as new—but they do not apply among strangers in public venues.

This includes airplanes, although Miss Manners could think of a humanitarian exception—offering food around if you happen to have some and are stranded on the runway for hours with starving passengers.

～ *Sharing Conversation* ～

DEAR MISS MANNERS:

When I travel alone on an airplane, all I want to do is to sit quietly and read a book or a magazine, fill out a crossword puzzle, or do some other such quiet, solitary activity. However, I often find myself seated next to someone who wishes to engage me in a lengthy conversation. People like this will inquire about my origin, my occupation, my love life, whether I am traveling for business or pleasure, or they relate to me their entire life histories. Once I sat next to a lady who, spontaneously and entirely un-encouraged by me, proceeded to describe to me at length the entire course of her amateur ballroom dancing career.

Being on a plane, I am, of course, trapped in these exchanges, perhaps for an hour or two at a time. Is there anything I can do, politely, to fend off these unwanted conversational advances? I may seem antisocial, but I don't wish to be rude. Some of my friends have suggested that I pretend to sleep or wear earphones and pretend to listen to music, but I would prefer to be left in peace and quiet without having to resort to such stratagems.

GENTLE READER:

Although Miss Manners sides with the victims of prying and hounding strangers, she begs you to remember that conversation among long-distance passengers was a great boon to travelers back when trips took even longer than airport delays. It was understood that the requirement for introductions was suspended so that people could be helpful and entertaining to one another.

This is no longer necessary. If people want to pour confidences and extract confessions from total strangers, they can go on the Internet. The polite way to discourage those who are not discouraged by vague looks and short answers is to say pleasantly, "Forgive me, I'm just not up to conversation now."

⌒ *Sharing Too Closely* ⌒

DEAR MISS MANNERS:

On a recent evening flight, seats were mostly empty. I busied myself with work, and kept my nose in my laptop for most of the flight.

Once my battery had died, I looked up and around me. I could not help noticing a rather telltale set of not-very-discreet-at-all motions coming from a couple barely six feet away from me, the only other occupants of my row.

While I am hardly prudish, I was truly shocked and disgusted. Even after several pass-bys of the flight attendants, even after a few clearings of my suddenly-itchy throat, the "frolicking" continued (to be a little clearer: this was far beyond the enthusiastic affections one might expect of honeymooners, for instance).

I avoided any kind of contact with them in those uncomfortable moments between landing and de-planing, and gladly went my own way after that. However, their rudeness left quite a sour pall over the rest of my evening, and I found myself really wishing I'd found something cleverly tart to say (actually, the click of a camera might have been perfect, as it seemed that exposure was their goal after all).

Usually I prefer to answer rudeness with silence, but for such extraordinary circumstances, I still wish I'd said something on behalf of the flight crew, other passengers, and myself. What might you have said or done?

GENTLE READER:

Miss Manners always brings a book, and never looks up. Perhaps that is just as well.

What did you have in mind? Tapping them on the shoulder—whosever shoulder happened to appear within reach—and asking to borrow their in-flight magazine? Expressing the hope that they were having a pleasant flight?

Miss Manners doesn't make citizen's arrests, even for indecency in transit. The only people with some authority over air-passenger etiquette are the flight attendants. You might have suggested that one of them approach the couple and order them to fasten their seat belts.

⌒ *Ships* ⌒

People who go cruising on ships worry a great deal about the niceties of etiquette. Actually, it is the people who do their cruising in shopping mall parking lots who should be worrying about their manners, in Miss Manners' opinion. Shipboard behavior is comparatively simple.

The principal activities in which passengers engage on cruise ships are eating, dressing, tipping and complaining. You will notice a similarity to pastimes in which many people engage on dry land. The difference is that on shipboard, you do a great deal more of each. There are also other options, such as seasickness and buying baskets in port (or port in baskets), but these are not bound by strict laws of the sea and tend to operate on an every-person-for-himself basis.

Miss Manners will assume that you have mastered the basics of each main activity at home, and will explain only the differences you may encounter at sea.

You have been taught to be friendly to whatever companions you find at the dinner table, to eat everything you are offered and to keep all foods confined to plates, the bowls or prongs of eating utensils or the mouth. None of these rules quite applies on a ship.

Ships serve the following meals: breakfast, elevenses, luncheon, tea, dinner and midnight supper. Most people attempt to eat them all, including all the many courses of each, on the logical grounds that they have paid for this access to unlimited amounts of food. This is a mistake. Many people find out just how bad a mistake it is, the hard way.

When you consider how time consuming it is to consume even some of this food, you will realize the importance of having compatible table companions. This is why the first thing you do aboard a ship is to get a table reservation—alone, with the people with whom you are traveling, or at a table to be arranged at the judgment of the dining room steward. If you choose the last, the second thing you do aboard ship is ask to be moved. This type of discreet snubbing may be applied to anyone on the ship except its captain. If you have the tremendous honor of being asked to sit at his table and can't quite bear his conversation, it is necessary to plead seasickness and to reassign yourself a table in your own cabin.

Spilling food is permissible aboard ship, if accompanied by a dark look over one's shoulder, to implicate the stabilizers and the ocean itself in this transgression.

Dressing on cruise ships has become Standard Tourist, which is to say sports clothes during the day and restaurant clothes at night. Miss Manners deeply regrets the general passing of wearing black tie to dinner, and applauds those few ships and passengers who steadfastly stick to the custom. Of course, one does not so dress the first night out, the last night out, the night before getting into port, nights when the ship is in port, or nights the ship is leaving port. On most cruises, this accounts for every night there is, but Miss Manners would still like to see evidence of the intention, such as a steamer trunk full of evening clothes in case the ship is unexpectedly stranded at sea.

Tipping, which most people fear, is actually easy, as all ship personnel are willing to tell you what is expected, and then some, complete with brochures on exactly how to distribute it to waiters, cabin attendants, wine stewards and bartenders and others. The percentages of the fare that they recommend are generous, but people on the receiving end of tips are always generous in their recommendations.

As for complaining, it is the general cost of cruising that inspires many people who are otherwise meek and patient with whatever life gives them to become highly critical of everything the ship has to offer. As cruising should be vacation time, Miss Manners recommends this constant harping only to those who find it relaxing. Personally, she prefers to sit in a deck chair and reread *Moby-Dick*.

DEAR MISS MANNERS:

I am a normal suburban woman who does not travel in "high society." This summer, my husband and I will be cruising on a ship and there will be a concierge available. Does a simple inquiry require payment, or does one just compensate a concierge for a favor performed for you, such as reservations or tickets?

GENTLE READER:

There is no such thing as high society. If there were, Miss Manners is afraid it would have to devise a better test of eligibility than knowledge of the expectations of hotel and restaurant staffs. Far from being an aristocratic secret, this information is distributed by shipping lines as guidance.

There is no such thing as a concierge either; perhaps this is what should be called the purser. One of the attractions of cruising is that there is a separation between helpfulness and compensation. You need not pay anyone for answering simple questions or making reservations, nor have your wallet out each time someone serves you food or cleans your cabin. Those who perform these and other tasks are tipped only at the end of the trip, and the purser would be included only if you had made special requests.

DEAR MISS MANNERS:

While I appreciate the friendliness of the crew on a seven-day cruise I took, I felt that having hands thrust at me to shake, from the ship's officers to the waiters in the lounges and even the cabin steward, was too much. I relayed my feelings to the ship's hostess who did not seem to think it a serious concern, stressing that she felt the friendliness of the crew was most important. She insinuated that I was being too old-fashioned and that everything had changed, including manners.

I still feel that a gentleman should not put a lady in the uncomfortable position of having to shake hands, whether she wants to or not, as in any situation, one should try not to do anything which might cause discomfort.

GENTLE READER:

If the ship's hostess is so devoted to friendliness, why is she blowing you off?

Miss Manners has long opposed using the term "friendliness" to mean a pleasant professional demeanor. It puts both service people and their clients in the undignified position of feeling they have social obligations, when both of them simply want to get a job done. But your story is not the first time she has noticed an inverse relationship between declarations of friendliness and a willingness to please.

Ladies are supposed to offer their hands if they want to shake hands, and should not do so to the staff, except when socializing with the ship's officers. More importantly, staff members who receive complaints should not lecture passengers about manners.

∼ Trains ∼

DEAR MISS MANNERS:

As a single woman who sometimes takes the train on a long (7 to 8 hour) journey, I enjoy sitting by the window to pass the time. Since I board at the beginning of the line, I usually get a window seat.

During my last trip, I was asked by the conductor to give up my window seat so that a couple who boarded at a later stop could sit next to each other. I refused, simply saying "No," and with, I am ashamed to say, a bit of eye-rolling.

I don't feel that my single status should make me the handmaiden of every married couple. How could I have politely but firmly gotten this message across?

GENTLE READER:

It is not a polite message. You are entitled to a window seat, but you are not entitled to generalize this request into a grudge against the married state.

Besides being unpleasant, it is ridiculous: Plenty of people traveling alone are married, and many people who want to sit together, whether to hold hands or to do business, are not. Travelers should try to accommodate one another if they can, without unduly inconveniencing themselves.

Miss Manners is glad to hear that you are ashamed of the curt refusal and the eye-rolling. She expects you to keep your eyes still while you say to the conductor, "Of course, I'd be glad to, but I especially wanted to sit by the window. Would you be good enough to find me another window seat? And then we could change."

⟨ Hotels ⟩

It is charming that people like to bring home small souvenirs to remind them of their holidays. Miss Manners would find it more charming, however, if they limited their mementos to items they bought or found on the beach, rather than little things they picked up while no one was looking.

It makes Miss Manners decidedly nervous to see, in someone's house, a towel, a bathrobe or a writing pad that bears the logo of public accommodations. Miss Manners tries her best to think charitably of such persons, in the style of a lady in a *Punch* drawing who, observing a towel marked "Victoria Hotel" in another lady's bathroom, suggested, "Perhaps it's her maiden name."

But Miss Manners does not succeed in distinguishing between stealing from individuals and stealing from corporations. Whenever she sees stolen goods in someone's house, she reminds herself not to invite them to come and be on terms of intimacy with her own monogrammed linens.

She even feels this way about seeing items belonging to the user's employer. When Miss Manners visited the house of an acquaintance who worked at the White House and found the place stocked with White House stationery, memorandum pads, pens and pencils—he had apparently overlooked only the possibility of bringing home a rug with the presidential seal woven into it—she had unpleasant thoughts about her taxes. But in that case there was, at least, the excuse that the employee needs such things because his work carries over to the home. Presumably, the President might call and not want his instruction copied on plain paper with the regular government-issue pen.

Travelers can make no such excuse. Towels, forks, miniature bars of soap and paper packets full of sugar are meant to be used by the customer on the premises only. They are not offered as compensation for high prices. A person who has blown his travel budget on one such establishment and wishes to get his money's worth of status from it may honorably spend his entire vacation writing on the hotel stationery to everyone he knows in the world. What he may not do is to stash away the paper and use it for communications from humbler quarters, including his own.

⟨ Recommending Hotels ⟩

DEAR MISS MANNERS:

Whilst in Paris for my yearly sojourn, I happened upon an elegantly unpretentious hotel—on the Right Bank, *naturellement*. It was an unmitigated delight and one which I am not eager to share with others.

However, during tea, my acquaintances often ask the name of my latest hostelry discovery. This occasions agitation in my otherwise placid circumstance. How, Miss Manners, may I decline to reveal my little secret and still maintain my impeccable reputation for frankness and amiability?

GENTLE READER:

No one is expected to remember the exact name of a Parisian hotel. It is enough to show your willingness to share your discovery with your friends, as follows:

"You know the Métro stop with the interesting entrance? Oh yes, you do, it's very famous, the one with the carvings, you see its photograph everywhere. Well, you get out there, and then go across the street and you'll see the—oh, what's its name?—the boutique, the one with the frightfully expensive things? They have one in Nice, and I think London and Palm Beach too, but I'm not sure. You'll recognize it. It has a silk scarf in the window, draped over a leather bag. Well, you go around the corner from that, and on the other side, about a block or two up, there's a *parfumerie*, and keep going and you'll come to a shop with rare books and prints, and that's where you turn left. Keep going until you get to the glove shop, and then it's right across the street. I think it's the Grand Something or the Petit Something, I'm not sure. You'll love it. And please remember me to Madame, who runs it. You'll be sure and remember that, won't you?"

∽ Hotel Beds ∽

DEAR MISS MANNERS:

My husband and I sleep in a double bed at home, and would like to do so when we travel. We always seem to be put in rooms that either have two single beds, or two double beds. The single beds are too small, and I get embarrassed to have the maid see that we use only one of the double beds, so I've even taken to messing the other one up to make it look slept in, which my husband says is silly. How can I get the kind of accommodations we want?

GENTLE READER:

By requesting them. If you find that this embarrasses the room clerk, you might introduce him to the hotel maid you think is also capable of embarrassment, and suggest that they both take up another line of work.

～ *Tipping in Hotels* ～

DEAR MISS MANNERS:

I'm looking for the proper etiquette in tipping room service deliveries. Sometimes I have even seen the bill stamped "Gratuity Already Included"—but there is always a blank line above the total that says "tip" as though there is still an expectation for more than what was already added in. I've never added in an additional tip on that line, but I'm wondering if there is any standard courtesy regarding this that I am unaware of.

GENTLE READER:

For goodness' sake, the built-in tip, or service charge, is supposed to relieve anxiety, not cause more. Miss Manners is a great proponent of abolishing payment by tip, because it brings out the worst in so many people, so please give it a chance.

If you keep fretting over how much is right to give, and the recipients keep fretting over how much they can count on (or if you plot how little you could get away with and the recipients plot how much they can get out of you), the purpose of the service charge—which is to pay for the service—is defeated. If you wish to leave more to recognize special service, by all means do so, but otherwise just eat your breakfast, knowing that the server has been paid the same way you probably are— fairly and reliably.

VACATION TRIPS

As a social inquiry, "Tell me all about your vacation" is in a category with "What does your baby do now?" and "How's that contractor coming with the repairs on your house?" Extreme caution must be exercised before interpreting such questions as the starting signal to tear off on a long-distance narration without looking back.

Miss Manners does not consider "But they asked me!" to be sufficient excuse for nonstop showing-and-telling. Of course people ask returned vacationers about their vacations. Despite warning signs that these people are bursting with stories to download, there is nothing else that can be said by way of acknowledging someone's return.

"Oh, have you been away?" shows too little feeling. "I missed you so much I cried myself to sleep every night" may be overdoing it, although it does get people's attention and distract them from describing all the restaurants they patronized while they were away, what they ordered, how it tasted and how much it cost.

It is therefore incumbent upon the vacationer to figure out what the question means before attempting a response. The basic assumption should always be that it is no more deeply probing than "How are you?" Literal-minded people are perpetually hurt to discover that this is not usually asked out of curiosity about their digestions and plumbing, but is simply a pleasant way of acknowledging their humanity. They are even more hurt when Miss Manners tells them that their answer, unless it is "Please call an ambulance, I'm hemorrhaging," must be limited to "Fine, thank you, how are you?"

The answer to "How was your vacation?" is "Great; you had one yet?" Even a follow-up question does not constitute permission to travelogue. The proper response to the traditional follow-up question, "I hope you had nice weather," is "Wonderful, but I bet it was hot here" or "Well, it rained a bit, but I'd brought along some books."

It is only by practicing such self-restraint that the returned vacationer is able to identify potential listeners who have some genuine interest. These are the ones who insist on setting a time when such a conversation can be held, and who say raptly and rashly "Okay, now tell me from the beginning, and I hope you brought pictures."

Even then, Miss Manners advises caution. These people have their reasons. Fondness for the individual and anticipation of amusing stories full of acute observations may be among them. But there is more motivation than that.

There is the shocking fact that they hope to talk, as well as listen. Rather than sitting silently, they cherish hopes of breaking into the conversation. This is why Miss Manners limits what-I-did-on-my-vacation talks to three anecdotes (with points to them) and one roll of film, with plenty of breaks.

If willing listeners have been to the same vacation spot, they need time to say things like "How could you miss the turtle zoo—it's world famous" or "I can't believe Doc turned the ice-cream parlor over to his daughter—boy, nothing's the same any more," or (the chief anxiety that tourists ask of other tourists) "I hear it's getting totally overrun with tourists." Even if they haven't been there, they need to be able to talk about any vacations they have had, and it doesn't matter how long ago. They still haven't found anyone to listen to the full story.

∽ Bringing Back Presents ∽

DEAR MISS MANNERS:

Where is it written that people always have to buy gifts for other people when they themselves are on vacation? It seems as if when people ask, "Did you buy us anything?" it's the same as if they were saying, "We don't care whether or not you had a good time, but you'd better have brought us something."

Now, if a person has buchu kopecks, there would be no excuse for not buying people some little remembrance. But for people like me who don't have big-spender status, the vacation cheer has to be limited to the vacation-takers.

If I sound a little short, it's because I haven't had a real vacation in over five years, and I'm due a good, long one. To my way of thinking, a vacation is for the person taking it, not for anyone else. Mostly it is a time to get away from the people that one is "supposed" to buy gifts for.

GENTLE READER:

Quick, go. Miss Manners will talk to you when you get back and are feeling better. Meanwhile, she wants to have a talk with those people you are so gratefully leaving.

Demanding presents is rude. It's rude if you claim that you just mean that you wish to be remembered, it's rude even if you are the traveler's beloved child or grandchild, it's rude no matter how rich the vacationer may be and it's rude even if that person always brings you something anyway.

The most Miss Manners will allow is "Send me a post card." She does not recall ever having written, in stone or any other substance, that vacationers must fork up when they get home. It may be a charming custom, but it is not obligatory. And the time to discontinue this custom is when it gets to the point that the would-be recipient of such generosity voices a demand for it.

~ *Sending Postal Cards* ~

Just when you think you have succeeded in getting away from it all, free of all questions of form because you are on holiday and don't even have to put your shoes on, let alone your manners, you will have a panicky thought about Miss Manners. The thought will be "Wish you were here."

This will have nothing to do with sympathy for your poor Miss Manners, stuck toiling away in the hot city. It will mean that you are in trouble. Big etiquette trouble. This will happen just after you have begun to wind down and relax. You will stop somewhere on the street, during a leisurely stroll, and purchase postcards. Or perhaps you will pick them up free from your hotel, or perhaps you will pick them up free from the lobby of a hotel more expensive than the one you are staying in.

Still calm and confident, you will make yourself comfortable at the beach, or at some foreign café, and go cheerfully to work, selecting which card should go to which person on your list, stamping and addressing them. Then you will stare hopelessly at a blank space, not three inches square, while you slowly realize that you have nothing intelligent to say on a postcard.

That is when you will wish for Miss Manners to explain correct postcard style. All year long, Miss Manners is asked about the complexities of writing letters of business, gratitude, condolence and congratulation, but the postcard, that staple of summer correspondence, is something people mistakenly assume they can manage for themselves. If you could just write "Wish you were here," not to Miss Manners but to all your friends, the matter would be simple. Unfortunately, this convenient message has gone out of fashion on the irrelevant grounds of being insincere.

The only easy thing about postcards is that they need not use any closing, or any opening either. The rest is difficult. Miss Manners' first solution is to prune your list. Like Christmastime, summertime is an opportunity to send brief greetings to people one does not otherwise remember. Just as at Christmastime, one tends to greet people who do not remember one. This is a reason to identify oneself clearly at the end of the postcard and not assume that its informality means that nicknames or initials will do. Postcards do not even give the clue of where the sender lives, only where he vacations.

Now for the message. The important thing to remember about a postcard is the wide audience it will receive. Reading someone else's letter is a high crime; reading someone else's postcard is in a category with jaywalking—not a good idea, but everyone does it and the chances of getting away with it are good. It should therefore be discreet, or at least ambiguous. "Lola and kids staying on—meet you Tuesday, Marshland Marriott" is not a good postcard message. Neither is the temperature or population of a foreign city, which is not only dull but sounds smug to a person stuck at home. "Prices here out of sight" is preferable, but not terrific.

Humor is out of the question. It looks terrible, when you get back to the office, to see something that was funny when you were full of piña coladas pinned on the bulletin board. Anyway, most postcard humor is unintelligible to the recipient, who forgets to look at the postcard picture on which the joke is based. Taking into account all these pitfalls, Miss Manners proposes the perfect all-purpose postcard message that can be sent to anyone: "Thinking of you." It can mean anything up to, and even including, "Wish you were here."

HOLIDAYS

The etiquette question that troubles so many fastidious people New Year's Day is: How am I ever going to face those people again?

Miss Manners recognizes that even the most well-bred person may be subject to a fit of bad behaving at holiday parties. One may suffer from an overdose, not necessarily of alcohol, but of frankness, cuddliness, reminiscences or other enemies of the social structure.

The simplest thing is merely to write a charming note of apology. "I'm sorry I drank all your wassail bowl and told you it was a mistake for you to get a divorce." A common complication, however, is that one doesn't know exactly what one should be sorry for. The major discomfort in what is designed as "remorse" is not shame, but the blind scrambling around an addled brain in search of the answer to "My God, what did I do?"

If you were lucky enough to have been accompanied by an intimate to the disaster-fiesta, you may hear the answer to this question. Without even asking it. This is unlucky. Miss Manners believes that the secret of an unhappy marriage is communication. A truly loving person volunteers nothing and, if pressed with "How bad was I?" replies, "Why, I thought you were cute."

This information is not so vital as one seems to think at the time. Socially, it is not useful until months later, when the adventure can be humorously recounted at a party and leave you basking in self-admiration. The worse you behave, the better the anecdote will then be.

In the meantime, one must resist the impulse to call up the hostess under the pretense of chatting, to measure in her tone of voice the size of the misdemeanor. She's too busy. She has to clean up the mess you left, and to think what to say to those people she asked especially to meet you. Instead, send her a small present. This does not incriminate you, as an apology would, and on the fat chance that she thought you were cute too, can be seen simply as a gracious gesture. However, it might help compensate her for the lamp or lifelong friendship of hers you don't remember breaking.

New Year's Day

DEAR MISS MANNERS:

Last year, I gave up eating between meals, and the year before, I gave up smoking. Can you suggest a New Year's resolution for me, for this year? It might be hard, not only because, as you can see, I am nearly perfect, but because, as you can also see, life is bleak enough for me without giving up any of my few remaining pleasures.

GENTLE READER:

Try giving up expecting the mechanics of life to work smoothly. For example, give up expecting a store to get your order right, or the car ahead of you to start when the light changes, or the mail to be delivered within a reasonable time. If you succeed in this, you will be deprived of nothing you had before except frustrating rage, and you will be contributing to the welfare of the world—not by improving it, but by ceasing to contribute to it your own dissatisfaction.

~ Valentine's Day ~

How many valentines did you get?

This question was the culminating touch of a Valentine's Day tradition once widely practiced at schools. That was before self-esteem got into the curriculum, and maybe it was how self-esteem got in. Being snubbed in childhood doesn't always turn one into a criminal; sometimes it turns one into a reformer.

Here is how the old system would go:

Pupils addressed valentines to their favorite classmates and stuffed them into a cardboard box they had decorated for the purpose. Everyone assembled and the teacher then pulled out the valentines, one by one, and read each name aloud. After each call, the recipient would come forward to collect that valentine, so some people made repeated trips, and others made few or none.

Beginning to perspire? Wait.

After the formal part of the program, the young people who had been called most often would amuse themselves by running around asking those who had been overlooked, "How many valentines did you get?"

Never mind that everyone involved knew the answers because it had all been conducted in public. "Oh, that's too bad," they would reply to shame-faced admissions or implausible exaggerations. Or worse, "Oh, well, I guess it doesn't matter."

Ultimately, this ritual was not as unfair as it seemed. In due time, the valentine-less were running around asking their tormentors what they got on their SAT scores and which colleges had accepted them.

Miss Manners, who never cared for the tactic of showcasing one's triumphs by a show of curiosity about the less fortunate, regrets to note that this technique managed to survive the withdrawal of educational sanction. There are plenty of people still running around asking such artless questions as:

"What kind of car do you drive?"

"Is your child reading yet?"

"Are you still in the same job?"

"Are you going abroad this year?"

Upon receiving answers, the questioners reveal that they have an expensive new car, a toddler who is reading *The Decline and Fall of the Roman Empire*, a handsome promotion and plans for a glamorous vacation. Then they point out the advisability of doing the same, as opposed to having an old car, a slow child, a pathetic income and a limited horizon.

They could also point out to Miss Manners that they are showing an interest in others by asking them questions and attempting to prompt general conversation. Simply to announce their own achievements would be bragging.

Nevertheless, there are forms of bragging that are more acceptable than this particular form of showing an interest in others. Among friends, one is allowed to announce an occasional triumph, provided it is done with such breathless excitement as to give the impression that this is a rare and unexpected stroke of luck.

Thus it is perfectly all right to go shout, "Guess what! I found a diamond ring in my lunch box! Wow! I can hardly believe it." Provided one does not inquire, "And what did you get for Valentine's Day?"

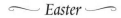

Easter

DEAR MISS MANNERS:

How about Easter? I suppose you have etiquette rules that apply to Easter Day?

GENTLE READER:

Certainly, and when the Day of Judgment comes, Miss Manners will have etiquette rules to apply to that as well. The chief rule in regard to Easter is that everyone must eat every egg given to him or her, or colored by him or her, and not unload it on someone else. This is because Easter eggs are delightful on Easter Sunday, fun to play with on Easter Monday and revolting on Easter Tuesday. They should be eaten before that, with a grain of salt.

DEAR MISS MANNERS:

I am taking my grandchildren to the Easter Egg Rolling at the White House, but they have asked me what egg rolling involves, and I don't know the answer. Also, do we bring our own eggs?

GENTLE READER:

"Rolling" must be interpreted in its political, rather than gravitational, sense, as in "logrolling." In other words, you had better look out for your own interests and bring your own eggs to feed your own family.

~ Beach Week ~

People keep trying to enlist Miss Manners' help in clearing beaches of people whom they find aesthetically displeasing. It can be the elderly, the fat, the skinny, the ugly or the disabled. "Don't they realize how awful they look?" they ask. "Why do they parade themselves around in bathing suits where everybody can see them?"

This question puzzles Miss Manners. She would have thought it well known that the reason everybody wears bathing suits to the beach is that they are better suited for swimming and suntanning than ski clothes, for example. However, Miss Manners has never been one to be hostile to dumb questions. What irritates her about the letters is their assumption, which is by no means confined to the beach, that the world should belong to young, comely people.

Naturally, it is absurd to speak of beauty, or even youth, as if there were a national standard by which fitness may be recognized. But if there were, the idea would still be unbearably ugly. Beaches, like other public places and institutions, are for any members of the public who wish to use them properly. Ogling people one finds attractive is not the proper use of beaches. This does not mean that, as with so many improper functions, it may not be practiced and enjoyed if done discreetly. It does mean that the rights of people who properly use the beach to swim and sun take precedence.

Observing the human scene—now that is another activity, and the one for which God made sidewalk cafés. The difference between this and ogling, since you obviously intend to bring that up, is that a moving crowd on a sidewalk does not permit the observer to stare at any one person for a long time and thus force him or her into the game. The other difference is in sophistication. Those who can find beauty in human beings of many ages and shapes do not dispute the rights of others. But Miss Manners is hanged if she will try to clear the beaches for those who specialize in watching only certain types of people, and probably only certain parts of the bodies of those.

Now you will have to excuse Miss Manners. She has gotten so hot and bothered over this that she is going to go and put on her bathing suit—the one with the billowing sleeves and sailor collar—and go and cool off.

∽ Hallowe'en ∽

"Whoo, it's a ghost!" well-mannered adults would say when a small thing in bedraggled white appeared on the doorstep at Hallowe'en, with a smaller, shyer companion hanging behind. "Oh, and a witch, too. I'm so frightened. What can I do?"

Hand it over, of course, but sometimes the apparitions' own manners kicked in, in spite of themselves, and a scary thing would reply, "It's okay, Mrs. Saddlebag, it's really me, Gary, see? I was only fooling."

It was an innocent routine, highly gratifying to both parties. It still occurs, festooned with security measures on both sides, but is no longer commonplace. Hallowe'en, Miss Manners has observed, has rapidly grown older and more immature.

First the big kids took over, playing at what they considered scary, which was not ghosts but street gangs. Good kids (a term that now refers to children who live in well-to-do neighborhoods and don't have long police records) began to see it as a safe day to dabble in vandalism. Sometimes they were joined by the real thing. Sometimes they turned into the real thing.

Householders began to meet them at their own level. Unfortunately, one response was to slip tricks into treats. The possibility of razor blades nestled in apples ensured a balance of fright on both sides of the ghost costume. Then the bigger kids—bigger by a decade or more—took over Hallowe'en. Adults, with their larger allowances, went in for elaborate costumes and decorations in a big way, making Hallowe'en into a major holiday on the scale of Christmas and Thanksgiving. Why they bother, Miss Manners can't imagine, considering that funny T-shirts, casual Friday and the absence of dress codes have made every day dress-up day.

This thought brings her back to the little children whose holiday has been co-opted. They still like to play dress-up, and to fool people with their outfits.

The children's clothing industry has come to their rescue. They have pushed the idea and produced the clothing making it possible for little girls to dress up as sluts and little boys to dress up as thugs. Furthermore, small children won't have to wait for a holiday to do so, because these are appearing in the form of school clothes.

Some adults are objecting. Miss Manners also sees a reason to object. As children have been passionately opposing the institution of dress codes at school on the grounds that they need to express their true selves in their clothing, would it not be reasonable for adults to take them at face value and believe that they are sluts and thugs?

She hopes not. Surely the kind thing to do is merely to pretend to go along, being careful to give them a chance to reveal the truth. As in:

"Oh, no, a streetwalker! In my neighborhood!"

"No, no, it's okay, Mrs. Middleforth (or more likely, "Ginny"), it's me, Emmeline. I was just fooling. I'm not really a streetwalker."

And by the way, Miss Manners knows how to institute a dress code that high school students will eagerly vie to obey. Put a neon sign with a chic-vulgar name over the school and a huge velvet rope in front of it, and hire a tough and pitiless young man to tell most of them, "No, not you. I don't like your look."

DEAR MISS MANNERS:

I would like people to see another side of teenagers' trick-or-treating. I understand the point about people not dressed in costumes with their cigarettes in hand wanting candy. But I am 17 years old, and when my two best friends, 17 and 18, and I go trick-or-treating, we could have been at a party where there may be drugs and alcohol. Why risk having a few drinks and then trying to drive home or getting busted by the cops? If we weren't supposed to go trick-or-treating, what were we supposed to do?

GENTLE READER:

What do you do the rest of the year? Do you have other ways of blackmailing people who if they don't entertain you, you'll get into serious trouble?

Come to think of it, however, that is the premise of trick-or-treating. Miss Manners will only remind you that even trick-or-treaters have responsibilities, and to entertain their victims by wearing costumes is the chief one.

~ Thanksgiving ~

Oh, go ahead. Have some more ceremonial eating. It's good for you.

Miss Manners is no longer so sure it is. The traditional holiday meal—emotionally nutritious and nutritionally aggressive—has taken a distasteful turn. Rather than going after the food while treating the people considerately, participants go after the other people while considering the food.

Every culture has its ritual feast. Everyone is expected to take part, dressing up not only their bodies, but their attitudes, for the occasion. Special food is prepared, the best table equipment is shined and starched and the setting is festooned with decorations. A prescribed procedure is followed at the table, to the extent that many of the utterances people make are traditional to the occasion.

As such things go, our Thanksgiving is cozy and simple. Relatives and friends gather around a table to eat turkey and seasonal produce, the chief requirement being that there be too much of it. As in the days when only fancy folk had dinner in the evening, it is an afternoon meal served from platters on the table. Daytime dress need be only formal enough to make everyone sit up smartly, and have to make furtive adjustments as the meal progresses.

Everyone is expected to praise the food and protest the amount. Children must be told that they are bigger, and adults that they are smaller. A groaning session is held toward the end of the meal, although discretion is advised when offering descriptions of digestive struggles. Help is offered that the hosts may or may not choose to accept. Everyone is supposed to depart before turning cross.

How hard is that?

And yet it seems to Miss Manners as if few people seem to manage it now without turning prematurely cross.

It starts with reluctance to attend and complaints about the guest list: "I didn't choose my relatives, I'd rather be with my friends. . . . If he's going to be there, you can count me out. . . . If you invited those children, keep them away from me. . . . I hope you don't expect me to be civil to people I can't stand. . . ."

Then there is rebellion against making any effort to dress: "That's stupid, I'm going to be comfortable. . . . I don't care what anyone else does. . . . It's just family. . . . You think I'm going to wear a tie? . . . No, I'm not wearing a skirt and that's final. . . . What do you mean, these are not real shoes?"

Finally, there is the conversation. You remember the traditional comments: "She got the drumstick last year, so it's my turn. . . . Nobody makes pie the way you do. . . . Since you insist, but only a little. . . . I'm going to burst. . . ." Now guests have taken to making unpleasant remarks about the menu and the habits of other guests: "Don't you know what that does to the system? . . . You don't really need that. . . . Yuck. . . . I hate that. . . . I'm not supposed to have that. . . . There's nothing here I can eat."

Come on, folks, it's a holiday. It won't kill you to look nice, it won't kill you to be nice, and if you think the food will kill you, please skip it without comment. It's a ritual, and we don't have that many of them.

DEAR MISS MANNERS:

My daughter is having Thanksgiving dinner at her home this year. She is planning on no TV football games during dinner and when the football game is on, the volume will be on mute. Is this correct? She also plans on having games. Help!

GENTLE READER:

Your daughter wants to have live conversation at the family holiday table, and afterward she expects people to play games with one another rather than all being slumped around separately watching strangers play games? Has she no sense of tradition?

As your daughter is the hostess, you must go along with her outrageous wishes. You may actually find yourself feeling thankful for this sociable treat. The only help an unsympathetic Miss Manners offers you is to suggest that the dinner be scheduled after the games—or before or after a particular game in which this crowd is most interested—and that the other guests be warned.

⌒ The Christmas Season ⌒

Here are some clues that you might be overdoing the holidays:

The neighbors' children are going to school bleary-eyed because the lights on your house are keeping them awake.

There is so much to be done in connection with your office celebrations that it is one of the most hectic work times of the year, although the service your company ordinarily performs has been all but suspended.

Your special wardrobe contains so many Christmas sweaters and items of jewelry with trees, bells and wreaths that you have to keep track of which you have worn where.

Not remembering who some of the people on your card list are and how they got there does not discourage you from sending them greetings.

Strangers show up at your holiday parties and open conversations with you by asking whether you can point out the host.

You are sending presents to a generation of relatives whom you have not seen since babyhood, and from whom you have never received acknowledgment.

People to whom you bring little surprise treats don't look thrilled and exclaim in pleasure; they look cornered and exclaim, "Oh, I meant to get something for you."

After you offer people good wishes, you find yourself having to urge them to get into the spirit of the season.

Your children get cranky when there are no more presents for them to open, partly because it doesn't occur to them to go on to the next stage of playing with what they received, but mostly because they are just plain exhausted from the task.

You press food on people after they claim to be sated by telling them how much work you put into making it.

You quiz people about their ancestry for the purpose of celebrating their particular holidays, even ones they don't celebrate themselves.

You end up being annoyed at everyone you were trying to please.

Normally, Miss Manners is an enthusiastic supporter of the cheerful and the festive, with little patience for those who claim that they find merriment depressing. She believes that traditions bind people together and that it is divisive, if not cruel, to scorn family observances. Her admiration for those who plan their holidays for others' pleasure, and not just their own, is boundless.

But she worries about people who, bless their hearts, get so into the holiday spirit that they go around spreading fatigue and obligation and, ultimately, their own disappointment that others fail to keep up with them.

They would do well to remember that there can be too much of a good thing:

An hour of generalized fellowship in an office is a delightful break, but the additional workload or assessment to support serious celebrations is a burden that should not be imposed.

There is no pleasure in receiving cards or presents from people one can't place, and no point in sending presents into a void from which there is no response.

Unexpected treats and presents should be on so modest a scale as not to leave the recipient with a surprise social debt. Giving is blessed, but force-feeding people presents or food beyond what they can handle is not.

Assuming that everyone celebrates Christmas may be insensitive, but so is assuming that everyone has a Christmas equivalent and wants help sharing it.

DEAR MISS MANNERS:

Miss Manners might suggest, before Christmas, that unless a specific invitation is being extended, Generous Souls—and others—refrain from asking people who are alone:

a. What are your plans for Christmas?
b. Did you have a nice Christmas?
c. What did you do for Christmas?

It saves painful embarrassment if the answer is:

a. None.
b. No.
c. Nothing.

GENTLE READER:

Conventional conversation is full of such questions, and one has to learn that they are only the meaningless devices of light sociability and not attempts to probe for information. Otherwise, an unhappy person could suffer fresh pain every time someone said "How have things been going?" or "I hope you have a pleasant weekend."

Miss Manners understands that the Christmas season's emphasis on family life may produce some melancholy in those who live alone. But she cannot go along with the suggestion of making other people censor their careless conversation so as to avoid adding to the pain, as one watches one's words in front of someone in the midst of an acute tragedy. This self-consciousness, prompted by pity, is helpful to avoid jarring the feelings of a person in crisis, but bad and patronizing in a long-term situation.

Questions a, b and c can all be answered by "Oh, the usual—what about you?"

The Computerized Christmas

Maybe your computer won't kiss you under the mistletoe this year, but it has been relieving people of the other loving acts they are supposed to perform at Christmas.

Miss Manners is all for everyone's gathering around the flickering hearth during the holidays. She is just surprised to find that the preferred ratio is now one person to each hearth. And she considers it a pity that modern flickering doesn't inspire sharing the warm memories one has been hanging onto, so much as hanging on hold for the hot line.

Nevertheless, there is always much to be done at this time, and she likes to see the whole household pitch in. The computer is eager to be of service.

For the exchange of holiday greetings, it will find or help design a card or write a seasonal letter, and keep track of who has sent any to you. It already has your list of names and addresses, which it is happy to sort for the occasion, and it will send any message right out without anyone's having to brave the weather. If you prefer greetings that can be propped on mantelpieces, it will still save you the trouble of addressing envelopes and perhaps of finding and licking stamps.

It is getting more and more enthusiastic about doing your shopping for you. It will save you the strenuous treks through malls or catalogues by showing you all kinds of wares to buy and accepting your credit information without wandering off to do something else while you wait. In fact, it is willing to do other people's shopping for you. It invites you to post your own Christmas wishes to alert shoppers you know who may be prepared to grant them.

It asks no thanks for itself, but should it occur to you to thank others, it will undertake to facilitate that job.

Miss Manners is not one to scorn offers of help, and she notices that people are taking increasing advantage of these opportunities. She is, however, grateful that a few of them are still asking whether doing so is not just easy but proper.

Sometimes, it is. You have only to ask yourself first "Why not?" (No, wait. "Why not?" is your family motto, isn't it? So make that: You have only to ask Miss Manners why not.) She can't think of a reason people shouldn't do their shopping on line if they prefer. But she can think of a whopper of a reason why they should not post their own holiday wishes: Christmas is indeed a time for charity, but those who are not in need should not apply. Besides, an adult advertising the hope that people will foot the bill for his or her shopping list lacks the appeal of a small child whispering to Santa Claus.

In greetings, the formula is calculated by measuring both style and content, with handwritten personal notes at the top of the scale and mass emailings at the bottom. (Yes, people can tell the personalized from the personal.) So a truly individually written email message would be more or less equivalent to a conventional greeting written out by hand. (But sending a card that ties up someone's computer to download is more or less equivalent to throwing festively colored toilet paper into someone's tree.)

Miss Manners is not as fussy as she might be about how envelopes are addressed, now that they are no longer hand delivered. But she is fussier than ever about letters of thanks being handwritten (and that those physically unable to do so include an apologetic explanation). This includes the Gentle Reader who argued that the small gift of homemade bread from a colleague was surely trivial enough to be acknowledged by email. But the bread was homemade, and hand-making a letter is easier than making a loaf of bread—even homemade with a bread machine. Miss Manners is not against mechanical help, but she insists on preserving the flavor.

(For more about cards and presents, please see p. 614.)

⌒ Christmas Day ⌒

Christmas is an important day for everyone to practice hypocrisy. Does that offend you? Miss Manners is so excessively polite that she rarely has the wicked pleasure of offending people, and you must allow her to relish the sensation for a moment before she explains what she means and spoils the effect.

There now. Miss Manners feels quite herself again and is prepared to discuss Christmas behavior with appropriate sobriety. What she means is that Christmas is an excellent time for people to forgo the honest expression of their true feelings and adjust—not to say dissemble—their behavior in order to cater to the feelings of others.

Take the difficult matter of midafternoon on Christmas Day. Everyone always feels cross then. This is perfectly understandable. They have been up too early. They have had little rest the night before, either because they have had visions of sugar plums dancing in their heads or because they were trying to put together a vision for someone else, which had some of the parts or the directions missing and should have been put together by the store, which refused to do so. Some people are cross because they did not get what they wanted, and some are cross because they did and are now tired of it or are feeling postpartum depression. Some people are stiff from sitting in church, and others are stiff from sitting on the floor with the electric trains, and some are both.

Those who have Christmas dinner at night are cross because they are starved, and those who have it at midday are cross because they are overstuffed, and all of them are beginning to wish they had not eaten the candy canes off the tree. Christmas hypocrisy requires that everyone conceal these feelings and behave kindly and patiently to others.

It is especially important on Christmas that children be reinforced in their hypocritical behavior. Children must be taught to express pleasure and surprise when they open presents, concealing their actual assessment of the acquisitions if this is inconsistent with the official emotions. They must be instructed to refrain from making such true statements as "I already have one." And they must be taught the unnatural act of reading the card before opening the package.

They must also be forced into another unnatural act, that of sitting down and writing letters of thanks immediately—letters that express enthusiasm and gratitude with the best artifice they can muster in order to make the emotion sound genuine. (This is, incidentally, an excellent midafternoon activity for calming down overexcited children. Their little eyelids will be drooping in boredom in no time, and there will be a merciful moment of quiet in the house.)

Even adults accustomed to faking verbal and written joy often need practice in Christmas hypocrisy. It is not easy to sound convincing when one is expressing a wish to "help." Everyone at a Christmas gathering should be falsely shining with the apparent desire to set the table, pick up the torn wrappings, go for a walk in the snow as far as the garbage can and fix the children's malfunctioning toys.

If you do not like the term "hypocrisy," Miss Manners will permit you to call it "doing unto others."

DEAR MISS MANNERS:

It's all very well to say that Christmas is too commercialized—nobody will argue with that. But how do you avoid the materialistic atmosphere that gets into even the coziest family gathering, when the most important part of the day is obviously open-ing the presents?

Every Christmas we go to my mother's, where we have a big meal with my sis-ter's family, my aunt and uncle, and their children and grandchildren. We are all on good terms, and it ought to be a lovely warm occasion. But the conversation among the children is about nothing but "What did you get?" and the grown-ups, too polite to do that, talk instead about food—"Have some more" or "I ate too much." We are not very religious people, and maybe that's the trouble. In my husband's family, they went to church on Christmas, so at least there was some time of the day not focused on appetite (for food or toys).

It's not that I'm trying to convert my family to stricter churchgoing habits, but I wish there were a way to make this Christmas just a tiny bit more—can I say it?—spiritual, or at least slightly less base.

GENTLE READER:

What you need, in a hurry, is some family tradition. Christmas Day was tradi-tionally filled with events—not only going to church, but caroling, visiting, and annoying the poor. One no longer drops in on other people's celebrations uninvited, and the poor have rebelled against being used as supernumeraries in others' Christmas pageants.

However, you can still organize your own activities among your own family. Reading aloud from the Bible or some Christmas-related book such as Charles Dickens' *A Christmas Carol*, singing carols, making the children who take music lessons play Christmas selections for the family, asking each person to tell what Christmas means to him or her—almost anything will do.

You just have to ignore protests that the activity is corny, or that you've all done it before. It is the simplicity and the repetition that make a tradition, and the chil-dren who have to be pried from their avariciousness to participate this year will look forward to it next year, and will remember it fondly all their adult lives.

~ *Presents* ~

DEAR MISS MANNERS:

We hold open house every Christmas, inviting some people in advance and bringing others back from church with us—just people we happen to see but hadn't thought of beforehand. It's just lots of eggnog and cookies, and people seem to enjoy it very much.

My question is about those who bring presents. They're not really supposed to, but a few people do. I'm always afraid of this embarrassing other guests, who might then think they were supposed to, and I also feel funny about accepting these presents because I'm not giving them anything (or I'd have to have something for everyone and the whole open house idea would be impossible).

Should I open the presents when they are given to me? Should I send those people presents afterwards? One other question: I invited some Jewish friends, and they said they couldn't come. Was it wrong to invite them—were they offended because they don't celebrate Christmas?

GENTLE READER:

Unless you can open the presents inconspicuously—and how can you, with other guests to greet?—it is better to put them aside and thank the people the next day, by note. You don't owe them presents; you gave them a lovely day. There is a whole range of reasons that your Jewish friends might have had for refusing your invitation—from not wanting to participate in a Christmas celebration to having another Christmas celebration to attend. But however differently Jews, Muslims or others may regard Christmas—from a religious holiday that they do not celebrate to a winter festival that they might—they are all aware that it exists, and it cannot be considered offensive to mention it.

At Christmas, as always, Miss Manners has a little something for everyone, in the way of advice:

For Children Planning to Come Home from College, at Great Social Sacrifice, to Visit Their Parents for the Christmas Holidays: Kisses first, dirty laundry later. The idea is to appear pleased to see the old couple that live there, rather than to rejoice exclusively in the creature comforts they have to offer.

For Primary-School Teachers: After you have set the holiday pageant and cookie party for two fifteen on a Wednesday afternoon, do not inform your pupils that "Now, we want to make sure all the parents come." This plants the dark thought in little minds that a parent who fails to show up to watch their own child in a non-speaking role is a callous villain who has abandoned their flesh-and-blood for personal fulfillment and creative gratification at a factory all day.

For Temporary Help in Department Stores: Granted that you cannot be expected to know the stock, be able to fill out the charge forms or have known just how unpleasant a task it was to deal with the general public, try to be patient and pleasant. Considering your qualifications, why else are you getting that miserable salary?

For Generous Souls, Who Always Invite the Elderly, the Orphaned and the Otherwise Abandoned to Christmas Dinner: When you get a refusal, suggest immediately one of the other three hundred and sixty four days of the year that this person could dine with you. It makes the motive for your Christmas invitation sound less like a penance.

For Multigenerational Families Who Gather for Christmas Reunions: Do not relax and be less than a thoughtful houseguest, or allow your immediate descendants to do so, on the grounds that these people are related to you. Blood is not necessarily thicker than water, and it generally helps at this time of year to have a little Scotch in both.

~ *New Year's Eve* ~

It is some time now since Miss Manners noticed that New Year's Eve is a great deal more fun in theory than in practice. Miss Manners has nothing against dressing up, drinking champagne, dancing through the night and indulging in a modest amount of free-lance kissing—provided she doesn't have to do all this too often. Once a fortnight would be about right.

However, this kind of luxurious leisure is not what New Year's Eve is about any longer. New Year's Eve has become the national quintessential Saturday night, set aside as a social occasion with built-in disappointments for everyone. There is nothing like an officially designated time of glamour and excitement for producing mass discontent and depression. This effect is best achieved by not having been asked to celebrate New Year's Eve with someone else, although you can also manage it if you have a date but no party to go to or a party but no date to go with or the wrong date or the right date in the wrong mood.

Even if you have a full set of invitations, you can still spoil the occasion by watching the people at your party depart for better parties from which you were excluded. New Year's Eve parties, being long and not carefully orchestrated—as, say, a dinner is—offer many opportunities for behaving badly, in ways one will suddenly remember with a sickening flash at breakfast the next afternoon. If you can't manage this yourself, you can always observe a loved one behaving badly.

Miss Manners' suggestion for coping with this mess is that everyone calm down and build a New Year's Eve suited to the actual purpose of the holiday. The reason we divide time into years is to give everyone a fresh start, not to mention a clean calendar. New Year's Eve, therefore, has two purposes: to practice the better, more graceful living one has promised oneself, and to pack in a last bit of wickedness before reforming forever. One celebrates in a way that is slightly more expensive, more fattening or more naughty than one can ordinarily afford to be. None of these requires the sort of franticness that ends in accidents, automobile or marital, and various numbers can play. The ideal New Year's Eve leaves one with the will to get through a New Year's Day.

DEAR MISS MANNERS:

I know that there is special license about kissing at New Year's Eve parties, but I have questions about who and how much. Are you obliged to kiss the person you brought to the party exactly at midnight? If so, can you then go around kissing anybody you want to? Can a woman refuse a kiss or make a scene about it? How long after midnight can the kissing go on?

GENTLE READER:

Miss Manners hopes that the New Year's Eve party you are planning to attend is a masked ball in a damp Venetian palace, so that, mysteriously disguised, you can slither about kissing whomever you choose until it is time for your flight home.

The ordinary New Year's Eve party does not permit quite such an exciting suspension of the rules. The custom is to seek out, just before midnight, the person with whom you came to the party, or at least the person with whom you plan to leave it. As midnight strikes, you may kiss or not as you choose, but if you plan to do some general kissing, this is the place to start. Oddly enough, the degree of passion one properly exhibits is in inverse proportion to that believed to be associated with the relationship. Thus, a long-married couple should kiss with tremendous enthusiasm, while a pair of crazed new lovers should barely touch lips or cheeks. Please don't ask Miss Manners to explain why; these are examples of good taste.

You may then turn to people nearby, but the type of kisses you offer must be of the chaste variety many people use as greetings. Don't tell Miss Manners that she is spoiling your fun. It is perfectly possible to press a thrill of meaning into a cheek kiss, if that is what you want, and you do not run the risk of beginning a fresh year in a melee. Miss Manners would consider twelve fifteen a good time to get back to the more decorous task of drinking champagne. After all, you have a whole year ahead of you.

10. *Death*

IT'S WONDERFUL how death transforms the spirit, so that everyone who is deceased becomes a self-effacing promoter of the comfort of the living. Or so one would assume from hearing surviving friend and relations saying things like "He would have wanted me to go out and enjoy myself on a day like this," "She would have preferred that I go to the football game instead of being glum at her funeral service" and "He would have told us to go ahead with our festival and not cancel it on his account."

Nonsense. Miss Manners' knowledge of human emotions tells her that he would have wanted you to be too overcome with grief to be capable of enjoying anything, and she would have wanted national mourning. Putting sentiments in the mouths of others is always offensive, but Miss Manners finds it particularly so in the case of those who are not around to speak for themselves.

When a person dies, those who cared about him or her have the obligations of attending the funeral service and family gathering afterward, and of offering assistance, writing letters, and paying condolence visits to the immediate family. The most graceful way of getting through all of these is to search one's mind until one has a supply of anecdotes about the dead person that are both favorable and believable. Foibles that can be told with admiration are particularly effective. These stories are crucial at a funeral in which eulogies are delivered by friends. Such services can be quite moving—and anything is better than a funeral at which the clergyman says, "I didn't have the privilege of knowing Jeff Perfect" (groans from friends because he was never nicknamed Jeff) "but I feel as if I did. He was someone who had a rare zest and love for life . . ."

They are also the proper conversation for wakes, postfuneral gatherings and other condolence visits, all of which should be bittersweet events in which one reminisces about the dead while consuming his liquor supply. Additional presents of liquor, along with the traditional offering of cooked food to the bereaved, are a way of keeping such events going. This is important to the immediate family. While you may not assume that the deceased is preoccupied with the convenience of his friends and their social calendars, you must act on the idea that he would have been concerned with the emotional welfare of his family. The formalities connected with death are designed with this in mind.

Honest mourning, Miss Manners has observed, is a matter for both laughter and tears; gloom unrelieved by happy memories is suspicious. Because this mixture of sudden hilarity and equally sudden depression is peculiar and unpredictable, it is customary for the recently bereaved not to attend ordinary social events.

This does not mean that they do not need, perhaps acutely, the company of others; and the services, gatherings, visits and letters serve this purpose, along with requiring much activity—arranging services, notifying people, accepting condolences, responding to letters—that helps distract the grief-stricken and postpones their dealing with the void left by the death. It is a mistake to think that the living are too grief-struck to notice who fulfills these obligations and who doesn't. So you must inconvenience yourself, if you wish to honor someone who has died. Believe Miss Manners—he would have wanted it that way.

DEAR MISS MANNERS:

Are there socially acceptable alternatives to expressing one's grief or sense of loss regarding the passing on of friends or relatives short of attending the wake or funeral? I guess what I am asking is if attending wakes and/or funerals is considered de rigueur?

For reasons even I do not understand, wakes and funerals cause me an undue amount of stress and anxiety. I don't handle them well at all and wonder if there are less stressful options for me when needing to convey my sense of loss regarding an acquaintance's passing.

GENTLE READER:

Miss Manners understands your reasons for disliking funerals, because everyone else shares them. You are not a special, sensitive case. Funerals focus on the horrible fact that someone connected to you is now gone, and the frightening fact that one day you too will die.

Nevertheless, it is no exaggeration to say that they are a defining element of civilization. We wouldn't think much of a society, no matter what its other achievements, that threw its deceased into a disposal like garbage. Funerals honor the dead, comfort the bereaved and give life a sense of meaning and continuity.

So get a grip on yourself and go. Yes, there are other ways of expressing grief and compassion—writing condolence letters, sending flowers, paying calls on the bereaved, establishing memorials—but these are additions rather than substitutes.

⌒ Notifying People ⌒

DEAR MISS MANNERS:

It is now six weeks since my father died, and we are just beginning to have the house free of the sickening smell of too many flowers—our church only permits one family wreath, and redirected the others here—and of the unpleasant telephone calls from people who demanded to know why we "didn't let them know" of the death. He was a man who hated any kind of fuss, although he touched many people's lives with his quiet kindness, and we did everything as privately as possible, to keep it in his style. But it didn't work. What should we have done?

GENTLE READER:

You have been following two rules of good taste that unfortunately apply to everything except funerals. Life's other milestones, such as births, graduations and weddings, are commonly rendered vulgar by people who try to use them to seek personal publicity and to manipulate their gift-giving potential. When someone dies, however, it is appropriate to inform the local newspaper and supply biographical material, and it is acceptable to inform people that flowers should be omitted—even suggesting another means of expressing sympathy, such as a charitable donation. This is acceptable because these things are not being done by the honoree.

Funerals

AS NO ONE ever chooses to put on a funeral, you might think that leniency would be granted in passing judgment on its taste and effectiveness as a public event. Lack of planning time could also be pleaded, and an absence of the social spirit. Nevertheless, it is probably the most harshly appraised type of gathering held, and there is not, as after a botched dinner party, the possibility of erasing the failure by doing it over again, right.

The only comforts Miss Manners can offer are that the simplest arrangements are in the best of taste, and that the responsibilities may be divided among the friends of the deceased and the bereaved, with the chief mourner charged only with policy and major decisions. For example, it is good to designate a friend, rather than an immediate relative, to make arrangements with those whose professional services are required. People in the funeral business naturally equate respect and love with elaborate furnishings and expensive fittings, and even those who know that these things are not related may not have the heart to conduct a skirmish on the subject.

Other assignments that may be made are:

- *Notifying people of the death.* Calls are made to those who are thought likely to be affected, and public notification is made by supplying the facts of the person's life to the newspapers.
- *Answering telephones and doorbells.* Someone with the instincts of a good butler in being able to judge and convey with gentleness which calls are convenient to be taken when, should be on duty in the house. He or she may also drop hints about the bereaved's being tired, if the sympathetic callers stay too long.
- *Supervising the kitchen.* The tradition of callers bringing food is a widespread one, and someone has to be in charge of putting things away and arranging them into meals for the family and lesser offerings to other callers.
- *Acting as pallbearers.* This is a position of great honor, offered only to those closest to the deceased, and cannot be refused unless one has a dire excuse, such as a plan to have one's own funeral in the near future.

- *Speaking at the funeral.* In these days when many people's formal religious ties are somewhat casual, a stranger sometimes gives the eulogy. One way to avoid this is to have selected people who did have the privilege of knowing the deceased say a few plausible but tasteful words at the funeral. This honor may be refused on the grounds that one is not a good speaker or is too overcome to get up and talk. (The excuse of not having anything good to say about the person is sufficient, but must be disguised.)

Friends who do not receive assignments are responsible for sending letters of condolence, paying condolence calls, attending the funeral and sending flowers or making charitable contributions.

This leaves the chief mourner, who has designated the tasks, to set the basic style and budget of the funeral, acknowledge the services and expressions of sympathy, readjust to life and inherit the worldly goods. He or she may be confident that his or her bearing under such weights is closely and mercilessly scrutinized by all. Consolation may be taken in the fact that at least the person most concerned need not suffer under society's judgment.

The Memorial Service

DEAR MISS MANNERS:
What is the difference between a funeral and a memorial service?

GENTLE READER:
Put bluntly, it is the presence or absence of the honored person. A funeral precedes a burial. A memorial service is held afterward, or instead, if there is no such event for mourners to attend.

Dressing for a Funeral

DEAR MISS MANNERS:
Does it matter what you wear to a funeral? I hardly ever see anyone wearing black anymore, except possibly the widow.

GENTLE READER:
Dark clothes should be worn to a funeral, although most people cherish the mistaken notion that the deceased would prefer them to be casual and comfortable, rather

than to make a special effort on his behalf. However, there is such a thing as ostentatious mourning. A mysterious woman who shows up at a funeral more droopily festooned in black than the widow is making what is known as a fashion statement.

⁓ Signing the Registry ⁓

DEAR MISS MANNERS:

How does one sign the registry book at a funeral home when one attends the funeral of one in the immediate family or a very close relative? Is it Mr. and Mrs. John Doe? Is it John and Polly Doe? Or is there another way? What is the most correct? Several people I have asked confess they do not know and I feel there are many who would like to.

GENTLE READER:

It is true that the usual form for funeral registry books has been "Mr. and Mrs. John Doe," but Miss Manners believes it should be "John and Margaret Doe." Note that nicknames should never be used and last names should always be included: This serves the purpose of the "Mr. and Mrs." form in making it clear how the bereaved should address these people. Miss Manners has two reasons for wishing the change. One is that the formal title seems cold, particularly in the cases you describe. The other is that Miss Manners believes that no one should write his own title under any circumstances. (Even Miss Manners does not do so. "Miss" is her given name.)

⁓ Funereal Demeanor ⁓

DEAR MISS MANNERS:

When I was recently attending the funeral of a close friend's relative, many folks from "the old gang" came out to give him support. A few hours after the service during the "reception" a couple of us were talking and laughing together because we hadn't seen each other in quite a while.

While our laughing was not obnoxious or loud, another friend suggested that a funeral reception isn't the place for humorous chatter at all. This sparked a lighthearted debate, and we've never come to a solid conclusion. Is humor in that particular time of sorrow considered rude or disrespectful? Or is it then when it is needed most?

GENTLE READER:

Yes, humor is acceptable after a funeral, and yes, your humor was disrespectful. And so, by the way, was your "lighthearted debate" about your own behavior.

A funeral, and the gathering of mourners afterward, is supposed to focus on the person who has died. It is not a party, and it is not a reunion. Miss Manners realizes that this is hard for people to grasp. There are refreshments, so it seems like a party. There are others present whom one has not seen in a long time, and so it seems like a reunion.

Nevertheless, it is bad form to be so easily consoled as to forget about the deceased and engage in ordinary socializing, including ordinary lightheartedness. To those who are more deeply afflicted, that offers a vivid illustration of how easily the person has been forgotten, even moments after his burial. The humor that is acceptable on such occasions, and may actually be consoling, is that which arises from affectionate recollections about the deceased.

DEAR MISS MANNERS:

My father passed away a couple of months ago after a long and brave battle with cancer. My immediate family saw a once vibrant man struggle each day with the disease. He died proudly with each of us at his bedside.

Many of our relatives came from out of town and, as with any funeral, there were inappropriate comments, etc. However, we had one cousin (my father's nephew) who took pictures of everyone and had that camera around his neck like he was on vacation. Several times, members of the family requested him to stop taking pictures.

Less than a month after my father's death, he sent my Mother a video of the entire funeral (with all the details). My Mother viewed the tape alone and needless to say it was a mistake. I live in another city and was not able to intercept the video.

Maybe this is the way of the future, but certainly consideration and respect should not be outdated. At a minimum, my cousin should have (1) told us about the video, (2) asked if we wanted to have a copy and (3) waited a respectable period of time before presenting it to the family.

I haven't seen the tape and don't want to relive one of the most painful events of our family's life. At least, not now. Please tell your readers to have some respect for the feelings of others.

GENTLE READER:

It wouldn't help. People who think of life—and in this case, death—as a photo opportunity will only ascribe to others their feeling that the souvenir of an event is more meaningful than the event itself. For this reason, Miss Manners finds it safer not to consult their own feelings, but just to tell them to cut it out. A discreet taping of the eulogies is about the limit for a funeral, and only then with the consent of the immediately bereaved.

Bereavement

THE GREAT ART of etiquette was invented to translate the incoherent jumble of human feelings to which we are all subject into something more presentable. When we cast it aside and let our emotions run around naked and exposed to public comment, as we have done by abandoning the formal customs of mourning, everybody suffers. And that saddens Miss Manners.

When someone dies, the bereaved are either grieved or they are not. Yet both true grief and the absence of grief are, in their natural states, socially intolerable. What we expect is quiet dignity, a kind of steadfast, restrained semblance of sorrow. Either joyous relief, or the ricocheting between hysteria and hilarity that is the natural reaction to deeply felt loss, is mistakenly perceived as an unnatural reaction.

Miss Manners approves of the return of the widow's veil, or its jazzier equivalent, the pair of oversized sunglasses, for funerals. She would like to see a more extensive return to formal mourning, in however modified a modern way, to protect survivors from public scrutiny of their inner feelings.

Before mourning was abolished, the deep crêpe veil was worn off the face for a year of deep mourning; a widower wore a black band on hat or sleeve. Clothes for both ladies and gentlemen were black, with dull surfaces rather than shiny—suede gloves, for example, rather than kid. No jewelry was permitted except for pearls, diamonds and black onyx. One did not go into society, and one's letters were written on black-bordered paper.

Second mourning, a year or sometimes two years after the death, consisted of lightening the all-black effect with touches of lavender, purple, gray or white.

Miss Manners can just hear the cries of how morbid this all is, and how life must go on. Of course life goes on. The strictest instructions about old-fashioned mourning always had to include the information that a widow should cease to wear mourning immediately upon selecting her second husband. Do you think the Victorians didn't understand the charm of woefulness, or how fetching many ladies look in black?

The value of mourning is not to remind people to be unhappy, but to relieve them of the necessity of acting out unhappiness for the benefit of others. The most deeply grieved people will have, even quite soon after a death, moments of merriment, sometimes based on memories of the deceased and some unrelated to the death. If these occur when the person is gaily dressed and out socially, they will be taken as indications of callousness. If, however, a person in those circumstances suddenly bursts into tears on no apparent provocation, which also can happen, the same critics will be annoyed at the lack of control and may go so far as to level a charge of hypocrisy.

If mourners stay away from other people's parties, they do not subject themselves to this criticism. They needn't isolate themselves, but simply conduct their social relations in their own homes, where they may choose companions who share or at least understand their behavior.

Wearing mourning—the modern version would be somber, conservative clothes, although not necessarily black—serves, like the black borders on letters, as a warning that this is a person taking a death seriously. Establishing that fact through symbols saves one the trouble of having to prove it.

You know, and Miss Manners knows, that whatever you may say about getting back to normal, there is nothing that the acquaintances of bereaved people enjoy more than being shocked at their behavior for seeming so—normal.

DEAR MISS MANNERS:

For the last seven years I have taken care of my mother, probably the sweetest, most adorable and lovable Alzheimer's patient in the world. She passed away last month, and I am amazed at the level of grief I feel.

I don't have a problem during the workday or otherwise accepting condolences from colleagues, friends, and associates. What I am finding difficult is my social unreliability. There are several invitations, milestones at that, for the extenders, which I accepted before Mom's sudden death. I'm having a hard time because these people have been very supportive, both during Mom's illness and after her death. What are my responsibilities to others in what has turned out to be the most difficult time of my life? I would be most grateful for your counsel.

GENTLE READER:

Your responsibility is to tell them that you are in mourning. Why modern society abolished such a sensible accommodation to the normal human response to the tragedy of death, Miss Manners cannot imagine.

The recently bereaved are excused from social activities, and should ignore ridiculous advice to keep up a pretense of cheerfulness. You should wish your friends well, express your regret that you cannot be with them and respond graciously to their condolence visits and letters.

DEAR MISS MANNERS:

When my husband died, I put a black ribbon on our front door, which is still there. It makes me sad every time I come home and see it, but I was told putting black bunting on your front door was the proper thing to do. I would like to know how long I should leave it on my door.

GENTLE READER:

Take it down now. While the custom is rarely practiced these days and Miss Manners can't imagine who told you that propriety demanded it, its function is to symbolize that the house is in mourning and thus discourage any frivolous approaches. When it makes you sad, instead of protecting you, it should be removed.

~ *Critiquing the Bereaved* ~

DEAR MISS MANNERS:

Was I out of line watching my boyfriend act like the grieving widower at his ex-wife's funeral, when for the past four years, I have heard him do nothing but bad mouth her? He claims his tears were for support of his son and his son's sister (not his daughter). We have been at odds with one another ever since the funeral. If you tell me I was wrong, I will apologize at once.

GENTLE READER:

Then Miss Manners wishes you would please do so right away. Critiquing someone else's grief, or even pretending to understand it, is not just out of line, but arrogant and cruel.

At best, your approach could be said to be logical: If he had bad things to say about her, he should be glad, or at least relieved, that she is dead. But Miss Manners suspects you of worse—of accusing him of disloyalty to you and citing his tears as evidence.

Human nature is more complicated than that. It is possible for him to have resented his former wife and to be completely loyal to you—and yet be grieved by the passing of someone to whom he was, after all, once married.

Now here is an uncomplicated aspect of human nature: Failure to understand and respect one's deep and perhaps noble feelings, and the humiliation of being asked to justify their inadvertent expression, are bound to have a dampening effect on love.

DEAR MISS MANNERS:

A few months ago my friend (let's call her Mary) was widowed. She lives halfway across the country so I did not attend the funeral but sent a letter of condolence.

Since then, we have emailed each other fairly often. Yesterday was her birthday so I decided to phone her, but I got her answering machine. I was stunned to hear her late husband's voice on the tape.

I know that some women living alone prefer to have a man's voice on their answering machine but Mary has two grown sons who I feel sure would be willing to re-tape the message for her. It was very disconcerting to hear her late husband's voice. Should I gently suggest a change or assume that others have already done so and that she has refused?

GENTLE READER:

Oh, a new way to bother widows. Just what we needed.

A new widow can count on receiving the following pieces of erroneous etiquette advice:

1. That if she has used "Mrs." with her husband's name, as in "Mrs. Hubert Willow," she may no longer do so, but must be "Mrs. Anastasia Willow."

In fact, a lady's name does not change when her husband dies, and if she has used the traditional formal form, she continues to do so. Furthermore, "Mrs." with a lady's first name is always incorrect, which is why "Ms." is so useful to divorcées, as well as to anyone else, married, unmarried or widowed, who uses her own full name.

2. That she must soon remove the engagement and wedding rings her dear husband gave her, and which she has worn and cherished all her married life.

Etiquette does not ask widows to hold out their hands so any lingering symbols from a marriage can be confiscated. The only time it is incorrect for a widow to wear her rings is when she is marrying another gentleman.

And now you want Miss Manners to throw in a third piece of mischievous misinformation. Why? Why do you care? You don't even call her often.

In any case, Miss Manners refuses to validate your feeling that your friend should erase her late husband's voice, which for all you know she takes comfort in hearing. All that etiquette requires of taped telephone messages is that they be succinct.

DEAR MISS MANNERS:

When a couple marries, each gives the other a ring to wear on the left hand ring finger signifying to all that each is a married person. I lost my beautiful wife just one year ago yesterday. We would have had our 55th wedding anniversary in June of this year.

I am still wearing the ring she gave me on my left hand ring finger. Since I'm now no longer married, but widowed, would it be proper to move the ring to the right hand ring finger or wear it around my neck on a chain, or just—what?

To clarify, I have no intention of ever marrying again, but I would like to find a companion with similar tastes for entertainment that I have that I could share with. I DO NOT WANT TO SHOW ANY DISRESPECT TO MY FORMER WIFE, AS I LOVED HER SO MUCH.

GENTLE READER:

Yes, yes, please don't upset yourself. This is one of the extremely rare cases in which etiquette forgoes its usual dictatorial ways and advises you to go by your own feelings. There is no rule requiring or forbidding the widowed to remove their wedding rings.

Lest you think Miss Manners is deserting you, she hastens to assure you that she does have something to contribute to the subject. Etiquette not only makes rules, but it presides over the symbolism system, so it is her job to explain the symbolic ramifications of whichever choice you make.

Your wedding ring symbolizes your marriage, which has sadly ended in your wife's death, so it would not be disrespectful to remove it. It also symbolizes your love for her, and that is why the widowed sometimes choose to keep wearing their rings.

However, others, as well as yourself, will be reading that symbolism. If you are seeking simple friendship, the rings would serve as notice that you mean nothing more and do not intend to remarry. If you are seeking a romantic attachment, it would be only polite to keep the ring from public view to avoid its reminding another lady (and everyone you both know) that she is of secondary emotional importance to you.

Condolences

IS IT TRUE that we now live in a world where there is more joy than sorrow? Miss Manners doesn't know how else to account for everyone's knowing how to wish fortunate people happiness, while expressing sympathy is so strange and frightening that many people will choose the rudeness of silence rather than even attempt it.

Statistically, it turns out, as many people as get married, die. In fact, more people die than marry, although, unlike marriage, they tend to do it once and for all. Yet no one ever refuses to go to a wedding, crying pitifully as an excuse, "I just wouldn't know what to say."

As you know, Miss Manners requires you, when someone you know has died, to write a letter of condolence to the family, attend the funeral or memorial service and pay a formal visit on the family afterward. So she will tell you what to say.

Say "I'm sorry." Or "I'm so sorry"—Miss Manners allows for individuality of expression. If you can't manage that much, simply press the person's hand, look meaningfully into the eyes (this is done by raising the eyebrows from the nose bridge) and arrange the lips in a weight-of-the-world smile (done by raising the central part of the closed mouth at the same time as the corners are slightly raised).

There is a great variety of interesting things not to say. There is practically no limit to what imaginative and ill-meaning people will think of to increase the suffering and impair the dignity of the bereaved.

For instance:

"It's all for the best."

"You mustn't carry on like this. She wouldn't have wanted you to grieve."

"Do you really think you ought to be going about like this so soon after?"

"Oh, well, you'll soon have another child (marry again/meet someone else)."

"I'm surprised to see you've changed things about so. I should have thought you would have wanted to leave the house as it was when he was here."

"Of course you feel terrible. You must have all kinds of guilt feelings about what you could have said or done differently before it was too late. Would you like to talk to me about it?"

"I don't want to interfere, but I notice that you've let the children go back to their play group. Don't you think it's a little early?"

"You must feel just awful. I know you're being brave, but you can let it out with me. Go ahead, cry. It must be a terrible strain for you to act as matter-of-fact as you do."

"It's really much better his way. You wouldn't have wanted her to linger on and deteriorate, and this way you can remember her at the height of her youth."

"At least you had many years together. It's not like what happened to me."

"Of course, you can do what you want. But do you really feel it's respectful to the dead?"

"Oh, dear. *What can I say?*"

～ The Condolence Call ～

DEAR MISS MANNERS:

Don't you think that nowadays, in modern life, the old-fashioned custom of the condolence call is out of date?

GENTLE READER:

Why is that? Is it because people don't die anymore, or is it because the bereaved no longer need the comfort of their friends? Miss Manners is always interested in hearing about how life has been improved by modern thinking or technology.

～ Sympathy Cards ～

DEAR MISS MANNERS:

What kind of sympathy card do you consider dignified? Does the sender need to do anything more than sign it? In that case, what is the proper response from the person who has received it? Also, would you give me the correct wording for a card for the family to send out acknowledging cards, flowers, visits and gifts of food?

GENTLE READER:

Miss Manners is going to have to be very stern with you, in spite of her presumption that you are already feeling burdened, as well as grieved. A death is one of the times when human contact among those who care is most important. No sympathy cards are proper. No acknowledgment cards are proper. Letters of condolence should be written by hand, as should the letters of thanks from the bereaved; two sentences will do. Writing these out by hand does not take a minute more than signing a card, but it makes the difference between a cold, canned sentiment and a fresh, warm one.

Email

DEAR MISS MANNERS:

What's the deal on email these days? Is it okay to express sympathy for deaths in the family, congratulations for promotions, etc. via email? I'm just not into snail mail at all any more and it seems weird to pull out the Crane's embossed. But being a fairly old coot, I sometimes feel guilt when I don't. Any guidelines?

GENTLE READER:

Yes: Please continue to feel guilty when you fail to do what is right. Miss Manners is happy to sort out your confusion and remind you of the correct thing to do, but she can't stand over you and make you do it. This is why you have a conscience.

Mind you, Miss Manners agrees that email is a wonderful thing. It allows us to blanket the entire world with the same endless collection of jokes, our bosses to find out what we really think of them, and perfect strangers to enjoy those intimate thoughts we don't want to tell our intimates.

However, it is a casual form of communication and thus unsuitable for deeply serious messages. Quick congratulations on a minor promotion and trivial etceteras, sure; condolence letters and serious etceteras, no.

Mentioning "Death"

DEAR MISS MANNERS:

Is it in bad taste to use the word "death" in condolence notes? I seem to have reached the stage of life in which the occasion to write such notes arises with increasing frequency, and I am uncomfortable with euphemisms like "passed on," or "passing," and even with "loss," which always makes me think of Lady Bracknell in *The Importance of Being Earnest*, who tells Jack Worthing that having lost both his parents looks like carelessness.

A death is a terrible loss. Is it wrong to name it when expressing sympathy? Many other people seem to prefer the euphemisms. Will I add to the pain of the bereaved if I write that I am sorry about the death of a loved one?

GENTLE READER:

As fond as Miss Manners is of Lady Bracknell, the dear lady was not known for her tact. Propriety, yes, but that is something else. Lady Bracknell did not knock herself out to ingratiate herself with orphans.

It is true that the word "death" has been considered too harsh for the newly bereaved, although the stalwart mourners of the past did not flinch from the reality of death. One might also imagine that modern society, which freely uses death in its graphic forms of popular entertainment, would also be inured to the word.

Nevertheless it is easily avoided. And although euphemisms should not be universally scorned, as delicacy often spares feelings, you need not resort to them. Condolence letters are supposed to focus on reminiscing about the deceased (would you rather Miss Manners say "of the corpse"?) and sympathizing with the survivors. It is unnecessary to point out that the person has died, because the recipient of the letter already knows.

~ Difficult Condolences ~

DEAR MISS MANNERS:

About a month ago, I had a prolonged, public argument with a friend within earshot of his wife. I've just heard that he has since died. Although we weren't on speaking terms recently, we'd been good friends in our time, so I feel I must express my sympathy. Writing letters of condolence is always awkward, but in this case, I'm finding it well nigh impossible. Should I apologize to the wife for the fight, or avoid the subject in favor of the usual banalities?

GENTLE READER:

Your friend has taken unfair advantage of you by putting himself beyond reach of settling the argument, but Miss Manners agrees that you ought not to hold it against him. She also agrees that conventional condolences will be received with irony. You need not go so far as to apologize for your position in the argument, unless you now believe it to have been in error, but it would be nice if you could bring yourself to say that you respected him in spite of your differences, and regretted the breach in your friendship, the former delights of which you can then stress.

DEAR MISS MANNERS:

My sister-in-law recently had a miscarriage, one of several she has had over the years. They have one child. Do I mention the miscarriage when writing to her and my brother, and if so, what do I say about it?

GENTLE READER:

A miscarriage requires a particularly tricky kind of condolence letter, as it concerns the mother's health as well as the loss of the baby. Miss Manners suggests you do it very simply, staying entirely away from the medical aspects of the situation. The jolly assurance that "you will have other children" not only does not compensate for the loss of this one, but may not be true for reasons your sister-in-law does not wish to discuss with you. It is also offensive to announce that it was "probably better" that a child who could have had problems not be born. Excessive family talk is inappropriate too, as it usually comes out sounding as if your side thought that if your brother had married the woman they fixed him up with, instead of getting carried away with this one, the line would have been better continued.

DEAR MISS MANNERS:

How does one properly express sympathy to someone who is determined to not acknowledge their own grief? I don't want my friend to think that I didn't hear her insist that her grandmother's death was a "blessing" that ended long suffering; but I don't want her to think that I don't see that she is grieving despite her protests.

GENTLE READER:

Miss Manners supposes you could back her up against the wall and rail at her about her loss until she breaks into tears. No doubt it would make you feel better.

But your friend has the nerve to hold a different idea of what makes her feel better. Miss Manners is afraid that you have to respect that. Presuming that you already made the proper expression of sympathy, which is to offer your condolences and to say anything kind you can about the deceased, all you can do is to make yourself available if she indicates a need for more comfort. You cannot force it out of her.

⌒ Acknowledging Condolences ⌒

DEAR MISS MANNERS:

I know that mourning customs have almost disappeared, but I have seen black-bordered stationery in a store, and I wonder if I should get it for my mother to answer our condolence notes. (My father recently died.) She has put off writing them at all, saying she doesn't feel up to it, but it seems to me unkind to people, many of whom wrote very nice letters about my father, just to leave their condolences unacknowledged or answered by an impersonal card. What would you advise? My mother says she is too depressed, but would probably do what I insisted on.

STB

Dear Mrs. Perfect,

I was so sorry to read your sad news. In the few times that I was privileged to meet Mr. Perfect, he came to represent, for me, the ideal of a gentleman whom I hope some day to emulate. Please accept my deepest sympathy.

Sincerely yours,

Sean Batchitt

A letter of condolence. A man's private writing paper, marked with his initials.

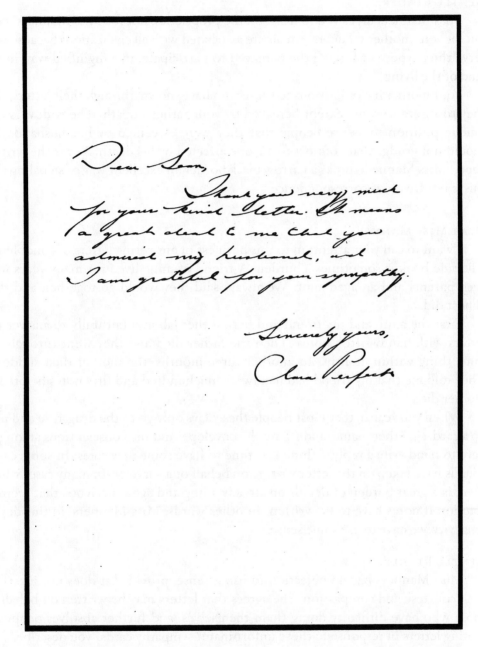

Dear Sam,

Thank you very much for your kind letter. It means a great deal to me that you admired my husband, and I am grateful for your sympathy.

Sincerely yours,

Clara Perfect

Letter of reply to letter of condolence. This is necessarily brief, because Mrs. Perfect has hundreds of them to write.

GENTLE READER:

Miss Manners urges you to insist on the proprieties, not for Miss Manners' sake, but for your mother's. Funeral rituals are associated with all civilizations because they serve the purpose of forcing the bereaved to participate, in a dignified way, in the land of the living.

Your mother has obligations to those who have shown, through their letters, that they too were to some extent bereaved by your father's death. The widow is in a unique position to assure people that they were esteemed by her husband. She should not grudge that comfort to anyone affected by his death. As for the writing paper, Miss Manners thinks a narrow black border an excellent way of signaling that this is not frivolous correspondence.

DEAR MISS MANNERS:

I want to call your attention to this business of answering letters of condolence. The rule book is sometimes a burden. A friend of mine lived for many years with aged parents and an aged aunt. We always said they would go together, and they almost did.

First the aunt, and my friend and her mother labored faithfully to answer the letters with handwritten notes. Then the father died and they went through the same thing within months. In another three months, the mother died suddenly. They told me that my friend had handwritten a hundred and fifty notes before her mother died.

When you realize that most people these days only go to the drugstore and pick up a card, sign their name, and stamp the envelope, and the conscientious among us have to handwrite a reply, I think it is time to have some new rules. In some cases, friends have taken on the letter writing on behalf of a survivor. In many cases where there is a great burden of details on already ailing and aged survivors, that seems a solution if notes have to be written. In other words, Miss Manners, in this day of longevity, we have to use some sense.

GENTLE READER:

Miss Manners has no objection to using sense, provided it does not interfere with courtesy and compassion. She agrees that letters may be written on behalf of those who have difficulty doing them themselves, and further absolves people of writing letters in response to those unfortunate "sympathy cards" you describe.

What Miss Manners considers important is that a personal expression of feelings about a death be acknowledged in an equally personal fashion, by, or on behalf of, the closest survivors. This may be done over a period of many months, but for anyone to send out form letters about a death—which is what printed sympathy cards or acknowledgments are—is callous. Burdensome as it may be, it offers the comfort of knowing that one is representing the deceased to those who cared about him.

DEAR MISS MANNERS:

My dear husband passed away last week, and I am concerned about doing the correct acknowledgments. Do I send acknowledgments to everyone who attended the funeral service? Do I acknowledge sympathy cards purchased in a card shop? Anyone who brought food to my house? Contributions? People who wrote me beautiful letters? I received about two hundred condolences—where do I draw the line?

GENTLE READER:

After you have written a letter to each person who wrote you or sent a contribution in your husband's name, however long that takes, you may draw the line. (Of course, you thanked donors of food as they brought it.)

The charitable contributions, of whatever size, were made on behalf of your husband and you must represent him in expressing gratitude. And any person who cares enough about him or you or both to write a letter should be appreciated, and answered in kind. "Thank you for your kindness. It means a great deal to me" will do, if it is in your own hand.

Miss Manners will then defend you from people who believe that funeral appearances or sympathy cards should be acknowledged—and some of these will attack, simply because people love to torture the bereaved on any excuse—on the grounds that attending the funeral is simply a mark of respect to your husband and an outlet for their own sorrow at his death, and that greeting cards are an impersonal and minimal form of communication.

~ Ending Mourning ~

DEAR MISS MANNERS:

Several doors up the street from my house is one of those street-side shrines—the memorials set up by friends and family at the site where someone has been killed.

It was set up over six months ago by high school students where one of their friends crashed his car and was killed. The offending telephone pole was decorated with a large Irish flag inscribed yearbook-style, votive candles, flowers, and many small mementos.

Never beautiful to my eyes, the display has been neglected and is now little more than a pile of trash. I walk past it several times a day and I'm tired of looking at it. I'd like to remove it, but . . .

Is there a standard period of tolerance for such displays? Though it's not in front of my house, do I have any right to remove it or must I persuade my neighbor to do so? Should I just forget it until the seniors have gone to college in the fall and won't be around to refresh it if it's removed?

GENTLE READER:

You do see the pathos, and not just the unsightliness, in these shrines, don't you? However miserable a heap of wrinkled balloons and rain-soaked teddy bears may appear, it symbolizes the anguish of the bereaved in wanting to assure the dead that they are not forgotten.

The problem, sad to say, is that the symbols, if not the people, are forgotten. Even the most assiduous mourners are not likely to attend to grave sites daily, which is why these should be located in dedicated places with custodial care. While Miss Manners will not allow you to refer to the display you mention as trash, she agrees that makeshift memorials abandoned in public space do take on that appearance and character.

To clean this up without violating the spirit in which it was built, she suggests notifying the high school that it is time for the students to collect what they want to preserve, and to think about a more lasting tribute to their friend.

⁓ Resuming Social Life ⁓

DEAR MISS MANNERS:

I would welcome instruction in the etiquette of bereavement, particularly in how the remaining member of a couple resumes relationships with couples who were friends before the mate's death. It is now three months since my wife passed away, and there are at least four couples with whom we had been friendly, couples who were solicitous during my wife's illness and who attended her funeral service, but who have made no effort since to get in touch with me.

I hesitate to get in touch with them. Indeed, I am under the impression that it is their social obligation to resume the relationship under the altered circumstances. Shouldn't they at least call to see how I am getting on, and perhaps invite me to come by for dinner or drinks or something sociable? I admit I am hurt and entertain the terrible thought that these people were friendly because they only liked my wife.

But rather than sulk and feel sorry for myself, I would like to bring my feelings in the situation under control. Is my experience an unusual one? Should I call them and see how they are getting on (but doesn't that look as if I am angling for an invitation)? Shall I invite them to come visit me? (But I hate cooking or preparing for guests. My wife did that.) I welcome your comments and suggestions.

GENTLE READER:

Miss Manners' comment is that your situation is a very usual one, and her suggestion is that someone—in your case, you—had better do something about it.

Often, with the refusal of the society to recognize forms for bereavement after the funeral, people simply do not know what to do. As there is no official mourning period agreed upon, they are afraid of intruding into yours with festive invitations. Another possibility is that these people have not discovered that it is impossible in modern society, for many reasons, to adhere to the once prevalent but always silly custom of entertaining only pairs and not individuals. Widows are more likely to be victims of this ridiculous notion than widowers, because women tend to live longer than men.

In either case, the social burden is put on the bereaved person, which is unfair because such a person is already in an emotionally weakened state. But shouldering it is, as you realize, better than the alternative, which is sulking.

In your normal state, you do not invent trouble for yourself by considering whether your friends will interpret your kindness in inquiring after them as angling for an invitation. Please cease that whole line of thinking. You can only flatter them by saying outright, "I am ready to see people again, and I've missed you."

You must also stop thinking that you cannot entertain people at home simply because you now have to do the work, instead of your wife. Hating to cook is an extremely poor idea for people who live alone. Your entertaining need not be as elaborate as was hers, but you can surely provide some sort of food and drinks to your friends. And if you can't, you can take them out. Miss Manners hopes that these problems will be considered when people start parroting the idea that formal customs of mourning—including a general recognition of when mourning ends—are barbarous.

DEAR MISS MANNERS:

Several times over the last ten years, we've invited the same couple to be our guests for a weekend during the summer. Unfortunately, this past winter the husband died. Now we'd like to invite the wife out for the weekend, but are afraid that a visit would bring up painful memories for her. On the other hand, we don't want not to invite her and have her think we don't want to see her any more. What should we do?

GENTLE READER:

You need not worry that you are in danger of reminding your friend that her husband is dead. Miss Manners can assure you that the lady remembers this perfectly well without your help.

However, you are bound to influence your friend's mood this summer, whatever you decide to do. One way would be to invite her as usual and provide her with the comfort of talking with her about her husband when she's feeling low, but also with the distractions of friendship and your usual summer activities. Alternatively, you could drop her, leaving her to spend the summer brooding that she has not only lost her husband but her friends—or people she assumed were her friends until she discovered that she was only welcome as part of a couple.

Just don't try to tell Miss Manners that you would do this lady a favor by cutting her from your visiting list. People who never mention the deceased to the bereaved, or who leave them alone with their pain, have an inflated sense of themselves if they imagine that the pain only exists if they mention it. They are equally deluded to think they can dispel it. What friends can do that is important is to offer their friendship.

～ Remembering ～

DEAR MISS MANNERS:

Three years ago (almost exactly), at my high school, four boys were killed in a car accident. I knew all four and wrote letters to their families and attended their funerals.

Today I was reminded of one of them by a song on the radio. It reminded me of how much I miss him and how I still think of him and of what a kind and funny person he was.

I was struck by the urge to write to his family again to tell them that he won't be forgotten, that people still think of him fondly. I was unsure as to whether or not this would be appropriate for many reasons—I don't want to dredge up more grief for them and I don't want to intrude on their loss, which still must be very painful. Please help me choose the correct thing to do!

GENTLE READER:

It is to sit down at your desk and write that letter immediately. Miss Manners can hardly think of anything more comforting to the family than knowing that the memories and grief they feel are still shared by others. Your misgivings are not only misplaced—they contribute to the wall of silence that makes the bereaved feel as if the person they lost is not only gone, but forgotten.

II. *Answers to Questions Nobody Asked*

EVERY SO OFTEN, Miss Manners goes balmy and starts answering questions that nobody asked. She asks your indulgence and your compassion. Those who know what it is to have a head full of information that never comes up in the conversation—old baseball statistics, the histories of minor characters in minor operas, the world's records for undistinguished feats—will understand.

Here are some samples of what is clogging up poor Miss Manners' brain:

The correct form of address by the Holy Roman Emperor when speaking of himself to others, or when addressing himself, for that matter, is "*Ma Majesté.*"

When giving a private ball in one's house, one must provide an awning and a red carpet from one's front door to the street.

Sable is the correct fur to wear when one is in mourning.

A gentleman may express his passion for a married woman in a letter, but the letter must not suggest that his love has been looked upon with favor in any way that would be intelligible to a jury of their peers.

When paying a formal call on someone one does not care to visit, a lady may have her chauffeur leave her card, but there must be a woman in the car, although it needn't be the lady whose card is being left.

It is permissible to dress one's chambermaids and parlormaids in the color theme of one's house in the morning, provided they change to their black uniforms with afternoon aprons, collars and cuffs for luncheon.

If a gentleman does not have a silk house suit to wear to dinner at home alone or with his family, he may make do with wearing an old dinner jacket.

If one has chartered a train for the convenience of one's wedding guests, one should enclose an engraved card, four and a quarter inches by three and a half inches, giving the times of arrival and departure of the "special train" and serving, when presented to the conductor, as the ticket.

The only circumstances in which a host and hostess may sit next to each other at their own dinner party is when they have a horseshoe-shaped table and sit at the outside center of its curve.

There is no known correct way to eat pistachio nuts. Nevertheless, they are delicious. The pistachio nut must therefore be Nature's way of teaching us self-control. If so, it doesn't work.

It is wrong to wear diamonds before dusk, except on one's marriage rings. Before, after and during breakfast, luncheon and dinner, it is vulgar to wear a mixture of colored precious stones. It is always a comfort to know that so many things one can't afford to do anyway are vulgar.

"The numbers at a dinner should not be less than the Graces, nor more than the Muses," stated the Roman formula, when guests lay three to a couch. If the Graces are busy, you could try the Fates, who are not asked out as often.

"Your good friend" is the letter closing used not only by sweet, old-fashioned children but by kings and queens when they write to presidents.

An official speech made in front of the British monarch should begin "May it please Your Majesty," but one should not expect reassurance at the end that it has.

Restaurants are not exempt from the rule that one never puts a filled plate in front of anyone, with the exception of the soup plate, but offers platters from which the person can serve himself. However, few restaurants in the United States realize this.

The only circumstances under which a lady can properly call upon a gentleman are if he is old and ill and has requested the visit. Whether he is also rich is irrelevant, but it never hurts.

If you habitually travel with a valet or maid, it is necessary to ascertain beforehand that your hosts will be able to accommodate extra servants.

A lady and gentleman who pay a call and find no one at home leave three cards— one of hers and two of his. Hers is for the lady of the house and one of his is for the lady and one for the gentleman. If this seems excessive, they can just go away and deny having ever been there.

An introduction made at a ball, for the purpose of forming couples to dance, does not count later. While other formal rules are going out of use, this one is actually being expanded. There are many instances nowadays of people who have been briefly in each other's arms but do not afterward recognize each other socially.

The title by which a sovereign is addressed is called his *petit titre*, but he may also have a *grand titre* and a *titre moyen*. The *grand titre* may include "the names of the fictitious as well as of the real dominions" he claims, which is to say that he can slip in all the places he used to have or thinks he is entitled to have. The *titre moyen* may be fairly long, but it is expected to be truthful.

The wide-tined fork is considered a more correct implement for eating ice cream than is the spoon, although the spoon is not actually incorrect. This leeway is permitted because any fool can see that ice cream will drip through the fork tines, however wide.

There now. Miss Manners feels better for having gotten all that out. Thank you for your kind patience.

Acknowledgments

DAVID HENDIN is the treasured colleague and friend to whom the author is most indebted for every stage of this book, beginning with the suggestion that it be written. She is also grateful to Angela von der Lippe, Kimberley Heatherington and those who worked on the first edition: Thomas A. Stewart, Diana Drake and Jennifer Georgia. Her Gentle Readers were kind enough to entrust her with their questions, for which she gives them thanks.

Index

ability, 177, 460, 737–38
academic institutions. *See* school
Academy Awards, 224, 717
accidents, 122, 565
   embarrassing, 556–57
Achilles, 184
acknowledgment of condolences, 815, 818, 819
acquaintances, 118, 142
   business, 206
   social, 206
actors, 764
address, forms of, 56–57, 99–100, 106–9, 113,
      119, 120, 128, 206, 502–3, 659, 690, 825
   on cards, 596–99, 610–11
   of ex-relatives, 659–60, 661, 666
   invitations to couples with different names,
      543–44
   of patients, 490
   on wedding presents, 433
   on writing paper, 594
address, street, 235, 272, 401
adjustment:
   of bra straps, 633
   of stocking seams, 633
adolescents, 52, 315, 321–23, 329–32
adoption, 63
adult. *See* grown-ups
adults, 75, 119, 177, 211, 305, 317, 318, 326, 404,
      669, 784, 786
   consenting, 111
advertisements, 143, 214
advice, giving of, 65, 286, 287, 793
   to pregnant women, 38
   unsolicited, 613
affair:
   getting over, 264–65
   having an, 262–66, 656, 661

age, 80, 86, 96, 97, 113, 150–51, 177, 209–10, 218,
      233, 307, 320
airplanes, 141, 766–70
   indecency on, 770
   meals on, 766, 768–69
alcoholic beverages. *See* cocktails; drinking;
      drinks
Alexander the Great, 694
Alexandra, Queen, 642
Alice in Wonderland (Carroll), 169
allergies, 124, 569, 590, 744–45
alumni, 309, 316
ambassadors, 707
America, manners in, 53, 99–100, 111–12, 141, 145,
      150, 161, 162–63, 172–73, 202, 328, 405,
      581–82, 687, 694, 707
American flag, the, 696
Americans abroad, 764–67
ancestors, 225
"and family," 358
   on invitations, 401
"and guest," 358, 386, 404, 543, 567
   on invitations, 401
anecdotes, 214, 287
animals, 132
ankles, 133
anniversaries, 254, 677–84
   fiftieth. *See* anniversaries, golden
   golden, 679, 680, 681, 682
   posthumous, 684
   presents, 679–80
   rings, 679–80
   silver, 679, 681, 683
   sixtieth, 679
   thirtieth, 680
   twenty-fifth. *See* anniversaries,
     silver

announcements, 47–48, 63
  anniversary, 683
  birth, 47–51, 61
  birth, formal, 48–49, 48 (example)
  birth, informal, 48–49
  divorce, 651
  graduation, 51, 309, 311–12
  illicit, 406
  of pregnancy, 38
  presents and, 431
  wedding, 51, 317, 369, 386, 394, 404–5, 672
announcing guests, 568
answering invitations. *See* invitations, replies to;
    replies
answering machines, 147, 237, 239–40, 809
answers. *See* replies
antifeminism. *See* sexism
apartments, 137–38, 139–40
Aphrodite, 741
apologies, 499, 500, 562–65, 566, 767
  accepting, 565
applauding, 123, 724, 730, 731
  for oneself, 733
appointments, breaking, 504
arguments, 256–58, 814
aristocracy, 460
arm rests, on airplanes, 767
arms, 341
Artemis, 741
art exhibits, shushing in, 726–27
artificial insemination, 40
ashtrays, 448, 454
assistance, 114, 119–21, 122, 792, 799
  at home, 268, 269, 520
at home cards. *See* cards, at home
attendants, 381–83, 419, 424. *See also* best man;
        bridesmaids; groomsmen; maid of honor;
        matron of honor
Austen, Jane, 145
authors, 719
automobiles, 147–49, 419, 696, 711, 736, 825
  mechanics, 490, 491
  opening doors to, 134–35
available people. *See* single people
awards, accepting, 717–18
awning and carpet, for a ball, 525

babies, 42, 58, 60–69, 346–47

  gender of, 41–42, 63
  names of, 56, 63
  nursing, 64
  see also showers, baby
baby-sitters, 67, 68–70, 275, 346, 384
bachelor's dinner, 378, 417
background music. *See* music, background
back packs, 150
bad moods, 258, 290
balls, 826
  charity, 525–26
  inaugural, 705
  private, 525, 825
banks, 333
baptism. *See* christenings
bar, 427, 450
bar and bat mitzvahs, 305, 529
Barber of Seville, The (Rossini), 724
bartenders, 421
bathing suits, 642, 644, 735, 783
  bikinis, 642
bath linens. *See* trousseau
bathrooms, 240, 249, 256, 278, 283, 553–54
beaches, 783
  suntan, 146
beards, 126–27
beauty pageants, 740–41
beauty salons, tipping in, 762
beaux, 620. *See also* boyfriends
bed linens. *See* trousseau
bedrooms, assigning, 277–78
beds:
  hotel, 775
  making, 94, 275
  receiving in, 272
beer, 479, 754
beloved, 620. *See also* lover
bequests, 289–90
bereaved. *See* mourners
bereavement, 344, 821
Berith Milah. *See* Bris
best man, 413, 417, 545, 674. *See also* attendants
Bible, the, 422, 792
bigotry, 18, 209
bills, 25, 70
  in beauty salons, 763
  checking, 761
  in restaurants, 755–56

wedding. *See* weddings, costs
birth, 268, 316, 381, 387, 415
    calling after, 269
    illegitimate, 49–50
    parties, 37
birth announcements. *See* announcements, birth
birth control, 218, 221
birthday, 661
    parties, 81, 89, 92, 429, 534, 684
    parties, for children, 87–91
    presents, 431, 618
birth defects, 42–43
black:
    wedding guests wearing, 414–15
    worn at christenings, 59
    see also mourning
black tie, 16, 413, 625, 630, 700, 771. *See also* dress,
    evening
blame, 498–500
blind persons, 119–20
blue jeans, 765
boasting. *See* bragging
bodyguards, 711
body language, 112
Bonaparte, Napoleon, 695
bonuses, 475–76, 481
booing, at the opera, 724
Book of Common Sense Etiquette (Roosevelt), 179
books, 151, 287, 328, 384, 719
    sending of, 123–24
bookstore-cafés, 759–60
bosom, display of, 642
boss, 462–63, 648, 473, 475, 480–81, 505
boss's wife, 261–62
bowls:
    cereal, 200
    two-handled, 449
bows, 687, 724
boyfriends, 134, 338, 345. *See also* gentleman friend
boys, 41–42, 51, 87, 305, 329–30
bragging, 173, 218, 222–23, 224, 225, 309, 315, 422,
    460, 526, 612, 744, 782
brassieres, 632, 633
"Bravo!," 724
bread, 513
    and butter, 169, 181–82, 513, 522, 582
    at formal dinners, 582
    as a pusher, 160–61, 167

    in restaurants, 582
    sopping sauces with, 167–68, 199
    at tea, 521
    toast, 199
bread-and-butter letters. *See* thank-you notes,
    from houseguests
breakfast, 145–46, 272, 278, 513
    on shipboard, 771
breaking an engagement. *See* engagements, broken
breaking up, 350–53
breastfeeding. *See* babies, nursing
Bridal Color Code, 673
bridal party. *See* wedding party
bridal portraits, 430
bridegrooms, 46, 371, 378, 381, 390, 391, 413, 417,
    423, 430, 672, 673
brides, 62, 318, 358, 362, 371, 378, 380, 381, 413,
    422, 423, 429, 430, 437, 480, 624, 672,
    673
    giving away of, 375, 665, 670, 673
    grown-up, 670
bride's luncheon, 417
bridesmaids, 368, 371, 374, 381, 417, 419
    dresses, 413–14
    presents, 384
    see also attendants
bridesmaids' and ushers' dinner, 417
bringing up children. *See* child rearing
Bring Your Own Bottle (BYOB), 518
Bris, 59–60
Britain. *See* England
Brith. *See* Bris
brothers. *See* relatives, brothers
buffets, 554–55, 579, 763
burping, 294–95
buses, 102–3, 123, 135–36, 141, 146, 149–51
business, 233, 459–61, 478, 487–88, 720–21
    cocktail parties, 478, 479
    colleagues, 16
    dinners, 166, 478
    entertaining, 477–81
    false friendship in, 493–94
    language, 659
    letters, 247, 480, 592, 605
    letter salutations, 482–83
    lunches, 166, 474, 478
    manners in, 25, 468
    personal, 595

business (*continued*)
  suits, 623, 628–30, 631–32
  telephoning, 484–87
businessmen, 468, 474
businesswomen, 468, 473, 474
butlers, 455, 465, 568, 589, 708–9, 710, 711, 802

cads, 137, 330, 331–32, 368, 370
cake, 60, 146, 182
  christening, 58
  tea, 521
  wedding, 377, 419, 425, 428
calculators, using in public, 761
California, 582
Caller ID, 236–38
callers, 802
calling cards. *See* cards
Callisthenes, 694
calls, paying, 269, 272–73, 317, 536
  on acquaintances, 268
  with condolences, 799, 802, 812
  formal, 49, 594, 811, 825
  on gentlemen, 826
  on new parents, 61
calls, telephone. *See* business, telephoning; telephone
call waiting, 239, 485
camera telephone, 245–46
candles, 568
candy, 182–83, 568. *See also* chocolate
candy dishes, 448
canes, 119
car. *See* automobiles
cards, 49, 55, 240, 268, 521, 592, 594, 596–601, 825
  acknowledgment, 815, 819
  of admittance, 700
  at home, 405–6
  business, 598
  for children, 600
  of formal invitation, 594
  "hold-the-date," 529
  informal, 441, 442, 592, 594, 596–98
  invitations on, 58
  menu, 568
  new informal, 592
  place, 568, 588
  reception invitation, 392, 399
  reminder, 594

  response, 399, 403, 421
  turning edges of, 268, 597
  in wedding invitations, 392, 399
  see also greeting cards; playing cards; writing paper
careers, 53, 214, 217, 226–27
carpooling, 148
Carroll, Lewis, 169
carving, 585
Casual Friday, 628–29
caterers, 358, 359, 368
celebrations, 651
  after first communion, 307–8
  after subsequent weddings, 670
celebrities, 17, 226, 713–23
cellular telephones, 118, 234–35, 242–45, 482–86, 501–2, 579–80
censoring music, 83
centerpiece, 568
ceremonies:
  divorce, 651–52
  graduation, 309
  wedding, 389–90
champagne, 58, 287, 426, 431, 450, 525, 588, 746, 748, 794
  at weddings, 359
changing babies. *See* diapering
chapel, 670
chaperones, 332, 382
chargers, 572–73
charitable donations, 614, 801, 803, 819
charity, 790
  soliciting for, 434–35
charm, 459
chauffeurs, 711
cheating, 738–39
checking coats, 751–52
  ladies', 751–52
checks:
  as presents, 682
  in a restaurant, 478
  splitting, 755–56
cheek stashing, 166
child rearing, 85, 89, 128, 172
children, 16, 27, 51, 57, 61–62, 68–70, 75, 80–81, 83–84, 85, 87–91, 93–94, 99, 119, 123, 124, 171, 177, 182, 209, 210–11, 218, 219, 228, 241–42, 265–66, 299, 305, 309, 316, 329,

343, 344, 345, 364, 367, 371, 480, 617–19,
641–42, 663–64, 675–76, 713, 759–60, 786
addressing adults, 502
arguments in front of, 257–58
artwork by, 454
censoring music of, 83
on Christmas, 791
conversing with, 207–8
correction of, 28, 75–76, 77–78, 90–91, 94–95,
179–80, 256–57
courteous, 88
divorce and, 652, 662, 663–64, 666–68,
675–76
of fiancé, 672
first, 50, 51
giving anniversary parties, 681–82
helping to serve, 586
illegitimate, 263–64
-in-law, 28
names for, 53–54
not inviting, 403, 404
at the opera, 728–30
at parents' weddings, 411, 422, 670, 674–75
prejudice against, 73–74
at restaurants, 94–95
second, 44–45, 50
served first at picnics, 172
small, 784
teaching of, 74–75
unrelated, 76–77
writing letters, 88–89
Children, The (Wharton), 660
china, 357, 433, 436, 448, 452, 520, 588
serving dishes, 449
see also trousseau
China, manners in, 161, 555
chivalry, 128–29, 131, 133–34
chocolate, 146
chocolate, hot, 521
choking, 294
christenings, 58–60
Christmas, 266, 505, 609–13, 787–89, 793–94
cards. *See* greeting cards, Christmas
caroling, 792
computerized, 789–90
dinner, 793
hypocrisy, 790–91
letters, 592, 609–13

lists, 787
open house, 792
pageants, 793
parties, 478
presents, 431, 475, 614, 618
traditional, 792
Christmas Carol, A (Dickens), 792
chupah, 420
church, 58, 106, 122–23, 308, 317
dress for, 637–38
cigarettes. *See* smoking
cigars. *See* smoking
Cinderella, 660
citizen participation, 298–99
city living, 137–38, 142, 144
class, social, 23–24, 31–32
classroom parties, 92–93
cleaning up, 172, 252, 710–11
cleaning women. *See* maids
clearing the table, 179
clergy, 58, 372, 417, 419, 421, 681, 799
-women, 106
clerks, 466, 499, 503
clothes. *See* dress
clubs, 197, 742–43
proposing members, 741
resigning from, 741–42
cocktail(s), 747
hour, 427
parties, 478, 513, 523–25, 629–30, 636, 672
coffee, 444, 447, 521–22, 560, 581, 588
cups, 449, 569
pot, 446
service, 445–46
tray, 586
coffee houses, 125–26, 244–45
cold, common, 66
cold voice, the, 23
colleagues, 122, 151, 474
consideration of, 471–72
college, 142, 217, 310, 311–12, 317, 323–24, 468–74,
475, 476, 479, 480–81, 485–86, 487–88,
509, 793
changing names at, 53, 54
comfort, 567, 626
commands, 205
commencement balls. *See* proms
commitments, 338–39, 357

communication, 16, 204–5, 213, 216, 220–21, 234–35, 246–47, 272, 780, 819
communion, first, 307–8
companions, 403, 711
company manners, 173, 249
competition, 740
complaints, 138, 171, 490, 771
compliments, 62, 86–87, 228–30, 307
  accepting, 230, 717–18
  giving, 228–29
computers, 789–90
  laptop, in restaurants, 758
concerts, 514, 550–51, 727–28
  children at, 728–30
  toe tapping at, 727–28
condescension, 138, 209
condolence calls, 269, 800
condolences, 779, 799, 800, 803, 811–15
  acknowledging, 803
confidence, 460
confirmation, 307–8
Confucius, 555
congratulations, 39, 230, 305, 366, 423–24, 779
  on pregnancy, 39–40
Congress, 687
containers, food, 161, 171–72, 757–58
conventions, political, 300, 523
conventions, social, 61, 86–87, 128, 143, 601–3
  of mourning, 821
  phrases, 206, 536
  wedding, 673
conversation, 65–66, 85, 119, 122, 144, 151, 171, 173, 207–8, 212, 213–16, 232–33, 241–42, 307, 469, 544, 551, 560, 569, 576, 663, 720
  art of, 221, 231–32
  at a ball, 526
  books and, 552
  boring, 233
  children's, 792
  conventional, 788–89
  at dinner, 578, 585
  distance between acquaintances, 112
  at family dinners, 252
  hazardous topics, 214–15
  hogs, 230–31
  with hospital patients, 287
  about oneself, 223–24
  openers, 214

pieces, 568
with pregnant women, 38
'round the hearth, 255–56
with strangers, 769
at the White House, 703
cooks, 576, 708, 709, 710
correcting:
  in letters, 605
  mistakes, 742
  others, 27–28, 107, 126–27, 163, 217, 232
correspondence:
  business, 107, 482–84, 592, 594, 605
  social, 441
  summer, 779
corsages. See flowers, wearing
cotillions, 317–18
coughing, 293–94, 724
couples, 128, 197, 345–46, 357, 570–71, 576–78, 665
  adult, 318
  bridal, 419
  engaged, 541
  homosexual, 103
  introducing, 104–5
  married, 128, 316, 401, 541, 677–78, 681
  names on cards, 594
  newly married, 394
  seated apart, 570, 577–78, 582
  unmarried, 459
courses, 146, 155, 513, 581 (full list)
  cheese, 445, 582, 588
  dessert, 161–62, 450, 585, 588
  entree, 582
  first, 449, 573, 580, 585
  fish, 162, 449, 585, 588
  fourteen, 581
  fourth, 585
  fruit, 157
  meat, 162, 170, 188, 450, 585, 588, 710
  salad, 162, 581–82, 585
  soup, 450
  third, 585
courtesy, 134
courtroom, 626–27
courtship, 325–53
  slow, 338
  suitors, 657
cousins. See relatives, cousins
co-workers. See colleagues

cracking knuckles, 297
cream, 446, 521
crispness, in business dealings, 460
criticism, 76–77, 750
cross dressing, 627–28
crossing one's knees, 133
crumbing the table, 585–86
crumbs, 126–27, 182
crystal, 433, 449, 450, 452
curtains, 211
curtsies, 687–90
customers, 491–95, 496–97, 501–2, 551, 750
cut, direct, the, 137
cutting remark, the, 137

dances, 332
   dinner, 305
   duty, 320
   private, 315, 320–24
   at school, 329–30
dancing, 307, 371, 514, 526, 794
   at weddings, 376, 419
dating, 70, 262, 325–26, 330–31, 332, 335–39,
      343–44, 347, 348, 469–70, 794
   first dates, 334
   Internet, 334, 343–44
daughters, 317, 320, 331, 346, 364, 367, 392–93
daughters-in-law. See in-laws, daughter
Day of Judgment, 782
death, 268, 381, 799–800, 813–14
   condolence calls, 269
   saying good-bye before, 288
   see also mourning
deathbed scene, the, 289–90
debutantes, 317–20, 687
   dresses, 408–9
debuts, 317
De Civilitate, 225
Decline and Fall of the Roman Empire, The (Gibbon),
   782
defining jobs, 129–30
degrees:
   academic, 105–6, 602–3
   honorary, 106
   medical, 602
delicate condition. See pregnancy
demitasse, 449
   cups, 447, 449

spoons, 445, 447
democracy, 23, 715
demonstrations, political, 300
demureness. See shyness
departure, of guests, 425, 555–56
depression, 259–60, 291, 292, 578–79, 719, 794,
      800, 815. See also bad moods
de-proving others, 26–27
dessert, 145–46, 156, 172, 586, 744, 746
   forks and spoons, 161–62, 575, 586
   plate, 575, 586
   service, 170
destination wedding, 387–88
diamond jubilee, 679
diamonds, 362, 645, 806, 825
diapering, 65
diaries, 259, 569
Dickens, Charles, 792
diet, 590
dignity, 121, 490
dining room, 521, 576, 584, 712
dinner, 67, 154, 164–65, 175, 334, 417
   breaking engagements, 545, 570–71, 703
   broken engagements, 368, 564
   Christmas, 793
   company, 626
   formal, 158, 179–80, 707
   formal, invitations to, 567–68, 582
   hour, 525, 546
   houseguests at, 275
   houseguests treating hosts to, 276
   to meet prospective in-laws, 363
   Noah's Ark type, 577
   parties, 157, 513–14, 528, 560, 576
   partner, 568
   perfect little, 513
   seated, 67
   on shipboard, 771
   singles at, 541, 578–79
   state, 703
   Thanksgiving, 785–86
   wedding rehearsal, 385–86, 391
   at the White House, 545, 699, 700–707
dinner-dance, 305
dinner jackets, 825
diplomacy, 263
diplomatic parties, 477
disabled persons, 110, 118–22, 148–49, 282

disasters, medical, 557–58
discipline, 75–76, 77–78, 89
discomfort, 171
discotheques, 526
discretion, 663, 783
divorce, 15, 264, 266, 345–46, 358, 362, 368, 381,
    387, 409, 430, 541, 606, 651–68
  changing names after, 53, 55, 659
  divorced parents at weddings, 392
  divorcée, 55, 659, 662
  reaction to, 655
  relationships after, 661–63, 666–67
doctorates, 100, 105, 106, 602–3
doctors, 100, 286, 490–91
  female, 104–5, 491, 602
  medical, 104–5, 602
  of philosophy (Ph.D.), 105, 106, 602–3
dogs, 124–25, 205
doilies, 588
doormen, 763
doors, 128, 527
  answering, 269–70
Double Insult, the, 76–77
double-sheet:
  letter paper, 592
  wedding invitation, 399
  writing paper, 592
Dr. *See* titles, Dr.
drapes, 211
drawing room, 445, 464, 569, 584–85, 588, 710,
    720
dreams, 221–22
dress, 16, 17, 82, 622–47
  afternoon, 521
  for anniversaries, 680
  for the beach, 647
  black, 803
  black on television, 722
  blue jeans, 622, 623, 634
  bridesmaid's, 413–14
  for business, 623, 461, 470, 628–30, 631–32
  categories of, 625
  children's, 83–84, 641–42
  cocktail, 629–30, 636
  codes of, 82–83, 528, 622–24, 628–29
  conservative, 806–7
  cutaway and grey trousers, 413
  daytime, 624, 637, 645

debutante's, 320, 408–9
  for dinner, 637–38
  for divorce, 652
  evening, 17, 624, 633–34, 673
  formal, 413, 624, 630, 631, 635
  formal daytime, 413
  at funerals, 803–4
  for high school reunion, 315
  informal, 624, 625, 628, 673
  for interviews, 461
  for jury duty, 626–27
  long, 377, 416
  for luncheon, 637–38
  men's, 623, 624, 632, 633–34
  men's shirts, 632
  morning, 627
  mother of the bride, 374
  optional, 625
  for picketing, 143
  for prom, 321–23
  semiformal, 625
  sports, 771
  street, 521
  suits, 413, 633–34
  summer, 624
  trains on, 641
  trouser suits, 631–32
  underwear, 632–33
  wedding, 427, 624, 673, 680
  for wedding guests, 413
  for weddings, 413, 414–15
  white, 639, 640
  at the White House, 700
  winter, 624
  women's, 470, 623, 624, 627–28, 631–32, 641
  see also mourning
dressing gowns, 252
dressing up, 514, 794
drinking, 323–24, 349, 427–28, 479, 635, 744, 748,
    794
  at business dinners, 478, 479
  at high tea, 522
drinks, 165, 546, 568, 576, 744
  mixed, 450
  watering, 749
drivers. *See* motorists
dropping in, 206–7, 269–71, 735
drugs, 743

Duchess of Windsor, 341
dueling, 136–37

Easter, 782–83
Easter Egg Rolling, at the White House, 782–83
eating, 145–46, 171, 523, 635, 724
    outdoors, 171–72
    pauses in, 171
    on shipboard, 771
    utensils, 160–61, 187–88
eavesdropping, 233, 758
education, 299, 315
elbows, 167
elderly persons, 121, 149, 210, 232–33
election parties, 523
elegance, 624
elevators, 113, 145, 152–53
elevenses, 771
email, 234, 235, 238, 246–47, 269, 279, 288, 313,
        314, 334, 343–44, 349, 438, 462, 463, 464,
        468, 482, 485, 487–88, 491
    of birth announcements, 47
    mass, 790
    spamming, 247–48
    see also Internet
embarrassment, 25, 82, 225, 254, 273, 460, 474,
        489, 503, 517, 556–57, 633, 775
emergencies, medical, 562
employees, 468–69, 470, 476, 478, 492, 505–6,
        508, 750
    of doctors, 502
    household, 465, 502–3
employer, 69, 455, 459, 461, 462, 464, 476, 505,
        508, 509
    of servants, 465, 502–3, 708–9
Employer Problem, the, 465
employment, name used in, 54
engagement party, 385
engagements, 268, 357, 657–58
    announcing to families, 672
    breaking social, 545
    broken, 368–70 (example of announcement),
        369–70, 545
    couples invited together, 541
    length of, 359
    parties, 672
    presents, 364
    previous, 539, 703

rings, 360, 361–62, 369, 643
England, manners in, 99–100, 163, 187, 368, 571,
        694–95, 765
English Gentlemen's Child, The (Sutherland), 589
engraving, 48–49, 358, 439, 592, 594
    partial, 594
    silver, 445
entertainers. See celebrities
entertaining, 67, 70, 138
    formal, 548–49
entertaining, business. See business, entertaining
entertainment, 145, 173
    adult, 91
    children's, 728–30
entourage, 714
envelopes, 399, 401, 592
    addressing, 601–3
    inner, of wedding invitations, 399
    outer, of wedding invitations, 401
equality, 134, 149, 478
Erasmus, 28, 225
escalators, 151–52
escorts, 578
ethnic jokes, 227–28
ethnic origin, and names, 53
etiquette:
    art of, 806
    of cultural centers, 729–30
    definition, 766, 806
    false definition of, 24–25, 115–16, 118, 154
    forms of, 31–33
    Procrustes School of, 372
Etiquette, Holy Subject of, 21–826
eulogies, 799, 803
euphemisms, 559
    for death, 813
    for women's underwear, 211–12
Europe, manners in, 112, 113, 141, 160, 163, 445,
        581–82
evening clothes, 143, 526, 643–44
    men's, 309, 413
    see also dress, evening
exchanging presents. See presents, exchanging
"Excuse me," 294, 737
excuses, 767
ex-husbands, 660–61, 665–66, 676
ex-lovers, 261, 349, 352–53
experience, 214, 460, 618

explanations, 346–47, 351, 562
ex-wives, 658, 659
eye contact, 112
eyeglasses, 411

falling asleep, 561
family, 62, 123, 177, 222, 249, 256–58, 264–65,
        275, 307, 316, 320, 357, 371, 389
    breakfast, 444
    of the bridegroom, 378, 388, 417
    at the deathbed, 289–90
    of the deceased, 799, 802, 812
    dinner, 159, 172–79, 200
    dinner, excusing children, 177
    discord in, 256–58, 264–66
    extended, 173
    formation of, 363
    gatherings, 289–90, 792
    at graduation, 309
    harmony, 174
    on invitations, 401
    loyalty, 82, 658
    manners, 249–50, 253
    multigenerational, 794
    names in, 53–54, 56
    news, 610
    nuclear, 659–60
    obligations to, 309
    shunning of, 266–67
    step-relatives, 660
    substituting business principles in, 254–55
    tree, 56
    at weddings, 371, 373
famine (and bad table manners), 164
fathers, 76–77, 394, 670, 673
    of the bride, 373, 419
    of the bridegroom, 419
    children's name for, 57
    courtesy towards, 173
    in divorce, 666–68
    divorced, 676
    of new baby, 49, 51
    passing on names, 56
    prospective, 38
    at showers, 46
    step-, 660
feelings, 61, 92, 147, 210, 213, 272, 284, 338, 340, 605
    fake, 290–91

    of others, 790
    wounded, 657
fiancé, 68, 363, 390, 672, 712
fiancée, 362, 645
fights, 132, 256–58, 357
filling in, 571
filling plates, 587, 826
finger bowls, 157, 575, 588
fingers, 160, 167–68, 172–73, 180–81, 186, 195
    licking, 172
fireplaces, 255–56, 748–49
"Fire Worship" (Hawthorne), 255
firing employees, 462, 505–7
first communion, 307–8
First Lady, 96, 687
first-name basis, establishing, 108. See also acquain-
        tances; names, first
fish. See courses, fish; food, fish
flatware, 444, 449, 588, 751
    placement after use, 170–71
    see also silver; table settings
flings, 653, 654
flirtation, 460, 479, 526
flower girl, 417, 674
flowers, 49, 58, 320, 350, 420, 549, 568, 572, 647,
        710, 711, 800
    enclosing cards with, 594
    at funerals, 801, 803, 812
    wearing, 320, 323, 647
    at weddings, 670
food, 69, 218, 252, 254, 792
    allergies, 94
    apples, 146, 189
    apricots, 189
    artichokes, 180, 581
    asparagus, 180–81, 581, 582
    bacon, 181
    for a ball, 525
    bananas, 146, 180, 189–90
    beautiful, 590
    berries, 190
    at business dinners, 478, 479
    butter, 164, 169, 195, 581
    canapes, 582, 584
    carry-out, 161
    cheese, 520, 581
    cheese snacks, 186
    cherries, 190

chicken, 173
Chinese, 161
chips and dip, 183
clams, 183–84, 581
at cocktail parties, 513
cookies, 513
corn-on-the-cob, 184
cucumber sandwiches, 426, 513
declining of, 168
dislikes, 94, 168–69
in drinks, 747
eclairs, 184
eggs, 185, 513, 522
fake, 185–86
finger, 173, 180–81
fish, 155, 187–88, 449, 581, 746
fish souffle, 576
for a formal dinner, 576, 581
french fries, 186
fried chicken, 146, 186
fruit, 143, 145–46, 189–90, 568, 588
fruits, 581
garlic, 198
garlic butter, 183, 184, 193, 199
garnish, 191
grapefruit, 146, 191
grapes, 190
hamburgers, 194
at high tea, 521–22
hot dogs, 186
ice cream, 191–93, 826
ice cream cones, 191–92
ice cream sodas, 192–93
ketchup, 186
kippers, 522
lobster, 193
meat, 146
nuts, 193–94
oranges, 190
oysters, 155
peaches, 190
pears, 146, 190
peas, 161, 194
pickles, 194
for picnics, 171–72
pineapple, 190
pizza, 161, 186
pomegranates, 195

potato chips, 196
potatoes, 164, 195
potatoes, baked, 195
poultry, 746
presents of, 515, 548
presents of, to mourners, 799, 802, 812, 819
prunes, 196
rejecting, in restaurants, 757
rolls, 169, 573, 582
salads, 513
sandwiches, 194, 197
sauces, 180, 202
sausages, 522
shish kebab, 198
shrimp, 198
sloppy joe, 186
snails, 183, 199
soups. *See* soups
spaghetti, 201–2
spareribs, 173
steak, 202
taffy, 202
for tea, 513
for tea parties, 521
television, 523
for Thanksgiving, 785–86
tomatoes, 203
veal, 746
vegetables, 145–46, 585
watermelon, 190
wedding, 426–27
see also cake
fools, 352
football, 732
footmen, 171, 240, 268, 465, 525, 568, 710
foreigners, imitation, 765
forgetting names, 97, 101–2
"forgive and forget," 565
forks, 160, 161–62, 165, 170–71, 172, 173, 174,
      180–82, 184, 185, 190–91, 194, 195–97,
      323, 571, 573, 747, 826
carving, 445
plastic, 171, 186
for snails, 199
and spaghetti, 201
use of, 158, 163
see also table setting, forks
formal dinner parties, 200

formality, 49, 109, 180, 189–90, 357, 396, 568–69,
     575, 626, 670
  vs. comfort, 626
formal service, 157, 196–97, 449. *See also* service, *à
     la russe*
four-letter words. *See* invective
fourth (or IV), 54–56
France, manners in, 272, 328, 569, 581
Franklin, Benjamin, 275–76
frankness. *See* honesty
free gift, 431
friends, 60–62, 68–69, 80, 81–82, 98, 99, 108,
     117, 118, 142, 225–26, 249, 259, 341–42,
     346, 349, 371, 461, 489, 507
  in business, 481, 764
  children as, 40, 93
  at christenings, 58
  at the deathbed, 289–90
  of the debutante's parents, 317, 320
  of the deceased, 802, 814
  after divorce, 653–54, 667–68
  dropping, 535
  dumping emotions on, 291, 292
  eligible, 578–79
  female, 349, 653, 657
  former, 661–62
  introductions to, 660
  new, 535
  old, 535
  at one's divorce, 651
  performances by, 229
  unmannerly, 276–77
  in the wedding party, 670
  writing to, 610–11
friendship, 120, 335, 382, 478, 481, 657, 822
  false, 493–95
Fry, Christopher, 222
full mouth, the, 165, 166, 172
funeral arrangements, 802
funerals, 25, 799–801, 802–5, 818, 819
  demeanor at, 804–5
  pallbearers, 802
  videoing of, 805
  see also services, memorial
fur:
  coats, 633, 752
  mink, 633
  during mourning, 825

gamekeepers, 711
garbage, 140
gardeners, 711
gay. *See* homosexuals
gender, 381–82, 544
gender-neutral terms, 129–30
genealogy, 56
generations, 53, 56, 77, 177, 255, 320, 617–18
  younger, 68–69
generosity, 436, 665, 683, 763
Generous Souls, 788
gentleman friend, 342. *See also* woman friend
gentleman of the household, 711
gentlemen, 17, 114, 121, 133–34, 135, 208, 209, 262,
     268, 320, 325–26, 330–31, 370, 459–60,
     467, 468, 521, 568, 633–34, 637–38, 641,
     652, 710, 719, 744 (definition)
  language of, 231–32
  presents from, 619
  young, 330–31, 634
  see also ladies and gentlemen
gentlewomen. *See* ladies
Germany, manners in, 100
gifts. *See* presents
girlfriends, 345, 348
  former, 261
girls, 51, 86, 87, 305, 317, 329–30
  young, 229, 317–20
given name. *See* names, first
giving away the bride. *See* brides, giving away of
glasses, 190, 747
  brandy, 450
  champagne, 450
  clinking, 748
  liqueur, 450
  plastic, 520
  sherry, 450
  smashing, 420, 748–49
  stemmed, 588
  unstemmed, 450
  water, 588
  wine, 450, 588
  see also trousseau
gloves, 16, 17, 521, 635–37, 700
  eighteen-button, 635, 636
  white, 635, 636
God, 26, 60, 106, 123, 174, 178, 183, 193, 201, 224,
     275, 338, 359, 420, 605, 638, 690, 783

godparents, 18, 58–60
gold diggers, 331
Good Behavior (Nicolson), 555
"good day," 207
"good morning," 207, 252
Googling, 248–49
gossip, 137, 214, 225–27, 272–73, 486
governesses, 711
grace, at meals, 165
graduate school, 317
graduation, 309
    announcements, 311–12
    balls. *See* proms
    invitations, 310
    presents, 431
    speeches, 312–13
grammar, 210
grandchildren, 346–47, 364, 617–18, 660
grandfathers, 371
grandmothers, 134, 218, 359, 361, 371, 662
grandparents, 177, 242, 371, 372, 377, 439, 441
    seated at wedding receptions, 419
grape scissors, 190
greed, 290, 615, 682–83
greeting cards, 594, 609–11
    Christmas, 609–13, 787
    sympathy, 812–13, 819
greeting guests, 526
greetings, 17, 109, 113, 140–42, 148, 151
grief, 799, 806, 812. *See also* mourning
grooms. *See* bridegrooms
groomsmen, 381, 417. *See also* attendants
grown-ups, 80–81, 172, 177, 209–10, 663, 669, 681–82
guest gift. *See* house presents; presents, from houseguests
guest list, 307, 528, 539–40, 570–71
    for a television party, 523
guest room, 275
guests, 62, 94, 197, 268, 495–96, 534, 709
    arriving early, 547
    in the bedroom, 272
    children as, 77, 89
    at christenings, 58–59
    classifying, 569–70
    at cocktail parties, 424–25
    difficult, 545

donating professional services, 384
at the family table, 177
first to arrive, 546–47
first to leave, 547
guests bringing guests, 543
leaving, 555–56
out-of-town, 417
overnight, 93–94
of parents, 83
passing food, 166
paying for drinks, 427–28
seating, 752
served first, 165
smoking, 745
uninvited, 403
unwanted, 532–33
watching television, 523
wedding, 670
at weddings, 358
guests of honor, 305
    at business dinners, 478
    first to leave, 556
    missing a dinner, 564
    at showers, 46
    at a tea party, 521
guilt, 25–26, 498, 562
gum, chewing, 298

hair:
    dyeing, 654
    long, 646
    pieces, 228–29
Hallowe'en, 784–85
Handel, George Frederick, 550
handicapped persons. *See* disabled persons
handkerchiefs, 294, 295–96, 298
hands, 109–10, 184, 186, 189–90, 194, 197, 341
    kissing, 111
    left, 162–63, 187, 195
    right, 162–63, 187
handshakes, 109–10, 695, 772–73
hats, 521, 637–38, 646
    during national anthem, 637, 697
    tipping of, 113
    wearing indoors, 637–38
Hawking, Stephen, 552
Hawthorne, Nathaniel, 255
Hayworth, Rita, 297

headphones, 734
heads of state, 695
hearth. *See* fireplaces
heirloom, 658, 662, 679
"hello." *See* greetings
helper, 584–85
"He would have wanted it that way," 799–800
hiccuping, 294
high heels, 626
hiring employees, 465
hold (on the telephone), 127, 503
"hold-the-date" cards, 529
holidays, 774, 784, 795
holiday trips. *See* vacations
Hollywood, California, 371
Holy Roman Emperor, 825
home, 193
    christening at, 58
homosexuals, 103, 277–78
    parents of the bride, 374–75
honesty, 272, 437, 462
honeymoon. *See* weddings, trip
honor, 262, 268
honors, accepting, 717–18
hope chest, 451
horses, 736
hospitality, 275, 277, 513, 515, 516, 528, 533, 553, 555
    acknowledging, 269, 280–81
    overnight, 431
hospitals, 59, 122
    patients, 272, 286–89
host, 26–27, 155–56, 169, 208, 275, 534
    alone, 587
    of deathbed gatherings, 289–90
    experienced, 569–70
    in the kitchen, 552
    parents as, 89
    served last, 585
    serving drinks, 584
    at weddings, 373
hostess, 89, 154, 157, 576
    angry, 560
    apologies to, 566
    ball-giving, 525
    leaving cards, 268
    with overnight guests, 327–28
    of a potluck supper, 514
    sending flowers to, 549

when served, 585
    signals to begin eating, 164, 589
    at a tea party, 521
    at weddings, 419
hotels, 157, 496, 550, 774
    property, 455
    tipping in, 763, 776
    writing paper, use of at home, 594
house, 137, 273, 308
    country, 712
    -work, 69
house guests, 275–76, 278, 279, 282, 327–28, 794
    assigning bedrooms, 277–78
    children as, 618
    impolite, 276–77
    length of stay, 275–76
    long term, 275–76
    perfect, 272–73, 279–80
household, 454
    equal opportunity, 710
    nonmarital, 346
    staffs, 708–12
housekeepers, in the large household, 711
housemates. *See* companions
house presents, 275, 276
house sitters, 282–83
housewarmings, 518–19
"How are you?," 291, 473
"How do you do?," 206
humiliation, 86, 351
humility. *See* modesty
husband, 46, 104–5, 128, 132, 252, 381, 420, 474, 568, 578, 652, 661, 678, 679
    errant, 259–61, 262–63
    taking name of, 53–55, 380, 596, 676
hyphenated names. *See* names, hyphenation of
hypocrisy, 233, 790–91

ichthyotomy, 187
identification, 120
illness, 284–88
    privileges of, 222
    quizzing on, 285–86
    visiting the sick, 269, 283
"I love you," 338
Importance of Being Earnest, The (Wilde), 813–14
improving others, 25–26

Impulse Rude, the, 22
"I'm sorry," 811
inaugurations, 305, 705
indecency, in airplanes, 770
infants. *See* babies
inferiors, 96, 478, 690
informal cards. *See* cards, informal
informal gatherings, 161
informality, 107, 189–90, 357, 466, 504, 625–26
    family, 252
    Miss Manners' version of, 521
initials, 53, 358, 393, 445
    on cards, 596
ink, 592, 594, 601, 610
in-laws, 625
    daughter, 210–11, 437, 660, 662, 658
    mother, 65, 210–11, 396, 399, 660
    parents, 380–81
    son, 381
    at weddings, 675
insanity, as a social excuse, 564
instant messaging, 249–50, 482
insults, 18, 75, 76–77, 80, 101, 118–19, 127–28, 131,
        136–37, 147–48, 172, 209, 211, 227–28,
        476, 559, 611, 622
Internet, 30, 246–50, 265, 285, 313, 314, 327, 331,
        620, 713
    dating, 334, 343–44
    Googling, 248–49
    instant messaging, 249–50
    spamming, 247–48
    see also email
internships, 462–63
interruptions, 87, 721
interviews:
    college, 17
    job, 459–61
    newspaper, 719
intimacy, 252, 262, 504, 603
    instant, 107–8
    in marriage, 252
introductions, 96–99, 100, 101, 107, 307, 345,
        346–47, 526, 578, 764
    of children, 99
    of servants, 98–99, 502–3
    of step-families, 660
invective, 86, 786
invitations, 46, 91, 128, 346, 480, 528, 542

acknowledging, 320
anniversary, 684
belligerent, 530–31
to business dinners, 478
cards, 592
to christenings, 58
to a "congruence," 340
to debuts, 320
declining, 716–17
to divorced couples, 541
formal, 536–37, 567–68, 592 (engraved cards),
    670
formal reply, 537 (example)
graduation, 309, 310
negative, 404
to office parties, 478
open-ended, 533
to prom, 320–24
for a reception "in honor of," 395 (example)
replies to, 358, 386, 396
secondhand, 531–32
to separated couples, 544
to showers, 44, 365–66
spoken, 546
spontaneous, 532–33
third person, 531–32
wedding, 369, 386, 391, 393 (example for a dou-
    ble wedding), 394–95, 396, 402, 404,
    665–66, 670, 671, 675
to the White House, 699, 700–705
written, 3990–91, 546
"ish" o'clock, 546
Italy, manners in, 161, 202, 644

Jackson, General, 700
James, Henry, 624
jealousy, 258–60, 290
Jefferson, Thomas, 700
jewelry, 384, 642–47, 658
    ankle bracelets, 647
    earrings, 633
    in mourning, 806
    pearls, 644–45
    symbolic value, 657–58
jewels, 218, 526, 642–47
Jewish traditions:
    bar and bat mitzvah, 305–7
    bris, 59–60

Jewish traditions (*continued*)
    Pidyon Haben, 60
    wedding, 373, 419, 420
job applicants, 459–60
job etiquette, 131, 205
job interviews, 309, 459–61
jobs, 462
jogging, 736–37
Johnson, Samuel, 276, 695
jokes, 227, 232–33
    dirty, 228
    ethnic, 227–28
journalists, 723
junior, 54–56, 596

Kafka, Franz, 351
Keim, De B. Randolph, 699
Kennedy, President John F., 733
kids. *See* children
killing. *See* murder
king. *See* royalty
kissing. 109, 254, 335, 336, 349, 469–70, 695, 793
    ceremonial, 359
    cheeks, 795
    on New Year's Eve, 794
    social, 111–12
kitchen, 552, 587, 710, 802
kitchen linen. *See* trousseau
knees, crossing one's, 133
knives, 162, 170–71, 173, 174, 180, 185, 190–91,
        194, 195
    carving, 445
    for grapefruit, 191
    plastic, 171
    see also table settings, knives
knocking before entering, 251

Labor Day, 639
ladies, 132 (definition), 133–34, 209–10, 268–69,
        297, 325–26, 330, 333, 459–60, 464, 568,
        637, 641, 643, 644–45, 652, 676, 825
    acceptable presents for, 619
    in the newspapers, 719
    old, 121, 150–51, 209–10, 660
    pregnant, 38
    single, 660
    young, 209–10, 260, 309, 317–20, 331–32,
        350–51, 352, 660

    see also women
ladies and gentlemen, 111, 113–14, 127–28, 131–34,
        135–36, 212, 259, 260, 323–24, 325–26,
        335, 337, 568, 622–47, 737, 826
lady friends. *See* woman friends
ladylike behavior, 132, 467–68, 719
lady of the house, 710
Lady's Not for Burning, The (Fry), 222
laptop computers, 125, 488–89
    in restaurants, 758
last names. *See* names, last
late arrivals, at the opera, 725
laughing, 557, 724, 799
laundresses, 711
laundry, 279–80
Leaflets, 143
Lear, Edward, 447
leaving:
    one's job, 507–8
    the table, 295–96
    the theater, 726, 730
    see also departure, of guests
lecturers, 719
left-handed, 166, 585
    handshakes, 110
Lehrer, Tom, 293
lesbians, parents of the bride, 374–75
letter closings, 439, 779
    "affectionately," 603
    "love," 484, 603
    "respectfully," 483–84
    "sincerely yours," 206
    "your friend," 603–4
    "your good friend," 826
    "yours sincerely," 207, 484, 603–4
    "yours truly," 206–7
    "yours very truly," 484, 603–4
    "yr. most obedient and humble servant," 484
letter paper. *See* writing paper
letters, 49, 251, 603, 604, 606, 670, 671, 742, 799
    acknowledging condolences, 800, 811
    of apology, 564
    business, 482–84, 779
    Christmas, 224, 592, 610. *See also* letters, hand-
        written
    closings. *See* letter closings
    of condolence, 799, 800, 803
    four-page, 259

handwritten, 391, 603–4, 667
of invitation, 58, 543, 671, 682
long, 604
love, 260–61, 569, 606, 710, 825
mimeographed, 610
of praise, 763
of recommendation, 461–62
of resignation, 742
of thanks, 17, 61, 442, 791
that should not be written, 604–6
see also cards, new informal
letter salutations, 603–4, 779
"Dear . . . ," 206
"Dear Friends," 483
"Dear Madam," 483
"Dear Sir," 483
"Dear Sir or Madam," 482
"Dear Sirs," 482
"Gentlemen," 482–83
"Madam My Sister," 695
"Mesdames," 483
"Sir My Brother," 695
libraries, 759, 760
limousines, 700
linens. *See* trousseau
lingerie. *See* underwear
lipstick, 761
liqueurs, 569, 581
listening, 85, 230–31
lists:
A, B and C, 569–70
paper for, 592
see also guest list
live-in, 128, 346
living alone, 788–89
living room, 552. *See also* drawing room
living together, 346, 366, 367, 411, 602, 775
location, for wedding, 387–88
look, of enthusiasm, 460
Louis XIV, king of France, 626
love, 16, 210, 257, 261, 328, 338, 339–40, 347–48,
    351, 357, 422, 460, 465, 470, 677
lovers, 128, 328, 338, 345, 350, 358, 381, 422, 541
illicit, 541
see also live-in
luggage, carry-on, 766
lunch, 58, 198, 200, 444, 451, 513, 771, 825
business, 478

wedding, 670
Lyly, John, 276

machines, 147–48, 152, 239–40
magazines, 251
Magic Flute, The (Mozart), 724
maid of honor, 394, 545, 674
job description, 383
see also attendants
maids, 98–99, 276, 502–3, 710–11, 826
chambermaid, 710, 825
hotel, 775
house, 495–96, 710
kitchen, 710
lady's, 710
parlor, 464, 710, 825
mail, 137, 402, 659
junk, 144, 611
reading others', 120, 259, 260–61
making love, 69, 263, 738
making others comfortable, 24–25
mandatory donation, 431
Mann, Thomas, 713
manners:
business, 25, 460
company, 249
family, 249–50, 363
guidelines, 33–34
Manners, Miss:
corrections from, 6
name, 691
patron goddess of social events, 429
maps, in wedding invitations, 396, 399
Margaret Rose, Princess, 368
marital status (or lack thereof), 56–57
marriage, 56–57, 68, 252–53, 268, 325, 338, 341,
    345, 357, 360, 363, 389, 413, 415, 425,
    639–40, 651–52, 663, 675–76, 677–78
changing names in, 53–55
essentials for beginning married life, 444
intimacy in, 252
previous, 675–76
proposal of, 360
on the rebound, 345
subsequent, 665–66, 669, 672–73
symbols of, 657–58
troubled, 262–63
see also weddings

married women. *See* women, married
Marshall, George, 312
mass emailings, 790
Master of Ceremonies, 421
matchmaking, 332–33
maternity clothes, 37
mates, 577–78
mating, 327, 335
matrimony. *See* marriage
matron of honor, 371, 394, 427. *See also* attendants
"may I present," 96–97. *See also* introductions
meals, 62, 252
medals, 646
meeting people, 331–32
meetings, public, 697–98
Memorial Day, 639–40
memorials, streetside, 819
memory, 101, 428–29, 566
men, 46, 96, 149, 318, 344, 468, 603, 637–38, 646, 665–66
    dress for, 16, 625
    wealthy, 645
    writing paper for, 594
menus, 120, 568, 528
    handwritten, 588
    ladies', 752–53
middle age, 261, 262–63
midnight supper, 514, 771
military salutes, 113
milk pitcher, 446, 521
ministers. *See* clergy
mink. *See* fur
minors. *See* children
miscarriages, condolences for, 814
mispronunciations, 232
Miss. *See* titles, Miss
Miss Lonelyhearts (West), 549
mistress. *See* roommate
Mitford, Nancy, 594
models, 751
modesty, 100, 222–23, 224, 230, 252, 315, 459
monarch. *See* royalty
money, 25, 307, 357, 363, 427–28, 441, 449, 460, 465, 5531, 615–16, 663
    conversation on, 220–21
    soliciting, 434–35, 436
money tree, the, 682
monograms, 384, 452, 571

on table linens, 451
on writing paper, 592
Monopoly, 739–40
mothers, 28, 41–42, 65, 69, 77, 87, 134, 371
    of the bride, 358, 368, 374, 414, 419, 436
    of the bridegroom, 358, 414, 419, 437
    divorced, 675–76
    dresses at wedding, 358, 359
    reluctant, 39–40
    single, 70
    step-, 660
    working, 793
mothers-in-law. *See* in-laws, mother
motorists, 147–48
mourners, 799–800, 802
    chief, 802
mourning, 799–822
    black-bordered writing paper, 592
    critiquing, 808
    deep, 415, 806
    ending, 819–20
    formal, 806
    modern, 806, 807
    second, 415, 806
Mouse, Mickey, 678
movies, 514, 729
movie stars. *See* celebrities
moving, 268
Mr. *See* titles, Mr.
Mrs. *See* titles, Mrs.
Ms. *See* titles, Ms.
murder, 182–83, 723
museums, shushing in, 726–27
music:
    background, 123, 125, 550–51
    talking during, 722
    for weddings, 384
musicians, 143
    in restaurants, 292–93, 751
mystery, 339

names, 101, 307, 358, 567–68, 569, 603, 718
    on cards, 594, 598, 600. *See also* cards, new informal
    changes in, 52–54
    changing of, 676
    dropping, 676
    first, 17, 57, 107–9, 252, 380, 466, 490, 502–4

full, 393, 401, 687
hyphenation of, 53, 56, 626
on invitations, 401
last, 53–54, 55–57, 98, 107, 108–9, 128, 380, 392, 401, 610–11, 625–26, 659, 687, 710
maiden, 54, 55, 56, 379, 380, 393, 445, 452–53, 659
married, 379–81, 439, 452
middle, 52, 380
nicknames, 52–53, 804
of parents, 57
proper, 228
remembering, 101, 568
wrong, 101, 127, 350
name tags, 102
naming babies, 60
nannies, 711
napkins, 145, 158–59, 170, 174, 184, 221, 521, 573–74, 588
cloth, 173
dinner, 451
folding, 573–74
linen, 449
luncheon, 451
paper, 159, 171–72, 449
rings for, 159–60
national anthem, 637, 696–97
natural behavior, 61, 118, 119, 284, 558
negligees, 618
neighbors, 124–25, 137–38, 139–40, 142, 270
calling on new, 269, 272–73
new, 272–73
newspapers, 123, 137, 214, 251, 719
obituaries in, 801, 802
New Year's Day, 780, 795
New Year's Eve, 794–95
New Year's resolutions, 780–81
Nicolson, Harold, 555
nightgowns, 618
"No, thank you," 115–16, 743, 744
nobility, 99–100
noblesse oblige, 715
"No" for an answer, 115–18, 120, 168, 287, 743
"no gifts, please," 435, 534, 683–84
noise, 123, 139, 551
in restaurants, 759
noises:
acceptable, 294
sympathetic, 293–94
unacceptable, 294
nomenclature. *See* names
nondairy creamer, 185
nonsmokers, 745
nose:
blowing one's, 295–96
cleaning one's, 296
picking one's, 296
wiping one's, 298
notes, 49, 603–4
of apology, 350, 780
handwritten, 396, 790, 818
see also thank-you notes
notification of death, 801
Not Stooping, 22
novels, 145
numerals, with names:
ordinal, 54–55
Roman, 54–56
nursery, 167, 168
nurses, 711
nursing, of babies. *See* babies, nursing
nursing homes, 503–4
nut dishes, 588
Nya-Nya Factor, the, 716

obituaries, 801, 802
occupations, 216–17, 570
women's, 268
offense, 127–28
offering a lady one's arm, 114
office, 122, 151
stationery at home, 594
office party, the, 478, 479
off the record, 720
ogling, 783
older people, 110, 210
one-night stands, 326–28
on-line shopping, 789
On Love (Stendhal), 328
opera, 514, 551, 724, 732
opinions, 214, 287
orchestras, 525
ordering, in restaurants, 752–53
outbursts, vocal, 301
overnight hospitality, 326
overtime, 477, 478

pallbearers, 802
panhandlers, 144
pants, 133
paper napkins. *See* napkins, paper
paramour. *See* significant other
parasols, 146
parents, 17, 61, 63, 68–69, 75–77, 89–91, 93–94,
        177, 192, 228, 257–58, 278, 307, 309,
        317–18, 347–48, 360, 371, 430, 793
    of the bride, 363, 374, 391, 417, 673
    of the bridegroom, 363, 377, 378, 379, 391
    at christenings, 58
    after divorce, 667–68
    in divorce, 666–68
    giving housewarmings, 519
    -in-law, 380–81, 675
    multiple, 371, 372
    names of, 57
    new, 61
    original, 371, 373
    in the receiving line, 419
    visiting, 603
    at weddings, 391–92, 669, 670
Paris, 624, 774
parking, 139–40
parking lot, 141, 147
    attendants, 466
parties, 138, 305, 309, 389, 513, 523, 556, 569, 680
    arriving early, 547
    arriving first, 546–47
    calling after, 268
    after christenings, 58
    holiday, 780
    large, 564
    leaving, 547
    New Year's Eve, 794–95
    within parties, 743–44
    prewedding, 367–68
    retirement, 305, 508–9
    sales, 516–17
    surprise, 517–18
    wine-and-cheese, 513, 520
party book, 569
party favors, 527
passion, 328, 335, 795, 825
patients, 119, 419. *See also* hospitals, patients
patronizing others, 490
paying, 70, 379, 388–89, 391, 417, 427–28, 474,

        533, 750
    for damage, 564
    for loss, 560
    in restaurants, 750–51
payment, presents as, 435
pearls, 521, 644–45, 806
peddlers, 269–70
pedestrians, 143, 736
peeling, 190
    fruit, 189–90
    shrimp, 198
peers, 100
People Who Still Entertain, 528
pepper, 197
performances, by friends, 229
personal conversations, 233
personal questions, 218–19, 424
personal remarks. *See* remarks, personal
person information, 119
perspiration, 297
pets, 124–25
photographers, 421
photographs:
    with celebrities, 714–15
    family, 455, 682
    posed, 429
    wedding, 428–30
physical appraisals, 86
physical compatibility, 364
physicians. *See* doctors, medical
picketing, 143
picking up, strangers, 333
picnics, 171–72
    baskets for, 171
Pidyon Haben ceremony, 60
pilfering, 774
pits (fruit), 196
pity stories, 496–97
place setting, 588
plants, 287
plates, 184, 195, 199–201
    bread-and-butter, 449
    dessert, 449
    dinner, 170–71, 448, 585
    empty, 588
    filled, 588
    fruit, 449
    luncheon, 448–49

oyster, 588
paper, 171, 186
place or service, 200, 572–73, 585, 588
salad, 449
for snails, 199
soup, 200, 449, 588
tea, 449, 521
underliners, 200
platters, 166, 569, 585, 588, 590, 826
Plautus, 276
play dates, 93
playing cards, 738–39
plays, 514
pleasure, faking, 791
Plutarch, 694
poker, 739
politeness, in the family, 177–78, 249
political flyers, 143
politics, 298–301, 560
conversation on, 220
popping corks, 748
popularity, 80–81, 329
secret of, 329
postcards, 326, 778–79
reading others', 779
post office, 401
potluck suppers, 514–15
pouring, 428
precedence, 145, 149
preference in forms of address, 54–55, 108–9, 128
pregnancy, 37–38, 41, 42, 149, 415, 425
announcement of, 38
unwanted, 39–40
presents, 57, 62, 290, 508–9, 531, 614–21
accepting, 614–15, 616–18, 619
acknowledging, 436, 594, 605, 606
anniversary, 679–80
announcements as bids for, 50–51
as apologies, 780
baby, 67
birthday, 59, 90, 308, 475, 618–19
brought to parties, 684, 793
cards with, 594, 600
certificates as, 616
christening, 59
Christmas, 59, 614, 618, 792–94
comparable value of, 347, 620–21
costs, 615

during courtship, 347, 619
for debutantes, 320
disappointing, 615, 616, 617, 619, 621
for a divorce, 652
engagement, 364–65
exchanging, 437, 615
expecting, 29–30, 435, 615, 683
expensive, 620–21
for first communion, 308
of food, to mourners, 799, 802, 812
graduation, 311, 313–15
hideous, 455, 614, 615, 619
to hospital patients, 287
from houseguests, 275, 276
of liquor, 799
of money, 441, 615–16, 682
notes with, 594
obligatory, 364, 431, 681, 683
personal, 620
as return for hospitality, 277
returning, 352, 443
from returning vacationers, 277–78
sending, 684
at showers, 44, 45, 46
for smokers, 745
soliciting, 434–35
for subsequent weddings, 669–70
wedding, 29–30, 254, 358, 365, 368, 386, 406–7,
432, 433, 434–36, 439, 441, 444, 455, 674,
681
for wedding attendants, 384
of wine, 548
President, the, 96, 422, 687, 695, 699, 706, 743
press conferences, 720
prices, 273, 751
on presents, 620–21
priests. See clergy
privacy, 66, 119, 122, 193, 275, 279, 291, 297, 396,
578, 743
invasions of, 283, 758
privilege of rank, 715–16
processional. See weddings, processional
procrastinators, 563
Procrustes, 372
profanity, 77, 212
professional hazards, 217
professional names, 53
professional titles, 105

professions, 217, 570, 718
professors, 217
profiting from others, 29–30
proms, 16, 309, 320–23, 624
property, 147, 282
proposal, the, 360
protocol, 703
pseudo engraving, 48–49, 358
public, 64, 143–44, 193, 291, 297–99, 340–41,
    395, 422, 425, 720, 783, 802
  meetings, 697–98
public balls. *See* balls, charity
public rebukes, 86
punch, 58, 427, 428, 581
purses, 752
put-downs, 22, 39, 142, 209

Queen Elizabeth, 113
Queen of England, 826
questions nobody asked, 825–26
quotations, 231–32

rabbi, 420
race, 363
radios, 171
rain, 146–47
raised printing. *See* pseudo engraving
raises, asking for, 463–64, 468
raising children. *See* child rearing
rank, 80–81, 96, 97, 104, 111, 132, 177, 209–10,
    478, 694, 703, 715–16, 751
  pulling, 715–16
reading, 792
  at table, 178
rearing children. *See* child rearing
receiving, 272
receiving lines, 307, 419, 423, 700–701
  at wedding receptions, 372, 373
  at the White House, 701
receptions, 59–60, 521
  delayed wedding, 394–95
  wedding, 673
recessional. *See* weddings, recessional
reciprocating, 535–36
refusals, 145, 337, 404
rehearsal dinner, 378–79, 385–86, 417
rejectee, 351
rejecting food, in restaurants, 757

relationships, 336, 341–42, 345–46, 347–48, 795
  business, 478, 720–21
  clandestine, 661
  letters as evidence of, 605
  among new in-laws, 363
  nonmarital, 346
  recognized by society, 345–46
  social, 478, 720–21
relatives, 60, 76, 77, 82, 96, 99, 172, 307, 377, 487,
    618–19, 651
  brothers, 377
  at christenings, 58
  cousins, 660
  giving showers, 45
  seating, 752
  sisters, 393
  step-, 660
  writing to, 610
religion, 363, 515
  conversation on, 220
religious callers, 269–70
religious services. *See* services, religious
remarks, 77, 172
  bigoted, 227–28
  careless, 40
  dirty, 222
  dumb, 208–9
  improper, 221
  personal, 38, 86
remembering names. *See* names, remembering
remembering the deceased, 822
removing foreign matter from the mouth, 187,
    196
removing plates, 585, 760
renewing vows, 677, 680–82
replies, 115–17
  to compliments, 86
  to formal invitations, 402, 537 (example), 568
  handwritten, 403, 537
  to invitations, 528
  to an offer to dance, 321
reporters. *See* journalists
reputations, bad, 226–27
requesting invitations, 287
reservations, 772
response, 166, 219, 229, 473
  to improper remarks, 221, 469
  to pregnancy, 39

responsibilities:
of bridegroom's parents, 363, 377, 379, 417
to children, 663–64
civic, 299
of debutantes, 318–20
of godparents, 59–60
of graduates, 309
on the job, 460, 465
in marriage, 262–63
of mourners, 802, 819
of parents for subsequent weddings, 673
religious, 305
restaurants, 135, 145, 164, 170, 185–86, 254, 307,
341, 455, 474, 478, 494–95, 545, 631,
750–51, 759, 760
children at, 94–95
finer, 157, 757
laptop computers in, 758
music in, 550
rejecting food in, 757
salad in, 581–82
stacking dishes in, 761
tea in, 521
tipping in, 762
retirement, 508–9
reunions, college, 315
Reverend, the. *See* clergy
ring bearer, 417, 674
rings, 657–58
anniversary, 679–80
dinner, 657
of a divorcée, 657–59
guard, 658
wearing on the right hand, 658
wedding, 657–59, 678
of widows and widowers, 809–10
Robert's Rules of Order, 215, 697
romance, 258, 259, 260, 325–26, 328, 331–32, 335,
340–41, 349, 360, 365, 470, 578, 677, 728
Roof Principle, the, 102–3
roommate, 94, 541
Roosevelt, Eleanor, 179
Royal Highness (Mann), 713–14
royalty, 56, 272, 692, 694, 826
numerals of, 54–55
R.s.v.p., 396, 404, 536
rudeness, 21–23, 25, 41, 75, 85, 107, 108, 114, 120,
125–26, 127–28, 132, 136, 139–40, 143,

145, 163, 165, 168, 169, 173, 186, 209, 249,
260, 272, 286, 287, 382, 396, 403, 422,
424, 435, 466, 487, 491–92, 500, 504,
506, 531, 551
abroad, 765, 766
avoiding condolences, 799
background music, 550
at cocktail parties, 524–25
in the family, 252
in marriage, 252, 253
to patients, 288–89, 490
professional, 711–12, 723
rules, 674
for children at table, 174–75
for children in divorce, 663–64
of competitive sports, 737–38
for debuts, 318–20
for family dinners, 173
of family etiquette, 251–52
for fish consumption, 187
for gossip, 225–26
for hat tipping, 113
for house sitters, 282–83
of jealous conduct, 259
for joggers, 736–37
of modern calling, 269
for opera-going, 724
for spending the night, 93–94
for Thanksgiving dinner, 786

salad, 581–82
bowls, 161
course, 161
plates, 161
platter, 585
see also courses, salad; formal service; table settings
salary, 465, 476
sales parties, 516–17
salespeople, 144, 493, 494, 499, 516
temporary, 793
saliva, removing, 298
salt cellars, 197, 588
same-sex weddings, 414
save-the-date letters, 385, 402
saying "no," 115–18, 743
Scandinavia, manners in, 581–82
scholarships, naming of, 718

school, 80, 83–84, 103, 105, 309
    changing names at, 52, 53
    private, 641–42
scratching, 297
screaming, 151, 558
seating:
    ladies, 135, 752
    in the theater, 726
seating arrangements, 576–78
    in restaurants, 751
    at wedding receptions, 372
    at weddings, 358
seating charts, 172, 568
seats:
    exchanging of, 726
    giving up, 128
second (or II), 55–56
second helpings, 169, 744
secretaries, 239, 240, 645
secrets, 81–82, 261–62
    family, 251, 276
    of unhappy marriage, 780
Seeing Eye dog, 119
self-admiration, 733
self-expression, of children, 85, 92
senior, 54–56
senior citizens, 210, 343
sentiments, 454
    handwritten, 610
separate checks, in restaurants, 755–56
separation, 262, 541, 657
Servant Problem, the, 464–65
servants, 268, 455, 464–65, 587–88, 708–12, 826
servants, introduction of. See introductions, of servants
servants, public, 465–66
service, 25, 145, 161–62, 465–66, 490–91, 750, 762
    à la russe, 569, 587–88
    family, 200
    at the family table, 177
    formal, 568–69, 572–73
    without help, 587
    from the left, 585
    passing food, 166
service jobs, 465–66
services:
    funeral, 799

memorial, 800, 803
    public, 551
    religious, 307–8
serviettes. See napkins
serving dishes, 161, 449
serving implements:
    asparagus tongs, 445
    cake server, 445
    grape scissors, 445, 448
    ladle, 445
serving oneself last, 177
sex, 39, 228, 326–27, 329, 337, 357, 422, 469, 663, 720
    of babies, 41–42
    conversation on, 220
    partners, 578
    see also gender
sexism, 45
sexual:
    affiliations, 103
    freedom, 334
    relations, 262
sexuality, 119
shaking hands. See handshakes
Shaming Them, 22
sharing, 767–70
    in restaurants, 756–57
Shaw, George Bernard, 604
sheets. See trousseau, bed linens
ships, 23, 103, 770–73
    table companions aboard, 771
shoes, 767
    cream-colored, 639–40
    high heels, 638
    white, 639–40
shopping, 550
    on-line, 789
showers, 46, 684
    baby, 44–46
    bridal, 45, 365–67, 383
    definition, 45
    divorce, 652
    wedding, 385, 386
showing off. See bragging
shunning, 266–67, 661–62
shushing, 726–27
shyness, 112
sick people, visiting, 286–88
sidewalk cafés, 783

sidewalk pamphleteers, 143–44
significant other, 345
signing:
  cards, 812
  funeral registers, 804
  names, 439, 610–11
silence, 219, 550, 551
silver, 59, 157, 161, 220, 357, 384, 433, 444, 521, 588,
    679, 683–84, 710, 745
  basic place setting, 444
  dishes, 448
  engraved, 571–72
  flatware, 444
  inherited, 571–72
  wine goblets, 572
  see also table settings; trousseau
sin, living in. See living together
single people, 326–27, 332, 531–32, 578–79,
    653–54, 773, 788–89
Sinking Feeling, That, 126–27
sisters. See relatives, sisters
"sit anywhere," 576–77
slacks. See pants
slops bowl, 521
slow jilt, the, 338
slurping, 190, 193, 200
small talk, 83
smiles, 763
  of constrained delight, 617
  demure, 368
  frosty, 227
  gooey, 119
  half-, 135
  knowing, 166
  mysterious, 360
  naughty, 551
  open-mouthed, 300
  patient, 309
  puzzled, 151
  radiant, 717
  regretful, 218, 293
  shy, 717
  social, 62
  sweet, 221
  weight-of-the-world, 811
smoking, 620, 635, 744–45, 780
  in the house, 745
  see also nonsmokers

smoking jacket, 620
smoking room, 620
snail tongs, 199
snappy comebacks. See put-downs
sneezing, 127, 294, 295
snobbery, 31, 105, 570
snooping, 259, 260–61, 551–52
snubs, 703
social disease, 350
social duties, 61, 288, 340, 677, 717
social intercourse, 26, 259. See also communication;
    conversation
social skills, 89, 115–17, 305
social terms, 206–7
society, 61, 75, 80, 86–87, 189, 317–18, 320, 526,
    626, 665
solitaire, 739
sommelier. See wine steward
sons, 320
soup, 199–200, 581, 582, 585
  bouillon, 521
  bouillon cups, 449
  bouillon spoons, 445
  bowls, 200, 449
  cups for, 200
  ladle, 445
  plates, 200, 449, 588
  spoons, 444
  tilting bowls, 200
  tureen for, 200
  see also courses, soup; slurping; table settings,
    soup spoons
South America, manners in, 112
souvenirs, 455, 774
Spain, manners in, 198
spamming, 247–48
speaking when spoken to, 113
speeches, 311–12
spending the night:
  adults, 326, 327–28
  children, 93–94
spilling food, 172, 771
splitting the dinner, 756–57
spoons, 161–62, 170, 173, 190–92, 195, 199–201,
    571, 826
  coffee, 446
  egg, 447
  grapefruit, 191, 445

spoons (*continued*)
    iced tea, 445
    runcible, 447
    serving, 445
    and spaghetti, 201–2
    see also table settings, spoons
sports, 732–39
sports parties, 523
spouses, 108, 144, 228, 358, 372, 480, 687
    at business dinners, 478
    invited alone, singles, 541
squeamishness, 284
standards of manners, 363
standing, 149
standing for ladies, 132–33
standing ovations, 724, 731
State Department, 707
stationery. *See* writing paper
steak knife, 157
stealing, 774
Stendhal (Marie-Henri Beyle), 328
stepmothers. *See* mothers, step-
stepparents, 371, 373, 374, 375–76, 392, 660, 675
stimulants, 561, 743
stockings, 633, 647
    seams of, 633
stood up, 127
strangers, 66, 97, 113, 136, 141, 142, 147, 260, 270,
        309, 327, 331, 334, 344, 493
    coming out among, 317, 318
    conversation with, 769
    dumping problems on, 291–92
straws, 193
street and sidewalk behavior, 113–14, 136, 140–44,
        146–47
    sidestepping, 114–15
subway, 128, 149–50, 151
sugar bowl, 446, 521
suitors. *See* courtship, suitors
suits, 670
Sunday Best, 626
superiors, 96, 478, 489, 687
Supreme Court, the, 687
    ʳnames. *See* names, last
    ʲse parties, 517–18
    nd, Douglas, 589
    ʲools, 275, 735–36. *See also* bathing suits
    ʲ. 409

sympathy:
    cards. *See* greeting cards, sympathy
    for divorce, 653
    see also condolences
tablecloth, 158, 184, 190, 449, 568
    damask, 451
table linens, 451–52. *See also* trousseau
table manners, 17, 132–33, 154–203, 707
    children's, 94–95, 174–75, 257
    European, 162–63
    family, 172–79, 257
    forks, 154–58
    for particular foods, 179–203
table mats, 451
tables, 155, 173
    A and B, 579
    two, 579
table settings, 176
    bread-and-butter plate, 169
    butter knives, 162, 169, 202
    dessert forks, 156–57, 161–62, 190
    dessert plates, 155–57
    dessert spoons, 156–57, 190, 200
    fish forks, 155, 187–88, 588
    fish knives, 162, 187–88, 588
    forks, 154–58, 163, 187–89, 588
    fruit forks, 157, 189, 588
    fruit knives, 157, 189, 588
    fruit plate, 157
    knives, 154–56, 169, 187–89, 202, 588
    luncheon plate, 169
    meat forks, 155, 588
    meat knives, 162, 588
    oyster forks, 155, 588
    plates, 155–56
    salad forks, 155, 157, 588
    salad knives, 162, 588
    soup spoons, 154–55, 199–200, 588
    spoons, 154–57, 190–91, 199–201, 444, 445, 588
    tablespoons, 444
    teaspoons, 200, 445
    see also silver
tact, 28, 126–27, 474
tails. *See* white tie
taste, 344, 454–55, 616, 670, 684, 801, 802
    bad, 642
    children's, 729

taxicabs, 763
taxi drivers, 466
tea, 58, 67, 127, 419, 444, 546, 720, 771
    afternoon, 520–22
    bags, 446, 447, 521
    caddy, 521
    cups, 449, 521, 522
    high tea, 522
    iced, 446, 450
    invitations for, 520 (example)
    -kettle, 446
    parties, 428, 444, 513
    -pot, 446, 521
    sandwiches for, 359
    service, 220, 445–46, 521
    strainer, 521
    -time, 520, 522
tears, 296, 799
teenagers. See adolescents
teeth, 126–27
    picking one's, 296–97
telephone, 51, 61, 145, 173, 238, 251, 259, 279, 325,
        344, 349, 402, 436, 491, 499, 568, 643, 710,
        802
    answering machines, 147, 237, 239–40, 809
    answering the, 236, 237–38
    business, 484–87
    busy signals, 250
    call waiting, 239
    camera, 245–46
    cellular, 118, 234–35, 242–45, 482–86, 501–2,
        579–80
    compared to correspondence, 605
    during dinner, 173
    before dropping in, 269
    ending calls, 241, 486
    hanging up, 239–40
    long distance calls, 276, 277
    multitasking on, 240, 242–44
    numbers, 272, 326, 598
    overhearing others' calls, 233
    personal calls at work, 460
    returning calls, 326–27
    speakerphone, 484–85
    unlisted number, 235
    wrong numbers, 238
television, 69, 172, 173, 268, 271, 523, 550, 719
    talk shows, 721–22

tennis, 737–38
Thanksgiving, 785–87
"thank you," saying, 94, 177–78, 204–5, 230, 275,
        276, 285, 338, 442, 476, 717, 763
thank-you cards, 441, 442
thank-you notes, 17, 61, 88–89, 269, 307, 311,
        314–15, 401, 437–38, 603–4, 605, 606,
        607, 684, 780, 791
    addressing, 603–4
    for dinner, 548, 607–8
    emailed, 438
    handwritten, 443
    from houseguests, 276, 280–81, 605
    overdue, 442
    for wedding presents, 358, 436–38, 439, 441,
        443
    see also letters, of thanks; notes, of thanks
Theory of Everything, The (Hawking), 552
third (or III), 54–56
thoughtlessness. See rudeness
tiaras, 646–47
tilted nose, the, 23
timing:
    the dinner hour, 568, 576
    one's arrival, 721–22
tipping, 260, 750, 751, 762–64
    owners, 762, 764
    on shipboard, 771–72
tissues, 295
    in wedding invitations, 399
titles, 99–100, 103–4, 401, 568, 690–92
    Ambassador, 687, 690
    baroness, 100
    on cards, 596
    contessa, 99–100
    Dr., 104–5, 392–93, 490–91, 502, 602–3
    duchess, 100, 690
    earned, 99–100, 690–91
    foreign, 690–91
    General, 687
    Governor, 687, 690, 692, 695
    grand titre, 826
    Honorable, the, 687, 692
    job, 687
    Judge, 687, 695
    Justice, 687
    loss of, 691–92, 695–96
    Madam, 104, 205, 483, 687

titles (*continued*)
  Madame, 659
  Mademoiselle, 659
  maharaja, 99–100
  marquess, 54–55
  Mayor, 687, 690
  Messrs., 401
  Miss, 57, 103–4, 105, 128, 205, 401, 659, 711
  Mr., 54–55, 99, 104, 105, 107, 109, 380, 381, 602, 687, 690, 710–11, 804
  Mrs., 53–55, 57, 103–4, 107, 108–9, 128, 380, 381, 659, 687, 711, 804
  Ms., 57, 103–4, 105, 108, 128, 659
  for parents, 57
  petit titre, 826
  President, 687, 695, 696
  professional, 104–5
  for relatives, 660
  Senator, 690
  social, 596
  Speaker, 687, 690
  titre moyen, 826
  Vice President, 687
  woman's medical, 602
toasts, 367–68, 748–49
  to oneself, 749
toddlers, on the telephone, 241–42
toe tapping, at concerts, 727–28
toilet paper, 249
toilet seats, 553
tongue, 189, 192, 298
  use of, 180
tourists, 763–67
towels:
  bath, 452
  face, 452
  guest, 553–54
  hand, 452
  linen, 452
  warm, 575
toys, 147, 792
tradition, 128, 358, 371, 372, 375, 378, 381, 385, 414, 422, 442, 502, 520, 521, 651, 792
  family, 672
  149–50, 641, 773
  d for weddings, 825
  n, 69
  123, 146, 149–51, 769

traveling abroad, 764–67, 774
traveling alone, 769, 773
Tree, Sir Herbert Beerbohm, 604, 605
trick-or-treating, 784–85
triumph, social, 665–66
trophies, 455
trousers. *See* pants
trouser suits, ladies', 631–32
trousseau:
  bath linens, 451, 452
  bed linens, 451, 452
  china, 448–49
  glassware, 449–50
  kitchen linens, 452
  table linens, 451
T-shirts, 623, 624, 634, 640, 641–42
turning cards. *See* cards, turning edges of
turning the table, 579–80
tutors, 711
tuxedo. *See* evening clothes, men's
typewriters, 591

umbrellas, 127, 146–47, 150–51
unannounced visits, 269–71
unconventional behavior, 309
underwear, 45, 620
  euphemisms for women's, 211–12
ungentlemanlike behavior, 297
uniforms, 641–42
United States. *See* America
unladylike behavior, 297
unlisted number. *See* telephone, unlisted number
unmarried women. *See* women, unmarried
unwanted attentions, 716–17
upper-class, 31–32, 225
ushers, 413
  presents, 384
  see also attendants

vacations, 229, 429, 455, 776–77, 783
  bringing back presents, 777–78
Valentine's Day, 781
valets, 710, 826
Van Buren, Martin, 700
van der Rohe, Mies, 428
vases, 213
vegetarian, 590
Vice President, the, 687

Victoria, Queen of England, 24, 694, 695
Victorian manners, 181, 187, 323–24, 710
videographers, 421
vigilantism, 148–49
villains, *See* cads
virginity, 409, 414
visiting cards, *See* cards
visitors, 61–62, 287
visits, paying, 61–62, 268–72, 792
   hospitalized acquaintances, 286–88
   sick friends, 269
   see also calls, paying
vocal outbursts, 301
Vulgar American Tourist, the, 764

wages, 465
waiters, 135, 171, 179–80, 421, 428, 466, 474,
    494–95, 631, 760, 764
waiting, 144–45
   to begin eating, 164–65, 589
   for dinner guests, 576
waitresses, 260, 428, 464, 493, 494, 710
wakes, 799. *See also* funerals
waking up, 278, 561
walking, 736
walking sticks, as weapons, 146
war (and bad table manners), 164
Warburg, Max, 555
Washington, George, 717
waste bowl. *See* slops bowl
watch chains, 646
watches, 645–46
   pocket, 646
   wrist, 643, 646
Water Music (Handel), 550
Waugh, Evelyn, 187, 521
wedding party, 681
wedding presents. *See* presents, wedding
weddings, 340, 359, 367, 389–455, 665, 669–76
   afternoon, 416, 419
   albums, 455
   announcements, 386, 404–5
   arrangements, 390
   breakfast, 419
   ceremony, 395–96, 411, 417
   costs, 388–89, 391, 417, 427–28, 673
   customary, 670
   customs, 385, 388, 422

   day, 305
   destination, 387–88
   dinner, 396, 419, 426
   divorced parents at, 373, 376
   double, 393–94
   dress, 320, 358, 369, 408–11, 414, 427
   evening, 413, 419
   fights concerning, 357–59
   first, 670
   food, 426
   formal, 369, 430
   giving the bride away, 373–74, 375–76, 422
   guests, 358
   hazards, 420–22
   invitations, 366, 369, 391, 392–93 (titles on),
     393 (example for a double wedding),
     394–95, 396, 399, 401 (example of address
     on), 402, 403, 404, 433
   Jewish, 420
   large, 670
   location for, 387–88
   morning, 419
   of one's daughter, 665
   original ceremonies, 422
   pew assignments, 371, 372
   photographs, 428–30
   presents, 29–30, 358, 386, 406–7, 432, 433, 439,
     441, 443, 672, 681
   processional, 417
   reception, 426, 427–28, 734–35
   recessional, 419
   rings, 362, 420, 658–59
   same-sex, 414
   small, 680
   Snicker-Proof, 670
   subsequent, 651–52, 669–76
   This-Time-We-Know-What's-What, 670
   throwing rice, 419
   throwing the bouquet, 419
   throwing the garter, 419
   trip, 358, 383, 387, 394, 432
   veil, 670
   walking down the aisle, 373, 392, 394
   watching sports during, 734–35
   see also presents, wedding
well-bred person, 75, 780
Welles, Orson, 297
West, Nathanael, 549

Wharton, Edith, 268, 660
"What did you bring me?," 617–19
"What do you do?," 216
"What-I-did-on-my-vacation" talks, 776–77
wheelchairs, 119, 121
Which Fork to Use, 154–56
white, wearing, 670
    christening dress, 58
    clothing on television, 721–22
    shoes, 639–40
    by wedding guests, 414–15
white dress, the, 408–11
White House, the, 300, 545, 700, 703, 774
    dinner at, 699–707
white tie, 413, 625, 700
widows, 657, 804, 806–7, 821
    names of, 809
    wearing veils, 806
wife, 46, 55, 123, 136–37, 252, 259–60, 399
wine, 60, 513, 746–47, 748
    bad, 746
    by the glass, 754
    covering your glass, 589
    as present, 515
    presents of, 548
    red, 746
    refusing, 589
    in restaurants, 754
    served by butler, 710
    sweet, 746
    tasting, 520
    white, 746
wine-and-cheese parties, 513, 520
wine steward, 746
Wishing Well Wedding, 436
withering look, the, 23

wives, 568, 578
    of officials, 687
woman friends, 262. *See also* beloved
women, 70, 96, 108, 131, 177, 209–10, 222, 228,
        258, 261, 333, 344, 360, 480, 568, 625–47,
        666, 670
    dress of, 16, 17, 470, 625, 644
    embittered, 666
    handshaking of, 772–73
    married, 128, 474, 596, 659, 825
    other, 260
    rivalry among, 665
    unmarried, 229
    writing paper for, 592, 594
    young, 317, 467, 468, 644
    see also ladies
women's liberation, 134
women's rights, 128–29, 132
work, 151, 205, 216–17, 226–27, 459–507, 522, 698
    conditions of, 69
    hours, 69–70, 465, 708
    quitting of, 507–8
    retiring from, 508–9
    strikes, 143
    women and, 131, 467–70, 474, 503
Worth, House of, 624
writing paper, 392–93, 403, 439, 592–94, 774
    black-bordered, 806, 815
    Christmas, 610
    colors for, 592, 600–601
    formal, 537
    stationery wardrobe, 592–94
    see also cards

young girls. *See* girls, young
youth, 96, 97, 110, 113, 210, 669, 783